opposing viewpoints

SOURCES

nuclear arms

opposing viewpoints
SOURCES

nuclear arms

vol. 1

David L. Bender, *Publisher*
Bruno Leone, *Executive Editor*
M. Teresa O'Neill, *Associate Editor*
Claudia Debner, *Assistant Editor*
Bonnie Szumski, *Assistant Editor*

Bernard S. Bachrach, Ph.D., *Consulting Editor*
Professor of History
University of Minnesota, Minneapolis

greenhaven press, inc.

577 Shoreview Park Road
St. Paul, MN 55126

"Congress shall make no law. . .abridging the freedom of speech, or of the press."

first amendment to the US Constitution

contents

foreward

"It is better to debate a question without settling it than to settle a question without debating it."

Joseph Joubert (1754-1824)

The Importance of Examining Opposing Viewpoints

The purpose of Opposing Viewpoints SOURCES is to present balanced, and often difficult to find, opposing points of view on complex and sensitive issues.

Probably the best way to become informed is to analyze the positions of those who are regarded as experts and well studied on issues. It is important to consider every variety of opinion in an attempt to determine the truth. Opinions from the mainstream of society should be examined. But also important are opinions that are considered radical, reactionary, or minority as well as those stigmatized by some other uncomplimentary label. An important lesson of history is the eventual acceptance of many unpopular and even despised opinions. The ideas of Socrates, Jesus, and Galileo are good examples of this.

Readers will approach this anthology with their own opinions on the issues debated within it. However, to have a good grasp of one's own viewpoint, it is necessary to understand the arguments of those with whom one disagrees. It can be said that those who do not completely understand their adversary's point of view do not fully understand their own.

A persuasive case for considering opposing viewpoints has been presented by John Stuart Mill in his work *On Liberty.* When examining controversial issues it may be helpful to reflect on his suggestion:

> The only way in which a human being can make some approach to knowing the whole of a subject, is by hearing what can be said about it by persons of every variety of opinion, and studying all modes in which it can be looked at by every character of mind. No wise man ever acquired his wisdom in any mode but this.

Analyzing Sources of Information

Opposing Viewpoints SOURCES includes diverse materials taken from magazines, journals, books, and newspapers, as well as statements and position papers from a wide range of individuals, organizations and governments. This broad spectrum of sources helps to develop patterns of thinking which are open to the consideration of a variety of opinions.

Pitfalls to Avoid

A pitfall to avoid in considering opposing points of view is that of regarding one's own opinion as being common sense and the most rational stance and the point of view of others as being only opinion and naturally wrong. It may be that another's opinion is correct and one's own is in error.

Another pitfall to avoid is that of closing one's mind to the opinions of those with whom one disagrees. The best way to approach a dialogue is to make one's primary purpose that of understanding the mind and arguments of the other person and not that of enlightening him or her with one's own solutions. More can be learned by listening than speaking.

It is my hope that after reading this anthology the reader will have a deeper understanding of the issues debated and will appreciate the complexity of even seemingly simple issues on which good and honest people disagree. This awareness is particularly important in a democratic society such as ours where people enter into public debate to determine the common good. Those with whom one disagrees should not necessarily be regarded as enemies, but perhaps simply as people who suggest different paths to a common goal.

The Format of SOURCES

In this anthology, carefully chosen opposing viewpoints are purposely placed back to back to create a running debate; each viewpoint is preceded by a short quotation that best expresses the author's main argument. This format instantly plunges the reader into the midst of a controversial issue and greatly aids that reader in mastering the basic skill of recognizing an author's point of view. In addition, the table of contents gives a brief description of each viewpoint, allowing the reader to identify quickly the point of view for which he or she is searching.

Each section of this anthology debates an issue, and the sections build on one another so that the anthology as a whole debates a larger issue. By using this step-by-step, section-by-section approach to understanding separate facets of a topic, the reader will have a solid background upon which to base his or her opinions. Each year a supplement of twenty opposing viewpoints will be added to this anthology, enabling the reader to keep abreast of annual developments.

This volume of Opposing Viewpoints SOURCES does not advocate a particular point of view. Quite the contrary! The very nature of the anthology leaves it to the reader to formulate the opinions he or she finds most suitable. My purpose as publisher is to see that this is made possible by offering a wide range of viewpoints that are fairly presented.

David L. Bender
Publisher

introduction

"Clearly it is meaningless to speak of victory in a large nuclear war, which is collective suicide."

Andrei Sakharov
February 1983

The real prospect of global nuclear war looms large in the world of the late twentieth century. Indeed, today, the world stockpile of nuclear armaments exceeds 50,000 warheads. This staggering figure roughly translates into 4 tons of TNT for every living human being. Since most of these weapons are controlled by the United States and the Soviet Union, the relationship between these two superpowers largely determines the world's future.

The nuclear arms buildup between the United States and the Soviet Union stems from conflicting ideologies; it is exacerbated by mutual distrust. Caspar Weinberger, Secretary of Defense, justifies US deterrence policy by explaining his belief that stockpiling nuclear arms deters a Soviet attack and is necessary to attain nuclear parity, or equality. He views the Soviet/American arms buildup as "an imbalance that. . .will only worsen if we do nothing to counter it." The Soviets in turn strive to attain their perception of a balance of that nuclear power. Andrei Gromyko, Soviet Minister of Foreign Affairs, sums up Soviet intentions: "Our policy. . .is to preserve at all costs the equality that has evolved over many years."

It may be argued that the deterrence policy has so far achieved peace because the pervading threat of a nuclear holocaust ensures that neither country will call the other's bluff. In defense of this poker game diplomacy, former US Secretary of State John Foster Dulles eloquently described the ability to be on the brink of war without actually getting into war "a necessary art." However, the arms race continues, even though nuclear disarmament talks receive worldwide importance and are given high priority by the United States and the Soviet Union.

Some organizations claim that before the US can opt out of the nuclear arms race, it must be freed of the Soviet threat of domination. According to groups such as the Committee on the Present Danger, the Soviet drive for dominance is the principal threat to the United States, to world peace, and to the cause of human freedom. They claim that no economic nor social sacrifice is too great to defend America against this danger. Others like Alan Wolfe, author of *The Rise and Fall of the Soviet Threat*, believe that it is not the Soviet threat that endangers the US "but the threat posed by those who would arm the United States to the teeth for reasons that have little to do with national security and much to do with politics."

The purpose of *Nuclear Arms* is to confront the reader with the complex issues and questions attending the worldwide proliferation of nuclear armaments. It is an anthology of opposing viewpoints concerning thirteen of the most important issues related to nuclear war and nuclear weapons. Each issue corresponds to one of the following chapter titles: The Soviet-American Debate, The Bomb and Its Effects, The Arms Race, Economics of the Arms Race, Missiles in Western Europe, The MX Missile Controversy, Nuclear Disarmament, The Nuclear Freeze, The Peace Movement, Paths to Peace, Catholic Bishops on War and Peace, The Morality of Nuclear Weapons, and High Frontier. The editors feel that if the reader grasps these issues, he or she will have a foundation upon which to form a personal opinion concerning nuclear arms in the current world.

"Our policy. . .is to preserve at all cost the equality, the principle of equality and equal security, that has evolved over many years."

The Soviets Must Arm Against America

Andrei Gromyko

This press conference was in a way prompted by statements made by the American President, mainly the latest of these. In them he touched upon a number of important issues of the international situation, the policy of the United States of America and the policy of the Soviet Union. In almost none of his speeches does the President miss the opportunity to speak about the policy of the Soviet Union. Some other questions that need to be elucidated have also accumulated.

What above all attracts attention in the recent speeches of the U.S. President and in his statement of March 30 and, I would say, in his April 1 statement, if one has European time in mind? The President said that in its foreign policy the United States, and, to be more precise, the present U.S. Administration, is guided by lofty moral values, pursues the aim of guarding and protecting the rights of peoples and that of adequately defending the interests of the United States of America regardless of what corner of the world these interests lie in.

But, of course, the U.S. President had and has his own understanding of the first, the second and the third. Lofty moral values cannot be defended by a state which is engaged in preparing for war, above all a nuclear war. If one asks whether it is possible to defend lofty moral values and at the same time to engage in preparations for a nuclear war in whose flames hundreds and hundreds of millions of people would die, every honest person will answer in the negative. A government engaged in preparations for a nuclear war, which, as many politicians and almost all scientists rightly say, would be a catastrophe for civilization on Earth, has no right to speak about defending lofty moral values in connection with its foreign policy activities.

American Interests

Apropos of defense of American interests. It would be

Andrei Gromyko, *Press Conference*, Moscow: Novosti Press Agency Publishing House, 1983.

a good thing if this meant defense of the legitimate interests of the United States of America, the defense of what really belongs to the U.S. But on the whole few people can be found in the world today who are not familiar with the way the formula "the defense of American interests" is understood in Washington. It appears that any corner of the world where Washington believes suitable conditions have been created for the U.S. to secure some moral, political, and especially military-strategic gains for itself, is proclaimed an area of American interests. Declarations are made that these should be defended with the utmost strength, including the force of arms. If one is to speak about all the specific facts, it would take a very long time.

Let each person think, for instance, about the Persian Gulf zone and adjoining waters. He will get a sufficiently convincing answer to the question as to how Washington understands "American interests," human rights and the rights of peoples. . . .

Soviet foreign policy is a policy of peace, a policy of friendship between peoples. It is a policy of non-interference in the internal affairs of other states. It is a policy aimed at easing tensions and defusing the tense international situation. Our policy aims at reversing the insane arms race. It is necessary, above all, to find ways to limit and reduce arms, and then to find ways to destroy arms. . . .

Soviet Proposals

The Soviet Union has proposed steps which nobody has a right to ignore without fully admitting his unconditional, open—I repeat, open—adherence to a militarist policy. What are these steps?

First. The Soviet Union has unilaterally assumed an obligation not to be the first to use nuclear weapons. It did not wait for the consent of other powers to that. This was a resolute and bold step. I think everyone present here will probably agree with this. The Soviet Union takes upon itself an obligation not to be the first

1

to use nuclear weapons, while the other nuclear powers did not even move a finger to advance in that direction. Yes, this is a bold and peaceloving step of ours. In the West they are not at all keen to speak of this. That is wrong.

Second. The Soviet Union and its friends and allies in the Warsaw Treaty decided at a meeting of the Political Consultative Committee to propose to the NATO countries that a treaty be concluded. On what? On the non-use of nuclear weapons and the non-use of conventional weapons, that is to say, on the non-use of any force at all in relations between the states of NATO and the Warsaw Treaty. Why was the proposal made in this form? Because there was a lot of demagogy in the West that the Soviet Union allegedly might launch an attack on a state or a group of states not necessarily with nuclear weapons but with conventional weapons. I repeat, this was, of course, demagogy. But those fabrications could mislead ill-informed people who are not conversant with foreign policy matters.

"Lofty moral values cannot be defended by a state which is engaged in preparing for war, above all a nuclear war."

The proposals put forward by the Warsaw Treaty member-countries undercut such arguments. We are prepared to sit at the negotiating table with the NATO countries even today and to discuss this issue, or, better still, to sign an appropriate document with reciprocal commitments not to use force against one another. . . .

Geneva Talks

I want to dwell on questions of nuclear weapons in Europe in connection with the talks now taking place between the Soviet Union and the United States. What is our view of their immediate prospects and of the present-day situation in this regard? To begin with, we would like to stress the fallacy of the claims made in Washington that, generally speaking, serious talks are being conducted in Geneva—that there is presumably no cause for alarm there, and the only thing to do is to pressure the Soviet Union and to strike a tougher posture, and then everything will be all right. They even claim: "The more pressure we put on the Soviet Union, the better the chances of agreement." This line is manifest in the specific proposals tabled at the talks.

The statements made in Washington contain many untruths, false assertions, misrepresentations and much juggling as regards factual data. It is necessary to dwell on this matter. To begin with, it is necessary to examine the assertion which has been formulated particularly explicitly in the latest statements of the U.S. President that his proposals with regard to medium-range missiles are a road to agreement, to peace.

This is wrong: they are not a road to peace and agreement. The gulf between agreement and these proposals will be even wider. Does everyone know that the President is leaving out whole components which are enormous both in importance and in scope? This relates to aviation, to nuclear delivery aircraft. They are not to be found in the statements and discourses of the American President. Neither politicians nor military leaders have the right to exclude this component from talks and agreements. What difference does it make to people what they die from—a nuclear warhead delivered by a missile or a nuclear warhead delivered by a plane? What was dropped on Hiroshima and Nagasaki was dropped from planes. And today planes can deliver even more horrendous weapons. How is it possible to exclude this entire component?

The delegations in Geneva have attempted to discuss this question. They tried to approach it. Nothing, however, came of that discussion. Why so? Because the U.S. representatives had instructions not to agree on that question. I shall cite an example.

They say: you see, medium-range planes can deliver not only nuclear weapons. They may serve a military and peaceful purpose. And for this reason, it is alleged, they cannot be included among nuclear weapons delivery vehicles. This would be the same as if someone described the most powerful and formidable ballistic missile, say, a land-based one, like this: it can deliver a nuclear warhead, but it can also be used for meteorological purposes, so it is better not to include it among those that deliver nuclear warheads. Absurdity? Yes, total absurdity. But it is essentially this position that is stated by official representatives expressing the opinion of the U.S. government.

Next. The United States has aircraft carriers and carrier-borne aviation. According to widely known data, at least six American aircraft carriers are especially fond of Europe. They are staying in the waters of Europe, in the Mediterranean, or near Europe—beyond the line which separates European waters from non-European waters and which they can cross in a matter of minutes. They are a tremendous force. Each aircraft carrier has about forty planes capable of carrying nuclear weapons. Yes, nuclear weapons.

Should we, the Soviet Union, close our eyes to this and not include the carrier-borne aircraft in the count? This is absurd. The intentions of a government which proposes we should close our eyes and not see this, are not serious. Therefore, any proposal which excludes a whole, we would say dreadful, component of the nuclear weapons delivery vehicles, such aircraft, from the count, is not serious. And it is impossible to look for agreement on this basis. . . .

Missiles in Western Europe

Britain and France have nuclear systems—missiles, nuclear missiles. The Soviet Union suggests that these be counted in the course of the talks. It is impossible to close our eyes to them, to believe they are non-existent and to seek agreement only on the American systems. For these missiles are a part of the common forces of the North Atlantic alliance. Many statements have been made on this score. There are hundreds—thousands if you want—of statements, most solemn ones, to the effect that the nuclear forces of Britain and France are an inseparable part of the nuclear forces of NATO as a whole. It is suggested that we seek agreements while leaving these nuclear forces aside. This is not a serious proposal. . . .

We envisage the possibility—this was mentioned by Yuri Andropov in making the well-known relevant proposal—that we might withdraw part of our missiles from Europe, from the European zone, to Asia, if an agreement were reached. This is our business and our right. And we are prepared to install them at sites from which they will not reach Western Europe. We have stated this at the talks and the U.S. Administration knows it. I repeat what we have said: we shall withdraw them to sites from which these missiles will not reach West European countries. But we are told: no, this is not enough. The arguments of the U.S. Administration and the President personally boil down to the demand that these missiles should be eliminated too. This demand alone precludes agreement.

Soviet Defense

These missiles pose no threat to European countries. But why are they needed? The Soviet Union needs them to ensure its security. It is common knowledge what a circle of American military bases surrounds the Soviet Union. Japan and the waters around it are stuffed with nuclear weapons and carriers for them. The island of Okinawa is a huge base of nuclear weapons. South Korea is a huge base or, rather, a complex of bases of nuclear weapons. The Indian Ocean, especially the Diego Garcia base, is bristling with nuclear weapons which can reach the Soviet Union. The Persian Gulf and adjoining waters are bristling with nuclear weapons. And, please note, I ask you to concentrate your attention: what is at issue is medium-range weapons. All these weapons can reach Soviet territory. Moreover—and if someone is not conversant with what I say, it will be especially interesting for him to know that—these weapons have within their range the whole of Siberia, the whole of the Asian part of the Soviet Union, even its northernmost part—the Taimyr Peninsula. And reference here is being made only to medium-range weapons. I do not mean here the U.S. strategic arms which exist and are deployed in the same areas that have been mentioned. Strategic arms are regulated by another agreement, an interim agreement, while it operates. The sides have agreed to extend the operation of that agreement. Consequently, only medium-range weapons are being taken into account. And so it is these

weapons that keep within their range the whole of the Asian territory of the Soviet Union. Doesn't the Soviet Union have a right, for the purposes of defense, to have something to match those weapons? It does have such a right.

They do not speak about all this publicly in the West, they do not tell the truth to the people. We are confident that if the people had been told the truth on the first, on the second and on the third questions, then people who are uninformed today would have changed their opinion—and most certainly not in favour of the U.S. Administration which is ignoring facts. But they simply do not talk about these facts; neither in the press, nor on the radio or over television are the facts mentioned, they are being hushed up. If you take the United States, their people hear from dawn till late at night only one and the same thing: the Soviet Union is a threat, it does not want to conclude agreements, it tables proposals which do not meet the U.S. line. And this instead of providing people with factual material to ponder over. No such material is provided. This may sound harsh, but one cannot help saying that in general it is deceptive propaganda that is being fed to the people, and that the picture that is being formed in these countries in the minds of the people, who are little informed through no fault of their own, is a totally distorted one.

"The Soviet Union has proposed steps which nobody has a right to ignore without fully admitting. . .adherence to a militarist policy."

As for the claim that the more pressure is put on the Soviet Union, the better are the chances of an agreement, it is also totally unserious. In a measure, it is, perhaps, explained by a lack of knowledge about the Soviet Union, a lack of knowledge, if you wish, about our character.

In short, the U.S. proposal is not a serious one. It is not designed to open up opportunities for an agreement with the Soviet Union. . . .

American Aggression

The line currently maintained at the talks in Geneva by the United States is not a line for rapprochement. It is a line of moving away from agreement, a line of complicating the situation, of whipping up the arms race even further, of worsening relations with the Soviet Union even further, securing an even faster growth of military budgets and containing the forces which favour finding a common language with the Soviet Union and resolving the problems of disarmament, to a greater degree. . . .

Thus, we may say in conclusion, having in mind the latest statements, mainly those by the U.S. President, that the "interim option," as the President has called his idea, is unacceptable, unacceptable for the following reasons.

First, it does not take into account the British and French medium-range nuclear systems, including 162 missiles.

Secondly, it does not take account of the many hundreds of American nuclear-capable planes based in Western Europe and on aircraft carriers.

Thirdly, the Soviet medium-range missiles in the Asian part of the U.S.S.R. would also be subject to liquidation, although they do not have any relation to Europe.

"The nuclear forces of Britain and France are an inseparable part of the nuclear forces of NATO as a whole."

On the whole, while at present NATO has a 1.5:1 superiority in medium-range nuclear warheads in Europe, in the event of the "interim option", as it is called by the President, being implemented, NATO would have almost 2.5 times as many such warheads as the Soviet Union. . . .It would be useful for everyone always to remember that our weapons, meaning medium-range weapons in Europe, cannot reach the territory of the United States. Such a task is not even set. As for the American weapons planned for deployment in Europe, each missile can reach the territory of the Soviet Union. This is a geographic factor. Whom does it favour? It favours the United States to the prejudice of the Soviet Union. But we do not ask for any compensation and we are not raising this question, although we could do so if we were working out the balance scrupulously and accurately. . . .

Nuclear Parity

Our policy on questions of both medium-range and strategic weapons, if one goes beyond the framework of Europe, is to preserve at all costs the equality, the principle of equality and equal security, that has evolved over many years. One may say that life itself has led to the principle of equality. This is not just the result of office work.

U.S. policy aims at breaking, destroying this principle. We shall do everything—with an agreement reached or without it—in order to preserve this principle. If it were violated as a result of the actions of the U.S. government and those of other NATO countries, then the Soviet Union would certainly—and there can be no two ways about it and no doubts in the mind of anyone—adopt such measures as are required to protect its legitimate interests so that this principle could continue to operate. And we will do it. For this, we have enough material and intellectual possibilities—there can be no doubt on this score. And we think that, properly speaking, those who bear the blame for the present situation also know this.

Andrei Gromyko is the U.S.S.R. Minister of Foreign Affairs.

"The Soviet Union has engaged in a relentless military buildup, overtaking and surpassing the United States in... acquiring...an offensive military capability."

America Must Arm Against the Soviets

Ronald Reagan

Last week I spoke to the American people about our plans for safeguarding this nation's security and that of our allies. And I announced a long-term effort in scientific research to counter, some day, the menace of offensive nuclear missiles. What I have proposed is that nations should turn their best energies to moving away from the nuclear nightmare. We must not resign ourselves to a future in which security on both sides depends on threatening the lives of millions of innocent men, women and children.

And today I would like to discuss another vital aspect of our national security—our efforts to limit and reduce the danger of modern weaponry.

We live in a world in which total war would mean catastrophe. We also live in a world that's torn by a great moral struggle—between democracy and its enemies, between the spirit of freedom and those who fear freedom.

In the last 15 years or more, the Soviet Union has engaged in a relentless military buildup, overtaking and surpassing the United States in major categories of military power, acquiring what can only be considered an offensive military capability. All the moral values which this country cherishes—freedom, democracy, the right of peoples and nations to determine their own destiny, to speak and write, to live and worship as they choose—all these basic rights are fundamentally challenged by a powerful adversary which does not wish these values to survive.

This is our dilemma, and it is a profound one: We must both defend freedom and preserve the peace. We must stand true to our principles and our friends while preventing a holocaust.

The Western commitment to peace through strength has given Europe its longest period of peace in a century. We cannot conduct ourselves as if the special danger of nuclear weapons did not exist. But we must

Ronald Reagan, speech delivered to the Los Angeles World Affairs Council, Beverly Hills, CA, March 31, 1983.

not allow ourselves to be paralyzed by the problem—to abdicate our moral duty.

This is the challenge that history has left us. We of the 20th century, who so pride ourselves on mastering even the forces of nature, except last week when the Queen was here. We are forced to wrestle with one of the most complex moral challenges ever faced by any generation.

Reducing Nuclear Danger

My views about the Soviet Union are well known, although sometimes I don't recognize them when they are played back to me, and our program for maintaining, strengthening and modernizing our national defense has been clearly stated. Today, let me tell you something of what we are doing to reduce the danger of nuclear war.

Since the end of World War II, the United States has been the leader in the international effort to negotiate nuclear arms limitations. In 1946, when the United States was the only country in the world possessing these awesome weapons, we did not blackmail others with threats to use them; nor did we use our enormous power to conquer territory, to advance our position or to seek domination. Doesn't our record alone refute the charge that we seek superiority, that we represent a threat to peace?

We proposed the Baruch plan for international control of all nuclear weapons and nuclear energy—for everything nuclear to be turned over to an international agency. This was rejected by the Soviet Union. Several years later, in 1955, President Eisenhower presented his "open skies" proposal: that the United States and the Soviet Union would exchange blueprints of military establishments and permit aerial reconnaissance to insure against the danger of surprise attack. This, too, was rejected by the Soviet Union.

Since then some progress has been made—largely at American initiative. The 1963 Limited Test Ban Treaty prohibited nuclear testing in the atmosphere, in outer space or under water. The creation of the hot line in 1963, upgraded in 1971, provides direct communication between Washington and Moscow to avoid miscalculation during a crisis. The Nuclear Nonproliferation Treaty of 1968 sought to prevent the spread of nuclear weapons.

In 1971 we reached an agreement on special communication procedures to safeguard against accidental or unauthorized use of nuclear weapons, and on a seabed arms control treaty which prohibits the placing of nuclear weapons on the seabed or the ocean floor. The Strategic Arms Limitation Agreements of 1972 imposed limits on antiballistic missile systems and on numbers of strategic offensive missiles. And the 1972 Biological Warfare Convention bans—or was supposed to ban—the development, production and stockpiling of biological and toxic weapons. But while many agreements have been reached, we have also suffered many disappointments. The American people had hoped, by these measures, to reduce tensions and start to build a constructive relationship with the Soviet Union.

Soviets Violate Agreements

Instead we have seen Soviet military arsenals continue to grow in virtually every significant category. We have seen the Soviet Union project its power around the globe. We have seen Soviet resistance to significant reductions and measures of effective verification, especially the latter.

And, I am sorry to say, there have been increasingly serious grounds for questioning their compliance with the arms control agreements that have already been signed, and that we have both pledged to uphold. I may have more to say on this in the near future.

Coming into office, I made two promises to the American people about peace and security: I promised to restore our neglected defenses, in order to strengthen and preserve the peace, and I promised to pursue reliable agreements to reduce nuclear weapons. Both these promises are being kept.

Today, not only the peace but also the chances for real arms control depend on restoring the military balance. We know that the ideology of the Soviet leaders does not permit them to leave any Western weakness unprobed, any vacuum of power unfilled. It would seem that to them negotiation is only another form of struggle.

Yet I believe the Soviets can be persuaded to reduce their arsenals—but only if they see it's absolutely necessary. Only if they recognize the West's determination to modernize its own military forces will they see an incentive to negotiate a verifiable agreement establishing equal, lower levels. And, very simply, that is one of the main reasons why we must rebuild our defensive strength.

All of our strategic force modernization has been approved by the Congress except for the land-based leg of the TRIAD. We expect to get Congressional approval on this final program later this spring. A strategic forces modernization program depends on a national bipartisan consensus.

Over the last decade, four successive Administrations have made proposals for arms control and modernization that have become embroiled in political controversy. No one gained from this divisiveness; all of us are going to have to take a fresh look at our previous positions. I pledge to you my participation in such a fresh look and my determination to assist in forging a renewed bipartisan consensus.

"We know that the ideology of the Soviet leaders does not permit them to leave any Western weakness unprobed, any vacuum of power unfilled."

My other national security priority on assuming office was to thoroughly re-examine the entire arms control agenda. Since then, in coordination with our allies, we have launched the most comprehensive program of arms control initiatives ever undertaken. Never before in history has a nation engaged in so many major simultaneous efforts to limit and reduce the instruments of war:

—Last month in Geneva the Vice President committed the United States to negotiate a total and verifiable ban on chemical weapons. Such inhumane weapons, as well as toxic weapons, are being used in violation of international law in Afghanistan, in Laos and Kampuchea.

—Together with our allies, we have offered a comprehensive new proposal for mutual and balanced reduction of conventional forces in Europe.

—We have recently proposed to the Soviet Union a series of further measures to reduce the risk of war from accident or miscalculation. And we are considering significant new measures resulting in part from consultations with several distinguished Senators.

—We have joined our allies in proposing a Conference on Disarmament in Europe. On the basis of a balanced outcome of the Madrid meeting, such a conference will discuss new ways to enhance European stability and security.

—We have proposed to the Soviet Union improving the verification provisions of two agreements to limit underground nuclear testing, but so far the response has been negative. We will continue to try.

—And, most importantly, we have made far-reaching proposals, which I will discuss further in a moment, for deep reductions in strategic weapons and for elimination of an entire class of intermediate-range weapons.

Commitment to Arms Control

I am determined to achieve real arms control—reliable agreements that will stand the test of time, not cosmetic agreements that raise expectations only to have hopes cruelly dashed.

In all these negotiations certain basic principles guide our policy:

—First, our efforts to control arms should seek reductions on both sides—significant reductions.

—Second, we insist that arms control agreements be equal and balanced.

—Third, arms control agreements must be effectively verifiable. We cannot gamble with the safety of our people and the people of the world.

—Fourth, we recognize that arms control is not an end in itself but a vital part of a broad policy designed to strengthen peace and stability.

It is with these firm principles in mind that this Administration has approached negotiations on the most powerful weapons in the American and Soviet arsenals—strategic nuclear weapons.

"Other countries' nuclear forces, such as the British and French, are independent and are not part of the bilateral U.S.—Soviet negotiations. . . .They are strategic weapons."

In June of 1982, American and Soviet negotiators convened in Geneva to begin the Strategic Arms Reduction Talks, what we call START. We have sought to work out an agreement reducing the levels of strategic weapons on both sides. I proposed reducing the number of ballistic missiles by one-half and the number of warheads by one-third. No more than half the remaining warheads could be on land-based missiles. This would leave both sides with greater security at equal and lower levels of forces.

Not only would this reduce numbers—it would also put specific limits on precisely those types of nuclear weapons that pose the most danger.

Counter Proposal

The Soviets have made a counter-proposal. We have raised a number of serious concerns about it—and this is important—they have accepted the concept of reductions. I expect this is because of the firm resolve that we've demonstrated. In the current round of negotiations, we have presented them with the basic elements of a treaty for comprehensive reductions in strategic arsenals. The United States also has, in START, recently proposed a draft agreement on a number of significant measures to build confidence and reduce the risks of conflict.

This negotiation is proceeding under the able leadership of Ambassador Edward Rowny on our side.

We are also negotiating in Geneva to eliminate an entire class of new weapons from the face of the earth.

Since the end of the mid-1970's the Soviet Union has been deploying an intermediate-range nuclear missile, the SS-20, at a rate of one a week. There are now 351 of these missiles, each with three highly accurate warheads capable of destroying cities and military bases in Western Europe, Asia and the Middle East.

NATO has no comparable weapon. Nor did NATO in any way provoke this new, unprecedented escalation. In fact, while the Soviets were deploying their SS-20's, we were taking 1,000 nuclear warheads from shorter-range weapons out of Europe.

This major shift in the European military balance prompted our West European allies themselves to propose that NATO find a means of righting the balance. And in December of 1979, they announced a collective, two-track decision:

—First, to deploy in Western Europe 572 land-based cruise missiles and Pershing 2 ballistic missiles capable of reaching the Soviet Union—the purpose to offset and deter the Soviet SS-20's. The first of these NATO weapons are scheduled for deployment by the end of this year.

—Second, to seek negotiations with the Soviet Union for the mutual reduction of these intermediate-range missiles.

In November of 1981 the United States, in concert with our allies, made a sweeping new proposal. NATO would cancel its own deployment if the Soviets eliminated theirs. The Soviet Union refused and set out to intensify public pressures in the West to block the NATO deployment, which has not even started. Meanwhile, the Soviet weapons continue to grow in number.

Agreement Standards

Our proposal was not made on a take-it-or-leave-it basis. We are willing to consider any Soviet proposal that meets these standards of fairness:

—An agreement must establish equal numbers for both Soviet and American intermediate-range nuclear forces.

—Other countries' nuclear forces, such as the British and French, are independent and are not part of the bilateral U.S.-Soviet negotiations. They are, in fact, strategic weapons and the Soviet strategic arsenal more than compensates for them.

—Next, an agreement must not shift the threat from Europe to Asia. Given the range and mobility of the SS-20's, meaningful limits on these and comparable American systems must be global.

—An agreement must be effectively-verifiable.

—And an agreement must not undermine NATO's ability to defend itself with conventional forces.

We have been consulting closely with our Atlantic

allies and they strongly endorse these principles. Earlier this week I authorized our negotiator in Geneva, Ambassador Paul Nitze, to inform the Soviet delegation of a new American proposal which has the full support of our allies.

We are prepared to negotiate an interim agreement to reduce our planned deployment if the Soviet Union will reduce their corresponding warheads to an equal level. This would include all U.S. and Soviet weapons of this class, wherever they are located.

Our offer of zero on both sides will, of course, remain on the table as our ultimate goal. At the same time we remain open, as we have been from the very outset, to serious counter proposals.

The Soviet negotiators have now returned to Moscow, where we hope our new proposal will receive careful consideration during the recess.

Ambassador Nitze has proposed and the Soviets have agreed that negotiations resume in mid-May, several weeks earlier than scheduled.

I'm sorry that the Soviet Union, so far, has not been willing to accept the complete elimination of these systems on both sides. The question I now put to the Soviet Government is, if not elimination, to what equal level are you willing to reduce?

The new proposal is designed to promote early and genuine progress at Geneva. For arms control to be truly complete and world security strengthened, however, we must also increase our efforts to halt the spread of nuclear arms.

Allies' Part

Every country that values a peaceful world order must play its part. Our allies, as important nuclear exporters, also have a very important responsibility to prevent the spread of nuclear arms. To advance this goal, we should all adopt comprehensive safeguards as a condition for nuclear supply commitments that we make in the future. In the days ahead, I will be talking to other world leaders about the need for urgent movement on this and other measures against nuclear proliferation.

Now that is the arms control agenda we have been pursuing. Our proposals are fair, they're far-reaching and comprehensive, but we still have a long way to go.

We Americans are sometimes an impatient people. I guess it's a symptom of our traditional optimism, energy and spirit. Often this is a source of strength. In a negotiation, however, impatience can be a real handicap. Any of you who have been involved in labor-management negotiations, or any kind of bargaining, know that patience strengthens your bargaining position. If one side seems too eager or desperate, the other side has no reason to offer a compromise and every reason to hold back, expecting that the more eager side will cave in first.

Well, this is a basic fact of life we can't afford to lose sight of when dealing with the Soviet Union. Generosity in negotiation has never been a trademark of theirs; it runs counter to the basic militancy of Marxist-Leninist ideology.

So it is vital that we show patience, determination and, above all, national unity. If we appear to be divided—if the Soviets suspect that domestic, political pressure will undercut our position—they will dig in their heels. And that can only delay an agreement and may destroy all hope for an agreement.

"Generosity in negotiation has never been a trademark of theirs; it runs counter to the basic militancy of Marxist-Leninist ideology."

That's why I have been concerned about the nuclear freeze proposals, one of which is being considered at this time by the House of Representatives. Most of those who support the freeze, I'm sure, are well intentioned—concerned about the arms race and the danger of nuclear war. No one shares their concern more than I do. But however well intentioned they are, these freeze proposals would do more harm than good.

They may seem to offer a simple solution. But there are no simple solutions to complex problems. As H.L. Mencken once wryly remarked, he said for every problem there is one solution which is simple, neat and wrong.

Freeze Dangerous

The freeze concept is dangerous for many reasons:

—It would preserve today's high, unequal and unstable levels of nuclear forces, and by so doing reduce Soviet incentives to negotiate for real reductions.

—It would pull the rug out from under our negotiators in Geneva, as they have testified. After all, why should the Soviets negotiate if they have already achieved a freeze in a position of advantage to them?

—Also, some think a freeze would be easy to agree on, but it raises enormously complicated problems of what is to be frozen, how it is to be achieved and, most of all, verified. Attempting to negotiate these critical details would only divert us from the goal of negotiating reductions, for who knows how long.

—The freeze proposal would also make a lot more sense if a similar movement against nuclear weapons were putting similar pressures on Soviet leaders in Moscow. As former Secretary of Defense Harold Brown has pointed out, the effect of the freeze "is to put pressure on the United States, but not on the Soviet Union."

—Finally, the freeze would reward the Soviets for their 15-year buildup while locking us into our existing equipment, which in many cases is obsolete and badly in need of modernization. Three-quarters of Soviet strategic warheads are on delivery systems five years old or less; three-quarters of the American strategic warheads are on delivery systems 15 years old or older. The time comes when everything wears out—the trouble is, it comes a lot sooner for us than for them. And, under a freeze, we couldn't do anything about it.

Our B-52 bombers are older than many of the pilots who fly them; if they were automobiles they would qualify as antiques. A freeze could lock us into obsolescence. It is asking too much to expect our service men and women to risk their lives in obsolete equipment. The two million patriotic Americans in the armed services deserve the best and most modern equipment to protect them—and us.

Presidential Dream

I'm sure every President has dreamt of leaving the world a safer place than he found it. I pledge to you, my goal—and I consider it a sacred trust—will be to make progress toward arms reductions in every one of the several negotiations now under way.

I call on all Americans, of both parties and all branches of government, to join in this effort. We must not let our disagreements or partisan politics keep us from strengthening the peace and reducing armaments.

I pledge to our allies and friends in Europe and Asia: We will continue to consult with you closely. We are conscious of our responsibility when we negotiate with our adversaries on conditions or issues of concern to you, and your safety and well-being.

"To the leaders and people of the Soviet Union, I say: Join us in the path to a more peaceful, secure world."

To the leaders and people of the Soviet Union, I say: Join us in the path to a more peaceful, secure world. Let us vie in the realm of ideas, on the field of peaceful competition. Let history record that we tested our theories through human experience, not that we destroyed ourselves in the name of vindicating our way of life. And let us practice restraint in our international conduct, so that the present climate of mistrust can some day give way to mutual confidence and a secure peace.

What better time to rededicate ourselves to this undertaking than in the Easter season, when millions of the world's people pay homage to the one who taught us peace on earth, good will toward men?

This is the goal, my fellow Americans, of all the democratic nations—a goal that requires firmness, patience and understanding. If the Soviet Union responds in the same spirit, we are ready. And we can pass on to our prosperity the gift of peace—that and freedom are the greatest gifts that one generation can bequeath to another. Thank you, and God bless you.

Ronald Reagan was elected President in 1980. U.S./U.S.S.R. relations have been a controversial topic of his administration.

"The purpose of the on-going nuclear arms race. . .is to back up U.S. uses of conventional armed forces overseas and to deter such uses of Soviet conventional forces."

Overview: The Nuclear Arms Debate from 1945

Randall Forsberg

What is the relationship of the nuclear arms race to the various roles of conventional military forces?

Most people in the United States believe that the purpose of US nuclear weapons is to deter a nuclear attack on the United States by the Soviet Union by threatening retaliation in kind.

This is undoubtedly one of the functions of US nuclear weapons, but it is not the only function, nor the function that motivates the continuation of the nuclear arms race between the United States and the Soviet Union.

The purpose of the on-going nuclear arms race, to the extent that there is any rational purpose, is to back up US uses of conventional armed forces overseas and to deter such uses of Soviet conventional forces. This connection between the roles of nuclear and conventional military forces is illustrated throughout the history of the nuclear arms race.

Initially, the United States developed nuclear weapons because we believed that there might be a nuclear program in Germany during World War II. We wanted to be able to respond to a potential nuclear threat with a nuclear response.

However, toward the end of World War II it became clear that Germany did not have a nuclear program; and that there was no nuclear threat to the Western allies. At that point the US nuclear program did not end. With great momentum, it continued right ahead.

During the four-year wartime Manhatten project, the United States produced enough fissionable uranium and plutonium to make just three nuclear bombs. We tested one of them in the desert, and we used the other two on Hiroshima and Nagasaki.

This use of nuclear weapons had nothing to do with deterring a nuclear attack on the United States or anyone else. The United States used nuclear weapons that had been produced for two reasons.

Randall Forsberg, "A Nuclear Freeze & Non-Interventionary Conventional Policy." Position paper available from, *Institute for Defense and Disarmament Studies*, 251 Harvard St., Brookline, MA 02146. Reprinted with permission.

One was to end a conventional war with, it was argued, less loss of life than would occur if the war continued. It was claimed that it might take 500,000 American lives to recapture all of the Pacific islands from the Japanese, in bloody, over-the-beach warfare. The bombs dropped on Hiroshima and Nagasaki killed, immediately, about 100,000 persons each. So nuclear weapons were seen as a means of decreasing death and violence and ending the war more quickly. They were intimately interrelated with the pursuit of conventional warfare goals.

The second reason probably played a great role in the dropping of the second bomb, on Nagasaki. For the bomb on Hiroshima should have been enough (if even that was needed) to make the Japanese sue for total surrender, which were the only terms permitted to them.

The function of the second bomb, if not the first, was to intimidate the Soviet Union: as a precedent for the post-war environment, to make clear that the United States not only had a nuclear monopoly, but was prepared to use it. The demonstration was intended to show that, if the Soviet Union used its conventional forces in a manner objectionable to the United States, the USA would not hesitate to respond with nuclear weapons. Thus, again, nuclear policy was inextricably intertwined with conventional war and power politics.

Post-War Nuclear Policies

During the period from 1945 to 1955 the United States continued to have a virtual monopoly on nuclear weapons. US policy in this period was called "massive retaliation." Its purpose was to deter Soviet uses of conventional military force by threatening simply to wipe out the major cities of the Soviet Union in response. In 1950 the United States had 300 nuclear bombs on 300 propeller-driven planes. Those were all the nuclear weapons in the world. They were not very many by present day standards; and they might well have been used against population targets because they were, relatively speaking, so few in number.

By 1960, the Soviet Union had acquired nuclear weapons and the means to deliver them to the United States. It had at that time 150 strategic bombers that could reach this country, together with several hundred nuclear missiles and about 500 bombers that could reach Western Europe.

"In 1950 the United States had 300 nuclear bombs on 300 propeller-driven planes. Those were all the nuclear weapons in the world."

In the interval, the United States had deployed 2000 strategic bombers, loaded, ready-to-go, and aimed at the Soviet Union: 600 B52s and 1400 shorter-range B47s stationed at overseas bases. The USA had also built up a force of about 10,000 tactical nuclear weapons. These are short-range nuclear weapons aimed primarily at military targets: anti-aircraft missiles with nuclear tips; antisubmarine torpedoes with nuclear tips; and surface-to-surface missiles to use on the battlefield against oncoming enemy tank formations, including missiles with a range of 400 miles that would go from West Germany to East Germany, as well as missiles with a range of 70 miles, missiles with a range of 30 miles, and even 8-inch howitzers with a range of 15 miles, for use on the battlefield in West Germany. (The neutron bomb is an antitank weapon that is designed to emit enough radiation not merely to kill the men driving the tanks but to make them die in a matter of minutes or hours rather than days or weeks.)

Accompanying the deployment of tactical nuclear weapons, the United States maintained the policy in effect since the end of World War II of posing a threat of first use of nuclear weapons. If the USA became involved in a conventional war with the Soviet Union, and the war was going against this country, we would be ready (on someone else's territory) to escalate up to the use of our tactical nuclear weapons against Soviet conventional forces.

Until the mid-1960s, the United States still had such a marked superiority in both intercontinental and Europe-oriented nuclear weapons that it could continue to pose this threat with some confidence. The USA built up its original strategic missile force much sooner than the Soviet Union did. Both on land and on submarines the main force of invulnerable US missiles was deployed between 1960 and 1967. At that time, the Soviet Union was still relying on its few intercontinental bombers and on 200 vulnerable ICBMs. Neither the Soviet bombers nor the ICBMs were ready to launch, and both could have been destroyed in a preemptive strike.

The Soviet Union first began to acquire nuclear forces that gave it an invulnerable, second-strike deterrent in 1965. This is when the USSR started building ICBMs in steel-reinforced concrete underground silos. The Soviet Union deployed 1400 such ICBMs over the period 1965-1971. It started building submarines with long-range missiles deployed in range of the United States only in 1967; and it built up a force of sixty-two strategic submarines between 1967 and 1977.

Thus, it is only in this last 15 years that US cities have become unavoidably hostage to a Soviet missile strike that could take place in half an hour. It is only because we failed to stop the arms race in 1960 that we are exposed to this threat today.

During the last decade there has been widespread recognition of parity betwen the USA and USSR in nuclear forces. What this means is not that the Soviet Union can match all the esoteric nuclear capabilities of the United States, but that, for the first time, it can match the all-important, "bottom-line" second-strike capability: it can retain the forces to obliterate the USA in a second strike, no matter what sort of counterforce attack the United States undertakes first.

While the Soviet Union was still building up its main generation of strategic missiles, between 1970 and 1977, the United States took out most of the missiles that it had on land and on submarines and replaced them with new missiles with multiple nuclear warheads or MIRVs (multiple, independently-targetable re-entry vehicles).

In 1976, in a program that was perfectly predictable, the USSR started doing the same thing: replacing its main ICBM and submarine-launched missiles with new MIRVed missiles. The Soviet MIRV program has now been completed on land but is still under way on submarines, where it probably will not be completed until 1985.

Effort to Recapture Superiority

The response of the United States to Soviet acquisition of an invulnerable deterrent force over the last 15 years is to try to recapture the clear superiority that it had until the mid-1960s. The attempt to do this is being made by developing and deploying the MX missile, which will have the ability to destroy Soviet ICBMs in their silos; and by adding a new submarine-based missile, the Trident II, and a new type of missile, the cruise missile, which will provide thousands of additional nuclear warheads with precision attack capability.

In addition to these new offensive nuclear forces, the United States already has an extraordinary antisubmarine warfare (ASW) capability built, as described earlier, in response to Soviet conventional submarines. The US ASW capability has been strengthened for operations against strategic submarines. The United States has large sonar towers off the coast of Norway, off the Azores, and off the Japanese Islands. These are attached by cable to a giant computer processing center, which can dampen out all of the other noises in the ocean and leave in only the noises of Soviet submarines. Under good conditions, Soviet submarines can actually be tracked all the way across the Atlantic by means of these sonar towers. Soviet submarines come out of narrow port exits. They are rather poorly designed and noisy. The port exits are surrounded by US, Japanese and British antisub submarines and aircraft.

As a result of this ASW capability, when the United States acquires the MX in the late 1980s, it will be back in a position similar to that of the 1950s and 1960s, when it could threaten a preemptive strike against most Soviet medium-range and intercontinental nuclear forces.

There will be very important differences, though, between the earlier situation and that in 1990. When the USA threatened a preemptive strike earlier, the number of targets (airfields and missile groups) that it would strike was relatively small, a few hundred; and the Soviet Union had no capability to launch its missiles on warning of an incoming attack. Today and in the future that will not be the case. The Soviet generals can now launch their missiles, just as the United States can, when their radar screens show that the opponent's missiles have been launched. In addition, current US counterforce attack scenarios provide for the use of several thousand nuclear warheads against the large Soviet missile forces. The Soviets could send back to the United States a retaliatory attack of equal magnitude.

The effect of even a limited counterforce exchange between the two superpowers, with nuclear warheads directed against the nuclear forces of the opposing side, has been calculated to be between three and twenty million dead in the United States and a like number in the USSR, simply from downwind fallout of the explosions on missile sites.

"It is only in this last 15 years that U.S. cities have become unavoidably hostage to a Soviet missile strike that could take place in half an hour."

This is the most easily predictable effect. No one has the faintest notion of what would happen to the global ecology if 4000-8000 nuclear weapons were exploded in a very short space of time. The ozone layer would be blown away. The fallout would increase the background level of radiation and darken the sky worldwide. Tremendous firestorms would be created. These things combined would create changes in the world's climate which could be cumulative and synergistic....

The main region for nuclear deterrence of conventional war is Europe. But this is a very stable region, in which conventional war between East and West is highly unlikely: both sides have too little to gain and too much to lose. Where conventional war remains

quite likely, and thus, where the nuclear backup may actually be believed to play an active role in shaping the course of events, is in the third world. In this sense, the purpose of the on-going nuclear arms race is, from the point of view of the USA, to give the United States greater freedom to intervene in developing countries without risking a conventional challenge on the part of the Soviet Union; and to inhibit Soviet conventional intervention. From the point of view of the USSR, the purpose of trying to match US nuclear developments is to nullify the nuclear factor in global power politics.

The US generals calculate that, if they can show on paper that a direct conventional confrontation between the two superpowers could escalate to a local or intercontinental nuclear exchange that would leave the US ahead by some measure, then the Soviet generals will not risk sending in conventional forces in the first place; nor will they feel free to intervene themselves in developing countries where Western stakes are high, which was not the case in Afghanistan.

Randall Forsberg is director of the Insitute for Defense and Disarmament Studies.

"Whatever position we eventually take on the subjects of arms and arms control, it is imperative that we begin to get a grasp on the weapons themselves."

Overview: The Nuclear Arms Debate in the 80s

Sheila Tobias and Shelah Leader

When we first began to learn about defense, we thought that we would give the weapons short shrift. Our interest was in military strategy and military spending. But we have since changed our minds. It is the weapons and what they are capable of doing that seem to drive military spending and to shape our national security options. Yet it is the weapons that are most awesome and difficult to grasp. On the frontiers of engineering design and applied science, they present us with an ever-increasing technological capability that seems impossible to stop. Thus, whatever position we eventually take on the subjects of arms and arms control, it is imperative that we begin to get a grasp on the weapons themselves.

The United States and the Soviet Union—to give some concrete examples—now have airplanes that can be programmed to reach a speed of 700 miles per hour and fly 50 feet off the ground, skipping over hillocks and telephone poles (the terrain being continuously "observed" by complex radar linked to computers); missiles whose accuracy over a 6,000-mile path permits a hit within 500 to 1,000 feet of their target from anywhere in the United States to anywhere in the Soviet Union (after passing through the earth's atmosphere twice and traveling at 20,000 miles per hour); armored tanks so massive that they can easily drive through a house; guided bombs and air-launched cruise missiles so accurate that they can be launched from planes flying hundreds of miles away; radar able to "see" for thousands of miles; air transport planes that are bigger than high-rise buildings, capable of hauling hundreds of soldiers and hundreds of thousands of pounds of equipment; not to mention massive aircraft carriers that hold 6,000 people, and nuclear-powered submarines cruising underwater for 60 to 70 days without having to surface for fuel, air, or supplies.

The amazing and continually evolving possibilities created by technology—as well as the drive to stay ahead or at least match the other side—increase the Pentagon's appetite for more and better weapons with which to defend the U.S. The new weapons systems represent about one-third of the annual Pentagon budget, and the President has mandated $615 billion for "weapons modernization" over the next six years; a staggering commitment of our total national resources directed to defense.

Part of the plan is to spend $78 billion for bombers and cruise missiles (small pilotless airplanes equipped with warheads); $51 billion for sea-based weapons; $42 billion for intercontinental ballistic missiles (guided missiles launched from an upright position); $22 billion for command, control, and communications; $29 billion for air and missile defense—most for new weapons to replace and supplement current ones.

For fiscal year 1983, defense spending is budgeted at more than double that of health, social services, and housing combined. It isn't just the advocates of human services who have criticized these plans. The *Wall Street Journal* points out that the 1983 military budget alone will exceed total corporate profits (after taxes) for any year in our history. It is about 50 percent larger than the combined federal outlays for health, education, job-training, agriculture, energy, environment, transportation, natural resources, and law enforcement. A single nuclear-powered submarine and its missiles will cost about the same amount as total yearly U.S. outlays for both cancer research and refugee aid.

How is all this weaponry supposed to make us more secure?

Some of our most terrifying and expensive weapons exist *not* to be used. Strategic nuclear missiles and bombs ("strategic" designating those that can reach the U.S. from the Soviet Union—and vice versa—or from submarines at sea) are neither offensive nor defensive but deterrent. This means that they can be used to at-

Sheila Tobias and Shelah Leader, "An Intelligent Woman's Guide to the Military Mind," *MS.*, July/August 1982. Reprinted with authors' permission.

tack and punish the enemy *after* he attacks. Unlike all previous weapons known in history, however, they cannot shield us; that is, they cannot prevent damage to the country and its population. Each side buys these weapons for the express purpose of keeping the other side from using theirs.

Since both the United States and the Soviet Union have more than enough nuclear warheads to destroy each other many times over (30,000 warheads and bombs for us, roughly 20,000 for them)—you're probably asking yourself: Why do we keep building more? The answer lies partly in technology and partly in doctrine. According to the theory of deterrence, several preconditions must exist. First, the enemy must know, roughly, how much and what kinds of nuclear weapons we have: what our "capability" is. Second, the enemy must believe in our willingness to use our weapons: we must have "credibility."

As one expert puts it, "It's not enough to have enough weapons. You must be *seen* to have enough."

Once this theory is understood, the drive toward increasing the number and effectiveness of our weapons follows. If we are to remain "credible," we have to be able to match or keep ahead of every advance in Soviet technology; and, since we don't want to be surprised by some new missile, bomber, or radar system that our rival produces, we have to continue to develop everything we can. As a result, despite an existing atmospheric test ban and some attempts to put ceilings on the number of nuclear weapons each side possesses, the total number of strategic nuclear weapons deployed by both sides has more than doubled in the past 10 years.

The typical nuclear weapon is either a bomb—carried on bombers—or a warhead, loaded on a land or sea-based missile. Each of these weapons is from three to 75 times more powerful than either of the two atomic bombs dropped on the Japanese cities of Hiroshima and Nagasaki. Together, the United States and the Soviet Union have 50,000 of these devices.

Many people argue that deterrence could work just as well with fewer nuclear weapons on both sides because we already have "mutual assured destruction" (MAD, as it's called) capability.

MIRVs

One reason for the enormous mutual increase in total explosive power has to do with a new technology called MIRVing. Most of our newest missiles (and those of the Soviet Union as well) are fitted with multiple independently targetable reentry vehicles (MIRVs), separate warheads that ride on the tip of the missile, called the "bus." All are programmed to fly off, each in a different predetermined direction, when the missile approaches enemy territory. They will then detonate at different (and very distant) locations. Because of MIRVing, many missiles in our arsenal (and in the Soviet's arsenal) are significantly more powerful than missiles used to be.

For many years, our mutual capacity to destroy one another—with each country's missiles targeted all the time on key military and industrial targets in the other—seemed a sufficient "assurance" that neither side would try to engage the other in nuclear war. But a second change in the mid-1970s, in addition to MIRVing, made both sides fear that its weapons were in jeopardy.

Where previous nuclear "delivery systems," as they are called, would land as much as a mile or more from their intended targets, today's accuracy permits both sides, for the first time, to hit the other side's "hard targets"—most particularly their underground missile silos (the concrete tubes in which land-based missiles are stored and from which they are launched). This new capability has given rise to new fears for the "survivability" of our retaliatory force. As a result, the military has come up with new doctrines for the protection and limited use of nuclear weapons.

"It is the weapons and what they are capable of doing that seem to drive military spending and to shape our national security options."

The new U.S. doctrine, sketched out in the summer of 1980 by President Carter's Presidential Directive Number 59, is called the "countervailing strategy." It calls for expanding U.S. capacity to fight a so-called limited nuclear war. The intent of this policy is to enhance deterrence by demonstrating the readiness of the U.S. to respond to limited nuclear attacks against some or all of our nuclear forces without having to escalate immediately to all-out nuclear war. The flaw in this logic, which was recognized by Carter's Secretary of Defense Harold Brown at the time, is that *any* use of nuclear weapons by the superpowers, especially against each other's homeland, is very likely to escalate to general nuclear war. Nonetheless, the Reagan Administration has also embraced such a limited nuclear war doctrine.

The United States' response to improvements in Soviet long-range missile accuracy includes another planning scenario that goes like this: with the Soviet Union's new accuracy, it has acquired the theoretical capability to knock out (in about 30 minutes) most of our 1,052 land-based missiles in their "hardened" (reinforced) silos, plus all of our long-range bombers not on alert; that is, not already in the air. This explains why President Reagan, while running for office in 1980, claimed we have a "window of vulnerability," and why the MX missile, with its mobile basing scheme, was proposed two years ago.

To make sense of all this, and to critically examine the current arguments for increased defense spending, we must begin with an overview of what this country currently has.

For nearly 20 years now our long-range intercontinental weapons have been cleverly dispersed not only geographically but also functionally in a so-called Triad. The Triad consists of: (1) land-based missiles (1,052 of them); (2) Air Force bombers (about 320); and (3) a fleet of nuclear-powered missile-bearing submarines (32). All told, they carry about 9,500 nuclear weapons. The Soviets, too, have a Triad, although somewhat different from our own: 1,400 land-based missiles; 150 bombers; more than 60 missile-bearing submarines. All told, theirs carry about 7,800 nuclear weapons.

"The amazing and continually evolving possibilities created by technology. . . increase the Pentagon's appetite for more and better weapons with which to defend the U.S."

In addition to these long-range or "strategic" systems, we have shorter range "tactical" or "theater" nuclear weapons positioned in Europe (and current plans call for replacing some of these with new longer-range weapons capable of hitting the Soviet Union from Europe).

To protect our stationary, land-based missiles from attack, we have relied in the past on their being in underground, hardened concrete silos. But the new accuracy of Soviet missiles means they might be hit so directly that they would be destroyed: "put in the crater" as it is said. Thus, our land-based missiles have begun—to some people—to look less like deterrents and more like vulnerable targets.

The MX Missile

To make them more resistant to this kind of attack, the Air Force came up with the idea in 1976 of building new and more powerful missiles (both in terms of their accuracy and the number of MIRVed warheads they can carry) that would be "untargetable" because they would be constantly moving from one missile shelter to another. This was the origin of the MX or "missile experimental." The plan was to hide 200 missiles among 4,600 underground bunkers over 12,000 to 15,000 square miles of Utah and Nevada. Each missile would "live" in a cluster of its own 23 bunkers and be moved at random among them. To further confuse the enemy (which has the ability to monitor all our weapons through satellite photography), we would have had to put 22 dummy missiles in each silo cluster. The media promptly dubbed the scheme the "shell game."

The costly mobile-basing-scheme (about $100 billion) aroused strong protests in the normally pro-defense states of Nevada and Utah. As a result, President Reagan has currently scrapped the scheme and decided to build the new missiles and for now put them into ex-isting silos. Critics point out that this doesn't solve the "vulnerability" argument. Others say the threat to land-based missiles has been grossly overstated anyway: the scenarios put forward are fine for weapons' analysts to play out on their computers, but hardly anything a sane political leader would contemplate, let alone undertake, because of the enormous uncertainties involved.

The B-1 Bomber

Nonetheless, the maddening "logic" of technology can also be seen in another current weapons controversy, this one involving the B-1 bomber.

One leg of our Triad, as we have seen, is airborne. For 30 years now, the Air Force has relied on B-52 bombers (the same ones we used in Vietnam), which carry both nuclear bombs and short-range attack missiles called SRAMs. The Air Force wants to replace the B-52 with a new plane, the B-1, at a current cost estimate of $200 million to $400 million each.

This sleek new plane has been designed specifically to evade new and improved Soviet radar. Owing to its shape, it has a "lower radar profile." But there is another way to evade Soviet radar and perform the same task (or "mission" in military jargon) and that is to keep the bombers at a distance from their targets and to have them launch so-called cruise missiles instead. In 1977, President Carter decided not to produce the B-1, but to upgrade the B-52s with cruise missiles. President Reagan has revived the B-1. Unless Congress votes it down in the course of the 1982 legislative session, 100 planes are now scheduled to be produced at a cost of $40 billion.

Some critics believe that by the late 1980s when significant numbers of B-1s are expected to be in service with the Air Force, the plane will have been made obsolete by a new aircraft called "Stealth." The Stealth bomber, with highly classified design features and special coatings, will be even more radar-invisible. It exists currently only on paper so we don't know if it will work. Reagan has, nonetheless, pursued all three paths. He has approved the B-1, authorized continued research on Stealth, *and* ordered 3,000 cruise missiles for the B-52.

The Nuclear-Powered Submarine

This Administration is also committed to expanding and improving our naval forces. This has fueled an intense debate over the kind and number of ships we need. One controversy surrounds the Administration's decision to build more (nuclear-powered) aircraft carriers. The aircraft carrier is more than a ship: it is a golden memory among military men because it won the war against the Japanese fleet in World War II. But as $3.5 billion each, with high vulnerability to the omnipresent cruise missiles, which all ships are now being equipped with, many say it is not a bargain at any price.

Of all the weapons now in our arsenal or soon to be added to it, none seems more modern and invincible than the sea-based leg of our Triad: the nuclear-powered missile submarine. We have 32 of these which, together, carry 520 long-range missiles bearing a total of some 4,700 nuclear warheads.

If you hadn't been following weapons developments over the past 20 years (as we had not), you may not have noticed that the submarine is no longer just an antiship weapon. Instead, it has become (since the early 1960s) a movable missile-launching pad. It is so quiet, fast and independent of surface supplies—and the missiles on any of our submarines are capable of reaching almost anywhere in the world—that some analysts argue that we no longer need a Triad of nuclear weapons, but only a fleet of missile-bearing submarines.

On the other hand, if the United States concentrates all retaliatory potential in submarines, the Soviet Union might devote its full research effort to submarine-detection devices that could make U.S. submarines vulnerable again in a few years' time. Technology has come to have a life of its own. The arms race is, in part simply an effort to keep up with the breathless pace of change.

"The submarine is no longer just an anti-ship weapon. Instead, it has become (since the early 1960s) a movable missile-launching pad."

Even conventional (nonnuclear) weapons have become increasingly complex, sophisticated, and expensive. Although they are highly "capable" by some standards, they are often unreliable because their complex components break down, and difficult to buy in large numbers because of their expense. This breeds further controversy over the advantages of buying such weapons. For example, 776 of the United States' latest tank, the M-1 (which is now in production), cost $2 billion, the same amount of money (in constant 1982 dollars) that would have purchased 6,000 tanks in the 1950s. It's not just inflation; it is complexity. The M-1 goes faster, has a special armor to protect it against one kind of antitank shell (but not another) and has an accompanying bulldozer type vehicle (dubbed by the press as its "valet") to dig holes for it. (Tanks sometimes fire from behind embankments for self-protection, much like soldiers using foxholes.)

The quest for "high performance" is part of the story of defense procurement and cost overruns and will be addressed in our next article. But the essential dilemma is the difficulty of getting off this technological treadmill. Even if we could agree with the Soviets not to pursue new technologies, such agreements depend on the ability of each side to verify to its own satisfaction that the other side is adhering to the agreement. But how can we "verify" what is going on in laboratories and in the heads of scientists? And how can we "limit" or "ban" technological innovations that haven't been thought of yet?

The possibilites of technology are almost limitless. We are now talking about "war in space" with antisatellite weapons, laser and particle beams. Still, the decisions about whether to develop, buy or use a given technology are *not* beyond our control; technology is the medium, but politics is still the message. An interested and better-informed citizenry can make itself felt: witness the current popular movement for a nuclear freeze.

But we must understand the dynamics if we are to change it.

This viewpoint has been published by William Morrow, Inc. in an expanded version as the book What Kind of Guns Are They Buying for Your Butter? A Beginner's Guide to Defense Weaponry and Military Spending *(1982). The book will also be available in paperback under the title* The People's Guide to National Defense.

"Let us not be duped by the Soviets' war of words. Let their actions be testimony to their real intentions in the world."

viewpoint **5**

The Soviets Are a Threat

William Broomfield

I want to share a few thoughts about the Soviet Union and its real intentions in the world. I believe that many of you will agree with me in saying that duplicity and threats characterize Soviet behavior in the international arena.

During the so-called period of detente, the United States honestly complied both with the letter and spirit of the understanding. We reduced American military expenditures and weapons modernization efforts. Our foreign policy became almost passive and inactive.

The Soviets, on the other hand, modernized weapons systems and introduced new ones. Their military budgets grew steadily. Their long-range and more aggressive foreign policy brought Soviet involvement and influence in Southeast Asia, Central America, Africa and the Middle East. Needless to say, their Cuban surrogates furthered the Soviets' objectives in many countries. Afghanistan and Poland are recent examples of the Soviets' expansionist policies. Unfortunately, detente is dead. Soviet duplicity killed it.

Destroyed Parity

During the period of detente, a rough nuclear weapons parity existed in Europe. While the Soviets talked peace, and stressed the importance of harmony in international relations, they installed more than 300 medium-range theater missiles in Europe. This effectively destabilized the previous balance of forces in the area. This deployment worried both the United States and our NATO partners.

In response to this new threat, NATO announced plans to deploy U.S. Pershing and cruise missiles in 1979. The Soviets immediately began a massive disinformation and propaganda campaign directed against this planned effort. The Soviets painted themselves as peace-loving while describing NATO and the United States as warmongers who would bring about the end of the world. The freeze movement quickly spread throughout Europe to the United States.

The Soviets directed a wilting propaganda barrage at Germany just prior to the recent election. When the Kremlin failed to sway the German people, they resorted to hard threats and intimidating statements against Germany and NATO itself. Even Japan, with modest military capability, was subjected to a formidable threat by the Soviets threatening to put Japan in its place if it did not behave.

To deflect attention away from the real issues, Soviet SS-20s in Europe and the Soviets' refusal to remove these weapons of destruction, the Kremlin began raising the tension level between the East and West. They accused the United States of stalling in the INF talks and of being intransigent.

In the early March, Soviet Central Committee Deputy Chief Zagladin said that if the Pershing and cruise missiles were deployed, the Soviets would "deploy missiles equivalent to Pershing IIs with an equally rapid flight time in the vicinity of the United States."

War of Words

On Swedish television, Soviet Gen. Chervov said that the so-called Soviet countermeasures would not only affect those European states where missiles are sighted, but U.S. territory as well.

Let us not be duped by the Soviets' war of words. Let their actions be testimony to their real intentions in the world. In spite of their promises during detente, they increased their military prowess. In spite of their claims to want peace, they invaded Afghanistan. In spite of their statements regarding arms parity in Europe, they deployed SS-20s.

During the House debate on the nuclear freeze question, they skillfully threatened to deploy missiles near our shores if we failed to acquiesce. Let us not be swayed by their well-orchestrated disinformation and

William Broomfield, "The Soviet War of Words," *The Washington Times*, March 29, 1983. Reprinted with permission.

19

propaganda efforts. Let us vote to keep America and our allies strong.

William Broomfield is a Republican Congressman from Michigan.

"The serious question is not what the men in the Kremlin dream of doing, but what they are actually capable of doing."

The Soviets Are Not a Threat

Joseph Harsch

According to President Reagan the Soviet Union of today is an "evil empire" engaged in "power projection" aimed at "eventual domination of all peoples of the earth."

This is strong stuff. Obviously, it is the kind of language Mr. Reagan and/or his advisers think is best calculated both to whip Congress into line behind the President's current and all-time high arms program and also to give his own Republican Party a political advantage over the Democrats come next election day.

The political angle is easy to work out. The Democrats are bound to cut back to some extent on that arms program, partly because they want the money for social programs and partly because they honestly believe that some of it is there not because the world situation justifies it but because Mr. Reagan wants to do a favor to the corporate makers of armaments.

Inevitably the Democrats will cut back on some of the arms program and inevitably most Republicans will vote for it. Then, come next election time, the President will apply to the Democrats a modern version of that old charge of being "soft on communism" which worked so well for the Republicans back during the times immediately after World War II.

The political advantage to the Republicans from maneuvering the Democrats into having to vote against some part of the arms program is so obvious that one can't help wondering whether the program was deliberately inflated just for that purpose.

Be that as it may, the important question for the ordinary citizen watching all this from the sidelines of the political arena is how frightened he ought to be by the President's alarming rhetoric. Are the Soviets really about to gobble up the world?

First let us take up the question of what the Soviets actually seek. Do they really aim at eventual domination of all the peoples of the earth?

Without doubt there are people in the Kremlin who daydream of some happy moment when the whole world would be communist and subservient to the will of Moscow. But that kind of dreaming is a characteristic of eager people around the throne of any great imperial power.

The Spaniards certainly dreamed of world dominion when their great Armada set sail for England. King Louis XIV of France had far-ranging ambitions. Napoleon had even farther-ranging dreams. He was perhaps the first to think in terms of possibly getting effective control over the entire world. Had he conquered Russia he would have had exactly that.

But wanting something like that and getting it are two different matters. There have been people in Washington in modern times who also dream of effective control over the world. Had the Soviet Union collapsed just after World War II the United States would have been in effective control of everything. One reason that there is so much friction between Moscow and Washington is that either one would be the effective world ruler were it not for the existence of the other.

Both in Washington and Moscow people yearn for total security. In both cases total security could come about were the other to disappear.

But then, neither the US nor the USSR is going to disappear; certainly not in the visible future. The two are likely to exist for quite a while, and continue to irritate, frustrate, worry, and frighten each other. And both will engage in "power projection," as both have been doing since they became the only two superpowers in the world.

Severe Limitations

The serious question is not what the men in the Kremlin dream of doing, but what they are actually capable of doing. On that, there are severe limitations.

For one thing, China went Marxist, and was briefly

under Moscow discipline, but has long since become Moscow's biggest concern next only to its concern over the US.

For another thing, in the news only this week we learn that the revolutionary government in Iran is barely on speaking terms with Moscow these days in spite of its strong dislike of the US. One would think that the Soviets could capitalize on Iran's break with Washington to get on good terms with the Ayatollah Khomeini. In three years they have failed.

"There is considerable evidence that U.S. estimates of Soviet and Warsaw Pact military expenditures are calculated incorrectly and are presented in a misleading way."

The Soviets engage in a lot of attempted "power projection," particularly where it irritates Washington the most—in Central America. But overall they are worse off today than when they had both China and Egypt on their side. They are actually on the downhill side of power projection.

So, much as they may dream of ruling the world, they are farther away from it today than they were 10 or 20 years ago.

This viewpoint originally appeared in the Christian Science Monitor, *a well-known national newspaper.*

"The chief purpose of our military establishment has been to win wars. From now on its chief purpose must be to avert them."

Nuclear Deterrence: A Historical Perspective

Fred Kaplan

Those who believe that deterrence should be the sole policy and that this requires only a small nuclear arsenal generally take their cues from the earliest writings of Bernard Brodie, the father of nuclear strategy, who in 1946, just months after Hiroshima, wrote:

> "The first and most vital step in any American security program for the age of atomic bombs is to take measures to guarantee to ourselves in case of attack the possibility of retaliation in kind. The writer. . .is not for the moment concerned about who will *win* the next war in which atomic bombs are used. Thus far the chief purpose of our military establishment has been to win wars. From now on its chief purpose must be to avert them. It can have almost no other useful purpose."

Brodie also said:

> "The number of critical targets is quite limited. . . .That does not mean that additional hits would be useless but simply that diminishing returns would set in early; and after the cities of, say, 100,000 population were eliminated, the returns from additional bombs would decline drastically. . . .If 2000 bombs in the hands of either party is enough to destroy entirely the economy of the other, the fact that one side has 6000 and the other 2000 will be of relatively small significance."

The Atomic Bomb

Yet only a few years later, Brodie himself, in a development not widely acknowledged or known by many of his celebrators, started to adopt a different standard for assessing atomic adequacy.

As the 1950s began, the Soviets had virtually no atomic bombs and the United States had a few hundred. The fear among the American military was not that the Soviets would attack the United States but that they would invade Western Europe, economically prostrate after World War II, physically unable to defend itself. Since the United States had no conventional forces to speak of, and certainly none that could quickly

Fred Kaplan, "Strategic Thinkers," *The Bulletin of the Atomic Scientists,* December 1982. Reprinted with author's permission.

be mobilized to Western Europe, the only hope for defense and deterrence was the atomic bomb.

Brodie was briefly consultant to Air Force Chief of Staff General Hoyt Vandenberg at the beginning of the decade, and was assigned the task of examining the atomic war plan. Brodie discovered that virtually no one had figured out precisely how the bomb was to push back or wipe out the Soviet military. The U.S. Strategic Air Command (SAC), according to the war plan, was simply to drop all of its bombs as quickly as possible on targets inside the Soviet Union, destroying as many key factories and—as long as they were close to other targets—military facilities as it could in a single volley. The Air Force called the strategy "the Sunday Punch," and saw it as the optimal way of "killing a nation."

Brodie had doubts. For one thing, the Soviets were in the process of acquiring their own atomic arsenal. If the United States responded to Soviet conventional aggression by "killing" the Soviet Union, the Kremlin would almost certainly retaliate in kind. Thus, to execute SAC's war plan would be tantamount to committing suicide. The nineteenth-century warrior-philosopher, Karl von Clausewitz, had said that "war is the continuation of politics by other means." Brodie, an admirer of Clausewitz, interpreted that to mean that wars must be fought to accomplish rational objectives and that the degree of destruction should be proportional to the value of the objective. National suicide, of course, was hardly a rational objective, whatever the value of the stakes. The SAC plan, therefore, was not only a fatuous war strategy; it might not even serve well as a deterrent, since the Soviets might suspect that no sane U.S. President would carry out such a self-defeating threat.

Brodie conceived an alternative plan: If the Soviets, say, invaded Western Europe, the United States should fire only a few of its nuclear weapons—perhaps against Soviet troops on the battlefield, certainly *not* against Soviet cities. The United States should also have weapons that survived. The most efficient way to accomplish this, according to the NAVWAG, was to have a relatively small number of nuclear-armed submarines stationed at sea at all times.

That was all we needed; no matter how many weapons the Soviets built, the United States would be in fine shape as long as the submarines were there. Building more bombers or land-based missiles would only guarantee an unending arms race.

Against this last point the Air Force had no argument. An arms race was exactly what they wanted—as long as they were given the money and weapons to win it. For them, the beauty of counterforce, was that—unlike finite deterrence—it prescribed no logical limit to the number of weapons that were "needed." As long as both sides kept building weapons—as they almost certainly would—there would be more and more targets, requiring more and more weapons with which to destroy them.

Controlling the Military

By the time John F. Kennedy took office in January 1961, the issues of nuclear strategy had become thoroughly intertwined with a major interservice rivalry over which branch of the military would receive the bigger budget. This Air Force-Navy competition would dominate the U.S. side of the nuclear arms race and the strategic debate through the 1960s.

When Robert McNamara became Kennedy's Secretary of Defense, he initially liked the idea of "finite deterrence." It provided a clear measure of how much was enough, and systematic guidance on how tightly he could rein in the military, over which he wanted to establish complete control. But McNamara had also hired some RAND strategists as his top assistants—most notably Charles Hitch as comptroller and Alain Enthoven as Hitch's deputy for systems analysis. Advocates of the counterforce philosophy, these two were distressed by McNamara's penchant for finite deterrence. They persuaded their boss to give William Kaufmann's views a hearing and set up an appointment for February 10, 1961.

A week earlier, McNamara had visited SAC headquarters in Omaha for a briefing on the Single Integrated Operational Plan (SIOP), the military's nuclear war plan. Basically, it was only a slight variation on the old SAC plan—kill and destroy as much as possible in the Soviet Union, Red China and Eastern Europe, as quickly as possible: there were virtually no provisions for more limited options. McNamara was appalled by the massive devastation called for, by the straitjacket in which it would strap a President in a crisis. He was looking for some way to give the President more options—and Kaufmann's briefing showed him how.

McNamara adopted the counterforce/no-cities strategy in his first few years as Defense Secretary, espousing its philosophy at Athens in a top secret speech to the NATO Defense Ministers in May 1962 and in a public commencement address at the University of Michigan the following June.

At the same time, however, McNamara was cutting Air Force programs by the handful—the B-70 bomber, various primitive cruise missiles, the Skybolt air-launched ballistic missile—and limiting the number of B-52 bombers and Minuteman ICBMs to be deployed. The Air Force had its counterforce strategy, but not the budget or the weapons for which it had adopted counterforce as a rationale. Top officers started to apply ferocious pressure on McNamara, all the while using his own endorsement of counterforce to support their demands for more money.

"It took two to play the counterforce game, and if the Soviets refused to go along, it made no sense at all."

The Secretary fought back by dispensing with the counterforce rhetoric. He and his systems analysts devised a new measure of nuclear adequacy called "assured destruction" which over the years became known as "mutual assured destruction" or MAD. It stated that the United States had enough nuclear weapons when, following a Soviet first strike, it could still kill one fourth of the Soviet population and half its industry. This task required—so went their calculations—the equivalent of 400 one-megaton bombs. McNamara extended this to note that there should be 400 "equivalent megatons" on each leg of the strategic Triad—the intercontinental ballistic missiles (ICBMs), submarine-launched ballistic missiles (SLBMs) and bombers—so that if two legs failed or were destroyed, there would still be one that could wreak the required devastation. Assured destruction thus would be met by 1,200 equivalent megatons surviving a Soviet attack.

McNamara's aides worked out this calculation most formally in 1964. As it happened, his five-year defense plan for that year—which recommended several hundred fewer nuclear warheads than the military wanted—provided enough weapons so that by 1969, after a fairly successful Soviet first strike, the United States could respond with exactly 1,200 equivalent megatons. The assured-destruction philosophy was, in essence, a political technique that appeared to give scientific justification to McNamara's own weapons plan in the face of Air Force opposition.

At the same time, McNamara was having genuine doubts about counterforce. A top secret study (since declassified), titled "Damage Limiting," was produced in 1964 by General Glenn Kent, under the auspices of Harold Brown's Directorate of Defense Research and Engineering. It suggested that even with a very good

U.S. counterforce strike—supplemented by air, anti-ballistic-missile (ABM) and civil defense—the Soviets, in a retaliatory strike, could still inflict tremendous damage. Moreover, if the United States spent a great deal more on these defensive efforts, the Soviets could nullify the additional expenditure much more cheaply by adding only slightly to their strategic offensive forces. Counterforce, in short, appeared to be a loser's game.

"By the late 1960s, the requirements of a successful counterforce mission had become inconsistent with the philosophy underlying that strategy."

In addition, it appeared from their own writings that the Soviets did not believe in using nuclear weapons as tit-for-tat instruments, or in carefully differentiating urban from military targets. It took two to play the counterforce game, and if the Soviets refused to go along, it made no sense at all.

Nevertheless, even as McNamara's disenchantment grew and as assured destruction became the *declaratory* strategy, the *actual* strategy—as reflected in the targeting plan at SAC—remained predominantly counterforce. And new weapons were built to accommodate it. As the Soviets built more and more ICBMs in the 1960s, the United States responded by building MIRVs (multiple independently targetable re-entry vehicles) that allowed a single missile to strike several different targets hundreds of miles from one another. As the Soviets began to follow America's prudent example of encasing their ICBMs in hardened silos, the United States built new inertial guidance systems that made its missiles—theoretically, anyway—more accurate.

MIRVs and improved guidance systems were approved by McNamara, mainly as part of a political trade-off in which the Air Force agreed to hold the line at 1,000 Minuteman missiles. It was, in retrospect, a short-sighted deal, for the two programs kept the flame of counterforce burning.

By the 1970s, a mismatch cropped up in U.S. strategic forces. The Soviets had built still more ICBMs and hardened their silos even further. The United States had continued to MIRV hundreds of Minuteman missiles and to improve the guidance systems. But it still wasn't enough: 1,650 warheads on 550 Minuteman III missiles could not destroy all 1,400 Soviet ICBM silos. (It is generally estimated that at least two warheads are needed to destroy a single hardened missile silo, since some will fall outside the "lethal radius" and some others will not work at all.)

So the Air Force, in 1973, asked for a new ICBM—the MX—which would have ten warheads and still better accuracy. With 200 MX missiles—or even 100 combined with the Minuteman IIIs—counterforce could be feasible once more.

Meanwhile, in the 1970s, the Navy had also equipped its submarine-launched ballistic missile force with MIRVs: Poseidon and Trident I. As a result, the Navy had more warheads than were required for assured destruction or for the NAVWAG-5's strategy. Yet not even in theory were these missiles accurate enough to destroy hardened silos. In the mid-1970s as the second Poseidon submarine went to sea—each with 16 missiles carrying up to ten warheads per missile—Admiral Gerald Miller, then deputy director of SAC's Joint Strategic Target Planning Staff, complained to an aide: "Hell, what are we going to do with all of those?" New targets had to be created for new weapons—not the other way around.

So the Navy had no objection when, in the late 1970s, Andrew Marshall, the RAND veteran who had become director of Pentagon net assessment, started lobbying for a program to improve SLBM accuracy to give it "hard-target-kill capability." The result was the Trident II missile, now in research and development, scheduled for operations in the late 1980s.

The Navy could now afford to get into the counterforce business, since the strategy was no longer a source of interservice rivalry. Even the Army grew cooperative when all agreed that the anti-ballistic missile, the Army's only piece of the strategic-nuclear pie, might play a part in helping to protect the MX from nuclear attack. The entire military establishment could comfortably close ranks around a common stake in counterforce. The link between strategy, force levels and higher budgets suited all.

Flaws in Strategy

However, several theorists—and a small number of military officers—were beginning to detect further problems with counterforce. The Soviet Union had built so many ICBMs (1,000 by 1967) that a full-scale U.S. counterforce strike would require firing at least 2,000 nuclear warheads. The problem was that the Soviets would probably be unable to distinguish such a massive strike from an all-out attack against their cities and would probably order full-scale retaliation. Thus, by the late 1960s, the requirements of a successful counterforce mission had become inconsistent with the philosophy underlying that strategy.

Thomas Schelling, a strategic theorist from RAND and Harvard, recognized this potential contradiction as early as 1960. His solution: If nuclear weapons are to be used, fire small-scale, shot-across-the-bow strikes. The idea was the same as that outlined by Brodie in 1951: Inflict pain, threaten more pain as a way of coercing the Soviets to stop their aggression, but do so in a way that deployed a highly secure, essentially invulnerable reserve force of nuclear weapons. After this limited strike, the United States should insist that the Soviets stop their aggression at once and threaten to use the reserve force against Soviet cities if they did not stop. The hope was that this carrot-and-stick combination would effect a Soviet surrender or, short of that, keep the battle limited to the battlefield.

In the early 1950s, neither the Air Force nor the rest of government paid much attention to Brodie's idea. Indeed, a few years later, President Eisenhower and Secretary of State John Foster Dulles proclaimed a policy of "massive retaliation" very similar to the SAC war plan.

"Deterring an enemy nuclear attack required having enough nuclear weapons so that in the event of an enemy first strike the United States could obliterate the urban-industrial society of the aggressor."

But Brodie did influence others. In 1951 he joined the RAND Corporation, an Air Force-sponsored "think tank" specializing in military research. There several other budding strategists were attracted by his ideas. One was Herman Kahn, who later explored nuclear-warfighting scenarios in three influential books: *On Thermonuclear War, On Escalation* and *Thinking about the Unthinkable.* Another was Andrew Marshall, since 1974 director of the Pentagon's net assessment office. Marshall later had a major role in drafting the controversial "Defense Guidance" by Secretary of Defense Caspar Weinberger, which calls for the ability to fight a "protracted" nuclear war.

Counterforce Strategy

Brodie had dealt more with what targets should *not* be hit with nuclear weapons than with those that should. An answer to the latter question presented itself—not so much to Brodie as to his colleagues—in 1953, when the Soviet Union detonated its first hydrogen bomb. The United States had exploded one a year earlier, with several times the power of the first Soviet effort. But the Soviet test indicated that they were much farther along than the United States in developing a hydrogen bomb that could be attached to an intercontinental ballistic missile (ICBM). Suddenly, America was entering a new state of vulnerability. And to some of the RAND strategists the appropriate target for Brodie's limited-strike strategy was clear: the Soviet strategic nuclear arsenal. Sparing Soviet cities in a nuclear attack might *induce* the Soviets to avoid American cities; knocking out their long-range weapons

would *prevent* them from doing so.

Thus, the tentative beginnings of what would later be known as a "counterforce/no-cities strategy" began to penetrate the strategic community at RAND. More systematic thinking about the issue was inhibited, however, by the concern that the United States would never be able to find all the Soviet military targets, making such a strategy unworkable.

By the end of the 1950s this obstacle collapsed. The U-2 spy plane and the impending development of the Discoverer reconnaissance satellite—which a few at RAND, including Marshall, knew about—made counterforce seem feasible. The theory was taken up again, most actively by a RAND historian and political scientist named William W. Kaufmann. Like his former teacher Bernard Brodie, Kaufmann had done a great deal of writing on limited (conventional) warfare in the mid-1950s.

For a few bright, ambitious officers in the Air Force staff, Kaufmann and counterforce came along at just the right time. The Air Force was facing, from the U.S. Navy, a fearsome threat, far more severe than any the Soviets had ever posed. This was the Navy's new Polaris submarine. Unlike SAC's bombers, which sat on airfields that were increasingly seen as vulnerable to attack, Polaris moved underwater, undetected. Its submarine-launched missiles (SLBMs) travelled at hypersonic speeds in a ballistic trajectory and were therefore invulnerable to Soviet air defenses as well. And Polaris could destroy Soviet cities and many other targets just as easily as the bombers could. Since SAC's war plan called for hitting urban and military targets simultaneously—with an emphasis on destroying industrial plants in enemy cities—SAC seemed dangerously on the edge of obsolescence.

A new strategy was needed at once, and RAND's counterforce/no-cities idea seemed just the thing. By late 1960, counterforce/no-cities became the official Air Force policy. The Air Force liked counterforce because one weakness of Polaris was that its missiles were dreadfully inaccurate; they could not be relied upon to strike military targets without hitting nearby cities as well. It was questionable whether SAC's bombers would be perfect at the task, either, but they would have a much better chance.

The Navy had its own "new strategy," designed to rationalize Polaris and further discredit SAC. Called "finite deterrence," its tenets were explained in a widely circulated but classified document called Naval Warfare Analysis Group (NAVWAG) Study No. 5, "National Policy Implications of Atomic Parity."

The idea was in essence a refinement of the strategy that Brodie had outlined 15 years earlier in *The Absolute Weapon.* Deterring an enemy nuclear attack required having enough nuclear weapons so that in the event of an enemy first strike the United States could obliterate the urban-industrial society of the aggressor with the avoids striking Soviet cities and thus compels the Soviets to keep the conflict limited.

The idea appealed to another RAND theorist, James Schlesinger, who elaborated on it in a series of RAND studies, done in association with the Air Force in the late 1960s, known as NUOPTS, or Nuclear Operations. By the time Schlesinger became Secretary of Defense in 1973, several officials in the national-security bureaucracy had become interested, and Schlesinger was determined to make it policy.

The result was a series of National Security Decision Memoranda, beginning with NSDM-242 in January 1974 and climaxing in 1980 with President Carter's controversial Presidential Directive 59. The 1982 "Defense Guidance" signed by Weinberger is only a slight elaboration of the strategy of counterforce and small-scale strikes first articulated in the 1950s.

Force requirements for this sort of nuclear strategy are less elaborate than for the full-scale counterforce plan, in that a military adopting such a strategy would not need so many weapons since it would not have to hit all of the adversary's counterforce targets. But they are more elaborate in that the weapons would have to be even more precise, and because the command-control-communications network would have to be almost unimaginably extensive and durable.

Both sides would need intelligence facilities—satellites and sensors—that could immediately inform their top officials of what targets were hit and what weapons remained. The links connecting the officials and the weapons would have to remain under firm centralized control for days, weeks or longer. This is practically impossible, given the inevitable confusion of large-scale organizations, the inherent unreliability of much military electronic gear and the vulnerability of this equipment to a wide array of nuclear effects, including blast, radiation and electromagnetic pulse. Indeed, these systems are so *inherently* vulnerable that after one or two nuclear "exchanges," chances are very high that escalation will slip completely out of anyone's control.

The strategy also shares certain problems with those of the counterforce philosophy: How do you get the Soviets to play according to the same rules? Does this combination of strikes and threats really coerce the other side? Couldn't the other side fire back equally small-scale strikes—or simply pretend to ignore our "signals"—and try to coerce us instead? Finally, how do you end such a war, on what terms, on what basis of shared trust? After the initial volley, strategy vanishes; only luck and prayer remain.

Some theorists have argued that Soviet surrender would be facilitated if the U.S. targeting plan were geared to destroy the political infrastructure of the Soviet Union; that we should "take out" command posts and other key facilities of the party and military apparatus; that then the Soviet Union would collapse. The real-life technicians of nuclear targeting—the Joint Strategic Planning Staff in Omaha—have considered these suggestions but have discovered no way to make them work. Furthermore by destroying the enemy's command-control network, we might be eliminating the only means by which the Kremlin could communicate with us and signal a desire to end the fighting. We would also be destroying the means by which the top Soviet political leaders could keep their own military officers under control. Authority to use nuclear weapons might automatically fall to some "mad marshal" or "crazy colonel," making further escalation and mutual destruction more likely.

Conventional War

Finally, there are those, mainly in Army circles, who talk of fighting a nuclear war on the battlefield. The idea goes back to the early 1950s, when a number of scientists and theorists—Bernard Brodie among them but more notably J. Robert Oppenheimer and later Henry Kissinger—wanted to avoid the holocaust of the hydrogen bomb and city-bombing by "bringing the battle back to the battlefield."

"Some theorists have argued that Soviet surrender would be facilitated if the U.S. targeting plan were geared to destroy the political infrastructure of the Soviet Union."

But after 30 years of thinking, nobody has devised a way of doing this. Towns in West Germany, where a theater nuclear war would probably be fought, are only two kilotons apart, so to speak. If tactical nuclear weapons were used on a militarily meaningful scale millions of West Europeans would die—and that assumes no Soviet retaliation. Moreover, pressure would logically build to "take out" Soviet SS-4, SS-5 and SS-20 missiles, the weapons that most lethally threaten Western Europe. Those missiles lie inside the Soviet Union; once Soviet territory is hit, American territory would almost certainly be next. Then the problems of the counterforce and small-strike strategies start all over again.

Fred Kaplan is the author of The Wizards of Armageddon, *the story of the nuclear strategists, published by Simon & Schuster in 1983.*

"The Soviets have matched their military buildup with military and political expansion into strategically important areas far from the Soviet periphery."

viewpoint 8

America Must Deter the Soviets

Caspar Weinberger

In my testimony last year I focused on the modifications that we had to make to the military strategy and defense posture that we inherited. In some cases, we found that the policies we inherited did not conform to the international realities we faced, and we had to make some changes. Today I want to discuss our entire policy from a broader outlook, considering both the reforms we have made, and the enduring principles from the past that together form the foundation of our current defense policy.

National Security Objectives

At the outset, it may be useful for us to recall that our overall national security objectives, in a very abbreviated form, are:
• To deter military attack against the United States, its allies, and other friendly countries.
• In the event of a conventional attack, to deny the enemy his objectives and bring a rapid end to the conflict on terms favorable to our interests.
• To promote meaningful and verifiable mutual reductions in nuclear and conventional forces.
• To inhibit further expansion of Soviet control and military presence.
• To avoid subsidizing or supporting the Soviet buildup by preventing, in concert with our allies, the flow of militarily significant technologies and material to the Soviet Union.

The Soviet Military Threat

In assessing our ability to achieve these national security objectives, we recognize that the Soviet Union poses, and for the foreseeable future will continue to pose, the most formidable threat to the United States and our interests. Of course, we recognize that some threats arise independently of the Soviet Union. But, more often than not, the magnitude and persistence of

Caspar Weinberger, statement before the Senate Armed Services Committee, February 1, 1983.

these other threats and our difficulties in countering them are greatly aggravated by Soviet policies, backed by the expanding reach of Soviet military power.

I want to emphasize that it is not our intention to match the Soviets tank for tank or aircraft for aircraft. Our intention is to regain an effective deterrent against either Soviet conventional or nuclear aggression. We recognize that other factors besides quantitative comparisons affect the military balance. One of the most important of these is that the Soviets have matched their military buildup with military and political expansion into strategically important areas far from the Soviet periphery. . . .

Soviet Expansionism

The 20-year Soviet military buildup, coupled with the collective failure of the United States and our allies to make a sufficient response, has resulted in a dangerous shift in the global military balance.

This global military balance has shifted against us because the Soviet Union has out-spent and out-produced us for a least a decade. Even when we include the allied efforts of each side, we find that the Warsaw Pact has out-spent and out-produced the NATO countries. . . .

This trend is even more worrisome when one considers that the Soviet Union has also upgraded the quality of its weapons—particularly in conventional forces. The Soviet Union has always fielded greater numbers of conventional weapons which we offset with smaller numbers of more capable equipment. But now we find that the steady growth in Soviet investment has allowed them to produce increasingly more sophisticated weapons such as the potent T-72 tank, accurate air defense weapons, and fighter aircraft capable of operating in all types of weather. . . .

The Soviet Union now has:

- Acquired security and cooperative agreements in Africa, the Near East, Southeast Asia and Southwest Asia.
- Undertaken massive arms deliveries to third world countries—double the amount we supplied from 1977-1981.
- Acquired Cuban, East German and/or Libyan military proxies in Central America and Africa.
- Greatly increased its power projection capabilities.
- Expanded its overflight and access rights to operating bases in key parts of the world.
- Occupied Afghanistan.

The cumulative effect of the Soviet military buildup and Soviet expansionism has been not only to change the type of attack we might confront and the areas in which we could be attacked, but also to increase greatly the effectiveness of such an attack. The increased size and quality of Soviet forces has enabled them to turn from a defensive force posture to one increasingly structured for offensive use. Their increased naval and power projection capability, coupled with their acquisition of critical footholds in strategic locations throughout the world, enables them to launch and maintain conflict in several theaters simultaneously. Their buildup of nuclear forces, particularly ICBMs, enables them to threaten to destroy a very large part of our force in a first strike, while retaining overwhelming nuclear force to deter any retaliation we could carry out.

Defense Strategy

Our defense strategy for dealing with this threat consists of a series of discrete but interrelated elements, some of which have endured for many years, others of which are more recent in origin. It incorporates three main principles:

- First, our strategy is *defensive*. That is to say, it excludes the possibility that the United States would initiate a war or launch a preemptive strike against the forces or territories of other nations.
- Second, our strategy is to deter war. The *deterrent* nature of our strategy is closely related to our defensive stance. We maintain a nuclear and conventional force posture designed to convince any potential adversary that the cost of aggression would be too high to justify an attack.
- Third, should deterrence fail, our strategy is to *restore peace on favorable terms*. In responding to an enemy attack, we must defeat the attack and achieve our national objectives while limiting—to the extent possible and practicable—the scope of the conflict.

To carry out this strategy we have emphasized three vital supporting policies.

First, the United States remains part of, and contributes to, *a collective defense* posture that incorporates the strength of our allies. The North Atlantic Treaty, the Rio Treaty, the Anzus Treaty, and our treaties with Korea, the Philippines, and Japan help provide for an effective common defense against external aggression.

Second, to buttress our collective security posture, we maintain *forward deployments* that, combined with the forces of our allies, provide the first line of conventional defense in Western Europe, Japan, and Korea. In the event of war, we would reinforce these forward-deployed units rapidly.

"The 20 year Soviet military buildup, coupled with the collective failure of the United States. . .to make a response, has resulted in a dangerous shift in the global military balance."

Third, we seek a *flexible force structure* that builds on our alliance commitments and forward deployments and provides us a variety of options for quickly responding to unforeseen contingencies in any region where we have vital interests to defend.

The Problems We Inherited

When the Reagan Administration took office, we found inconsistencies between the existing strategy and the forces available to carry out that strategy. Furthermore, that defense program held little promise of providing either the strategy or the force posture necessary to maintain deterrence in future years in light of the changing Soviet threat. Therefore, we had two simultaneous tasks to accomplish. We needed to make our forces ready to fight immediately, should conflict be forced upon us. We also needed to begin long term improvements to our defense posture so that we would be prepared to meet threats that might arise in the future. . . .

The Defense Budget

Before I conclude, I want to correct some misconceptions regarding the defense budget.

First, the defense budget has *not* been sacrosanct—it too has taken its "fair share" of cuts in the Reagan Administration. As this chart shows, when the Reagan five-year defense budget was unveiled in March 1981, we planned to add $116 billion to the Carter Administration budget for the same period. Now, less than two years later, that figure has been reduced by more than half. And we must also recall *why* it was necessary for the President to ask such a large increase for the 80's. It was because our neglect of our armed forces in the 70's coincided with the vast increases in the U.S.S.R. military strength described earlier.

But, the cuts we have made in the President's defense spending plan have not sacrificed readiness for modernization. Since we took office over 100 marginal weapons or equipment programs have been eliminated, reduced or merged.

Third, cutting back on defense is not the solution to this nation's very real deficit problem. The increase in defense spending has not produced these large deficits, and a decrease in defense spending, while it could endanger American security, would not cure them. . . .

Finally, I want to address those who say "I am for defense, but. . ." and those who say "I don't know anything about the defense budget, but. . .
- we must cut it to reduce the deficit, or
- we must cut it in fairness to other programs, or
- we must cut it for a myriad of other reasons."
I must emphasize to them that we simply cannot reduce defense spending any further without undermining the security of the United States. We cannot afford a situation in which legitimate and necessary defense spending becomes the "whipping boy" of those who look only at budget or deficit numbers or forget that the Soviets are driven by no such constraints. We must not forget that defense needs must be determined by the threat to our national security that we face.

Facing the Threat

We must therefore develop a responsible and balanced understanding of the real meaning of the threat we face. The detailed facts are clear enough. But there is great resistance to accept the real meaning of these facts, because to do so is to accept the need for a major sustained response. Confronted as we are by all manner of other real or apparent needs, there is a temptation to argue away even the most overwhelming evidence, with misplaced hope that we can continue as usual, putting off or canceling unpopular military necessities, and increasing our spending on more politically popular domestic programs. Instead, the regrettable fact is that, in view of the threats posed to our national security, this course is no longer open to us.

"The cumulative effect of the Soviet military buildup and Soviet expansionism has been not only to change the type of attack. . .but also to increase greatly the effectiveness of such an attack."

We must also recognize that the commitment to deterrence and defense is neither easy nor inexpensive. When it confronts an opposing coercive "offensive." strategy, it requires continued vigilance to maintain. When deterrence succeeds, it is easy to attribute the maintenance of peace not to the contribution of the defense that enforces the deterrent, but to a host of more facile assumptions—some imagined new-found "peaceful intent" of the opponent, the spirit of detente, growing economic interdependency, and so forth. When deterrence fails, however, and the opponent has

deliberately weighed the risks and still decided to attack, the dividends of a viable defense are unquestionable. But unless such a defense is acquired, is in being, and is maintained at the ready, it is too late to try to regain it after war begins.

We simply cannot wait to restore our military strength—we must do it now, this year, in this budget. The rapid and continuous growth of Soviet offensive military power does not allow us the option of waiting until after the economy fully recovers, or waiting until an emergency develops.

The past decade of inadequate defense spending has forced us to accept "double duty." We must increase the basic readiness and sustainability of our forces to be prepared for an immediate crisis, should one occur. At the same time we must make up for lost years of investment by undertaking the research and development, and force modernization—including the modernization and strengthening of all three parts of the strategic TRIAD—that are needed to meet threats that are likely to arise in the future. To do one at the expense of the other or to stint on either would be to undermine the security of the United States and that, ladies and gentlemen, I, and I hope you, are not willing to do.

Caspar Weinberger is the secretary of the defense under the Reagan administration.

"I do not believe that at any time there has been any evidence to suggest that the Soviets were planning to launch a military attack on the U.S. or Western Europe."

Deterrence of the Soviets Is Unnecessary

Gene LaRocque

We are witnessing in the United States today a period of unprecedented ferment on nuclear issues. Never before has such widespread attention been paid to nuclear weapons and nuclear war. The public is involved, the media are involved, the congress is involved, and even the Reagan Administration has reluctantly responded. The movement for a bilateral U.S.-Soviet nuclear freeze arose unexpectedly and quickly gained mass support in all parts of the country. And during the last year over 100 books were published on nuclear weapons and nuclear war. As nuclear weapons become more commonplace and as we and other nations plan, train, arm and practice for nuclear war, public concern mounts.

Why is this happening? After all, we have lived with the bomb for more than 35 years, and the basic parameters of U.S. nuclear policy were elaborated in the late 1950's and early 1960's. Nuclear weapons explosions in the atmosphere and the very close shave we had with nuclear war over Soviet missiles in Cuba caused a brief flurry of public concern, but when the nuclear tests were hidden underground and Cuba receded, public interest waned. The Vietnam war occupied the nation for over ten years while plans for nuclear war proceeded swiftly and imperceptibly to keep pace with dramatic improvements in nuclear weapons technology.

The newfound American and worldwide interest must be credited to President Reagan and his close associates. Without his effective exposition of good old fashioned American jingoism wrapped in the flag, it is doubtful if the martial spirit which pervades the United States today would have occurred. In actuality he and his Administration changed very little but were more explicit, more open than previous Administrations about our plans and preparations for nuclear war. They called a spade a spade. Plans for a huge buildup of U.S. nuclear weapons and specific statements about fighting and winning and prevailing in a nuclear war and firing "warning" shots with nuclear weapons got peoples' attention. Polarization at home and abroad occurred immediately.

When Ronald Reagan was elected in 1980 on a defiant cold war program, few guessed his actions would generate such strong public currents countering his fondest programs.

I have been concerned for many years that Americans do not appreciate the danger of nuclear war. For decades governments have cloaked the dreadful reality of nuclear war and nuclear weapons in reassuring and soothing language. Many Americans, including political leaders and military men, have failed to understand the tremendously destructive nature of nuclear weapons and have approached the accumulation of military power in the nuclear age much as in earlier times—the more the better. Many Americans have come to believe that a war with nuclear weapons could be controlled, won, and survived. It was Robert McNamara, early in his career as Secretary of Defense in 1962, who articulated the generally accepted view of nuclear war as an extension of previous wars. Mr. McNamara said:

> The U.S. has come to the conclusion that to the extent feasible, basic military strategy in a possible general nuclear war should be approached in much the same way that more conventional military operations have been regarded in the past.

Mr. McNamara, evidently, later came to understand that there was little that was "feasible" about this.

Revolution in Warfare

Failure to appreciate the revolution in warfare and international affairs brought about by nuclear weapons has been and still is a fundamental problem, although in recent years there has been a salutary increase in public education about the nature of nuclear weapons and the consequences of nuclear war. More people are aware that a nuclear war would be unlike any other

Admiral Gene LaRocque, "America's Nuclear Ferment: Opportunities for Change," *The Annals*, Vol. 469. Copyright © 1983 by the American Academy of Political and Social Science. Reprinted with permission.

war in American history. Many are beginning to realize that we will not go to war next time—it will come to us. While most know that a nuclear war would be a war without winners, the majority of Americans support the construction of thousands of new weapons each year. Paradoxically, there is a growing demand among informed people to slow, stop, and reverse the nuclear arms race.

This demand is a positive development. I find it very encouraging. On the nuclear issue the public here and in Europe are ahead of their governments and many so-called experts. It has been our objective at the Center for Defense Information since it was founded in 1972 to educate the public and the media with the facts on nuclear war. This was the purpose of our First Nuclear War Conference carried on national television in 1978, and of our Conference on Nuclear War in Europe held in the Netherlands in 1981.

But, I fear that the shift in public attitudes has yet to make any substantial impact on the thinking of those who are currently in charge of the U.S. military establishment. Official policy remains enamored of nuclear weapons and continues to be based on attempts to pursue military advantage in the nuclear age. The fuzzy ideology of deterrence is proclaimed in public while strenuous efforts are made to prepare to try to fight and win a nuclear war.

This is not new with the Reagan Administration. The dominant thrust of U.S. military policy for decades, whether Republican or Democratic, liberal or conservative, has been to tie the U.S. ever more closely to preparation for nuclear war.

Generals Against Nuclear Weapons

There have been from the beginning of the nuclear age a small number of distinguished military men speaking out forcefully against nuclear weapons and the illusions that accompany them. Lord Mountbatten of Great Britain jolted many of his former military colleagues when he said:

> As a military man who has given half a century to active service I say in all sincerity that the nuclear arms race has no military purpose. Wars cannot be fought with nuclear weapons. Their existence only adds to our perils because of the illusions which they have generated.

General Douglas MacArthur also turned against nuclear weapons:

> Global war has become a Frankenstein to destroy both sides. No longer is it a weapon of adventure—the short-cut to international power. If you lose, you are annihilated. If you win, you stand only to lose. No longer does it possess even the chance of the winner of a duel. It contains now only the germs of double suicide.

Many, if not most, military men are uncomfortable with nuclear weapons and frustrated by the inability to use them militarily. It is the job of the professional military in every country to prepare for war and to prepare to win. Nuclear weapons complicate the job

tremendously. But despite these complications and uncertainties, the fact is that in both the United States and the Soviet Union, the armed forces have been almost totally nuclearized. From top to bottom, the Army, the Navy, and the Air Force in both countries are armed to the teeth with nuclear weapons. We and they are constantly practicing and preparing for nuclear war. Nuclear weapons are the life and blood of the American military. We have built our military power around nuclear weapons and depend upon their use to wage war against all prospective opponents.

"As a military man who has given half a century to active service I say in all sincerity that the nuclear arms race has no military purpose."

Attempts are sometimes made to minimize the extent of our dependence on nuclear weapons by saying, as Secretary of Defense Weinberger did recently, that less than 15% of the annual military budget goes for nuclear weapons. A more complete accounting of all the funds expended on nuclear forces (including all personnel and R&D costs) brings the total to nearly 25%. But even that figure understates the degree to which preparations for nuclear war dominate military planning in the U.S. and the Soviet Union. Almost every warship and submarine in the U.S. Navy carries nuclear weapons. Current planning makes nuclear weapons central to the conduct of combat operations in Europe by U.S. Army, Air Force and Navy forces.

The U.S. has about 30,000 nuclear weapons. The Soviet Union has about 20,000. Any war between the two countries will be a nuclear war. Most military planners realize that and plan accordingly.

The United States first acquired nuclear weapons and used them to win the war with Japan. Then we hoped for a nuclear monopoly and consolidated our new post-war position of worldwide military dominance. We developed theories of deterrence to help justify our nuclear weapons and explain what we might do with them. These theories of deterrence connote restraint and a defensive attitude which helped promote public confidence in the wisdom of those in control of nuclear weapons.

Views of Soviet Union

I believe we are at a point now where we should critically reassess some of the major assumptions for the use of nuclear weapons to achieve our national objectives. The acquisition of more nuclear weapons to deter Soviet actions can only be valid if we continue to be persuaded it will be effective and is necessary. Deterrence is totally dependent upon the mental attitude of the Soviet government officials and hence we must clearly understand what motivates the Soviets.

The major assumption underlying U.S. foreign policy since 1945 has been the devil image of the Soviet Union. We have assumed the Soviets to be diabolically aggressive and a malevolent force in the world. We have seen our role as that of the good guys containing the bad guys, the protectors of Western civilization from the communist menace. We have assumed that but for our powerful military forces, the Soviet Union would take over the world through military conquest. We have assumed that Soviet officials understand only brute military force, ours or theirs. Our people and our government officials have shared a profound distrust and even hatred of the Soviets. This distrust and hatred lead to fear which has dominated our foreign policy. Any temporary departure from this anti-Soviet stimulus has always been a brief aberration.

President Reagan's rearticulation of the image of the Soviet Union as "the focus of evil in the modern world" may strike some as crude but I believe it accurately reflects both popular and official attitudes. We do consider ourselves in every way to be better than, and superior to, the Russians. We believe it is our manifest destiny to protect the world from the Russians.

George Kennan and a few others have attempted to make Americans reflect critically on their traditional attitudes toward the Russians. I believe many of our assumptions about the Russians are erroneous and we need to reassess them quickly if we are to protect ourselves from the potentially disastrous consequences of our current misperceptions. We and the Russians must learn to live together on this planet, or we will surely die together. "We are doomed to coexist" with the Soviet Union, as Henry Kissinger said in 1976. I do not believe we can survive or prevent nuclear war if we persist in our devil view of the Soviet Union. War is inevitable sooner or later if we believe our contest with the Soviet Union is one of good versus evil. We will think it worth dying for in a nuclear war (and we will die) if such is our conception of our purpose. But in my view, there is no issue between the U.S. and the U.S.S.R. that requires nuclear war.

"The Soviets have consistently sought economic relations with the West which would bring desperately needed goods and services to the Soviet Union."

I do not believe that at any time there has been any evidence to suggest that the Soviets were planning to launch a military attack on the U.S. or Western Europe. There is no time in their history when the Soviets would have had anything to gain from an attack on the U.S. or Europe, nor can I visualize any set of circumstances when it would be to their advantage. Soviet officials have never evidenced any illusions about the mortal danger they would put themselves in by such action. They have never shown any confidence that Soviet military power is such as to even raise the prospect of success in such a war.

More important than these negative factors, however, is the positive value that the West holds for the Soviets. The Soviets have consistently sought economic relations with the West which would bring desperately needed goods and services to the Soviet Union. They need our grain. They need our technology. They need our trade.

I must point out, of course, that rejection of the devil image of the Soviets does not convert them into angels or render them militarily harmless. Even though they have not had intentions of attacking the West, they have since the 1930's (*not* just since the 1960's, it should be emphasized) sought to build a very large military establishment. The Soviets, in fact, are obsessed with national defense. But Soviet officials are not insane and the Soviet people have no stomach for aggressive military expansion. They have not shaped their military effort around plans for highly risky military attacks that would be suicidal.

Reassessing Deterrence

American military policy in the years since World War II has been articulated chiefly in the concept of deterrence. Most recently, Defense Secretary Caspar Weinberger stated, in March 1983, "We are simply maintaining the calculus of deterrence." Deterrence has a reassuring sound to it. It is evoked on any and all occasions.

George Orwell would be impressed with what the concept of deterrence has accomplished: it has anesthetized public perception of the reality that lies behind it. A former State Department official recently wrote in *The New York Times* that "Nuclear weapons are not weapons of war, but instruments of deterrence." Everyone knows that deterrence has "worked."

But it is far from clear what we mean by deterrence or whether deterrence is an accurate description of our policy. It may not even be a good policy, particularly as we have been pursuing it.

Dictionary definitions may provide a starting point. To deter is "to discourage or restrain from acting, as through fear." The Joint Chiefs of Staff's *Dictionary of Military and Associated Terms* (JCS Pub. 1) defines deterrence as:

> The prevention from action by fear of the consequences. Deterrence is a state of mind brought about by the existence of a credible threat of unacceptable counter action.

The most striking aspect about deterrence is that even though everyone talks about it, nobody can say what it consists of. Who knows what is necessary to deter? Who knows how much is enough? No one knows, and in part for this reason, we (and the Soviets) have accumulated essentially unlimited nuclear arsenals and work constantly in a very determined way to acquire still more new weapons, new means of delivery, with new stratagems to use these weapons.

Deterrence is such a vague term that it can be used, and has been used, to justify everything we do. It is now purely a slogan. It has no real value as either a guide to what we *should* do or to what we actually do in our policy toward the Soviet Union.

Deterrence has been a useful concept for public relations purposes because it sounds good, just as the word "defense" sounds good, as in Defense Department. Remember that we once had a *War* Department. No one can oppose buying more weapons for the purpose of deterring war or to provide defense.

Deterrence has always been a small part of the U.S. military effort. Military men have always been unsatisfied with the limitations of a purely deterrent policy which strikes them as too passive, too inflexible, too limiting, too demoralizing, and even too immoral. Military men have wanted to make nuclear weapons manageable tools of warfare, weapons like any other weapons which can be used to prevail in battle over the enemy. Military men have always sought an edge and resisted the self-limitations of deterrence.

In part for these reasons, the version of deterrence pursued by the U.S. over the years has been remarkably elastic, all-encompassing, and ambitious. The policy of nuclear deterrence pursued by the U.S. versus the Soviet Union has had almost unlimited goals of deterring any Soviet actions that we do not like. Inherent in our deterrent strategy is an overt willingness to "use" our nuclear weapons. That is, to attack and destroy the Soviet Union and kill its people. Of equal importance to our strategy of nuclear deterrence is the relegating to ourselves of the sole right to decide when deterrence has failed and requires use of nuclear weapons. This understandably appears to the Soviets as very one-sided, threatening, and coercive.

Soviet Threat?

Actions we have taken in the name of deterrence have almost invariably been perceived by the Soviets as threatening and provocative and have resulted in stepped-up military response by them. One man's deterrent is another man's threat.

It is interesting to conjecture how we Americans would feel if the Soviets officially proclaimed a "deterrent" strategy to prevent the U.S. from taking military actions around the world. There need be no limit on the size of such a force because, like the U.S. "deterrent force," it would be a matter for the Soviets to decide on the basis of what they perceived to be necessary to deter us. Certainly, there could no longer be the criticism from the U.S. and other NATO countries that such a "deterrent force" was larger than was needed. I never have understood why the Soviets did not follow

the open-ended U.S. policy of building deterrent forces, unless perhaps they really do see their military posture as defensive.

Of course, nearly everything the Soviets do in the military arena is perceived by our side as threatening and never characterized as contributing to a Soviet "deterrent." It was as early as 1950 in the NSC-68 report that American officials began proclaiming the discovery that Soviet military forces exceeded the requirements of defense: "The Soviet Union actually possesses armed forces far in excess of those necessary to defend its territory." As no American official has ever bothered to define what he thinks a Soviet military establishment that met the requirements of an adequate Soviet defense posture would be, I think we are forced to conclude that such statements by U.S. officials serve only propaganda purposes.

"It is interesting to conjecture how we Americans would feel if the Soviets officially proclaimed a 'deterrent' strategy to prevent the U.S. from taking military actions around the world."

It is interesting to observe that while U.S. Department of Defense officials regularly point out that the Soviet military is larger than needed for defense of the U.S.S.R., there is never any mention of the fact that only about 10% of the U.S. Department of Defense budget is for the direct defense of the United States.

Because there never have been any reasons advanced for the U.S.S.R. to invade Western Europe or launch a nuclear first strike on the U.S., the constant invoking of these alleged Soviet intentions by American officials has been viewed by the Soviets as more reflective of U.S. aggressive intentions toward them. The fear and mistrust that Americans have toward the Soviet Union is exceeded only by the fear and mistrust that Russians have toward the United States. It needs to be experienced to be believed. They have attributed to us the same expansionist, aggressive intentions that we have habitually pinned on them. It serves no useful purpose to dismiss Soviet concerns as "standard Soviet disinformation that's been poured out for years," as Mr. Weinberger recently said.

If we were seriously attempting to implement a policy of deterrence, we would pay much more attention to Soviet attitudes than we do. American officials often describe "deterrence" as our ability to influence the Soviet mentality. The Joint Chief's definition of deterrence refers to "a state of mind." But we have little competence to measure Soviet attitudes and little interest in doing so. Mr. Weinberger recently said that "it's very hard to get inside the Soviet mind. I have not attempted to do that." He does not seem conscious of how contradictory that is for a deterrent policy. Of course, reference to "the Soviet mind" is usually an excuse for making the most simplistic and self-serving assumptions about Soviet intentions and the matter is left at that. We do not care to dig deeper.

The sad state of Soviet studies in the United States reflects our basic indifference to learning what the Soviets are really thinking. It speaks eloquently for the emptiness of our deterrent philosophy. Few diplomats bother to learn Russian. Fewer and fewer students are being taught Russian. Fewer and fewer graduate students are pursuing Soviet studies. There are not enough jobs even for the handful of Americans who have sought to prepare themselves for careers in Soviet affairs.

Dr. Robert Legvold of the Council on Foreign Relations summed up the situation:

> The gaps in our knowledge are enormous. And they are growing....In the absence of serious, carefully researched studies, our view of the Soviet Union is shaped increasingly by popular impressions, a prior analyses, built from superficial reflections on the Soviet actions that most catch the eye, and traditional habits of thought.

For Americans, apparently, it has been enough to know that the Russians are the bad guys and we are the good guys and all that matters is being tough and spending more money on the military.

"Ronald Reagan and Caspar Weinberger. . .genuinely believe that the Soviet Union is following the path of Hitler Germany."

If we are to improve the security of the United States, we should place first priority on improving our understanding of the Russians both in and out of government. Clearly there are various views of the Russians. There is no monolithic truth on the subject. And there is no panacea in simply learning more about the Russians. But we start from a position of such abysmal ignorance that any improvement would be good. There needs to be intensive contact at all levels between Russians and Americans. Officials of both countries should be in constant communication. Few members of the U.S. Congress have visited the Soviet Union, although they vote every year for hundreds of billions of dollars for weapons to deter the Soviets.

A Retaliatory Policy

Where should we go from here? The two major contending forces on the American scene seem to be the Reagan Administration's policies and those Americans who say we have enough weapons on both sides. Personally, I believe the U.S. and the Soviets should reach agreement to stop the production, deployment, and testing of nuclear weapons in our mutual interests. It would only be the first step in a more comprehensive effort to bring the nuclear arms race under control in order that the Soviet Union and the United States could redirect their activities away from war and destruction.

But it is clear that the Reagan Administration is bent on other priorities. Ronald Reagan and Caspar Weinberger model themselves on Winston Churchill. They seem to genuinely believe that the Soviet Union is following the path of Hitler Germany and that it is their mission to lead a Western crusade against the totalitarian menace. They believe that their domestic critics are appeasers. They seem to believe that there is a good chance of war unless the U.S. engages in a huge military buildup and moves militarily around the world to snuff out Soviet subversion.

I do not take seriously President Reagan's recent speech announcing his plan to set a national goal of developing a perfect defense against Soviet nuclear weapons. President Reagan is attempting to rescue his military budget and his nuclear buildup from mounting opposition. Advocates of a big U.S. military expansion such as Fred C. Ikle (now Under Secretary of Defense) have long attempted to use a moral attack on assured destruction as an expedient vehicle for justifying new weapons. It is essential to note that President Reagan did *not* couple his announcement of a future expensive program to defend against nuclear weapons with any diminution of the even larger existing program of acquiring new offensive nuclear weapons. Defense is not being substituted for offense. Reagan made no changes in the U.S. plans to build 17,000 new offensive nuclear weapons in the next ten years.

I interpret Reagan's recent speeches as primarily political ploys, as attempts to again make the Russians look bad and immoral, and to draw attention away from those who would slow, stop, and reverse the arms race. Once Defense Department officials realize that they are not going to get all the money they are hoping for in future years, the star wars fantasy will begin to lose its attraction. There is not enough money in the U.S. to build a perfect defense, just as there is not enough money to build an effective first strike counterforce capability in either the U.S. or the U.S.S.R.

All these new programs are justified by invoking the name of deterrence. No military man can tell you how many of what kinds of weapons are required for deterrence. No one knows. There are no experts on this subject. We are left with the fundamental fact that nuclear weapons exist, and that they have enormous destructive power.

In our nuclear weapons policies I think we can do no better than maintaining a nuclear retaliatory force. A retaliatory force is a much more concrete and quantifiable thing than a deterrent force which in fact has no measurable dimensions. A military man can tell you, within approximate measure, how large our forces need to be to survive an opponent's first strike and retaliate with devastating effect. That quantity is much less than we have today. In the 1960's McNamara attempted to quantify the approximate level of strategic forces required for retaliation and assured destruction. His calculations were in the range of 400 large nuclear weapons. McGeorge Bundy has argued that even the prospect of a few nuclear weapons exploding on major cities would be enough.

When Jimmy Carter was first elected it is reported that he briefly explored the possibility of a much lower level of U.S. strategic weapons but then abandoned this because it would have been too radical a break with established practice. It *would* be a wrenching change but I think that an American President could implement a drastic reduction in nuclear weapons and a reorientation of U.S. military policies away from obsessive building of new weapons. Many military men would go along with this. Vice Admiral Gerald E. Miller, former Deputy Director of the Joint Strategic Target Planning Staff, observes:

> The simple fact is that nuclear weapons are not very realistic tools for the military commander. Any commander basing the success of his campaign on the use (first use or last) of nuclear weapons has taken a major step toward defeat. . .The Joint Chiefs of Staff, if left to themselves without all the political and diplomatic constraints, would probably give up plenty of the arsenal. And they could do so without reference to the Soviets. It is the harnessing of our actions to the Soviets that presents the complications, the restrictions on unilateral actions.

Our thinking about nuclear war and nuclear weapons has been almost exclusively on the technological plane. We have fallen in love with paranoid scenarios of speculative future developments. Our nuclear theories are arid, void of realistic political and social content. Our impulse to constantly refine our weapons and accumulate newer and better ones, all in the name of deterrence, brings us no peace of mind or enhanced security.

We can deemphasize nuclear weapons and planning for nuclear war and improve our security. But aggressive presidential leadership will be required for this. A President can also inform the American people of the actual Soviet and American strengths and weaknesses. He can dampen the false alarms that have so distorted our government decision making and public support in recent years.

New Approaches

In the current conditions of public and official ferment over nuclear issues, openings have been created for major departures from traditional approaches. The new opportunities have arisen unexpectedly but at least for the next few years it should be possible to mobilize broad political support for containing, limiting, and

nearly eliminating the nuclear arms race. This is a real opportunity for practical action, not an idealistic delusion. The Reagan Administration itself has ironically played the major role in making possible these changes.

But at the same time as we move forward with arms negotiations we need to start dealing with the basic issue of how to facilitate peaceful coexistence between the United States and the Soviet Union. Fear and mistrust are at the heart of the nuclear arms race. They are at the heart of our deterrence policy theories which assume an aggressive intent on the part of the Soviet Union. We cannot go far toward slowing the nuclear arms race if the current level of fear and tension continues. Even at greatly reduced numbers of nuclear weapons, the world will not really be much better off if we and the Soviets continue to engage in hostile confrontation.

A concerted effort is required to identify areas of possible U.S.-Soviet cooperation and understanding. Europeans can serve as a bridge between the two superpowers, rather than serve as a battlefield again. In the early 1970's the U.S. and the U.S.S.R. made initial steps toward setting up a comprehensive program of cooperation in many areas. The Apollo-Soyuz space linkup in 1975 was one result. But these initial efforts foundered on the U.S. defeat in Vietnam and American self-doubts.

We need to get back on the path originally devised by Dwight Eisenhower and Nikita Khrushchev and then followed by Richard Nixon and Henry Kissinger. Peaceful coexistence is possible between the U.S. and the Soviet Union. It is not a vacuous slogan but a necessity.

Looking ahead, if the Soviet Union, Europe, and the U.S. are to avert a nuclear war, we must embark on a dynamic program to enhance cooperation and understanding. In preparing for the 21st Century we ought to devote the last years of this century to measures that will improve the understanding and cooperation among the peoples and governments of the U.S., the Soviet Union, and Europe. If these nations understand each other, cooperate, and prosper, Latin America, Asia and Africa would all benefit.

Gene LaRocque is the director of the Center for Defense Information. The Center supports a strong defense but opposes excessive expenditures on forces. It believes that strong social, economic and political structures contribute equally to national security and are essential to the strength and welfare of our country.

"It explains why we have had no direct attack on the developed nations since Hitler's gamble failed. Nuclear deterrence works."

Nuclear Arms Make Deterrence More Effective

Raymond English

Potential aggressors are deterred by the probability of unacceptable damage to their own territory—such is the general theory of nuclear deterrence. However, another aspect of nuclear deterrence comes into focus if the subject is viewed in historical perspective.

From that perspective it is clear that the most tempting region for the conquest and exploitation in our time is Western Europe, whose wealth, skilled work force, industrial efficiency, and uncertain will to resist make it the obvious target for despotic and economically inefficient regimes. Many Western European intellectuals seem convinced that it is only a matter of time before their countries succumb to Soviet power; to use Toynbee's terminology: the internal proletariat is prepared to collaborate with the external proletariat. The intellectuals appear to agree with Voltaire: "The nation which makes the best use of the sword will always subjugate the nation which has more gold and less courage."

Yet, while much of the world has been ravaged by wars and violent upheavals, Western Europe—the one area that would repay its conqueror with loot on a fabulous scale—has remained immune. Surely it is not a coincidence that Western Europe is also the one region of the world (apart from the two superpowers) that has been sheltered by the threat of nuclear war. Thus, those who bewail the invention of nuclear weapons, who wish that the djinn would go back into the bottle, or who blindly demand unilateral nuclear disarmament are wrong. Nuclear weapons, if exploited skillfully, offer the remedy for mankind's persistent failure to build on and expand the achievements of high civilization.

Again and again history records the psychological or physical inability of developed, pluralistic, civilized (and often relatively free) societies to muster the will and energy to resist envious, loot-hungry barbarians.

Sumer, Babylon, Assyria, and Indus Valley civilization, even Egypt with its natural defenses, Persia, Greece, Rome and (at recurrent intervals) Chinese civilization collapsed when their armies could no longer withstand the pressure from the economically underdeveloped, but militarily vigorous, peoples on the fringes of civilization.

The record of failure did not end with Rome. The great civilization of Islam rose and fell; medieval Europe—still barbarous—played its part in destroying both Islamic achievements and the remnants of Byzantine civilization; the vigorous and greedy British and French overwhelmed the decadent civilized states of India and Southeast Asia; Russia led the drives to dismember the Ottoman empire (the "sick man of Europe") and to partition Poland (a more developed nation than Russia).

If history shows the creation of empires through the conquests of less developed peoples by more developed, it also shows the reversal of the process when the more developed civilization reaches a high point of cultural, economic and political achievement—the point at which the West stands today.

Whether civilized people are effete and deserve to be swept into the dustbin of history is a question that only God, or Hegel, or Marx can answer. Yet it seems wasteful for societies to repeat *ad infinitum* the slow, difficult climb to complex social and economic organization, prosperity, and personal and political freedom, only to succumb to a barbarous tide of invasion, conquests, and tyranny. Alexis de Tocqueville remarked about the tragi-comedies of history that he could not believe that our creator placed us on earth to have us repeat endlessly the same mistakes.

Barbarism

The term "barbarian" is used here to describe economically less efficient and militarily more aggressive states in contrast to states with advanced

Raymond English, "Civilization, Barbarism and Nuclear Deterrence," *The Washington Times*, September 23, 1982. Reprinted with permission.

economic development and political freedom. The Soviet Union, with its tyrannical and adventurist rulers, qualifies as the leading barbarian power today. Ambassador Averell Harriman warned President Truman before the end of World War II to expect a "barbarian invasion" of Europe by the Soviet Union.

The American monopoly of the atom bomb, coupled with the establishment of NATO, blocked the invasion of Western Europe, but came too late to preserve Eastern Europe from the barbarian tide. There can be little doubt that without the nuclear deterrent not even NATO's conventional forces would have prevented a later Soviet takeover. But for the nuclear umbrella, the Soviets would today control Eurasia and the Middle East and have much of Africa at their mercy.

> "Almost certainly there will be no need for the defenders of freedom and civilization to use nuclear weapons, as long as they have the option to do so."

Sir Halford Mackinder's pre-nuclear prophecy would be fulfilled:
Who rules the Heartland
          commands the World-Island;
Who rules the World-Island
          commands the world.
Why has the nuclear threat changed the pattern of history? It seems that massive barbarian armies, even when equipped with the latest conventional armaments, and even when in possession of nuclear weapons, can no longer gamble on the conquest of the free, highly cultured, and unbellicose populations of civilized societies in order to seize their economic resources. *If the barbarians resort to nuclear war they destroy the territory and loot that beckon them. If the defenders use tactical or even strategic nuclear weapons, they destroy only things that they have not envied and do not want.* Almost certainly there will be no need for the defenders of freedom and civilization to *use* nuclear weapons, as long as they have the option to do so. The nuclear threat may change the dreary, cyclical pattern of history.

Four German statesmen, in their response to the proposal to renounce the first use of nuclear weapons in Europe, identified the break in the historical pattern in a single perceptive sentence:

"Wherever nuclear weapons are present, war loses its earlier function as a continuation of politics by other means." (Nuclear Weapons and the Preservation of Peace," by Kaiser, Leber, Mertes, Schulze, *Foreign Affairs,* Summer 1982, page 1157.)

Precisely. A land and people devastated by nuclear warfare are little use to anyone, and least of all to predatory barbarians.

Nuclear deterrence is thus an unprecedented factor that may bring rationality into relations between "have" and "have-not" powers—between the envied and the enviers. This explains why we have had no direct attack on the developed nations since Hitler's gamble failed. Nuclear deterrence works, which is frustrating for contemporary Genghis Khans and Attilas, and confusing for contemporary Mahatmas.

Raymond English is a vice president of the Ethics and Public Policy Center in Washington.

"If there are no winners, then no rhetoric can disguise the endless death upon which deterrence policy is based."

Nuclear Arms Make Deterrence Obsolete

Kermit D. Johnson

We should examine the underlying rationale for the arms race: the policy of nuclear deterrence. To "deter" means to "frighten" or to "strike terror." We must have sufficient nuclear capability to frighten a possible aggressor into acting rationally. The aggressor must be convinced he is calling sure and certain retaliatory destruction down on his head. Or, in the words of the U.S. Military Posture Statement for Fiscal Year 1983: "Deterrence depends upon the assured capability and manifest will to inflict damage on the Soviet Union disproportionate to any goals that rational Soviet leaders might hope to achieve."

But what is a "sufficient" nuclear capability? How many of what kinds of nuclear weapons will create the precise degree of fear to promote rational behavior in an aggressor? How much fear is enough? Which psychologist can define it? Which technician can meter it? At what point will *too much* fear shatter rationality? When Soviet missiles were being deployed in nearby Cuba, we were willing to risk all. Will the Soviets take a similar gamble when we cut the missile flight time to the Soviet Union from 30 to under eight minutes by basing Pershing II missiles in Europe this winter? And what of the MX and Trident II first strike capability? At what level does the creation of fear become an irrational act in itself? Who's terrifying whom?

Deterrence and Trust

And we speak of not being able to trust the Russians! Our very policy of nuclear deterrence is *founded* on trust, trust that they will be infused with "rational fear," but not succumb to blind, irrational terror. Who among the hard-headed realists and bottom-liners can tell us what requirements meet the needs of a doctrine based, not so much on reality, but on perceptions of reality? The sober answer is that no one knows. We know only that nuclear deterrence will likely continue

to be the only game in town. As a four-star general once told me, asking the military to relinquish nuclear deterrence is like asking unions to forego their right to strike or the clergy to renounce their doctrine of Divine punishment.

The very imprecision inherent in nuclear deterrence lessens the weight which can be given to the technician's task of calculating and comparing the quality and quantity of weapons systems. Measuring the effects of additional weaponry in an overkill world is a dubious proposition at best, much less projecting how Soviet leaders will perceive those effects. Nuclear deterrence may masquerade as military science, but at bottom it is little more than an ideological rallying point for "true believers." One must *believe* that U.S. and Soviet technology and technicians will not trigger accidental war. One must *believe* the "inescapable paradox" that arms build-ups magically lead to drawdowns. One must *believe* that the nuclear arms race will not end suddenly in mutual annihilation or slowly in mutual suicide through moral, emotional and economic dissipation.

Mr. Weinberger credits our "credible nuclear deterrent" for the "uncomfortable form of peace" we experience, where "major world powers have not fought each other for 37 years." He concludes that nuclear deterrence "is the best way we have found" and "we must not forget that it has been totally successful thus far." Employing this logic, he might as well guarantee that there will be no cataclysmic California earthquake solely because we haven't had one for 77 years. The history of deterrence includes not only the few wars-which-never-were, but also a long and terrible trail of carnage. In the past, even failed deterrence left nations with the possibility of recovery. Today, there will be no second chance. The theology of nuclear deterrence is based on a perfectionist view of human nature, which holds that human beings will not make "one more mistake."

Kermit D. Johnson, "Nuclear Deterrence as Ideology," *The Defense Monitor*, Vol. XII, No. 3, 1983.

Unwinnable War

However, when Mr. Weinberger speaks of "a war that was never fought because we were prepared to fight it, *and to win it*" (my emphasis), he is obviously considering the possibility of failed deterrence. This stated intention to "win" doubtless accounts for this administration's equation of deterrence with "war-fighting." If peace through preparation is the military's first principle, then victory through war if peace fails runs a close second. General Douglas MacArthur's "There is no substitute for victory" are hallowed words. As are Vince Lombardi's: "Winning isn't everything, it's the only thing."

"The theology of nuclear deterrence is based on a perfectionist view of human nature, which holds that human beings will not make 'one more mistake.'"

This drive to win is reflected even in the unsporting realm of nuclear doctrine when Mr. Weinberger speaks of "prevailing." But what does it mean to "prevail" in an "unwinnable" nuclear war? How does this square with President Reagan's words: "I don't think there could be any winners."

If there are no winners, then no rhetoric can disguise the endless death upon which deterrence policy is based. Asking mere mortals to exercise perfect restraint while threatening to destroy one another is more than an irony. It is an irrational drive toward death.

Major General Kermit D. Johnson was Chief of Chaplains in the U.S. Army until his retirement in 1982. He is currently Associate Director of the Center for Defense Information.

The Nuclear Bomb: How It Works and Its Effects

Peter Goodwin

Make no mistake about it, nuclear bombs are quite totally different from any other form of weapon. To begin with, their explosive power can be millions of times greater than the biggest conventional (high explosive) bombs; to add to this destructive capability they also generate dangerous radiation which could kill and maim even more victims than the stupendous blast and heat which is produced.

The bomb which destroyed Hiroshima in 1945 was a comparatively modest nuclear weapon by today's standards. Nevertheless it killed 80,000 people—more than the number killed by bombs in Great Britain during the whole of the Second World War. Many survivors of the Hiroshima blast died later from injuries, burns and infections, their bodies weakened by radiation which, in some, caused fatal illnesses such as leukemia years later.

In the shorthand jargon of nuclear weaponry the Hiroshima bomb was rated as a 12.5 kiloton (or kt) weapon, i.e., it was equivalent to 12,500 tons of TNT high explosive. Many present-day weapons have explosive powers of several magatons (or Mt)—equivalent to several *million* tons of TNT. The most powerful bomb ever known to have been exploded (experimentally) was over 50 magatons in yield. To say that nuclear bombs are millions of times more powerful than conventional bombs, however, is still not enough to convey their dreadful effects, for the huge concentration of energy within the nuclear fireball created at the point of explosion has other lethal effects.

Converting Matter into Energy

Until the twentieth century it was thought that matter could neither be created nor destroyed. The same was thought to be true of energy. But Albert Einstein realized that it is possible under special circumstances to convert matter into energy, or energy into matter. Normally this never happens, but when scientists started to experiment

Peter Goodwin, *Nuclear War*, London: The Rutledge Press, 1981. Reprinted with permission.

with atoms they proved that matter from the innermost parts of the atom *could* be converted into energy, and a huge new source of power could be tapped. When the Second World War began, it became a matter of urgency to develop bombs which derive energy from splitting the atom.

Nuclear Bombs

There are two basic types of nuclear bomb. In the first, called a 'fission' or atom bomb, atoms are split apart. This can only happen to very large atoms such as those of the element uranium. The nucleus breaks up into two smaller pieces and several neutrons, releasing energy while the disintegration takes place.

The hydrogen or 'fusion' bomb, works by fusing atoms of light elements together—particularly hydrogen, which then forms helium. This process also releases large amounts of energy by the destruction of matter within the nucleus.

Nuclear Fission

The heaviest element found in nature, uranium, has 92 protons within the nucleus of every atom. But there are several different isotopes of uranium. More than 99 percent of the natural element consists of uranium 238, which has 146 neutrons in the nucleus together with the 92 protons. Nearly all the remaining natural uranium consists of isotope 235, which has only 143 neutrons in each nucleus. This difference turns out to be vital because neutrons are involved in the processes by which the nucleus is held together and prevented, under normal circumstances, from disintegrating. A few neutrons added to or subtracted from a nucleus can make a great deal of difference to an element's stability.

Uranium 235 is less stable than uranium 238; in a lump of uranium 235 containing millions of atoms, a few disintegrate spontaneously at any one moment. Each nucleus splits, or fissions, into two smaller parts forming different elements. When fission takes place neutrons are also released from the nucleus together with pure energy in the form of gamma rays.

Because each fissioning nucleus releases neutrons, these in turn can cause fission in other uranium 235 nuclei nearby. A chain of fission reactions can occur if there are enough fissionable nuclei in the vicinity (a 'critical' amount). If the chain reaction is allowed to proceed an explosion can take place in a tiny fraction of a second. This is what happens in a fission bomb.

The smallest amount of fissionable material needed to produce a chain reaction is called the critical mass. A few pounds of uranium 235 can form a critical mass. If compressed by an explosion—one of the means by which some bombs are triggered—even smaller amounts can become critical. This is because the nuclei are much closer together than in the uncompressed state. An alternative means of detonation is suddenly to bring together two pieces of uranium which are each individually less than the critical mass but which equal or just exceed this amount when brought into contact.

"Although a clear distinction cannot truly be made between...different categories [of weapons], strategic arms are the only ones strictly limited by international agreement."

Heavier elements than uranium can be produced artificially. Uranium 238 absorbs neutrons inside nuclear reactors, becoming a different isotope—uranium 239. This is not stable, but releases two electrons (beta particles) from the nucleus. The residue forms the element plutonium, which then has 94 protons in each nucleus as a result of two neutrons within the nucleus being converted into protons by the release of the two beta particles. All nuclear reactors produce plutonium as a by-product. Like uranium 235, plutonium is also fissionable and works very well in fission bombs. Since it is more readily obtainable than uranium 235, it is of immense importance in the making of nuclear weapons.

Fusion Bomb

When nuclei of the lightest element, hydrogen, are fused together to form nuclei of helium, matter is converted into energy and, as in the fission of uranium or plutonium, a great deal of energy is released. The hydrogen isotopes deuterium and tritium react with each other to produce the most energy of all the fusion reactions.

The fusion reaction will only begin, however, if the temperature of the mixture of hydrogen isotopes is raised to tens of millions of degrees centigrade. To do this, a fission bomb is used as a trigger for the fusion bomb. Hence fusion bombs always combine fission with fusion.

Hydrogen (fusion) bombs can be more powerful than a simple fission bomb because fusion of a mixture of deuterium and tritium can produce nearly three times as much energy as fission of the same weight of uranium or plutonium. In addition, however, large amounts of deuterium and tritium can be stored in the bomb before detonation without any risk of the mass becoming critical, whereas in a pure fission bomb it is difficult to keep large quantities of material sufficiently separated to prevent the chain reaction from starting.

Delivery Systems

Nuclear warheads can be delivered to their targets by means of shells, bombs or missiles. They can be fired from silos, aircraft, submarines and even huge guns. A distinction is sometimes drawn between 'strategic', 'theatre', and 'tactical' nuclear weapons. It is approximately true to say that strategic weapons are those which can be delivered to a very distant target, one in another continent, whereas tactical weapons are for exactly the opposite purpose: for fighting battles between armies. Normally tactical weapons have much shorter ranges, from hundreds down to only a few miles, and have lower yields.

Theatre weapons are intermediate in range: they are intended for fighting a campaign in a particular region, or theatre, of the world in a war which does not spread across the globe. Although intermediate in range between strategic and tactical weapons, they are not necessarily intermediate in explosive yield: some are just as powerful as the strategic weapons. (The words 'theatre' and 'tactical' are often used interchangeably.)

Although a clear distinction cannot truly be made between these different categories, strategic arms are the only ones strictly limited by international agreement. The Strategic Arms Limitation Talks (SALT) between the Soviet Union and the United States have limited the number of weapons described as strategic, but have not controlled theatre or tactical arsenals.

Ballistic Missiles

The ballistic missile has transformed the nature of war because of its great speed. It consists fundamentally of one or more warheads mounted on a space rocket. Because the rocket is shot out of the earth's atmosphere it can accelerate to about 15,000 miles per hour (24,000 km/h) without having to push against the air which at lower altitudes would make such a high speed impossible. So strategic missiles can fly between continents in about 20 minutes. Theatre missiles can reach targets several miles away in just a few minutes.

Accuracy

The word ballistic implies that the missile is 'thrown' to its target. The rocket motors only operate for the first acceleration, which takes the missile out of the atmosphere. After that it simply flies like a bullet, a method needing considerable accuracy. This is provided by computers (on the ground and in the rocket) connected to 'inertial navigation systems'—devices such as gyro-compasses—linked electronically so as to detect every acceleration the rocket makes and thus to keep track of its precise location. While the rocket motors are still burning, the inertial navigation system establishes whether the missile is on course and makes any adjustments necessary to improve the accuracy of its flightpath.

Despite tremendous navigational advances, doubts are still raised about the targeting accuracy of ballistic missiles. Areas of improvement in missile guidance systems are, understandably, closely guarded military secrets, but it is known that mid-flight correction could be made, for instance, by mounting a telescope on the missile capable of taking a 'fix' from one or more stars. So-called 'terminal guidance' (for recognizing the individual target and correcting the missile flightpath yet again to bring the warhead on to it) could be achieved by a number of possible methods such as radar capable of recognizing terrain in the target zone. But all of these methods are fraught with difficulties.

Because a missile can only be expected to have a chance, not a certainty, of striking the target, estimates of the accuracy of any particular system result in a figure called the circular error probable, or CEP. This is the radius of a circle (the centre of which is the target) within which half of the missiles targeted are likely to fall. Even when missile systems are thought to have quite small CEPs no claims are made about the likely landing sites of the 50 per cent of warheads which fall outside the CEP radius so that you could expect some missiles to land off course, introducing yet more uncertainty into any actual nuclear conflict.

The Nuclear Explosion

The nuclear fireball is as hot as the sun, indeed its immense power is derived from nuclear reactions similar to those happening continuously within the sun. The very high temperatures cause a blinding flash of light and heat to radiate out from the explosion. Anyone looking at the fireball could be blinded for several minutes or hours, or severely damage their eyes. Within a few miles from the explosion exposed skin and flesh might be charred and burnt from the bone and houses could burst into flames. A whole city could ignite within seconds and might even become engulfed in a 'fire storm'—a ranging inferno which sucks in air from the surrounding area and would not abate until everything was burnt.

When the bomb is exploded in the atmosphere, the fireball is almost spherical. In less than a thousandth of a second after detonation, the fireball from a 1-Mt explosion grows to more than 300 feet (100 metres) wide, and is nearly 6,000 feet (2 km) wide after ten seconds. At the same time, it rises like a hot-air balloon, at about 300 feet every second.

Air Bursts and Surface Bursts

If the fireball does not touch the ground (detonation having taken place in the atmosphere) the explosion is described as an air burst. For a 1-Mt bomb, for example, the explosive point would have to be more than half a mile (1 km) above the ground to be classed as an air burst—higher than the greatest radius of the fireball.

"The nuclear fireball is as hot as the sun, indeed its immense power is derived from nuclear reactions similar to those happening continuously within the sun."

When the height of an explosion is greater than about 100,000 feet (30 km) it is called a high altitude explosion, being above most of the earth's atmosphere. The effects on the ground would then be different from lower bursts within the atmosphere.

Detonation on the ground, or close enough for the fireball to touch the surface, is called a surface burst.

Heat Effects

About one-third of the nuclear fireball's energy is radiated as intense heat. In clear weather the heat flash could instantly set fire to objects and harm people.

Air bursts can cause greater heat damage than ground bursts because the heat rays can travel further without getting absorbed by buildings, hills and other surface features. The more powerful the weapon, the longer the pulse of heat (over three seconds for a 25-kt). Most substances would be less likely to be damaged by a particular amount of heat if it were spread out over several seconds than they would be if it were delivered in one sudden flash. Calculations show that within a range called the fire zone, most combustible materials would be ignited in clear, dry weather.

Eye Damage

A brief, direct glimpse of the fireball could cause temporary blindness lasting from a few minutes to some hours (called flash-blindness) or permanent eye damage (retinal burns) which could impair vision, though not necessarily cause total blindness. A 100-kt weapon exploding at a height of 50,000 feet (15.2 km) could cause flash-blindness even in daytime (when the eye is adapted to bright light) at a distance of over 20 miles (32 km). The same explosion would cause retinal burns at a distance of 27 miles (43.2 km) in daytime, and at more than 70 miles (112 km) distance at night (when the iris is dilated to improve vision in low-light conditions).

Air Blast

The enormous pressure which builds up within a fraction of a second at the point of explosion is the source of a high-pressure blast wave, capable of striking property and people like a giant hammer blow. The blast wave travels outwards from the centre of the explosion at approximately the speed of sound (1,100 feet per second/330 metres per second), so it takes about five seconds to travel 1 mile (three seconds to travel 1 km). When an explosion occurs the first effect is the blinding flash of light, accompanied by an invisible 'flash' of radiation (which would be lethal if you were close enough). But there is no noise until the blast wave arrives, just as thunder follows lightning.

If you could count the seconds between the light flash and the arrival of the blast wave you might estimate your distance from the point of detonation. Knowing this distance could help you to survive in some circumstances.

Drag Effects

The blast wave pushes air bodily outwards from the point of the explosion causing tremendously strong winds. Although the blast pressure could crush huge buildings, as much damage might be caused by loose objects (such as cars, trucks, people and flying debris) being blown by the hurricane-force winds. Winds from a 20-Mt bomb exploded over Kennedy Airport could reach 200 miles per hour (320 km/h) on the East Side of Manhattan. Survival would be practically impossible for anybody caught out in the open; people indoors would probably be trapped beneath tons of fallen masonry.

Afterwinds

Following the initial outward rush of wind accompanying the blast wave, a gentler afterwind blows back inwards towards the point of explosion. This is not likely to be dangerous in most circumstances.

How Blast Damages Buildings

Before the blast wave arrives the pressure over the building is normal atmospheric: 14.7 pounds per square inch (psi). The blast wave itself consists of an advancing 'slice' of air which is compressed to over normal atmospheric pressure, a so-called 'over-pressure'. Not only does a wave of compression move outwards from the explosive point, but air also moves itself, causing very strong winds. So there are two kinds of pressures exerted suddenly on buildings in the path of this blast wave: the sudden overpressure and the drag pressure caused by the wind.

"Blast pressures capable of destroying a house could leave humans physically unharmed."

Vertical walls, particularly those directly facing the on-coming blast wave (i.e., towards the explosive point) reflect the overpressure blast wave like a racket reflecting a tennis ball back down the court. A force of twice the overpressure is felt on the side of a building because of this reflection. But when the wind drag effects are added the total reflected pressure can rise to much more than twice the blast overpressure. If the blast wave does not squash the building flat, therefore, the 'hammer blow' of

such reflection effects could demolish a wall.

There are several different ways in which the unequal distribution of pressure can crush a building. If not many doors and windows were open it might simply be crushed flat because the pressure outside was much greater than that inside. If they were strong enough, however, the sides and roof not facing the blast might withstand the maximum overpressure, but the wall facing the shock wave might not because of the increase in pressure caused by reflection, and most if not the whole of the building could collapse. Thirdly, the blast wave from the explosion of large nuclear bombs can take several seconds to pass completely, so the maximum overpressure and wind speed may persist for this period. If there were enough doors and windows open (or blasted out), the extra pressure would force air into the building and as soon as the wave had passed, it would explode. About 10 miles (16 km) from a 10-Mt explosion, for example, the blast overpressure would take about eight seconds to pass. At this range the overpressure could reach about 4 psi above atmospheric pressure. This is quite enough to flatten most buildings, but the tremendous pressure built up in the eight seconds of the blast wave's passage would cause most buildings which remained standing to explode.

Blast Effects on People

Blast pressures capable of destroying a house could leave humans physically unharmed. The body is flexible and small. It bends on impact, and when squashed the internal pressure quickly rises to equal the external pressure.

An overpressure of 5 psi could possibly rupture eardrums, though not if the ears were protected. Ten psi overpressure (enough to bring down even earthquake-resistant reinforced concrete buildings) might cause slight bleeding in the lungs. Up to 30 psi pressure could cause severe lung hemorrhage and 40 psi could kill. (But anybody close enough to an explosion to experience 40 psi overpressure would almost certainly be killed by other bomb effects.)

The main danger to people in the open air at the time of an explosion would be being struck by flying glass and debris, or being thrown bodily by the wind pressure against hard objects. Five miles (8 km) from a 1-Mt air burst, for example, the blast overpressure of up to 4 psi would destroy houses but leave people uninjured. But many would be killed or smashed by being dragged along in winds of up to 130 mph (210 km/h) and hurled into solid objects, or they would be severely lacerated by flying glass.

Calculating Blast Destruction

The testing of nuclear weapons has made it possible to make detailed predictions about the amount of damage done at different ranges from explosions of various weapon powers. An invaluable reference for precise details is the US Government's publication *The Effects of*

Nuclear Weapons, in which full documentation of the types of damage and possible mechanisms are given. Inserted into the back cover of the book is a Nuclear Bomb Effects Computer: a circular slide rule which enables you to make quick accurate calculations of all of the main effects. It is *very important* to note, however, that many factors could change these effects: a bomb might not explode properly, so that only a fraction of its energy was released; hills could reflect blast and heat and channel winds, and many aspects of the weather—rainfall, visibility, temperature of different air layers and winds—could all change the effects of nuclear weapons. So it is only possible to give *approximate* figures for the amount of damage which might occur in *average* places under *average* conditions.

The amount of blast damage depends almost exclusively on the blast overpressure produced by the explosion. This is highest at or below the explosion ('ground zero').

The Fire Threat

The risk of the outbreak of severe fires after a nuclear explosion can hardly be overstated. Cities could burn very easily following a large scale nuclear attack, as would forests and other vegetation including farm crops. Fire could not only devastate urban civilization, it could also threaten the life of farm livestock and the natural habitat of many wild animals and plants. A 'fire zone' could extend 5 miles (8 km) in all directions from the explosive point of a 1-Mt bomb. It would be possible to convert every city in Europe, the United States and the Soviet Union into a fire zone using only a small fraction of the present day nuclear arsenal. Work out the risk for yourself: draw circles of 5-mile (8-km) radius over towns and cities on a map. Not many such circles are needed to account for the greater part of civilized habitation in the world.

Fire Storms

Hiroshima was engulfed in a fire storm following the explosion of the atom bomb above it in 1945. So many fires were started by the heat flash that they all joined together in the central area and raged away like an enormous blow-torch, sucking air from outside until everything combustible was burnt. Firestorms also happened in some German cities bombed during the Second World War. Once a fire storm had begun, nothing could stop it until everything was burnt. It would not only destroy buildings and property, but also burn up oxygen from the air, so that even people in deep, heat-resistent shelters could die of suffocation.

Nobody knows for certain how easily nuclear explosions would cause fire storms: Nagasaki did not suffer from one although there was widespread burning.

Conflagration

Whether or not fire storms did occur, however, fires could start which spread out of control. Called conflagrations, these could extend to and devastate regions far removed from the areas of the other weapon effects. This is what happened in Nagasaki: the distribution of buildings and the hilly terrain prevented a fire storm but favoured a conflagration. Especially with the radiation hazards of nuclear weapons it would be unlikely that any effective fire-fighting could be carried out. Huge numbers of people could be burnt to death and many others could die from the effects of less severe burns.

Burns

Because so much of the nuclear bomb's energy is generated in the form of heat the most common injuries among survivors would probably be burns. Victims 23 miles away from a 20-Mt explosion standing in the open could suffer from charred skin (third degree burns) on parts of the body not covered by clothes. The same effect could be produced 8 miles away from a 1-Mt explosion and at this range many fires would be started by the heat flash.

"All effects of nuclear weapons are uncertain by large factors, so it is by no means definite that because a weapon of a particular yield is targeted to a particular point a known sequence of events will take place."

The medical problem of treating hundreds of thousands of burn victims on the fringes of each explosion would be insuperable. Most would die painfully because of lack of medical facilities.

Sources of Uncertainty

All effects of nuclear weapons are uncertain by large factors, so it is by no means definite that because a weapon of a particular yield is targeted to a particular point a known sequence of events will take place. In fact the actual events may be completely different from those suggested by the theory. One reason is that the bomb may not reach its target: it may miss by hundreds of feet or several miles. The effects of a near miss could be totally different from a direct hit if, for example, a hill stood between the intended target and the actual point of impact. Secondly the bomb might not explode efficiently: the fission and fusion reactions might not proceed fully, so a 10-Mt bomb might only produce an explosion equivalent to a much smaller device or no explosion at all. Most uncertain of all is the weather: heavy rainfall would almost completely eliminate the hazard of serious fires even though some could start. Fog or low cloud could prevent light and heat radiating out from the fireball, and strong winds could produce at least two effects: they could help push the warhead off-course, and they would blow fallout and debris. You could be just a few miles upwind of ground zero in a strong gale and torrential rain with low clouds and be saved by the weather from heat, some of the blast, light-flash and fallout. Yet another uncertainty is terrain: hills and tall buildings reflect blast and cast shadows shielding other places from light and heat in a way which could greatly change the bomb effects.

Radiation

Radiation is one of the most fearful aspects of nuclear warfare. Invisible, it is also undetectable by the other human senses, and yet it is lethal. The explosive energy of nuclear fission and fusion processes produce huge numbers of fast neutrons. At the same time the immense release of energy generates x-rays and gamma rays: both are electromagnetic waves, similar in basic nature to light waves and radio waves, but far more energetic (having very short wavelengths) and therefore penetrating and dangerous to humans. The flash of radiation produced at the time of explosion is called initial radiation. The fallout radiation, which continues to be a hazard after the explosion, is called 'delayed radiation'.

Initial radiation is harmful within only a limited range because as the gamma rays and neutrons travel outwards from the explosion they become weakened by spreading out and becoming absorbed in the atmosphere. The x-rays are absorbed even before leaving the fireball.

"The feature which makes nuclear bombs uniquely powerful...also creates the hazard of fallout radiation which is not encountered with ordinary explosives."

But the larger weapons (a few hundred kilotons upwards in power) would produce so much blast and heat that anybody close enough to receive lethal amounts of initial radiation would almost certainly not survive death by blast injury or burning. If people were exposed to low-yield weapons, however, they might be killed by initial radiation. The 12.5-kt Hiroshima bomb inflicted initial radiation damage on many people. Modern weapons of 1 kt designed for use on the battlefield could kill victims far beyond the range of heat and blast effects by exposure to neutron and gamma radiations.

Delayed Radiation: Fallout

The feature which makes nuclear bombs uniquely powerful, the fission and fusion of nuclei, also creates the hazard of fallout radiation which is not encountered with ordinary explosives. When fission takes place uranium and plutonium nuclei do not all split into the same types of fragments. More than 300 different isotopes—the fission products—may be formed. Some of these—those which exist normally in nature and whose nuclei are identical with those of atoms found widely in ordinary materials—may be stable. But many of the

fission products are very unstable. Their nuclei can erupt like volcanoes, spewing forth electrons and gamma rays with great vehemence. These are 'radioisotopes' which can fall to earth as fallout. Not every unstable nucleus erupts at the same moment. If this happened all the radiation would emerge in an instant and there would be no remaining fallout hazard. Each nucleus has a statistical chance of decaying by ejecting radiation within a period of time (which differs for each isotope). But at the end of that time some will have decayed whereas others will continue holding on to their pent-up energies.

Half-Life

The 'half-life' of any particular radioisotope is the length of time taken for half of the atomic nuclei in a particular sample of the isotope to erupt and transform themselves into the nuclei of other atoms by emitting radiation. After two half-lives, only one-quarter of the atoms will be left, after three half-lives one-eighth and so on.

Range of Half-Lives

Some fission products have half-lives of just a few minutes so all of their atoms disappear soon after the explosion. But the full range of the many different radioisotopes produced by a nuclear explosion includes those which have half-lives of thousands of years.

The shortest-lived isotopes are the most hazardous soon after the explosion, because most of their atoms erupt and produce radiation. The long-lived isotopes produce smaller amounts of radiation in a given length of time but continue to do so for many years. They can create a serious long-term risk to health and life by entering the environment and the food chain and getting trapped within the body.

Reduction of the Hazard with Time

All atoms of radioisotopes in fallout have a statistical likelihood of decaying and becoming stable substances not hazardous to life as the amount of radiation emitted by fallout decreases as time goes by. Many of the isotopes have very short half-lives and tests have shown that seven hours after an explosion the amount of radiation is only one-tenth as much as one hour after detonation. This is sometimes called the seven-tenths rule. Extending this to a period of 49 hours (7 x 7 hours) the rate of radiation dosage is reduced to one-hundredth of its initial value. After two weeks (7 x 7 x 7 hours) it has fallen to one-thousandth. This factor of 1,000 is sufficient to reduce the radiation dose rate to relatively safe levels. This is why two weeks is often quoted as 'the shelter period'.

Warning: Although the seven-tenths rule demonstrates dramatically how quickly radioactivity can fall off as time passes, there is no substitute for actually measuring the strength of radiation with instruments such as radiation dose-meters and Geiger Counters. Fallout can be far more concentrated in some places (such as where heavy rain has fallen) than others and even though the radiation decreases with time it could begin at a very high level in such a 'hot spot'. A further reason for caution is that the seven-tenths rule should not be taken too literally: it was worked out from tests and calculations taking note of the quantities and half-lives of all isotopes likely to be present in most nuclear explosions, but nobody can be sure whether an explosion would proceed as the textbook says it should. Special weapons could even be used with extra elements designed to *increase* fallout contamination with selected isotopes.

How Fallout is Made

In air-burst explosions the fallout consists of a very fine dust which is a mixture of fission products, bomb construction materials, atoms of air and other substances in the atmosphere such as water vapour and pollutants. Surface bursts draw huge quantities of earth and other material into the fireball. This vaporizes, collects fission products, then cools, forming larger fallout particles, some as big as snowflakes and marbles, which fall to earth much more quickly than the fine dust of an air burst. In addition to this, the original surface materials become radioactive themselves (by absorbing fast neutrons) and add to the concentration of radiation produced by the fission products.

Thus fallout would be a far more severe local problem if a surface burst took place.

Global Fallout

All nuclear explosions in the earth's atmosphere cause distant fallout, however, because some of the fission products inevitably take the form of very fine dust which can stay at high altitude for long periods of time. For weapons with explosive yields from 100 kt upwards such particles rise into the stratosphere more than 30,000 feet (10 km) and can remain there for many years because this is above the altitude up to which particles can be 'scoured' by rainfall (most rain clouds are below this altitude). This stratospheric pollution with radioisotopes causes a global fallout hazard, with longer-lived isotopes, such as strontium 90 (half-life: 28 years), gradually falling to earth in widely dispersed places over many years. Global fallout would affect all countries, including ones which might not have been attacked with nuclear weapons. If enough of the bombs *already in existence* were ever to be exploded it is possible that the global fallout would reach dangerous levels for everybody on earth, and the prospect of a polluted world in which everybody surviving is exposed to hazardous levels of radiation after a nuclear war is entirely possible.

How Radiation Affects People

The danger from radiation cannot be stressed too much. You cannot see, hear, smell, taste or feel radiation and yet it can deliver a lethal blow in seconds. It is not even a kind killer. Death from radiation is almost always excruciatingly painful and protracted.

When radiation fails to kill, it can leave its mark on your body: sterility, leukemia, cancer, inherited disorders, birth defects and many other conditions may result from the destructive effect radiation has on living cells.

Because radiation is such an effective killer, it is even possible that in a nuclear war it could be used as the primary weapon. The neutron bomb is specifically designed to kill people by neutron radiation. Other nuclear weapons can be specially 'salted' with elements which can inflict additional radiation damage. Even defensive antimissile systems can consist of guided nuclear bombs which explode near an incoming missile—releasing fallout close to the defending country. There would be, indeed, no escape from the radiation problem if nuclear war began.

Harmful Radiation

Not all radiation is harmful. Heat and light are forms which normally do no damage at all. The unique, distinguishing feature which makes nuclear radiation so dangerous is that it causes 'ionisation', or static electricity, among the atoms of any material it passes through. This happens when electrons are torn away from their positions surrounding atoms. Atoms consist of a nucleus charged with positive electricity surrounded by electrons charged with negative electricity. When the ionising radiations separate these charges by removing electrons, atoms and free electrons react swiftly with other atoms or collections of atoms (molecules). In so doing they can greatly damage living tissue.

Our bodies are built up from billions of cells. Although each cell is no bigger than a hundredth part of a millimetre it contains a complex structure of atoms. Cells have the remarkable property of being able to reproduce themselves, and each human cell contains a set of instructions, a blueprint which specifies the structure of the cell. All of our bodily characteristics, hair colour, height, skin colour and so on, are coded like a computer programme in the genetic blueprint contained within each and every cell of the body. In theory it is possible to grow an entire human being (a clone) from a single human cell.

"All nuclear explosions in the earth's atmosphere cause distant fallout....Some of the fission products inevitably take the form of very fine dust which can stay at high altitudes for long periods."

The entire, beautiful form of a living cell is held together by electrical forces. The tiny attractions between atomic nuclei (which are positively charged) and the electrons (negatively charged) cement the different parts of the cell together. Although atoms and electrons within the cell move about to some extent, this motion is so tiny that the basic formation is very rarely disturbed. Imagine, therefore, what happens when a high-speed nuclear particle or energetic gamma ray enters the cell. The effect is devastating because the energies or ionising radiations far surpass the energies binding the cell parts together.

Cells can be so badly damaged that the elegant order is completely destroyed and the cell dies. If less radiation damage is incurred the cell may stay alive but have its chemistry so totally altered by the impact that it loses its original pattern. It may thus live on to become a cancer cell, endlessly reproducing itself in a grossly abnormal form. Very slight radiation damage may possibly be repaired, and in such circumstances normal cell life resumes.

"Not all radiation is harmful. Heat and light are forms which normally do no damage at all."

It is unfortunately true, however, that for reasons which are not understood even tiny amounts of radiation damage to cells can sometimes produce serious ill health. So no amount of ionising radiation, however tiny, can be dismissed as harmless.

Types of Radiation

Some forms of ionising radiation are beams of pure energy, rather like light but capable of penetrating materials. Others consist of particles: minute, invisible pieces of matter, some carrying electrical charges, others not. The most important types of ionising radiation are described below:

X-rays consist of waves, like light waves but much shorter, carrying more energy. They are used in medicine because of their ability to penetrate the body, particularly the fleshy parts, and reveal internal abnormalities on x-ray photographs. Even medical x-rays are dangerous to a slight extent.

Gamma rays are similar to x-rays but have a shorter wave length and are more energetic and more damaging. The fireball of a nuclear explosion produces an intense pulse of gamma rays. Fallout dust emits gamma radiation continuously and this is the most severe risk after a nuclear attack.

Beta particles are electrons which have been freed from the nuclei of atoms. They can only penetrate a few millimetres of human flesh. The main risk from beta radiation occurs if fallout producing it is accidentally swallowed or inhaled. In this way a radiation dose can be delivered continuously to sensitive internal organs rather than to skin, which is not very sensitive to radiation.

Alpha particles are the nuclei of helium atoms, stripped bare of electrons. They are heavy, carry an electric charge, and penetrate less than 1 millimetre through body tissues. Alpha particles outside the body are of little importance. But if fallout which contains isotopes releasing alpha particles is swallowed or inhaled, the radiation dose to internal organs can be dangerous.

Neutrons: One of the basic particles out of which atomic nuclei are made, a neutron carries no electricity and this helps it penetrate deeply within body tissues because it is unaffected by the positive and negative charges in the matter through which it passes. If it is absorbed by the nucleus of another atom, however, it can make that atom unstable and radioactive, forming an additional radiation hazard. Fallout produces few neutrons. The initial fireball of a nuclear explosion produces many. The neutron bomb is designed to produce as much neutron radiation as possible.

Exposure to these harmful radiations from the fireball and from fallout can cause radiation sickness and long-term effects.

Radiation Sickness

The symptoms of radiation sickness usually occur when a person has received at least 150 r of whole-body radiation over a short period of time, i.e., up to a few days.

Immediate Symptoms

A person receiving a dose of 450 r has, on average only a 50 per cent chance of surviving. This is called the 'LD 50 dose', and the symptoms of radiation sickness described below are those which result from radiation doses at about this level. A dose of about 600 r will kill almost anybody exposed to it but, as with almost any case of radiation sickness, death may be delayed for days or weeks.

Within a few hours of exposure to doses at about the LD 50 level, a person might feel nausea, vomit (possibly repeatedly) and develop diarrhea. These symptoms could could begin within half an hour of exposure, or could be delayed for several hours. If they disappeared after one or two days, the person might survive. If the symptoms continued with vomiting and diarrhea increasing, the person could develop exhaustion, fever, perhaps delirium and might die a week or so after exposure.

Victims who recovered from the early symptoms of sickness and diarrhea might feel fairly well, though tired, and have little appetite, but tests would show a fall in the number of white cells in the blood. After two weeks, new symptoms could arise: hair might start to fall out; then, from about the third week onwards, small hemorrhages might be noticed in the skin and the mucous membranes of the mouth. These areas could have a tendency to bruise easily and there might be bleeding from the gums. Ulcerations could develop in the mouth and throat and in the bowels, causing diarrhea again. Complete loss of appetite, loss of weight and high fever might follow. People as ill as this would not be able to eat and healing wounds would break down and become infected.

At this stage the number of red cells in the blood would be below normal and this condition of anemia would increase until the fourth or fifth week after exposure. The fall in the number of white cells (first noted two days after exposure) would have progressed, impairing the body's ability to fight infection. Evidence from Nagasaki and Hiroshima shows that infections of all kinds were rife among victims of the bomb. Many of those affected would die at this stage, a month or so after exposure. Those who survived would recover very slowly and, even after recovery, they might die suddenly from an infection which would cause a minor illness in a healthy person.

How Radiation Causes These Symptoms

As we have seen, the principal effect of ionising radiation is to inject sudden, excessive energy into living cells and thus to damage them. Cells have the ability to reproduce themselves, but some do this more quickly than others. Rapidly dividing tissues are very much more sensitive to radiation than tissues where the cells are reproducing more slowly. The human gut is an area of rapidly dividing tissue and radiation damage there would lead directly to the symptoms of nausea, vomiting and diarrhea. Damage to the gut could also allow bowel contents to enter the bloodstream and cause infection. Hemorrhages might appear at the site of gut damage as well as in other radiation-damaged tissues, leading to loss of blood and anemia.

Bone marrow cells are also rapidly dividing and sensitive to radiation. They manufacture most of the white blood cells with which a healthy person combats infections. Destruction of the bone marrow thus would make the victim vulnerable to a wide range of infections against which he or she no longer had adequate natural defences.

Some of the white cells in the bone marrow are also responsible for manufacturing the blood cells called platelets. In a healthy person these help the blood to form clots which stop severe hemorrhage at wounds or other sites of damage. Killing bone marrow cells removes the platelets' source and the victim could more easily bleed to death.

Some of the body's white cells for fighting infection, the lymphocytes, are manufactured in the lymph nodes and spleen. These organs also make the natural chemicals called antibodies, another of the body's weapons against disease. Radiation damage to the lymphatic system could thus impair still further the body's defences against disease.

How to Treat Radiation Sickness

Radiation can destroy vital organs so there can be no wonder cure for radiation sickness. Some drugs given *before* radiation exposure could limit the damage to a slight extent, but care after exposure would normally be limited to easing the symptoms and supporting the patient by good nursing. In many cases this could make all the difference between life and death. If, for example, only one per cent of the bone marrow's cells remained undamaged after exposure these could reproduce and eventually replace the cells which had died. If the patient were nursed carefully he or she might thus survive.

Without hospital facilities the best help you could give victims of radiation sickness would be to keep them warm and comfortable in bed. You could give pain killing drugs if you had them, taking care not to overload the patient with drugs which the disturbed metabolism might not be able to tolerate. Vitamins and mineral tablets could help replace vital nutrients which had been lost because of vomiting and other symptoms. If you had access to them, antibiotics could be used when infections developed.

Patients might find it impossible to eat, but it would be important to try giving them as much water as they could comfortably drink to combat the dehydrating effect of the stomach and gut symptoms.

"Radiation can reduce the fertility of men and women and if the dose is large enough make them permanently sterile."

If you were lucky enough to get the patient to a working hospital he or she could be fed intravenously, and there is a possibility that bone marrow transplantation could be of some help, though this is not by any means an easy to trouble-free treatment. Blood transfusions could be given to replace lost blood and thus combat anemia. Drugs which control shock symptoms and medicines to reduce bleeding could also be used. Whether any of the treatments mentioned could actually save many lives is open to question. Death might be delayed, but if the underlying damage were severe enough the patient will still die.

Long-Term Effects

Those who survived the initial onslaught of radiation sickness resulting from short-term doses greater than 150 r or thereabouts would nevertheless face the risk of a wide range of possible long-term complications. People who had been exposed to less than about 150 r of radiation would also face the same long-term hazards, though to a lesser degree (so far as is known). And radiation doses as low as 1 r per week are thought to contribute to ill health many years later.

Evidence from Hiroshima and Nagasaki shows that radiation victims (who had received large, but not lethal doses) were four times more likely to suffer from leukemia than other people. Even so the risk is still quite small: on average, about one person in 100 who are heavily exposed will develop the disease. When they do, the disease begins a few years after exposure.

Nearly all of the early pioneers of radioactivity (the scientists who discovered x-rays and first learned to use them in medical diagnosis) developed cancer later in life. Generally this was 20 or 30 years after their exposure to radiation. The early uranium miners (at the end of the last century) often developed 'mountain sickness', later shown to be lung cancer, as a result of inhaling radon, the radioactive gas which comes from uranium ores. Cancer commonly affected factory workers who painted radium onto watch and clock faces to make them luminous (particularly those who licked their brushes while working). Medical treatments and diagnosis using x-rays have also been known to cause cancer in many people. All of these activities are now carefully controlled but it is clear that large-scale contamination with radioactive fallout from nuclear warfare would produce major epidemics of cancer 20 or even more years later.

High doses of radiation can cause the lens of the eye to become opaque—a condition called cataract. This would be likely to happen in people who had survived near-lethal doses. Even then, not all vision might be lost.

The early x-ray pioneers handled radioactive materials frequently, receiving large doses of radiation to the hands. This led to reddening of the skin, warts, running sores, extreme pain, gross deformities and often cancer at the site of radiation injury: the full list of these ailments took many years to develop in different victims. Fallout dust which stuck to the skin, clothes and hair could cause skin burns, especially from beta radiations which would then be close enough to have an effect, adding to the dose from gamma rays produced by fallout. It would be extremely important to wash off any fallout and to remove contaminated clothes.

Radiation can reduce the fertility of men and women and if the dose is large enough make them permanently sterile. A dose of about 500 r delivered to the ovaries or testes would be likely to produce permanent sterility. Similar doses could produce temporary sterility which lasts for several years. Women are born with their full complement of unfertilised eggs. These eggs are all targets for radiation. In men sperms are manufactured constantly, so although existing sperms might be damaged, future sperms would be spared, provided the organs that manufactured them were undamaged.

An unborn child in its mother's womb is more susceptible to radiation than adults or even children. Radiation exposure during the few weeks immediately after conception (before embryonic limbs and other organs had begun to take shape) could easily cause an abortion. The fetus is at the most vulnerable between the second and sixth weeks following conception. If the fetus suffered radiation exposure then, when the organs were first being formed, a wide range of birth defects could result—such conditions as cleft palate, short limbs, fusion of the ribs and similar deformities, right through to severe disturbance of the central nervous system leading to mentally retarded babies.

Many diseases are thought to be caused by defects in the body's inheritance mechanisms. We inherit characteristics from our parents by means of the complex DNA molecules within each cell of our bodies. The DNA molecule is like a long string with 'beads' on it. Collections of beads form what are called genes, and it is these which tell our body whether to make, for example, blue eyes, black hair and all other bodily characteristics.

If the DNA molecules in human egg or sperm cells were damaged by radiation, however, a completely different gene, a mutation, could be formed. Most mutations produce harmful characteristics such as an increased tendency to contract particular diseases. Although some mutations can be beneficial and lead to stronger, healthier offspring, the harmful mutations are far more common. Because of this there is a great fear that nuclear warfare could lead to vastly increased mutation rates and to a wide range of genetic diseases. Just how severe this risk is has not been established because not enough people have yet been heavily exposed. But the genetic hazards of radiation could turn out to be as important and as devastating as any of the other effects in the very long term.

Background Radiation

No amount of ionising radiation, however small, can be said to be harmless. Even a dose of one r per week has been found to depress the number of white cells and just a few roentgens to the fetus can cause birth defects. But even in peacetime we cannot escape exposure to very small amounts of ionising radiation which bombard us continuously throughout our lives. These come from cosmic rays (high-speed nuclear particles coming from the stars and other bodies in space), radioactive elements in the ground and in our food, and from medical x-rays. The growth of nuclear power has led to a very slight increase in this natural background radiation because of minute quantities of radioisotopes released from nuclear power stations. A much more significant increase has been from the fallout injected into the atmosphere by the many experimental explosions of nuclear weapons.

Tolerance to Low Doses

Although such background radiation may cause damage it is an historical fact that humans are capable of tolerating it. Each person on earth receives no more than a few tenths of a roentgen of background radiation each year. It is only when the dose rises significantly above this figure that we have cause for concern. There is a great deal of argument about the precise level or dosage at which radiation can be said to be harmful, but there is unanimous agreement among doctors that the dose rates resulting from nuclear weapons exploded on inhabited countries would be very harmful indeed.

Peter Goodwin is author of the book, Nuclear War, The Facts on Our Survival.

"Were the Soviets aware that the American people are able to survive an attack, they would be much less likely to take the risk of initiating a conflict."

Civil Defense Is Needed

Edward Teller

Educating people about the nature and actual perils of nuclear weapons would not be easy under any circumstances. It is almost impossible when elementary facts are guarded by strict regulations of secrecy. Given such conditions, dangerous myths develop and proliferate.

The reality of nuclear weapons is grim enough. Exaggerations about them are apt only to paralyze us. Some of the current myths have grown from misinterpreted scientific studies; others seem to be based on simple wishful thinking. They all have one common characteristic: so long as they are believed, they obstruct an accurate assessment of our problems and will prevent the development of workable plans to preserve peace.

Myth 1: The Soviet and American nuclear stockpiles are close to identical. A nuclear freeze would stop the arms race and offer improved mutual protection.

Neither the United States nor the Soviet Union publishes information on its current arsenals, and secrecy laws prevent me from discussing even the available estimates. There is, however, an officially released fact: between 1966 and 1981 the total megatonnage of the American nuclear arsenal was *reduced* to less than one-half its former size. The Soviet arsenal has rapidly increased in yield, accuracy and diversity during the same period and currently includes a total nuclear explosive power in excess of what the United States *ever* had.

The Soviets have built the most powerful single weapons ever constructed. Militarily such weapons have very limited value, but as a blackmail threat against free-world cities, they seem to be quite effective. Weapons of such immense size are most likely to cause damage to the earth's ozone layer (which acts as a shield against lethal amounts of ultraviolet radiation) and lower the global temperature. A movement that

Edward Teller, "Dangerous Myths about Nuclear Arms," *Reader's Digest*, November 1982. Reprinted with author's permission.

says "freeze the current arsenals as they are" grants acceptability to these extraordinarily destructive Soviet weapons when they should be vigorously opposed.

By comparison with the Soviet Union, we have but a small fraction of the world's existing nuclear megatonnage. We do have sufficient power to create great damage, particularly to the Soviet industrial plant, *if* our retaliatory forces are safe from the first strike. They are not safe, however, and their deterrent effect has become doubtful.

Myth 2: Each nation has the power to destroy the other totally. Mutual destruction can most surely be avoided by disarming.

Our nuclear defense strategy, Mutually Assured Destruction, has the most appropriate acronym of MAD. The theory: if the Soviet Union and the United States have their urban populations at risk, then neither will attempt a first strike.

The Soviets have never agreed to the ideas on which MAD is based. The landmass of the U.S.S.R. is more than twice that of the United States; its urban concentration proportionately much lower. The Soviets' civil-defense planning may well enable them to lose fewer people in a nuclear conflict than the 20 million or more casualities they suffered in World War II.

Disarmament (as opposed to simple surrender) must be based on openness or trust. The extreme reticence of the Soviets to allow on-site inspections has been a continuing problem since 1958. Our basis for trust has not grown since. Recently declassified information offers an example of our problems. Since silos but not missiles can be counted by aerial surveillance, the SALT treaty limited silos. The obvious objective was to limit the number of deliverable missiles. The American silos are not reloadable. The Soviet silos are. This is not a breach of the treaty. American negotiators, neglecting the possibility that the Soviets might not have an equal urge to disarm, failed to insert an essential clause.

We have negotiated for 25 years, and the results are

readily visible. Why would a totalitarian empire that depends on military force to maintain its power voluntarily disarm itself?

Myth 3: Stopping U.S. weapons research and development will help make the world safer from the destructive effects of nuclear weapons.

For more than 25 years the primary purpose of U.S. weapons laboratories has been to make nuclear weapons *less* indiscriminately destructive. Cleaner bombs (with less fallout) smaller, more militarily effective weapons, and neutron bombs useful for battlefield defense (with less civilian damage than that created by a conventional artillery barrage) are among the results.

Furthermore, extremely important research is being conducted on systems to defend against incoming nuclear missiles. For example, exploding a very small nuclear bomb near an attack missile as it enters the upper-to-middle atmosphere over our nation would have no effects on the ground and negligible effects on the atmosphere, but could totally *disarm* the incoming missile without *detonating* it. Such a system, used to protect our vulnerable missile silos, could be an important first step in improving both our current retaliatory position and directing our policy toward defense. The nuclear-freeze movement would end further work on what could be the best defense systems.

The Soviets have already deployed an antiballistic-missile system around Moscow. We have the right to deploy a similar system but have not done so. The Soviet-American antiballistic-missile treaty is now being reviewed. We should change our policy and emphasize defense rather than retaliation.

Myth 4: If a large number of nuclear weapons were exploded, fallout would pollute food and water supplies, making combatant countries uninhabitable. The spread of radioactive fallout throughout the world would end life on earth.

Fallout is part of many myths, and one of the common misunderstandings has to do with the durability and extent of its effects.

The radioactivity of fallout declines rapidly. For example, if 1000 rems per hour (a lethal dose) were released by a bomb, seven hours later the dose would be 100 rems per hour (far below lethal). In 49 hours radiation from this fallout would be reduced to 10 rems per hour. In 100 days the radiation would be 0.1 rems, comparable to the amount received from a chest X-ray.

The amount of radioactivity produced by a bomb, contrary to myth, is finite. Radiation from fallout of the intensity described would be limited to the immediate vicinity of the explosion and the adjacent areas downwind. People in these areas could move to uncontaminated regions. (Decontamination is feasible if we prepare for it.)

Fallout in the vicinity of a nuclear explosion is a visible material, an ash. It can be wiped or washed off cans, wrappers, skin or any other surface. It can be easily filtered out of water. Food exposed to fallout is not harmed by the radiation. In fact, radiation is used commercially for food preservation. The only risk connected with food is if the fallout itself is eaten in the food or through some part of the food chain.

Skin contact with fallout is not necessarily fatal—depending on the intensity of the radiation and the precautions taken. Injuries can be reduced simply by washing off the ash. Through tragic miscalculation, 23 Japanese fishermen were covered with fallout from the multi-megaton test at Bikini Atoll in 1954. The fallout reached their boat three hours after the explosion and continued for an additional 4½ hours. They made no effort to brush or wash off the ash. All suffered skin lesions, most had appetite loss, some experienced nausea and vomiting. One died shortly afterward, and two others died 20 years later of liver disorders that may have been associated with the fallout. The rest have survived. Simple knowledge on how to deal with fallout would practically have eliminated the effects.

"Fallout is part of many myths, and one of the common misunderstandings has to do with the durability and extent of its effects."

There would be numerous dreadful real consequences if a nuclear exchange occurred. Preventing war—in particular, nuclear war—is our single most important task. Should nuclear war occur in spite of every good effort, the number of people killed would be truly terrifying, but many more would survive. Perhaps this is the most frightening thing about our current myths: the misconceptions that exist currently would intensify the fear and suffering of survivors needlessly.

Myth 5: The explosion of nuclear weapons in the atmosphere will bring an end to life on this planet by damaging the ozone layer.

This new doomsday myth is gaining popularity. What we know today about the ozone layer suggests that if weapons larger than half-megaton bombs—such as only the Soviets possess—were exploded in the atmosphere, they would generate considerable amounts of nitrogen oxides at high altitudes. These oxides continue to destroy ozone over a protracted period. If the ozone were depleted, more ultraviolet radiation would reach the earth.

Assuming a worst-case scenario—a nuclear attack in which 5,000 weapons, all of 1-to-20-megaton size, were exploded in the atmosphere—there would probably be a 50 per cent decrease in the ozone layer over the Northern Hemisphere during the following year. (In the next few years, the ozone layer would return to about 80 per cent of normal.) If this occurred, people would suffer rapid sunburn and a significant increase in skin cancer. Some ultraviolet-sensitive species could be extinguished, and some serious ecological changes might follow. However, our survival can be considered certain.

More detailed scientific information about the ozone layer is needed and should be gathered on an international basis. In the meantime, limiting the explosive power of all individual nuclear weapons to 400 kilotons would effectively eliminate the possibility of any significant damage to the ozone layer. Such a limitation should become an important part of disarmament talks.

"We could accomplish so much for so little were we to spend only one percent of our defense budget on civil defense."

Myth 6: Civil defense is without value in saving lives and may actually increase the risk of war.

This is perhaps the most dangerous myth of all.

Today some Soviet nuclear missiles may carry an explosive force a thousand times greater than the 15-kiloton Hiroshima bomb. However, while the vertical force of the explosion increases a thousand times, the horizontal distance over which such bombs produce equal damage increases much more slowly. For example, a one-megaton bomb, while almost 70 times more powerful than the Hiroshima bomb, produces equal damage over only about four times the distance.

Few people realize the following facts about the effects of the Hiroshima and Nagasaki bombings. Earth-covered conventional bomb shelters practically under the airburst atomic bombs were essentially undamaged even though blast and fire destroyed all other buildings in the area. In Nagasaki, people in caves survived one-third of a mile from ground zero. In Hiroshima, a well-built wood-frame house one mile away from ground zero was badly damaged but stood. The day after the blast, bridges were open to traffic; the second day, trains ran; the third day, streetcars were operating. The people of these cities were without any knowledge of how to protect themselves. Yet 1.6 to 3.1 miles from ground zero, 98 per cent of the inhabitants—283,000 people—survived. Among this group in the past 33 years, about 500 more deaths from cancer have occurred than would be predicted in an unexposed similar group of people.

What about predictions of genetic damage? Detailed analyses have been made of about 35,000 children born to atomic-bomb survivors. So far, no evidence of genetic damage has been found. This does not mean that none exists. However, genetic damage compared with the other horrors of nuclear war is practically negligible. Radiation during pregnancy—especially in the early stages—is very harmful to the fetus. More than one

quarter of the infants born five to nine months after the bombing suffered from retarded growth, including mental retardation. About seven per cent of those born in the four months following the bombing also suffered these defects. Yet the myth suggests that all fetuses tragically exposed by nuclear war will suffer developmental malformation. The actual effects of atomic weapons are ghastly enough. Exaggeration discourages reasonable measures to protect those most vulnerable.

Under Soviet civil-defense plans, nonessential city workers would be evacuated if the immediate danger of war (or intent for a Soviet, first strike) arose. The evacuees would build crude but effective shelters in the countryside according to well-prepared instructions. (Tests of the Soviet shelter plans at Oak Ridge National Laboratory show them to be excellent.) With optimum conditions, these plans would allow the Soviet Union to protect all but about 5 to 10 per cent of its people from a full retaliatory strike. Well over 50 per cent of the unprepared U.S. population would die in a nuclear attack. This need not be so. Comparable civil-defense planning in the United States could save 100 million more lives.

War has always been more terrible than words can describe. Nuclear war would create immense suffering. Surely taking out some insurance against increased suffering is neither wasteful nor inhumane. We could accomplish so much for so little were we to spend only one per cent of our defense budget on civil defense.

Planning the evacuation of urban residents and stockpiling food already owned by the government in the corresponding evacuation areas is a most important cheap insurance policy. Were the Soviets aware that the American people are able to survive an attack, they would be much less likely to take the risk of initiating a conflict. And can you really believe that civil defense will make the American people or our government more likely to risk nuclear war?

Our first step toward stability, toward improving the prospects for peace and for the security of all people, must be the replacement of myths with knowledge. Only then can we approach the best possible solutions. They will not be perfect. But they will offer the chance for improvement—of changing mutually assured destruction into a decent chance of survival, of maintaining sufficient military strength to coax Soviet leaders toward real detente. If our salvation is to be real, it must be based on fact, not fantasy.

Dr. Edward Teller is a physicist, was instrumental in the development of the H-bomb, and is currently a Senior Research Fellow at the Hoover Institution at Stanford University.

"Civil defense in the nuclear age serves to delude federal officials and a few members of the populace into thinking that nuclear war can be waged with relative impunity."

Civil Defense Is Unrealistic

Karen Steingart and Diane Meier

"A crisis exists. . . .You should relocate. . . .This is a guide. . . ." In case of nuclear war, the government has a plan. Affected persons will find advice in an insert in the newspaper, including detailed instructions regarding what to bring — credit cards, toothbrush and extra underwear — and what not to bring — the pet dog, drugs, liquor and handguns; where to go — west for those on the westside, east for those on the eastside; and what is to be done once evacuees get to their destination — start digging.

Civil defense for nuclear war: Will it save lives? Does it increase the chances of a nuclear war? Does civil defense planning escalate the arms race?

In recent months, the civil defense controversy has come to Portland's front yard in the forms of the U.S. Civil Defense Council's national meeting in the city and the City Council debate of the merits of evacuating Portland in the event of a nuclear attack.

The U.S. Civil Defense Council national meeting Oct. 11-14 in Portland attracted from across the country local emergency planners, whose jobs include preparations for floods, earthquakes, volcanoes, toxic waste spills and nuclear war.

Natural disasters — known for generating a high degree of cooperation among those involved — cannot be compared to nuclear war. A natural disaster is a time-limited event affecting a local area, with the comforting knowledge that the outside world will provide relief sooner or later. In a nuclear war, all urban areas are likely to be equally devastated; there will be no outside help.

Nobody, it seems, is in favor of a nuclear war, but there are proponents of civil defense planning for nuclear war. T.K. Jones, deputy undersecretary of defense for strategic and theater nuclear forces, stated

Karen Steingart and Diane Meier, "Flaws Bury Feasibility of Civil Preparedness for Nuclear War," *The Sunday Oregonian,* December 12, 1982. Reprinted with permission.

earlier this year that the United States would recover from an all-out nuclear attack in just two to four years given an adequate civil defense program.

In a January 1982 interview with Robert Scheer of *The Los Angeles Times*, Jones had this to say on the subject: "Everybody's going to make it if there are enough shovels to go around. . . .Dig a hole, cover it with a couple of doors and throw three feet of dirt on top. It's the dirt that does it."

Proponents of nuclear war civil defense planning wonder if any harm is done by being prepared on the grounds that if even a few lives are saved, the effort is probably worth it. The Federal Emergency Management Agency, the agency charged with overseeing nuclear war civil defense planning, has published a pamphlet that includes this statement: "FEMA hopes the U.S. will never see such a crisis, but feels nuclear civil protection, including crisis relocation planning, is needed insurance in an uncertain world."

Opponents respond that any preparations for civil defense amount to preparation for nuclear war and may increase the chances of one occurring, that the belief that survival is feasible lowers the threshold for nuclear war by lulling people into a false sense of security, and that those saved by initial civil defense measures would likely succumb to long-term effects of a nuclear war.

"Just as we regard Russian civil defense posturing as threatening evidence of preparation for nuclear attack, so do they regard ours," retired Adm. Noel Gayler has warned. "In this way, it generates a mind set favorable toward nuclear war."

Civil Defense Delusion

In the words of Dr. Jennifer Leaning of Physicians for Social Responsibility: "Civil defense in the nuclear age serves to delude federal officials and a few members of the populace into thinking that nuclear war can be waged with relative impunity."

Since 1978, the FEMA has been charged with the development of a civil preparedness plan in the event of nuclear war. Because of the prohibitive expense of in-place blast and fallout shelters, the agency has opted for a crisis relocation plan that requires evacuation of urban dwellers to small towns at safe distances from the blasts. Sheltering from radiation, food supplies, sewage handling, medical care and the details of the evacuation of 145 million people from 250 cities are in the planning stages. Assumptions of the crisis relocation plan include these considerations:

1. A three-to five-day warning period during a time of heightened international tensions, and during which time evacuation could take place.

2. An evacuation could take place in an orderly and controlled manner.

3. Small towns would welcome the arrival of millions of refugees.

4. Adequate food, water, sewage facilities, medical care and protection from radiation would be available for the required 30-day sheltering period.

5. That those emerging from the shelters into the post-attack world could survive to rebuild the nation's economic and political system.

The FEMA working scenario assumes a deliberate, pre-emptive first-strike by the Soviets on military and industrial targets (that is, the cities) of the United States of 6,559 megatons — 524,720 times the explosive power of the Hiroshima bomb.

Since an intercontinental ballistic missile takes approximately 30 minutes to reach this country from the Soviet Union, expecting a three- to five-day grace period may be somewhat optimistic. In addition, today's weapons are so accurate that the attacking country could rapidly retarget its warheads to strike the evacuating population.

"U.S. civil defense planning promotes an atmosphere of false security, and leads people to believe that they could rebuild a normal life after a nuclear war."

Furthermore, calm, organized cooperation in such a terrifying situation is unlikely as people are told to wait their turn for evacuation while the bombs are expected to strike at any minute.

In a nuclear war, refugees could be expected to panic as parents frantically seek lost children and violence erupts at gasoline pumps. Psychiatrist Judith Lipton has likened an evacuation under the proposed crisis relocation plan to the "last traffic jam."

Assuming the evacuation process succeeds, the FEMA plan calls for sheltering millions of people for 30 days against lethal radiation. Days to weeks would be required to dig adequate shelters for the relocated

millions, but radiation travels with the speed of the wind. Shelters require a 3-foot wall of dirt in all four directions for adequate protection from radioactivity. People would be required to move many cubic yards of earth.

"Deep shelters would become deep tombs," Gayler has said. "How long can you and your family live under two doors covered with 3 feet of earth? How do you dig around New York or Chicago or Moscow in the frozen ground of winter?"

Once in the shelter, each person would have an estimated 2-by-3-foot space in which to live for one month. Sanitation, food supplies, uncontaminated water, care for the sick and disposal mechanisms for human corpses would not exist.

Even if FEMA attained maximum success in its effort to evacuate and shelter 145 million urban Americans, survivors would face overwhelming problems. The FEMA scenario assumes an 80 percent survival rate for those evacuated, including 50 million injured and sick persons still alive at the end of the 30-day shelter period. The major urban centers would be flattened. Radiation exposure in those areas would be lethal — 10,000 rads per hour immediately after an attack in cities, declining to 500 to 3,000 rads per hour in outlying evacuation areas. The lethal dose for humans is 500 rads.

The FEMA scenario further assumes the destruction of approximately 90 percent of hospitals, 90 percent of industries producing medication, 70 percent of fuel and transport facilities and 70 percent of grain stores.

Effects of a Nuclear War

Given these estimates, what level of survival can be expected after the war? Leaning has defined the term survivability as the ability of a population to reproduce. She named five factors which would influence negatively this process after an attack.

1. Prolonged low-dose radiation exposure can be expected to have multiple detrimental effects. Data drawn from Japanese victims demonstrates that 20 to 50 rads per week led to decreased sperm production and infertility in 60 percent to 90 percent of the men examined for as long as one year after the bombings. Many Japanese women experienced anovulatory periods and spontaneous abortions for several years after the explosions. These same low-level exposures to radiation led to decreased lymphocyte counts — to 10 percent of normal — which increases susceptibility to infection. Depression, decreased appetite and diminished immunity may also be expected.

2. Food and grain stockpiles, including grain reserved for planting, are predictably available for only about a six-month period after an attack. Almost 80 percent of this nation's food-processing capacity is located in high-risk areas and would be destroyed. Distribution of food would be difficult without fuel or roads. Planting and

harvesting by persons with little or no experience in farming will be complicated by large numbers of radiation-resistant insects and predators, and the lack of fertilizers, machinery and pesticides.

3. A weakened, malnourished and depressed population will be more susceptible to infectious disease. The resurgence of diseases such as plague and smallpox that are now rare in North America can be expected. Chronic low-dose radiation exposure, malnutrition, psychological shock and lack of sanitation facilities will increase the chances of epidemics. The means of production of antibiotics and vaccines will have been destroyed. Surviving physicians will not be able to halt the spread of disease.

4. The ecological consequences of nuclear explosions include climatic changes, ozone layer depletion, production of huge amounts of dust, soil erosion, death of small plant and animal life at the base of the food chain, and radioactive contamination of soil and water across the globe.

5. The psychological will to live that is crucial in assuring continuation of the species is likely to be at a low ebb following a nuclear war. "Death in Life," a study by Robert Jay Lifton, concludes that survivors of the Hiroshima bombing experienced pervasive guilt, believing that they had failed those who died. They were found to feel permanently contaminated and lacking in dreams, hope and meaning in their lives. The willingness to bond, to fall in love and to bear children depend in great part upon a secure and healthy environment and expectation of a safe future.

"Nuclear war is not in any humane or civilized sense survivable and civil defense planning for nuclear war is delusionary behavior."

The cumulative effects of these five factors on death and birthrates are likely to decimate the post-attack population, so much so that they will negate any gains in survival due to crisis relocation. The FEMA plan cannot and does not provide for these long-term consequences.

Beyond the fact that FEMA's plan is unlikely to save lives in the long run, it is strategically, psychologically and economically dangerous. The Soviets view this nation's commitment to a strong civil defense as preparation for a pre-emptive first-strike, a threatening and destabilizing move on our part that increases the chances for an outbreak of war. The official commitment to an unworkable civil defense plan — which includes instructions from FEMA to fill out change-of-address cards and to remember to take credit cards along in an evacuation — undermines the credibility of the U.S. government in the eyes of the American public

and the world. If federal officials really believe in crisis relocation as an effective way to save lives, they will be less fearful of initiating nuclear war.

These issues and related ones are under consideration by a task force established Oct. 13 by the Portland City Council. The task force is charged with examining the FEMA crisis relocation plan, its desirability for Portland, and its fiscal impact. Meetings are held at 5 p.m. Wednesdays in City Hall and are open to the public.

Meanwhile, several questions are worth considering.
— Will civil defense save lives?

No. Even if evacuation and sheltering of 150 million people is successful, a large percentage of the post-attack survivors will likely succumb to the combined effects of radiation, infection, starvation, major ecological shifts and loss of the will to live.
— Does civil defense increase the chances of a nuclear war?

Yes. U.S. civil defense planning promotes an atmosphere of false security, and leads people to believe that they could rebuild a normal life after a nuclear war. A populace or a government that believes a nuclear war could be fought, won and survived is much more willing to get involved in one. In addition, civil defense planning diverts efforts and attention away from the real problem: prevention of nuclear war.
— Does civil defense capability escalate the arms race?

Yes. The crisis relocation plan has strategic as well as local impact. Just as the United States perceives Soviet civil defense planning as preparation for nuclear war, the Soviet Union is equally threatened by this country's recent massive budget increases for crisis relocation planning. If the United States were to initiate massive evacuation of its cities at a time of heightened international tensions, the Soviet Union would logically fear a pre-emptive first-strike, and might be tempted to launch one of its own.

Leaning summed up the problems with FEMA's plan in the following statement, delivered in March to the Senate Foreign Relations Committee: "It is important for us to realize that the problem with civil defense planning in the setting of nuclear war is not with the specific plan, but with the concept of survivability. . . .our cities in rubble, our land burned and contaminated, our friends and relatives gone, (our) future grimly foreshortened by prospects of famine and disease. Civil defense cannot change what the weapons can do. . . .Nuclear war is not in any humane or civilized sense survivable and civil defense planning for nuclear war is delusionary behavior. All our efforts must be directed at prevention."

Drs. Karen Steingart and Diane Meier of Portland are members of Physicians for Local Social Responsibility, a non-profit organization devoted to the education of the public on the medical consequences of nuclear war.

"Unless we demonstrate the will to rebuild our strength and restore the military balance, the Soviets—since they're so far ahead—have little incentive to negotiate with us."

viewpoint **15**

The US Must Achieve Nuclear Parity with the USSR

Ronald Reagan

The prevention of conflict and the reduction of weapons are the most important public issues of our time. Yet, on no other issue are there more misconceptions and misunderstandings. You, the American people, deserve an explanation from your government on what our policy is on these issues. Too often the experts have been content to discuss grandiose strategies among themselves and cloud the public debate in technicalities no one can understand. The result is that many Americans have become frightened, and, let me say, fear of the unknown is entirely understandable. Unfortunately, much of the information emerging in this debate bears little semblance to the facts.

To begin, let's go back to what the world was like at the end of World War II. The United States was the only undamaged industrial power in the world. Our military power was at its peak, and we alone had the atomic weapon. But we didn't use this wealth and this power to bully; we used it to rebuild. We raised up the war-ravaged economies, including the economies of those who had fought against us. At first, the peace of the world was unthreatened, because we alone were left with any real power, and we were using it for the good of our fellow man. Any potential enemy was deterred from aggression because the cost would have far outweighed the gain.

As the Soviets' power grew, we still managed to maintain the peace. The United States had established a system of alliances with NATO as the centerpiece. In addition, we grew even more respected as a world leader with a strong economy and deeply held moral values. With our commitment to help shape a better world, the United States always pursued every diplomatic channel for peace. And for at least 30 years after World War II, the United States still continued to possess a large military advantage over the Soviet Union. Our strength deterred—that is, prevented—aggression against us.

This nation's military objective has always been to maintain peace by preventing war. This is neither a Democratic nor a Republican policy. It's supported by our allies. And most important of all, it has worked for nearly 40 years.

What do we mean when we speak of nuclear deterrence? Certainly we don't want such weapons for their own sake. We don't desire excessive forces, or what some people have called "overkill." Basically, it is a matter of others knowing that starting a conflict would be more costly to them than anything they might hope to gain. And, yes, it is sadly ironic that in these modern times it still takes weapons to prevent war. I wish it did not.

We desire peace, but peace is a goal not a policy. Lasting peace is what we hope for at the end of our journey; it doesn't describe the steps we must take, nor the paths we should follow to reach that goal. I intend to search for peace along two parallel paths—deterrence and arms reductions. I believe these are the only paths that offer any real hope for an enduring peace.

And, let me say, I believe that if we follow prudent policies, the risk of nuclear conflict will be reduced. Certainly the United States will never use its forces except in response to attack. Through the years, Soviet leaders have also expressed a sober view of nuclear war; and if we maintain a strong deterrent, they are exceedingly unlikely to launch an attack.

The Military Imbalance

Now, while the policy of deterrence has stood the test of time, the things we must do in order to maintain deterrence have changed. You often hear that the United States and the Soviet Union are in an arms race. The truth is that, while the Soviet Union has raced, we have not. As you can see from this U.S. line on the "Defense Spending" chart, in constant dollars our

Ronald Reagan, address to the nation broadcast from the White House, November 22, 1982.

defense spending in the 1960s went up because of Vietnam, and then it went downward through much of the 1970s. Now, follow the line which is Soviet spending. It has gone up and up and up. In spite of a stagnating Soviet economy, Soviet leaders invest 12%-14% of their country's gross national product in military spending, two to three times the level we invest.

DEFENSE SPENDING

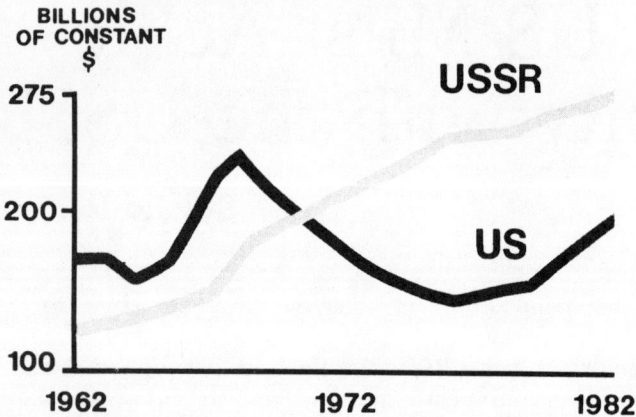

I might add that the defense share of our U.S. Federal budget has gone way down, too. Watch the U.S. line on the "Defense Share of Federal Budget" chart. In 1962, when John Kennedy was President, 46%, almost half of the Federal budget, went to our national defense. In recent years, about one-quarter of our budget has gone to defense, while the share for social programs has nearly doubled. And most of our defense budget is spent on people, not weapons.

DEFENSE SHARE OF FEDERAL BUDGET

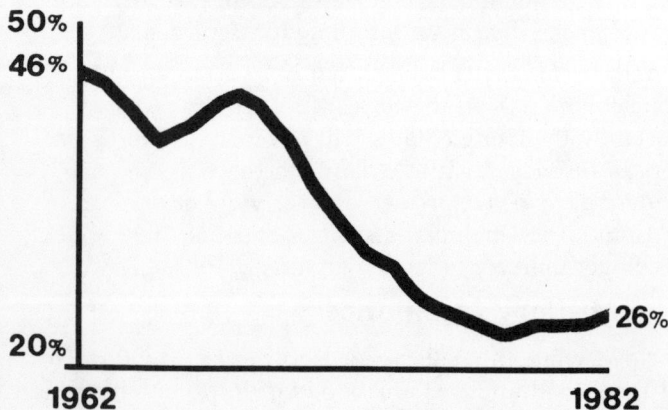

The combination of the Soviets spending more and the United States spending proportionately less changed the military balance and weakened our deterrent. Today, in virtually every measure of military power, the Soviet Union enjoys a decided advantage.

The "Strategic Missiles and Bombers" chart shows the changes in the total number of intercontinental missiles and bombers. You will see that in 1962 and in 1972, the U.S. forces remained about the same, even dropping some by 1982. But take a look now at the Soviet side. In 1962, at the time of the Cuban missile crisis, the Soviets could not compare with us in terms of strength. In 1972, when we signed the SALT I [Strategic Arms Limitation Talks] Treaty, we are nearly equal. But in 1982, well, that Soviet bar stretching above the American bar tells the story. . . .For example, the Soviet Union has deployed a third more land-based intercontinental ballistic missiles than we have. Believe it or not, we froze our number in 1965 and have deployed no additional missiles since then.

STRATEGIC MISSILES AND BOMBERS

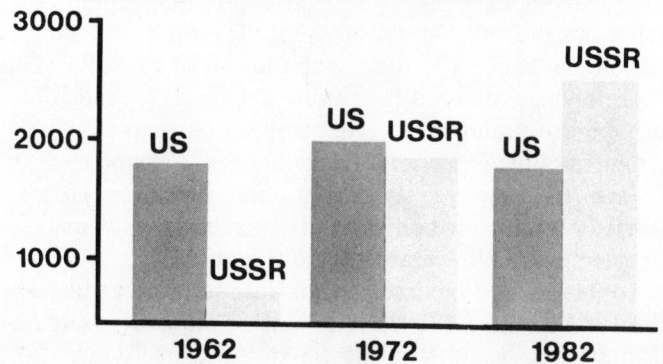

The Soviet Union put to sea 60 new ballistic missile submarines in the last 15 years. Until last year we hadn't commissioned one in that same period. The Soviet Union has built over 200 modern Backfire bombers and is building 30 more a year. For 20 years, the United States has deployed no new strategic bombers. Many of our B-52 bombers are now older than the pilots who fly them.

The Soviet Union now has 600 of the missiles considered most threatening by both sides—the intermediate-range missiles based on land. We have none. The United States withdrew its intermediate-range land-based missiles from Europe almost 20 years ago.

The world has also witnessed unprecedented growth in the area of Soviet conventional forces; the Soviets far exceed us in the number of tanks, artillery pieces, aircraft, and ships they produce every year. What is more, when I arrived in this office, I learned that in our own forces we had planes that couldn't fly and ships that couldn't leave port, mainly for lack of spare parts and crew members.

The Soviet military buildup must not be ignored. We've recognized the problem, and, together with our allies, we have begun to correct the imbalance. Look at the "Projected Defense Spending" chart of projected real defense spending for the next several years. Here's the Soviet line. Let us assume the Soviets' rate of spending remains at the level they have followed since the 1960s. The line is the United States. If my defense proposals are passed, it will still take 5 years before we come close to the Soviet level. Yet the modernization of our strategic and conventional forces will assure that deterrence works and peace prevails.

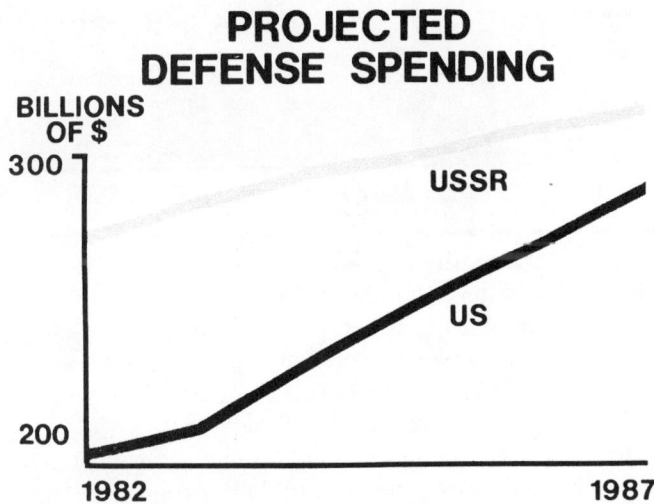

PROJECTED DEFENSE SPENDING

BILLIONS OF $

300

USSR

US

200

1982   1987

Proceeding with MX

Our deployed nuclear forces were built before the age of microcircuits. It's not right to ask our young men and women in uniform to maintain and operate such antiques. Many have already given their lives in missile explosions and aircraft accidents caused by the old age of their equipment. We must replace and modernize our forces, and that is why I have decided to proceed with the production and deployment of the new ICBM [intercontinental ballistic missile] known as the MX.

Three earlier Presidents worked to develop this missile. Based on the best advice I could get, I concluded that the MX is the right missile at the right time. On the other hand, when I arrived in office, I felt the proposal on where and how to base the missile simply cost too much in terms of money and the impact on our citizens' lives.

I have concluded, however, it is absolutely essential that we proceed to produce this missile, and that we base it in a series of closely based silos at Warren Air Force Base near Cheyenne, Wyoming. This plan requires only half as many missiles as the earlier plan and will fit in an area of only 20 square miles. It is the product of around-the-clock research that has been underway since I directed a search for a better, cheaper way.

I urge the Members of Congress, who must pass this plan, to listen and examine the facts before they come to their own conclusion.

Arms Reductions

Some may question what modernizing our military has to do with peace. Well, as I explained earlier, a secure force keeps others from threatening us and that keeps the peace. And just as important, it also increases the prospects of reaching significant arms reductions with the Soviets, and that's what we really want. The United States wants deep cuts in the world's arsenal of weapons.

But unless we demonstrate the will to rebuild our strength and restore the military balance, the Soviets—since they're so far ahead—have little incentive to negotiate with us. Let me repeat that point, since it goes to the heart of our policies. Unless we demonstrate the will to rebuild our strength, the Soviets have little incentive to negotiate. If we hadn't begun to modernize, the Soviet negotiators would know we had nothing to bargain with except talk. They would know we were bluffing without a good hand, because they know what cards we hold—just as we know what's in their hand.

You may recall that in 1969 the Soviets didn't want to negotiate a treaty banning antiballistic missiles. It was only after our Senate narrowly voted to fund an antiballistic missile program that the Soviets agreed to negotiate. We then reached an agreement.

We also know that one-sided arms control doesn't work. We've tried time and again to set an example by cutting our own forces in the hope that the Soviets will do likewise. The result has always been that they keep building.

I believe our strategy for peace will succeed. Never before has the United States proposed such a comprehensive program of nuclear arms control. Never in our history have we engaged in so many negotiations with the Soviets to reduce nuclear arms and to find a stable peace. What we are saying to them is this: We will modernize our military in order to keep the balance for peace, but wouldn't it be better if we both simply reduced our arsenals to a much lower level?

Let me begin with the negotiations on the intermediate-range nuclear forces that are currently underway in Geneva. As I said earlier, the most threatening of these forces are the land-based missiles, which the Soviet Union now has aimed at Europe, the Middle East, and Asia.

The "Missile Warheads" chart shows the number of warheads on these Soviet missiles. In 1972, there were 600. The United States was at zero. In 1977, there were 600. The United States was still at zero. Then the Soviets began deploying powerful new missiles with three warheads and a reach of thousands of miles—the SS-20. Since then the bar has gone through the roof—the Soviets have added a missile with three warheads every week. Still you see no U.S. on the chart. Although the

Soviet leaders earlier this year declared they had frozen deployment of this dangerous missile, they have, in fact, continued deployment.

We also seek to reduce the total destructive power of these missiles and other elements of U.S. and Soviet strategic forces.

MISSILE WARHEADS
INTERMEDIATE RANGE · LAND BASED

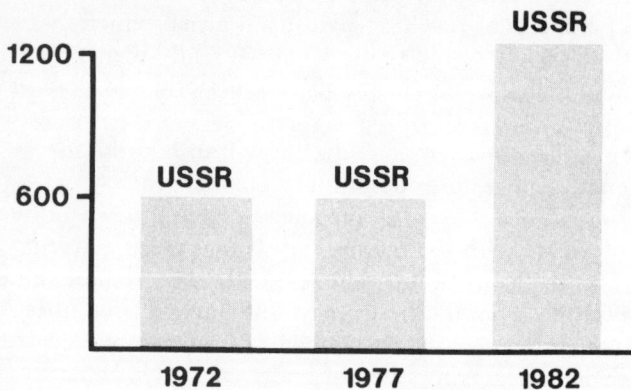

STRATEGIC BALLISTIC MISSILES

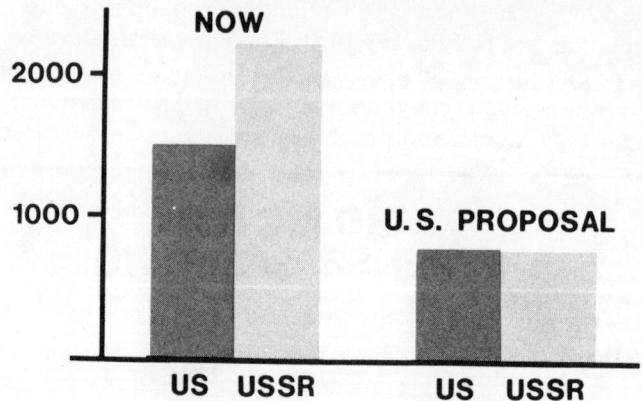

Last year, on November 18, I proposed the total, global elimination of all these missiles. I proposed that the United States would deploy no comparable missiles—which are scheduled for late 1983—if the Soviet Union would dismantle theirs. We would follow agreement on the land-based missiles with limits on other intermediate-range systems.

The European governments strongly support our initiative. The Soviet Union has thus far shown little inclination to take this major step to zero levels. Yet I believe and I am hoping that—as the talks proceed and as we approach the scheduled placement of our new systems in Europe—the Soviet leaders will see the benefits of such a far-reaching agreement.

This summer we also began negotiations on strategic arms reductions, the proposal we call START [Strategic Arms Reduction Talks]. Here we're talking about intercontinental missiles—the weapons with a longer range than the intermediate-range ones I was just discussing. We are negotiating on the basis of deep reductions. I proposed in May that we cut the number of warheads on these missiles to an equal number, roughly one-third below current levels. I also proposed that we cut the number of missiles themselves to an equal number, about half the current U.S. level. Our proposals would eliminate some 4,700 warheads and some 2,250 missiles. I think that would be quite a service to mankind.

The "Strategic Ballistic Missiles" chart shows the current level of U.S. ballistic missiles, both land and sea based. This is the Soviet level. We intend to convince the Soviets it would be in their own best interest to reduce these missiles. Look at the reduced numbers both sides would have under our proposal—quite a dramatic change.

In 1977, when the last Administration proposed more limited reductions, the Soviet Union refused even to discuss them. This time their reaction has been quite different. Their opening position is a serious one, and even though it doesn't meet our objective of deep reductions, there's no question we're heading in the right direction. One reason for this change is clear. The Soviet Union knows that we are now serious about our own strategic programs and that they must be prepared to negotiate in earnest.

We also have other important arms control efforts underway. In the talks in Vienna on mutual and balanced force reductions, we've proposed cuts in military personnel to a far lower and equal level. And in the 40-nation [U.N.] Committee on Disarmament in Geneva, we're working to develop effective limitations on nuclear testing and chemical weapons. The whole world remains outraged by the Soviets' and their allies' use of biological and chemical weapons against defenseless people in Afghanistan, Kampuchea, and Laos. This experience makes ironclad verification all the more essential for arms control.

Accident and Misunderstanding

There is, of course, much more that needs to be done. In an age when intercontinental missiles can span half the globe in less than half an hour, it's crucial that Soviet and American leaders have a clear understanding of each other's capabilities and intentions.

Last June in Berlin and again at the U.N. Special Session on Disarmament, I vowed that the United States would make every effort to reduce the risks of accident and misunderstanding and thus to strengthen mutual confidence between the United States and the Soviet Union. Since then, we've been actively studying detailed measures to implement this Berlin initiative.

Today, I would like to announce some of the measures which I've proposed in a special letter just sent to the Soviet leadership and which I've instructed our ambassadors in Geneva to discuss with their Soviet counterparts. They include but also go beyond some of the suggestions I made in Berlin.

The first of these measures involves advance notification of all U.S. and Soviet test launches of intercontinental ballistic missiles. We will also seek Soviet agreement on notification of all sea-launched ballistic missiles as well as intermediate-range land-based ballistic missiles of the type we're currently negotiating. This would remove surprise and uncertainty at the sudden appearance of such missiles on the warning screens of the two countries.

> *"The Soviet military buildup must not be ignored. We've recognized the problem, and, together with our allies, we have begun to correct the imbalance."*

In another area of potential misunderstanding, we propose to the Soviets that we provide each other with advance notification of our major military exercises. Here again, our objective is to reduce the surprise and uncertainty surrounding otherwise sudden moves by either side.

These sorts of measures are designed to deal with the immediate issues of miscalculation in time of crisis. But there are deeper, longer term problems as well. In order to clear a way some of the mutual ignorance and suspicion between our two countries, I will propose that we both engage in a broad-ranging exchange of basic data about our nuclear forces. I am instructing our ambassadors at the negotiations on both strategic and intermediate forces to seek Soviet agreement on an expanded exchange of information. The more one side knows about what the other side is doing, the less room there is for surprise and miscalculation.

Probably everyone has heard of the so-called hotline, which enables me to communicate directly with the Soviet leadership in the event of a crisis. The existing hotline is dependable and rapid with both ground and satellite links. But because it is so important, I've also directed that we carefully examine any possible improvements to the existing hotline system.

Now, although we've begun negotiations on these many proposals, this doesn't mean we've exhausted all the initiatives that could help to reduce the risk of accidental conflict. We'll leave no opportunity unexplored, and we'll consult closely with Senators Nunn, Jackson, and Warner, and other Members of the Congress who've made important suggestions in this field.

We are also making strenuous efforts to prevent the spread of nuclear weapons to additional countries. It would be tragic if we succeeded in reducing existing arsenals only to have new threats emerge in other areas of the world.

Reaffirming America's Destiny

Earlier I spoke of America's contributions to peace following World War II, of all we did to promote peace and prosperity for our fellow man. Well, we're still those same people. We still seek peace above all else. I want to remind our own citizens and those around the world of this tradition of American good will, because I am concerned about the effects the nuclear fear is having on our people. The most upsetting letters I receive are from schoolchildren who write to me as a class assignment. It's evident they've discussed the most nightmarish aspects of a nuclear holocaust in their classrooms. Their letters are often full of terror. This should not be so.

The philosopher Spinoza said, "Peace. . .is a virtue, a state of mind, a disposition for benevolence, confidence, justice." Those are the qualities we want our children to inherit, not fear. They must grow up confident if they are to meet the challenges of tomorrow, as we will meet the challenges of today.

Ronald Reagan was elected president in 1980.
U.S./U.S.S.R. relations have been a controversial topic of his administration.

"The point is that Washington has now set itself the aim of disrupting the parity and achieving military superiority."

The US and USSR Have Achieved Nuclear Parity

Dmitri Ustinov

Question: Comrade Minister, what can you say about US President Ronald Reagan's statement that the Soviet Union has military superiority over the United States?

Answer: US President Ronald Reagan indeed makes this claim. In his speech on November 22 he said that "today in virtually every measure of military power the Soviet Union enjoys a decided advantage." Such claims do not accord with the facts. Their aim is to deceive the public and they serve to justify the unprecedented military programmes and aggressive doctrines of the United States. It is regrettable that the leader of a great power, whose very position presupposes realism and a sense of responsibility in assessing the facts, should resort to such attempts to persuade people of the existence of what is totally non-existent.

The balance between the USSR and the US in the sphere of strategic armaments was thoroughly checked after nearly seven years of negotiations by both sides to draft the SALT-2 Treaty and it was confirmed by the heads of state at its signing. That was in 1979. Can one really conceive of a "decided" superiority being achieved in the space of two or three years, as the US President asserts, in strategic systems on whose development and deployment many years are spent? Or, maybe, something unexpected of which the United States was previously unaware, has come to light? No, nothing new has happened. And Washington is well aware of this. How come that the leaders of the previous Administration James Carter, Harold Brown and Cyrus Vance were admitting in 1979-1980 that there was an approximate parity in the sphere of strategic armaments between the USSR and the US, but President Reagan and Defense Secretary Weinberger on taking office started claiming as early as in 1981 that no such parity exists? It is obviously not because the objective situation in the world has changed or because the Soviet Union has surged ahead in armaments. The point is that Washington has

Dmitri Ustinov, *The Existing Parity Must Not Be Destroyed*, Moscow: Novosti Press Agency Publishing House, 1982.

now set itself the aim of disrupting the parity and achieving military superiority. Even an approximate deadline for achieving this, the year 1990, is mentioned. This is the nub of the matter.

And if one considers the military might of the sides in other than strategic arms, it is wrong to compare the forces and weapons of just the USSR and the United States. It is the armed forces of NATO and of the Warsaw Treaty which face each other. Therefore to make an objective assessment one must compare the forces of these two military alliances.

In the sphere of medium-range nuclear arms an approximate balance of forces has existed in Europe for many years now. Each side has approximately a thousand such delivery vehicles deployed. In the number of nuclear weapons delivered to their target in one launch —a very important index—NATO already has a 50 per cent superiority at the present time.

US Misleading Public

The head of the US Administration is misleading the public when he makes it a question only of the ground-based medium-range missiles of the USSR and the United States. Since for several reasons in the past 20 years the United States has not had this type of weapons in Western Europe, the Soviet Union must, according to Washington's logic, abolish its missiles. But the US forward-based systems are to remain intact. And this contrivance that cannot be taken seriously is called "zero option", as if it were something simple and fair. I do not dispute its simplicity. What can be simpler than to destroy the Soviet Union's defense system at one go. But as for fairness, there is not a trace of it in such an approach. The American-style "zero option" is motivated by the same striving for superiority and by nothing else.

The real picture is that Soviet medium-range missiles and bombers face the nuclear arms of this type that exist in Europe: US nuclear-capable aircraft stationed at air bases in several West European countries, nuclear-capable aircraft on board US aircraft carriers cruising in seas washing Europe, and the land-based and sea-based medium-range ballistic missiles and bombers of a corresponding type belonging to Britain and France.

Can one really ignore these weapons when determining the composition of medium-range forces, as the United States is striving to do at the talks in Geneva? Of course, one cannot. For these are not tactical nuclear weapons, as the United States would like to depict them. The above-mentioned weapons have a range (action radius) of from 1,000 to 4,500 kilometres and are capable of dealing blows at targets on USSR territory right up to the Urals.

The Americans' attempt to compare the forces of the sides only in respect of Soviet and American ground-based missiles, excluding the weapons of their allies and the United States air force deployed in Europe, and to serve up to the public monstrous figures of the USSR's superiority over NATO aims at intimidating Western Europeans and getting them to agree to the "supplementary armament" of Europe with new American nuclear missiles. But it is clear to anyone who has a regard for facts that such an arbitrary approach does not accord with the principle of equality and equal security. It is an American attempt to prove what cannot be proved.

Sowing Distrust

At the same time in the President's speech an attempt was made to sow distrust of the Soviet Union's stand. He declared that the Soviet Union was violating the unilateral moratorium it had announced on the deployment of its medium-range missiles in the European part of the USSR. I declare quite categorically: the USSR is true to its word. It is not deploying the above-mentioned missiles in the European part of the USSR and is unilaterally even reducing them considerably. That is the truth. And Washington will not succeed in casting doubt on our policy.

As regards assessment of the relation between the conventional armed forces of the sides, this is a more complex matter, because the Warsaw Treaty has more forces and weapons of some types and NATO has more of others. But according to the basic indices the picture is as follows: the NATO bloc is superior to the Warsaw Treaty in overall numerical strength, in the number of combat-ready divisions and in anti-tank weapons, and is approximately equal to it in the quantity of artillery and armour. NATO is somewhat inferior to the Warsaw Treaty in the number of tactical aircraft. But on the whole an approximate balance of forces exists in respect of conventional arms, too.

Thus, if one assesses the correlation of military forces of the Warsaw Treaty and the NATO bloc objectively, on the basis of the facts, one will have to acknowledge this: whether you take strategic nuclear arms or medium-range nuclear weapons in Europe, or the con-

ventional armed forces of NATO and the Warsaw Treaty—in every case approximate parity exists between the sides. There is no "decided Soviet advantage" whatever.

In this parity of the armed forces facing each other we see embodiment of the principle of the equal security of the sides. Moreover, it is our firm belief that the application of this principle must find expression not in the endless building up of armaments and armed forces but in joint and co-ordinated efforts to reduce the levels of military confrontation. Precisely this is what the USSR is striving for at the current talks with the United States on military matters.

Question: President Reagan claims that the Soviet Union is leading the arms race. In support of this, he alleges that the US armed forces have remained at the same level since 1962 while the armed forces of the USSR have for 20 years been continually increasing. Is this claim true?

"If one assesses the correlation of military forces of the Warsaw Treaty and the NATO bloc objectively. . .in every case approximate parity exists between the sides."

Answer: On November 22 the master of the White House said: "The truth is that while the Soviet Union has raced we have not." Let us see who is really the initiator of the arms race. Who, one may ask, first developed atomic weapons and used them against the population of Hiroshima and Nagasaki? Who first built thousands of heavy nuclear-capable bombers, began to mass-produce and deploy intercontinental missiles, and increased the number of nuclear-powered ballistic missile submarines? Who first equipped ballistic missiles with multiple independently targetable reentry vehicles? Who started to produce neutron and binary chemical weapons? Who is now trying to spread the arms race to outer space? One only has to ask all these questions for it to become clear that it is precisely the United States that has been throwing down a challenge to the Soviet Union for more than thirty years. Starting from the 1950s the United States forced an arms race upon us in respect of all weapons of intercontinental range. Already in the early sixties it had about 2,000 heavy bombers and by 1966-1967 it had deployed over 1,000 ground-based intercontinental ballistic missiles as well as 41 nuclear submarines carrying 656 ballistic missiles, that is to say, it had reached the present level of strategic arms in respect of the number of delivery vehicles. At that time the USSR had a little over 600 strategic delivery vehicles of all types.

US Seeks Superiority

These are the facts. Why did the US President not say

who first developed strategic nuclear forces on an unprecedented scale and threatened the world? He did not do this because this is not to the advantage of the United States. That is why he speaks only about what the USSR was doing in the seventies. But the truth is that the Soviet Union was faced with the need of responding to the actions of the United States and taking steps to maintain its own defense potential. Only this, and nothing else, was what we were doing in the sixties and the seventies. The USSR was concerned with parity and never thought of having military superiority over the United States.

The US President was evidently counting on creating impression to his own advantage by alleging that US strategic arms have for 20 years remained unchanged either qualitatively or quantitatively. But he again was going against the facts.

In actual fact there was a continuous build-up of US strategic arms. In the first half of the past decade alone new weapon systems were deployed in large numbers: Minuteman-1 missiles were replaced by 550 Minuteman-3 intercontinental ballistic missiles each having three independently targetable warheads. At the same time work proceeded to increase the yield of the warheads and to equip Minuteman-3 missiles with a system of the remote re-targeting of missiles. Thirty-one nuclear-powered missile submarines were equipped with 496 Poseidon C-3 ballistic missiles, each having 10 to 14 warheads.

"The truth is that the Soviet Union was faced with the need of responding to the actions of the United States and taking steps to maintain its own defense potential."

Nearly 270 heavy bombers were equipped to carry 20 SRAM nuclear missiles each. Starting in the late seventies new nuclear submarines with Trident missiles began to be introduced in the navy; the development, production and deployment of long-range Cruise missiles—air-, sea- and land-based—continued throughout the decade.

The implementation of its plans for developing strategic arms in the seventies, together with President Reagan's well-known "strategic programme" for the eighties and Washington's desire to achieve at all costs the "supplementary armament" of Western Europe with new medium-range nuclear missiles, as well as with the colossal level of military spending, a level unwarranted by any defense needs, shows that it is the United States, and it alone, which is at the present time too the initiator of the arms race. By strengthening its armed forces the Soviet Union was only responding to the military preparations of those who threatened our country. At the same time it was repeatedly proposing to the United States that the development of new systems of weapons of mass destruction should be renounced. But all our proposals remained without an answer, although it was a question of undertaking mutual obligations. . . .

Question: What do you think the decision announced by the US President on deploying MX missiles and further building up the strategic potential, in particular, through the deployment of new US medium-range nuclear missiles in Western Europe, may lead to?

Answer: The planned deployment of MX missiles on US territory and of medium-range missiles in Western Europe is Washington's programme for abolishing the existing military balance and achieving superiority over the USSR on a global and regional scale. It is an extremely dangerous spiral in the nuclear arms race. After all, 100 MX ICBMs are one thousand highly accurate independently targetable nuclear warheads of 600 kilotons each. This means that the yield of each warhead is 30 times greater than that of the atomic bomb dropped on Hiroshima. MX missiles are a weapon destabilizing the overall strategic situation.

Current Negotiations

It should also be recalled that simultaneously with these missiles the deployment of new Trident ballistic missiles on submarines, of strategic bombers and of long-range Cruise missiles of all basing modes, as well as the use of outer space for military purposes are envisaged. By 1990 the United States counts on having up to 20,000 nuclear warheads in its strategic nuclear forces alone. All this taken together can hardly be assessed as anything but a programme of preparations for a general nuclear war.

The implementation of NATO's plans to deploy about 600 new American medium-range nuclear missiles in Western Europe would also lead to a dangerous change in the situation for the Soviet Union and other countries of the socialist community. All these missiles installed close to Soviet frontiers would be a direct supplement to the US strategic nuclear potential deployed on the American continent.

We have ever increasing doubts about the sincerity and seriousness of the United States' intentions to reach a mutually acceptable agreement at the Geneva talks on medium-range weapons. One cannot help arriving at the conclusion that the American side, using the "zero option" as a screen at the talks, is in actual fact pressing for the full-scale deployment of its new missiles in Europe.

The question arises: what is the United States doing all this for? It claims that its new missiles are intended to counter Soviet SS-20 missiles and to defend West European countries. But this is to deceive West Europeans. Western Europe will not be more secure if new

American missiles are deployed. On the contrary, the nuclear threat to Europe will increase. The American missile with their 2,500-kilometre range are a first-strike weapon and are designed for waging nuclear war in Europe. As the Pentagon document "Fiscal Year 1984-1988 Defense Guidance" points out, these missiles will be targeted primarily at government and military command centers in the USSR, as well as at our intercontinental ballistic missiles and other strategic targets. The flight time of the Pershing-2 missile will be about six minutes, you see, and so the aggressor calculates that it will be difficult to take counter-measures within this space of time. So it is a question not of the simple arithmetical addition of 600 missiles to the US strategic potential but of a qualitative change in the strategic situation in favour of the United States. This is a fact the Soviet Union cannot help reckoning with.

USSR Concludes

The appropriate conclusions are being drawn in the Soviet Union both from the ever-mounting anti-Soviet propaganda campaign and attempts to distort our peace initiatives, as well as from the prospect of a growth of the real threat to our country should these US plans begin to be implemented. The US Administration will not succeed in intimidating the USSR by creating "super-protected" MX strategic missiles and deploying Pershing-2 and Cruise missiles in Western Europe. The US Administration should not hypnotise itself with the possibility of achieving military superiority over the USSR. Nothing will come of it. If, flouting common sense and defying the will of the peoples for peace, the present White House leadership throws down a challenge to us and starts deploying MX missiles, in response to this, a new intercontinental ballistic missile of the same class will be deployed in the Soviet Union and its characteristics will be in no way inferior to those of the MX missile. The USSR will, if need be, be able effectively and promptly to counter other threats, too, from Washington.

"The planned deployment of MX missiles on U.S. territory. . .is Washington's pro-gramme for abolishing the existing military balance and achieving superiority over the U.S.S.R. on a global and regional scale."

The aggressive designs of the United States and NATO are compelling us together with the fraternal socialist countries to concern ourselves seriously with maintaining our defense capability at the due level. But we are against military rivalry. For that very reason we are calling upon the United States to renounce its nuclear build-up plans and not to destroy the existing balance of forces. On this point Yuri Andropov, General Secretary of the CPSU Central Committee, has stated with absolute clarity: "We are for seeking a sound basis, acceptable to all sides, for settling the most complex problems, and above all, of course, the problems of curbing the arms race in both nuclear and conventional arms. But let no one expect unilateral disarmament with us. We are not naive. We do not demand unilateral disarmament from the West. We are for equality, for taking account of the interests of both sides, for honest agreement. We are ready for this."

Dmitri Ustinov is the Marshal of the U.S.S.R. and the Minister of Defense.

The Arms Buildup Is Necessary

James P. Mullins

Few would deny that the world today is becoming increasingly more dangerous—dangerous to you, your children, and the democracy and freedoms we all enjoy.

Since yesterday, the Soviet Union has built eight more warplanes, 144 new missiles, 48 more tanks or armored vehicles. . .and has produced enough new hand weapons to equip an additional 1,400 infantrymen.

One would think from this feverish pace, that the Soviets are "just catching up." The fact of the matter, unfortunately for us, is that they caught up years ago. . .during years when we argued incessantly about the value of national defense.

Today the Soviets have almost 1,400 ICBMs. . .we have just over 1,000. Today the Soviets have 1,000 sea-launched ballistic missiles. . .we have about 575. Today the Soviets have some 4.8 million people in uniform. . .we have just over 2 million.

But that's not all. They have more than 7,000 fighter aircraft. . .we have fewer than 4,000. They have 220 attack submarines. . .we have fewer than 100. And they have 46,000 tanks, while we have just 11,000.

One must ask, at this point, just what the Soviets have in mind? Why do they continue to subordinate their hard-pressed economy to the acquisition of even more war-making capability?

Frankly, I don't think the Soviets are very fond of our democracy. . .because I think we're standing in the way of Soviet world domination. We're a very large thorn in their side. . .a thorn that, ultimately, they plan to remove!

Just during the time I am speaking with you today. . .just during these few minutes. . .the Soviets will build another two missiles. . .missiles I believe they will aim at our ultimate destruction.

Facing up to that threat will not be easy. In fact, if history is any guide, it will be very difficult for us even to admit to ourselves just how much trouble we're in—to admit that the threat is greater today than ever before in our history—and to admit that, because of past neglect, our arsenal isn't what it used to be.

Historically we've always denied the unpleasant— we've always looked the other way—and somehow we've pretended it didn't exist.

In 1921, President Woodrow Wilson left office a broken and unpopular president. . .not because of any scandal . . .not because of any incompetence. . .but because he dared to attack America's denial of reality.

Isolation Engendered War

He dared to chip away at the wall of isolation we were building. . .a wall designed to protect us from the world's unpleasantries. And he dared to look at what his country didn't want to see. . .yet he was utterly rejected by those he tried so desperately to help.

The dangers Wilson foresaw, of course, did not go away. In fact, a decade later, from the ruins of worldwide depression, the seeds of Nazi tyranny were planted. . .yet we still did not want to see. And as the tentacles of imperialism began spreading, there were cries of warning. . .yet we still did not want to hear.

On September 1st, 1939, Hitler started World War II by attacking Poland. Two days later, both Britain and France declared war on Germany. Yet we pretended it was not happening. By the end of the month, Poland had been crushed by the German blitzkreig. . .and Nazi plans called for a systematic annihilation of Poles. . .an extermination of some 5 million lives. Yet, we said, "surely this can't be true," and we went about our business as usual.

On November 13, 1939, the first bombs fell on British soil. And within a few weeks, food rationing began in Great Britain. But we had all we wanted to eat. . .and no bombs seemed to threaten our serene lifestyle.

We just couldn't admit to ourselves that we were threatened. . .we just couldn't come to grips with the unpleasant reality we faced. . .the unpleasant truth of those cold December days in 1939.

James P. Mullins, "The Price of Freedom," *Vital Speeches of the Day*, August 1, 1983. Reprinted with permission.

But as we all know, not admitting this reality didn't make it go away—and for us, those days late in 1939 quickly turned into a December 7th day late in 1941—a day when we were taught a painful lesson about the realities of life—and about the realities of death. Fortunately, then, we had the industrial might—we had the time to rearm—and we were able to see the conflict through to victory.

"Many are morally outraged that we spend what we do to maintain our nuclear arsenal. . .yet they accept without comment the Soviets' larger nuclear arsenal we must defend against."

During those terrible years, we all learned a valuable lesson—we all learned that you can't ignore a "1939"—and that if you do, it will quickly become a "1941." But apparently there are many who believe that, as in 1941, we'll have time to rearm America, because I see that same lack of preparedness, that same denial of reality throughout our country today as we saw in 1939. But the sad reality is we will not have time to get our act together—to mobilize and rearm. Modern weapons technology has seen to that.

One need only look at Czechoslovakia and Poland to see clear manifestations of tyranny's expansion. One need only consider the flagrant use of chemical and biological agents in Afghanistan, agents the Soviets have sworn never to use. . .agents that indiscriminately subject even the most innocent child to a cruel and inhumane death. . . .

One need only consider the Soviet's use of these weapons to correctly gauge the value of their assurances. . .the trustworthiness of their sworn oath. . .the hostile intent of their leardership.

Soviet Arsenals

Many in this country caution against overreacting to Soviet provocations. . .yet they somehow forget to condemn the provoker. Many are morally outraged that we spend what we do to maintain our nuclear arsenal. . . yet they accept without comment the Soviets' larger nuclear arsenal we must defend against. We need only open our eyes to see the reality we face.

For example, each year the Soviets produce more warplanes than we and all our allies have totally committed for the defense of Europe. Yet many argue about the cost of defending Europe. . .they argue whether such defenses are really needed. . .they argue whether this is really any of our business. . .in fact, they argue and argue and argue some more. . .yet they never face up to the unpleasantness they want so desperately to deny.

Just consider the tremendous concern today, both in government and private sectors, over the size of the federal budget. . .and in particular, the defense budget. Many condemn the increases in defense spending as the cause of our economic ills.

Yet they fail to look at the facts. . .they fail to see that until fiscal year 1982 defense spending, as a function of "real dollars" has been lower than 1962 levels. In fact, except for the Vietnam buildup and in spite of the increases in fiscal years 1981 and 1982, on the average the defense budget declined from 1962 to 1982.

Many look back at the "golden day" of the late Kennedy and early Johnson years, and yearn to go back. . .yearn to return to that time when, they believe, we had our priorities straight. . .when we had defense in its proper, subordinate place.

Well, I'd like to go back to those years too, because we spent a much greater share of our nation's resources for defense then than we do now. In fact, between 1964 and 1979 we reduced defense spending from 8 percent to 5 percent of our nation's GNP. During those same years, however, we increased our federal non-defense spending from 11 percent to 16 percent of GNP. In other words, while we were chopping away at our national security, we were funneling more and more money into non-defense programs.

The Soviets, of course, were not sitting idly by. They took advantage of our desire to deny the unpleasant. . . our fascination with only the nicer things in life. . .and they undertook an unprecedented buildup of warmaking capability. During the decade of the '70s, the time when we were underfunding our defense programs, the Soviets were increasing their defense spending dramatically.

There were many weapons systems we didn't buy during that period. . .weapons we should have bought. . .weapons we must now buy at today's inflated prices. For example, we should have bought the B-1 then, but we didn't. Now we must rely on our fleet of aging B-52s, an airplane which, in many cases, is older than the crews who fly it.

It's going to take a great deal of time and money to replace just those B-52s, but we have no choice. Just as we did in the 1930's, we've ignored an unpleasant reality in the '70s. Now it's 1939 all over agian. . .now it's time for us to pay the price while we still can afford to pay it!

The United States Air Force has an aging inventory of airplanes, an inventory where three-fourths of the fleet that must deter war. . .that must keep you free. . .threefourths of that fleet is over nine years old. By contrast, 30 years ago, only 14 percent of our fleet was over nine years old.

Inability to go to War

But it's not only the fleet that has suffered. The cumulative decrease in military spending has directly impacted our ability to go to war—and thereby, our ability to deter war.

We haven't been able to give our aircrews the flying hours they should have had, we haven't been able to do much of the maintenance we should have done, and we haven't been able to purchase many of the munitions and spare parts we should have purchased.

Additionally, we've had to underfund some of our "people programs"—we've too often capped pay and removed benefits, and we've seen many of the well-publicized problems in morale and retention develop as a direct result.

The decade of neglect has also taken a terrible toll on our defense industry. We've starved out many of our most important suppliers, we've lost many of our most talented people, and we've allowed our industrial base to become outdated and less competitive. So we're in the unenviable position today of needing more, needing it quickly, but not having the capability to produce it.

Fortunately, with this administration's recognition of the problem, our industrial base is now beginning to show signs of recovery. And fortunately, with the real growth we've started the process of restoring strategic balance, restocking spares and munitions for readiness, and modernizing our aging forces.

But we must recognize that this will be a long-term effort, one requiring substantial sacrifice and resolve on the part of both the government and industry. For we're not actually increasing our forces yet—we must first catch up from past neglect before we can do that. In fact, our aircraft procurement programs remain well below levels needed to cope with greatly expanded Soviet capabilities. And it still takes years even to produce a few landing gear parts.

Now getting back on the right track is going to be expensive, but the point is that we can afford it. In reality, we'll spend more on alcoholic beverages today than we'll spend equipping and operating our Air Force. And Americans will spend more on recreational activities this year than we'll have in the entire Air Force budget.

Sometimes we just don't seem to function with good common sense—and I think one of those times is now. We don't argue about the cost or value of alcoholic beverages, and we don't argue about the cost or value of recreational activities. But we do constantly argue about the cost and value of defense. And we often defer long-term considerations to the myraid of short-term gains and comforts that tempt us.

Here's an example of what I mean. When we think of our defense budget, we often forget what it would cost us in dollars alone if we were unable to deter war. We're not even talking here about loss of life or loss of freedom. We're just talking about money.

In World War II, where our way of life was clearly threatened, we spent about 542 billion dollars to fight the war and survive. Now this includes 54 billion for veterans benefits which we're still paying today, and 200 billion for interest on war loans.

But have we considered what it would cost to fight that same war today? Assuming just a five percent inflation rate annually since World War II, one would find that the cost today would exceed four trillion dollars. That's almost 19 times the defense budget for FY 1982.

In fact, if you took out a mortgage today at 15 percent for 30 years on a four trillion dollar loan, your payments would be 50 billion 600 million per month. And you know, that's about how we'd have to finance such a war today. If we made the mistake of weakening our deterrence, and thereby could not avoid a war, we'd have to mortgage the future of our businesses and families to pay for it.

Nuclear Threats

To deter war, we must have a military capability which can clearly deal with those who threaten us. Now therein lies our greatest challenge, yet therein also lies our greatest opportunity to preserve the peace. In 1939, after years of neglecting our defense industries, our enemies failed to gauge correctly the ability of America's private sector to produce war material. Had they known that in 44 months we could turn out 310,000 aircraft, 88,000 tanks, 27 aircraft carriers, 211 submarines, 358 destroyers, 900,000 military trucks, and 411,000 artillery pieces—had they known we had this capacity for productivity, World War II may have been avoided.

"Defense is our greatest social program—for it has allowed us to think about doing all those other 'nice things' in life."

But our potential adversaries just didn't believe we had it in us—they were not deterred—and war became a reality. Now today, how do you suppose our potential adversaries gauge our defense industry's capability? How credible is that aspect of our deterrent? And how important is revitalizing our defense industry, even at the expense of other programs.

It's important to remember that defense, by keeping us out of world conflict, gives us the freedom and resources to do many other things. In this regard, defense is our greatest social program—for it has allowed us to even think about doing all those other "nice things" in life. But what good will our social programs be if we fail to deter war—or even worse, if we fail to keep this nation free? What good will urban development be if conquering armies are marching through our city streets?

These are questions we'd better start asking, because, it's 1939 again. The threat to our way of life, to our own well-being and to the well-being of our future generations grows relentlessly around us, even as I talk with you now.

We've got to wake up, we've got to stop bickering among ourselves, we've got to get away from our near-sighted infatuation with short-term profit and comfort—and we've got to get on with the deadly serious business of deterring war with a strong defense. And nowadays, that means a defense that is substantially in being, with a back-up, long-term production capability if that is needed.

That also means spending what we need to spend—and it means producing what we're technologically capable of producing. The great arsenal of democracy is unique among many of the world's arsenals, because it's almost totally comprised of private industry. That has been our greatest strength, for it has made possible our unique diversity, and it has encouraged our "yankee ingenuity." This has allowed us to achieve what we have achieved. And I'm confident that in the future, this same strength will allow us to do what we need to do!

"Whatever the costs involved, whatever the price we pay. . .if we manage to keep this democracy intact, if we manage to keep this country free—then our defense will have been a bargain."

In conclusion, let me just say that it really doesn't matter how expensive an adequate defense will be—it's really not important how many short-term concerns we have to deter. In the final analysis, all that matters is that we do what needs to be done, that we sacrifice whatever it takes to pay the price of freedom. We must honor the obligation of being free people, we must do for our future generations what prior generations have done for us.

For whatever the costs involved, whatever the price we pay, if we manage to meet the challenges we face, if we manage to keep this democracy intact, if we manage to keep this country free—then our defense will have been a bargain.

Thank you.

James P. Mullins is a commander in the U.S. Air Force Logistics Command.

"Listening to the pessimists, one would never know that the U.S. spends almost three times as much as the Russians per soldier."

The Arms Buildup Is Unnecessary

Franklyn D. Holzman

Many thoughtful observers in America believe that the military might of the Warsaw Pact nations, especially the USSR, has been increasing relative to that of the NATO nations, especially the United States, and that, as a result, the Warsaw Pact nations have achieved military parity with NATO, or have pushed ahead. This military buildup, moreover, is taken as prima facie evidence that the Warsaw Pact nations have aggressive intentions vis-a-vis their neighbors.

What explains such a momentous shift of positions in the arms race? The usual answer is that the Soviet Union has increased military spending to a greater degree than the United States has. To reverse this dangerous trend, naturally, the U.S. and its allies have been contemplating similar increases. As President Reagan put it in his State of the Union message on February 18, 1981;

> I believe my duty as President requires that I recommend increases in defense spending over the coming years. Since 1970, the Soviet Union has invested $300 billion more in its military forces than we have.

In the two and a half years since that address, the President's apprehensions about Soviet aggressiveness have been reflected in the sharp rise in U.S. military expenditures, our steadfast opposition to the Soviet-Western European gas pipeline, and a steady deterioration of relations in practically every other area in which the two nations interact.

But there is considerable evidence that U.S. estimates of Soviet and Warsaw Pact military expenditures are calculated incorrectly and are presented in a misleading way. With proper calculation and interpretation, the military-spending gaps that favor the Soviet bloc largely disappear. This leads one to question the magnitude of the Soviet bloc's military buildup and to view skeptically the claims of the Administration that the buildup is necessarily offensive rather than defensive.

Franklyn D. Holzman, "Are We Falling Behind the Soviets?", *The Atlantic,* July 1983. Reprinted with permission of author.

Several factors help to explain what may be a distorted view of Soviet-bloc military expenditures. Perhaps most important is the tendency of bureaucrats, politicians, and the press to summarize complicated computations with a few simple figures. Two such figures are the CIA annual estimates, widely quoted, that the USSR is currently outspending the U.S. on defense by 50 percent, and that over the decade 1971-1980 the USSR outspent us by $420 billion (an update of President Reagan's $300 billion).

CIA Estimates

Once these figures surface, they begin to have a life of their own; rarely mentioned are the numerous qualifications attached to them by the CIA when they were first released. While the two figures presented may have validity for some purposes, even without qualifications, for other purposes they are misleading and inappropriate. For example, the CIA's 50 percent figure is based on an estimate of Soviet military spending that, when converted into rubles and expressed as a percentage of Soviet GNP, reveals the so-called burden of defense spending, providing an indication of the military drain on Soviet resources. Currently, the CIA estimates that burden at between 12 and 14 percent of GNP. Conceptually speaking, this is a valid use of the CIA's estimate.

Suppose, however, we want a figure that represents the confrontation between the United States and the USSR. President Reagan clearly used the related $300 billion figure in this way in his State of the Union address. For that purpose, the 50 percent and $420 billion gap figures are inappropriate, because a large part of Soviet military spending is irrelevant to the superpower confrontation. For example, the Soviet Union maintains an army of roughly 750,000 men on the long Sino-Soviet border. According to Harold Brown, former secretary of defense, in his 1979 annual report, the Soviets "have felt obliged to allocate up to about 20 percent·of their total defense effort to the Far East and the PRC [People's Republic of China]." In various statements in the past few years, the CIA has estimated the same figure at between 12.5 and 20 percent.

Money spent by the Soviet Union to support its large army across 5,000 miles of inhospitable terrain has thus not been available to build tanks, planes, and missiles that might be used against the U.S. and its NATO allies. If 15 percent of Soviet expenditures is subtracted from the total (the CIA estimate is $1,535 billion for the years 1971 to 1980), the current gap is reduced from 50 percent to 27.5 percent and the 1971-1980 expenditure gap is reduced by $230 billion—that is, from $420 billion to $190 billion (all in 1979 dollars).

Thus, both the current and the ten-year spending gaps are roughly halved by removing expenditures directed at China. The appropriateness of removing these expenditures is supported by the Department of Defense's practice of excluding U.S. expenditures on Vietnam when comparing NATO and Warsaw Pact total defense costs.

"If contributions by our allies and the Soviet Union's allies are factored in, the imbalance between NATO and Warsaw Pact military spending is sharply reversed."

Finding a true estimate of the gap between Warsaw Pact and NATO "confrontation" spending requires another major adjustment. The CIA restricts its published estimates to comparisons of military spending by the U.S. and the USSR. This establishes a framework for virtually all governmental and media discussions of military spending. In effect, these discussions imply that the U.S. and the USSR confront each other without allies. If the contributions of the NATO and Warsaw Pact nations (other than the U.S. and USSR) were either inconsequential or of roughly equal magnitude, this mode of calculation would make sense. However, as Harold Brown put it in the same annual report, "We are fortunate in having prosperous and willing allies who can help counterbalance the Soviet effort. The Soviets are not so fortunate." According to the authoritative International Institute of Strategic Services, in London, America's NATO allies spent $94.9 billion in 1980, or almost six times more than the $16.7 billion spent by Warsaw Pact nations other than the Soviet Union. In fact, France, Great Britain, and Germany each spent more than all "other" Warsaw Pact nations added together.

If contributions by our allies and the Soviet Union's allies are factored in, the imbalance between NATO and Warsaw Pact military spending is sharply reversed. As of 1980, NATO was still outspending the Warsaw

Pact—over the decade, by more than $250 billion, despite the huge USSR-U.S. dollar gap calculated by the CIA. The $250 billion difference in NATO's favor makes no correction for Soviet expenditures directed at China. If we take into account the $230 billion dollars that the Soviets are estimated to have directed at China, the total difference in military spending between NATO and the Warsaw Pact nations rises to $480 billion.

Currency Adjustments

Another major distortion in comparisons of East-West military spending stems from the practice of relying on dollar valuations to compare the two defense establishments. As the CIA acknowledges:

> Dollar cost calculations tend to overstate Soviet defense activities relative to those of the United States. . . .Given different resource endowments and technologies, countries tend to use more of the resources that are relatively cheap—and less of those that are relatively expensive—for a given purpose. A comparison drawn in terms of the prices of one country thus tends to overstate the relative value of the activities of the other.

This so-called index-number effect is not difficult to understand. The Soviets pay their soldiers a very low wage and, perhaps partly for this reason, have more than twice as many men and women in uniform as we do. When we value their 4.5 million military personnel on the basis of *our* average annual pay, which is close to $20,000, the result is a very high estimate of Soviet spending. The *reductio ad absurdum* of this methodology is the recently revealed (though unofficial) CIA estimate of Chinese military spending in dollars, which purports to show that the Chinese government is currently mounting a defense effort equal to our own. This bizarre conclusion arises from a calculation of the cost of mobilizing the enormous Chinese army at U.S. pay scales.

The usual, and proper, procedure when comparing real costs in two different monetary systems is to calculate expenditures in the currencies of both nations, in this case in rubles as well as in dollars. The dollar estimate provides an upper limit of Soviet expenditures, the ruble estimate a lower limit (since it exaggerates U.S. expenditures by putting a very high ruble price on our more advanced military technology). An average of the two, usually a geometric mean, can be calculated if one wants a single figure. In most of its other U.S.-USSR comparisons, the CIA follows this procedure. For example, almost two years ago, the Joint Economic Committee of Congress released a CIA study that compared consumption expenditures in the USSR with those in the U.S. and other nations. In the "overview," on the first page of that study, was this statement:

> In 1976, real per capita consumption in the Soviet Union was 34.4 percent of that in the United States: this value is the geometric mean of comparisons in rubles (27.6 percent) and in dollars (42.8 percent).

The CIA currently makes defense estimates in both dollars and rubles. However, the ruble comparison, once presented, is thereafter ignored, and the geometric mean is not presented at all. The reason for this practice is not difficult to discern: until a few years ago, the Agency did not know the costs in rubles for many Soviet weapons or other defense material. The CIA now claims to have many more prices, and should, therefore, be able to present the geometric mean of the dollar and ruble comparisons as the official estimate. Since the dollar comparison shows the Soviets outspending us by 50 percent and the ruble comparison reduces the difference to 30 percent, the geometric mean works out to 39.6 percent. If this change in the CIA's USSR-U.S. comparison is combined with an adjustment for forces on the Chinese border, the current difference between U.S. and Soviet "confrontation" spending shrinks to below 20 percent, and the ten-year gap between U.S. and Soviet military spending is reduced to roughly $100 billion (from $420 billion). It also widens the NATO-Warsaw Pact ten-year gap to roughly $550 billion, in *our favor*.

Exaggerations

Before we leave index numbers, three more points need to be clarified. First, while we know more about the costs of Soviet armaments than we did in the 1970s, ruble prices for most military products are still unavailable. What this means is that when making ruble estimates, one has to assign value to most weapons first in dollars and then in rubles, using as a basis for conversion the few available ruble prices of other weapons. But ruble comparisons are thus in large part dollar comparisons, and therefore they still exaggerate Soviet military spending. While no precise estimate of the exaggeration is possible, the CIA's estimate that the USSR outspends the U.S. by 30 percent in a ruble comparison is clearly much too high. An adjustment for this distortion would reduce still further Soviet and Warsaw Pact military spending as discussed above.

Second, American advocates of larger military appropriations for equipment procurement point out that the Soviet equipment buildup is made possible by the very low wages the USSR pays its soldiers. As William Perry, former undersecretary of defense for research and engineering, put it in a 1982 review of James Fallow's book *National Defense*, "they can devote half of their budget to equipment procurement while we devote less than a quarter of ours to equipment. . . ." While Dr. Perry's statement is true as far as it goes, it neglects the fact, as put by Stansfield Turner, a former director of the CIA, that "military hardware is much more expensive than manpower in the Soviet Union, while in the United States manpower is relatively more expensive than hardware. . . ." So, the Russians need to spend a greater percentage of their military budget on equipment; we need to spend a greater percentage on manpower.

Third, if Soviet military expenditures vis-a-vis the United States are exaggerated, U.S. estimates of the percentage of Soviet gross national product that is devoted to those expenditures are also likely to be exaggerated. They are—but for reasons other than those already mentioned. The proper way to measure Soviet military expenditures in relation to GNP for the year 1982 would be to value both in 1982 rubles. Unfortunately, the most recent set of ruble prices for military equipment available to our intelligence establishment is for 1970. So, for lack of a better alternative, the CIA is forced to measure Soviet military expenditures and GNP for the years since 1970 in so-called "constant 1970 ruble prices."

"While many. . .view the Soviet Union and its allies as outspending us on defense, the Soviet Union probably views the spending competition. . .as unfavorable to itself."

If trends in ruble prices of military equipment were representative of GNP as a whole, then it would not make much difference whether 1970 or 1982 prices were used in the estimate. In fact, however, because of rapid technological advances in Soviet weaponry, the price of any given weapon's capability over the 1970-1982 period must have fallen relative to Soviet prices in general. In this respect, Soviet weapons are like American computers, whose prices have dropped enormously over the past decade, in spite of inflation in the rest of the economy. The more advanced military equipment being produced for Soviet armed forces today would have cost many times more rubles to produce in 1970 than at present. So the most recent CIA estimate (12 to 14 percent) of the percentage of Soviet GNP (for 1980, but in 1970 prices) devoted to military expenditures is certainly an exaggeration, and would undoubtedly be several percentage points lower in 1982 Soviet prices.

Military Buildup Compared

The view of the military spending gap just outlined appears to be greatly at odds with the conventional wisdom that the USSR and its allies have been engaged in an enormous military buildup that has enabled them to reduce or eliminate NATO military superiority, and that this has been accomplished by virtue of increased defense expenditures. If the facts reveal no military spending gap in favor of the Warsaw Pact countries, how can this be reconciled with the Soviet bloc's alleged military buildup?

First, perhaps the military buildup, and the degree to which the Soviets have caught up with us, have been exaggerated. A military effort has many dimensions, and those who sound dire warnings tend to concentrate their attention on areas in which Soviet progress has been most rapid. Further, the emphasis is usually on numbers—quantity rather than quality. Some experts have testified that the U.S. defense effort represents, in part, a sacrifice of quantity for quality. This view was recently echoed by a CIA spokesman before the Senate Armed Services Committee. He stated that U.S. military equipment tends to be produced with "more sophistication, more quality and better performance. . .[more safety], more quality control. . .a more highly designed product" than Soviet equipment. Apparently General John W. Vessey, Jr., chairman of the Joint Chiefs of Staff, feels that this is a good thing. On May 11, 1982, after admitting that the Soviets had a quantitative superiority in many weapons, he testified to the Senate Armed Services Committee: "But, overall, would I trade with [Soviet Chief of Staff] Marshal Ogarkov? Not on your life."

Listening to the pessimists, one would never know that the U.S. spends almost three times as much as the Russians per soldier in training and maneuvers, or that our missiles are more accurate, or that our subs are superior to theirs, and so forth. One cannot doubt that the Soviets have been catching up, but the degree to which this is true may well have been overstated.

Second, if the Soviets have been catching up, how has this been possible if, as has been shown, the actual military-spending gap is much smaller than official estimates suggest? Military-expenditure comparisons measure cost but not effectiveness and not the wisdom of the expenditure choices. If the United States has been spending money less wisely in terms of our needs than the Soviets have in terms of theirs, then the Soviets could catch up without outspending us.

"It hardly makes sense to throw hundreds more billions of dollars into defense . . .without drastic revision of the military."

Much has been written in the past few years regarding the waste and the misdirected expenditures in our defense program. Some general categories of wasteful spending often mentioned are so-called gold-plating of weapons (for example, air-conditioning and power steering in tanks); introducing some technology that is so complex (and expensive) that it can be neither easily operated nor properly maintained by our servicemen; introducing too many competing models and changing models too often, both of which prevent reduction of costs; allowing weapons suppliers very high profits and cost overruns not caused by inflation; maintaining facilities and programs that no longer serve a military function but are good for some congressman's constituency. Further evidence of inefficiency may be adduced from the fact that the balance of forces in Europe does not appear to reflect NATO's much higher levels of military spending.

What are the policy implications of the foregoing? If the view of the military-spending gap presented here is correct, the USSR is not as far ahead of the United States as the Reagan Administration and others contend. Moreover, if the USSR is catching up owing to waste and inefficiency on our part, it hardly makes sense to throw hundreds more billions of dollars into defense, at the expense of so many of this nation's major civilian priorities, without drastic revision of the military decision-making processes. Preventing the waste of $50 billion in cost overruns, misguided programs, and the like is as good a way to finance our military buildup as legislating $50 billion in new taxes or accepting a $50 billion increase in the national debt.

Finally, while many in this country view the Soviet Union and its allies as outspending us on defense, the Soviet Union probably views the spending competition in the terms just outlined—that is to say, as unfavorable to itself and its allies. If that is the Soviet view—and in fact the USSR views itself as having to take on almost singlehandedly the whole Western industrial world, plus China and Japan—then the motivations behind its buildup may well be less ominous than the Administration believes.

Franklyn D. Holzman is a professor of economics at Tufts University in Medford, Massachusetts.

"Soviet weapons are made especially to destroy American weapons—to defeat America while killing very few Americans and leaving our economy intact."

The Arms Buildup Will Prevent a Soviet Takeover

Americanism Educational League

If the Soviet Union were to inflict a nuclear first strike upon the United States, well over 90% of the American people would read about the attack in their newspapers or hear about it on radio or TV. Only a small percentage of Americans would see, hear, or feel any effects of the attack, and considerably less than 1% of us would become casualties.

Designed to Defeat

This is not wishful thinking, but rather a sober, detailed appraisal of the effects of the Soviet nuclear weapons which exist or are being built, if they were used according to the military strategy which the Soviet Union has been teaching to its forces since the beginning of the nuclear era. Soviet weapons are made especially to destroy American weapons—*to defeat America* while killing very few Americans and *leaving our economy intact.*

Simply put, the Soviet Union is not out to destroy us, but to defeat us. We can take no comfort in this, because the Soviets have made tremendous strides toward being able to achieve this goal, and because, after being defeated by the Soviets, most Americans might wish that Armageddon had come instead!

All of this, of course, is contrary to the picture of nuclear war which has been propagated by most American politicians, academics and publicists for a generation. According to their view, nuclear war would be a spasmodic exchange. Both the U.S. and the U.S.S.R. would shoot everything they had at each other's centers of population, literally bombing each other back into the Stone Age.

Criminally Stupid

Neither country could or would take any care, before or during the conflict, about limiting damage to itself. Each would strive only to annihilate the other even as it was being annihilated itself. This popular American

Americanism Educational League, "The Danger Is Defeat, Not Destruction." Available for 5¢ from the Americanism Educational League, Freedom Center, PO Box 5986, Buena Park, CA 90622.

picture of nuclear war has always been *utter nonsense.* Nonetheless, the technological advances of recent years have made it even more criminally stupid.

Since the early 1970's, it has been beyond dispute that the Soviet Union has a superior ICBM force built for one primary mission: destroying American missiles in their silos. By so doing the Soviet Union can diminish the United States' ability to strike back with its population-killing weapons.

Thus while American policies have aimed at producing dead Russians but leaving intact Soviet strategic weapons, the Soviet Union has never targeted our population. As a result of our misperception, we have been worrying needlessly about being burned to a crisp, or about dying of radiation sickness.

Irrational Fear

We have worried ourselves so irrationally about a far-fetched danger that we have rendered ourselves incapable of doing anything about the present danger—*the Soviet Union's growing ability to defeat us and to do to us what it has done to other peoples it has conquered.*

"We Don't Understand"

At least 326 of these missiles are SS-18's. These carry 10 independently targeted warheads, each of which has a yield of about one megaton—one million tons of TNT. (This is a highly tentative estimate, because the United States really does not understand how Soviets build nuclear weapons.) These 3,000+ Soviet warheads carry more explosive power than the entire American missile force put together! These warheads by themselves are also sufficient to cover every American "hard target" twice over.

The United States has less than 1,500 such sites overall, each able to resist pressures of 1,000 lbs. per square inch. Russia's SS-18 warheads are accurate enough to place their megaton within about one-tenth of a mile of the target—close enough to be quite sure of killing it. The

SS-18's alone can go a long way toward disarming the United States.

The Soviet Union either has deployed or is now deploying 500 SS-17's and SS-19's. These missiles carry four and six warheads respectively. Though not quite so accurate as the 18's, these 2,500 magaton-size warheads could kill "hard targets." But they could also be used to destroy "soft" military targets such as air bases, or be kept in reserve to threaten cities.

Over 2,000 Warheads

In addition, there are almost 600 SS-11's, each carrying one megaton. The Soviet Union has also deployed some 900 missiles aboard submarines. Almost half of these are longer range than anything aboard American subs, and about 200 of these carry multiple warheads. By the early 1980's, the latter's number will rise to about 500. The Soviet submarine force should be expected to have over 2,000 warheads, each of which would yield between 500 kilotons and one megaton. Such warheads, however, are only accurate to within a half mile. Therefore they can be used to attack air bases or to threaten cities.

"While American policies have aimed at producing dead Russians but leaving intact Soviet weapons, the Soviet Union has never targeted our population."

The Soviet heavy bomber force is small—less than 150 operational Bears and Bisons. Yet it can easily be augmented by 200 Backfire medium to long-range bombers, or even by cargo aircraft. The reason is simple: Soviet aircraft seeking to drop bombs on the United States need not use speed, low altitude, or deception to counteract American air defenses, *because none exist.* They have been dismantled over the past two decades. Even civilian cargo planes could be used to bomb the United States!

Four Huge Radars

The Soviet Union, on the other hand, has deployed 6,500 air-defense radars, 10,000 interceptor missiles, and 2,600 interceptor aircraft. It practices air-defense constanly. It has also built four huge phased-array radars which can be the core of a nationwide defense against ballistic missiles. The other components of such a defense already exist.

The Soviet Union has but to mass produce them— which, for all we know, it may be doing—in order to have a respectable defense. To back up its active defenses, the Soviet Union has an expanding civil defense, featuring hard shelters for about one-fourth of the urban population, protection for vital industries, and sheltered food supplies.

American defenses are practically non-existent. The old Distant Early Warning (DEW) line of arctic radars is obsolete. Once a Soviet pilot gets through that line, he can be confident of flying to his destination undetected. Even if he were detected, little could be done. The United States had only 300 old F-106 interceptors, and no surface-to-air missiles deployed to defend the country.

The United States has developed excellent technology by which to defend against ballistic missiles, but has renounced its use. According to American strategic doctrine, safety lies in *mutual* vulnerability. So far do American officials adhere to this doctrine that the United States is wholly without civil defense!

Basic Differences

It is clear that the biggest difference between the Soviet and the American force concerns the purposes for which the weapons may be used. Soviet military writings refer to deterrence quite differently from American ones. Whereas American Defense intellectuals see the weapons as scarecrows by which to ward off attack on American cities, the Soviets see them as tools by which to achieve their ends. Thus, for them, deterrence is an offensive concept: That is, to keep the Americans from thwarting Soviet purposes. For them, deterrence is achieved by the ability to win the war.

The Soviets expect that the United States would be deterred from doing anything serious to stop the ultimate triumph of the Marxist "Socialist Commonwealth" by the following prospect:

If pressed too far, the Soviet Union could launch its force of SS-18's and therewith destroy nearly all American land-based missiles and bombers. At the same time, Soviet ships or aircraft would mine the harbors where half of the American Polaris-Poseidon submarines lay. This would put the submarines out of action, and keep them where they could be destroyed at will by ICBMs, quite without killing Americans. Reduced to some 2,500 40-kiloton warheads, what could the United States do? The U.S.S.R. would still have about 7,000 warheads—all invulnerable.

"Air Bases Bombed"

If the United States chose to strike back, it could not thereby reduce the threat to itself. At this point, the United States would have suffered militarily, but in no other way. The 3,000 Soviet megatons which would already have exploded over places such as Davis-Monthan Air Force Base, Arizona and Warren Air Force Base, Wyoming, would have killed less than a quarter-million Americans—5 years' traffic fatalities!

But if, at this point, an American President ordered a strike at Soviet cities, he would risk a Soviet attack on America's population. At this point, negotiated surrender would make far more sense. Moreover, even if the President of the United States, or several submarine crews acting on their own, were to launch Polaris-Poseidon missiles on the Soviet Union, they could do relatively little damage. The Soviet civil defense system would have been on alert. The key industries would have shut down, "hardened" their machinery, and sheltered their workers. The rest of the urban population, the non-essentials, would have been placed in lesser shelters or sent to outlying areas.

Finally, the incoming American warheads would probably be met by some kind of antiballistic missile system. That fraction of the American warheads which arrived—probably far less than 100—would knock down a lot of buildings. *The future would belong to the Soviet Union!*

Frightened the U.S.

That fear has helped to convince American policymakers not to assist America's beleaguered friends in places like Iran. In 1973, the threat of Soviet intervention in the Middle East led the United States to stop Israel from consummating its victory against Soviet-supplied Arab armies which had attacked her on Yom Kippur. The same prospect frightened the United States into submitting to virtual expropriation of its oil production equipment in the Middle East and the quadrupling of the price of oil.

As the Soviet Union's arsenal becomes more fearsome, it will become more logical for the Soviet Union's friends around the world to be bolder, and it will be more logical for the United States and its friends to suffer more to avoid antagonizing the Soviets.

The decisive defeat of the United States in the world—a defeat which would leave no doubt in anyone's mind who ruled the world—could be accomplished easily, given the "cover" of decisive nuclear superiority. On October 1, 1979, the pro-Soviet government of Panama became legally sovereign over the whole Panama Canal Zone. Anytime thereafter it can abrogate the treaties which preserve a residual role for the United States. Then it can ask the Soviet Union to send troops to "help protect the Canal from the United States."

Loss of the Canal

Of course, the United States would enjoy local military superiority. But, given the Soviets' ability to carry out a disarming nuclear strike on the United States, and our inability to disarm the Soviet Union, would the United States actually risk killing Russian soldiers? It would be more reasonable to absorb the loss of the Canal and of the last shreds of American influence in the world.

Such losses could not help but jar the United States into realizing that strategic inferiority to the Soviet Union can lead only to enslavement. But surely, by the mid-1980's, this realization would come too late. *Surely the United States would begin to build the weapons it should have built during the 1960's and 1970's.*

But how would the United States respond to a Soviet declaration that the continuation of such an American build-up would be regarded as an act of war, for which the United States would bear full responsibility? If the United States chose to disregard the warning, the Soviets could look forward to losing their supremacy in a few years. Why should they not use it while they had it?

The Rape of America!

Subjugation of the United States would open new and more violent chapters in the history of the world. The rape of the United States would be swift. Russians have never been very farsighted in the husbanding of golden geese. The history of postwar Eastern Europe indicates the Soviets would set unrealistic reparations quotas and try to squeeze blood from stones. They would attempt to rid the economy of "parasitic" occupations—and to rid the earth of "useless mouths." All would be made even harsher by the inevitable campaigns against religion, the family, and other ancestral enemies of Communism. Those given power would be the most reliable. Reliability would be proven by harshness. Unfortunately, this is not speculation, but dreary experience. The history of Soviet rule consists of little else.

"These 3000+ Soviet warheads carry more explosive power than the entire American missile force put together."

The United States is not doomed to defeat. The Soviets have not built their nuclear forces by peculiar genius. The United States possesses technology to build weapons of the same kind that are even better. More important, the United States possesses the technology to build weapons of altogether different kinds, weapons which are likely to safeguard both our freedoms and our lives. Of course, to build these things at all we would have to change the way our officials have been thinking about war and weapons.

"We Want to Survive..."

Much would happen, however, if the American people transmitted one simple message to their officials: *"We want to survive any war with our freedoms intact!"*

With such a mandate, the President of the United States should begin by ordering the U.S. Air Force to remove the Minuteman II's and III's from their silos, to place them inside their factory canisters, and to keep them on the move aboard trucks, whence they could be launched. This would end the Soviet Union's ability to target and destroy these missiles. With that gone, the Soviet Union would lose a large part of the military incentive for a first strike.

The Americanism Educational League conducts a sustained campaign on behalf of private ownership of property, strong national defense, strict crime control, and limited government conducted within balanced budgets.

"Does the United States need to engage in a strategic buildup in order to deter nuclear war, prevent threats. . .or gain Soviet cooperation in arms control?. . .It does not."

Soviet Aggression Is No Excuse for the Arms Buildup

George W. Breslauer

"God knows, it's been frustrating to read some of these stories and not be able to say, 'That's untrue! Here's what the actual facts are. . . .' It's just been frustrating the hell out of me."

—Cyrus Vance

In recent years, we have heard a great deal about how detente was a one-way street, how the Soviets used arms control for unilateral advantage, and how U.S. security would be better enhanced by a strategic buildup than by arms control. Some of these arguments are accompanied by heavy documentation regarding Soviet capabilities, intentions and past behavior. Others are based primarily on assumptions or contentions about the psychology of deterrence and the logic of bargaining.

If the Strategic Arms Reduction Talks (START) and Theater Nuclear Force negotiations now under way prove fruitless, all these arguments will again be voiced, at still higher volume. Concerned citizens should therefore examine the assumptions behind arms-racing, preparing themselves now for future political debates.

It seems to me that the arguments in favor of a return to the arms race have, for the most part, been specious. My purpose here is to discuss several propositions used to justify it. I will indicate what basis they have in fact—none of them is totally groundless—and then summarize why I consider them to be wide of the mark. What I am addressing here are *strategic nuclear* questions, not the premises underlying calls for a conventional U.S. military buildup or Soviet actions in the conventional sphere.

The Soviets cannot be trusted to honor their treaties. There are many reasons that our leaders give credence to this proposition, over and above a general predisposition to believe the worst about the Soviets. One is the

Soviet obsession with secrecy, which creates the belief that perhaps they have something to hide. Another is the Soviet tendency to undertake all feasible programs not prohibited by treaties, coupled with their policy of testing the limits of all elastic clauses and ambiguities in agreements. In addition, there were specific incidents during the 1970s that raised grave suspicions: an outbreak of anthrax in the Soviet Union, as well as the discovery of certain toxins in South East Asia, raised questions about Soviet compliance with the chemical and biological warfare conventions of the early 1970s. Similarly, several incidents of telemetry encryption during Soviet missiles tests struck U.S. observers as violations of SALT I verification rules.

Yet the verdict is far from clear. Neither Soviet secrecy, nor their testing of ambiguities, nor the Soviet military buildup constituted violations of SALT I. There were minor violations on both sides which were smoothed out to mutual satisfaction in the Standing Consultative Commission established for precisely this purpose. The telemetry encryption episodes were just that—episodes—rather than a pattern. Moreover, they were not clear violations, and many complex discussions ensued in an effort to establish mutual understanding about what did and did not constitute an violation. The anthrax and toxin charges are more serious, but the last word has not been spoken on them. And there is evidence to support the view that these were not incidents of Soviet perfidy.

Soviet Behavior

What is more, Soviet behavior on these matters does not necessarily reflect their behavior in the strategic nuclear field. The Soviets have always taken less seriously multilateral conventions produced by international organizations. Bilateral deals with the United States, in the strategic nuclear field, are something else. On balance, U.S. arms control negotiators have been satisfied that the Soviets have adhered to the treaties they have hammered out with the United States: The Test-Ban Treaty (1963); The Nuclear Non-Proliferation Treaty (1967); SALT I (1972) and, thus far, the unratified SALT II. It is primarily those who did not like the terms of those treaties who have claimed Soviet perfidy. The negotiating experience of the 1970s suggests that the Soviets are neither benevolent partners nor unalterable antagonists. Rather, they are tough, pragmatic negotiators, who take seriously the nuclear arms control treaties they forge with the United States.

The Soviets are striving for strategic superiority in order be able to face us down through the Third World. The several components to this proposition all have some basis in fact. The Soviet buildup of offensive capability, reinforced by a military doctrine that lacks "defined standards of what constitutes enough," makes it difficult to discern whether the Soviets are truly committed to numerical parity. At the same time, the vast expansion of Soviet conventional capabilities, coupled with their much-expanded use of the military instrument in Third World competition with the West, stimulates the worst fears about their ultimate intentions worldwide. Also, under Soviet military doctrine, nuclear strategic forces are indeed used as a cover for conventional military activities in peripheral areas. Finally, Soviet official rhetoric exudes a surface optimism about the "correlation of forces" in the world shifting decisively to the advantage of socialism at the expense of capitalism. All of which stimulates profound fears that the Soviets view the world as a zero-sum game, at the end of which they will bury us.

Distortions and Exaggerations

Although we cannot penetrate the inner recesses of Soviet leaders' minds, we can rebut each of these propositions because they distort the content of Soviet behavior and doctrine. First, one should not exaggerate Soviet capabilities. Their crash program to add MIRVs to their strategic forces was part of an effort to catch up in an area where the United States held a commanding lead. Much of our fear comes from the loss of this lead rather than from an actual condition of inferiority. Moreover, we far exceeded the Soviets in numbers of warheads deployed during the 1970s. And while the Soviets were undeniably modernizing faster than we in most areas of strategic weaponry, we were moving faster in research and development of the most advanced weaponry: MX, Pershing II, Trident II, cruise missiles, Stealth bombers, the Mark 12A warhead. The situation today remains one of essential equivalence in overall strategic capability.

A second reason to avoid worstcase conclusions relates to our estimate of Soviet intentions and reliability in the face of their strategic buildup. The Soviet buildup violated no treaty or formal understanding with the United States. Indeed, at the May 1972 summit, Leonid Brezhnev explicitly told then-President Richard Nixon that the Soviets would build up in those areas

allowed by SALT I. Most especially, this meant MIRVs, which only the United States then possessed, but which we are unwilling to bargain away in SALT. Then too, the Soviets were eager to ratify SALT I, which would have placed restraints on further buildup. Finally, Soviet political doctrine does not emphasize the advantages of achieving strategic superiority, but rather the importance of denying strategic superiority to the United States through Soviet attainment and maintenance of strategic parity.

> *"Strategic parity ensures the permanence of Soviet status as a global power by denying the United States the ability to drive them out of the Third World."*

Undeniably, there has been a large Soviet conventional buildup, engendered not just by defensive considerations but more importantly by a commitment to becoming a global power, able to compete with the United States for influence and allies throughout the world. This does not prove, however, that the Soviet intent is to encircle us and run us out of the Third World. Put differently, it does not mean that they view global power competition as a zero-sum game. They have shown meaningful restraint in several ways:

• They have periodically signalled their interest in superpower collaboration to defuse certain Third World problems.

• Their use of the military has typically been in places like Angola, Ethiopia, South Yemen or Afghanistan, which could not plausibly be defined as primary Western security or political spheres. In contrast, their actions have been much more restrained, and their respect for Western concerns more obvious, in places such as Rhodesia, Saudi Arabia and Iran.

• The Soviets have often resorted to military means only after such resort by "the other side," for example, after the South African invasion of Angola, or the Somali invasion of the Ogaden.

Reluctance to Take Risks

Another half-truth resides in the U.S. perception of Soviet strategic nuclear weapons as a "cover" for these conventional military activities. Soviet doctrine does *not* stress the need for strategic superiority to provide such a cover; the offensive component in their calculations is not that strong. Rather, the doctrine emphasizes that Soviet attainment of strategic parity with the United States now prevents the United States from overreacting to Soviet victories in the Third World—that is, from threatening nuclear war. Thus, strategic parity ensures the permanence of Soviet status as a global power by denying the United States the ability to drive *them* out of the Third World.

Indeed, Soviet doctrinal literature limits Soviet risk-taking by emphasizing the high probability of escalation once nuclear weapons enter a conflict and the consequent importance of being highly selective in choosing areas to be defended by the threatened use of nuclear weapons. The Soviet "nuclear umbrella" is restricted primarily to the homeland and Eastern Europe. It does not even cover Vietnam and Cuba, much less Angola, Ethiopia and South Yemen. (Presumably it does cover the Red Army in Afghanistan, were it seriously threatened by a great power counter-invasion.) Thus, the main Soviet emphasis is on the function of *denial*: denying the United States the ability to use a perception of its own strategic superiority to prevent the Soviets from acquiring their place in the sun as a global power.

The final component of this proposition relates to Soviet optimism. Allegedly, the Soviets are both cunning and optimistic, as evidenced by their official statements and doctrine. This too is a half-truth. Optimism has been a constant feature of Soviet political culture, but with great variations in type and degree. And it is these variations that determine the current mindset of the Soviet leadership.

When the Soviets look out on the world today, they are not as optimistic as they were in the early 1970s, and far from being as optimistic as they were in the late 1950s. They have witnessed the decline of detente, a U.S. remilitarization, a U.S.-China embryonic strategic alliance, Poland in disarray, and their own agricultural economy in shambles, making them more dependent than ever on external sources of grain. They have long feared that U.S. technological breakthroughs would lead us away from arms control and back to arms racing—a fear that may be coming true. In contrast, most Soviet "wins" in the world—and in Africa in particular—have been in areas of tertiary interest for them.

"The process and politics of arms control negotiations are not attuned to a bargaining-chip approach. It might work in an isolated case. . .how would they know they had it?"

The Soviet "correlation-of-forces" doctrine is often pointed to as proof that the Soviets are highly optimistic about the demise of capitalism and the victory of socialism. In an abstract sense, this is true: Marxist-Leninist ideology and the propaganda with which the Soviets mobilize their population both stress the historical inevitability of victory. But such ritualized generalities do not directly inform Soviet foreign policy, nor do they determine the current mind-set of Soviet policy-makers.

There is a second, more functional component to the correlation-of-forces doctrine. This doctrine, first touted in 1959, delivered the message to the United States that "you won't have the Soviet Union to kick around anymore." Consolidation of socialism in the Soviet Union and Eastern Europe, Premier Nikita Khrushchev argued, was now irreversible. Moreover, decolonization plus the victory of socialism in China and elsewhere meant that world imperialism was on the defensive; it could no longer claim that time was on its side. When coupled with Soviet acquisition of nuclear weapons *and the means to deliver them*, it meant that the United States could no longer deal with the Soviet Union by fiat, or from "positions of strength."

On this issue, the Soviets have been consistent and determined. The rhetoric of rollback, containment, massive retaliation and so on stuck in their throat. According to the correlation-of-forces doctrine, such policies could not be successfully prosecuted. It did *not* claim, however, that the Soviets were now in a position to dictate terms to the United States—and that is a crucial difference.

The Soviets only negotiate seriously from a position of potential inferiority; a U.S. strategic buildup makes sense, because it provides bargaining chips to trade for major Soviet concessions. From the standpoint of those who believe in arms control, this is the "best case" interpretation of the Reagan Administration's current motives. There is something to be said for the logic behind the proposition. We know, for example, that Soviet motivation to negotiate seriously during SALT I was heavily influenced by their desire to head off U.S. development and deployment of the Safeguard nationwide ABM (anti-ballistic missile) system. A major tradeoff in SALT I was Soviet willingness to place quantitative limits on their offensive missile buildup in exchange for U.S. willingness to forego this system. We also know that the Soviets today are very worried about a variety of new U.S. weapons systems, and that they have long been concerned about impending U.S. technological breakthroughs. Hence, we have good reason to believe that they would be willing to make serious tradeoffs to avert these developments.

Arms Control

The main arguments against this proposition derive less from the study of Soviet intentions than from studies of the arms control process itself and of U.S. foreign policy decision-making. The process and politics of arms control negotiations are not attuned to a bargaining-chip approach. It might work in an isolated case, but overall, it is apt to backfire.

I have three reasons for believing this.

• The process of negotiating arms limitations is a protracted one. SALT I and SALT II combined spanned a decade and achieved what they did only by deferring the resolution of the knottiest issues to SALT III. During lengthy negotiations, it is quite likely that our bargaining chips will become instead non-negotiable "building blocks" of our strategic posture—and that they will be matched by the Soviet Union.

• The pace of technological advance is currently outstripping the capacity for verification of arms limitations. Many of our bargaining chips fall into that category (submarine launched cruise missiles, for example). Thus, the difficulty of figuring out how to verify compliance can actually prolong negotiations. Yet the longer the negotiations, the greater the probability that bargaining chips will evolve into building blocks.

• The process of justifying the research, development and deployment of bargaining chips is a political one. It requires the creation of both an atmosphere of grave threat and an image of total resolve. A bargaining chip is ineffective if the Soviets believe you are bluffing. Yet that same political process of justification plays into the hands of those who have a bureaucratic, ideological or material stake in avoiding arms control and returning to unilateral means of ensuring U.S. security. And while this is going on, those forces within the Soviet political establishment which have a similar interest are being strengthened in the claim that the United States is actually seeking strategic superiority.

We must build up our strategic forces because of the imminent "window of vulnerability," which will tempt the Soviets to launch a first strike. Fears of this sort began to grow back in 1967, when the Soviets unveiled a new rocket—the SS-9—that was a blockbuster. Its sheer size and the megatonnage it could carry, led U.S. strategists to wonder whether the Soviets were building toward an arsenal capable of destroying our land-based missile arsenal before we could respond. These apprehensions grew steadily throughout the 1970s, and Soviet missile development and deployment did little to dispel them. Ultimately, those fears helped to block ratification of SALT II, and now reign over U.S. strategic planning.

"Even if the Soviets had the ability to destroy our strategic capability. . .how would they know they had it?"

The credibility of this proposition, however, hinges less on interpretations of Soviet intentions than on assumptions about the political psychology of deterrence. For even if the Soviets had the ability to destroy U.S. land missiles before they got off the ground, nobody claims the Soviets have, or will have, the ability simultaneously to destroy our submarine launched ballistic missiles and our Strategic Air Command bombers, either of which could easily destroy the Soviet Union as a functioning society.

Vulnerability Uncertain

The whole notion of vulnerability on this issue defies logic. Even if the Soviets had the ability to destroy our strategic capability on land, sea and in the air, how

would they know they had it? This is obviously not something that can be tested, and there are many eminent physicists who argue that it is a logical impossibility. But even if the physicists were wrong, the political psychologists could step in. Consider the situation from the viewpoint of the decision-maker. The level of uncertainty about the capabilities and reliability of the technologies is so high, and the cost, if he miscalculates, is so immense that only a madman would contemplate launching a first strike. Soviet leaders are tough, ambitious and expansionist; but they are not madmen. They do not believe that nuclear war is winnable. Indeed, the final irony associated with this proposition is that, if they actually were demented, no amount of U.S. arms buildup would suffice to deter them.

There is a second variant of the "window of vulnerability" argument which goes as follows: The problem is not that the Soviets would make a calculated decision to take out the ICBM force in an attempt to coerce or destroy the United States. Rather, they might be tempted, during a severe international crisis, to consider using their very potent counterforce capability. Stress and fear might lead them to grasp at the thought that they could get away with something they wouldn't even consider in calmer times.

At first glance, this formulation appears more plausible than the other. Yet it too is fundamentally flawed in its assumptions about the psychology of nuclear deterrence. Even in times of crisis and stress, Soviet leaders still know that only one leg of the U.S. strategic triad—land-based missiles—is vulnerable to a first-strike takeout. They also know that, even if such a take-out were successful, retaliation would be sure and swift, in the form of nuclear-equipped submarine launched ballistic missiles and bombers. If they were willing to strike first despite these odds, it would not be out of a sense of confidence that the vulnerability of our land-based missiles gave them some sort of advantage. It could only be if they had concluded that they themselves were about to be attacked by an irreversible U.S. first strike. Yet if they decided on a preemptive strike, they would be just as likely to do so whether or not a "window of vulnerability" existed.

A third formulation argues that the "window of vulnerability" gives the Soviets the political-psychological edge in Third World crises. Knowing they have some sort of strategic advantage, they will be more likely to try to face us down by engaging in nuclear threats—and we will be more likely to cave into those threats. This proposition is subject to all the arguments advanced against the proposition that the Soviets are striving for strategic superiority so that they can face us down in the Third World. Briefly, there is nothing in Soviet past behavior, current perspectives or doctrine about the use of force in international relations to suggest that a partial vulnerability in the U.S. strategic triad will allow them to use nuclear threats more easily than we, in order to gain decisive advantage in crisis behavior. Moreover, the history of the past 35 years of U.S.-Soviet confrontations belies the notion that the state of the strategic balance determines the outcomes of crises. Finally, this proposition is both frustrating and dangerous, for it can easily become a selffulfilling prophecy. U.S. policy-makers, in order to get their favored strategic programs through Congress, claim that without such programs they themselves will be more likely to succumb to nuclear threats; and that the Soviets, perceiving this, will be more likely to make such threats. This is a classic case of what has been called "the perceptions trap."

Maintaining Deterrence

The Soviet Union remains a formidable adversary of the United States. In light of this, I believe the maintenance of nuclear arsenals on both sides is probably the best deterrent to their going to war with each other over the real issues that divide them. But the key question is: how much is enough? Does the United States need to engage in a strategic buildup in order to deter nuclear war, prevent threats to our vital interests, or gain Soviet cooperation in arms control? The answer is: it does not. My reading of Soviet behavior, perspectives, and capabilities, along with my views on the logic of arms control negotiations and the political psychology of deterrence, lead me firmly to believe that another spurt in the arms race is neither desirable nor necessary.

George W. Breslauer is associate professor of political science at the University of California, Berkeley. His most recent book is Khrushchev and Brezhnev as Leaders.

"The substance of Washington's position is that it is aimed not at reducing strategic armaments but at legalizing ...their race in the hope that the U.S. would get...advantages."

U.S. Arms Reduction Proposals Are Self-Serving

Andrei Gromyko

Question: Everywhere in the world people's attention is rivetted to the task of preventing a nuclear war and, in this connection, to the problem of nuclear arms limitation and reduction. What in your view is preventing a solution of this problem which is daily growing more acute?

Answer: The problem of nuclear arms limitation touches the very core of states' security. It is not an easy problem to solve. But it must be solved and no difficulties of an objective or subjective nature can justify procrastination.

As experience shows, questions of curbing the nuclear arms race are quite amenable to solution given goodwill and a desire to seek agreement on the basis of the principle of the equality and equal security of the sides. In the sixties and seventies a certain amount of progress was made. Suffice it to recall the treaties on banning nuclear weapon tests in three media, on the non-proliferation of nuclear weapons, on limiting the ABM systems, the agreement on measures to reduce the threat of a nuclear war between the USSR and the United States, the interim agreement on certain measures in the field of strategic offensive arms limitations and, finally, the SALT II Treaty signed in 1979.

At present, however, advance in this exceptionally important direction has halted. And the blame lies with Washington which has set itself the aim of destroying the existing parity of forces in order to give the United States military superiority. Incidentally, this aim is not kept secret. And its material expression are the multibillion programmes for building up the US military arsenal and the various doctrines for waging nuclear wars—from "limited" to "protracted" ones.

It is this that determines the sharply negative attitude of the United States towards questions of arms limitation and disarmament. Suffice it to cite some major facts. The United States refuses to follow the Soviet

Union's example and assume a commitment not to be the first to use nuclear weapons. It refuses to agree on the non-emplacement of weapons of any kind in outer space. It has derailed the SALT II Treaty. Pointing in the same direction is the US refusal to continue talks on the total banning of nuclear tests.

One could go on listing examples of this kind. The principal conclusion is that the US is after military superiority at any price. This line is not designed to achieve agreement.

One cannot fail to perceive the dangers Washington's policy bodes for the peoples, including the American people. And the sooner the US Administration gets back onto the ground of reality and realizes that agreement on nuclear arms limitation and reduction is needed by the US no less than by the Soviet Union, the more it will be possible to make rapid headway in solving these questions which are of vital importance for the whole of mankind.

Question: What is, in these conditions, the position of the USSR?

Answer: Our approach has been consistent and not subject to fluctuations of expediency. It reflects the principal line of our policy—that of strengthening peace and eliminating the threat of a nuclear war. The Soviet Union does not strive for military superiority, does not advocate limited or protracted nuclear wars and regards the unleashing of a nuclear war as the gravest crime against mankind. It is ready to adopt the most far-reaching measures to limit the nuclear arms up to and including their total liquidation.

When there were still fresh ruins left by the Second World War whose juggernaut ravaged scores of countries, the Soviet Union tabled a proposal to declare the use of nuclear weapons incompatible with the conscience of mankind, and to ban and destroy nuclear weapons for all time. That was a step of outstanding importance on the part of the Soviet Union, which instilled in people's hearts the hope that the tragedy the

Andrei Gromyko, *People Should Know the Truth*, Moscow: Novosti Press Agency Publishing House, 1983.

world had just lived through would not be repeated.

No First Use

Today the Soviet Union is the world's only nuclear power to have taken a clear-cut and unequivocal commitment not to be the first to use nuclear weapons and proposed that other nuclear powers follow its example.

The difference in our approach and the US approach to the problem of nuclear arms limitation is a difference of principle that has also determined the specific positions of the sides at the Geneva talks now being held.

The Soviet Union seeks a real solution to these issues. It is prepared to reduce and limit nuclear arms on a mutually acceptable basis. It tables specific and far-reaching proposals to this effect. Washington, for its part, is by its deeds demonstrating its unwillingness to give up the policy of escalating the arms race and destroying the agreements already reached.

Question: What is the stumbling block at the Geneva talks on strategic arms and on nuclear arms in Europe?

Answer: If one is to speak about the chief obstacle, it is that Washington is seeking unilateral disarmament by the USSR and does not even want so much as to touch its own programmes for the development of the most advanced nuclear weapons intended to give it military superiority. This position is lopsided, egoistic and imbued with the spirit of overweening imperial ambitions. In the process references are made to allegations that the Soviet Union has upset the current balance, while the United States is only striving to restore it. But this is a deception. And those resorting to it know this themselves.

Nuclear Parity Exists

An objective analysis of the existence of a parity has repeatedly been given in statements by Soviet leaders, including their most recent statements. Well known are statements made to this effect by the General Secretary of the CPSU Central Committee Yuri Andropov. Until quite recently the existence of this balance was recognized—and on several occasions—by the US Administration itself. Incidentally, it is worth recalling that a resolution of the latest session of the UN General Assembly also states in no uncertain terms that parity does exist. And no other conclusion can be drawn if one bases oneself strictly on the facts and does not resort to falsehoods or juggling with facts.

Take the 1979 SALT II Treaty. That Treaty spells out in great detail the parity in strategic arms, painstakingly verified and recognized by the highest political and military authorities of the USSR and the United States. As is known, the Soviet Union has done nothing since then that could upset that parity. Even the present US Administration has publicly admitted that the USSR did nothing that would be at variance with the SALT II Treaty.

As regards Europe, the situation here too is quite clear. The USSR and the NATO countries have about 1,000 medium-range delivery vehicles on each side—missiles and aircraft. Nobody can refute this fact. We have cited data to this effect: both aggregate figures and with a break-down for types and kinds of weapons. Not a single aircraft or a missile has been invented by us in that balance. They all exist in reality. In the US capital they can, of course, try to go on further denying facts and juggling with numerical data. This will not change the truth, however. The Soviet Union seeks no military advantages for itself. This must be understood by every individual in the countries of Western Europe, by each family in those countries and in the United States itself. The fact is that in those countries people are daily, and one can even say, hourly, under the influence of false propaganda regarding the policy and intentions of the Soviet Union.

"The United States refuses to follow the Soviet Union's example and assume a commitment not to be the first to use nuclear weapons."

Question: Could you sum up briefly the basic contents of the proposals of the USSR and those of the United States at the talks in Geneva and what is the situation there today?

Answer: The essence of the Soviet position expressed in concrete parameters was set out by Yuri Andropov. The Soviet Union suggests that the strategic armaments of both sides be cut approximately by 25 per cent to equal levels. The number of nuclear warheads on these arms would also be reduced substantially to equal agreed-upon ceilings. All channels for the continuation of the strategic arms race would be closed: it would be prohibited to deploy long-range Cruise missiles and other new types of strategic weapons, and the ability of both sides to compete in qualitative improvement of armaments would be restricted to the utmost.

Naturally, all these limitations and reductions would be subject to verification. The Soviet Union is then prepared to advance further, to even more far-reaching reductions.

At first glance it seems the US side also suggests reductions. But it suggests the cuts not in all types of strategic armaments but selectively, in a way that would suit the United States. It is suggested that the Soviet Union should destroy a large part of its land-based intercontinental missiles while the United States would be implementing, unhindered, its plans to create new strategic weapon systems: MX missiles, Trident missiles, as well as new types of heavy bombers. The United States would in general preserve multiple, yes, multiple, superiority in heavy bombers. Likewise, Washington does not want to hear of any limitations of such a dangerous new type of nuclear armaments as long-range Cruise missiles.

Thus, the substance of Washington's position is that it is aimed not at reducing strategic armaments but at legalizing, and at a rapid pace, their race in the hope that the United States would get unilateral advantages.

A similar picture is observed also at the talks on nuclear arms limitation in Europe. The Soviet Union suggested reaching agreement on the renunciation of all types of nuclear armaments meant for hitting targets in Europe, both medium-range and tactical armaments. But Washington pretends that this proposal of the USSR does not exist. In other words, it does not accept it.

The Soviet Union also advanced another proposal the implementation of which would reduce to a third the number of medium-range nuclear weapons in Europe on both sides.

And finally, as Yuri Andropov said, we would be prepared for the USSR to keep in Europe only as many missiles as Britain and France have, not a single missile more. The number of the medium-range nuclear-capable aircraft kept in the region by the USSR and the NATO countries would be reduced to equal levels on both sides.

Just Proposal?

Is not this a just proposal? No one would get any unilateral advantages if it were implemented. And Europe's security would gain, for medium-range nuclear arms in the area would be reduced altogether by over 1,300 units. After these reductions the number of launchers of our medium-range missiles in the European part of the USSR and the total number of warheads they are armed with would be less, I repeat, less than in 1976, that is *before* the Soviet Union *started* to *modernize* its medium-range missiles.

"Washington is seeking unilateral disarmament by the USSR and does not even want to touch its own. . .nuclear weapons intended to give it military superiority."

All these constructive proposals have found reflection in the detailed draft treaty which the Soviet delegation tabled at the negotiations. The draft treaty is now lying on the table in the White House.

What does the United States propose? It continues to stick to its false "zero option", the whole point of which is to eliminate Soviet medium-range missiles in both the European and eastern parts of the USSR while not a single aircraft and not a single missile would be reduced on the side of the United States and NATO. They propose "zero" to us while leaving intact

everything they have. Can one speak at all of such a proposal as a serious one? Of course, not.

That is a brief summary of the positions of the sides as they are today. I think it is clear who is looking for accords and who is conducting negotiations in Geneva for appearance's sake.

From this it is also clear that no headway is being made at the negotiations. People should know the truth which obviously does not suit Washington. Propaganda there propounds the idea that things are not going too badly at all at the negotiations. The aim is to soothe the general public, above all people in Western Europe, who are really worried by the question of whether the problem of nuclear arms will be solved or will the nuclear arms race unfold on an even greater scale.

At the same time the idea is being instilled that if the United States departed from its present stand, this would only worsen the chances of reaching an accord.

All that is a deliberate and in fact threadbare propaganda device which is designed to dull people's vigilance. Serious negotiating partners do not resort to such methods.

Question: How could one assess the attitude of the other NATO member-states, apart from the United States, towards nuclear arms in Europe?

Answer: This question is undoubtedly in the focus of attention of the West Europeans and here there are different points of view. There is also awareness of the formidable danger which deployment of new US missiles in Western Europe would bring, and of the need to prevent such a course of events. This awareness is gaining in strength and scope.

Official spokesmen of several NATO countries often outwardly pay tribute to this awareness, state their desire to settle the question at the negotiating table and lay the emphasis on that part of NATO's 1979 decision which speaks of a possible agreement as an alternative to the deployment of US missiles in Western Europe.

At first glance this looks logical: if there is an agreement in Geneva there will be no need for US Pershing-2 and Cruise missiles. But what kind of agreement? After all, simultaniously support is expressed for the US "zero" intended for the Soviet Union, the "zero" by means of which Washington is evading an agreement. So the pronouncements of spokesmen of NATO countries do not somehow tally. Falsity strikes the eye.

"Zero Option"

It turns out that their statements in favour of an accord are one thing and their actual stands are quite another thing. To come out in favour of the US "zero option" means to support the deployment of new US nuclear missiles in Europe. This must be clear to every unbiased person.

I think West European states have no right to play the role of outside observers, let alone, popularizers of the present US stand. Western Europe can have its own say in favour of a just solution to the problem of medium-range nuclear weapons, in favour of peace. This would be an indicator of the political maturity of the stands of those countries.

Question: There has been talk in Western Europe lately that the US "zero" is, so to say, the initial stand and that the Americans may put forward some other "intermediate" versions. There was allegedly a hint to this effect in the recent pronouncements by US Vice-President George Bush. What would you say on that score?

Answer: Indeed, there is such talk. This is a definite indication that for Washington and other NATO capitals it is becoming increasingly difficult to defend the present American position. Regrettably, in the deliberations on this score so far there is no sign of any shift toward greater realism. In the final analysis everything boils down to the original position which is in one way or another to implement the NATO plan and to foist new US missiles on Western Europe.

"It continues to stick to its false 'zero option', the whole point of which is to eliminate Soviet medium-range missiles."

One can absolutely definitely state that no proposals meeting the principle of equality have so far emanated from the United States or NATO. The NATO states are still working on the assumption that the block has to have military advantages in Europe, a military edge. That is why the propaganda campaign alleging the possibility of some qualitatively new proposals does not square with reality.

Moreover, people are being indoctrinated to believe that deployment of the new US missiles would not be at variance with the objective of the Geneva talks now being held: deployment of missiles would begin while talks would proceed as if nothing were happening.

This is a delusion. The appearance of new US missiles in Western Europe would result in a qualitatively new situation. The total responsibility for the consequences of this would rest with the United States and NATO as a whole.

They cannot but know in the NATO capitals that by deploying its new missiles the American side would in fact undermine the nuclear arms talks.

Question: Is there a possibility of reaching specific agreements at the Geneva talks?

Answer: Objectively, such a possibility does exist. The Soviet proposals are geared precisely to the attainment of agreement. We are for an agreement in accordance with the principle of equality and equal security. And if Washington stops counting on destroying the parity and adopts a constructive approach, there will then be no doubt that agreement is possible. So it is now for the US to speak up.

Andrei Gromyko is the U.S.S.R. Minister of Foreign Affairs.

The US Is Serious about Arms Control

George Bush

No city has done more than Geneva to advance man's oldest, yet seemingly most elusive, dream—to live at peace with his neighbors. This is the city of Rousseau, who taught us that man is born both free and good, a concept that has had the most profound effect upon my country and many others as well. It was near here that Voltaire made his home when his incisive, but often irreverent, mind brought down upon him the displeasure of his king. After the calamity of the First World War, the League of Nations was established and housed in this very building, in the hope that here in the free city of Geneva this embodiment of man's best intentions might prosper.

Today, the world's hopes for peace are once again focused on this city. Two vital bilateral negotiations are underway here with a single aim: to make significant reductions in the nuclear arsenals of the United States and the Soviet Union and thereby to strengthen international stability and to increase the security of all states. And, in this committee, multilateral efforts are in train to deal with other urgent arms control issues: how to eliminate chemical weapons from the world's arsenals; how to effectively verify limitations on nuclear testing; how to approach the question of possible further arms control measures affecting outer space.

My message to you is simple and unequivocal: The United States will do all that it can to create a foundation for enduring world peace through arms control and through agreements that enhance international security and stability. This task is the President's highest priority, and he has asked me to tell you that we will pursue sound and workable arms control initiatives with the utmost determination. But we will not hesitate, nor should we, to differ with approaches which are not sound or do not hold out the prospect of effective, verifiable agreements.

What are the prospects for progress here in Geneva? I

would like to set forth the views of the United States on the status of our efforts—both bilateral and multilateral—to advance the cause of peace by reaching agreement on effective arms control measures.

President Reagan assumed office at a time of increasing concern among the American people over the behavior of the Soviet Union and its allies. In its foreign policy, as well as in the relentless buildup of its military forces, the Soviet Union has appeared determined to advance its own interests at the expense of everyone else's. This determination was reflected in the invasion of Afghanistan, in the suppression of human rights in Poland, in the use of chemical and toxin weapons in Southeast Asia and Afghanistan in violation of customary international law and existing international conventions, and in the steady accumulation of vast amounts of modern weaponry far beyond any reasonable requirements for defense.

Clearly, this behavior required a revitalization of our own defenses, which in many measures of military power had been outstripped. The United States has undertaken this effort not with a view toward conquest or intimidation but rather to maintain our ability to deter aggression and thus to defend our vital interests and those of our friends and allies against threat or coercion. I know that President Reagan would much prefer to spend our resources on other pursuits. But we will do—we must do—what is necessary to defend our interests and preserve the peace.

U.S. Arms Control Efforts

But providing the means of defense is only one aspect of insuring one's security. The Reagan Administration believes that arms control measures can be a vital part of our national security and that equitable and effective verifiable arms control agreements can increase that security. One of the first actions taken by President Reagan was to launch the most thorough review of our arms control policy ever undertaken by any new Ad-

George Bush, remarks to U.N. Committee on Disarmament, February 4, 1983.

ministration. A new approach to arms control was necessary to deal with the changed situation in which the United States found itself as a result of Soviet actions over a decade. Arms control had not become less important. Indeed, effective arms control had, if anything, become more important, since the military balance, at all levels, had become more unstable.

"In its foreign policy, as well as in the relentless buildup of its military forces, the Soviet Union has appeared determined to advance its own interests."

President Reagan announced the general principles which guide our arms control efforts in a statement on November 18, 1981. They are worth repeating here.

First, the United States seeks to reduce substantially the number and destructive potential of nuclear weapons, not just to freeze them at high levels as has been the case in previous agreements.

Second, we seek agreements that will lead to mutual reductions to equal levels in both sides' forces. An unequal agreement, like an unequal balance of forces, can only encourage aggression.

Third, we seek agreements that will enhance the security of the United States and its allies and that will reduce the risk of war. Arms control is not an end in itself but a vital means toward insuring peace and international stability.

Fourth, we will carefully design the provisions of arms control agreements and insist on measures to insure that all parties comply. In other words, we will insist that agreements must be verifiable. Otherwise, the parties cannot have confidence that all are abiding by the provisions of an agreement. This is particularly important in the nuclear area, where we have proposed deep cuts in the U.S. and Soviet arsenals. It is also vital to our efforts in this committee to ban chemical weapons and to develop effective limitations on nuclear testing.

Based on these objectives, my government since then has advanced a dynamic program of arms control initiatives: in our bilateral negotiations with the Soviet Union, in the work of this committee, and—together with our allies—in the negotiations at Vienna on mutual and balanced force reductions in Europe. Let me now deal with those which are of particular interest to the members of this committee.

U.S. Proposals

The problem of achieving reductions in the world's nuclear arsenals is our most important challenge. The United States has met this challenge by developing what President Reagan has called the most comprehensive program of nuclear arms control ever proposed by

my country. These proposals are on the negotiating table here in Geneva—in the intermediate-range nuclear forces, or INF, negotiations and in the START talks on reducing strategic nuclear forces.

The point I want to stress here is that the U.S. proposals in the START negotiations entail deep and significant cuts in U.S. and Soviet nuclear arsenals—a 50% cut in our strategic ballistic missiles. In the INF negotiations, we have proposed the elimination of an entire class of weapons. The proposals do so in a way which is balanced and which reduces the risk of war. This is, after all, what these negotiations are all about. Stability and security could be greatly enhanced if both sides thus reduced their arsenals, and it is precisely because of this that we are proposing such major reductions.

In the INF negotiations, there is now on the table a far-reaching U.S. proposal which would, at a stroke, ban an entire class of U.S. and Soviet longer range INF missiles, the systems of greatest concern to both sides. The Soviet Union now has over 600 such missiles with some 1,200 warheads, while the United States has none—zero. Under our proposal, the Soviet Union would be required to eliminate all of its ground-launched missiles of this type. These missiles—of the type referred to in the West as SS-4, SS-5 and SS-20—are in place now. The United States would be required to forgo the deployment of its roughly comparable missiles. As you know, they are scheduled to be deployed in Europe beginning this year under the decision taken by the NATO alliance.

The United States believes that any such agreement on nuclear forces must be effective and balanced; it must genuinely reduce the nuclear threat to both sides; it must enhance stability; and it must lessen the risk of conflict. Our proposal meets these criteria. Indeed, it strikes to the very heart of the problem.

Thus far, the proposals advanced in these negotiations by the Soviet Union have been designed to leave it with significant advantages, indeed, with a monopoly over the United States in longer range INF missiles. Indeed, the ideas recently advanced by General Secretary Andropov continue to have this as their aim. We will, of course, continue to give the most serious consideration to any constructive Soviet proposal. Ours is not a take-it-or-leave-it proposition. However, we think the Soviet Union must recognize our legitimate security concerns in these talks.

We think ours is a moral—a moral—position. What is wrong with eliminating from the face of the Earth an entire class of new, deadly missiles? The only argument I have heard as to why we cannot eliminate this whole generation of INF missiles is that the Soviet Union opposes it; it simply says, "We're against it." I simply don't believe, in this awesome nuclear age, that that's good enough. So our challenge to the Soviet leadership is: Come up with a plan to banish these INF missiles, and let's consider openly and in frank dialogue initiatives that will achieve that moral goal.

As in the case of the negotiations on intermediate-range missiles, we are emphasizing in the START negotiations real and significant reductions in the levels of strategic armaments on both sides, down to equal ceilings. As President Reagan has pointed out, our proposals in these negotiations would eliminate some 4,700 warheads and 2,250 missiles from the combined nuclear arsenals of the United States and the Soviet Union.

We have been encouraged by the fact that the Soviet Union is negotiating seriously—we have said that publicly, and I am very pleased to repeat it again today—and has accepted the concept of reduction, although we do not find the proposal it has tabled sufficient. It fails to focus on the more destabilizing elements of strategic forces, ballistic missiles, and particularly ICBMs, and it does not go far enough in making the kind of deep reductions in ballistic missile forces that we believe to be necessary. However, we believe that the approaches provide a basis for negotiation, and we intend to explore avenues for achieving such reductions and to pursue the negotiations seriously and constructively. Indeed, our President, upon hearing of a proposal by Mr. Andropov, recognized this seriousness of purpose. And I think this was appropriate, and people should understand that.

I will be meeting during my visit here in Geneva with the U.S. and Soviet delegations to both these critical negotiations. My purpose in doing so is to emphasize the great importance which the United States—and President Reagan personally—attaches to a successful outcome in both of them. I will pass on to our negotiators the President's hope that they will press forward with speed and energy and his wishes that their efforts will meet with success. I know that all of you deeply share this hope.

I will also, as I have in other stops on this trip of mine, make clear that I am not a negotiator. The negotiators are here in Geneva, seriously talking with their Soviet counterparts now.

Banning Chemical Weapons

Let me now turn to the work directly before this committee, to which we also attach the highest importance. The committee is confronted with numerous important issues. None has a higher priority for the United States than the efforts to ban forever an entire and different class of weapons from the world's arsenals. As President Reagan has stated, the goal of U.S. policy is to eliminate the threat of chemical warfare by achieving a complete and verifiable ban on chemical weapons.

The nations of the world have already prohibited the first use of chemical and biological weapons in the Geneva protocol of 1925 and have outlawed the possession of biological and toxin weapons in the 1972 biological and toxin weapons convention. Like most other nations at this table, the United States is a party to these treaties; and, like most others, we are in full compliance with their provisions. Beyond the provisions of these treaties, there is an even broader moral prohibition against the use of these weapons. President Franklin Roosevelt perhaps expressed it best when he said that their use "has been outlawed by the general opinion of civilized mankind."

All forms of warfare are terrible. But these weapons are particularly to be feared, because of the human suffering they can inflict. This is why the civilized world has condemned their use. Sadly, mankind has, nonetheless, had repeated demonstrations of the cruelty and horror wrought by the use of these weapons. And now, chemical and toxin weapons are being used in Afghanistan and Southeast Asia in violation of international law and international arms control agreements. These violations are made all the worse by the fact that their victims have neither the means to deter the attacks against them nor to defend or protect themselves against these weapons.

The United States presented conclusive evidence to the world community of the facts surrounding the use of chemical and toxin weapons. Others have presented evidence as well. We did not come to our conclusions seeking confrontation or rashly, but only after the most exhaustive study. The implications that flow from the use of these weapons are so serious that many would prefer to disbelieve or simply to ignore them. But we have to face the facts.

The world's progress toward more civilized relations among states has been doggedly slow and beset at every turn by fears, ambitions, and rivalries among the nations. We cannot, therefore, allow the progress which we have made to be destroyed. To do so would be to begin a relentless slide back to a new dark age of mindless barbarism. This is what is at stake, and this is what we must prevent.

"The United States believes that any such agreement. . .must be effective and balanced; it must genuinely reduce the nuclear threat to both sides."

So what must now be done? The United States has already called upon the Soviet Union and its allies to stop immediately their illegal use of these weapons. I repeat that call here today. And I urge the Soviet Union and all other members of the committee to join the United States in negotiating a complete and effective and verifiable ban on the development, production, stockpiling, and transfer of chemical weapons, a ban that will insure that these horrors can never occur again.

A complete, effective, and verifiable ban on chemical weapons is long overdue. My government, therefore, would like to see the work of this committee accelerated and negotiations undertaken on a treaty to eliminate the threat posed by chemical weapons.

A number of key issues, of course, must be resolved if we are to be successful in negotiating such a treaty. In the coming days, the U.S. delegation will present to this committee a new document containing our detailed views on the content of a convention we believe could effectively—more specifically, verifiably—eliminate the chemical weapons threat. We undertake this initiative with the aim of further advancing the work of the committee and to encourage contributions and cooperation from others as well.

"The elimination of the threat of nuclear war is clearly of paramount importance to all of us, and the United States fully accepts its special responsibilities in this area."

The key to an effective convention—one that could eliminate the possibility of chemical warfare forever—is the firm assurance of compliance through effective verification. This principle is fundamental. Effective verification, as the world's recent experience with the use of chemical and toxin weapons shows, is an absolute necessity for any future agreement. This is why the United States seeks a level of verification that will protect civilization, ourselves, our allies, and, indeed, humanity itself. For today, the threat of chemical warfare has increased. And until an effective agreement can be achieved, the United States, just as others, must continue to insure that it can deter the use of chemical weapons against its citizens and friends. If we are to expect nations ever to forgo the ability to deter chemical warfare, those nations must have confidence that others who accept the prohibition cannot circumvent their obligations and later threaten the peace with chemical weapons. They must be certain that they will not be attacked with such weapons by any state which, like they have, has foresworn chemical warfare. In short, for us, the verification and compliance provisions of a comprehensive chemical weapons treaty must be truly effective.

We know that most of the members of this committee, like we, are dedicated to accomplishing this important task. To do so will require more than our dedication; it will require greater willingness and flexibility on the part of the Soviet Union and its allies to work seriously and constructively on resolving the key outstanding issues—especially pertaining to the verification and compliance side. And such issues must be resolved if we are to expect to make genuine progress. For although some may argue that progress could be made by concentrating on the "easier" issues, or even by drafting treaty texts on them, this would be a fruitless exercise if the verification issue cannot be resolved. We will not support such a diversion of effort here.

I urge all members of this committee to begin negotiations in this session to resolve the key issues that face us in this area and to join with us in achieving a complete and verifiable ban on chemical weapons.

Eliminating the Threat

The committee is also faced with a number of nuclear arms control issues. The elimination of the threat of nuclear war is clearly of paramount importance to all of us, and the United States fully accepts its special responsibilities in this area. We are recognizing this responsibility in the most effective way we know—here in Geneva, in good faith, across the negotiating table from the Soviet Union.

At the same time, this committee has its role to play in the area of nuclear arms control. One of the major issues before it is that of a comprehensive ban on nuclear tests. Such a ban remains a long-term goal of U.S. policy, and we will continue to work toward its achievement. The work already done in the committee by the group of scientific experts on developing a worldwide system for monitoring of nuclear explosions has been valuable. Moreover, at the suggestion of the United States, this committee formed a working group last year to study issues of verification and compliance surrounding a nuclear test ban. Verification is one area, in particular, in which the United States believes greater progress must be made if we are to make progress toward a ban on nuclear tests. Therefore, we would hope that the committee will continue its work in this area this year.

My government believes that the negotiations in this body on a convention to ban radiological weapons offer the prospect of a modest but real, genuine step forward, a step that could eliminate a potentially very dangerous type of weapon. We should take it as a cardinal rule of this committee that when there is the prospect for real progress toward an agreement, we should pursue it to its conclusion. While there are a number of issues yet to be resolved, we believe that an agreement is within the committee's grasp and that we should move ahead with all due speed to conclude the negotiations on this treaty.

I should also like to say a word about further arms control measures affecting outer space. The United States has been the leader in the peaceful exploration and use of outer space. We intend to continue this leadership. Some of these activities in outer space are important to our national security and that of our allies. They help to monitor the peace, to warn of the threat of war, to insure proper command and control of our armed forces worldwide, to preserve our deterrent capability, and to assist in the verification of arms control agreements. The Limited Test Ban Treaty, the 1967

Outer Space Treaty, the Environmental Modification Convention, and the Antiballistic Missile Treaty, which is one of the SALT I [Strategic Arms Limitation Talks] agreements, all have important arms control provisions affecting outer space. Some are now asking whether additional measures might be called for and, if so, what kind? The United States does not have a simple answer to this question, and we are continuing to study this issue. Clearly, the conditions do not exist which would make negotiations appropriate. We are, however, prepared to exchange views with other members of this committee, and believe the committee should address the matter in a more systematic way than it has in the past. . . .

Conclusion

There is, in closing, one thought which I would like to leave with this committee, a thought which underlies our approach to arms control and to the issues before this committee. And that is that the achievement of effective arms control agreements is difficult work. It requires dedication, persistence, tolerance, a respect for the views of others, and, above all, a faith that conflict can be prevented and that solutions, no matter how difficult, can be found. The most dangerous view for mankind, particularly in this nuclear age, is that war is inevitable. I reject this view entirely, because such a belief merely increases the inclination to make it a self-fulfilling prophecy. Let us rededicate ourselves in this committee, and in every other available forum, to the hard and serious work which is absolutely essential to prevent war.

George Bush is the vice-president of the US. He and President Ronald Reagan were elected in 1980.

"If the President and the American people are to be united on the question of arms control, the principle of unity must be: Freeze first, then reduce."

The Key to Arms Control: A Bilateral Freeze

Randall Kehler

The Freeze Campaign itself is now active in all 50 states of this country and in a majority of Congressional districts. American citizens from all walks of life and from every political persuasion are becoming aware of the enormous risks posed by the continuing nuclear arms race between the United States and the Soviet Union. These millions of citizens are voicing one very simple straightforward demand. That demand is, Stop the nuclear arms race! No more testing, no more production, no more deployment. Enough is enough!

The day has passed when Americans simply ask their elected representatives to do something about this problem. History clearly shows that experts and government officials have forfeited their right to lead the way to nuclear disarmament and thus to national and international security. Thus far, this elite corps of decision-makers has led us only to greater rounds of dangerous nuclear escalation. Perhaps it is true that governments are not *capable* of disarming themselves and that people must disarm governments. Thus, we have reached a point where the American people are now taking the initiative on their own. Instead of waiting for the government to come up with effective policy, they are now *telling* their elected representatives what that policy should be.

If those millions of Americans who support a bilateral nuclear weapons freeze could be here today to evaluate, themselves, the various arms control proposals that have been discussed during the course of these hearings, they would have no trouble doing so. There is one very simple yardstick that they would use: Will this proposal stop the nuclear arms race? It is with this question in mind that the National Committee of the Nuclear Weapons Freeze Campaign strongly endorsed the Kennedy-Hatfield Resolution, which is, by far, the clearest expression of the Freeze Campaign's goal. Similarly, our National Committee has gone on record opposing the Jackson-

Randall Kehler, testimony before the US Senate Committee on Foreign Relations Subcommittee on Arms Control, May 13, 1982.

Warner Resolution, which is nothing more than an endorsement of the Administration's plans to build more weapons.

The same yardstick must be applied to the President's START proposal, which was announced this past Sunday at Eureka College, in Illinois. The fact is, the President's proposal falls far short of stopping the nuclear arms race. Even if the Soviets agree to negotiate on the basis of the President's proposal, which is not likely, given the imbalances implicit in the proposal itself, the result would be a dangerous new round of destabilizing weapons, built and deployed on both sides while the negotiations are taking place. Does the START proposal call for a halt to the MX missile? The new Trident II missile? The Cruise or Pershing missiles? Or the B-1 bomber? No, it does not. All of these weapons, according to the President's proposal, would be built. Rather than providing the Soviets with an incentive to reduce their own weapons, these new weapons on the U.S. side will certainly provide the Soviets with an incentive to build their own new generation of weapons.

To call for negotiations on reductions while going ahead full steam with a massive weapons build-up is pure folly. Trying to reduce nuclear arsenals without first halting their growth is like trying to go on a diet before you quit overeating. The inevitable result is escalation.

Assumptions Impede Arms Control

The Administration's approach is not helpful or constructive because it is based on several faulty assumptions. First, it is not true that the Soviet Union enjoys an advantage over the United States in terms of overall nuclear forces. While preoccupied with the question of land-based ICBMs, particularly those of intermediate range, based in Europe, the Administration chooses to ignore the decisive U.S. advantages with regard to submarines and bombers. If this Administration is so concerned about achieving parity, are they willing to allow the Soviets to catch up in these two areas? Are the American people supposed to believe that Secretary of Defense Brown, the Joint Chiefs of Staff, and a number of other high officials were somehow misinformed, or else lying, when they stated less than a year and a half ago that U.S. and Soviet nuclear forces were roughly equal? Or are we supposed to believe that the situation has suddenly changed within that short period, when it is well-known that it takes not months but many years to develop and deploy nuclear weapons systems.

"Trying to reduce nuclear arsenals without first halting their growth is like trying to go on a diet before you quit overeating."

Equally faulty are the Administration's various nuclear war scenarios, which would have us believe that a disarming Soviet first-strike is plausible. What Soviet leader would possibly risk the devastation of his entire country and all its inhabitants when the uncertainties of any kind of nuclear exchange are so great?

The Administration also talks about the potential for Soviet "blackmail" as a result of alleged Soviet advantages with regard to particular weapons systems. This kind of talk rests on the faulty assumption that advantages in nuclear weapons produce corresponding political advantages. Historically, this is simply not the case. How many concessions was the United States able to extract from the Soviets during the past 30 years when we enjoyed a clear advantage in nuclear weapons? Did our nuclear advantage prevent the Soviet Union from invading Hungary in 1954? Or Czechoslovakia in 1968?

Finally, the President's START proposal rests on the misguided assumption, as stated by senior Administration officials, that arms control proposals can be used to deflect the public's concern about nuclear weapons. To do so is not only to cheapen any given proposal, but also to offend the principles of democracy upon which this country is based.

Fortunately, the millions of people across the country who support the Freeze will not be diverted by such proposals—proposals which make no pretense of halting the nuclear arms race and thus of limiting or reducing the risk of nuclear war.

Bilateral Freeze Halts Buildup

In contrast, the proposal for a bilateral freeze on the testing, production, and deployment of nuclear weapons by the U.S. and the Soviet Union is a genuine proposal for halting the nuclear arms race. Its principal virtue is that it would break the vicious cycle of escalation that we have seen over the past 30 years, an escalation scarcely hampered by proposals for reductions that have come from both sides. Because most Americans are not experts and are not politicians, they have the splendid

capacity to see the forest for the trees. They can clearly see that the risks of freezing the nuclear arms race, whatever they may be, are far less than the risks of continuing it. They can also see that there is far more logic in moving from a freeze to major reductions than trying to move from a massive build-up to major reductions. Furthermore, they see no sense in wasting vast amounts of our resources in building new weapons when the stated purpose of this build-up is to reduce the total number of weapons....

Every major national poll during the past few months has indicated that the great majority of Americans favor a bilateral freeze on the testing, production, and deployment of nuclear weapons between the U.S. and the Soviet Union. According to the Yankelovich Poll of March, 1982, this majority includes 66% of those who consider themselves Republicans and 65% percent of those who voted for President Reagan in 1980.

You should know, however, that support for a comprehensive, bilateral Freeze amounts to more than a number of opinion polls. There are now more than 80 city councils across the nation which have publicly endorsed the Freeze, including Philadelphia, Cleveland, Minneapolis, Des Moines, Baltimore, Detroit, Pittsburgh, and Chicago. Three hundred fifteen towns in New England have also passed Freeze resolutions. One or more branches of the state legislatures in 11 states from Maine to Oregon have passed Freeze resolutions. Campaigns are now underway to put the Freeze on the ballot statewide in Michigan, New Jersey, Delaware, Arizona, Oregon, Wisconsin, and California.

One hundred thirty-five Catholic bishops have endorsed the Freeze, along with representatives of every major religious denomination in this country. Sixty-nine national and international organizations have also endorsed the Freeze, including the YWCA of the USA, the U.S. Conference of Black Mayors, and the United Food and Commercial Workers International Union, the largest affiliate of the AFL-CIO.

All of this support, by millions of American citizens, is rooted in a deep-seated fear and, in many cases, in an outrage over the situation we are in. It is also based on a growing understanding that there is only one way to stop the nuclear arms race and that is to stop it. It is not that people who support the Freeze are opposed to reductions. Far from it. It is simply that we are convinced that there will be no genuine reductions unless first preceded by a comprehensive bilateral Freeze.

If the President and the American people are to be united on the question of arms control, the principle of unity must be: Freeze first, then reduce.

Randall Kehler is the National Coordinator of the Nuclear Weapons Freeze Campaign.

"We would advance our prospects better by seeking...to understand our opponents."

The Key to Arms Control: Better US/USSR Relations

Charles McC. Mathias, Jr.

Lord Carrington used this year's Alastair Buchan Memorial Lecture to make a timely and well-reasoned appeal to the West to take a new approach to East-West relations. He reminded us that:

> The West must be true to its own values. It is the Leninist tradition which is one of conflict and not cooperation.
>
> Our own tradition must be for the peaceful resolution of potential conflict through energetic dialogue. The notion that we should face the Russians down in a silent war of nerves, broken only by bursts of megaphone diplomacy, is based on a misconception of our own values, of Soviet behavior, and of the anxious aspirations of our own peoples.

Americans should pay particular attention to Lord Carrington's sensible advice—for American interests are particularly poorly served, and even endangered, by practices which limit our dealings with the Soviets to the most difficult aspects of our common superpower roles. If you think no spoon is long enough to permit us to sup with the Devil, you should read no further. The premise of this essay is that we must share our planet with a dangerous and despised adversary for the foreseeable future.

That being so, we should seek, at a minimum, to develop some functioning rules for our co-tenancy. To arrive at such an arrangement and to keep it working, we need to explore and maintain the widest variety of contacts, the broadest and most diffuse forms of engagement. Instead of restricting our discussions to the gravest and least tractable problems of arms control, we should be pushing our way down paths of less resistance, looking continually for limited openings, marginal advances, small opportunities to create a measure of understanding and shared interest.

Weary Work

It will be weary work. It should not be undertaken with the hope of spinning a restraining net around the Soviet Union. That exercise, attempted a decade ago,

Charles Mc.C. Mathias, "Habitual Hatred, Unsound Policy," reprinted by permission of Foreign Affairs, Summer 1983. Copyright 1983 by the Council on Foreign Relations, Inc.

failed because it took too little account of the competing forces which shape American foreign policy, and because it assumed that significant areas of Soviet policy at home and abroad could be affected by what we had to offer or withhold in areas of less significance. The policy patronized a nation which wants, almost more than anything else, to be treated by America as an equal. We assumed that Soviet leaders could be made to respond—as we ourselves would not—both to bribes and threats. The idea was unsound. The practice was unconvincing.

A better approach, less illusory in its promise and more manageable in its application, must begin by defining our goals in terms of our ability to attain them, not just in terms of their desirability. From the start we have to rule out policies premised on the imminent collapse of the Soviet empire. Survival in power seems to be the highest good the Kremlin leadership sets itself; much as we may want to see that wish frustrated, and soon, we invite only confrontation if we make the extinction of our adversary our overriding ambition. There may be subtle ways to play on the grave strains within the communist system, and we should not neglect opportunities to do so. But we should expect no more than partial progress on that front, and should not ask either our people or our allies to commit vast energies to an effort certain to be painfully slow and likely to be inconclusive.

At the other extreme we would be foolish to revive either the notion of superpower condominium—never officially admitted but nonetheless feared by others on occasion—or the dream of superpower convergence, a more popular but equally naive reverie. We have far too many profound conflicts of interest with the U.S.S.R. to suppose that we can bury our disagreements in a joint stewardship of the globe. And beyond the unnatural acts such a pairing would require, we have only to consider the reactions of lesser but still sovereign powers to understand that the idea would not fly in Peoria, or

Peking, or Paris.

The other myth has more appeal but no more substance. Yes, we and the Soviets are all human beings, parents, lovers, fellow travelers on "Spaceship Earth." And we have technocrats, bureaucrats and, to a degree, Socrates in common. But the separation of geography, history, culture, political values and socioeconomic systems is vast. We have not yet bridged similar disparities with Mexico. We should not set ourselves the impossible dream of discovering and developing common traits and attitudes in a far more distant and disagreeable climate.

How then do we get through this inevitable marriage of inconvenience? Since annulment can come only through mutual annihilation, we have to face the facts presented above and see if, based on a realistic appreciation of both the dangers we face and the limits under which we operate, we cannot keep to the path John Kennedy described 20 years ago, the search to "help make the world safe for diversity." He said then what we should never forget: "We can seek a relaxation of tensions without relaxing our guard.... [W]e are willing and able to engage in peaceful competition with any people on earth."

"Just as we would not show or recognize America in a monochrome portrait, we should not insist on painting the U.S.S.R. in a single color."

To sustain that competition, we need to be clear in our view of our rival and precise in the formulation of our priorities. Only policies which serve America's long-term interests will command the long-term support of Americans. To be effective in a race that has no defined finish line, we must be as persistent as our rival and, hence, as united by the consent of our people as the Soviets are by compulsion. In the pages that follow I offer an assessment of the Soviet Union recognizable, I hope, to most Americans. And based on that assessment I recommend a renewed effort to engage the Soviet government and—to the extent we can reach it—Soviet society in a protracted but pacific competition based on mutual interests.

Moral Conviction

The official Reagan Administration view of the Soviet Union, precisely and repeatedly stated by the President, has one consistent characteristic: moral conviction. In the course of the 1980 campaign, Mr. Reagan told a *Wall Street Journal* reporter, "[T]he Soviet Union underlies all the unrest that is going on. If they weren't engaged in this game of dominoes, there wouldn't be any hot spots in the world." Almost three years later, in a speech this March to the National Association of Evangelicals, the President urged prayer "for the salvation of all those who live in a totalitarian darkness" but added that until salvation came:

[L]et us be aware that while they preach the supremacy of the state, declare its omnipotence over the individual man, and predict its eventual domination of all peoples of the earth—they are the focus of evil in the modern world...

So in your discussions of the nuclear freeze proposals, I urge you to beware the temptation of pride—the temptation blithely to declare yourselves above it all and label both sides equally at fault, to ignore the facts of history and the aggressive impulses of an evil empire, to simply call the arms race a giant misunderstanding and thereby remove yourselves from the struggle between right and wrong, good and evil...

I believe we shall rise to this challenge; I believe that Communism is another sad, bizarre chapter in human history whose last pages even now are being written. I believe this because the source of our strength in the quest for human freedom is not material but spiritual, and, because it knows no limitation, it must terrify and ultimately triumph over those who would enslave their fellow man.

On April 1, 1983, President Reagan told the Los Angeles World Affairs Council:

We live in a world in which total war would mean catastrophe. We also live in a world torn by a great moral struggle—between democracy and its enemies, between the spirit of freedom and those who fear freedom. In the last 15 years and more the Soviet Union has engaged in a relentless military buildup, overtaking and surpassing the United States in major categories of military power, acquiring what can only be considered an offensive military capability. All the moral values which this country cherishes—freedom; democracy; the right of peoples and nations to determine their own destiny, to speak and write and live and worship as they choose—all these basic rights are fundamentally challenged by a powerful adversary which does not wish these values to survive....

Today, not only the peace but also the chances for real arms control depend on restoring the military balance. We know that the ideology of the Soviet leaders does not permit them to leave any western weakness unprobed, any vacuum of power unfilled. It would seem that to them negotiation is only another form of struggle....

Generosity in negotiation has never been a trademark of theirs; it runs counter to the basic militancy of Marxist-Leninist ideology....

Such rhetoric is recurrent. At his first White House press conference the President declared that Lenin had established "that the only morality they [Soviets] recognize is what will further their cause—meaning they reserve unto themselves the right to commit any crime, to lie, to cheat, in order to attain that, and that is moral, not immoral...." In the March 8 speech to the Evangelicals, Mr. Reagan specified that "their cause...is world revolution." And in Westminster Hall, during a June 8, 1982, address, he spoke of "totalitarian forces in the world who seek subversion and conflict around the globe to further their barbarous assault on the human spirit."

There is too much genuine fervor in these black-and-white depictions of our adversary to permit the suspicion that the President employs them simply to inflame passion and solidify domestic support. His language—even assertions such as the one on October 16, 1981, that the Soviets "have already got their people on a starvation diet of sawdust"—reflects a coherent analysis of Soviet purposes, strengths and weaknesses which is, however, too narrow to translate into any coherent policy beyond sustained confrontation. While President Reagan has managed on several occasions to state American aims in words meant to dilute the threat of conflict, he is both consistent and insistent in describing the Soviet challenge and ways to meet it in two dimensions: moral and military.

"The arrangement did not work because both parties brought to it unreasonable expectations."

America needs to use a wider lens in order to see the Soviet Union whole. Along with Moscow's "aggressive impulses" we must consider its defensive reflexes, its security obsessions, its self-preservative instincts and the less-than-uniform record of its expansionist conduct. The Kremlin's "evil empire" is also a diverse one, subject to internal strains, economically stagnant, technologically backward and—in Poland and Afghanistan—beleaguered. The Soviet Union today is still recognizable as the land Nikolai Nekrasov apostrophized more than a century ago:

> Wretched and abundant,
> Oppressed and powerful,
> Weak and mighty,
> Mother Russia!

American Exaggerations

Just as we would not show or recognize America in a monochrome portrait, we should not insist on painting the U.S.S.R. in a single color. It is a nation of 270 million people, but it is also a society in which the death rate per thousand persons rose from 6.9 in 1964 to 10.3 in 1980, where male longevity is dropping, and where the incidence of typhoid is 29 times as high as in the United States. The Soviet Union possesses vast economic potential, but whereas it was the world's second largest economy in 1980, it has slipped now to third place, behind Japan, and ranks sixth in the world by a measure of gross national product per capita that puts the wealth of an average Soviet citizen at less than half that of a Frenchman, and only twice that of a Brazilian. It is a naval power without a warm-water port, a political colossus which must station occupying forces on the territory of its nearest allies, and a revolutionary force which abhors the tiniest pressure for uncontrolled change at home. It is, in short, a welter of contradictions.

Those stresses are significant without being—except in some now unforeseeable internal cataclysm—fatal. They work in ways we do not understand to shape the policy universe of the Kremlin leadership and they impose both real choices on those leaders and concrete limits on the choices themselves. What remains fixed in that universe is not the early Utopian goal of world revolution, nor the target Khrushchev set in 1960 of besting the West in economic achievement, but a narrower, less inspiring and still all-consuming priority: the retention of control by the leaders over the people, by the Soviet Union over Eastern Europe and by the Soviet Communist Party over Communist parties it has nurtured in other lands. While the aim can be stated in three parts, its achievement appears to depend more and more on a single instrument: military power, applied directly by the Red Army or indirectly through Cuban proxies, East European surrogates or, under attenuated supervision, terrorist groups.

Thus, what makes the Soviet Union a danger to John Kennedy's hope of a "world safe for diversity," or, in President Reagan's terms, to "all the moral values which this country cherishes," is the Kremlin's conservatism and the armed might which is simultaneously its one reliable support and its most effective expression. The issue for Western policymakers is not the inherent evil of such a system, nor a mythical "master plan" that must be countered. The threat comes not from Soviet dynamism but from the kind of reactionary outlook which gave momentum to Czar Alexander I in constructing and maintaining the Holy Alliance after Napoleon's defeat. We should not fear the giant we face so much as the deformities which cripple all but his sword-bearing arm.

This disproportionate influence of military men and military considerations is the thinly concealed reality of Soviet politics. In Poland even the fig leaf has vanished. In both nations, however, the uneasy occupants of the throne of bayonets face problems to which regimentation and martial discipline provide only stop-gap answers. To retain control—over ambitious rivals in the first place, over a sullenly acquiescent populace in the second—the Soviet leaders must also project a certain degree of dynamism, enough to suppress doubts within the elite, above all, about the inevitability of Soviet progress. Unable to achieve such advances in economic development at home, the Kremlin has been limited to demonstrating and thus reconfirming its power abroad. Soviets do not necessarily pursue that path by preference. Rather, their course has become increasingly a product of restricted choice.

To some extent Western policy is responsible for narrowing Soviet options. The achievement of military parity with the United States more than a decade ago opened vistas of political equality as well, and Moscow's rulers looked to Washington to confer on them the status and legitimacy—in addition to economic stimulus—that would be convincing proof of their success and right to hold power. That bargain was struck first with General de Gaulle and Willy Brandt and, in 1972, with Richard Nixon. By the time it was reconfirmed at the August

1975 signing of the Helsinki Accords, however, the deal was already unraveling. It is worth looking back over the erosion of detente to see why the dike failed and the tide of East-West relations swept away from cooperation.

US-Soviet Trade Questioned

The record of events is familiar. The "Great Grain Robbery" of 1972 made Americans question the supposed benefits of expanded U.S.-Soviet trade. Moscow's conduct in relation to the Yom Kippur War of 1973 aroused not just a high level of temporary tension but a deep suspicion of Soviet selectivity in the practice of international restraint. The expulsion of Aleksandr Solzhenitsyn in February 1974 displayed the unchanged face of intolerance in a society Westerners had hoped was mellowing. The Jackson-Vanik and Stevenson amendments adopted at the end of that year confirmed a Soviet view of America's subversive intent.

"We should acknowledge that we need contacts with a widening range of Soviets simply for the insights we can gain through them into their system and the course it is taking."

There followed the 1975 Soviet airlift of Cuban troops into Angola, North Vietnam's triumph in Saigon and expansion into Kampuchea, the Soviet shift to the side of Ethiopia against Somalia, Cuban aid to the radical faction of the Sandinista Revolution in Nicaragua, the invasion of Afghanistan, and the suppression of Solidarity by the imposition of martial law in Poland. Paralleling and sometimes responding to such developments, the United States showed itself unable to move rapidly from the Vladivostok understandings of 1974 to a SALT II treaty, intensified its courtship of China, cut grain shipments twice (in 1975 and 1980), stepped up the decibel level of its human rights concerns in 1977 to a pitch the Kremlin found intolerable, invited Moscow back into the Middle East peace process and then withdrew the invitation, mounted the boycott of the Olympics to damage Soviet prestige in 1980, curtailed cultural, commercial and consular relations and, under President Reagan, sought not only to conduct a battle of epithets against the Soviet Union but also to strong-arm West Europeans into economic warfare against the oppressors of Poland.

To list the incidents in this spiral is not to analyze the reasons why the bargain of the early 1970s failed nor even to argue that it was an impossible agreement to maintain. The chronicle shows only that detente collapsed, not that failure was inevitable. What it does suggest, however, is that the arrangement did not work because both parties brought to it unreasonable expectations. Soviets assumed that the United States was prepared to accept not just the legitimacy of Communist

rule where it already was entrenched but the right to perpetuate that regime unmolested at home and to project its interests as a superpower abroad. Americans appeared to think, instead, that they were obtaining both the leverage to modify internal Soviet behavior, albeit gradually, and Soviet willingness to impose self-restraint in the conduct of foreign affairs. The Kremlin interpreted the deal as a ratification of past Soviet achievements and a *nihil obstat* to their extension. We preferred to read the implied contract as a promise of Soviet evolution toward moderation in all things.

One expectation was held in common. Both Americans and Soviets thought that the injection of Western industrial know-how and capital goods into the Soviet economy would stimulate greater efficiency and modernization of management and attitudes as well as production. Technology, it was believed, would generate not just economic change but sociopolitical reform. No horse could pull such a heavy cart, especially not from behind. The rigidities of Soviet economic planning and practice were too great and too resistant. The manpower, infrastructural and resource deficiencies of the U.S.S.R. could not be overcome or bypassed by improvements in communication or quality control. And the United States, which had helped Stalin's forced-pace industrialization in the 1930s, would not, for political reasons, make the long-term commitments on which Brezhnev's negotiators insisted.

The failure of these hopes, both the conflicting and the shared ones, has left the relationship in a shambles. To the extent that we continue to interact, we have been forced to pursue a single subject—arms control—that is simultaneously the most vital and the most difficult. In a poisoned political atmosphere we have narrowed what might be an extensive range of contacts to a set of limited negotiations more likely to stimulate paranoia and propaganda than progress. To the deformed Soviet giant we speak only of the shackles we would like to place on its one sound limb. And by addressing a militaristic society only on the strongest ground it occupies, we limit the influence we can have, the alternatives we can pursue.

Without question, arms control is a crucial pursuit. With little question, it is also an area in which the United States and the Soviet Union can formulate their separate interests in a compatible fashion based on their mutual concern to avoid Armageddon. Nevertheless, it is far from being the only potentially productive item on the superpower agenda, and it is at least possible that by exploring other subjects, even marginal ones, we can reduce some of the tension at the center. We would not automatically smooth the way toward stability in our vast nuclear arsenals, but we could make the tough talk about destructive power somewhat easier by setting it within a framework of a broader and possibly more constructive engagement.

Unilateral Beginnings

Such an effort to open and widen our contacts with Moscow has to proceed from a calculation of the American interests it could serve. It cannot be based on the assumptions we found faulty in the first exercise of trying to build better relations. And it must take account of an awkward political fact: the particular barriers we would have to lower are largely ones we raised ourselves, especially in 1980 after the Soviet invasion of Afghanistan. Thus, the first gestures would have to be unilateral American ones, an uncomfortable prospect. To make such actions palatable, we would require not just prearranged Soviet responses in kind but a solid conceptual rationale for reversing course.

The initial price is high. It cannot be discounted by investing in vague hopes of improved mutual understanding. While that is a benefit to seek, even eventually to realize, it is no better ground for a new beginning than was the old illusion that the Soviet appetite for cultural, scientific and commercial exchanges was so large that we could condition their continuation on good Soviet behavior either in emigration or in Africa. Instead, we should try to develop such joint activities for the value they hold for the United States, and be prepared to suspend or drop them when the cost is excessive or the return too low.

The basic test for an agreement to pass is that of America's interest. Are we better served by having a consulate in Kiev than by having no window on the Ukraine? Is our presence in the second largest Soviet republic worth the price: establishing a Soviet consulate in New York, where hundreds of Soviets already work at the United Nations? I would answer in the affirmative to both questions and try to revive the arrangement that was aborted in 1980.

"An effort to open and widen our contacts with Moscow has to proceed from a calculation of the American interests it could serve."

As for the 12 bilateral science and technology exchange accords which date from the Nixon era, there is greater controversy. In the late 1970s, especially, they came under two kinds of attack: the charge that Soviets were using these channels to sweep up American scientific secrets without imparting significant knowledge of their own; and the more demonstrable accusation that trips to American universities and laboratories were doled out only to loyal *apparatchiks*, making us partners in a system that reinforced Party control over Soviet science and diminished real freedom.

To the first complaint, the Americans who had been hosts to Soviet visitors or had been visitors themselves told a National Academy of Sciences review panel in 1977 that the United States "gains a lot scientifically" through the exchange (60 percent), that there should be more joint research (84 percent) and that Soviet visitors included "experts" who "suggested new research procedures, introduced new ideas" and "imparted new knowledge" (80 percent). Assessing the scientists' experiences, the panel concluded that "although American science is, on the whole, stronger than Soviet science, there is still a genuine scientific gain for the United States in having such exchanges....And even in those fields where it is clear that the United States teaches more than it learns, it is important for Americans to know what the Soviets are doing."

On the political issue, Loren Graham of the Massachusetts Institute of Technology noted in 1979, "The exchange programs are presently helping us to learn about repressive conditions in Soviet scholarship and we are able to make more informed decisions about the proper response....If joint programs no longer existed, what would irritated American scientists have to walk out on?"

New Trade Negotiations

Of the agreements in operation when Professor Graham wrote, three—an overall protocol on science and technology exchanges, and programs for cooperation in space and in energy research—have lapsed without renewal. Two more, on atomic energy and transportation, are up for renewal this year, and in the remainder—exchanges of graduate students and professors, cooperation between the two academies of science, and activities dealing with the environment, with medicine and public health, with agriculture, with housing and with world oceans—there are estimated to be only about one-fourth the number of participants there were before 1979. In addition, a long-standing cultural exchange agreement broke down before 1979, although the concert performance by pianist Emil Gilels in New York this spring suggests a Soviet interest in reviving the traffic without, it is hoped, attempting to extract an American pledge to return would-be defectors to Soviet authorities.

Each of the original scholarly exchanges should be examined on its merits. The space accord, which gave us the 1975 Apollo-Soyuz flight—occasionally referred to at the time as the "grain deal in the sky"—probably holds little attraction now, but a number of the others were of benefit once and could be again. American and Soviet scientists were cooperating in cancer research before there was a formal blessing for their work. As the work itself remains important, the blessing should be renewed.

More broadly, we should acknowledge that we need contacts with a widening range of Soviets simply for the insights we can gain through them into their system and the course it is taking. We need such social and political intelligence, far beyond what our diplomats can gather on their restricted rounds, because we need to understand the U.S.S.R. well enough to deal with it steadily. At issue is our self-interest. An unusual reading of our self-interest in giving the Soviets wide exposure to American thinking came from an American mathematician would threaten U.S. security far more than any exchange program in mathematics. Such a decline, he argues, could leave the Soviet Union unable to appreciate the catastrophic potential of the weapons we and they are able to develop. Nor should we underestimate the subliminal effect exposure to our vast network of superhighways may have on Soviet visitors used to the potholes, pitfalls and perils of the two-lane road linking Moscow with Leningrad. And, as Lord Carrington mentioned in his lecture, "it is worth recalling the impact on [Khrushchev] of the sight of an American grain field."

Mutual understanding, leading to the erosion of Soviet rigidity through the contagion of exposure to freedom, is a distant dream reachable, if at all, by very small steps. "[A]fter 30 years of almost constant interaction," former Senator J.W. Fulbright remarked in 1979, "we have still not made up our minds about what the Russians are really like." We cannot reduce that uncertainty by maintaining an aloof and disapproving distance. We may help ourselves, most of all, by expanding our opportunities to learn more of both the frustrations and pleasures of dealing with Soviets in limited, cooperative ventures.

Economic Advantages

We can also help ourselves in obvious, economic terms by selling more produce and products to the Soviet Union. Our national interest in such trade, however, cannot be measured simply in the jobs it sustains or the hard currency it moves from Soviet control to our own. Just as there was a strategic justification for restraining commerce throughout the cold war period, there must be a policy rationale for managing its expansion as a means of dissipating confrontation.

Again, old illusions must be discarded. Buckwheat and blue jeans may make communists plumper or prettier, but they will not subvert—indeed, they may reinforce—Party control over Soviet consumers. Nor is dependence on Western imports likely to reach such proportions that threats to stop the flow can be expected to make Moscow reverse its international course or significantly modify its domestic conduct.

While imports now account for roughly 15 percent of Soviet GNP, two-thirds of that volume comes from its socialist allies or from developing nations unlikely to forego sales on a point of political principle. Only for its purchases of food must Moscow rely heavily on a relatively few Western suppliers, but we know from our own 1980 grain embargo exercise that neither American farmers nor Canadian, Argentinian, Australian and European producers are prepared to withhold their supplies from the Soviet market in a period of world grain surplus. And as long as we sell foodstuffs to the invaders of Afghanistan, we lack the moral and political

authority to command our allies not to ship bootlaces for military shoes or compressors for natural gas pipelines.

Nonetheless, the profit motive cannot be our only guide to setting U.S.-Soviet trade policy. Such commerce is not politically neutral either in real or symbolic terms, and if we are to incur some costs from trade expansion, we must be clear as well about the political advantages we expect it to bring.

"Only over the long term can we expect a stable, growing trade with the Soviets to produce political plusses in the bilateral relationship."

The most immediate benefits would come in our relations with our allies. By moving closer to their outlook, we would diminish a major irritant, narrow an opening the Soviets have been adept at exploiting, and further the chances of implementing an effective common policy of credit and technology controls on Western exports. The discussions before and at the Williamsburg Summit give at most incomplete evidence of such progress. As long as international credit is generally tight, it is easier for all of us to hold East bloc borrowing on a short rein. But we clearly need closer consultation in this area on a permanent basis, so that the "foreign policy criteria" we have unsuccessfully tried to impose on technology transfer can be incorporated in a different fashion into bargaining with the Soviets simultaneously on economic and political issues.

Within the Coordinating Committee (COCOM) of the Western allies there needs to be an American admission that some goods are more strategic than others. We are now asking COCOM to police such a broad range of high technology that we cannot expect it to act effectively. An alliance agreement to bar export licenses for militarily significant machinery and know-how is in our common interest, but to make it work, we must define military significance in a way that facilitates enforcement rather than invites contempt.

Only over the long term can we expect a stable, growing trade with the Soviets to produce political plusses in the bilateral relationship. Having anticipated too much a decade ago, we should now realize that there are limits to the political price we can extract either from a single deal or continuing commerce. We cannot, however, be certain of the leverage available unless we engage in trade and attempt, in the process, to exert whatever pressure the traffic will bear. Nor, without coordinating an active trade policy with our partners, can we hope to extract the best mix of political and economic terms. For our part, we must begin by questioning the wisdom, in terms of U.S. interests, of continuing to withhold Most Favored Nation status from the Soviet Union when we grant it to almost every country in the world, including several where both free expression and free emigration are denied.

Over a long period of years, trade can open some now-closed doors and minds in the Soviet Union. In the meantime, in commerce as much as in diplomacy, science, scholarship and culture, we should maintain as wide and continuous an effort at broadening our contacts as our own self-interest justifies. To contain Soviet power more positively, we should not isolate ourselves from Soviet society but should seek, instead, to engage it in the most varied ways on the widest of fronts.

Those of us who periodically on his birthday have to read George Washington's Farewell Address to an empty Senate chamber perhaps have more occasion than most to reflect on his broad vision. His counsel in that address is sound policy for all times:

> The nation which indulges toward another an habitual hatred or an habitual fondness is in some degree a slave. It is a slave to its animosity or to its affection, either of which is sufficient to lead it astray from its duty and its interest. Antipathy in one nation against another disposes each more readily to offer insult and injury, to lay hold of slight causes of umbrage, and to be haughty and intractable when accidental or trifling occasions of dispute occur.

We should be the servants only of the priorities we set for ourselves. Our goal in dealing with the Soviets is to deter conflict, oppose threats to our freedom and our allies, and wait, as patiently as our adversary, for decay within the U.S.S.R. to slow and alter its character and conduct. On the margins, through an expansion of constructive engagements, we may find paths of less resistance along which we can hurry history a bit. The balance to pursue is the one spelled out by Bertrand Russell: "[R]esistance, if it is to be effective in preventing the spread of evil, should be combined with the greatest degree of understanding and the smallest degree of force that is compatible with the survival of the good things we wish to preserve."

In the past—indeed in the present—we have relied too exclusively on force. We would advance our prospects better by seeking, first of all, to understand our opponent and second, where possible, to conclude durable understandings with him.

Charles McC. Mathias, Jr. has been a Senator from Maryland since 1969, and sits on the Senate Foreign Relations Committee. From 1961-1969 he served in the U.S. House of Representatives.

"We should improve our procedures by determining goals at the outset...and then deciding on the strategy and tactics to achieve those goals."

The Key to Arms Control: A Coherent US Strategy

Ralph Earle II

It is an honor and pleasure to be here to deliver one of the Ogden lectures. I am truly grateful for the invitation—in part, because many of the previous lecturers were my colleagues and are my friends; in part, because I have a special feeling for Brown from which one of my children graduated and with which I am affiliated on a part-time basis; and, in part, because the subject which I will address is of such over-riding importance to our nation and to the world.

My topic tonight is "Arms Control: Its Role in the Future," but, reminded of the legend on the building in Washington which houses our national archives, "What is past is prologue." I think it necessary to talk to some extent about the past.

The recent history of arms control is not a particularly happy or successful one. In fact, many informed observers and participants now cite that history to demonstrate failure and urge that new and fundamentally different approaches be taken with respect to the issue; some even suggest that efforts toward arms control should be abandoned. For instance, Henry Kissinger in a recent article advocated a new approach toward strategic arms, urging what he called "not. . .a new proposal [but] a fresh concept." And the newly confirmed Director of the Arms Control and Disarmament Agency is reported to have called arms control negotiations "a sham."

What is the basis for this pessimism and lack of confidence? As I said, the recent history is not good. Let me give you a few examples.

Historical Example

—In 1972, the U.S. and the Soviet Union entered into the so-called Interim Agreement, which, in effect, froze the number of strategic land-based and submarine-based missile launchers of each side for a period of five years.

Ralph Earle II, "Arms Control, Its Role in the Future," *Vital Speeches of the Day*, August 26, 1983. Reprinted with permission.

Both sides committed themselves to a follow-on agreement within that period. It was not achieved, although the sides continue to abide by the Agreement's provisions.

—In 1974, President Nixon and General Secretary Brezhnev signed the Threshold Test Ban Treaty, limiting underground nuclear weapons tests to a maximum of 150 kilotons (all tests in the atmosphere, under water and in outer space having been previously banned by the Limited Test Ban Treaty of 1963). Again, although the sides have agreed to abide by its limitations, the Threshold Treaty has not been ratified by the U.S. (and ratification would bring into effect a number of helpful verification provisions).

—In 1976, President Ford and Brezhnev signed the so-called "PNE" or Peaceful Nuclear Explosions Treaty which also placed 150 kiloton limits on underground nuclear explosions for peaceful purposes. This Treaty has not been ratified.

—In 1979, President Carter and Brezhnev signed the SALT II Treaty which placed significant limitations on strategic nuclear delivery vehicles, the numbers of their warheads and even required the dismantling and destruction by the Soviets of almost 300 of their intercontinental weapons. This Treaty has not been ratified.

—In 1977, negotiations seeking a total or comprehensive ban on all nuclear testing began among the U.S., the Soviet Union, and the United Kingdom. Considerable progress was made, and the parties were on the verge of concluding such a treaty, albeit for a limited period of time, when those negotiations were terminated after the invasion of Afghanistan. They have not been renewed.

—In 1978, the two superpowers began discussions aimed at limiting or banning the development and deployment of anti-satellite weapons. Here again, real progress was made until the Afghanistan incursion. These negotiations too have remained in limbo—and it appears that they will stay there given Mr. Reagan's "Star Wars" speech last month.

—More recently, we have been talking with the Soviets in Geneva regarding limitations on and reductions of both intermediate range nuclear weapons and intercontinental weapons. But, when the chief negotiators briefed the Senate Foreign Relations Committee a few weeks ago, the reports were of little, if any, progress and one Senator commented that it was the most depressing briefing on arms control he had heard in his four years as a senator.

"Arms control as it has been 'practiced,'... has not been a failure...The failure has been. . .the ability to face up to what is good and right for the country and pursue it to a conclusion."

And not only does my list of examples demonstrate failure to come to positive results in the particular areas under consideration, but it undermines other areas in which there have been part successes. Most important, these examples strike at the basis of the Non-Proliferation Treaty. That Treaty, completed in 1968, and which now has well over 100 nations-parties, in effect was a compact between the nuclear "haves" and the nuclear "have nots." The former agreed to take steps to reduce their existing nuclear arsenals—"to achieve at the earliest possible date the cessation of the nuclear arms race and to undertake effective measures in the direction of nuclear disarmament"—in return for the latter's commitment not to acquire nuclear weapons. I had the bad luck to chair our delegation to the NPT Review Conference in 1980, and I can assure you that the non-nuclear nations represented there—some 85 or 90—were open and sometimes abusive in their view that the U.S. and the Soviet Union had not lived up to their NPT obligations, and in some cases there were implied and even express threats to withdraw from the Treaty and its obligation not to develop nuclear weapons of their own. If they felt that way in 1980, imagine their views today!

Infusing Political Will

So, given this litany of failure or not, at least, lack of success, it is not surprising that even those most in favor of arms control are prone to seek another, different approach to the issue. However, and here I come to the principal point of my remarks, I am not one of those. I believe that arms control as it has been "practiced," if that's the right word, in the past has not been a failure—in fact, I believe that the process has been a success—the failure has been one of political will—that is, the ability to face up to what is good and right for the country and pursue it to a conclusion. Change in method will not instill political will, but political will can bring

success to the process.

By political will, I mean presidential determination, but I do not limit it to that office. It is necessary to have it on the part of the Congress, and it is necessary to have it on the part of the public. Ideally, leadership in an area such as arms control should come from the President, but it can also come from the people and filter up. Perhaps the current widespread support of the nuclear freeze movement is a manifestation of the latter—I hope so. The resolutions for a nuclear freeze may be somewhat impractical and difficult, even impossible, to negotiate, but they reflect a broad-based, widespread drive on the part of the American people that something be done about the nuclear arms race and arms control. And perhaps it will be heeded by those in Washington.

Returning to my point that it was not the process that failed, let us look again at the examples I cited earlier.

The Interim Agreement of 1972 was followed by another agreement on strategic offensive arms—SALT II.

The Threshold Test Ban Treaty and the Peaceful Nuclear Explosions Treaty could have been ratified and could still be ratified. President Carter chose not to push for them as he feared the Senate should not subsequently accept a comprehensive test ban. And President Reagan does not push for them because they are not good enough. Classic examples of the best being the enemy of the good.

SALT II could, in my view, have been ratified had Carter continued his support. But it was 1980, an election year, with the Soviets in Afghanistan, the hostages in Tehran, and Ronald Reagan coming strongly from the right. It could still be ratified, but President Reagan has called it "fatally flawed"—and continues to abide by its provisions and complains bitterly when there is alleged evidence that the Soviets have violated its terms.

A comprehensive test ban treaty could, as I have noted, been completed. But again, it was 1980, and now Mr. Reagan has formally said we would not return to the table—at least until CTB and PNE have been improved.

I also believe that we could have—and still can have—an agreement which prevents outer space from becoming the next battlefield.

And, finally, I believe that successful agreements can be achieved in the negotiations in Geneva—if certain fundamentals are accepted and respected.

Military and Political Perspectives

First, I think it important to bear in mind that strategic arms negotiations (and their product—agreements) have to be considered from two perspectives: military and political.

From a military point of view, the arms control policy and implementation is a part of overall national security considerations. A simple guideline would be that the negotiators should not give something away until and unless a judgment had been made at the highest level that such an agreement would not jeopardize our national security. An obvious example: the U.S. should not have agreed to limit its ABM systems without the same commitment from the Soviet Union (and it did not).

The political aspect is far more complex and far more difficult to deal with. Shortly before Jimmy Carter was to be inaugurated as President, he met with the Joint Chiefs of Staff and, inter alia, asked them how many missiles did we need to deter the Soviets—in other words, could we do with fewer, perhaps many fewer, than we then possessed. I believe that the correct answer, from a purely military point of view, would have been in the affirmative. But, when word of this meeting with the Chiefs leaked to the press, Carter was severely criticized by many for even asking the question. Some of the criticism came from the uninformed, and some of it came from political opponents who chose to see it as a sign of weakness or pacifism. But some criticisms came from more thoughtful people, their reasoning being, and not without substance, that if in fact his question led to unilateral reductions which placed us in a numerically inferior position to the Soviet Union, even though our deterrent would be maintained, it could or would be seen by the rest of the world as an American acceptance of Soviet superiority. Put another way, if the Soviet Union could destroy the U.S. twenty times over and we could destroy them only twice over, then the Soviets would be considered ten times as strong as the U.S.; this in turn could result in increased Soviet political and economic leverage all over the world. So political considerations of this sort must be taken into account.

Second, any strategic arms agreement should be tested with respect to strategic stability. Strategic stability, by my definition, is a situation in which neither side is capable of attacking the other without assurance of receiving unacceptable damage in return, and neither side perceives either that it can make successful—that is, unanswered—attack, or that the other side can make such an attack. And here the perception is just as important as the reality. Does the particular agreement under scrutiny maintain or, preferably, enhance strategic stability?

A third, and much disregarded, fundamental is that consideration must be given to the asymmetries between the sides. These asymmetries are largely or entirely immutable and therefore are relevant to any negotiation between the super-powers.

One is geography. We have long coastlines with total access to non-ice-bound passages. The Soviet Union, although a huge land mass, has far fewer ports, and most of those lie behind so-called "choke points"—for instance, their submarines must transit close to Norway, Great Britain, Iceland, Japan, and so forth—ours are in the open sea the moment they leave, for instance, Charleston, South Carolina, Guam, or Bangor, Washington. This is a major reason why the Soviets have emphasized land-based missiles and we have put more effort into our submarine force. At the same time, we have a far larger percentage of our population on or near the coast which makes us more vulnerable to short flight-time SLBMs.

Second, the two powers have very different alliances. The Soviet allies are to one degree or another subject nations and without strategic capability of their own. On the other hand, our allies are free, with great economic potential, and two of them, Great Britain and France, are nuclear powers with their own missile-bearing submarines and, in the case of France, with their own land-based missiles.

There is also the matter of third countries. The Soviets are faced with a major threat over a border of thousands of miles long from one billion Chinese—who also have nuclear weapons. As someone noted, the Soviet Union is the only nation in the world surrounded by unfriendly Communist countries. We have no such strategic problem.

A fourth, and also often-neglected, fundamental is that we should in our negotiations with the Soviets, or anyone else for that matter, try to keep in mind their perceptions of the current situation, their perceptions of history, and their resultant attitudes and beliefs—these all affect the relationship. For instance, we see, understandably, the Soviet Union as an agressor (e.g. Afghanistan), a trouble-maker (e.g. Angola) and a nation seeking the spread of its own brand of Communism (e.g. Cuba).

"It must never be lost from sight that there is an almost infinite difference between a nuclear and a non-nuclear world."

Soviet Perceptions of U.S.

But how do they see themselves—and us? They see the Soviet Union in a world in which five nations have nuclear weapons and four of them have these weapons aimed at Moscow. They see what they call "U.S. adventurism" in Korea, Vietnam, Lebanon, and so forth, and they see us as the first and only nation to use the atomic bomb.

Let me make it clear—and I am not defending the Soviet Union or condemning the U.S.—I am simply saying that we can deal better with our adversary if we understand him and his perceptions.

Another rule for our future negotiations—let us not let the best be the enemy of the good. Do not ask for too much too soon. Let me give you some examples of what I mean.

In March, 1977, Secretary Vance travelled to Moscow to put foward the so-called "comprehensive proposal" which called for dramatic reductions, especially in land-based weapons. From the American point of view, it was a position which made good sense and would have contributed greatly to an enhancement of strategic stability. But the Soviets saw it very differently—as an effort to weaken their strength—land-based ICBMs—and in effect make them re-structure their forces at great cost and with no assurance that they would be equally secure after such restructing. As a result, they rejected that proposal almost immediately. It was not a major setback for SALT, but it does demonstrate my point.

Subsequently, in considering the resultant SALT II Treaty, critics complained that we "let the Soviets have 308 heavy ICBM launchers" and the U.S. could have none. There was an implication in this criticism that the U.S. had somehow made a gift of these launchers to the Soviet Union. In fact, they had had them for a decade and had tacitly agreed at Vladivostok in 1974, four and a half years before, that they would stop pressing for limits on the U.S. forward-based systems in Europe in return for maintenance of these launchers. And the very critics who claimed that the Treaty should not be ratified because of this alleged flaw were in fact advocating a no-treaty world in which the Soviets could have 3,008 or 30,008 heavy launchers.

And on the other side of the coin, as I mentioned earlier, those who support a freeze at this time may be asking for too much. Personally, I am very sympathetic to the freeze movement as it reflects a massive public support for doing something about the nuclear arms race. But is a freeze really attainable? I would assume that all of you want any future agreement with the Soviets to be verifiable. But how long would it take, for instance, to negotiate a truly verifiable ban on the production of nuclear weapons? Such a goal is obviously desirable in the long run, but would its pursuit not divert us from getting something almost as good in the near term?

One final fundamental: it must never be lost from sight that there is an almost infinite difference between a nuclear and a non-nuclear world. Winston Churchhill would have been ecstatic to have had an air defense against German bombers which was 95 pèrcent effective. If today we could achieve a 99 percent effective defense against Soviet missile warheads, and given the fact that they have approximately 7500 warheads, we would still lose 75 cities in an all out Soviet attack. A nuclear world is indeed different!

Arms Control Suggestions

Earlier I defended the process—but this does not mean that it cannot be improved. A few suggestions for the future:

First, we ought to decide what it is we really want. We ought to plan a strategy for carrying it out. We should learn from our experiences and our past mistakes. What do we want from arms control? Our objective is to enhance our national security. We ought to be and feel safer with it than without it. More specifically, this means that an arms control agreement should:

—Limit the Soviet threat to the United States and our forces.

—Improve the survivability of U.S. forces if possible. At a minimum arms control should not prohibit or inhibit the U.S. from steps required to maintain a survivable strategic deterrent.

—Improve our ability to monitor Soviet forces. Our uncertainties about Soviet forces and programs should be reduced as a result of arms control.

The U.S. should emerge from negotiations as a successful competitor and negotiator. This means that an agreement

—Must be and be seen as equal.

—Must be clear and without loopholes.

How will this come about? We should first decide on the acceptable outcome. Then, the United States must develop a broad bipartisan consensus in favor of arms control. Our goals must be clear, understandable and reasonable. This cannot be accomplished unless the administration develops and propagates its foreign policy objectives in a way that includes the role of arms control. This also means that the administration must acknowledge that the centers of power and influence are many in the United States and make sure that it does what it can to keep various groups informed and part of the process.

We must not exaggerate our expectations. The Congress and the American people appreciate candor. For example, there is little that arms control can do to save our fixed land-based missiles. We must not oversell arms control.

We must find a streamlined way to develop detailed negotiating positions based on our overall foreign policy and security goals. Past ways of developing positions and responses to negotiating have been slow and cumbersome and permitted relatively low ranking officials in one department or another to sidetrack high level decisions. This leads to long internal negotiations in which positions are overtaken by events, and, in the case of SALT II for example, those who started it were not responsible at the finish. In fact, so much time elapsed that those who sired that Treaty were able to disinherit it without cost.

In short, we should improve our procedures by determining goals at the outset, asking and answering the hard questions early, and then deciding on the strategy and tactics to achieve those goals.

And finally, if our leaders are unwilling or incapable of giving us the leadership necessary or the political will required to go forward to meet these criteria, we the electorate should use every possible means of persuasion to instill that leadership and will.

Ralph Earle II is the former Director of the Arms Control and Disarmament Agency and Chief of the United States Delegation at SALT II.

"One-half of 1 percent of a 2.5 trillion GNP is still a tidy sum, but. . .if doubling that expenditure would measurably reduce the probability of war, it would be a bargain."

viewpoint **26**

The Soviet Threat Justifies a Higher Budget

Kelly Burke

The great nuclear freeze debate—in all its manifestations—rages on in the United States as well as in many of the Western European countries. Regrettably, there is no discernible evidence of a comparable drive among the citizens of the only other nuclear superpower, the Soviet Union.

Unfortunately, for those who view debate as a mechanism to marshal facts and sharpen logic, the nuclear freeze controversy has seen precious little of either. Instead, the protagonists on both sides have, for the most part, offered a steady drumbeat of emotional rhetoric and ad hominem attacks against their opponents.

But leave it to Gov. Jerry Brown to reach new heights of hyperbole and new lows of campaign demagoguery. Brown, a Democrat, lost a hard-fought campaign for the seat of retiring Sen. S.I. Hayakawa. His Republican opponent was Pete Wilson, currently mayor of San Diego.

One of Brown's campaign gimmicks was a television ad that sought to translate the substantial emotional appeal of the nuclear freeze movement into votes. The ad opened with Ron Cey of the Los Angeles Dodgers baseball team saying, "I want to keep on playing baseball." He is followed by conductor Leonard Bernstein who wants "to go on making music." Then, actress Candice Bergen says, "I want to go on doing it all."

Next, the screen is filled with the unmistakable mushroom shape of the fiery nuclear explosion, and then a small boy saying plaintively, "I want to go on living."

No Simple Solutions

The ad concludes with a shot of Brown, presumably projecting peacefulness and goodwill, while an announcer delivers the not-too-subtle appeal to the voters: "Pete Wilson opposes the nuclear arms freeze. Jerry

Kelly Burke, "Arms Control in the Real World," *Union Leader*, January 11, 1983. Reprinted with permission.

Brown supports it. Vote for your life. Elect Jerry Brown to the U.S. Senate."

Now that's really getting down to basics: "Vote for me and you live, vote for my opponent and you die."

Would that life were that simple and that the issues we face could be reduced to such simplistic formulations. But they can't be, and certainly the nuclear freeze question can't be boiled down to a pithy one-liner.

Nor does it seem likely that those who question the desirability or practicability of a nuclear freeze (whatever that means) are motivated by a belief that any nuclear war is apt to have a happy ending. It is equally unlikely, as some have suggested, that all supporters of the nuclear freeze movement are communist sympathizers, if not outright card-carrying members of the Communist Party.

Expenditures Regrettable but Necessary

It's no bad thing that hundreds of thousands, perhaps millions, of people in this country are giving reasonably serious thought to the nuclear issue. All of us ought to view the prospect of nuclear war with absolute horror. All of us ought to regret the necessity of the large expenditures required to maintain the nuclear balance (but no more than we should deplore the much higher cost of the nonnuclear arsenals). Having done that, we then must carefully assess the few real alternatives that might provide us peace and security in this dangerous and disorderly world.

There is an old, shopworn axiom which holds that war is too important to be left to generals. Certainly that is true. But certainly the pursuit of peace is also important enough to warrant the time and attention of all of us.

In considering nuclear issues, it is useful to reflect on the world as it is. It is also useful to reflect on the world as we would wish it to be. But it is dangerous to confuse those two worlds.

A few millennia have passed since Isaiah prophesied

a time when man would beat his swords into plowshares. It is a sad commentary on mankind that there has been little if any progress in the direction of Isaiah's vision. While all of us can lament that it is so, few, if any, can doubt man's continuing proclivity to settle disputes with violence. In such a world—regrettably the real world in which we live—force remains the final arbiter, and nuclear forces the absolute, the ultimate, arbiter.

Need to Deter Soviets

Another unpleasant but inescapable fact about the real world is that we share it with a powerful and not-very-friendly competitor, the Soviet Union, a country that has shown an inordinate enthusiasm for acquiring military force and at least a cautious willingness to use that force in the pursuit of its political goals.

In such a world it would be a fundamental and perhaps fatal mistake for America to adopt any form of nuclear freeze that could lead it to a position of unambiguous nuclear inferiority. This is not to argue that on the day the Soviets calculate they're ahead by 10, 20, or even 100 percent, they will push the nuclear button and annihilate us. Given the complexity and unpredictability of nuclear exchange calculus, even a relatively small nuclear force has a reasonable prospect of deterring a much larger one.

"If we are to succeed in negotiating the right kinds of arms control. . . we must first convince the Russians that we are determined to match them."

But before airily dismissing the likelihood of nuclear war, it is well to reflect on the history of war. More often than not, wars begin in irrationality and confusion, frequently to divert attention from internal problems. Hence, our nuclear forces must be sized and shaped not just to deter war or nuclear war in relatively normal and placid times but in times of extremes, times when perhaps the Soviets are in danger of losing control over their people and their empire is crumbling. That is the correct test of the adequacy of our deterrent.

Maintaining Nuclear Balance

Even aside from deterrence of war, the nuclear balance is a dominant theme in another important context in this real world in which we live. Nuclear superiority, if attained by the Russians, can be and certainly would be converted to political leverage. The nuclear balance and the perceptions of that balance permeate world affairs today. That balance affects the behavior of not only the two superpowers but of the rest of the world as well.

To the extent that the Russians see themselves as ahead in this competition—and there is evidence that

they do believe themselves somewhat ahead at this point—they will tend to be even more adventuresome and opportunistic than they have been in the past. The other side of that coin is, of course, that to the extent we see ourselves as behind in the nuclear balance, we will tend to be more timid and less willing to interpose ourselves between the Russians and their objectives, no matter how much we may deplore those objectives. This is the first and immediate danger of allowing any major imbalance to develop.

Damon Runyon, a great American philosopher who liked to masquerade as a writer, once wrote: *"The race is not always to the swift nor the battle to the strong, but that's the way to bet."* Runyon would have looked very dubiously at nuclear freeze proposals that could lead to the Russians becoming stronger and swifter than us.

Maintaining the nuclear balance is important. Striving to reduce the level of weapons on both sides in a balanced way is also important. But even more important than simply reducing the overall numbers of weapons is to reduce specifically those weapons and those conditions that would add to instability in time of a confrontation between ourselves and the Soviets.

In particular, we should aspire to reduce, if not eliminate altogether, weapons that are at once highly threatening and highly vulnerable. That is, of course, a good description of silo-based missiles with multiple warheads. That is why the first goal of our strategic force planning should be to provide an adequately survivable basing system for the MX missile, and the first goal of our arms control negotiations should be to reduce the number of 10-warheaded Soviet SS-18 missiles.

Commonly, the pursuit of a strategic arms control agreement is justified on three grounds: first, to reduce the cost of maintaining our nuclear forces; second, to reduce the consequences of a nuclear war, should one ensue; and, third, to reduce the probability of war.

There is a dangerous tendency to confuse the relative importance of these three goals when, in fact, the last—reducing the probability of war—is so transcendental as to completely overshadow the other two. It is easy to deplore the expenditures of large sums for these awful and awesome weapons, but it is well to remember that over the past decade or so we have spent on the order of one-half of 1 percent of our gross national product on strategic nuclear forces. To be fair, one-half of 1 percent of a $2.5-trillion GNP is still a tidy sum, but it is also obviously an affordable sum. If doubling that expenditure would measurably reduce the probability of war, it would be a bargain.

Reductions in Arms Unrealistic

It is also easy to favor reductions in the overall number of nuclear weapons with a view toward substantially lessening the consequences of war should it come. Unfortunately, in the real world, in which the

Soviet Union is free to act in what it perceives as its own best interests, reductions of that magnitude do not appear attainable. Should we miraculously negotiate a treaty that reduced the nuclear inventories of both sides by 90 percent, the consequences of an exchange with the remaining 10 percent would still be calamitous beyond our ability to contemplate.

The nuclear freeze movement continues that same unfortunate tendency, a tendency to embrace wishful thinking and simplistic solutions instead of doing the hard thinking about the hard choices which exist in this real world. To borrow from Samuel Johnson, much of what propels the nuclear freeze movement is "a triumph of hope over experience." The danger is that in opting for the immediate and seductively appealing nuclear freeze proposals, we will lose patience and interest in those real, and terribly important, arms control negotiations now underway between ourselves and the Russians. That would be tragic.

No one who has done business with the Russians doubts that they are tough-minded, hard-nosed negotiators. They do have an interest, in many ways stronger than our own, in reducing nuclear armaments. But the oldest rule of diplomacy is that "peace treaties merely confirm the realities of the battlefield," and surely the realities of the current and projected military balance must dominate any arms control agreements we are able to negotiate with the Russians.

Arms Control Expensive

Negotiated arms control reductions are important, perhaps vitally so. If we are to succeed in negotiating the right kinds of arms control treaties—that provide a stable balance of forces—we must first convince the Russians that we are determined to match them at whatever higher level they insist upon. Once they truly believe that we are so committed, they have every reason to join with us in reducing the threat of war.

Unfortunately, this approach will necessarily require both time and money. But as another American philosopher, H.L. Mencken, who posed as a newspaperman, once said, "There's always an easy solution to every human problem—neat, plausible, and wrong." Nuclear issues are too important for such a solution.

Kelly Burke is the former Air Force Deputy Chief of Staff for Research, Development & Acquisition.

"The real fight in Washington is not over the size of the defense budget but over differing views of the Soviet Union."

viewpoint **27**

The Soviet Threat Is No Excuse for the Defense Budget

Charles William Maynes

The Reagan administration continues to take the country's breath away with its extraordinarily ambitious plans for defense spending. As virtually all other items in the federal budget were being slashed, the administration projected military outlays of $1.553 trillion from 1983 to 1988, or only $55 billion less than the amount it was intending to suggest a month ago.

Even this $55 billion figure did not represent the kinds of savings that result from real program cuts: Nearly $30 billion was the result of optimistic assumptions about the future course of inflation. Another $5.5 billion was found by lowering the estimates for fuel costs or other minor savings. The rest the administration found by freezing military pay for a short period.

Defense Budget Larger

In reading the fine print, an astonished Congress saw that everything in the proposed defense budget seemed higher than ever. The figure for nuclear arms was up more than 36 percent. The controversial MX would swallow $6.6 billion. The disputed B1 bomber would require another $7 billion. The navy would expand by 100 ships during the five-year period. And nearly 40,000 new recruits would enter the service in 1984.

There is, however, an unavoidable truth about the administration's defense budget that even its harshest critics try to run away from. The defense budget is not too high but too low—provided one accepts key assumptions, thus far inadequately challenged, that undergird the administration's requests.

In May 1982, the administration completed a five-year defense plan that was promptly leaked to the *New York Times.* A few months later, Gen. David Jones, former chairman of the Joint Chiefs of Staff, confirmed, in effect, that the central premises of the leaked documents were guiding, and in his view distorting, U.S. military planning.

Charles William Maynes, "Debate Soviet Threat, Then Arms Budget," *Minneapolis Star and Tribune,* February 9, 1983. Reprinted with permission from Charles William Maynes, editor, *Foreign Policy* Magazine.

The first premise is that U.S. nuclear forces "must prevail and be able to force the Soviet Union to seek earliest termination of hostilities on terms favorable to the United States." There can be, in other words, nuclear war that does not lead to the final holocaust.

The second premise is that the United States must devise plans to defeat the Soviet Union at any level of conflict from insurgencies to nuclear war. In the words of the document, "U.S. forces might be required simultaneously and in geographically separate theaters." The document speaks of using saboteurs, commandos and other forces in Eastern Europe.

The document asserts that although the United States has 16 army divisions, it will need 17 by 1988 and 25 by 1991. Navy carrier battle groups should rise from 13 to 22 by 1991, it says, and air force tactical fighter wings should increase by more than 50 percent. It adds that ICBMs should rise from 1,053 to 1,254.

Need for More Defense

The report admits that the goals are "probably infeasible," but on the basis of its premises one can reach a single conclusion: Defense Secretary Caspar Weinberger is correct in asserting that he needs more for defense, not less.

Behind this determined effort to impose a "Mission Impossible" on our armed forces is a conception of international politics that is the real issue in the current debate over the size of the American military. During the last presidential campaign and during his first weeks in office, Reagan voiced views about the Soviet Union that stood in sharp contrast to the more measured caution of earlier presidents.

Reagan first contended that the Soviet Union was behind virtually every event on the international scene adverse to American interests. Then in his first press conference he suggested that Soviet leaders could be expected to lie, cheat and steal in their effort to promote world revolution.

117

Reagan has not forgotten those early declarations, despite some apparent moderation. On at least three occasions he has reinserted them into speeches that the American far right considers the essence of the Reagan Revolution. In Reagan's speech before the British Parliament, his address to the U.N. General Assembly, and his comments to a group visiting the White House on Captive Nations Day, he repeatedly returned to those themes.

Differing Views of Soviets

Lenin is condemned for "resorting to all sorts of stratagems, artifices, maneuvers, illegal methods, evasions, and subterfuges." Reagan suggests the Soviet system is headed for the "ash heap of history."

"The best way to clarify the defense budget debate. . .would be to conduct a comprehensive set of congressional hearings designed to establish what kind of foe we face."

Most American scholars of the Soviet Union would not agree with the president's characterization. They would see the Soviet Union as dangerous but less inclined to take risks than the president believes. But these more traditional views are now having less impact on U.S. foreign policy than at any time in the postwar period.

The real fight in Washington is not over the size of the defense budget but over differing views of the Soviet Union. These differences of view lie behind the administration's difficulties with its NATO partners as well as its conflicts with Congress over the role of nuclear weapons.

The best way to clarify the defense budget debate—and issues of U.S. foreign policy—would be to conduct a comprehensive set of congressional hearings designed to establish what kind of foe we face.

Charles William Maynes is the editor of Foreign Policy *magazine.*

"The President's. . .defense budget reflects our continued commitment to maintaining and enhancing the current operating force. . .and to ensuring this Nation's future security."

Defense Spending Increases US Security

Caspar Weinberger

The President's FY 1984 defense budget reflects our continued commitment to maintaining and enhancing the current operating forces of the military and to ensuring this Nation's future security. It has been developed based on an honest and realistic reassessment of our existing and long-term military capabilities in the face of a growing threat. The costs are stated clearly. It is economically productive and provides for a controlled growth rate. The management initiatives undertaken during the first two years of this Administration to ensure the efficient execution of defense plans and programs are continued and considerably strengthened. The achievement and maintenance of improved levels of readiness and sustainability continue to receive a high priority. Force modernization and expansion programs are planned to meet the ever-present and growing Soviet challenge.

This budget, shown in Table II.A.1, proposes Total Obligational Authority (TOA) of $274.1 billion for FY 1984. The tables in Appendix B provide budget data by appropriation title and by mission area in current and constant FY 1984 dollars. The chapters in Part III of this report provide details on specific programs.

TABLE II.A.1
Department of Defense—Military Functions
($ Billions)

	FY 1982	FY 1983	FY 1984
Current Year Dollars			
Total Obligational Authority (TOA) 1/	211.4	240.5	274.1
Budget Authority (BA) 2/	213.8	239.4	273.4
Outlays 3/	182.9	208.9	238.6
Constant FY 1984 Dollars			
Total Obligational Authority (TOA)	229.2	249.3	274.1
Budget Authority (BA)	231.8	248.2	273.4
Outlays	197.6	216.4	238.6

Caspar Weinberger, Annual Report to Congress, Fiscal Year 1984.

This request represents an increase of $33.6 billion over FY 1983. About 25% of the increase will go to pay for inflation—a significant component of any program cost growth. The remaining 75% of the increase will provide a balanced approach to the already established goals for strategic force modernization, readiness and sustainability, airlift and sealift enhancement, and tactical force expansion.

Operating costs represent about 52% of the DoD budget in FY 1984. This category includes our payments to military and civilian personnel and military retirees as well as allocations for maintenance and repair of equipment and for utilities, medical costs, training, petroleum and lubricants, and spare parts.

The remainder of the budget largely represents funds for investment in research and development, procurement of weapon systems, and military construction and family housing. These are the programs that suffered the most neglect following the end of the Vietnam war. Throughout the decade of the 1970s, the cumulative decline in DoD investment was more than 30% in real terms.

During the past year, DoD has used commercially available models of the U.S. economy to study economic effects of changes in the level of defense spending. The comments made here reflect the results of that work and results obtained by leading private economists.

Federal Deficit and Defense Spending

Proposed defense budgets have been increasingly discussed in terms of the large federal deficits projected for the next several years. It has been argued that the size of the projected deficits, and the implications of these deficits for the economy, present a strong case for cutting defense spending. This argument does not consider the national security concerns that justify the levels of defense spending proposed by the Administration. Moreover, strictly on economic grounds, even drastic cuts in the proposed Five-Year Defense Program would not produce dramatic reductions in the deficit.

The total obligational authority (TOA) for acquisition of major weapon systems is paid out over a period of several years. Consequently, large cuts in TOA would produce only relatively small reductions in outlays in the current budget year.

"This argument does not consider the national security concerns that justify the levels of defense spending proposed by the administration."

Monies appropriated for pay, operations, and maintenance are paid out much more rapidly than are appropriations for procurement. But the costs of cuts in terms of readiness of our forces are also quickly felt and could be severe.

It is also important to recognize that cuts in defense spending would not reduce the deficit on a dollar-for-dollar basis. They do not for two reasons. First, and most important, cuts in defense spending tend to reduce revenues because:

—A large part of DoD expenditures becomes income to firms and individuals, some of which comes back to the government in taxes; and

—The ripple effects from defense spending tend to stimulate growth in GNP, which also increases total tax revenues.

Defense Spending Stimulates Economy

Second, because defense spending stimulates the economy, cuts in defense spending tend to increase unemployment and therefore are offset partially by increased government unemployment compensation payments. This effect is quite small, but still large enough to show up on the economic model used in the DoD analysis.

Analysis done by DoD shows that each dollar cut from defense spending reduces the deficit by about 50 cents in the year in which the cut is made. If defense spending remains at a lower level, the effect on the deficit becomes even smaller over time.

The projected federal deficits cannot be attributed simply to the proposed increases in defense spending. The federal budget last ran a surplus in 1969. During each of the following seven years 1970-76, the Consumer Price Index increased 47% (more than twice the increase of the preceding seven years) and the federal budget went from a surplus of $3.2 billion in 1969 to a $66.4 billion deficit in 1976. In real terms, DoD outlays will be less in FY 1983 than they were in FY 1969, the year of the last budget surplus.

Employment Effects of Defense Purchases

The budgets proposed by the Administration imply significant shifts in the composition of federal spending. In real terms, transfer payments remain constant over the FY 1981-85 period, while defense spending increases and "all other" spending decreases. Because of these compositional changes, there has been substantial attention paid to the question of whether DoD outlays create more—or fewer—civilian jobs than other forms of government spending.

Critics have argued that other government programs create more jobs per $1 billion of outlays than does defense spending. One study has even claimed that defense spending reduces employment.

In March 1982 DoD estimated that each $1 billion in DoD non-pay outlays creates 35,000 civilian jobs. This estimate is an average effect across different DoD budget accounts (excluding military and civilian pay and retired pay). The estimate includes:

—Direct employment by DoD prime contractors;

—Employment, below the prime contractor level, involved in production of goods and services used in production of defense goods;

—Employment involved in production of added demands for consumer goods (and their inputs) that stem from wages and salaries of individuals directly and indirectly employed in defense production.

Some parts of DoD outlays have larger employment effects than do others. For example, each $1 billion in military pay goes to about 49,000 servicemen and women. The same is true of other major categories of government spending. Consequently, comparisons of employment multipliers for narrowly defined categories have little significance.

DoD has examined the employment effects of DoD purchases of goods and services and the employment effects of non-defense federal purchases of goods and services using the models of three leading economic forecasting firms. Each of these models projects that, in current economic circumstances, increases in defense purchases outlays increase civilian employment. Furthermore, there does not seem to be much difference in the employment effects of defense procurements and other federal government purchases. It is also worth noting that transfer payments tend to create fewer jobs than either defense or non-defense procurement since they are less stimulative to the economy than purchases of goods and services.

Caspar Weinberger is the secretary of defense under the Reagan Administration.

"Excessive military expenditures. . .are silent killers, taking lives as wantonly as if the weapons they produce had been put to use."

Defense Spending Does Not Increase US Security

Ruth Leger Sivard

The images of modern war haunt our memories: the ashes of Hiroshima, London in flames, a napalmed child running in silent agony, the countless scenes of indiscriminate terror and destruction that shock and repel.

An arms race, by contrast, has no visual identity. It moves along quietly, impersonally, a complex phenomenon seemingly remote from daily life and best left to the experts. The financial burden, if we occasionally feel its weight in the tax bill, is to be borne for peace and security.

In its impact on world society, however, today's arms race is neither remote nor benign. The excessive military expenditures demanded by this malign competition are silent killers, taking lives as wantonly as if the weapons they produce had been put to use. The extreme poverty endured by one-third of humanity—the deteriorating cities, the young people without hope of jobs, the children with distended bellies for want of adequate food—is one by-product of an arms race gone wild. It is the ever-present human cost of an obsessive drive for security through weapons.

The first priority of central governments today is military power, and as a whole they spend more on military defense than on any other responsibility to the public. The world's military expenditures in 1982 will exceed $600 billion; on the average, they take $1 in every $6 paid in taxes. But the financial outlay gives only a partial picture of the scope of the military activity. These budgets now support 25 million men in the regular armed forces, another 22 million in the paramilitary forces, and 24 million in the reserves. With an additional 25 million civilians employed in military-related jobs, the world military population has reached an unprecedented number for a time when no major war is being fought. It is larger than the combined populations of Mexico and Canada.

Ruth Leger Sivard, "The High Cost of Insecurity," *The Nation,* June 17, 1978. *The Nation Magazine,* Nation Associates Incorporated © 1978.

Throughout the world, the power of the military bureaucracy extends into all branches of government. In central governments, its workers outnumber all other public employees and account for a major share of public payrolls. They also administer the largest slice of government revenues. In a growing number of governments, military officers hold the key positions of power; more than 40 percent of developing nations are under military control.

The official military power structure has its counterpart in industry. Purchases of increasingly complex military equipment have made the arms-producing industry one of the largest and richest in the world, and the only one with such a sizable representation within government itself. Nor is arms production any longer a monopoly of the industrialized nations—it is the new growth industry of the developing world. An estimated one-fourth of developing nations have acquired indigenous production facilities for arms, some as sophisticated as fighter aircraft and missiles. A growing number of these developing nations have in turn become suppliers to other nations.

Several factors operate to keep this military-industrial-political complex in perpetual motion, spiraling steadily upward in size and strength. To a striking degree, rivalry and antagonism between the United States and the Soviet Union have shaped the military competition in the postwar period. Although representing only 11 percent of the global population, these two nations alone spent about 60 percent of the world's military outlay between 1960 and 1980. Their dominance has diminished somewhat over the years, economically as well as militarily, but in 1980 they still accounted for over half the global military budget.

The arms race has been propelled by an exceptionally heavy investment in weapons research. Between 1960 and 1977, an estimated $336 billion went into research and development of new weapons, almost 80 percent of it spent by the two superpowers. The technological drive among the major military powers has also spurred military budgets and spread weapons across the world. The export of arms—primarily by the United States and the USSR, but also by France, the United Kingdom, and other industrialized nations—was encouraged as a way to ease the balance of payments, spread costs, and maintain the pace of military development. In this competition, governments themselves became the new "merchants of death." By the end of the 1970s, the arms manufacturers were doing a yearly export business of $25 billion, a rapidly growing proportion of it with the developing nations.

"There is no evidence that this vast expansion of destructive power has made any area of the world more secure."

The push for the newest in weapons came from the buyers as well as the sellers. Jet fighters of national prestige, and even nations without the technical personnel to operate them were ready to mortgage their foreign exchange to acquire them. Rapidly rising oil revenues accelerated the buildup of arms in the Middle East, the region where by far the largest buyers were to be found. However, sophisticated weapons have been shipped to every corner of the globe. In 1979, 98 developing nations imported arms, and more than one-fifth of them were among the world's poorest nations, with per capita income averaging less than $200 a year. The military expenditures of developing nations as a whole have increased much more rapidly than has the economic base to support them.

Threat of Annihilation

In military terms, the effect of the arms race of the 1960s and 1970s is a sharply elevated destructive potential everywhere on the globe, and an increased threat of global annihilation. The nuclear-weapon nations now include the United States, Russia, Great Britain, China, France, India, and possibly Israel and South Africa. The first two have between them over 16,000 strategic nuclear warheads, enough to destroy every city in the world seven times over, and an estimated 30,000 battlefield and intermediate-range nuclear weapons. Among the other states, there are an estimated 1,000 additional nuclear weapons. But overkill is no longer confined to nuclear stockpiles. The so-called conventional arms, on which 80 percent of military budgets have been spent, have increased dramatically in kill power as well as numbers. Napalm, binary nerve gas, antipersonnel cluster bombs, and other such weapons have narrowed the gap between the destructiveness of nuclear and conventional weapons.

Meanwhile, there is no evidence that this vast expansion of destructive power has made any area of the world more secure. Any national monopoly of modern weapons technology has been short-lived, since a technological advance by one nation is promptly duplicated by its adversary. Change is constant, instability increases, and the whole world has been made hostage to military forces of incalculable power.

In cost to society, the consequences of the arms race have been far-reaching and ruinous. No weapon need be fired: The profligate expenditure of resources for nonproductive use has been enough in itself to undermine the economy and seriously weaken the fabric of society.

Fuel for Inflation

One result has been the spiraling inflation that bedevils every nation. Heavy military spending generates buying power without producing an equivalent supply of economically useful goods for the market. The excess of disposable income adds to pressure on prices and in time becomes a prescription for intractable inflation. A disproportionate number of its many victims are among the weakest members of society: The old suffer more than jobholders, the poor with marginal incomes more than the rich.

The $3 trillion that had been poured into military programs in the 1960s and early 1970s was a significant cause of the 1973 boom in world prices, although the abruptness of the break was attributed to the oil embargo. In that year the worldwide rise in consumer prices accelerated to 11 percent from the annual average of 4 percent that had been common in previous years. In 1974 the jump was 15 percent over 1973 levels. Stimulated by the continuing military strain on resources, the year-to-year increase has fluctuated between 10 and 15 percent ever since.

Productivity gains are slowed as military spending vies with civilian investment for the technology and capital goods that insure growth. It is a competition in which the bargaining power of the military is strengthened by cost-plus contracts. Innovation for civilian needs lags far behind the dramatic advances in weaponry. Military and space programs absorb more public research funds than do all civilian needs combined. As long as military requirements have priority, essential research that could yield new sources of energy, increase food production, provide better housing, improve health, foster employment, and in general improve the conditions of life generally will languish.

Sluggish Economy

The sluggish U.S. economy and the deterioration of the dollar may illustrate these consequences more effectively than would global data. From 1960 to 1979, while U.S. military expenditures grabbed 7 percent of gross national product (GNP) and investment was 14 percent of GNP, productivity grew less than 3 percent per year. In six other major industrialized countries for which data are available, the military burden was less; in all six, investment was higher and productivity rose more rapidly. Japan provided the most striking contrast: only 1 percent of its GNP went to military expenditures in this period; the rate of investment was double the U.S. rate and the growth of productivity over three times as fast.

Unemployment is another side effect of the arms race. As military purchases restrict investment and growth in the civilian economy, they limit the civilian job opportunities that are essential for an expanding labor force. Military-related jobs do not provide an adequate alternative. Government spending on weapons yields only half as many jobs as would equivalent funds spent on houses, schools, transit systems, and health services. Weapons production is capital intensive, and the relatively few jobs that it does provide tend to be concentrated in the higher-skill categories. For these reasons alone, weapons production puts an especially heavy burden on developing countries, which typically have large labor surpluses but relatively few trained workers.

Price inflation, a slower growth rate, and rising unemployment give only a partial picture of the impact of the arms race on society at large. Since they compete for finite government resources, military expenditures also have a direct and immediate effect on the allocation of funds to meet human needs. They divert resources from education, health, nutrition, and other basic needs of society, and severely reduce the aid that richer countries make available for the development of the poorer.

As a result, the gap between the rich and the poor of the world is widening at an alarming rate. The children for whom there are no schools, the adults who are illiterate, the people who suffer from chronic malnutrition, unclean water, a shortage of housing and medical care, are present in steadily growing numbers. In a world rich enough to spend $600 billion a year on an oversupply of military power, one person in three lives in painful poverty.

The developed world has one-fourth of the global population and over three-fourths of the global product. It also spends over three-fourths of the world's military budget. The economic aid that the rich, developed nations provide to the poor, developing ones is equivalent to about 6 percent of those rich countries' military expenditures. But in the developing countries, too, budgets are skewed in favor of military programs. Overall, the military outlay of developing nations is almost as large as all their public investment in the education and health care of their 3.2 billion people.

The Social Deficit

While governments worldwide give priority to military defense, the social deficit grows ever larger. The number of children requiring education increases faster than the schools to house them. An estimated 500 million school-age children are not in school. Among adults, there are more than 800 million in the world who can neither read nor write. The backlog of facilities for health care is even more pronounced. In developing nations only one person in five has access to medical care; most rural areas are without a single doctor. On the average, the rate of infant mortality is five times greater in developing than in developed nations; in some of the poorest countries it is 20 times greater than in the richest. Life expectancy ranges from 40 years in some of the poorest nations to 75 years in some of the richest.

Perhaps most shocking today of all unmet basic needs is adequate food for all humankind. Malnutrition is still the single most important public-health problem in the developing nations. An estimated 500 million people lack sufficient food to meet their minimum daily requirements of calories. In many areas two-thirds of the children are undernourished.

"As military purchases restrict investment and growth in the civilian economy, they limit the civilian job opportunities that are essential for an expanding labor force."

It is not only in the developing nations that millions are trapped in conditions of extreme want. The United States itself illustrates the appalling dimensions of a social deficit that leaves no nation untouched. In America 32 million people live below the poverty line, 8 million are unemployed, 1 million adults are illiterate, 10 million children are without basic health care. Among Western countries the United States has an exceptionally high crime rate. The death rate due to homicides is several times higher than in other developed nations. Public surveys in 1973 and 1974 indicated that 45 percent of Americans are afraid to walk alone in their neighborhoods at night.

In military strength the United States is the most powerful nation in the world. . . .Only eight nations can boast a total national income larger than the budget we devote to military defense. Yet we have been unable to buy national security, despite an investment in weapons unparalleled in history. Indeed, no nation has managed to buy security with military spending. On the contrary, by straining the world economy and fostering the neglect of social needs, the arms race has amplified instability and insecurity. It has itself become the major threat to international security.

Ruth Leger Sivard is now director of World Priorities, a nonprofit research organization. She was formerly chief of the economics division of the US Arms Control and Disarmament Agency.

"Many federally funded social programs now being cut—such as job training, higher education, child welfare and urban development programs—are direct investments in. . .our people."

viewpoint **30**

The Defense Budget Destroys Jobs and Social Programs

Coalition for a New Foreign and Military Policy

Real national security involves more than military strength—it also requires a realistic and sensible foreign policy, a healthy economy, and social policies that are fair and just. We need military strength as insurance against extreme threats, but bankrupting ourselves in the face of exaggerated fears undermines our security.

The huge sums being invested in new weaponry will not resolve the international challenges which we face. As Vietnam demonstrated, we invite disaster when we overestimate the usefulness of military force. Military posturing did not end the Arab oil embargo in 1974. The Shah's powerful U.S.-backed military could not save his rule. Clearly, the challenges we face internationally require a better political strategy, rather than simply more overkill.

In some ways, greater military spending increases the risk of war. We are now beginning to produce a whole new generation of accurate nuclear weapons, ushering in a dangerous new stage in the arms race.

More and more citizens are now actively opposing this new stage of the nuclear arms race and the huge transfer of federal funds out of social programs into the military. . . .

Taking Action

Of the 435 Congressional Districts, 306 lose jobs when the military budget goes up.

So 70% of the U.S. Senators and Representatives can be faced with the fact that a vote for a high military budget is a vote to wipe out jobs in their state or Congressional District.

Members of Congress know that there is no more potent issue than jobs. Any challenger in either a primary or a general election who can prove to the voters that the incumbent has been costing his or her District jobs is in a very strong position to win the election. . . .
Military industry is very capital intensive. This means

"Creating a Real National Security," Coalition for a New Foreign and Military Policy.

that military contractors buy a lot of elaborate machinery instead of hiring people. Civilian industries hire many more people. So each transfer of money from civilian industry to the Pentagon reduces the number of jobs generated in our economy.

Military Spending Means Fewer Jobs

If $1 billion was transferred from military industry to civilian industry, 9,000 more jobs would be created. One billion dollars used by state and local governments to hire teachers, firemen and police instead of military personnel would create 35,000 more jobs.

Women are particularly hard hit by high military spending. Since only 1% of the female work force are military personnel or work on military contracts, increases in military outlays create very few women's jobs. But women are more than one-half of those employed in services and state and local government—the two sectors which suffer most from military spending. Therefore, each transfer from these civilian sectors to the Pentagon dramatically reduces women's job opportunities.

The Social Costs of Unemployment

While undermining our economic vitality, unemployment strains the health of both families and communities. Individuals are forced to make choices between their basic needs: food or medicine, heat or clothing. A Congressional study by Dr. Harvey Brenner of Johns Hopkins University found that a sustained 1% increase in unemployment results in a 4% increase in the rate of homicides, suicides, and prison and mental hospital admissions. Overall mortality increases 1.9%. Thus, the 2% increase in unemployment during the 1981-82 recession led to an estimated 75,000 more deaths.

Unemployment shatters the hopes, self-regard and initiative of once productive citizens, and destroys the futures of many young people. It is a central cause of child abuse, domestic beatings, and the abuse of drugs and alcohol.

Unemployment places the burden of misdirected national priorities upon those who have worked hard to build our economy and society.

Strategy for Full Employment

Decades of high military budgets have placed heavy burdens upon our economy and our citizens.

By drawing scarce capital, resources, and skilled workers from the civilian economy, high military spending has undermined our ability to modernize our basic industries. Our nation is becoming non-competitive in automobiles, steel, textiles, and a host of other major industries.

We have already lost our international competitive edge. While we spend hundreds of billions of dollars each year on military programs, our economic competitors are investing their capital in new factories and technologies. Figures from the UN show that the United States is now only 7th among industrialized countries in per capita income, exceeded by Switzerland, Luxemburg, Denmark, Germany, Sweden and Belgium.

"If $1 billion was transferred from military industry to civilian industry, 9,000 more jobs would be created."

We cannot solve our economic problems by mining wilderness areas, and by giving tax breaks to corporations and the rich. We cannot rely on the unfounded myth of "trickle-down" economics. The solution is more sensible and more basic. We must act now to get our people back to work—rebuilding our industries and railroads, making more efficient cars and producing new sources of energy.

Our country's most productive asset is its working people. Right now, the skills and talents of many working people are being wasted. Millions are unemployed. Others are doing unproductive work in military industries. The skills and talents of these people could be more productively employed in the civilian economy.

Our economic situation is serious. If we are to reverse our economic decline and maintain our standard of living, we must create productive jobs. Economic recovery strategies that ignore the burdens placed on our economy by the endless demands of the Pentagon simply will not work.

Converting the Work Force

By reducing the role of the military in our economy we could create more stable jobs for American workers —and more jobs for all. Working people and their communities would no longer be subject to the "boom-bust" cycles of military build-ups. As a nation, we would be free to use our resources to address the pressing industrial, technological and social needs of our society.

Conversion from military to useful civilian production requires planning. But numerous government and private studies show that, since our most troubled industries require the same skills which are now being used in military industry, conversion can be successful.

Railroads

In a comprehensive report on the railroad industry, the Department of Transportation has projected that national rail demand will more than double between 1975 and 1990. The report concluded that, without a $145 billion investment in new rolling stock and railroad facilities, we will not be able to meet this demand.

The required investment in new rolling stock alone would create over 56,000 jobs each year over that 15-year period. 19,000 jobs would be created for semi-skilled workers (precision metalworkers, machine operators and welders) who are now employed in military industries. 13,000 jobs would be created each year for skilled workers, such as machinists, mechanics, and tool and die makers. The same investment in missile systems or ordnance would create only 15,400 semi-skilled and 9,700 skilled jobs each year.

Wind and Solar Energy

A major study by the Mid-Peninsula Conversion Project of California's defense-intensive "silicon valley" shows that the production of wind and solar energy systems would demand basically the same skills now used in military aerospace programs. Investment in wind and solar energy would create jobs for sheet metal workers, machinists and precision machine operators, as well as for mechanical design engineers, drafters and technicians.

Construction

Between 1980 and 1985, the Department of Defense will be spending at least $35 billion on the construction of **new** military facilities. Military contractors are employing significant numbers of building trades workers. These workers could be constructing new homes and mass transit systems, and installing solar heating systems, rather than constructing ever more military facilities. $35 billion could build 440,000 new homes at $80,000 apiece.

The Myth About Social Programs

Contrary to the rhetoric used by those supporting bigger military budgets, there is nothing wasteful about social programs. Many federally funded social programs now being cut—such as job training, higher education, child welfare and urban development programs—are direct investments in the health, productivity and happiness of our people.

Programs like Food Stamps, when added to Social Security and AFDC, have made a big difference in improving the health of our citizenry. Since 1970, largely due to better nutrition, infant mortality among the poor has been reduced by 33%, and outbreaks of diseases related to poverty and malnutrition are down by 50%.

In FY 1983, President Reagan wants to cut the childhood immunization program by $2 million, eliminating immunizations for 50,000 children at risk. At the same time he seeks to spend $1.4 million on shots and other veterinary services for the pets of military personnel.

"Economic recovery strategies that ignore the burdens placed on our economy by the endless demands of the Pentagon simply will not work."

Where is the real source of government waste?

Unemployment, economic decline and the chance of war threaten the security and the standard of living of America's working people. That is why we must reduce military spending and use our energy and talents to address our real security problems here at home.

The Coalition for a New Foreign and Military Policy supports a demilitarized, humanitarian, non-interventionist foreign policy for the US.

"We cut back and introduced all of our massive social programs, so that today we have more 'tax eaters' than we have taxpayers."

Social Sacrifice Must Be Made for Defense

Thomas H. Moorer

When World War II ended, three things should have been evident that would affect our defense and foreign policies in the years ahead. They were:

(1) Nuclear weapons had imparted a new dimension to warfare, which meant that the United States would no longer be able to stand behind the world's two largest oceans and prepare for a war *after* it had started. We would have to be ready *before* it started;

(2) In the future, wherever a crisis occurred, the United States would be involved, because the world had changed drastically. . .our Britain and French allies were fast losing their world-wide bases of power, leaving us virtually alone to shoulder responsibilities around the globe;

(3) The Soviets, before the guns ceased firing in 1946, were embarked upon a grand scheme of world conquest. They fomented trouble in Europe. . .they strongly supported the North Koreans in the Korean War and the North Vietnamese in the Vietnam War—simply because they wanted to make the maximum number of problems for the United States as they advanced their scheme of conquest.

Americans Bad Negotiators

After World War II, we had a national policy called "Containment", but in Lyndon Johnson's administration, we began to talk about strategic arms limitation, and to negotiate. But unfortunately, in my opinion, Americans are the world's worst negotiators!

This is because we are an impatient people, and when given a job, we want to get it over with in a hurry! So we always have a fallback position. . .and then another fallback position, and another. Finally, we lose sight of the objectives of the negotiations and begin to think they are for the purpose of making an agreement rather than to protect the interests of the United States of America!

Thomas H. Moorer, "A Realistic Look at National Defense," *Americanism Educational League.*

In any event, as we negotiated, and even as the Russians began to expand, we were making radical cuts in our defense budgets and our forces. When I was Chief of Naval Operations—1967-70—we had over 900 U.S. Navy ships; today we have less than 500. We were spending 43% of the federal budget on defense; today, it's less than 25%. We were spending about 9-1/2% of gross national product on defense; now it's under 5%.

Added Social Programs

Yes, we cut back and introduced all of our massive social programs, so that today we have more "tax eaters" than we have taxpayers. And what have the Russians been doing over those same years?

Today the Soviets have seven new types of missiles, built while we were building one. They have a fine air defense system, and we do not. They have a very disciplined Civil Defense system, and we do not. They have a quick-acting decision-making process, while our process is enmeshed in endless red tape. They have an excellent intelligence system, while in recent years ours has been almost destroyed.

Soviet military personnel are recruited and paid virtually on a slave-labor basis, as compared to our standards, so that over 70% of their defense budget can go for hardware as contrasted with less than 50% of ours. In addition, the Soviets have established a world-wide presence through strategically located bases, while the number of bases we have access to has been reduced in a few years time from 130 to less than 30 today.

Russia Wants WW III

In my opinion, Russia is already fighting World War III. In Africa, they are fighting a resource war, maneuvering to gain control of the vast, unprotected resources of that huge continent. In Central America, we have given up our Canal in Panama; Nicaragua is now completely Communist; the Soviets are inciting revolution in Guatemala; on the island of Grenada, they are building a 15,000-foot air strip. . .to control the access and approaches to the Panama Canal!

The Middle East is also under Soviet attack, and it is vitally important to the U.S.A. and to our allies, because so much of our oil comes from that region. Our foreign policy in the Middle East is in effect an energy policy. . .and we are tragically weak today in our ability to project a strong presence in that area.

"I learned recently in New York City that you can now send your kids to see a matinee of Hansel and Gretel *for $34. If the American people can afford that, they can afford to build a proper defense!"*

With the Indian Ocean to worry about now, as well as the Atlantic and the Pacific, we are trying to handle a *three-ocean* problem with a *one-and-a-half* ocean Navy. . .and that's most difficult to do!

Must Make Personal Sacrifices

The cold fact is that we absolutely have got to turn this whole situation around if we are to continue to be the kind of country we've all known and loved. We will have to make real sacrifices—personal sacrifices—if we are going to restore the position of our country to where it should be.

For example, I learned recently in New York City that you can now send your kids to see a matinee of *Hansel and Gretel* for $34. If the American people can afford that, they can afford to build a proper defense!

Admiral Thomas H. Moorer was Chief of Naval Operations from 1967-70 and Chairman of the Joint Chiefs of Staff from 1970-1974, when he retired.

"When it's guns or butter we're a pretty fat country and survival comes before feeding your face."

viewpoint 32

A Larger Budget Will Improve the Military

Ray Saidel

In support of the administration's defense budget it seems necessary to point up the obvious and basic. While it is impossible to judge exactly how many dollars are needed to provide the essential tools for defense, it is far better to err on the plus side. The nuclear missile age makes "too little" and/or "too late" a formula for disaster.

Despite near unanimous accord (last year) on this need, there now seems a great likelihood that defense expenditures will be seriously cut and security endangered. Some of these reasons have been previously addressed, some not.

Defense has been endangered by an incompetent secretary of defense—Caspar Weinberger. The former Bechtel Corporation executive may have been great guns working with the Arab oil cartel, but he has been a bust as head of the U.S. defense establishment. If Weinberger had developed a comprehensive defense policy, if he had pressed for restructuring the joint chiefs (a general staff would seen more appropriate today), if he had shown more procurement costing—if, if, if—then we might not have had the public, press and politicians clamoring for cuts.

But Weinberger is a defense official with an axe to grind. He visualizes himself as the secretary of state, and often appropriates that job. His particular obsession is Middle East policy and he uses the full power of the Defense Department to press Israel in a manner that must bring much cheer to his friends in Saudi Arabia—where his heart lies. This reversal of U.S. policy will, in the end, cost us our only effective democratic ally in the region.

Threat to Civilization

And then, there is the press/TV induced public failure of will. Has the Korea/Vietnam/Desert One no-win syndrome so sapped our national vitality that we are not

willing to bear the cost for survival of this still best yet hope of humankind—our threatened Western civilization? Truly this may be an underlying, subconscious reason for much of the West's illogical hostility toward Israel's courageous and successful defense of its interests (i.e., resentment that a tiny country dared to inflict a defeat on a Soviet client—the only defeat suffered by the communist bloc since World War II. Can they be allowed to do what the great and powerful haven't the energy or principle to do?). . .Have we sunk this low? Is the "yellow-ribbon" and the "candle-in-the-window" (Vietnam and Poland) our best American response to aggression? Is this deterrence?

History is replete with examples of societies, advanced for their age, which were able but unwilling to inconvenience themselves sufficiently to bear the "high cost" of adequate defense—they preferred defense on the cheap. Invariably they were defeated, destroyed.

Inflation Is 'Small Potatoes'

President Reagan, and I oppose him vigorously on many matters, is dead right on his defense budget. Unfortunately, many others who just a short time ago seemed to see the light of reason—the snowballing Soviet threat—now sniff election winds and find defense dollars not so desirable (political winter soldiers are few). They natter about future inflation. But America's future existence is the issue and inflation is small potatoes when balanced against survival. Either we need a viable defense or we do not. It should not be an "economic" decision. Besides, economic problems will not be solved by defense deferrals that will raise tomorrow's needs and costs to impossible levels.

The argument is put that there is waste in defense. Certainly, and it is huge. But there is also enormous waste in social services, in public works and in other worthy endeavors. That is no reason to wash one's hands of them. Too often we take the easy way, throw the baby out with the bath water, and cry later.

Ray Saidel, "Defense Budget This Time Will Be a Test of Our National Will," *Union Leader*, March 24, 1983. Reprinted with permission.

131

It's difficult to write on this subject without cliches because the truths are eternal and should be self-evident. If we value our freedom, that is, if we really understand what it is to be free, the responsibility, and if we really recognize the fantastic degree of freedom we truly enjoy then it should be easy to keep priorities in order.

When it's guns or butter we're a pretty fat country and survival comes before feeding your face. When it's build now or defer defense purchases to a later time (defense as a convenience), that's a recipe for disaster. When it's defense or jobs (a phony issue) the poor value freedom too, friend.

Need and National Will

The issue is need and national will. The Soviet threat is obvious. It has been so well and frequently documented by independent experts, as well as defense and intelligence services of the free nations, that I refuse to review it here. Anyone still not convinced never will be—in time. So it is up to those who do understand the immediacy of the danger, and the tragedy of another (and possibly final) reversal of defense policy in this critical decade, to rally to the aid of the President in this debate. For the sake of country, children and self-respect we must not shirk this responsibility. To paraphrase Sidney Hook—those who make economic survival their supreme value are declaring that there is nothing they will not betray.

Ray Saidel is a research associate at The Center For International Security at Washington DC.

"Inflated military budgets encourage the Pentagon to design and buy ever more complex and questionable weapons."

A Larger Budget Will Not Improve the Military

Steven L. Canby

There is a clear answer to those punishing federal deficits and high interest rates: drastic cutbacks in outyear defense increases. To voice this is to be unpatriotic. Certainly we all want strong defenses. But is more defense really being obtained?

Inflated military budgets encourage the Pentagon to design and buy ever more complex and questionable weapons. We all know the amusing story of aircraft becoming so costly the Air Force can buy but one per year. We all know too the wasteful infighting among the services.

Now the military chiefs themselves are calling for reform of the Joint Chiefs of Staff. Implicit is that the present system leads to poor planning and poor use of resources. The first was apparent on the desert of Iran. The second is apparent in the Navy seeking more carriers for a task which could be done on the cheap by retrofitting B-52s for a long-range maritime air force.

Waste in the military is pervasive. NATO outspends the Warsaw Pact by 10 percent when measured in dollars and at least 25 percent when measured in rubles (CIA estimates). NATO has equal numbers under arms in peacetime. In Central Europe, in the Mutual Balanced Force Reductions guidelines area plus France, NATO actually has 200,000 more personnel in its air and ground forces.

Yet with less strength, the Warsaw Pact has three times the combat numbers and equipment.

NATO is simply being out-organized. The US Army requires three times more men to field a division than the Soviet Army. The US Air Force requires four times the men per combat aircraft than the Swedish and Israeli air forces.

For that matter, the Air National Guard is three times more cost-effective than the active Air Force. With this type of *structural* waste, is there any wonder the US

gets so little bang for the buck?

The administration's defense program does not address these issues. In 1987, the US will be no better off militarily than today. We still lose in NATO, Korea and the Gulf. At sea, we may have two additional carrier groups and we may sink the Soviet surface fleet more quickly. Little else will have changed.

Costly But Ineffective Defense

Our carriers remain vulnerable to antiship missiles and the carriers remain only marginally useful in other missions *vis a vis* the USSR. Where the carriers are most useful in force projection, only a few are needed at any one time. (Yes, the British needed big carriers in the Falklands. Two would have done nicely, thank you.)

The conclusion is inescapable. America's defense is costly but ineffective. For what we are paying *now*, we could in fact be obtaining (conventional) military superiority in Europe, Korea, and the Gulf. Similarly, at less cost, we could attain more relevant capabilities at sea.

The NATO imbalance has always been in ground forces. The US does not have the requisite divisions. Even if it did, only a few could be stationed permanently in Europe. Most could never arrive in time to be relevant.

Worse, the very attempt to do so allows the Europeans to opt out of their responsibilities. They have the resources to defend themselves. They even have the trained manpower in their reserves. But they have never organized them into divisions; nor bought the equipment for them (as they have done in the past).

The Europeans could triple their divisions at a steady state cost of $9 billion per year, which is a 15 percent increase in continental defense budgets. Alternatively, the money could be obtained by reducing continental air and naval forces by one-third. A 400-plane reduction could be readily replaced from the pool of 3,500 aircraft the US does not deploy to Europe in a NATO conflict.

Steven Canby, "Strong Defense Does Not Need More Money," *The Christian Science Monitor*, August 23, 1982. Reprinted with author's permission.

133

In this manner NATO could at no additional cost nearly triple its divisions (in the same manner as the Russians) while holding air power constant and eliminating the need for early reinforcement across the North Atlantic.

In Korea the deficiency is purely due to the design of the defense. Every European army learned in World War I that forces on forward slopes of hills will be smashed by an opponent having heavy artillery. Nor in mountainous terrain is a cordon (linear) defense feasible without strong reserves. These are not available until after mobilization. In the interim, holes can be smashed in South Korean defenses and light infantry passed through to collapse the defense while North Korean main forces move up and their tanks preempt further organized resistance. The US and South Korean military have still not absorbed the lessons of the Korean War—though excellent foreign discourses exist.

"The conclusion is inescapable. America's defense is costly but ineffective."

For the Rapid Deployment Force and the Persian Gulf, the deficiency is again the design of American forces. We are using standard infantry when specialized light infantry is required. Standard infantry was designed for warfare in the open flatlands. Its use in mountainous terrain (e.g., Italy in World War II and Korea) has been limited and distinctly inauspicious.

Ensuring Defense

Yet there is a much-tested method of combat in mountains. Adoption of widely used foreign tactics (e.g., British tactics in the Falklands and Israeli para infantry) would allow the US to defeat a Soviet invasion through Iran at a *third* of the size now being projected precisely because Soviet forces are so tank heavy.

It is these practices—there are many more—that explain the high cost and low effectiveness of Western military forces, US forces in particular. More money is not needed. Different practices and strategies are needed. Present military practices are bankrupt. For these should we now bankrupt our economies as well?

The present course ensures neither defense nor economic recovery. President Reagan's announcement of true military reform would lead to the biggest Wall Street rally ever!

Steven L. Canby is an economist and Washington-based defense analyst.

"A war would end very soon if any nuclear weapons, however small, were actually to be detonated by any side on any target."

European Nuclear Weapons Are Meant to Be Used

Edward N. Luttwak

Now that the United States is belatedly acting to restore a tolerable balance in forces nuclear as well as conventional, a vast chorus of protest has been heard from those who hold that deterrence is a policy not merely dangerous but irrational, and who therefore demand an immediate "freeze." Others have made a narrower protest, against the reliance of the United States and its allies on nuclear deterrence to dissuade a Soviet invasion that might be accomplished by the great non-nuclear forces of the Soviet army. And then there has been the broadest of claims, in which pastors and priests, rabbis and bishops, have been most prominent: that nuclear deterrence, and indeed nuclear weapons as such, are in themselves immoral.

Along with the arguments and the claims there has been a great outpouring of horrific imagery of Hiroshima and its victims, of mushroom clouds and radiation burns—imagery abundantly relayed in the complaisant press and in the visual media. The purpose has been to frighten those whom the arguments have not persuaded, so that the electorate which deliberately rejected Carter's strategy of weakness might now be terrorized into repudiating Reagan's strategy of strength.

Yet instead of reaffirming its strategy, the Reagan administration has for the most part responded to the arguments and the claims, to the words and the manipulative imagery, by appeasing the protesters, the churchmen, and the media. From those who once could explain quite lucidly the fundamental and unchanging reasons for the inevitable failure of arms control, we now hear much talk about the virtues of that very process. From those who started off resolutely determined to explain strategic realities, we now hear only great declarations of their love for peace, their revulsion against war, and their sincere dislike of nuclear weapons. Outside the Administration, too, all manner of

people once very attentive to the delicate texture of strategy have now come forward to mollify protest by offering schemes and plans designed to reduce the role of nuclear weapons in our defense, sometimes offering a non-nuclear substitute, and sometimes not.

And yet every one of the claims which sustain the protests large and small is false; each of the arguments, both strategic and moral, can be utterly refuted.

The "front" that the North Atlantic Treaty Organization sustains against the Soviet Union and its client-states divides not nations but political systems. On the one side there is the system of production, of individual welfare and social amelioration, while on the other side there is a system that proclaims those same goals very loudly, even while subordinating them to the preservation of totalitarian control and the accumulation of superior military power.

If nuclear weapons were now disinvented, if all the hopes of the nuclear disarmers were fully realized, the Soviet Union would automatically emerge as the dominant power on the continent, fully capable of invading and conquering Western Europe and beyond if its political domination were resisted.

Comparing Conventional Power

But why should that be so in a non-nuclear world? After all, our side has all the men and all the means that would be needed to outmatch the conventional forces of the other side. Already now, by the storekeeper's method of making up an inventory, the forces of NATO can appear as strong as or even stronger than those of the Soviet Union and its not-necessarily-reliable client-states. Compare, for example, total manpower in uniform, on active duty: 4.9 million for NATO and the United States versus 4.8 million for the Soviet Union and its client-states (and remember that out of that total the Soviet Union must provide the large forces deployed against the Chinese). Compare total manpower in ground forces: 2.7 million for us ver-

Edward Luttwak, "Western Europe Needs a Nuclear Option," *Commentary*, August 1982. Reprinted from *Commentary* August 1982, by permission; all rights reserved.

sus 2.6 million for them (with the same Chinese qualification, to make us feel even better). Compare total ground forces in Europe itself: 2.1 million on our side and only 1.7 million on the other (and one must make allowance for Polish, Hungarian, and other client-state troops that prudent Soviet military planners would not want to rely upon except to add sheer mass to a successful offensive). In naval forces, the U.S.-NATO advantage is large in almost every category, even if ships are counted by the prow, as in Homer, and not by tonnage (in which Western superiority is still greater).

If one delights in these comparisons, one can come up with more numbers that are comforting. But there are also some other numbers that are less reassuring. Tanks: 17,053 for NATO in Europe (U.S. included) versus a total of 45,500 on the other side, including 32,200 in reliable Soviet hands (Hitler had only some 3,000 in 1941 for "Barbarossa," the German invasion of Russia); artillery pieces: 9,502 versus 19,446; surface-to-surface missile launchers: 355 versus 1,224 for the Soviet camp (all the nuclear warheads are in Soviet hands exclusively); antitank guns (a rather antique category by conventional wisdom): 964 versus 3,614.

"If nuclear weapons were now disinvented. . .the Soviet Union would automatically emerge as the dominant power on the continent."

As for combat aircraft in Europe, the numbers go the same way: 2,293 fighter-bombers for NATO-Europe versus 3,255 in Soviet and Warsaw Pact air forces (but predominantly Soviet); fighters: only 204 on the NATO side (the U.S. Air Force believes in heavier multipurpose aircraft) versus 1,565 on the other side; interceptors (another depreciated category): 572 on the part of NATO versus 1,490 in Pact air forces.

The Real Story

Each set of numbers means little in itself. But ignoring all the details, there is one very striking fact that emerges—a fact that begins to tell us the real story about the "military balance" on which there is so much controversy now that McGeorge Bundy, George F. Kennan, Robert S. McNamara, and Gerard Smith have jointly proposed that NATO should renounce the "first use" of nuclear weapons to deter a nuclear invasion. That fact, indeed very remarkable, is that the rich are seemingly armed as poor men are armed, with rifles, while the poor are armed as rich men, with heavy weapons. Recalling that comparison of "total ground forces in Europe" in which NATO is shown with 2.1 million troops on active duty versus a mere 1.7 million for the Warsaw Pact—a ration of 1.27:1 in favor of our side—we now discover that the ratios for the major

weapons which modern ground forces need go the other way, in favor of the Soviet side: 2.65:1 for tanks; 2.05:1 for artillery; 3.45:1 for missile launchers; and so on.

More remarkable still, the poorer and less advanced have more combat aircraft, by ratios of 4.5:1 (bombers), 1.4:1 (fighter-bombers), 7.67:1 (fighters), 2.61:1 (interceptors), and so on. Never mind that on each side one should sort out old aircraft in each category, and never mind also that Soviet aircraft are judged inferior to their U.S. counterparts (though to take Israeli-Syrian combat outcomes as an index is totally misleading, since Soviet aircraft would do very nicely in Israeli hands, just as they performed quite well against our own fighter-bombers in Vietnam, and also in Indian hands against the Pakistanis). In spite of all qualifications large and small, the fact stands, and it is a great fact: the poor are far more abundantly armed, even in air power, which is the quintessential arm of the rich.

How can this be? What does this mean? How and why have the rich come to be poorly armed as compared with the Soviet Union (whose gross national product is now 60 per cent of the American and a mere 25 per cent of the U.S.-NATO total)? There is, of course, a very simple answer revealed by the statistics themselves. That famous number, the count of NATO ground forces in Europe in the amount of 2.1 million (as compared to 1.7 million for the Pact), is actually made up of 980,000 men in the armies of Western Europe and another 922,000 men in the Greek, Italian, and Turkish armies which mainly consist of lightly armed infantry disqualified by location, training, and equipment from fighting seriously against Soviet-style armored divisions.

But that too is no more than a circumstantial fact: it is not the ineluctable consequence of unalterable limits. NATO *could* have forces much larger *and* better equipped *and* in the right places, for it has a much larger population than the Pact, and also a far greater production. Why then do our richer allies in Western Europe fail to remedy the imbalance? Is it greed that dissuades them from spending enough, or is it perhaps defeatism? Both are in evidence in some degree. But the decisive reason is strategic: those in Europe who understand such matters know that an increased effort would not improve the balance unless it were truly huge, because there are two fundamental military factors at work which make NATO weak and the Soviet Union strong—and these are of such powerful effect in combination that they would nullify the benefits of any marginal increase in defense spending, just as they already outweigh every one of the disadvantages that afflict the Soviet Union, including the unreliability of some of its East European subjects, the hostility of China, and the technical inferiority of some Soviet weapons. Much more than the numbers, it is these two factors that truly determine the present military imbalance in nonnuclear strength.

NATO Is for Defense

The first of the two fundamental military factors is, quite simply, that NATO is a defensive alliance—defensive not just in declared intent, as all self-respecting alliances will claim to be, but rather in actual military orientation. Specifically, the forces of NATO on the "central front"—the 600-kilometer line running from the Baltic Sea to the Austrian border—are incapable of offensive operations on a large scale. There are no plans for a NATO offensive against East Germany; there has never been suitable training, or any army-sized exercises for offensive action. In spite of the abundant claims to the contrary in Soviet propaganda at its most implausible, Soviet military planners must know that NATO could not launch an offensive against their front. The notion that Belgian, Dutch, British, German, and U.S. forces would suddenly march across the border to invade is quite simply fantastic.

This means that the Soviet high command can concentrate its own forces for offensive action without having to allocate significant strength for defense. To be sure, many Soviet divisions are either deployed on or assigned to the very long Chinese border. But there too the Soviet Union need not disperse its forces to provide a territorial defense, since the Chinese, for all their millions of troops and tens of millions of rifle-armed militiamen, have no real capacity to mount significant offensive operations. At the very most, at a time of great opportunity such as a Soviet attack upon the West might present, the Chinese could mount a very limited and very shallow move against some segment of the Trans-Siberian railway where it runs near their territory.

> "What the European system. . .needs is a preclusive method of protection, not ultimate victory after much destruction and millions of deaths."

The Soviet army, which was greatly diminished in size during the 1950s but which has grown again during the last two decades, can now mobilize so many divisions that it can cover the Chinese border very adequately; provide more divisions to maintain a threat against Iran, Eastern Turkey, and Pakistan; keep the forces now in place in Afghanistan; and still send more divisions against the "central front" than NATO could cope with.

A Soviet Offensive

Not counting at all the divisions of the East European client-states (even though some at least could in fact be used), the arithmetic runs as follows: if 10 more Soviet divisions are added to the Chinese "front" (in addition to the 46 stationed there already); and if a further 18

divisions are kept in reserve to deal with all the contingencies that a prudent and well-provided military leadership can imagine; and if there is no reduction in the generous allowance of 26 divisions now deployed on the Soviet Union's "southern front" (opposite the under-equipped Turks, the chaotic Persians, and in Afghanistan); then finally, the Soviet Union, upon mobilization, could launch 80 divisions against NATO in Central Europe—that is, against the West German border. And since NATO is a defensive-only alliance, the Soviet army could concentrate its forces in powerful offensive thrusts aimed at narrow segments of that front.

By another estimate, produced by the International Institute for Strategic Studies, the Soviet army could send a total of 118 divisions against NATO, the greater number being obtained by assuming that no central reserve is maintained at all (the Soviet Union does after all keep 500,000 KGB and MVD troops, which are heavily armed) and that no reinforcement would be made to the Chinese "front."

As against this, NATO can claim a total of 116 divisions, only two fewer than the higher estimate of the Soviet divisions that could be sent against it—and actually 36 divisions more than the Soviet total estimated more conservatively.

But that is truly a hollow number, since NATO's 116 divisions include more than 16 American National Guard divisions that would have to be mobilized remanned, re-equipped (with what?), trained for weeks or months, and then transported to Europe by way of ports and airfields benevolently left intact by Soviet forces. The 116 divisions include more than 29 Italian, Greek, and Turkish divisions that are stationed far from Central Europe and are neither trained nor equipped to fight on that front. And they include 9 other divisions of foot infantry of various kinds. Once all these make-weights are removed from the count, we discover that against 80 Soviet divisions, NATO might field no more than 58 divisions of its own, including more than 12 French divisions whose participation in a fight is uncertain but whose scant armament for such combat is, unfortunately, not in doubt.

In fact, we might estimate even more truly by measuring NATO forces in terms of *Soviet* division-equivalents, whereupon we obtain 35 divisions upon full mobilization and with the transfer of all earmarked U.S. forces. The numerical imbalance thus finally emerges as a sharp one indeed: 80 Soviet divisions versus 35 for NATO. And then the defense/offense asymmetry intervenes to make the true combat imbalance even greater, since the Soviet divisions can be concentrated during an offensive against a few narrow segments of the front while NATO's divisions must defend all along a 600-kilometer border.

A Soviet Armored Blitzkrieg

Under any circumstances, the numerical imbalance in

real capabilities would make things very difficult for NATO. But it would not be decisive were it not for the second great factor that makes NATO weak, which arises from the very nature of armored warfare. Nowadays, there is only one army in the world that has actual hands-on expertise in the reality of armored warfare, in the combined use of large numbers of tanks, troop carriers, and self-propelled artillery to stage offensives of deep penetration, whereby enemy forces are not merely destroyed piecemeal by fire-fights but are defeated by being cut off and forced into surrender—and that, of course, is the Israeli army. But if there is one army in the world that seriously strives to overcome its lack of recent and relevant combat experience, it is the Soviet army. It is the only one which stages vast army-sized exercises to educate its officers and men in the broad art and the detailed craft of armored warfare.

"If NATO could not hold the front by non-nuclear combat, it would warn the Soviet Union that (small-yield) nuclear weapons would be used."

The Soviet army would not be lined up unit by unit along the 600 kilometers of the German frontier, there to fight it out in head-on combat with the forces of NATO similarly arrayed (hence the worthlessness of inventory comparisons which imply such front-to-front combat). Instead, its 80 divisions would be formed into deep columns and multiple echelons poised to advance by swift penetrations of narrow segments of the front. Having learned the art of armored warfare in the hard school of war itself, at the hands of the best masters, and having made the method at once simpler and much more powerful by employing the sheer mass of great numbers to relieve the need for fancy German-style maneuvers, the Soviet army would not employ its forces to launch a set-piece offensive on a preplanned line of advance (which would be detectable and vulnerable), but would instead seek to advance opportunistically, just as water flows down a slope, its rivulets seeking the faster paths. Initially, the advance regiments would probe for gaps and weak sectors through which a swift passage might be achieved. Any Soviet forces that could make no progress would be left in place, to keep up the threat and prevent the NATO commands from switching their forces to strengthen the front elsewhere. But Soviet reinforcements would only be sent where successful advances were being achieved in order to add to the momentum. First more regiments, then divisions, then entire "armies" would thus be channeled forward to keep up the pressure and push deep into the rear of the NATO front.

By feeding reinforcement echelons into avenues of

penetration successfully opened, the Soviet high command could obtain the full effect of the classic *Blitzkrieg* even without having to rely on the skill and initiative of regimental officers, as the Germans once did. Instead of a fluid penetrating maneuver obtained by free improvisation, theirs would be an advance just as fast, achieved by mass and momentum directed from above.

Soon enough, advancing Soviet columns would begin to disrupt the entire defensive structure of NATO, by cutting across roads on which Western reinforcements and resupply depend by overrunning artillery batteries, command centers, supply depots, and finally airfields—until the very ports of entry on the Atlantic shore would be reached. With NATO's front cut in several places, with Soviet forces already in their deep rear, the choices open to NATO formations in such non-nuclear combat would be either to stand and fight for honor's sake even without true military purpose, or else to retreat—thus opening further gaps in the front. In any case, the relentless advance would soon enough impose a broader choice at a much higher level of decision, for the Germans first and the others not much later: capitulation or military destruction.

Thus in the absence of nuclear weapons, it is not the numerical imbalance in itself that would bring the dismal results, but rather the fact that the Soviet army has a valid method of offensive war, while NATO for its part has no valid method of defense. For obviously the envisaged attempts to block Soviet advances by switching defensive forces back and forth along the line (right in front of Soviet forces which would have every opportunity to disrupt such lateral movement by fire and by their own thrusts) must fail. Indeed, it can be said that even if NATO had a perfect numerical equality, it would still find it impossible to match Soviet concentrations with its own, in order to block their advance right at the front line itself. The reason for this inherent defect is not any lack of military expertise on the part of NATO commanders and planners (although their unfamiliarity with modern armored warfare does show when some pronounce on the military balance by the bookkeeper's method). The defect rather is caused by the combination of NATO's defensive-only orientation and the character of large-scale armored warfare.

A Nuclear Option is Vital

In the face of an offensive threat by an armored-mobile army (unless the defenders are *vastly* superior in sheer strength), one of two conditions must obtain to make a successful defense possible: either the defenders must be ready and willing to attack first, in order to disrupt an offensive preemptively; or else the defense must have considerable geographic space in which to maneuver and fight in a defense-in-depth strategy. If NATO had the political will, the training, and the organization to strike first in the face of massing Soviet forces, the latter could not safely form up in deep columns for the attack and would instead have to dilute their strength to form a defensive array of their own.

This option is purely theoretical in NATO's case. It is impossible to imagine that so many diverse governments would agree to let their national forces engage in a preemptive attack to anticipate a Soviet invasion before the outbreak of war. More likely, in the face of a Soviet mobilization and a build-up of divisions opposite NATO, there would be demands for negotiations to settle the crisis by what would no doubt be called "political means," i.e., eager concessions.

As compared with a wholly unrealistic strategy of preemptive attack, the second opinion, a defense-in-depth, may seem a feasible alternative; and it would offer the possibility of a very powerful defense indeed for NATO. Under such a strategy, Soviet invasion columns would *not* be intercepted by NATO's main defensive forces right in the border zone. Instead, advancing Soviet forces would encounter only a mere border guard along the frontier itself, thereafter being harassed, delayed, and clearly revealed by light and elusive forces as they continued to advance, being steadily weakened by the loss of momentum imposed by time, distance, breakdowns, mined barriers, multiple obstacles at river crossing points, canals, and towns—and also by successive battles with strongholds along the way. Then too, NATO air forces operating quite freely over their own territory, where Soviet air defenses would be very weak, could attack advancing Soviet forces heavily and frequently. Only then would the major combat on the ground finally take place, with fresh NATO divisions maneuvering to strike at the stretched-out and by then ill-supplied Soviet columns (air strikes would do much more damage to supply vehicles than to the Soviet armored forces themselves).

"A better response to such a Soviet threat would be possible if by then NATO had acquired its own theater nuclear forces."

In such a setting, with a thin line of NATO covering forces on the border itself, with multiple barriers and strongholds in depth, and with the main line of resistance 100 or 200 kilometers to the rear, NATO could indeed have a very solid non-nuclear defense, and one which could moreover deter non-nuclear invasion all by itself—since any competent Soviet planner would have to estimate that defeat would be the most likely outcome. And that, of course, would be a defeat which would deprive the Soviet army of one-half of its divisions, and thus the Soviet empire of much of its gendarmerie as well as all of its prestige, no doubt triggering unrest at home and perhaps outright insurrection in the client-states.

But to imagine such a defense in depth for the NATO central front in Germany is not to consider a live op-

tion. It is, rather, to indulge in sheer fantasy—and malevolent fantasy at that. For that zone of deep combat happens to correspond to the territory where tens of millions of Germans live. Quite rightly, what the Germans demand is not merely an eventual ability to defeat an aggression at some ultimate point in time and in space, but rather an actual provision of security for themselves, their families, their homes, and their towns. The British, French, or Americans might obtain satisfaction from the defeat of an invading Soviet army in the depth of West German territory, but such a victory would be of little worth to the Germans themselves. What the European system of peaceful construction needs is a preclusive method of protection, not ultimate victory after much destruction and millions of deaths.

In the absence of an offensive capacity by NATO and a lively willingness to preempt invasion, such protection can only be assured by nuclear weapons—or more precisely, by the architecture of nuclear deterrence which is now in place. If the Soviet Union does attack, its offensive would be met in the first instance by a non-nuclear defense of the forward areas close to the border. If NATO could not hold the front by non-nuclear combat, it would warn the Soviet Union that (small-yield) nuclear weapons would be used to strike at the invading Soviet forces. And then it would strike with such weapons if the warning went unheeded.

At that point the Soviet Union would realize that the alliance was standing up to the test, that it did have the will to defend itself in its moment of truth. One Soviet reaction might be to call off the war—a quite likely response if the invasion has been launched out of some hope of gain, but much less likely if it were the desperate last act of a crumbling empire.

Another Soviet reaction might be to respond to the threat by a wider threat against the cities of Europe, or else— and more likely—to reply in kind. With its own forces weakened by nuclear attack, it might employ nuclear weapons to make its invasion easier, by blasting gaps through the NATO defenses. Or else, the Soviet Union might want to avoid the intermediate steps, and try to impose a capitulation by threatening to attack European cities if any more battlefield nuclear weapons were used.

An Answer in Kind

Such a verbal threat might in turn be averted by being answered in kind, in the first instance perhaps by the British and the French—assuming that their cities had also come under the threat. But a better response to such a Soviet threat would be possible if by then NATO had acquired its own theater nuclear forces which, like the Soviet forces that already exist in considerable numbers, would be suitable to threaten not merely cities indiscriminately, but rather such specific targets as political and military command centers, airfields, nuclear storage sites, and even large concentrations of ground forces—that threat being all the more credible for being less catastrophic.

Much more complex exchanges and many more variations can be envisaged. But by far the most likely outcome is that a war would end very soon if any nuclear weapons, however small, were actually to be detonated by any side on any target. The shock effect upon leaders on both sides—but especially on the Soviet leaders who had started the war—and also the devastating psychological impact upon the forces in the field, would most likely arrest the conflict there and then. It is fully to be expected that military units whose men would see the flash, hear the detonation, feel the **blast, or merely hear of such things, would swiftly.** disintegrate, except perhaps for a handful of units particularly elite, and also remote from the immediate scene. The entire "software" of discipline, of morale, of unit cohesion and *esprit de corps* and all the practices and habits that sustain the authority of sergeants, officers, and political commissars, are simply not built to withstand such terror as nuclear weapons would cause—even if at the end of the day it were to be discovered that the dead on all sides were surprisingly few.

The time has come to deal forthrightly with the antinuclear agitation. To do as the Reagan administration has done, to concede and appease, is highly dangerous. Because if the false argument is admitted, sound strategy is thereby delegitimized and then in due course policies of weakness will inevitably follow through congressional decision and public pressure.

If, for example, the Bundy-Kennan-McNamara-Smith proposal is accepted on the argument that it is good public relations to do so, and that only a verbal change would be involved, it will soon be discovered that once NATO's "first-use" policy is renounced it will be impossible to obtain approval for the upkeep of battlefield nuclear weapons. Why, it will be said, should we keep those nuclear-capable guns so near the border if we no longer seek to deter a non-nuclear invasion by nuclear deterrence? Thus the nuclear shells of the artillery will be withdrawn—they being the smallest of our nuclear weapons, and yet very likely the most powerful for deterrence because of their immediacy and the circumscribed effect that makes use credible.

Similarly, if the principle of arms control negotiations for this or that class of weapons is once accepted, **actually for purposes of public relations but ostensibly** for the sake of peace and survival, how will the demand for more concessions be resisted? After all, it will be said, what petty diplomatic concern, what minor strategic advantage, is more important than peace and survival? Not to stand and assert the truth in the war of ideas means to suffer delegitimization now, and then eventual defeat in the practical realms of policy and strategy.

Edward Luttwak is a senior fellow at the Georgetown University Center for Strategic and International Studies. Among his books are Coup d'Etat *and* The Israeli Army.

European Nuclear Weapons Are for Deterrence

Leon Wieseltier

The degradation of Western strategy by the doctrine of use, and the degradation of Western values by the doctrine of unilateralism, mar the debate about Europe, too.

The deployment by NATO of theater nuclear forces—the Pershing II and cruise missiles—may be justified in two ways. The first is that NATO needs these weapons in order to fight a limited nuclear war in Europe. The second is that NATO needs these weapons in order not to fight a limited nuclear war in Europe.

The first view has been championed forthrightly by Edward Luttwak. He considers the conundrum that NATO will face in the event of a Soviet attack. Its conventional defenses may fail, he observes correctly, and it may be forced to resort to the use of battlefield nuclear weapons. The Soviets, presumably, will respond in kind, but they can also raise the stakes by threatening the cities of Europe with theater nuclear weapons, the intermediate range SS-20s, that are already abundantly in place. How could NATO meet such a threat? "A better response to such a Soviet threat," he writes,

> would be possible if by then NATO had acquired its own theater nuclear forces which, like the Soviet forces that already exist in considerable numbers, would be suitable to threaten not merely cities indiscriminately, but rather such specific targets as political and military command centers, airfields, nuclear storage sites, and even large concentrations of ground forces—that threat being all the more credible for being less catastrophic.

Once again, the counterforce chimera. It is even more of a chimera in the European setting, where the population is all around; there is no Nevada desert to make a counter-military strike look clean. And a counter-political strike is dirty everywhere. The military action contemplated by Luttwak will accomplish not the defeat of an army but the demise of a society. It is hard to understand the sense in which such an action will be

"less catastrophic." Less than what? And for whom? "U.S. scenarios for limited war in the European theater do not amuse us," E. P. Thompson has complained. "This is where we happen to live." That they do. Arguments like Luttwak's only win sympathy for arguments like Thompson's.

Luttwak's Strategy

But let us stay with Luttwak's strategy. The Russians have attacked, and the Pershings are there. They are used. And suddenly, according to Luttwak, it is an age of reason. "By far the most likely outcome is that a war would end very soon if any nuclear weapons, however small, were actually to be detonated by any side on any target." No theory of victory here, at least. Still, no man has been given this much to know. In the matter of the outcome of a nuclear war there are no experts. Luttwak is only speculating. He believes that a nuclear war will limit itself, and that this is "likely." But it is just as "likely" that it will not. The threshold, after all, will have been crossed. The unthinkable will not only have been thought; it will have been done. Surely, then, it may be done once more. It is impossible to predict the actions of statesmen and soldiers at such a terrible time, but this much seems evident—that each missile that will be launched will make it easier to launch another. If the difference between conventional weapons and nuclear weapons is not respected, there is no reason to believe that the difference between one type of nuclear weapon and another will be. The greater escalation makes the lesser escalation more likely, not less likely. Luttwak, however, argues the other way around. The use of nuclear weapons will end the use of nuclear weapons, he maintains. Such reasoning is not reassuring.

What makes Luttwak so certain that the war will stay limited? "The shock effect upon leaders on both sides—but especially on the Soviet leaders who had started the war." This is a surprising endorsement of

Leon Wieseltier, "The Great Nuclear Debate," *The New Republic*, January 10-17, 1983. Excerpted from an article in *The New Republic*, © 1983 The New Republic Inc. An expanded version of the article has been published as a book by Holt, Rinehart and Winston.

the good sense of the Soviets. That the Soviets would stay cool in a nuclear situation is to be wished. But it is, once again, a belief in reason when the hour is late. The Soviets, in any case, have made it known that they would interpret an attack by NATO as an attack by the United States. It is the official policy of the Russians to turn a theater nuclear war with Europe into a strategic nuclear war with the United States. If Luttwak does not believe that this is their intention, he must show why not. If he does believe that this is their intention, however, he must admit that after the Atlantic alliance has fired its Pershings, the limitation of the war to Europe is out of its hands.

Psychological Impact

Luttwak offers another reason for his sanguine scenario for nuclear war in Europe.

> The devastating psychological impact [of the use of nuclear weapons] upon the forces in the field would most likely arrest the conflict there and then. It is fully to be expected that military units whose men would see the flash, hear the detonation, feel the blast, or merely hear of such things, would swiftly disintegrate, except perhaps for a handful of units particularly elite. . . .The entire 'software' of discipline, or morale, of unit cohesion and *esprit de corps*. . .are simply not built to withstand such terror as nuclear weapons would cause—even if at the end of the day it were to be discovered that the dead on all sides are surprisingly few.

This last remark refers, presumably, to the casualties caused by tactical nuclear weapons; theater nuclear weapons would leave no such surprise for the day's end. Unfortunately it is not the case that battlefield nuclear weapons would bring a halt to the hostilities. In an admirable essay on "The Human Face of Deterrence," John Keegan has shown that troops may continue to fight even in the aftermath of such an attack. Keegan cites the remarkable resilience of German infantry at Cassino and at Normandy, where they were subjected to bombings so intense that they approached the level of a tactical nuclear burst. To the astonishment of the Allies, the enemy troops continued to fire their guns. Keegan attributes this perseverance to the durability of "instinctive habits of obedience" acquired as a result of countless drills in training. Keegan's skepticism may be carried further. The efficacy of tactical nuclear weapons depends upon their early use. If they do not stop the advancing Warsaw Pact army at once, they will quickly become too costly to use, because as the adversary army continued its advance it would come closer to NATO forces, and to the civilian population that these forces are present to protect. Tactical nuclear weapons used at that point in the fighting would turn upon their users.

Battlefield Nuclear Weapons

There is no guarantee that battlefield nuclear weapons will limit the war. They cannot be counted upon to stop all the soldiers. Thus, it is said, NATO must have theater nuclear weapons waiting in the wings. But these weapons do not discriminate between soldiers and civilians, particularly not in the counter-political manner that Luttwak proposes they be used. They will destroy not the *esprit* but the *corps*. The "theater" will become a charnel-house. In short, such a war cannot, in good conscience, be called "limited." The United States, it is true, will be outside its "limits," though probably not for long. But for the people of Europe who are within its "limits," limited nuclear war is total nuclear war.

"The military action contemplated by Luttwak will accomplish not the defeat of an army but the demise of a society."

Like the conception of counterforce at the strategic level, the conception of counterforce at the theater level claims the cachet of deterrence. Luttwak concludes his argument for a war-fighting strategy for Europe with a short disquisition on deterrence. "Deterrence does not rest on the theoretical ultimate of all-out population destruction," he observes. "Whether nuclear or not, the workings of deterrence depend on threats of punishment that others will find believable. This requires that the act of retaliation be in itself purposeful, and less catastrophic than more." Luttwak's remark about "all-out population destruction" sounds a little like Rostow's remark about the resilience of the human race. It is true that deterrence does not work because everybody will die. Everybody will not. But the certainty that somebody will survive is hardly a warrant for fighting a nuclear war. Luttwak is arguing against a straw man. Nobody ever said that deterrence rests on the possibility of "all-out population destruction." What it rests on, rather, is the possibility of vast undifferentiated devastation. Yet the devastation imagined by a war-fighting strategy is highly differentiated. Military targets are differentiated from political targets, and both these targets are differentiated from civilian targets. Tactical nuclear weapons are differentiated from theater nuclear weapons, and both these weapons are differentiated from strategic nuclear weapons. The aim of all these differentiations is to weaken the compunctions of military commanders, to make a war that is without limit and without purpose seem "limited" and "purposeful." Deterrence, then, may be less than "all-out population destruction," but it is more than "purposeful" nuclear use.

The possibility of undifferentiated devastation, moreover, is perfectly "believable," in Luttwak's term; it is made believable by the power of an intermediate range missile to destroy its target by destroying the entire place where its target is to be found. The requirement that deterrence be "believable" is frequently **used** as an excuse for counterforce planning. In fact, deterrence does not require your enemy to believe that you will strike back; it requires only that he not believe that you will not. Deterrence does not, in other words, require certainty. Doubt is quite enough.

The Pershing

Deterrence is the real reason for the installation of the intermediate range missiles by NATO—deterrence, to be precise, at all levels. Deterrence at all levels does not now exist, and it is this that makes the use of theater nuclear weapons in Europe more likely. The peace movement, in other words, has it backward. It is in order *not* to fight a nuclear war limited to Europe that the missiles will be delivered to NATO this year. The last thing that the United States should do, if it intends to limit a nuclear war to Europe, is to put missiles in Europe that can reach the Soviet Union.

The decision to deploy the Pershing and the cruise was based upon a sound understanding of the political dangers posed by the present military balance in Europe. The Soviet superiority in theater nuclear weapons threatens Western Europe with political domination or physical destruction, because it discourages the United States from coming to Western Europe's defense. In the event of a confrontation between NATO and the Warsaw Pact, the Warsaw Pact can inflict upon NATO a nuclear blow for which NATO cannot retaliate in kind. The security of Europe rests on the readiness of the United States for suicide. And that, obviously, is no security at all. The Pershing and the cruise were developed as a solution to this problem. In the words of Michael Howard, they are designed "to assuage the fears of Western Europeans that, confronted by a threat that did not extend to their own continent, the Americans would be effectively deterred from intervening." These missiles lower the cost of retaliation for the United States, and raise the cost of attack for the Soviet Union. They will be there not to be used, but to prevent their Soviet counterparts from being used. There is, after all, one way that nuclear war may be limited, and that is by the firing of the SS-20s at states that have no Pershings and cruise. Such a war will indeed be limited—to Western Europe.

These missiles make possible retaliation without escalation. In a word, they deter. They restore the mutual hostage relationship in which deterrence is said to consist; the present predicament may be characterized as a single-hostage relationship, with Western Europe as the hostage. Still, the problem of the alliance is not solved. The new weapons with which NATO will be furnished make it less probable that the United States will be laid waste for the sake of Europe, but only less probable. They do not make it impossible. It is easy to defend the NATO missile decision against the illusions of the peace movement, but it is hard to defend it without bitterness. For the Pershings and the cruise, as the governments of Western Europe freely admit, are still a way of tying America to Europe's fate; and this is

necessary, as they do not freely admit, because Europe is not prepared to take responsibility for its fate on its own.

If the United States ever fights a nuclear war with the Soviet Union, it will almost certainly not be because the Soviet Union attacked the United States. It will be because the Soviet Union attacked an ally of the United States. The war will not begin with a strategic nuclear exchange, but it will probably escalate to it. The defense policy of the Atlantic alliance is based upon the inexorability of escalation. The official metaphors for escalation are "chain of deterrence," "web of deterrence," "continuum of deterrence"; the new missiles will be installed to complete this chain, this web, this continuum. Deterrence must hold at all levels, if the worst nuclear fear of the age is not to come to pass.

"Deterrence at all levels does not now exist, and it is this that makes the use of theater nuclear weapons in Europe more likely."

Thus, conventional warfare must be abjured, lest tactical theater nuclear weapons be used; tactical nuclear weapons must be abjured, lest theater nuclear weapons be used; theater nuclear weapons must be abjured, lest strategic nuclear weapons be used; and strategic nuclear weapons must be abjured. The promise of escalation is what stays everybody's hand. When there is peace, it is a promise of good. But when there is war, it is a promise of evil. The metaphors of deterrence are, after all, metaphors of entanglement. When deterrence fails, it may fail at all its levels. That is its dark side. The United States has remorselessly declared its intention, in its famous policy of "first use," to rescue Europe's armies by the use of nuclear weapons, that is, to raise a conventional war to a nuclear war. And the Soviet Union has declared its intention to interpret any nuclear attack by NATO as an attack by the United States—that is, to raise a theater nuclear war into a strategic nuclear war.

Inadequate Conventional Defenses

But it is not only doctrine that will make escalation inexorable. It is the real situation on the ground. The single most decisive fact about that situation is the inadequacy of our allies' conventional defenses. NATO and the Warsaw Pact are roughly equal in manpower, but the Warsaw Pact has particularly large advantages in tanks (2.64 to 1), artillery pieces (2.07 to 1), land-based bombers (4.83 to 1), fighters (5.07 to 1) and interceptors (7.14 to 1); and its supply lines are less of a problem than NATO's. (These figures are drawn from *The Military Balance 1982-83* of the International Institute for Strategic Studies, which concludes that "the

143

numerical balance over the last 20 years has moved slowly but steadily in favor of the East," while "the West has largely lost the technological edge which allowed NATO to believe that quality could substitute for numbers.") If a war goes badly, for this reason, there is escalation. A "first use" is really a last resort. In order to make a nuclear defense more credible (not least to the citizens of the democracies to be defended), the destructive consequences of first use were concealed for a time behind the doctrine of "flexible response," according to which the most horrible nuclear strikes would be averted, or in any case saved for last. The deficiencies in the doctrine of flexible response, however, have been amply documented. The less horrible strikes are pretty horrible. And the nuclear strikes would have to begin at once, as we have observed. But "political leaders would never sanction such early use of nuclear weapons," according to Lawrence Freedman (the author of *The Evolution of Nuclear Strategy*, the best single book about strategic studies that I have read). Freedman concludes, instead, that "Western European leaders have long considered the real virtue of theater nuclear forces, e.g., the Pershing and the cruise, to be the link the weapons provide to the U.S. strategic arsenal."

"For the people of Europe who are within its 'limits,' limited nuclear war is total nuclear war."

The defense of Europe, then, requires a readiness for nuclear war. Rostow, in a speech at Yale, made the point plainly. "There is no way to build an impermeable wall between the use of nuclear and conventional weapons," he said. "The President of the United States must never be put in a position where he would have to choose between abandoning a vital American interest and launching a nuclear war." Of course this has been precisely the position of every President since 1945; nuclear war in Europe has been avoided not because we were unwilling to launch it, but because political means for the resolution of crises have not yet failed. The weakness of NATO determines not merely its policy on defense, furthermore, but its policy on arms control as well. Rostow made the connection clear. "In order to prevent the unthinkable horror of nuclear war, we must enforce the rules of public order against all forms of aggression, conventional and nuclear." Or, more simply, "in order to eliminate nuclear war, you must eliminate war itself."

Now, one of the interesting things about Rostow's view is that it is shared by Schell. "In the present global political system," writes Schell,

> a leader of a nuclear power who comes to believe that his nation's vital interests are being threatened by another nuclear power faces a pair of alternatives that

never confronted any statesmen of pre-nuclear times: he can acquiesce in the aggression. . .or he can threaten to unleash a holocaust in which the life of mankind might be lost.

And there are implications for arms control, also much like Rostow's, only given more grandiloquently:

> For the world, in freeing itself on one burden, the peril of extinction, must inevitably shoulder another: it must assume full responsibility for settling human differences peacefully. . . .Nuclear disarmament cannot occur if conventional arms are left in place. . . .If we are serious about nuclear disarmament—the minimum technical requirement for real safety from extinction—then we must accept conventional disarmament as well.

Of course these men reason differently. Since we must fight wars, we must fight nuclear wars, reasons Rostow. Since we must not fight nuclear wars, we must not fight wars, reasons Schell. But there is, in the dystopia of Rostow and the utopia of Schell, a common assumption, which is that we no longer can fight conventional wars.

No First Use

Can we? According to the four distinguished architects of deterrence who proposed that the United States adopt a policy of "no first use," we can.

No first use makes no sense in the context of the current conventional balance, as Bundy, Kennan, McNamara, and Smith almost acknowledged; no sooner had they pitched the idea than they were arguing "on behalf of strengthened conventional forces." They acknowledged, too, that "no one on either side could guarantee beyond all possible doubt that if conventional warfare broke out on a large scale there would in fact be no use of nuclear weapons." The Soviet Union, always on the alert for propaganda opportunities, made a declaration of no first use at the United Nations in June, shortly after the article in *Foreign Affairs* appeared. The United States, quite correctly, did not at all modify its policy as a result of the Soviet declaration. "We could not make that assumption about the Soviet leaders," the "Gang of Four" wrote in a premonitory passage;" and we must recognize," they continued, at great cost to their argument, "that the Soviet leaders could not make it about us. As long as the weapons themselves exist, the possibility of their use will remain."

And yet the notion of no first use was greeted with great enthusiasm in the United States, despite the rather obvious fact that it struck at the foundation of European defense at a time of real conventional weakness. The reason for this enthusiasm is not far to seek. The notion of no first use spoke for a hope that the United States has hidden for the entire history of the alliance—the hope to which Secretary of State Haig referred when he retorted that no first use would "make the world safe for conventional warfare." The world, of course, has always been safe for conventional warfare. No first use dares to suggest that it still is. It denies the most dangerous discontinuity of the nuclear age. There is a thrilling thesis about history in no first use, which is that there remains before us not the choice between peace and extinction, which is the conventional wisdom about the nuclear age, but the choice between peace and war. No first use, in other words, is a proposal for the normalization of the nuclear world. For the nuclear world will be normal when wars may be waged between states that have nuclear weapons without their being used. In such a world, escalation is no longer inexorable. The defense of Europe no longer asks the sacrifice of America. No first use is addressed to America's nerves, which have been sorely exposed by NATO.

Fantasy of the Firebreak

No first use owes its popularity to what may be called the fantasy of the firebreak. The firebreak is the technical term for the difference between conventional war and nuclear war; it is the opposite of escalation. The firebreak is a worthy objective. It is not hard, in the nuclear age, to praise conventional war. The smaller scale of the catastrophe is, of course, what most recommends a conventional war. But there are other such recommendations. Nuclear weapons do not deter anything except nuclear weapons; the years since 1945 have been riddled with confrontations and conflicts. Moreover, nuclear weapons are a military deterrent, but not a political deterrent. Perhaps the best proof of this is the postwar period in Europe. The Soviet Union created its empire in Eastern Europe in the very years that the United States enjoyed not merely nuclear superiority but a nuclear monopoly. Insofar as it warns against too great a reliance upon a nuclear defense, then, no first use is a constructive suggestion.

"If these missiles are ever launched against the Soviet Union, deterrence will have failed not only for Europe, but for the United States."

Except for the Europeans. They hate no first use. "How will we fight back?" asks the editor of *Die Zeit.* "Given a renunciation of first use," four fearful West German defense specialists remind us, "conventional war in Europe would once again become possible." It is true that as you decrease the possibility of nuclear war, you increase the possibility of conventional war; but this would seem worth the gamble, especially for Germany, which would probably be annihilated by the nuclear conflagration in question. The Germans, however, prefer the possibility of annihilation to the preparedness for something less. This has been the case since the 1950s, when a nuclear bias was introduced into the force structure and the defense doctrines of

NATO. Since then it has been fatalistically assumed that NATO will never be able to match the Warsaw Pact in conventional strength. This fatalism, however, is related to finance. The recovery of conventional parity by Western Europe, it is commonly believed, demands an increase in defense spending so great that it might place the entire economies of these countries on a different footing. This is an exaggeration; according to General Bernard Rogers, the Supreme Allied Commander at NATO, the Soviet advantage can be offset by an increase of only 1 percent in the member states' defense spending. The general is probably too sanguine. Still, for the Europeans that is 1 percent too many. They prefer the nuclear peril to higher taxes. That is what is so galling about the defense policy of the Atlantic alliance. It is not only themselves that our allies place in jeopardy. Their economic objection to a conventional defense has consequences for the United States as well. Their pleas for the American nuclear guarantee mean that they would sacrifice us for the sake of their standard of living.

Not America's Fault

If the firebreak is a fantasy, it is not America's fault. Nor is it America's fault if doubts about the alliance are heard on this side of the Atlantic. (Intellectuals as different as Ronald Steel and Irving Kristol have voiced such doubts.) It must be understood, in the matter of NATO, who is dragging whom to their doom. E. P. Thompson cries that he is "not ready to accept the obliteration of the material resources and inheritance of this island, and of some half of its inhabitants, in order to further the strategies of NATO." This is sheer effrontery. The world is the other way around. It is the material resources and the inhabitants of the United States that will be obliterated in the defense of NATO, not the material resources and inhabitants of NATO that will be obliterated in defense of the United States. The installation of the Pershing and the cruise—which Thompson opposes, of course—will correct the apportionment of risk within the alliance, but only slightly. If these missiles are ever launched against the Soviet Union, deterrence will have failed not only for Europe, but for the United States, too. Against E.P. Thompson, who portrays NATO as a collection of small nations cowed by the United States into serving its interests, NATO must be defended as a community of principle. But along come the West German defense specialists and they do not speak of a community of principle. They speak only of "a community of risk." This, too, is sheer effrontery. They are asking the United States to do for them what they will not do for themselves. (The conservative goverment of Helmut Kohl proposes to spend less on defense than the liberal government of Helmut Schmidt.) And they are asking the civilization of Europe to countenance its own end so that they may compete in the world's markets.

NATO is a security arrangement based upon a common morality. For moral ends the United States has made an extraordinary commitment to Europe. It has "extended" deterrence. No first use would undermine that commitment. It would take deterrence back; it would, therefore, weaken NATO as a security arrangement. Still, no first use is a noble idea, refuted by an ignoble reality. It intends to put nuclear weapons out of play. But nuclear weapons can be put out of play in only two ways—deterrence and disarmament. No first use cripples deterrence but does not call for disarmament. And it encourages the delusion that words will do away with the nuclear danger, when only deeds will. For deterrence to work, weapons must have been made. For disarmament to work, weapons must have been unmade. The announcement that the weapons are there but there is no need to worry means nothing.

Leon Wieseltier is a senior writer at The New Republic *magazine.*

European Missiles Will Enable a First Strike

Soviet Committee for European Security and Cooperation

Europe of the early eighties faces a choice between a new round of the nuclear arms race, which may lead to disaster, and a firm rejection of this policy. The overriding question in East-West relations is confrontation or cooperation for peace?

Though, quite obviously, the right choice is the one of peace, the West is taking one decision after another that are augmenting the war threat to Europe and the rest of the world. The "two-track" NATO decision on deploying Euromissiles is a classic example. NATO propagandists want us to believe that the arms buildup is a policy stabilizing the situation, consolidating peace, and lessening the "threat to Europe" which, they allege, comes from the East....

The situation immediately related to European security, as all of us can see, is developing continuously. Its new aspects—including the continuing preparations of NATO countries for deploying new US nuclear missiles in Europe beginning at the end of 1983—call for an objective examination....

QUESTION. President Reagan maintains that the arms race is being initiated by the Soviet Union. He says that the US strategic nuclear forces have been the same since 1962, while those of the USSR were being continuously built up in these twenty years. Is this true?

ANSWER. Responding to these contentions of Ronald Reagan and other members of the US Administration, Marshall Dmitry Ustinov, USSR Minister of Defense, set forth the true state of affairs in his replies to a TASS correspondent published on December 7, 1982. He said, in particular: "Ever since the 1950s, the USA has been imposing an arms race on us in all intercontinental weapons. At the beginning of the sixties the USA already had nearly 2,000 heavy bombers, and by 1966-1967 had deployed more than 1,000 ground-based intercontinental ballistic missiles and 41 nuclear-powered missile submarines with 656 ballistic missiles. That is, it had

How to Avert the Threat to Europe, Moscow: Progress Publishers, 1983. Reprinted with permission.

reached the present level of strategic armaments in number of delivery vehicles by that time, while the USSR had just a few more than 600 strategic delivery vehicles of all types." Spokesmen of the US Administration speak only of what the Soviet Union did in the 1970s because they want to conceal the truth. And the truth is that the Soviet Union was confronted with the necessity of countering the moves of the United States and taking steps to maintain its defense capability. "This and only this was what we did in the 60s and 70s," the Soviet Defense Minister said. "The Soviet Union was only concerned about parity and never gave a thought to military superiority over the USA." To achieve parity, the Soviet Union was compelled to catch up with the United States. And the one who is catching up has always to move faster in order to draw even with the one who is ahead, and doubly so because the latter does not mark time, and keeps on moving.

QUESTION. But the initiative of developing Euromissiles belongs to the USSR. Don't the SS-20 missiles prove this? Yet those are the missiles which impelled the present growth of the nuclear threat to Europe. Isn't it the necessity for neutralizing them that is compelling NATO to deploy its own Euromissiles?

ANSWER. No. Here, too, the initiative belongs to the United States and NATO. First, it should be borne in mind that the Soviet Union acquired medium-range missiles only as a reaction to the appearance of US forward-based nuclear weapons in the 1950s, that is, weapons stationed in Europe and trained on the USSR and its allies. This causality is valid to this day.

Second, the West learned about the SS-20 missile only in 1976, and began referring to it in 1977 (Helmut Schmidt's well-known statement in London in the autumn of 1977). But references to new US Euromissiles began much earlier—at the junction of the 60s and 70s.

In February 1969, the US firm of Martin-Orlando concluded a contract with the Pentagon to develop a new theatre missile. In May 1971 and January 1972 new

147

contracts were concluded. By then the allocations were already running into millions. In the US army budget for fiscal 1975, the development of Pershing II missiles was already singled out as an independent programme. The crash development of the Tomahawk cruise missile was already underway at that time. The first contracts for its development were concluded with General Dynamics in 1972.

Would you call that a NATO "response" to the deployment of SS-20 missiles? It is no "response" but one more US initiative in the arms race.

"All claims that the Soviet Union has an...advantage in Eurostrategic weapons...does not stand up to criticism."

SS-20 missiles were developed and deployed for a number of reasons. On the purely technical plane, it was necessary to replace missiles which had served out their time. We must also bear in mind the many statements of US and NATO leaders that they may resort to nuclear weapons first. Attention was called to the fact that the old Soviet medium-range missiles "took a long time to get started", which made them "vulnerable to pre-emptive attack by NATO's QRA (Quick Reaction Alert) forces". Furthermore, as we have noted above, the USA and NATO had long since developed and begun to carry out plans for an intensive buildup of their medium-range nuclear potential in Europe. In the circumstances, it would have been a great risk for the USSR not to modernize its medium-range nuclear potential.

There were also definite political reasons why the Soviet Union had to modernize its medium-range weapons. It had repeatedly called for the inclusion of US forward-based nuclear weapons in the Soviet-American negotiations on the limitation of strategic arms. If this had been done and the problem had been settled by an appropriate agreement, it is quite safe to say that the Soviet Union would not have had any cause to modernize the weapons which were the counterweight to the US forward-based weaponry. But every time the USSR made such a proposal, it was brushed aside by the United States.

QUESTION. All the same, didn't the SS-20 missile give the Soviet Union superiority in medium-range weapons in Europe?

ANSWER. Not at all. In correlating the nuclear forces of the sides one must not consider some single type of weapon in isolation, such as ground-based missiles or some single characteristic of these missiles. The nuclear potentials must be considered as a package, taking into account all quantity and quality indicators. That is the only way in which the principle of equal security can be observed. If we take the European nuclear potentials of both sides as a package, we will see that they balance

out, that parity was in no way upset by the deployment of SS-20 missiles.

A rough parity in medium-range nuclear weapons in Europe has existed between the USSR and the USA, and their allies, for already a number of years—each of the sides has roughly a thousand delivery vehicles.

In the case of the USSR, this number includes ground-based missiles the West calls SS-20, SS-4 and SS-5, plus medium-range bombers.

In the case of the Atlantic Alliance, this number includes the US forward-based nuclear force (FB-111A, F-111, and F-4 aircraft, and A-6 and A-7 carrier-based aircraft) and, in addition, the nuclear armaments of Britain and France (ground-based S-2 and S-3 missiles, submarine-launched Polaris and M-20 ballistic missiles, and Vulcan and Mirage bombers). All these systems have a range (action radius) of 1,000 to 4,500 kilometres, and can reach targets on Soviet territory. This means that the West already has missiles analogous in capacity to the Soviet SS-20 (64 submarine-launched ballistic missiles with multiple warheads in Britain and 80 submarine-launched and 18 ground-based ballistic missiles in France).

It is especially important to stress that the medium-range delivery vehicles of the Atlantic Alliance are already now able to lift 50 per cent more warheads in one launch/sortie than the corresponding vehicles of the Soviet Union.

The Western states have more than once modernized their medium-range nuclear armaments. They are also doing so at present (improved Polaris A-3TK SLBMs with six warheads—and Trident-2 SLBMs in the longer term—are replacing Polaris A-3 SLBMs in Britain, and France is replacing its single-warhead M-20 SLBMs with seven-warhead M-4 SLBMs and its ground-based single-warhead S-3 missiles with seven-warhead S-4 missiles). US forward-based weaponry is also being upgraded.

QUESTION. But if we take only the Soviet-American nuclear balance in Europe, President Reagan says that the Soviet Union has a 6:1 advantage over the United States in medium-range weapons. Is this true?

ANSWER. Certainly not. One can only regret that the President saw fit to use a tendentious, incorrect method of counting. By the way, the NATO countries have used the same method to obtain other ratios of "Soviet superiority"—3:1, 2:1, and the like. How do they arrive at these figures?

Their method is inaccurate because, first of all, they count weapons with a range of just a few hundred kilometres along with the Soviet medium-range weaponry which, by definition, has a range of 1,000 kilometres and more (but below intercontinental range). This erodes the very concept of medium range, and leads to all sorts of misconceptions.

Their method is also inaccurate because much of the weaponry with a range of more than 1,000 kilometres is usually left out of the Atlantic Alliance figures, and, what is more, the nuclear potentials of Britain and France are totally ignored. Not counted, too, are some types of NATO aircraft that can reach deep into the air space of Warsaw Treaty countries, including the Soviet Union (e.g., the FB-111A). Also totally left out of the count are the US planes based on aircraft carriers patrolling waters in the proximity of European shores.

Under more or less close scrutiny, all claims that the Soviet Union has a six-fold, three-fold or two-fold advantage in Eurostrategic weapons, therefore, do not stand up to criticism.

QUESTION. Through its proposal to establish parity in medium-range weapons by reducing hundreds of Soviet missiles, the USSR has in effect admitted that there is no such parity at present, that there is Soviet superiority. Isn't that so?

ANSWER. This view of the Soviet proposal is specious because it completely overlooks one of its essential parts. By offering a "missile limit" in Europe within the bounds of the medium-range weapons of both sides subject to reduction, and the reduction of tens of the most sophisticated Soviet missiles, the Soviet Union does not, either directly or indirectly, admit any current superiority in medium-range weapons. For it has at the same time proposed that an appropriate limit should also be set on the number of aircraft carrying medium-range nuclear weapons. In that way the continental nuclear equilibrium will not be upset, but its level will be lowered.

QUESTION: The Soviet Union is not modernizing, but radically upgrading its medium-range weaponry, and this has alarmed the West. Many people think that the SS-20 is capable of a first strike or can at least serve as a means of political pressure on the West. What can you say on this score?

ANSWER. The Soviet Union has not engaged in any radical upgrading, and has merely modernized its medium-range missiles. That is not the same thing. It stands to reason that the new missiles are better than the old ones. But their combat characteristics are essentially the same: the range is the same as that of the old SS-5 missiles, and the aggregate yield is even less. As for the number of delivery vehicles, the Soviet Union did not upset the nuclear balance in Europe when it substituted the new missiles for the old. When stationing a new SS-20 missile, it removed one or two old missiles, which were dismantled and were not deployed in other areas.

This replacement of missiles led to no change in their combat mission, and did not upset the balance of nuclear strength in Europe. The new missiles have the same mission as the old: to counterweigh NATO's medium-range weapons in Europe. What is still more pertinent is that owing to their technical characteristics they cannot strike at the territory of the United States.

The attempt to portray Soviet medium-range missiles as a first-strike weapon is a perversion of the facts that is intended to frighten people. Soviet medium-range missiles are no first-strike weapon, because they cannot reach US territory and put US intercontinental ballistic missiles out of commission.

No less groundless are the attempts to portray Soviet medium-range weapons as a means of political pressure or blackmail vis-a-vis Western Europe or the United States. First, the entire history of Soviet foreign policy shows that it is wholly inimical to any policy "from strength", to obtaining political or economic concessions from other countries by the threat of armed force. Second, even if we made the false assumption (widely exploited by Western propaganda) and imagined that the Soviet Union might use its military power in this fashion, then, too, it would have to have military superiority for such an action to succeed. Yet the Soviet Union has no superiority in the military field, and does not want it. Third, for more than twenty years the Soviet Union has had medium-range nuclear weapons and has never used them (despite the ceaseless predictions of the inventors of the malicious fib of a "Soviet threat") for political pressure or blackmail against other countries, because these weapons have an entirely different purpose: to make sure of the security of the USSR and its allies in face of the threat created by the nuclear weapons of the USA and its allies. Lastly, the Soviet Union has declared quite clearly that it is renouncing first use of nuclear weapons.

QUESTION. All the same, despite all these arguments it is still a fact that the Soviet Union has sophisticated medium-range missiles, while NATO in Europe has none. Why, in that case, should NATO not modernize its arsenal and not have the same kind of weapons as the Soviet Union?

"America's main scheme, evidently, is to try and soften the retaliatory strike against US territory."

ANSWER. To begin with, it is not true that members of the North Atlantic Treaty have no missiles in Europe of the same capacity as the Soviet SS-20 missiles. They have such weapons, and in no small numbers. As we have already said, Britain and France have a nuclear-missile force totalling 162 delivery vehicles (ground-based and submarine-launched missiles).

So, if we take the whole NATO medium-range arsenal, including the US forward-based weaponry, then the addition of 572 new missiles provided for in NATO's "two-track" decision will abruptly upset the existing equilibrium in favor of the West.

According to available information, NATO has set out to condition public opinion to a "transformation" of its December 1979 decision with the purpose of boosting the number and upgrading the quality of the US missiles earmarked for deployment in Europe.

Eugene Rostow, former Director of the US Arms Control and Disarmament Agency, said in an interview to *Der Spiegel* in July 1981 that the figure referred to in the 1979 NATO decision was meaningless. "We had not fixed on any definite number in these negotiations," he said. "We will see...."

"The stationing of...US missiles in Western Europe is conceived as a means of strengthening the US potential for...a 'decapitation' strike."

The London *Times* of August 14, 1982 reported that NATO is planning to deploy something like 150 additional Pershing-2, Polaris and Trident-C4 missiles for attacking the rear of the Warsaw Treaty countries. The report says, admittedly, that their warheads will not be nuclear. But how can anyone check what kind of warheads they will really have and whether the missiles can or cannot be swiftly converted into a nuclear weapon in the event of a crisis? In October 1982 there were reports that it is being planned to deploy 385 instead of the originally specified 108 Pershing-2 missiles. All this cannot fail to put us on our guard.

NATO's "two-track" decision is also to be "transformed" in terms of the quality of the new US missiles. When the decision was being taken, Western propaganda went out of its way to stress that all the missiles planned for deployment would have one warhead. Gradually this theme was played down, and soon hushed up altogether. And here is why: on July 28, 1981 *Die Welt* reported that "the United States is considering the question of fitting the new medium-range Pershing-2 with multiple warheads. Well-informed quarters report that the requisite technical weapons research has already been successfully completed."

Unlike the Soviet medium-range weapons, their new American counterparts are, in fact, equivalent to strategic weapons because they can reach the territory of the USSR. This is no "Soviet propaganda ploy" but an objective characteristic, which is consciously or unconsciously admitted in NATO quarters. In an interview to the Italian newspaper *Il Manifesto* of November 18, 1980, Reagan's foreign policy adviser Robert Pfaltzgraff noted that the "modernization" of theatre nuclear weapons in Europe is "directly related to the strengthening of US strategic forces." And at a press-conference on February 27, 1981, Kurt Becker, an FRG government official, said: "It is, of course, quite clear that the Eurostrategic missiles will be an addition to intercontinental strategic missiles."

While maintaining officially that the new missiles are designed for the defense of the West European countries, Washington is really intending them for preventive strikes against Soviet intercontinental ballistic missiles and vitally important targets in the Western part of the Soviet Union. America's main scheme, evidently, is to try and soften the retaliatory strike against US territory in the event of an aggression against the USSR. It is not at all concerned about European security.

It is also important to note that the new Pershing-2 missiles can reach their targets in a matter of 5 or 6 minutes after launching. This will make the situation in Europe much more unstable and explosive. Their ability to deliver a surprise blow is not all, however. Pershing-2 missiles are highly accurate, and can hit targets with a radius of just 30 or 40 metres—a radius just one-tenth of the Pershing-1A accuracy factor. What does that mean? There can be only one answer: the United States wants to have weapons in foreign territory that can be depended upon to hit and destroy hardened military targets. And that is a first-strike function.

Indeed, Eugene Rostow made no secret of this mission of Pershing-2 missiles. "These intermediate-range missiles," he said, "with their enormous speed and destructive capacity are first-strike weapons or can be certainly."

Cruise missiles, too, are capable of a first strike. They have a long range (up to 2,600 kilometres) and can penetrate the air defense system flying at low altitudes (of some 60 metres), eluding discovery until they are close to target, and striking with pinpoint accuracy. Consequently, like Pershing-2, the cruise missile is also a first-strike weapon. The claim that it is "not dangerous" and introduces nothing new into the strategic situation because it is relatively slow, is therefore entirely false.

At present, the United States is planning to fit out its armed forces with thousands of cruise missiles. Can this large-scale build-up of US nuclear capability be called modernization? Certainly not. What we see is a US and NATO drive to create a new type of strategic weapon that can change the prevailing balance of strength in their favor both regionally and globally.

It should be borne in mind that the stationing of qualitatively new US missiles in Western Europe is conceived as a means of strengthening the US potential for what may be called a "decapitation" strike, that is, a nuclear strike that is meant to instantly destroy the centres of political and military leadership, and command and communication centres. As conceived by the authors of this concept, it must disrupt the enemy's entire military system and preclude retaliation or, at least, reduce it to a minimum.

It follows that the stationing of new US nuclear missiles in Western Europe is meant to achieve strategic superiority over the USSR, and not at all to "contain" the Soviet SS-20 missiles. Besides, US doctrine does not necessarily relate the timing and direction of the strike to events in the region where the weapons in question are stationed. This is why the new US missiles should be considered a strategic weapon in relation to the USSR. The USSR cannot afford to overlook all these aspects of the possible deployment of a US Eurostrategic potential in Western Europe.

QUESTION. Can you cite more specific data about the balance of conventional forces in Europe?

ANSWER. According to trustworthy international sources NATO is not behind but even slightly ahead of the Warsaw Treaty in armed forces strength in Europe. This is confirmed by the annual of the London Institute of Strategic Studies, *The Military Balance 1981-1982.*

Numerical Strength of Armed Forces

	NATO	WTO	Ratio
	thousands		
Total regular armed forces	4,998	4,821	1.04:1
Total ground forces	2,720	2,618	1.04:1
Ground forces in Europe	2,125	1,664	1.28:1

Numerical strength of combat-ready divisions. Combat-ready divisions can go into action without additional mobilization measures. Bear in mind that the complement of a deployed US and West German division is greater than that of a Warsaw Treaty division. The total number of Soviet ground troop formations is greater than that of the United States. And this is wholly justified, considering the far more complicated geostrategic position of the Soviet Union, to which we have already referred. But in Europe, the 89 divisions of the Atlantic Alliance (if Spain comes in there will be 94) are faced by 78 divisions of the Warsaw Treaty countries. Here, too, consequently, NATO is ahead of the Warsaw Treaty.

Tanks. The Warsaw Treaty countries have 25,000 tanks in Europe, and NATO has more than 17,000 directly in active units, and in addition some 1,500 American tanks and 6,500 tanks of West European NATO countries are stocked in reserve.

Aviation. Balance of strength in tactical aviation (NATO:WTO):
—in combat aircraft—1:1.2
—in bomb payload deliverable within 185 kilometres—3:1
—in helicopters—1.8:1

As we see NATO has an advantage in air support capability and in the number of helicopters. But the Soviet Union is making no "problem" out of this, as NATO does in the case of the WTO "tank threat."

QUESTION. Considering the Soviet naval buildup, is it seeking superiority on the seas?

ANSWER. Though people tend to consider the Soviet Union a land power, its nearly 47,000 kilometres of seashore and outlets to three oceans also make it a major ocean power, which legitimately requires an appropriate navy. But this navy is not intended for any "global spread of Soviet military power."

Here are a few facts about the balance of naval strength between the USSR and the USA, the Warsaw Treaty and NATO. The navies of the USA and other NATO countries have nearly thrice as many nuclear-capable battleships, cruisers, destroyers and frigates than the Warsaw Treaty countries. NATO's 3:1 superiority in combat ships of the basic types is compensated by the edge the Warsaw Treaty countries hold in submarines. The NATO navy has 26 aircraft carriers and air-capable ships (21 of them American). The Soviet Union has only two air-capable ships (and no aircraft-carriers). Tonnage: USA—over 4.5 million tons, USSR—about 2.6 million tons. US naval aviation surpasses Soviet naval aviation 2.5 times in number of aircraft, and still more considerably in striking power. More than 520 US nuclear-capable carrier-based attack aircraft can reach Soviet territory. Soviet naval aviation, on the other hand, is intended for repulsing sea-borne forces and not for striking the American continent. The US marine corps (190,000 men) exceeds the strength of the Soviet marines (12,000 men) 16 times over. In displacement and capacity US landing ships are far superior to the Soviet ships.

"The navies of the USA and other NATO countries have nearly thrice as many nuclear-capable battleships...than the Warsaw Treaty countries."

All this shows quite clearly that there is absolutely no need for compensating the spurious superiority of the Soviet Union in conventional armaments by building up Western nuclear arms.

The above viewpoint was authored in the Soviet Union by select members of the Soviet Committee for European Security and Cooperation and the Scientific Research Council on Peace and Disarmament.

"Renouncing the nuclear component of...NATO...would gravely undermine the West's ability to deter conflict or intimidation."

European Missiles Will Prevent a First Strike

US Department of State

Membership in the North Atlantic Treaty Organization, a coalition of sovereign Western countries formed and sustained to defend the interests and values of the Atlantic democracies, is the centerpiece of U.S. security efforts. The alliance is based on the principle that Western security is indivisible and that the defense of the political independence and democratic systems of the European allies against the threat posed by the Soviet Union is vital to the health and even survival of the United States.

Security in Europe

Throughout the postwar period, the central problem of NATO security has been shaped by two fundamental geographic realities:
- The nations and defense resources of the West are divided by the Atlantic Ocean;
- The Soviet Union emerged from World War II in control of a contiguous landmass extending from Asia into the heart of Europe.

The United States, the single most powerful Western nation, is separated from Europe by 3,000 miles of open water. Even within Europe, the nations of the West do not form a single contiguous landmass. Although the United States and its NATO allies together have more population, larger economies, and are more highly developed than the Soviet Union and East European states, the geographic division and distance always have posed special challenges to collective efforts to guarantee Western security. NATO always has had to contend with the risk that the Soviet Union, for military or political purposes, could bring superior force to bear on a particular vulnerable point.

Not only does the Soviet Union maintain the largest single army in Europe, but its direct land lines of communication permit it to reinforce those forces easily and rapidly from elsewhere on its own territory.

Security and Arms Control: The Search for a More Stable Peace. Washington, DC, US Department of State, Bureau of Public Affairs, 1983.

Moreover, its internal lines of communication allow it to choose the point of political attack or pressure on the West.

For the United States and other Western nations, it was clear in the late 1940s that these geographic realities could be overcome only on the basis of the closest possible alliance between Europe and North America. Memories of the 1930s—when a lack of effective solidarity prevented the democracies from checking the rise of aggressive dictatorships without recourse to war—were still fresh. The Soviets' seizure of Eastern Europe and their attempt to starve out the free city of Berlin were more immediate reminders of the dangers faced by a prostrate Europe and a demobilized United States. It was evident that only a policy of collective security would preserve the peace and protect the independence of the Western peoples. Only the commitment by the Western democracies to a common defense could deter military aggression or political pressure against any one of them.

Twice in this century the United States has intervened to defend democracy in Europe and restore a stable equilibrium of power. In the years following World War II, the test has been to see if American policy could be formulated and carried out in order not to win a new war in Europe but to prevent a conflict from ever recurring.

To this end, NATO was established in 1949 as the formal embodiment of the commitment to a security partnership of equals. From the beginning, NATO has been a defensive alliance, committed never to use force except in response to aggression. NATO's basic strategy has been to demonstrate the political will and military strength needed to deter aggression or intimidation.

Strategy of Deterrence

Deterrence is the basis of U.S. and NATO security policy. It requires that a potential aggressor be convinced that the costs of aggression outweigh any possible gains it might hope to achieve. Maintaining deterrence for more than three decades has been a difficult and dynamic process. The United States and the other members of the alliance have had to adapt to technological progress, to the growth and modernization of Soviet military power, and to political and economic change at home and abroad. In particular, they have had to offset repeated Soviet efforts to exploit their geographic advantages and divide NATO in order to dominate Western Europe.

"The purpose of this balance of forces is to permit a flexible range of responses capable of meeting any aggression."

At the outset, deterrence depended heavily on America's superior strategic nuclear power. The U.S. lead over the Soviet Union in nuclear capabilities allowed the West to offset substantial Soviet advantages in conventional strength, maintain the peace, deter aggression, and insulate Europe from Soviet intimidation.

As the Soviet Union developed its own nuclear forces, however, it became apparent that the threat of nuclear retaliation alone would not suffice to provide credible deterrence under all circumstances. Increasingly, on both sides of the Atlantic, it was recognized that stability could be assured only if the nuclear deterrent was supplemented by a more robust conventional force capability. Thus, in the 1960s, the alliance developed the military strategy of "flexible response," which continues to this day.

The basis of this strategy is that NATO must deter and, if necessary, counter military aggression of varying scales in any region of NATO. This objective can be secured only through the maintenance of a wide range of forces. The purpose of this balance of forces is to permit a flexible range of responses capable of meeting any aggression by direct defense at a level judged appropriate to defeat the attack and of escalating the level deliberately if defense at the first level selected is not effective. This strategy relies on strong conventional and nuclear forces, and the linkage between them, to convince the Soviet Union that NATO could and would counter any aggression and that the risks to the Soviet Union would far outweigh the potential gains from an attack at any level.

NATO Triad of Forces

To implement this strategy, NATO fields an interlocking array of forces:

Conventional forces, including, for example, armored and mechanized divisions, tactical aircraft, and naval forces;

Intermediate-range and short-range nuclear forces, based in Europe, with delivery systems operated by the United States and by its allies; and

Strategic forces, including intercontinental ballistic missiles (ICBMs); submarine-launched ballistic missiles (SLBMs); and heavy bombers, based in the United States.

This triad confronts a potential aggressor with great uncertainty as to the level and nature of a Western response. This uncertainty is essential to effective deterrence, since any aggressor must assume that an attack on NATO would incur incalculable risks, up to and including strategic nuclear retaliation.

All three elements of the triad play essential roles in the maintenance of an effective deterrent. They provide NATO with the capability to counter aggression at a variety of levels, threatening an aggressor with escalation if that is necessary to restore the peace and cause the aggressor to withdraw. The effect of the three elements working together is more than the sum of the individual parts. Conventional defense alone would not provide political confidence or military deterrence against the Soviet Union. Similarly, a nuclear force by itself would not be a credible deterrent in all possible contingencies and might, in fact, invite political pressure and limited military adventure. Together, however, this combination of conventional and nuclear forces has proved to be an extremely effective mechanism for preserving peace.

The key is the firm links among the elements. An aggressor must never be given the impression that risks could be safely limited in a conflict and, therefore, that an attack against NATO might be an attractive proposition.

Ultimately, the most important link is that between forces in Europe—both conventional and nuclear—and the U.S. strategic deterrent. It is this crucial coupling which gives concrete form to the indivisibility of American and European security and which ensures that the Soviets could not attack Europe without risking strategic retaliation against their own territory. Given its importance, it is not surprising that the way to maintain the linkage between Europe and North America has been the single most discussed element of NATO strategy over the years and that weakening the link has been a consistent Soviet objective.

The Current Debate

In recent years, the U.S. strategy of deterrence has been criticized from a variety of perspectives. For some, the cost of maintaining conventional forces has seemed too great, particularly in a time of economic difficulty. To these critics, it has appeared far easier to move back toward the simple strategy of an earlier era, relying on the threat of massive nuclear retaliation to provide an inexpensive deterrent.

For others, the risks of nuclear weapons have appeared too great. They believe that the effectiveness of nuclear weapons as a deterrent is less important than their unquestioned destructiveness if they were ever employed. They argue that the answer lies in reducing the role of nuclear weapons and perhaps even in renouncing their first use. Some of the proponents of such a course say that they would be prepared to increase sharply the expenditures for conventional defense to offset this change.

The United States and its allies cannot return to a doctrine based solely on massive nuclear retaliation, such as existed more than two decades ago. In an era of reciprocal nuclear vulnerability, the threat of massive nuclear retaliation alone is not suited to all or even most contingencies. A solely nuclear posture would leave the West able to respond only to one contingency—the worst one—and with no credible means of dealing with all the other possibilities, from political and economic pressure to various forms of limited aggression.

Conversely, to remove nuclear weapons from the deterrent, or to declare a policy of no-first-use, would allow an aggressor to plan actions with the certainty that risks could be limited. It would, in practice, make Europe safe for conventional war by guaranteeing to the Soviet Union that the West would not escalate to the nuclear level if faced with defeat by conventional forces. Renouncing the nuclear component of the NATO triad would gravely undermine the West's ability to deter conflict or intimidation.

"The Soviet Union has no hesitation in translating military power into political pressure."

Such a limitation also would be profoundly damaging to the unity of the alliance. It would mean that the commitment to defend all areas of the alliance, including those most exposed to Soviet threats, could not be effectively implemented. It is not surprising that the Soviet Union has made the question of nuclear no-first-use a primary propaganda theme over the years. And it is equally unsurprising that NATO has consistently rejected it while maintaining its own substantive arms control agenda.

There are some in the West who maintain that the defense of Europe is unnecessary or impossible. Those who hold the former view no longer consider the Soviet Union even a potential threat and do not believe that Soviet military advantage in Europe could be translated into political gains. Those who accept the latter believe opposition to the Soviet Union to be futile and suicidal and support, instead, a process of one-sided accomodation.

Clearly, however, recent history shows that the Soviet Union has no hesitation in translating military power into political pressure: witness, for instance, its behavior toward Poland since 1981. Nor are the Soviets averse to using force to achieve their political objectives, as demonstrated in East Germany, Hungary, Czechoslovakia, and most recently in Afghanistan. On the other hand, more than three decades of transquillity in Western Europe demonstrate that through collective efforts, the Western democracies can secure both peace and freedom.

The above viewpoint is excerpted from a publication of the United States Department of State, Bureau of Public Affairs.

"If we do not modernize the ICBM leg of the TRIAD, and maintain those important capabilities. . .restoration of a strategic balance will not be possible."

viewpoint **38**

The MX Buildup Will Improve Security

Caspar Weinberger

Since the end of World War II and the dawn of the atomic age, the United States has maintained peace and preserved its freedom, and that of its allies, by means of an inherently defensive policy—deterrence. This policy, and the strategic capability to back it up, serves as a clear indication to potential aggressors that the West has the will and the means necessary to resist aggression. By maintaining the ability to retaliate against a potential aggressor in such a manner that the costs we will exact will exceed substantially any gains he might hope to achieve through aggression, we can prevent any aggressor from coming to believe that he could profit from or win a nuclear war.

We, for our part, are under no illusions about the consequences of nuclear war. We know there would be no winners in such an exchange. But this recognition on *our* part is not enough to maintain deterrence. The *Soviet* leadership must understand this as well. The President's Commission on Strategic Forces made this point eloquently in their report.

> "Deterrence is not an abstract notion amenable to simple quantification. Still less is it a mirror image of what would deter ourselves. Deterrence is the set of beliefs in the minds of the Soviet leaders, given their own values and attitudes, about our capabilities and our will. It requires us to determine, as best we can, what would deter them from considering aggression, even in a crisis—not to determine what would deter us."

U.S.S.R. Military Aggressive

Unlike the United States, the Soviet Union seems to believe that under certain circumstances a nuclear war could be fought and won. Today we see that the number, the explosive power, and the accuracy of Soviet nuclear weapons are far greater than would be needed simply to deter attack. In addition, the Soviets have developed a refiring capability for some of their larger ICBMs, which could allow them to reload their

Caspar Weinberger, statement of the secretary of defense on MX basing before the Senate Armed Services Committee, April 20, 1983.

delivery systems several times. They have given us indications that *they* think they could fight a protracted war by hardening their silos and protecting key targets with elaborate air defenses. Their writings, military doctrine, and exercises all emphasize the kind of nuclear warfighting policy which we in the United States have rejected—and which we must deter. We must, therefore, make sure that the Soviet leadership, in calculating the risks of aggression, recognizes that an effective American response exists, and understands that, consequently, there can be no circumstance where the initiation of a war at any level would make sense.

Explaining the TRIAD

To this end, we have maintained over the last two decades a strong and interdependent force, known as the TRIAD, which consists of land-based intercontinental ballistic missiles, sea-based ballistic missiles, and manned strategic bombers. This multiplicity of forces provides three significant benefits.

First, each of the strategic components of the TRIAD acts in concert with the others to complicate Soviet planning, making it more difficult for the Soviet Union not only to plan and execute a successful attack but also to defend against retaliation.

Second, each of the legs of the TRIAD acts as a hedge against a possible technological break-through that could threaten the viability of any single strategic system. By maintaining a TRIAD we force the Soviet Union to disperse their resources among three components, preventing them from concentrating their considerable resources on defeating two or only one U.S. strategic system.

Finally, only a TRIAD of three unique systems can provide us with all the elements necessary to provide a strong, secure deterrent. The strengths of each system not only complement the strengths of the other two but also compensate for their weaknesses. To deter successfully all types of nuclear attack, our forces *as a whole* must possess a number of characteristics and capabilities—including survivability, prompt response, mission flexibility and sufficient accuracy and warhead yield to retaliate against hardened Soviet military targets. No single weapons system can incorporate all of these capabilities. Submarines are less vulnerable, but less accurate. Bombers are accurate, and retrievable, but thay are much slower. ICBMs are easier to command and control, faster, and more accurate, but they are more vulnerable than submarines and, once launched, irretrievable. But all three systems together can incorporate all those elements necessary to deter against all types of attack.

Soviet Buildup

For many years it was our good fortune to possess a TRIAD whose effectiveness could be assured well into the future. Unhappily, due to the massive, and largely unmatched, strategic build up that the Soviets have sustained since the 1960s, those days are gone. That build up has created substantial vulnerabilities in our strategic TRIAD which in turn have altered the strategic balance and reduced the effectiveness of our deterrent capability.

Over the past two years the President has instituted, and the Congress has supported, a number of initiatives to rectify the TRIAD deficiencies this build up has created, including production of the Trident submarine and development of a new, more capable SLBM, the D-5; production of the air-launched cruise missile, development of the B-1B and 'Stealth' bombers; improvements in the U.S.-Canadian Air Defense network; and improvements in the effectiveness and reliability of our command, control, communications and attack warning capabilities. I know this committee shares our conviction that such a strategic modernization program is vital to preserving deterrence and enhancing the prospects for arms reduction.

But one very serious weakness in our TRIAD has yet to be resolved—the modernization of the ICBM force. The United States made a conscious choice during the 1970s to restrict its nuclear weapons developments so as not to present the Soviet Union with a first strike threat. However, the Soviets showed no such restraint. During the 1970s the Soviet Union deployed more than 600 powerful SS-18 and SS-19 ICBMs with nearly 5,000 highly accurate warheads; at the same time they hardened their missile silos and key command and control facilities to resist attack. These Soviet developments have simultaneously endangered the survivability of our ICBM force, and substantially reduced the retaliatory effectiveness which lies at the heart of our strategy of deterrence.

Modernizing ICBMs

Without a viable ICBM force our TRIAD would lose several qualities that are crucial to deterrence: extremely high peacetime readiness rates, rapid and reliable communications with command authorities, and prompt counter military capability.

But, even more important, indeed at the heart of the current U.S.-Soviet strategic force imbalance, is the Soviet monopoly of prompt hard target kill capability. This gives them a twofold advantage over the United States. First, it enables the Soviets to launch a very high confidence first strike attack on our land-based ICBM, while expending only one third of their ICBM force in the process. The large store of remaining ICBMs would then enable them to divert weapons to other essential targets in a first-strike attack and still maintain a large and effective reserve force to conduct follow-on attacks. Second, the fact that we lack a prompt retaliatory capability against very hard targets allows Soviet planners to consider the possibility that, for the crucial first few hours of a nuclear conflict, the bulk of their ICBM force and supporting command and control structure would remain largely immune to U.S. retaliation. This would eliminate one of the major sources of uncertainty that is such an important element of deterrence—the unpredictable effects of U.S. retaliation on Soviet war plans. Without this crucial uncertainty exerting an influence on Soviet war planners, their confidence in their ability to fight and win a nuclear war is reinforced.

Dangerous Development

This development is too dangerous to be allowed to continue unchallenged. If we do nothing, we will face the very real danger that the Soviets could at some point come to believe that they could use, or blackmail us by threatening to use, nuclear forces to gain their military or political ends. . . .

"Unlike the United States, the Soviet Union seems to believe that under certain circumstances a nuclear war could be fought and won."

But the President's plan also has a wider, more long-term impact. The peacetime, day-to-day, decisions that collectively make up the behavior of the United States, the Soviet Union and all other nations are influenced by perceptions of the U.S.-Soviet strategic balance. The greater the imbalance, the more conscious we become of the limits to our options in international affairs and the greater the chance that we might be forced to compromise our interests to avoid crises that might overburden our capacity to deter conflict. In the same vein, the greater the imbalance, the greater the tendency of the Soviet Union to embrace ever more ambitious definitions of what constitute legitimate Soviet interests; the greater their tendency to view the risks of crisis as an acceptable price to pay for the satisfaction of their political aims. The behavior of other nations is affected by perceptions of the strategic balance too. The greater the imbalance, the greater the tendency to view Soviet aims as interests to be accommodated; the greater, also, their tendency to view U.S. aims as interests to be ignored or challenged.

U.S.S.R./U.S. Strategic Imbalance

Today, we are confronted with just such a strategic imbalance; an imbalance that, in the face of the continued enhancement of Soviet power, will only worsen if we do nothing to counter it. There are many things we can do to reestablish a strategic balance, some of which we are doing already. However, if we do not modernize the ICBM leg of the TRIAD, and maintain those important capabilities unique to the ICBM, restoration of a strategic balance will not be possible. As my predecessor, Harold Brown, wrote recently: ''. . . .we said in the early 1970s that we would modernize with a new missile in the late 1970s. In the mid-1970s we said that we would do so in the early 1980s, and in the late 1970s that we would in the mid-1980s. We have failed so far to do any of those things, even while the Soviets were deploying over 600 new ICBMs, each with a payload equal to or greater than that of MX, and with accuracies now matching those of the most accurate U.S. ICBMs.

To say that the United States will modernize in the early 1990s with a small warhead missile will just not be believable. The Soviets would be justified in calculating that any new U.S. ICBM system will be aborted by some combination of environmental, doctrinal, fiscal, and political problems.''

Arms Reductions

Finally, there is the important consideration of arms control. While a strong and viable deterrent is essential to the maintenance of peace, our search for a durable foundation that can support a lasting peace must also incorporate significant and verifiable reductions in the size and destructive potential of existing nuclear arsenals. The President's ICBM modernization plan is fully consistent with, in fact, necessary to, such arms reductions. As you are all aware, the President has proposed a strategic arms reduction proposal, START, which would reduce by one third the overall size of both sides' deployed ballistic missile warheads, with even greater reductions in those weapons systems that are potentially the most destabilizing—land-based ballistic missiles. Whether the President's START proposal is successful will, in large measure, depend on Soviet perceptions of this nation's determination to maintain its deterrent capability in the face of the persistent growth of Soviet military power. Because the ICBM modernization plan is essential to our deterrence capability, the Soviets will undoubtedly perceive this nation's decision on whether to support it a litmus test of the extent of that determination. If the American people and its Congress give their support, the Soviet Union will come to the realization that the United States understands the current strategic realities and fully intends to meet the national security obligations these realities impose. By reinforcing this perception of American determination, vigorous ICBM modernization will discourage the notion that a continuation of the Soviet arms build up will afford the Soviet Union any strategic advantage and encourage Soviet cooperation in bringing strategic arms under control. Conversely, failure to modernize will serve only to foster a Soviet belief in the soundness of their policy of seeking unilateral strategic advantage through the continued deployment of ever more powerful weapons in ever greater numbers.

"A strategic modernization program is vital to preserving deterrence and enhancing the prospects for arms reduction."

Until this issue is clearly resolved in favor of a modernized ICBM force, we can expect little cooperation from the Soviet Union in Geneva. We have learned the hard way that the Soviet Union is impressed not by self-restraint, but by determination. For the first time they have proved willing to sit down at the negotiating table to discuss arms reduction; let us give them the incentive to stay there and reach fair, equitable, and verifiable agreements.

Let me make one final point about the centrality of our ICBM modernization plan to arms control. This Administration has sought to move away from arms control agreements that confine their restrictions to such limited measures of strategic capability as launchers and missiles, and emphasized instead those elements of strategic capability that threaten to upset stability. . . .

President's Plan

The President's modernization plan supports this concern with stability by holding out the promise, over the long-term, of channeling ICBM forces into more stable directions. Such stability can be enhanced by deployments that distribute the total number of warheads contained in the ICBM forces over a larger number of smaller missiles, thereby reducing the target value of individual ICBMs. In reducing the value of individual strategic assets, we reduce the attack incentive of a potential aggressor. If this promise is to be realized, we must pursue the two-step process provided by the President's plan.

First, we must deploy the Peacekeeper missile to end the current, destabilizing advantage the Soviet Union enjoys in critical prompt hard target capability. The Soviets will not voluntarily give up their current strategic advantage. If we do not take this first step, they will have no incentive to move toward ICBM deployments that are more stabilizing. Deployment of the Peacekeeper will act as a necessary foundation and catalyst for a restructuring of U.S. and Soviet ICBM forces.

Second, we must vigorously pursue small, single warhead missile technology and operational concepts to determine the technical, operational and fiscal feasibility of moving to an ICBM structure that increases the emphasis on the deployment of ICBMs that individually are of less value as targets.

The report issued by the President's Commission reflects the dedication and patriotism with which this bipartisan group of distinguished Americans responded to the task given them. Let me end, then, by quoting from the end of their report:

> "If we can begin to see ourselves, in dealing with these issues, not as political partisans or as crusaders for one specific solution to a part of this complex set of problems, but rather as citizens of a great nation with the humbling obligation to persevere in the long-run task of preserving both peace and liberty for the world, a common perspective may finally be found."

Caspar Weinberger is the Secretary of Defense for the Reagan administration.

"Several members of the government have stated repeatedly that we are inferior to the Soviet Union in strategic weapons. . . .In my opinion there is no such inferiority."

The MX Buildup Will Not Improve Security

Hans A. Bethe

My name is Hans A. Bethe. I have been a Professor of Physics at Cornell University since 1935. In 1967 I was awarded the Nobel Prize for studies of nuclear reactions in the stars. I was Leader of the Theoretical Division of the Los Alamos Scientific Laboratory from 1943 to 1945 when that Laboratory developed the first atomic bomb. I have consulted for the Laboratory at least once a year. I was a member of the President's Science Advisory Committee from 1957 to 1960, and remained a member of its Strategic Military Panel until 1969 when the Panel was dissolved. In 1958 I participated in the Experts Conference in Geneva which discussed the verification of a ban on nuclear weapons tests, and led to the Partial Test Ban Treaty in 1963. I am testifying on behalf of the Union of Concerned Scientists of Cambridge, Massachusetts, but the ideas expressed in my testimony are my own.

Several members of the government have stated repeatedly that we are inferior to the Soviet Union in strategic weapons, and that we need to build up our weapons. In my opinion there is no such inferiority. We have more nuclear warheads than the Russians, and I consider this to be the most important measure of relative strength. In addition, as Dr. Kissinger stressed many years ago, at the present level of strategic armaments superiority in numbers or megatons has no meaning.

We are told that there is a window of vulnerability because the Russians might use their large ICBMs to destroy our land-based ICBMs. It is generally agreed that this is not possible *now*, but with the improving accuracy of Russian missiles it might become possible in a few years. Leaving the question of the technical feasibility aside, I claim that such a first strike would give no significant military advantage to the Russians.

The reason is that ICBMs make up only ¼ of our strategic nuclear forces, as measured by the number of

Hans A. Bethe, statement presented to the Senate Committee on Foreign Relations, May 13, 1982.

warheads. One-half of our force is on invulnerable nuclear-powered submarines, and another ¼ is on bombers, many of which can take off from their widely dispersed airfields in case of an alert. We would therefore have ample striking force left even if *all* our ICBMs were destroyed.

An attack on our ICBMs would surely arouse the will to fight in the American people. The fallout from such an attack would kill millions of Americans. This would have an even more profound psychological effect than Pearl Harbor, but would have less military consequences than Pearl Harbor did.

Russian Accuracy

It is sometimes argued that our submarine-based nuclear missiles do not have sufficient accuracy. However, if a Russian attack on our ICBMs is to make any sense at all, it would be accompanied by a massive invasion of Western Europe. The military installations for such an attack (airfields, munitions and fuel storage depots), and the staging areas for an invasion, are all soft targets for which our submarine-based missiles would have plenty of accuracy. Therefore, a hypothetical first-strike against our ICBMs would have practically no effect on our war-fighting capability. Therefore the window of vulnerability does not exist.

It is also often claimed that the Russians have introduced many new weapons of great power, such as the SS-18, -19, and -20, while we have done nothing. The latter statement is not true. While the outer envelope of our Minuteman ICBM has remained the same, we have progressed from Minuteman-1 to 2 to 3, and in the latter we have introduced MIRV, a development which the Russians imitated, and which led them to their great striking capability. More important, on our submarines we have progressed from the Polaris warhead to the Poseidon, and then to Trident I. The latter represents very significant progress: The range of Trident I is 4000 miles, compared to about 2000 for

Poseidon. This permits our submarines to operate over most of the North Atlantic, and to still hit Russia. Submarines at sea are very difficult to find. Now that they can roam over such a vast area of ocean, they are far more elusive. This greatly enhances their invulnerability. The U.S. has not stood still in nuclear weapons deployment.

The Cruise Missile

The most important addition to our arsenal is the cruise missile, which is being deployed on our B-52 bombers. The cruise missile can penetrate into the Soviet Union: No defense system against it exists. The elaborate and costly Russian air defense system has been made obsolete by the cruise missile, 3000 of which are to be installed on our bombers. In short we have, and will continue to have into the foreseeable future, two completely independent and essentially invulnerable strategic forces.

Because the cruise missile can penetrate the Soviet Union as no bomber can, and because it has extreme accuracy, we do not need a new bomber, the B-1, and even less its follow-up, the STEALTH. Perhaps the B-52 will eventually have to be replaced, but I cannot see why this replacement should have elaborate electronic equipment to penetrate into Russia, equipment which accounts for the enormous cost of B-1 and STEALTH. Penetration can be achieved much more effectively and cheaply by the cruise missile.

"We would have ample striking force left even if all our ICBMs were destroyed."

The government has stated that we need parity in strategic forces in every category. If this means that we need parity also in ICBMs, I disagree. With the increasing accuracy of missiles, on both sides, all land-based weapons will become vulnerable. I cannot think of any deployment on land which will be secure, and in my opinion the deployment of MX is a futile expenditure of money. We should maintain the emphasis on submarine and bomber forces; this makes our forces largely invulnerable, and thereby superior to those of the Soviets. If anyone has a window of vulnerability, it is the Soviet Union.

As I have said, several of our weapons programs are unnecessary: the B-1, the STEALTH, and the MX. But the submarine program deserves our full support, especially the further improvement of secure communication links to our submarines, as has been rightly emphasized by this Administration. Also, if we wish to decrease our dependence on nuclear weapons in Europe, a goal which I strongly support, our conventional forces must be built up, especially by exploiting our available high-technology in anti-tank weapons.

Threatened by Possibility

We are not inferior to the Russians in strategic armaments. But we, the Russians, and Western Europe, are severely threatened by the possibility that the enormous arsenal of nuclear weapons on both sides may some day be used. Our only hope lies in substantial reduction of these armaments. A good first step would be the ratification of the SALT II agreement by the Senate. The advantages of doing so have been persuasively demonstrated by Senator Hart in the *New York Times* of May 2. Among other things, if SALT II had been ratified in 1980, the Russians would now have 250 fewer strategic missiles than they actually have, and they could not continue their buildup. . . .

Arms Control

Negotiations with the Russians are difficult and lengthy in any case. The SALT II treaty took 6 years to negotiate. We cannot wait that long. We must stop the arms race by measures which are not subject to such long delay. I find most attractive the proposal by George Kennan, the famous expert on the Soviet Union, which has recently been revived by Admiral Gayler in the *New York Times Magazine* of April 25. The plan calls for similar reductions by both superpowers, let's assume by 5% of the existing force per year. Each side would choose the weapons it wants to retire, and compliance could easily be verified by our satellites. This plan is so simple that it might be agreed on with very brief negotiation, like the Limited Test Ban in 1963. But it would, in fact, not require any agreement; we could make such a reduction, and challenge the Russians to do the same. If they do so, we would make another similar reduction the following year, and so on. This would not require any treaty, and it would enhance our security.

Such mutual reductions could not replace a negotiated treaty, which has a permanence far beyond the bilateral reductions which I just proposed. Furthermore, a treaty could optimize the balance and invulnerability of the two strategic forces. This would remove the threat of pre-emptive strikes, and the current hair-trigger readiness that could lead to nuclear war by accident or miscalculation.

To summarize:

—our strategic forces are, if anything, superior to the Soviet's;

—our national security, and that of our allies, is most threatened by the grotesque size and continuing growth of both nuclear arsenals.

These are the basic facts. Once they are recognized, the essential features of a sound national security policy become apparent.

Hans A. Bethe is a John Wendell Anderson Professor of Physics Emeritus and a member of the Union of Concerned Scientists. The UCS is opposed to the nuclear arms race.

"Soviet planners would have to account for the possibility that MX missiles in Minuteman silos would be available for use, and thus they would help deter such attacks."

The MX Is a Defensive Weapon

President's Commission on Strategic Forces

In our effort to make a strategy of deterrence and arms control effective in preventing the Soviets from political or military use of their strategic forces, we must keep several points in mind.

The Soviets must continue to believe what has been NATO's doctrine for three decades: that if we or our allies should be attacked—by massive conventional means or otherwise—the United States has the will and the means to defend with the full range of American power. This by no means excludes the need to make improvements in our conventional forces in order to have increased confidence in our ability to defend effectively at the conventional level in many more situations, and thus to raise the nuclear threshold. Certainly mutual arms control agreements to reduce both sides' reliance on nuclear weapons should be pursued. But effective deterrence requires that early in any Soviet consideration of attack, or threat of attack, with conventional forces or chemical or biological weapons, Soviet leaders must understand that they risk an American nuclear response.

Similarly, effective deterrence requires that the Soviets be convinced that they could not credibly threaten us or our allies with a limited use of nuclear weapons against military targets, in one country or many. Such a course of action by them would be even more likely to result in full-scale nuclear war than would a massive conventional attack. But we cannot discount the possibility that the Soviets would implicitly or explicitly threaten such a step in some future crisis if they believed that we were unprepared or unwilling to respond. Indeed lack of preparation or resolve on our part would make such blackmail distinctly more probable.

Effective Deterrence

In order to deter such Soviet threats we must be able to put at risk those types of Soviet targets—including

Excerpted from the report of the President's Commission on Strategic Forces, issued April 1983.

hardened ones such as military command bunkers and facilities, missile silos, nuclear weapons and other storage, and the rest—which the Soviet leaders have given every indication by their actions they value most, and which constitute their tools of control and power. We cannot afford the delusion that Soviet leaders—human though they are and cautious though we hope they will be—are going to be deterred by exactly the same concerns that would dissuade us. Effective deterrence of the Soviet leaders requires them to be convinced in their own minds that there could be no case in which they could benefit by initiating war.

Effective deterrence of any Soviet temptation to threaten or launch a massive conventional or a limited nuclear war thus requires us to have a comparable ability to destroy Soviet military targets, hardened and otherwise. If there were ever a case to be made that the Soviets would unilaterally stop their strategic deployments at a level short of the ability seriously to threaten our forces, that argument vanished with the deployment of their SS-18 and SS-19 ICBMs. A one-sided strategic condition in which the Soviet Union could effectively destroy the whole range of strategic targets in the United States, but we could not effectively destroy a similar range of targets in the Soviet Union, would be extremely unstable over the long run. Such a situation could tempt the Soviets, in a crisis, to feel they could successfully threaten or even undertake conventional or limited nuclear aggression in the hope that the United States would lack a fully effective response. A one-sided condition of this sort would clearly not serve the cause of peace.

In order, then, to pursue successfully a policy of deterrence and verifiable, stabilizing arms control we must have a strong and militarily effective nuclear deterrent. Consequently our strategic forces must be modernized, as necessary, to enhance to an adequate degree their overall survivability and to enable them to engage effectively the targets that Soviet leaders most value....

Need for Modernization

There are important needs on several grounds for ICBM modernization that cannot be met by the small, single-warhead ICBM.

First, arms control negotiations—in particular the Soviets' willingness to enter agreements that will enhance stability—are heavily influenced by ongoing programs. The ABM Treaty of 1972, for example, came about only because the United States maintained an ongoing ABM program and indeed made a decision to make a limited deployment. It is illusory to believe that we could obtain a satisfactory agreement with the Soviets limiting ICBM deployments if we unilaterally terminated the only new U.S. ICBM program that could lead to deployment in this decade. Such a termination would effectively communicate to the Soviets that we were unable to neutralize their advantage in multiple-warhead ICBMs. Abandoning the MX at this time in search of a substitute would jeopardize, not enhance, the likelihood of reaching a stabilizing and equitable agreement. It would also undermine the incentives to the Soviets to change the nature of their own ICBM force and thus the environment most conducive to the deployment of a small missile.

Second, effective deterrence is in no small measure a question of the Soviets' perception of our national will and cohesion. Cancelling the MX, when it is ready for flight testing, when over $5 billion have already been spent on it, and when its importance has been stressed by the last four presidents, does not communicate to the Soviets that we have the will essential to effective deterrence. Quite the opposite.

Third, the serious imbalance between the Soviets' massive ability to destroy hardened land-based military targets with their ballistic missile force and our lack of such a capability must be redressed promptly. Our ability to assure our allies that we have the capability and will to stand with them, with whatever forces are necessary, if the alliance is threatened by massive conventional, chemical or biological, or limited nuclear attack is in question as long as this imbalance exists. Even before the Soviet leaders, in a grave crisis, considered using the first tank regiment or the first SS-20 missile against NATO, they must be required to face what war would mean to them. In order to augment what we would hope would be an inherent sense of conservatism and caution on their part, we must have a credible capability for controlled, prompt, limited attack on hard targets ourselves. This capability casts a shadow over the calculus of Soviet risk-taking at any level of confrontation with the West. Consequently, in the interest of the alliance as a whole, we cannot safely permit a situation to continue wherein the Soviets have the capability promptly to destroy a range of hardened military targets and we do not.

Fourth, our current ICBM force is aging significantly.

The Titan II force is being retired for this reason and extensive Minuteman rehabilitation programs are planned to keep those missiles operational.

The existence of a production program for an ICBM of approximately 100 tons is important for two additional reasons. As Soviet ABM modernization and modern surface-to-air missile development and deployment proceed—even with the limitations of the ABM treaty—it is important to be able to match any possible Soviet breakout from that treaty with strategic forces that have the throw-weight to carry sufficient numbers of decoys and other penetration aids; these may be necessary in order to penetrate the Soviet defenses which such a breakout could provide before other compensating steps could be taken. Having in production a missile that could effectively counter such a Soviet step should help deter them from taking it. Moreover, in view of our coming sole reliance on space shuttle orbiters, it would be prudent to have in production a booster, such as MX, that is of sufficient size to place in orbit at least some of our most strategically important satellites.

These objectives can all be accomplished, at reasonable cost, by deploying MX missiles in current Minuteman silos.

In the judgment of the Commission, the vulnerability of such silos in the near term, viewed in isolation, is not a sufficiently dominant part of the overall problem of ICBM modernization to warrant other immediate steps being taken such as closely-spacing new silos or ABM defense of those silos. This is because of the mutual survivability shared by the ICBM force and the bomber force in view of the different types of attacks that would need to be launched at each....In any circumstances other than that of a particular kind of massive surprise attack on the U.S. by the Soviet Union, Soviet planners would have to account for the possibility that MX missiles in Minuteman silos would be available for use, and thus they would help deter such attacks. To deter such surprise attacks we can reasonably rely both on our other strategic forces and on the range of operational uncertainties that the Soviets would have to consider in planning such aggression—as long as we have underway a program for long-term ICBM survivability such as that for the small, single warhead ICBM to hedge against long-term vulnerability for the rest of our forces.

The President's Commission on Strategic Forces, headed by Chairman Brent Scowcroft, completed its report on April 6, 1983 at the request of President Reagan. In the previous three months the commission held 28 conferences and talked to over 200 technical experts to examine the future of the ICBM forces and to recommend basing alternatives.

> *"The MX is an improvement upon the Minuteman only if you have offense in mind."*

The MX Is an Offensive Weapon

The New Republic

The ground is not steady beneath the nuclear forces of the United States. The problem is not modes of basing but modes of thinking. The traditional strategy for our nuclear arsenal is shaken by a war of ideas about its purpose, perhaps the most decisive war of ideas in its history. The purpose of the arsenal, at least until now, has been deterrence. The classic formulation was by Bernard Brodie, who wrote in 1946, "Thus far the chief purpose of our military establishment has been to win wars. From now on its chief purpose must be to avert them." Military planners and military intellectuals have been glossing Brodie's dictum ever since. Now things seem to be changing. Deterrence is everywhere besieged. In the Pentagon it is challenged by concepts of nuclear use. In the peace movement it is challenged by perfectibilian schemes for disarmament. The days may be gone when arguing for deterrence was like arguing for motherhood. Its merits are no longer obvious. Consider only the nuclear debate of recent weeks—the influential interventions of President Reagan's speech of November 22 and of *The Challenge of Peace: God's Promise and Our Response,* the pastoral letter on war and peace of the National Conference of Catholic Bishops.

"What do we mean when we speak of nuclear deterrence?" the President asked. Not "excessive forces," he replied, "or what some people have called 'overkill.'" The natural complement of deterrence, moreover, is arms control. They are, he said, "parallel paths...the only paths that offer any real hope for an enduring peace." And deterrence, he explained, is a policy of defense: "The United States will never use its forces except in response to attack." Sufficiency, not superiority, in the quantity of nuclear weapons; negotiations to control and reduce them; the renunciation of any intention to employ them except in retaliation, exactly as the theory of deterrence mandates—this is the sweet voice of reason. Then the President turned the page.

"While the policy of deterrence has stood the test of time," the equivocation began, "the things we must do in order to maintain deterrence have changed." There followed his now famous charts, the first national security video game: blue for the United States (the President's thesis was that the United States has reason to be blue), and red for the Soviet Union (color-coordinated, again); and the chaste white background stood silently for the chaste planet earth, which the lethal lines on the graph are disfiguring. The charts showed, with a very selective marshaling of evidence, that the Russians are ahead. "In virtually every measure of military power the Soviet Union enjoys a decided advantage." The conclusion drawn from this demonstration was what the President called "modernization," and "modernization" meant the MX.

Explosive Yield

The MX is a missile that is seventy feet long, weighs ninety-six tons, and carries ten warheads, each of which may have an explosive "yield" of more than thirty times that of the bomb that destroyed Hiroshima. Each of these warheads may be independently targeted; they are already accurate enough to hit very "hard" and very small targets, such as missile silos, with only a small "delivery error," and the experts are confident that during the next decade the "error" will be virtually abolished. The Reagan Administration wants to develop and deploy one hundred of these things. (There is some good news here: the Carter Administration had set its heart on two hundred. Of course Congress would not hear of such grandiosity; still, it is heartening to see Ronald Reagan lower a number.) They will be deployed in a manner known as "dense pack." That is, all one hundred will be planted in a single field near Cheyenne, Wyoming, and will be defended from Soviet missiles by the Soviet missiles themselves, which will create a

Editorial, "In Defense of Deterrence," *The New Republic*, December 20, 1982. Reprinted by permission of THE NEW REPUBLIC, © 1982, The New Republic, Inc.

nuclear hurricane that will knock them off course. This is the effect known, anthromorphically, as "fratricide."

In brief, this is the plan for the new missile, which will be called "Peacekeeper." (We defer, on this, to Johnny Carson, who said, "Soon they'll rename napalm 'Crazy Foam.'") The President's justification for the program was the famous "window of vulnerability," the exposed condition of the United States's land-based missile force. The problem of ICBM vulnerability—the President is correct that it exists—is also the problem of ICBM survivability: the United States must be certain that enough of its ICBMS will survive a Soviet strike to strike back. It is the capacity for a second strike that we are trying to secure—the capacity, in other words, to fulfill the requirements of deterrence. So goes the President's explanation. But a trick is being played on the American people.

The "Pindown"

The problem of ICBM vulnerability has nothing to do with the kind of ICBM that is vulnerable. What determines the safety of these missiles is the manner of their basing. The MX would be exactly as unsafe as the Minuteman in the dispersed silos, and the Minuteman would be exactly as safe as the MX in the dense pack. Assuming, of course, that the dense pack works. We have already expressed our doubts about this ("Window Pain," TNR, October 18), though we can't be sure that it won't work, and neither can the Russians. We can be sure, however, that "dense pack" will not work for very long. The Soviets can immobilize our entire MX force with what is called a "pindown"—exploding a sufficient volume of warheads at an appropriate altitude above the "dense pack," thus making it impossible for the marvelous MX to get through. "Pindown" is mentioned nowhere in the White House's background statements on the subject, unless that is what it means by "Soviet countermeasures" that are "no more than technical dreams." But "pindown" is no dream. It is true that the Russians do not yet possess the precise megatonnage to pin us down, but even the Air Force general in charge of MX admits that it will "drive [them] to development of new warheads larger in yield." According to Henry Jackson, the honest hawk, the Russians could have such warheads in four years. Up, then, goes the window. (Enter ABM, stage right.)

Mr. Reagan's analysis of our strategic situation epitomizes the mixture of patriotism and panic that may be found also in the present Pentagon. But neither the President nor the Pentagon has provided the answer to a rather simple question: if the Russians can destroy our entire land-based missile force, why don't they? The answer is that they probably can't, because unless they did away with all our missiles, they would be punished for the attempt by those that remained; and that even if they could, they won't, because we have missiles at sea and in the air which would avenge our ICBMs by destroying Soviet forces or Soviet society or both. The

deterrence scenario, after all, always envisaged something like the SS-18s—that is, it envisaged a Russian first strike. The sincerity of that scenario is now being tested. Did we mean what we said about desiring only to deter? If we did, we are still just as safe. If it is really a second strike for which we wish to prepare, we are prepared. The vulnerability of land-based missiles is not the same thing as the vulnerability of the United States. It is, however, a permanent fact of life; and it endangers the Russians more than it does the United States, because three quarters of their Strategic Rocket Forces are land-based. Our ICBMs are vulnerable; we are not. Indeed, as Lawrence Freedman has written, "the fact that ICBM vulnerability provided the greatest cause for concern [in the early 1980s] could be taken as a symptom of the underlying stability of the strategic balance."

MX Is Vulnerable

The MX, in other words, is not invulnerable. Nor is it necessary for the purpose of a second strike; there exists the unjustly vilified Minuteman III for that. (This weapon is not exactly a slingshot, as recent Administrations would have us believe. Some of the Minuteman IIIs are even good against Soviet missile silos; they are, that is to say, counterforce weapons, which is their dirty little secret.) From the point of view of deterrence, then, the MX is not justified. It is justified only from the point of view of counterforce. The MX is an improvement upon the Minuteman only if you have offense in mind. When the President declared that we will never strike first, and then went on to introduce the MX, he was deceiving the public, because the MX is supremely a first-strike weapon. The adoption of the MX by the American government represents not only the perfection of a technology but the transformation of a strategy.

---

*"Only if we wish to fire **our** ICBMs at **their** SS-18s—that is, only if we wish to start a nuclear war—do we need the MX."*

Does the United States need a first-strike weapon? The Pentagon says yes, because the Russians have one. James Schlesinger, when he was Secretary of Defense, used to call this "essential equivalence." But, once again, if the Russians will fire their SS-18s at our ICBMs, they will pay with a big part of Russia. Only if we wish to fire *our* ICBMs at *their* SS-18s—that is, only if we wish to start a nuclear war—do we need the MX. Our planners appear to believe that there are circumstances in which it would be in our interest to start a nuclear war. These conditions are usually referred to as "grave crises," in which, according to one specialist, "resorting to intercontinental nuclear attack would likely be the result of a conviction that a nuclear exchange had become inevitable, and that some advantage would obtain from going first." What the advantage might be is unclear. If we go first, they will go second. Who cares who goes third? Such brinksmanlike behavior, moreover, might also occur to the Russians. Indeed, once we have the MX, it will almost certainly occur to them. "Peacekeeper" is the best reason for preemption the Russians will ever have.

Mockery of Deterrence

Militarily, then, the MX is a mockery of deterrence, and makes the world a more dangerous place. Other justifications, however, are given for it. The fear of a Soviet breakthrough in antisubmarine warfare, for example. It is argued that conceding the vulnerability of our land-based missile force to the Russians will enable them to concentrate all their resources upon research and development at sea. This is not terribly persuasive. The Soviet disadvantage at sea is staggering, and it will be many, many years before they catch up. The United States, moreover, is not exactly devoid of the power to make the Russians fear for their own ICBMs. Their SS-17s, SS-18s, and SS-19s add up to about 820 counterforce targets, and three hundred of our Minuteman IIIs are outfitted with three warheads each, which adds up to nine hundred counterforce weapons. Not a perfect counterforce capacity, to be sure (military planners commonly allocate two warheads for each target); but not so imperfect that the Russians can sleep soundly.

> *"The MX is a mockery of deterrence, and makes the world a more dangerous place."*

The only argument for the MX that makes any sense is the argument from arms control—such is the perversity of the nuclear world. There may be a tactical value in proposing it, and in beginning to build it. The MX will be the Soviets' only incentive to reduce, limit, or dismantle their SS-18s, and it is the most urgent task of the United States in strategic arms talks to act upon the SS-18s. This makes the MX missiles the most expensive bargaining chips in history—about $300 million a chip. (The MX is the perfect counterbudget weapon.) This is also expecting the Russians to cut into the best and largest part of their forces, which may be expecting too much. Still, if they are persuaded of the American intention to become a first-strike superpower, they may make a deal. If they do, the sums spent in researching and developing the MX will have been a sound investment in ridding the world of these disgusting devices. We believe that the President is sincere when he maintains that he needs to take the MX to Geneva. *Si vis pacem, para bellum,* the old Roman adage sternly warns. If you want peace, prepare for war. But we have our doubts, however, that the planners in the Pentagon who invented and peddled this missile did so for the sake of arms control. They want us to have the MX, and maybe to use it. They think that it improves our political and military position. If you want war, prepare for war. So it is a gamble. If we win, a dimension of danger will disappear. If we lose, we will live forever by our nerves.

The New Republic *is a weekly opinion magazine.*

"You need MX to leverage the Soviets to get an arms control agreement."

The MX Is a Bargaining Chip

Michael Getler

An irony of President Reagan's MX victory in the House is that the pivotal figure on the administration's side was not a senior Republican but a liberal Democrat who made his first mark in Congress as a Pentagon critic.

Rep. Les Aspin, D-Wis., 44, is a sharp-minded, glib, former Pentagon "whiz kid" with a master's degree from Oxford and a doctorate in economics from the Massachusetts Institute of Technology who was elected to Congress 13 years ago.

Last Tuesday, on the eve of the House vote, Reagan quoted Aspin at length in a signed article in *The Washington Post* in support of the MX intercontinental ballistics missile, a testimonial to the importance of Aspin's voice and to his transition from maverick to man of the center on arms questions.

"Aspin carried a lot of intellectual water for us," a White House aide said.

Aspin was sharply criticized by some Democrats for his position on the MX, and agreed in an interview that the decision to support the president on the missile represents a unique and risky experiment for liberals such as himself. But it would have been worse for Democrats and for achieving arms control agreements with Moscow to oppose the president at this time, Aspin said.

Aspin described the vote on the MX as part of a bargain: The president got the missile, and gave a far more explicit pledge to seek arms agreements with the Soviet Union. The MX, Aspin said, may well give Reagan the "leverage" to succeed in those talks.

He agreed that he and other Democrats who supported the MX could wind up with egg on their faces if the bargain with Reagan falls through. Once started, big weapons systems are hard to stop, Aspin said, and there is no guarantee that Congress will stop the MX in future

Michael Getler, "Aspin says Stand on MX Part of Bargain by Reagan," Reprinted with permission of *The Washington Post*.

funding votes if the president fails to fulfill his promises on arms control.

Difficult Experiment

"What really is going on is a difficult experiment," Aspin said. "We've had experiments before, like the Social Security Commission, where you have a bargain between the legislature and the executive. But it's usually a one-shot deal, where they come together for one vote, one piece of legislation, Democrats and Republicans.

"But what you are talking about here," in the arms field where almost any action takes many years, "is something that has to continue over several congresses and several administrations," Aspin said. "I don't know of anything that's been done like this before, where you are talking about a deal that you're trying to hold together over such a period of time."

As to the genuineness of the president's intentions, Aspin said "we are about to find out" as Reagan studies changes in the U.S. negotiating position at the strategic arms reduction talks (START) with the Soviet Union scheduled to resume in Geneva June 8.

Several such changes—along with deployment of 100 MX missiles now and work on a new and less threatening small missile for the future—were all recommended earlier this year by a bipartisan presidential advisory commission headed by retired Gen. Brent Scowcroft. Reagan named the commission when Congress rejected the MX last winter and has endorsed all its recommendations.

The political risk is not so much in any immediate electoral terms, Aspin said, but because many of his liberal colleagues who broke with him on this issue are ready to say "I told you so" if there is no arms control agreement as the 10-warhead MX missiles are deployed.

"If the administration goes ahead and does its thing, makes a good faith effort and nobody sandbags the small missile and the arms control process and the

Russians simply don't buy it, well, we tried. We made an effort. But if this thing gets done in because somewhere along the line the Air Force makes sure the small missile doesn't work or somebody makes sure that our negotiating position is absurd'' there could be serious political repercussions, Aspin said.

Aspin said he voted for the MX for three reasons.

Serious Long-Term Threat

First, he said he believes it will help Reagan bargain with Moscow because the combination of highly accurate MXs and the Navy's new Trident II missile poses a serious long-term threat to Moscow's land-based missile force, and maybe the Soviets ''will be willing to make some accommodation to that.

''The second reason is that I'm convinced it would be a bad position for the Democrats to be against the Scowcroft commission recommendations. If MX had lost because Democrats had opposed it, then comes November, 1984, (and) Ronald Reagan can say, 'Well, I certainly might have gotten an arms control agreement, but the Democrats in the House didn't give me the tools I needed...even after I appointed a bipartisan commission and lots of Democratic experts on defense said this was a good thing.'''

''The MX...will help Reagan bargain with Moscow.''

With those Scowcroft recommendations approved, Aspin said, ''I think Democrats are now perfectly within their right to hold (Reagan) accountable and say, 'OK, we gave you everything you said you needed, now where's your agreement?' The standard story is that the Democrats have two issues to run on against Reagan. One is economics, and that may be fading. The other is arms control, and I think you have to vote for the Scowcroft commission recommendations to keep that one alive.''

The third reason, Aspin said, ''is that this thing (the MX) isn't going to go away. Big weapons like this don't go away. Even if you had the votes to kill it now, a year or two from now the Russians will do something like invade Afghanistan and the right wing will ride back into town saying that the Soviets did it because they feel emboldened and politically daring because they've got an advantage on us. And bang, we're back to building MX and God knows what else and at what cost, and we'd probably wind up with 200 or 300 rather than 100 missiles,'' he said.

''That's what happened with the B-1 bomber. Carter killed it at $100 million apiece, and Ronald Reagan brought it back at $200 million apiece.''

Nuclear Hair-trigger

And what of the argument that putting the MX in existing missile silos vulnerable to Soviet attack will put a hair-trigger on nuclear war?

''I think it does,'' he said, ''at least in the short run. Those missiles are vulnerable as hell. But all you can say is that you just hope a crisis doesn't reach those proportions,'' and that the overwhelming force on both sides will convince the super-powers it is better to bargain than to fight.

''We've got a potentially dangerous situation,'' Aspin said, but it would be dangerous even without the MX. He said he believes the oft-cited White House contention that the Soviets would not have agreed to an anti-missile defense treaty in 1972 if it were not for the U.S. threat to build one.

''I felt no interest in voting for MX,'' Aspin said, adding that his colleague, Rep. Albert Gore Jr., D-Tenn., ''definitely did not want to vote for MX.'' Yet both lawmakers and some other liberals supported the missile. The key difference that separated these liberals from their colleagues such as Rep. Thomas Downey, D-N.Y., who opposed the MX, ''was the belief that you needed MX to leverage the Soviets'' to get an arms control agreement.

Michael Getler is a reporter for The Washington Post.

The MX Is Not a Bargaining Chip

Gary Hart

Yesterday the president argued on this page that the only way to arms control is through strategic arms buildup. I am deeply troubled by the twisted logic that turns black into white, arms buildup into arms control, and the threat of war into the potential for peace. George Orwell is alive and well and living in Washington, on the eve of 1984.

The president's statement is correct that the votes in the House yesterday and the Senate today on the MX constitute "a question of vital concern which will affect the world our children inherit." But that is why the MX must *not* be developed or deployed.

This weapon will add nothing to the survivability of our land-based missile force. It will divert tens of billions of dollars from genuine human needs, as well as from the strengthening of our conventional forces—for which there is truly a broad-based consensus in America. It will help keep arms control right where it is today—dead in the water. And it will, in conjunction with Soviet deployments, move both nations inexorably closer to nuclear war. This is the real "bargain" the president offers, and it is no bargain for America.

First, the basing mode finally selected for the MX makes no sense. It is the worst of all worlds—the most attractive target we could present to Soviet missiles in the most vulnerable location we could devise. Virtually every expert group, including the Scowcroft Commission, has come away with one common message—heavily MIRVed missiles in existing silos are vulnerable threatening and inviting targets. One hundred missiles can be easily targeted and overwhelmed by the Soviets. As long as this administration refuses to seek ratification of the SALT II Treaty and fails to achieve new limits on Soviet warheads, this condition will remain.

Second, if our nation is serious about building a small mobile single-warhead missile to combine modernization,

Press release on the MX missile from the office of Senator Gary Hart, May 25, 1983.

increased stability and arms control in a single consensus package, then we should move on it now, not push it off until after the MX. By pursuing two missiles at once, bureaucratic pressures, diminishing funds and the desire for bigger rather than better will keep the smaller missile always a step out of reach in the future.

Enormous Diversion

Third, the MX represents an enormous diversion of defense resources from either a smaller new mobile missile or from improving our conventional forces. Already we are beginning to see the effects on defense spending as the president's unprecedented budget deficits bring closer and closer the day of reckoning for every segment of our society, including national defense. Each MX we build will mean less emphasis on truly survivable alternatives to today's vulnerable land-based missiles. Each MX we build will mean fewer ships, fewer tanks, fewer fighters and less readiness to face the threats before us around the globe, so that the first rifle shot could mean we would be forced to escalate to nuclear war simply because we are unable to meet aggression with appropriate power.

Fourth, the MX is no bargain for arms control. Secretary of Defense Caspar Weinberger said as much when he stated recently that President Reagan's letter to Congress on the MX and arms control commits him to "nothing basically new." The Reagan administration has repeatedly said that the MX will not be bargained away in negotiations. I fail to see how a vulnerable missile—that could easily be targeted by the Soviets, that will not be bargained away—can be a bargaining chip. The president has turned logic on its head.

Additionally, the record of this administration gives me no confidence that the arms control part of the MX "bargain" will be kept. This administration has refused to seek ratification of the Salt II Treaty. It delayed for many months any negotiations at all on nuclear arms—and then only went to the table when prodded by public pressure. It has abandoned the goal of a comprehensive nuclear test ban. It is launching a major "star wars" arms race in space—with no effort to stop this race before it gets started. What now should give us confidence that this administration is serious about nuclear arms control? What now should give us confidence that this administration will summon up the *statesmanship* and the *dedication* that can bring fewer weapons and safer weapons in a very difficult time?

False Argument

But the most pernicious and false argument raised in favor of the MX is that the MX is needed to demonstrate national will so the Soviets will negotiate seriously. Unlike the president, I believe in America's strength and in our will as a people to bear any sacrifice to remain free. If the issue is national will, we should put our defense dollars where they count—*not* on a vulnerable missile that all agree cannot be defended. If the issue is national will, then continually running down our arsenal before our people and the world is not the way to demonstrate it. Confidence is essential to deterrence, and we have good reason to be confident.

Finally, the MX is a step toward nuclear war. Because its power and vulnerability provide compelling reasons for the Soviets to strike it first, the MX, from a military point of view, is useful only as a first-strike weapon, or as a weapon to be fired the moment *we think* the Soviet missiles are on their way. In fact, the Joint Chiefs of Staff testified in April that we must have the MX so we can threaten Soviet missile silos and command posts. We have truly arrived at 1984 and "Newspeak" a year early when such a missile can be called "Peacekeeper."

"The most pernicious and false argument raised in favor of the MX is that the MX is needed to demonstrate national will so the Soviets will negotiate seriously."

Even if the MX is not used as a first-strike weapon, it would lead to a situation where both sides, despite their best intentions, could be tempted to fire their nuclear missiles in an extreme crisis. This was confirmed recently by Weinberger and John Vessey Jr., the chairman of the Joint Chiefs, who have said the United States might adopt a "launch under attack" policy of firing our missiles to counter pre-emptive attack.

The future, thus, will not be peace. The future will be both nations poised with fingers on hair-triggers ready to use their weapons rather than lose them.

I was born in Kansas, and although a Democrat, I grew up admiring and respecting another Kansan, Dwight D. Eisenhower, who stood for everything we as Americans have been raised to revere. Twenty-seven years ago last month, he wrote in a private letter: "When we get to the point, as one day we will, that both sides know that in any outbreak of general hostilities, regardless of the element of surprise, destruction will be both reciprocal and complete, possibly we will have sense enough to meet at the conference table with the understanding that the era of armaments has ended and the human race must conform its actions to this truth or die."

That day has long since come, and now more than ever we must face *seriously* the nuclear threat to our security and survival. The MX serves neither. It is a step into quicksand in the search for firmer ground.

Gary Hart, Democrat Senator of Colorado, is a member of the Senate Armed Services Committee.

"In...explaining his decision to build the MX missile, President Ronald Reagan painted a picture of the US-Soviet military balance that...contained elements that were misleading."

Reagan Is Misleading America on the MX

Fred Kaplan

In his speech explaining his decision to build the MX missile, President Ronald Reagan painted a picture of the US-Soviet military balance that—while not false—contained elements that were misleading.

In the past decade, Reagan said, the Soviets have rushed ahead in an arms race, but "we have not." As a result, he continued, "in virtually every measure of military power, the Soviet Union enjoys a decided advantage."

The measures he picked to illustrate this claim, however, were selective.

One chart he displayed indicated that, when measured in dollars, the Soviet military currently outspends that of the United States by about one-third. However, Reagan omitted three considerations that make such a chart somewhat less scary.

First, the CIA estimates that 25 percent of Soviet weapons and manpower are deployed on the Chinese border and, therefore, do not now threaten the United States or its formal allies.

Second, according to the Defense Intelligence Agency, the combined defense budget for 1982 of the United States and its NATO allies (just over $300 billion) is greater than that of the Soviet Union and its Warsaw Pact allies (about $260 billion).

Third, dollar comparisons mean little in any event. Such a technique calculates the Soviet defense budget by asking how much it would cost the United States to build the Soviet military machine. Thus, for example, US military wages are assumed, even though the Soviet conscript is really paid the equivalent of about $6.50 a month. Likewise, inflation in the US defense economy, by this technique automatically sends the Soviet defense budget spiraling upward.

A few years ago, the CIA conceded in congressional hearings that "the dollar-cost estimates cannot be used to draw inferences about relative military effectiveness... Nor can [they] be used to draw conclusions about the burden of defense on the Soviet economy." When these factors are taken into account, the Soviet defense budget does not appear to loom so far above that that of the United States.

Reagan also noted that the Soviets have more "strategic missiles and bombers" than the United States. This is correct, but the President made no reference to the number of each side's warheads and bombs. As Henry Kissinger once said, it is warheads and bombs—not their delivery vehicles—that kill people and destroy targets. The United States has about 9700 of these weapons; the Soviets have about 7800.

Doubled Arsenal

Reagan also said that the Soviets have one-third more land-based ICBMs than does the United States, and that the United States has built none since 1965. It is true we stopped at 1000 Minuteman ICBMs that year. However, beginning in 1970, Washington replaced 550 of them with the all-new Minuteman III, which has three warheads that can be aimed at separate targets (instead of just one) and better accuracy than the older models. Thus, without building a single additional missile, the United States doubled its arsenal of land-based warheads.

Reagan might also have said, but did not, that the United States has more than three times as many submarine-launched missile-warheads as the Soviet Union—5000 to 1600. These submarines are virtually invulnerable to attack, an important point, one would think, in an age of what Reagan calls an impending "window of vulnerability."

About the submarines, the President did say the Soviets have built 15 new ones in the last 15 years, while until last year the United States had commissioned none. Again, this is true, but in the past decade Washington has added Poseidon and Trident I missiles to its subs (each carrying 8 to 10 warheads—not enough to deem it

Fred Kaplan, "The MX and Arms Balance," *The Boston Globe*, November 24, 1982. Reprinted courtesy of The Boston Globe.

an "intercontinental" machine.

At the same time, the United States has spent several billion dollars modernizing its B52 bombers, with electronic countermeasures, weapons, navigation gear and so forth. It is hardly the same plane that it once was.

In another arena of nuclear competition, Reagan said Moscow has 600 intermediate-range ballistic missiles, whereas Washington has none, having withdrawn them all 20 years ago. This is true, but the United States chose to withdraw them because they were judged too vulnerable to Soviet attack and because nobody could figure out what missiles of intermediate range could do that ones of intercontinental range—based back in the United States—could not.

Even so, the President omitted a great deal from this calculation: the 180 French nuclear missiles and roughly 1000 or more US and allied nuclear-equipped airplanes—in Europe and on aircraft carriers—well within striking range of the Soviet Union; the several thousand shorter-range nuclear weapons that can obliterate Russian soldiers that might break through NATO defenses; and the 400 US Poseidon submarine-launched missile warheads that are explicitly dedicated to NATO's defense.

"The situation is not so lopsided as Reagan made it seem."

When similar airplanes and missiles are added to the Soviet total, the Soviet Union still has more, but the situation is not so lopsided as Reagan made it seem.

But there is a much broader issue, going beyond the numbers games. That concerns what nuclear weapons are for. If they ever have to be used, they are there to destroy targets—military facilities, war factories, industrial plants and so forth. What is important is not who has more missiles or warheads. Rather, it is whether each side can accomplish its strategic aims—which, in the nuclear realm, must primarily be whether it can threaten to retaliate with such horrendous destruction (or, if it wishes, with discriminating pinpricks) that the other side would have to be mad to attempt a first strike.

On this score, Defense Secretary Caspar W. Weinberger and others in the Administration have contended the MX will make the Soviets less willing to start a nuclear war. However, this thesis depends on two assumptions: first, that the closely spaced basing plan for the MX really will markedly improve the missile's prospects of surviving an attack in the long run; and, second, that the Soviets are not so deterred by the immense destructive power in the US submarines and bombers—and the (at least few) land-based missiles—that would survive an attack.

On these two crucial points, Reagan said nothing.

Fred Kaplan is the author of The Wizards of Armageddon, *the story of the nuclear strategists, published in 1983 by Simon and Schuster.*

"With such Soviet hara-kiri a few of the American MXs would remain intact, ready to take off for chosen Russian targets."

viewpoint **45**

Reagan Is Not Misleading America on the MX

John Chamberlain

Critics of the MX missile are having a field day at the expense of the so-called dense-pack plan for deploying 100 of the monster weapons in hardened underground silos 600 yards apart for 14 miles of Wyoming territory.

The theory is that incoming missiles from a Soviet first atomic strike would commit "fratricide," with the earliest arrivals causing such a detonating celestial ruckus that they would destroy the follow-on weapons. With such Soviet nuclear hara-kiri a few of the American MXs would remain intact, ready to take off for chosen Russian targets.

The point, as it is being made in congressional offices as these words are written, is that nobody has the least idea whether the "fratricide" of Soviet weapons at an anticipated Wyoming rendezvous would happen in accordance with the forecast. But M.I.T. scientists are already speculating that the Soviets might use missiles able to penetrate the ground before exploding. They could be timed to go off simultaneously with the later arrivals. Since not even the nuclear scientists know what sort of changes may be in store before the MXs can be built and stored in dense-pack arrangement, the confusion that is manifest on Capitol Hill is understandable.

It could be that practically everybody, whether he be hawk or dove, is missing the point about the MX. My own theory is that, even if it is built, it will never figure in an actual war. Yet Ronald Reagan needs it, or at least the threat of making it, for simple public relations reasons.

MX Is a Symbol

The MX, for better or worse, has become a symbol. If we refuse to build it, or something close to it, the agitation in Western Europe against putting Pershing II intermediate missiles in West Germany will grow to unmanageable proportions. The subsequent Finlandization of Western Europe will be easy enough to understand if the MX is cancelled.

We need the promise to build the MX if only to give credibility to our arms reduction negotiators at Geneva. If the Soviets don't think we are serious about matching their atomic capabilities, they will do nothing to cut back on the number of warheads they can aim at American silos.

The whole business is, of course, ineffably silly from any rational standpoint, but international politics in a world of radically clashing systems is not rational. I don't want to get into any debate about the possible "winability" of an all-out atomic war. It seems to me that if both sides let go at each other with the big explosives, there would be pockets of humanity left to carry on. But it would be in a world of complete disorder. Communications would be so disrupted that nobody would be able to make overtures to anybody else.

The so-called weaker nations in the Southern Hemisphere would suddenly emerge as the strongest powers on the globe. The winners in the war might be Paraguay, Chile—or even South Africa. Liberals would just love it.

The impossibility of envisioning what might happen if the Soviets and the United States were to engage in a series of first and second strikes is so obvious that we may be sure that nobody in either Moscow or Washington will press a first button. But this does not mean that the contest of the grisly symbols can be ended unilaterally.

If we don't go ahead with the MX in some basing mode, the West Europeans won't accept the protective Pershing IIs or the cruise missiles on their soil. Lacking the evidence that the United States is ready to preserve the reality of the nuclear protective umbrella, the West Europeans will be ready to deal with Moscow.

It's terrible to be ruled by considerations of public relations. But that is where we are in a world that missed its opportunity to throttle Bolshevism when it didn't have the nuclear bomb.

John Chamberlain, "Why Reagan Needs the MX Missiles," *The Union Leader,* December 18, 1982. Reprinted with permission.

John Chamberlain writes regularly for the Union Leader, *a daily newspaper published in New Hampshire.*

"Only [the MX's] capability, in the chess game of deterrence, can keep the Soviets reliably at bay."

The MX Is a Peacekeeper

M. Stanton Evans

The most important thing about the MX missile is the least often mentioned—the strategic problem it is meant to solve.

The report of the President's commission on the subject, headed by Lt. Gen. Brent Scowcroft, spells out this problem with disturbing clarity. Its sober discussion and conclusions are the more compelling because the members and counselors to the commission include a bipartisan array of brass from the last four national administrations. And what they tell us, in a nutshell, is that we are in a heap of self-inflicted trouble.

The features that make the MX missile desirable from the standpoint of our strategic planners are its augmented striking power and accuracy—both well in advance of our existing missiles. These qualities are needed, supposedly, to penetrate super-hardened targets in the Soviet Union in the calamitous event of nuclear exchange. Only such a capability, in the chess game of deterrence, can keep the Soviets reliably at bay.

> As matters presently stand, according to the commission, the Soviets could conceivably take out our missile force, as well as other targets in the U.S., but we couldn't do the same to them. The vulnerability of our weapons, and their inadequate striking power, might tempt the Kremlin to attack us. Only by going to the MX, and doing some other things besides, can we correct this dangerous imbalance.

As the commission sums it up, the Soviets now have 1,400 ICBM launchers with more than 5,000 warheads—compared to 1,047 launchers, with 2,250 warheads, for the United States. More than half of the Soviet missiles have been deployed since the last American ICBM was deployed. In addition, the Soviets have hardened missile sites and other defenses, and have deployed air and missile defenses to guard against U.S. attack.

Accordingly, says the commission, the Soviets "probably possess the necessary combination of ICBM numbers, reliability, accuracy and warhead yield to destroy almost all of the 1,047 U.S. ICBM silos, using only a portion of their ICBM force. The U.S. ICBM force now deployed cannot inflict similar damage, even using the entire force.

"Only the 550 MIRVed Minuteman III missiles in the U.S. ICBM force have relatively good accuracy, but the combination of accuracy and yield of their three warheads is inadequate to put at serious risk more than a small share of the many hardened targets in the Soviet Union. Most Soviet hardened targets—of which ICBM silos are only a portion—could withstand attacks by our other strategic missiles."

Unnerving Imbalance

In layman's terms, what this means is that the Soviets could take out all our missiles, and still have plenty left to counter any retaliation we might attempt from missile-firing subs—or aging bombers. Such an imbalance may not be sufficient to lure the cautious Soviets into striking, but it is unnerving to have U.S. survival hanging by the thread of Soviet caution. Defending ourselves would seem to be more prudent, and the MX is thought to be the way to do it. As the commission observes:

"A one-sided strategic condition in which the Soviet Union could effectively destroy the whole range of strategic targets in the United States, but we could not effectively destroy the whole range of strategic targets in the Soviet Union, would be extremely unstable over the long run. Such a situation could tempt the Soviets, in a crisis, to feel they could successfully threaten or even undertake conventional or limited nuclear aggression in the hope that the United States would lack a fully effective response. A one-sided condition of this sort would clearly not serve the cause of peace."

Behind all this—touched on only lightly in the commission report—is how the United States got itself into such a fix. How did a nation that not too long ago was incontestably the greatest military power in history

M. Stanton Evans, ''The Meaning of the MX Missile,'' *Human Events*, May 14, 1983. Reprinted with permission.

reach a point of serious concern that the Communists might take out its missile force—and that we would be unable to retaliate?

Chilling Answer

The chilling answer to that question is, quite simply, that we have done it to ourselves. In obedience to the mumbo-jumbo of detente and arms control, we have marked time, or actually moved backwards, while the Soviets have been pressing forward in relentless fashion. We have deferred development of new bombers and missiles, dismantled missile-bearing subs, phased out our air and missile defenses, and bound ourselves with the constraints of SALT.

"Only by going to the MX...can we correct this dangerous imbalance."

The underlying premise of this policy was that the Soviets, impressed by our forbearance, would go and do likewise. Instead, with a powerful assist from our technology (provided by detente), they have worked unceasingly to build their military arsenal, both nuclear and conventional. The result is the strategic impasse that we face today. When the hare lies down to take an indefinite snooze, even the most ungainly tortoise can eventually overtake him.

Incredibly, despite the bipartisan findings of the Scowcroft commission, there are those who want America to keep on snoozing. Not only are we beset by nuclear freezeniks, but there are plenty of people in Congress who want to kill the MX and any other such U.S. initiatives—while the Reagan regime itself continues abiding by the ruinous terms of that SALT II agreement.

The lesson of the MX, in short, is that we are the victims of self-inflicted weakness. Unless corrective steps are taken soon, it could turn out as well to be our epitaph.

This article by M. Stanton Evans appeared in Human Events, *a weekly conservative newspaper.*

"We can keep the peace with what we have."

The MX Is Not a Peacekeeper

James Kilpatrick

President Reagan was at his best last week in arguing a case for deployment of the MX missile. He laid out the ominous facts on the Soviet Union's buildup of arms; he emphasized the relative obsolescence of our "antique" weapons. His reasoning was persuasive.

But with deference to the president and his military advisers, I find the case not yet convincing. In principle Mr. Reagan is right. He is following policies at least as old as the Antonines; as Gibbon tells us, "They preserved peace by a constant preparation for war." That is sound doctrine.

The president's case rests upon these assumptions—that his new "dense pack" configuration will work, that the projected $27 billion cost is bearable, and that unless the United States goes ahead with the project the Soviets will not feel sufficiently "deterred" from atomic adventurism. Specifically, the Soviets would perceive no incentive toward serious negotiations on arms reduction and control.

The dense-pack plan calls for installing 100 of the MX missiles in underground silos just 600 yards apart. The idea is that the Soviet Union might launch a surprise first strike intended to nullify our land-based missile system. Under the pending theory, the tight spacing would frustrate such an attack because the Soviet missiles would knock each other out. No one knows for certain whether the theory is sound. On technological grounds alone, a high degree of skepticism can be justified.

Any discussion of costs has to begin with this fundamental proposition: National security comes first. We must spend whatever has to be spent—whatever is truly necessary—to maintain adequate defenses. But after we have crossed that threshold point, it is equally proper to observe that our resources are not infinite, that appalling deficits are projected for the next five years and that prudent fiscal policies also are a part of national

security. Could this $27 billion be spent more effectively on something else? It is a lot of money to pour into 100 holes in the ground.

It is the president's third assumption that causes the most trouble, for here we deal with the whole misty spectrum of perceptions and conjectures. How much deterrence is enough deterrence? On this point reasonably minded men may disagree.

Tons of Destruction

Depending upon how these infernal weapons are counted, the United States possesses about 9,000 to 9,500 warheads carrying a destructive capacity of 3,500 megatons. These missiles are deliverable from bombers, from submarines, from the old Titan and Minuteman silos. We are talking of 3.5 billion tons of destruction—enough to obliterate every conceivable target in the Soviet Union.

How much is enough? If the Soviets are not deterred by the prospect of retaliation in this awesome degree, would they be significantly more deterred by the proposed MX deployment? It seems highly unlikely. Would such a show of determination by the United States galvanize the Soviets into signing a verifiable bilateral agreement for arms reduction? No one can say with certainty. It is equally plausible that the president's plan, once it were accepted by Congress, would spur the Soviets to even more furious efforts to push ahead in the arms race.

In the end, it is not a perception of arms that will deter the Soviet Union. It is a perception of will. Against a Soviet first strike, would we retaliate? The answer, taking full account of the terrible implications, has to be: Of course. It is not possible for the human mind fully to envision the consequences of a nuclear Armageddon, but some part of the free world would survive. Some roots of freedom would remain, and in time these roots would grow again.

My own judgment, for whatever it may be worth, is that this dense-pack deployment is not needed. In a nice stroke of public relations, Mr. Reagan named the missile the ''Peacekeeper.'' My thought is that we can keep the peace with what we have.

James Kilpatrick is a syndicated columnist out of Washington, DC.

The Case for Unilateral Disarmament

Paul Walker

The current START (Strategic Arms Reduction Talks) proposals offer little hope for serious nuclear weapons reduction. The US offer is based primarily on a one-third reduction in long-range ballistic missile warheads. But it does not constrain new weapons—missiles, bombers, warheads, and bombs; specifically excludes all bombers and cruise missiles; suggests a ceiling on land-based warheads some 450 higher than the current US arsenal; requires the Soviets, on the other hand, to reduce their land-based missiles by some 900; and in many ways represents no more than a formalization of current US weapons production and retirement plans.

It is clear that past arms control agreements have promised more than they have actually delivered. While their accomplishments should not be underestimated, bilateral and multilateral negotiations have largely been self-serving exercises in diplomacy and public relations. They have represented positive steps toward peace if only for the international atmosphere of cooperation and information-sharing which they engender, yet they have grossly lacked substantive achievements toward real disarmament of the nuclear arsenals. And, in cases such as the 1963 Limited Test Ban, treaties have undermined further efforts for disarmament—in this case, banning all nuclear tests.

At best, past arms control negotiations have limited spending on ineffective and unnecessary weaponry; at worst, they have not slowed the pace of nuclear weapons modernization, research and development, and may have, in certain instances, even accelerated the arms competition through redirecting research and demands for "bargaining chips."

Case of the MX

The case of the MX is illustrative of the limitations of Soviet-American nuclear arms negotiations. The weapon was developed simultaneously while SALT II was being

Paul Walker, "Seizing the Initiative: First Steps to Disarmament," 1983, Fellowship of Reconciliation and the American Friends Service Committee. Reprinted with permission.

negotiated, 1972 to the present; it progressed uninhibited by SALT talks; it was not limited in the SALT II agreement, which, in fact, specifically stated that "each party may flight-test and deploy one new type of...ICBM;" its large size may have been maximized to meet SALT constraints; its latest basing designs may even violate SALT agreements; and it may require an anti-ballistic missile system which could violate the ABM Treaty. In fact, MX—renamed "Peacekeeper" by President Reagan—is now being argued as a "bargaining chip" for the START negotiations.

This is not a success story of parties seriously interested in limiting and reducing the burgeoning stockpile of nuclear weapons. Through both an inability to mutually agree and through intentional obstinacy on Soviet and American sides, arms control negotiations have failed to slow the quickening pace of the nuclear arms competition. While serving useful functions in regulating the competition, *treaties exhibit a singular lack of success in reversing the drift towards nuclear holocaust.*

Why? The reasons are many, depending on one's perspective, and interrelated. But they include the following: the "arms race" phenomenon whereby one side always lags behind the other in some area of nuclear systems development and deployment, thereby providing argument for being "behind" or "inferior;" the clear goal of negotiating parties to preclude obstacles to expanded research and development, in order "never to be surprised" by the opponent with a technological breakthrough; the ongoing demand for accumulating "bargaining chips" on both sides of the table, ostensibly to enhance one's negotiating position; and the continuing lack of public understanding, participation, and thereby pressure in arms negotiations. Fundamental to all these problems which continue to undermine fruitful results from arms control negotiations is the clear lack of political will, commitment, and courage by both Soviet and American elites to slow or reverse the nuclear competition.

SALT I required two and one-half years to negotiate, sign, and ratify; SALT II has now dragged on for 10 years and still sits unratified in Washington while the Reagan Administration debates whether or not to abide in spirit to its limits. Given the parochial starting proposals from both the Soviets and Americans in the START talks and European missile negotiations, there appears little hope for any solutions reasonably soon. Other talks have fared no better: talks on Mutual and Balanced Force Reductions (MBFR) in Europe have stumbled forward for ten years with neither party able to agree on the numbers of Warsaw Pact troops from which to start negotiating.

And the nuclear arms race grinds on: 5000 Soviet and American strategic nuclear warheads in 1966, 16,000 by 1980, approaching 18,000 today, and upwards of 30,000 in the combined arsenals by the end of the decade. Time will not wait for START or for any other negotiating forum, languishing over details necessary for formal agreements but unnecessary for reversing the arms race. The time is both ripe and urgent for new, innovative initiatives in arms *reductions* in addition to arms *regulations:* the Soviets have recently produced a new generation of long-range missiles, with several more on the drawing boards, while the Americans are just launching their newest spurt of weapons deployment. There is an overall balance between the two sides in nuclear weaponry, an appropriate time for strict limits. Both sides voice their concern and interest in halting an increasingly expensive and dangerous marathon with no finish tape in sight; only results in the very near future will prove the seriousness of their intent.

"Unilateral initiatives should...initially not reduce a nation's capacity to inflict unacceptable nuclear retaliation."

Unilateral, reciprocal initiatives, that is, steps taken outside of negotiating forums with the hope and expectation that the other side will respond in a positive manner and maintain the momentum of arms reductions, are one potentially very productive way to break the arms competition. They would not preclude START or other arms forums, but would rather complement ongoing negotiations and help to build confidence between parties.

The idea of unilateral initiatives is not a new or novel one. Individuals have long argued on religious, moral, and pacifist grounds for unilateral disarmament: W. H. Ferry, Victor Gollancz, Lewis Mumford, Bertrand Russell, Stephen King-Hall, C. W. Mills, Erich Fromm, and most recently, Alva Myrdal, among others. Fromm wrote, for example, an essay over twenty years ago entitled, "The Case for Unilateral Disarmament," in which he acknowledges a growing concensus for the need for unilateral initiatives:

> ...to risk the life of the human race, or even the results of its best efforts in the last five thousand years, is immoral and irresponsible. As warfare becomes at once more senseless and more devastating, the convergence between religious pacifist, humanist, and pragmatic opponents to nuclear armaments grows.

Seeds of the Freeze

In the 1950s and early 1960s, both East and West raised proposals for major nuclear reductions. Although such grand designs for both nuclear and conventional disarmament are viewed historically now with much cynicism, the nuclear initiatives contained the seeds of today's "Freeze" debate. For example, a Soviet proposal of June 2, 1960, included the recommendation that "all means of delivering nuclear weapons...be destroyed and their manufacture stopped...." The US counterproposal three weeks later included the statement that "agreed categories of missiles, aircraft, surface ships, submarines, and artillery designed to deliver nuclear and other weapons of mass destruction shall be destroyed or converted to peaceful uses." Both these proposals also made reference to the need for adequate "control measures," to include on-site inspectors to "verify destruction of existing stockpiles" and studies "to effect cessation of production of nuclear weapons."

Defense analysts such as Thomas Schelling also suggested in 1961 that "informal arms understandings" might offer more results than drawn-out negotiations:

> Maybe limited measures of arms control can be arrived at by quite indirect and incomplete communication; maybe they will take the form of a proposal embodied in unilateral action (or abstention from action) which continues if matched by corresponding action on the other side...Maybe instead of *arguing* about what we should do, we will simply do it and dare the other side to do likewise, or do it to suggest that we would like to keep it up, but only if they find it in their interest to do something comparable.

GRIT Strategy

Perhaps the best known proposals for unilateral initiatives are those of psychologist Charles E. Osgood at the University of Illinois. He has argued for Graduated and Reciprocated Initiatives in Tension-reduction—the "GRIT strategy." Osgood argues that unilateral initiatives should, among other things, initially not reduce a nation's capacity to inflict unacceptable nuclear retaliation and thereby maintain the system of deterrence; should be diversified; must be communicated to emphasize sincere intent; must be identified as part of a deliberate attempt to reduce tensions; should include explicit invitations for reciprocation; and must be performed on schedule and over time. Osgood states that such steps would overcome "the present climate of fear and distrust [where] it is hard to see how bilateral commitments of any significance can be reached."

The debate among the unilateralists has always been a broad one. The more "marginalist" participants, such as Amitai Etzioni, argue for "gradualism," a sequence of stages of confidence-building measures eventually developing into real reductions. Etzioni points out that, should gradualism not be reciprocated, the alternative of an accelerated arms race is always available. Robert Levine describes the other side of the debate as "systemists," those reluctant to condition their disarmament recommendations on reciprocation by the opponent. Mulford Sibley, for example, in his Quaker pamphlet, "Unilateral Initiatives for Disarmament," advocates a determinist policy:

> ...unilateral initiatives and eventually unilateral disarmament are ways of seeking a more effective defense than military weapons can any longer provide...If... preliminary agreements were not forthcoming within a reasonable period (six months, for example), the government would proceed with its planned unilateralist policy....once launched there would be no hope for success apart from a continuing determination to see things out to the finish and never go back to the prison house of nuclear deterrence.

"Fresh approaches are needed now more than ever, before it is too late."

More recently, the European Nuclear Disarmament (END) movement argued in 1980 that the two superpowers unilaterally "withdraw all nuclear weapons from European territory" in order "to free the entire territory of Europe, from Poland to Portugal, from nuclear weapons, air and submarine bases, and from all institutions engaged in research into or manufacture of nuclear weapons." Also the World Council of Churches included "independent initiatives" and "reciprocal actions" prominently in a 1981 study: "There is no nuclear-weapon state which could not make a start either by reducing existing arsenals or by halting announced plans to modernize."

One Belief

Regardless of their individual slant, past and present advocates for unilateral initiatives in nuclear disarmament share one belief: well-founded dissatisfaction and impatience with the lack of real progress towards reversing the arms race through formal bilateral or multilateral negotiating channels; and the conviction that fresh approaches are needed now more than ever, before it is too late.

The range of possibilities for unilateral alternatives by both the Soviets and Americans in nuclear and conventional forces is practically infinite; they also do not differ significantly from proposals bandied about through formal channels with one exception: they can be implemented immediately and reciprocated immediately, without endless delay for detailed, negotiated revisions and updates every six months as

weapons technology progresses. But *only sufficient political will, foresight, and courage combined with public participation and pressure will allow such proposals to be fulfilled.*

Without addressing each option in depth, I will list here a range of possibilities in no particular priority. The implementation of any single initiative may very well be affected by whatever initiatives precede or accompany it. The initiatives might include reductions in weapons arsenals, limits on research, development, testing, and evaluation of weapons, limits or bans on proposed weapons, and/or genuine confidence-building measures. Any initiative should have the following characteristics:

(1) represent a genuine disarmament step which does not seriously endanger national security; in other words, it must be a real cutback, limitation, or ban on weaponry which will help to stabilize military balances, dampen arms competition, and represent more than a phasing out of obsolete systems;

(2) be a unilateral action, independent of formal negotiations, but with the hope and expectation that the other side will reciprocate in an appropriate way so that the action-reaction process of limits and reductions might continue; and

(3) allow sufficient time, six months or more, for the other side to react before any definitive judgments are reached on its efficacy in international disarmament.

Paul Walker's pamphlet was published jointly by the Fellowship of Reconciliation and the American Friends Service Committee, both of which favor unilateral disarmament by the United States.

"If we...think of our undertaking unilateral nuclear disarmament, we can see that Soviet officials would be very unlikely to follow our lead."

The Case Against Unilateral Disarmament

George I. Mavrodes

Let us assume that the Soviet Union undertakes unilateral nuclear disarmament. Let's not worry now about why they might do that or whether it is likely that they will do that. For the present, this is just a thought experiment.

I want to discuss what may be called the "logic" of unilateral nuclear disarmament. At the end of the discussion, I will mention some considerations which lie outside of what I'm calling that logic.

I want to conduct much of the thought experiment in what may seem to be an inverted manner. In this country, we are likely to think of the pros and cons of disarmament in terms of *our* disarming, or at least in terms of *our* starting the disarmament process. Sometimes, however, it is useful to look at a problem "upside down," as it were. And that's what I want to do here.

I have proposed, therefore, to start by considering this very implausible scenario: the Soviets destroy all of their nuclear weapons, large and small. And they also dismantle their manufacturing facilities for nuclear armaments. Furthermore, let us assume that we have no doubt at all about what they have done. They invite our engineers and military people to monitor and inspect the whole operation. And we are satisfied that they really have gone through with it, a complete unilateral disarmament.

Reasonable Response

And now, what would be a reasonable response on our part? In particular, would it be plausible for us to match them with a complete nuclear disarmament of our own, thus moving toward a world free of nuclear weapons? To me, that response does not seem plausible for at least three reasons.

First, if the Soviets were to scrap their nuclear arsenal, then a major reason for our own interest in disarmament would disappear. When two antagonistic superpowers have atomic weapons, nuclear war is a danger. That is, both sides may choose to use those weapons. And such a bilateral exchange might not be limited. It is likely to escalate into an enormously destructive fusillade that might possibly destroy the world or at least the Northern Hemisphere. This danger is, as I see it, one of the main reasons for seeking nuclear disarmament, arms limitation, and the like. A unilateral nuclear disarmament completely eliminates the danger of a nuclear war (the bilateral exchange of nuclear strikes). If the Soviets have no nukes, then they cannot fire any at us, and that danger is gone.

However, unilateral disarmament does not eliminate the possibility of a unilateral nuclear strike by the other side (the United States, in this case). But in contrast with a bilateral exchange, such a unilateral strike could easily be limited and almost surely would be. But it is hard to see why, if the Soviet Union had no nuclear weapons, U.S. leaders would themselves fire off so many weapons as to destroy the world. The main reason for our own interest in nuclear disarmament would therefore be gone.

Furthermore, unilateral disarmament greatly reduces the danger of an *accidental* firing of nuclear weapons and minimizes the consequences if such an accident does occur. Half of the places where such an accident could have originated would be shut out. And what about our side? We now maintain a lot of weapons in a high state of readiness, poised to respond instantly to a Soviet attack. But if we knew that the Soviets had no nuclear capability, then we could ease off on that hair trigger. We could take plenty of time to check the facts before firing. The danger of an accidental firing would be cut way down.

Besides, if a weapon were somehow fired accidentally, that accident could not lead to a nuclear exchange. It would be a tragedy, of course, but a limited one.

George I. Mavrodes, "The Logic of Disarmament," *TheOtherSide*, October 1982. Reprinted with permission from TheOtherSide, 300 W. Apsley St., Philadelphia, PA 19144. Copyright © 1982.

Limited Bombing

And now for the second reason. If we retained our arsenal while the Soviets scrapped theirs, then we could actually use a nuclear threat—and, if necessary, a limited nuclear strike—to accomplish something. Maybe even to accomplish something good. We might demand, for example, that the Soviets withdraw their troops from Afghanistan and threaten to drop an atomic warhead on some Black Sea naval base if they do not. They would probably withdraw, but if not, then we could actually do that limited bombing. No doubt that would result in a withdrawal, which would mean survival for some Afghan soldiers and their families. Or we might secure some measure of freedom for Poles, Czechs, Hungarians, or even the remnants of the Baltic people.

A unilateral disarmament, then, provides an opportunity for the remaining nuclear power to use its capability effectively and with small risk—and for a good purpose if it so chooses. It might well be unwise, or even morally indefensible, for us to abandon that opportunity if we had it.

The third reason is, I suppose, a special case of the second, but important enough to mention separately. Bilateral disarmament carries with it a greater risk of a future nuclear war than does unilateral disarmament. Consequently, if we want to reduce the risk, and if the Soviet Union were to disarm, then we should not. Let me explain that.

Suppose the Soviets scrap their nuclear stockpile, and we follow suit. What happens after that? The world will not be put into a freezer. Time will go on, and things will change. In particular, the decision to renounce nuclear arms may not be an eternal decree. It is quite possible that some later Soviet administration would decide to rebuild their nuclear arsenal. We probably could not prevent that, but we might feel impelled to match that rebuilding. The world would thus come again to a state something like that of the present, with the consequent risk of nuclear war.

If, on the other hand, we retained our nuclear power while the Soviets abandoned theirs, then we could prevent their taking the first steps to rebuild such a capability. We could demand inspection privileges throughout the Soviet Union, require the dismantling of any facility producing weapons-grade material, and so on. We could, in short, prevent the occurrence of any further nuclear showdown. If such prevention would be of value, it would be a powerful reason against our own disarming.

For these reasons, then, it would seem implausible for us to dispose of our nuclear arsenal if the Soviets got rid of theirs.

Reduce the Arsenal

It would, on the other hand, make sense for us to reduce our arsenal under those circumstances. We would have no need of the many nuclear-tipped rockets which we now aim at Soviet nuclear silos. When those silos are empty, we may as well do away with those missiles of our own. And we now justify much of our overkill capacity with the fear that a Soviet first-strike could knock out many of our missiles. If the Soviet Union no longer had any nuclear capacity at all, we would have no need for all that excess firepower. So it would make sense for us to reduce our nuclear arsenal, though not to eliminate it.

Now, someone may object that in this thought experiment I have cast the United States as the good guys and the Soviet Union as the bad guys. Well, I guess I have done that. It seems to me that, relatively speaking, that corresponds to the facts. But for our purposes here it doesn't matter much, and so it would not be useful to get into any dispute over this point.

The arguments I've used aren't very difficult, and we can expect that, for better or worse, Soviet planners will think of their own version of them. Maybe they think of themselves as the good guys? Yes, maybe they do. And if they do, then I suppose they will construe their own nuclear power as a means to accomplish their version of good in the world. That explains, in part, why the Soviet Union is unlikely to undertake a unilateral disarmament. More importantly, it explains why a unilateral disarmament on our part is unlikely to be a first step toward a nuclear-free world.

So far I have talked as if only the United States and the Soviet Union were involved in this thing. But of course that's not so. Several nations already have small nuclear arsenals, and still others are on the verge. So it isn't just the United States versus the Soviet Union. How does this complication bear on the question?

"Even a complete and multilateral nuclear disarmament is unlikely to result in a nuclear-free world for long."

Well, if the Soviet Union were to disarm and we followed suit, then we would open ourselves (and others also) to nuclear threats and extortion by Pakistan, South Africa, Brazil, France, China, and so on. That seems like an implausible thing to do, and I don't know of any reason to think it would be a good thing to do.

For one thing, it would give some of those other nations both incentive and room to become major nuclear powers themselves. From Paris to Peking, from Karachi to Capetown, governments would scramble to build more and bigger bombs. And what reason is there to suppose that the world would be better off with, say, France or China or Brazil, rather than the United States, as a major nuclear power? The fact that the nuclear situation is multilateral seems to provide an additional argument against our disarming even if the Soviet

Union did so. And it makes even more remote the hope that our disarmament could lead to a nuclear-free world.

And so, if we turn our problem "right side up" again and think of our undertaking unilateral nuclear disarmament, we can see that Soviet officials would be very unlikely to follow our lead. Their principal incentive for disarmament would be gone, and they would have a powerful incentive for not abandoning their nuclear weapons. For they would see a clear opportunity to use those weapons to impose their vision of a world order.

Our disarmament, then, would eliminate the danger of a nuclear war between ourselves and the Soviet Union, but it would make actual (though limited) use of nuclear weapons much more likely than now. And nuclear threats, coercion, and extortion would probably be commonplace.

Unilateral nuclear disarmament, then, seems unpromising. It is very unlikely that the Soviets will initiate it. And it is implausible to suppose that our doing so would lead to any good consequence.

Proliferation of Weapons

Of course, at one time the United States alone had atomic weapons, and that situation developed into the present multilateral proliferation of weapons. So you might ask, haven't we already tried only one nation having nuclear arms—and found that it didn't work out at all as you have suggested?

That seems to be true. What little experience we've had with nuclear monopoly does suggest that it doesn't last. And I haven't so far taken sufficient account of that fact.

But that fact has to be evaluated in context. For we have also had experience with a world completely free of nuclear weapons. What did that lead to? Just forty years ago, well within my own lifetime, not a single nation in the whole world had so much as even one atomic bomb. Not a single engineer or technician had ever assembled a nuclear weapon.

In only forty years that situation has led to the present: half a dozen nations in the "nuclear club," with another six or eight about to enter; tens of thousands of atomic warheads around the world; missiles, planes, and submarines ready, armed, and waiting. And so our experience, for whatever it is worth, suggests that even a complete and multilateral nuclear disarmament is unlikely to result in a nuclear-free world for long.

And next time it would no doubt take less than forty years. The "hands-on" knowledge and experience of how to build nuclear weapons is already in ten thousand brains and muscles.

I myself think that our experience with both a nuclear-free world and a nuclear monopoly is significant. Probably neither of these situations can be expected to be stable (though I suspect the monopoly might have a little more chance than the other). And so very probably the world will not again be free of nuclear weapons for any extended time. Within that context, foreboding as it may be, we and our children will probably have to make our lives.

There is another real possiblity. Neither unilateral nor multilateral disarmament is likely to get rid of atomic weapons for long, but it would be another story if producing and maintaining nuclear weapons became impossible—I mean physically and technologically impossible. Ironically, the most likely thing to bring that about would be a massive nuclear war.

"In some situations, all the alternatives are bad. Maybe the world is now in such a position."

Such a war is likely to destroy most of the world's present industrial base, forcing the survivors to adopt a much more "primitive" style of life. Then it might really be impossible for a long time—maybe many generations—to build nuclear weapons and their delivery systems. Such a scenario, rather than any disarmament scheme, might lead to some extended time in which the world was free from a nuclear threat.

No Matching Action

Well, where does that leave us? We should not kid ourselves. If we do scrap our nuclear arms, we should not expect the Soviets to match our action. They would have strong reasons against such a response. That seems, to me at least, to be the logic of the situation.

But that is not in itself a conclusive reason against disarming. Possibly, for example, we have a duty to renounce nuclear weapons regardless of the consequences—for ourselves or others—of that renunciation. Or it might be that eliminating the risk of nuclear war is a value so great that it is worth any price (though it may be hard to imagine why a Christian should think so). Or (despite world history since 1945) we might guess that Soviet leaders will have little interest in outside meddling. And so on. Perhaps a case can be made for disarmament along such lines—but not in terms of a vision for a nuclear-free world.

Someone may argue that since unilateral disarmament involves such dreadful dangers, there must be a better way to resolve the situation. Such an argument would be fallacious. That a certain course of action is bad, even very bad, does not at all guarantee that a better one is available. For in some situations, all the alternatives are bad. Maybe the world is now in such a position.

Nuclear arms, it is said, have not made us secure. That is true. Unilateral disarmament will not make us secure either. Very probably we do not have a choice between security and danger. We can choose only among various sorts and levels of terrible dangers. The choice between security and danger would have been easy. But perhaps (is it the providence of God?) we are left only with the hard choice.

George Mavrodes teaches philosophy at the University of Michigan.

"The act of will that is currently thought of as disarmament would present the final blow to a crumbling military-industrial edifice."

Bilateral Disarmament Is Realistic

Mary Kaldor

Stopping cruise missiles is not just a matter of convincing the politicians. Time and time again, the statesmen of the world have met together in international fora and expressed lofty and commendable ambitions for peace and disarmament. Yet hardly anything of practical value has ever been achieved. New and more deadly kinds of weapons continue to be acquired; war and militarism continue to characterize international relations. It appears as though disarmament, which is viewed as an international act of will, is quite unrelated to armament, which is a national process involving people, money, and institutions deeply embedded in the fabric of our society.

If the campaign for European nuclear disarmament is to succeed, we need to see it, not just as a campaign to change the political will of Europeans—important as that is—but, more profoundly, as the first step in a process which reverses the process of armament. The aim would be to undermine the ideas and institutions which foster the arms race, to rechannel the energies which are currently devoted to militarization into other new directions, and create, so to speak, a vested interest in socially productive as opposed to destructive ends. The act of will that is currently thought of as disarmament would present the final blow to a crumbling military-industrial edifice, the last and perhaps least act in a series of events which totally transforms the current political, social, and economic environment of armaments.

Every armament process has its time and place. The culture which invented the stirrup was quite different from the one which developed the gun. The capitalist armament process and what is more or less its mirror image in the centrally planned economies has its own unique properties. This essay is an attempt to sketch out these properties and to see what they imply for disarmament....

Mary Kaldor, "Disarmament: The Armament Process in Reverse," in *Debate on Disarmament*, edited by Michael Clarke and Marjorie Mowlam. London: Routledge & Kegan, 1982. Reprinted with permission.

Western Countries

The prime contractors are among the world's largest companies. Since World War II, between forty and fifty U.S. companies have regularly appeared on *Fortune's* list of the top 100 companies and on the Pentagon's list of the 100 companies receiving the highest prime contract awards. Their stability, in both America and Europe, has been widely noted. Firms have been amalgamated or nationalized, especially in Europe, but basically there has been very little rationalization. The plants which receive prime contracts from major weapon systems have remained much the same, under different names, for thirty years. There has been more specialization and an increased amount of subcontract work both among the prime contractors and the outside firms, especially in the electronics industry. Also, the composition of subcontractors has varied enormously along with changes in technology and the business cycle— thousands of subcontractors regularly go bankrupt during recession. But among the prime contractors, there have been few, if any, actual closures in the postwar period. Equally, there have been no new entries into the major weapons markets. The consequence is that a specific mix of skills and physical equipment, and a specific set of relationships with customers (the military units) and suppliers (the subcontractors), has been preserved—in effect, a specific manufacturing experience which corresponds to a specific military experience....

The designers are the products of their military-industrial environment. The *competition* between prime contractors propels technology forward as each corporation attempts to offer something better than its competitor and something the military, at least in the U.S. can justify to Congress. And yet this technology dynamism is confined within certain limits—limits that are defined by the *stability* of military and industrial institutions, a stability which is guaranteed by the

189

planning system. The result is an entirely introverted form of technological change, something which has been described as "trend" or "routinized" innovation.

Trend innovation has found its characteristic form in the follow-on imperative. The form and function of the weapon system have not changed much since 1945. Technical change has largely consisted of improvements to a given set of performance characteristics. Submarines are faster, quieter, bigger, and have longer ranges. Aircraft have greater speed, more powerful thrust, and bigger payloads. All weapon systems have more destructive weapons, particulary missiles, and greatly improved capabilities for communication, navigation, detection, identification, and weapon guidance. Each contractor has designed, developed, and produced one weapon system after another, each representing an incremental improvement on the last. For Boeing, the Minuteman Intercontinental Ballistic Missile followed the B-52 strategic bomber, which followed the B-47. Between 1952 and 1979, Newport News's yards have produced no fewer than nine aircraft carriers, each bigger, and better than the last, bow to stern in the best follow-on tradition. And in Europe, Dassault has produced the famous series of Mirage fighters; Westland has manufactured one helicopter after another; and the submarine which the British propose to construct in order to launch the American Trident missile is likely to continue a tradition at Vickers Barrow that goes back, with interruptions, as far as the 1890s.

"As weapon systems approach the limits of technology, they become increasingly complex and costly."

The idea that each weapon system must have a follow-on has become self-perpetuating. Each corporation has a planning group whose sole function is to choose suitable successors for weapons currently being produced and which maintain close contact with consorts in the military. The planning procedure is supposed to be an exercise in prediction. In actual fact, because of the intimate relationship with the armed services it becomes a self-fulfilling prophecy. Even so the system has not worked smoothly, and it has taken periodic industrial crisis to initiate the full range of new projects. Such was the crisis which followed the winding down of the Vietnam war in the early 1970s. The pressure on the defense budget which we are now witnessing is partly the result of projects initiated during that period.

Bigger and "Better" Arms

Each follow-on is bigger and "better" than its predecessor. As weapon systems approach the limits of technology, they become increasingly complex and

costly. It becomes harder and harder to achieve incremental improvements to a given set of performance characteristics. Although the basic technology of the weapon platform may not have changed much, such improvements have often entailed the incorporation of very advanced technology, e.g., radical electronic innovations such as microprocessors, or nuclear power for submarines, and this has greatly increased the complexity of the weapon system as a whole. And as the weapon system becomes more complex, more labor and materials are required for development and production, greatly increasing the total cost.

The weapon systems of the 1970s represent what one might describe as a quantum leap in expense and grotesque elaboration. The monstrous MX missile with its ludicrous race-track system will cost somewhere from $33 billion (the official figure) to over $100 billion (an estimate made in April 1980). It will involve the biggest construction program in the history of the United States. The obese Trident submarine, which is too big to get out of the channel where it was built, will cost much the same. The real cost of producing the British-German-Italian Multi-Role Combat Aircraft will be slightly greater than the entire production costs of the Spitfire before and during World War II. A recent U.S. General Accounting Office report concluded:

> The cost problem facing the US military is growing worse and no relief is in sight. The so-called "bow wave" of future procurement costs is growing beyond the point of reasonableness. Current procurement programs are estimated to total about $725 billion. If these costs are spread over the next ten years (a conservative projection) the annual average of $72.5 billion will be more than twice the current funding levels.

Basis of Modern Strategy

Yet many people, and not just those who question the whole basis of modern strategy, are beginning to wonder whether the extra money will buy any real increase in military utility. A number of strategic writers have come to criticize the criteria for technical improvements to weapon systems. Many of the indicators of military effectiveness are thought to be no longer relevant to modern warfare. For example, the development of naval aircraft and submarines has meant that speed is no longer important for surface ships. Likewise, aircraft speed is only of advantage in fighter roles. The cost, complexity, and size of modern weapon systems consequent upon the so-called improvements in performance characteristics may turn out to be a positive liability. In the hostile environment of the modern battlefield, where the accuracy and lethality of all munitions have greatly increased, size and vulnerability go hand in hand. Complexity greatly increases unreliability, reduces maneuverability and flexibility, and creates enormous logistic problems. The U.S. Air Force's First Tactical Air Wing, whose motto is "Readiness is our Profession," recently failed a test given by the Air Force's Tactical Command to see if it was ready to mobilize for a war in the Middle East. Only twenty-three of the sixty-six F-15 aircraft were "mission capable" because of engine and parts failure, lack of spares, shortages of skilled technicians, etc.—and these problems are not untypical of Western weapon systems in general. Likewise, cost is a disadvantage because of the high attrition rates of modern warfare and because budgetary limitations lead to savings on such essentials as ammunition, fuel, spares, military pay, training, etc. The huge support systems and the overburdened centralized command systems associated with the modern weapon system are very vulnerable and could be easily disrupted in a war. Indeed, the experience of war in Vietnam and the Middle East—the problems of vulnerability, logistics, communications, etc.—has called into question the whole future of the weapon system. Destructiveness and effectiveness are no longer synonymous—if they ever were.

"Armaments in the Soviet Union are privileged products…the armament sector is the only sector in the Soviet system which enjoys consumer sovereignty."

The degeneracy of the weapon system is not without its effects on Western economy and society as a whole.…

In so far as they guarantee the stability of military-industrial institutions, of the major corporations, armaments can help to alleviate crises. But capitalist crises produce change. That same stability has the effect of freezing industrial structure and postponing change. In so far as armaments are themselves subject to the capitalist dynamic they can also drag the economy along their own technological cul de sac, passing on the degeneracy of overgrown trend innovation. In effect they can preserve and even extend industries that would otherwise have declined and at the same time fetter the emergence of new dynamic industries. This is one reason for the persistence of mechanical engineering and shipbuilding in Britain or the automobile and aircraft industries in the United States. The absorption of resources by these declining sectors, the distorting effects of armament-induced ways of thinking about technology on new as well as older industries, are among the factors which help to explain the backwardness of arms-intensive economies like Britain and the United States compared with, say, West Germany and Japan.

The Soviet Union

There is a remarkable parallel to be drawn with what happens in the Soviet Union. The armament sector in the Soviet Union could be described as the inverse of the Western armament sector. On the supply side, arms are produced by the same kinds of enterprises that characterize the centrally planned economy as a whole. Unlike those in the West, research institutes, design bureaus and production plants are organized as separate entities under the control of nine different defense ministries. The stability of these institutions, together with their suppliers, is guaranteed by the system of planning and budgeting. Unlike in the West, where competition, the pressure for technical advance, the winning or losing of contracts may lead to the amalgamation of design teams and prime contractors and to massive shifts in the composition of subcontractors, the various industrial organizations are assured of a steady flow of work. If the stability of the prime contractors slows down the process of industrial change in the West, then this same tendency for conservatism and continuity is typical of the Soviet economy as a whole.

On the demand side, however, armaments are characterized by competitiveness (with the West). Armaments in the Soviet Union are privileged products; it is often said that the armament sector is the only sector in the Soviet system which enjoys consumer sovereignty, and this is evident in the priority system. The armament sector receives the best machinery and parts; it can commandeer scarce materials; defense employees earn higher incomes and obtain better nonmonetary benefits; requests and orders from the administration tend to be dealt with more quickly. Many commentators have remarked on the unusual degree to which the consumer can ensure that specifications are met and can overcome resistance to demand-induced changes. From time to time, the leadership has imposed new solutions for forcing technology in order to initiate such programs as nuclear weapons, jet engines, missiles, etc. In general, these programs were a response to developments in the West, which was always one technological step ahead of the Soviet Union.

Hence, because of the degree of consumer sovereignty, the armament sector can represent a mechanism for change in the Soviet system. This was certainly the case in the 1930s, when military competition with Germany could be said to have been the overriding objective of the Soviet planning system. It can be argued that it was through the armament sector that the economy was mobilized. The armament sector continues to transmit new technology into the Soviet system; however, precisely because of the nature of the Western armaments, technologically induced change of this kind may prove distorting and not progressive.

Disarmament

The weapon system is the basis of modern military organization. It holds together the two great military alliances and divides East from West. And yet, paradoxically, the sector which produces the weapon system is also the conceptual *link* between the two societies. For it introduces an element of planning into the capitalist system; it thus helps to stave off crisis but, at the same time, slows down change. And it introduces an element of competition into the Soviet Union, inserting a mechanism for change.

In the past, the armament sector may have worked quite well in blunting some of the contradictions of each society. This is no longer true. The declining military effectiveness and growing cost of armament are gradually undermining the political weight of the superpowers and sapping their economic strength. The crisis of the armament sector has thrown up new forms of conflict and protest. New political and economic rivalries in the West, and consumer dissatisfaction, dissidence, and increased repression in the Soviet Union are all elements of a wider breakdown in the postwar international system of which the armament sector is a central part. The crisis has drawn a response from within the armament sector, as well as elsewhere, from soldiers ill-prepared for new forms of conflict (as in Vietnam), and from workers in the defense industry, concerned about employment. The new situation represents an opportunity for change. It entails the risk of war and of rearmament. But it could alternatively initiate a process of disarmament by channeling the new protests into positive directions.

Reversing the Armament Process

Most disarmament efforts are aimed at the role of armaments as objects of use. To reverse effectively the armament process, we also need to undermine their role as objects of production. We need to campaign against cruise missiles. But we also need to change the military-industrial culture which created them.

Industrial conversion is one way of achieving this. In a sense, any form of economic development represents a continual process of conversion—of finding new products and phasing out old ones. The conversion from arms to peaceful production would be merely one aspect of this process. Different societies have different mechanisms for conversion. The capitalist economy depends on the market as a method of allocating resources. It involves anarchy, dislocation, structural unemployment, and periodic crisis. The alternative is the central planning mechanism of the socialist countries which leads to rigidity because biases in government reflect vested bureaucratic interests. It thus avoids crises but, at the same time, is much more resistant to change than is the capitalist system.

The conversion from war to peace needs to be seen *not* as the *technical* process of converting swords to ploughshares, but as a *social* process of finding a new mechanism for the allocation of resources. Mere technical conversion from war to peace could never be sufficient. In a sense, we have already experienced this in the nonmilitary products of the arms companies—the

U.S. and Soviet space programs, Concorde and the TU-144, nuclear energy, various American rapid urban transit systems and environmental products. These have become what one might call quasi-weapon systems— similarly elaborate and expensive, with, in the end, similar economic consequences. Further, these products could never provide perfect substitutes for armaments since they do not command the same urgency. It would be difficult to justify increased expenditure on space or artificial hearts in times of economic recession.

"We need to campaign against cruise missiles. But we also need to change the military-industrial culture which created them."

Conversion needs to be seen as a way of creating a new economic system which would minimize those problems that create opportunities for conflict and the pressure for armaments. Such a system would combine the positive elements of planning with positive elements of free enterprise, instead of, as in the armament sector, the negative elements of both. The Western armament system, as we have seen, is characterized by planning on the demand side and competition on the supply side. The Western form of military technical change, the outcome of this system, is transferred to the Soviet Union through the consumer sovereignty that is the unique characteristic of the armament sector in the Soviet Union. What is needed is a system of consumer sovereignty in which the consumer is not a military establishment engaged in a competitive arms race but an ordinary person—in other words, planning, under democratic control. How is this to be achieved in practice?

Interest in Conversion

A sturdy democracy originates in popular movement, even though such movements must eventually find an institutional expression. Already, trade unions in the defense industry in Britain, West Germany, the United States, Italy, and Sweden have begun to express interest in the idea of conversion. This interest has proceeded farthest in Britain, where the workers of Lucas Aerospace and Vickers have earned a worldwide reputation for their proposals and campaigns to achieve socially useful production.

Marrying Social Need to Resources

The principle that underlies the Lucas Aerospace Corporate Plan, the Vickers pamphlets, and various proposals from workers in other companies, including Rolls-Royce ("Buns Before the Gutter"), BAC, and Parsons, is the simple but revolutionary idea that in a society where there are substantial unfilled needs it

192

makes no sense to put people, who could be making products to fill those needs, on the dole or into arms manufacturing. Neither the market mechanism nor central planning has proved very efficient at marrying social need to available resources. The alternative is to propose products which emanate from direct contacts between producers and consumers. This is the basis of the various worker plans.

In developing their ideas, the unions found it necessary to develop links with unions in supplier industries and with consumer organizations. Partly, this was in order to establish technical and social feasibility. For example, proposals by Rolls-Royce workers for gas turbine propulsion for merchant ships turned out to be an oversophisticated, marginally useful suggestion. More importantly, it provides a more effective method of putting political pressure on management and the government. Many of the ideas clash with priorities currently established by the government, which tend to reflect existing vested interests. Hence the shop stewards proposed energy conservation equipment and alternative forms of energy based on wind and waves; yet official energy priorities stress North Sea oil, coal, and nuclear energy. They also proposed new kinds of rail vehicles or ways of revitalizing Britain's canal system; yet transport policy places the emphasis on roads rather than railways or canals. The workers have consequently joined forces with organizations like the antinuclear energy movement or Transport 2000, which lobbies against the unplanned growth of the automobile infrastructure. On more mundane levels, unions in British Leyland pressed their management to purchase a scrap metal baler, one of the ideas put forward by the Vickers Shop Stewards. Lucas Aerospace Shop Stewards at Burnley worked closely with the local council with the idea of meeting local needs. These informal alliances between producers and consumers could provide the basis for future planning agencies which would reflect a different sort of social priorities from those that currently hold sway.

"Any campaign for disarmament must join forces with workers in the defense industry in demanding conversion."

Ideally, these links should be international, for there is always the risk that social criteria for resource allocation could turn out to be national, and hence divisive on a global scale. At both Vickers and Lucas Aerospace, some international links have been forged. Vickers workers have visited India (where they helped to establish a tank factory) and Iran (where they were shocked to hear of the way Chieftain tanks had been used). They have proposed various kinds of equipment for irrigation and for water purification. Lucas

Aerospace workers have discussed the possibility of adapting a road/rail vehicle they have invented for use in Tanzania and Zambia with the governments of those countries.

The Lucas Aerospace workers have actually achieved some success in pressing their management to undertake the manufacture of socially useful products. For the first time, workers are inserting their own criteria, as both producers and consumers, into the choice of products. They are, in a sense, developing a new mechanism for conversion, which, if it spreads, could change the composition of power in existing institutions—local councils, regional development councils, the Industrial Manpower Commission, the Atomic Energy Commission, for example—and which could eventually be embodied in a new set of planning institutions which set priorities according to the social needs of consumers and which guarantee stable, although mobile, employment.

Campaign for Disarmament

Any campaign for disarmament must join forces with workers in the defense industry in demanding conversion. Conversion—along with other more traditional disarmament issues—could build upon the growing fissures within the armament system and direct current frustrations toward disarmament rather than war. It could help to initiate a process of conversion which would precede disarmament. Conversion would thus be seen as a way of achieving disarmament rather than a thorny problem to be solved after the politicians had finally willed the reduction of armaments. Conversion would not just be a matter of turning swords into ploughshares. It would be a matter of creating a new mechanism for the wider process of economic conversion, matching the desperate needs of the modern world with resources that are either misused or not used at all. It could thus undermine the political and economic basis for armaments in advanced industrial countries and it would help to overcome the structural problems, weaknesses, and divisions of different economic systems. Hence it could help to remove the causes of war.

Mary Kaldor is Research Fellow at the Science Policy Research Unit, University of Sussex, and author of The Arms Trade with the Third World, The Disintegrating West *and* The Baroque Arsenal.

"We have long passed the point at which putting the weapons physically out of reach would make us much safer."

Bilateral Disarmament Is Not Realistic

Richard J. Barnet

The danger of nuclear war in the 1980s is awesome. Not only are inherently more dangerous weapons being built—vulnerable missiles with built-in pressures to "use them or lose them"—but nuclear weapons are being inevitably drawn into life-and-death struggles around the world. The first Cold War, we can now see in retrospect, was a relatively peaceful affair. Despite the cosmic ideological issues over which the U.S. and the Soviets occasionally threatened to blow up the world, the half-dozen men or so in Russia and America with a finger on the button never had any compelling reason to push it. The perceived need to avoid nuclear war was greater than either side's concern over the outcome of any particular confrontation.

This is not necessarily so for other beleaguered political figures of our time. The rulers of South Africa, sworn to maintain the domination of fifteen million blacks by four million whites on a black continent, are obvious customers for the technology of nuclear mass terror. Whether they actually have the bomb or, as is perhaps more likely, are in a position to acquire it whenever they wish is a detail. The threat of a nuclear Masada hangs over southern Africa as well as the Middle East.

The list of flashpoints for nuclear was is a long one. A statesman on the order of Idi Amin or some other despot with a ravaged brain; terrorist groups, with or without a cause; sophisticated criminals engaged in private-enterprise blackmail: all have plausible reasons to acquire, or to make the world believe they have acquired, nuclear weapons and the will to use them. The materials and technology for creating nuclear weapons are ever more widely available.

These developments greatly increase the likelihood of new U.S.-Soviet confrontations. In future confrontations we cannot always count on the Soviets backing down;

Richard J. Barnet, *Real Security*, copyright © 1981 by Richard J. Barnet. Reprinted by permission of SIMON & SCHUSTER, Inc.

their record of restraint in a crisis (even those they provoke) is a reflection of their relative military weakness in the past. Having achieved rough parity with the U.S. in military power, their national-security managers are now much more likely to think like their U.S. counterparts: "We can't afford to back down and be exposed as a pitiful, helpless giant." Thus the happy accident that the world has survived the first thirty-five years of the nuclear era is unimpressive evidence that we can avoid nuclear war in the coming era, for world power relationships are changing faster than we can comprehend and the arms race has become an entirely new game. The impending new stage of the military competition is likely to make the world of the 1970s look in retrospect like a Quaker village.

"Zero Nuclear Weapons"

It is evident that in the present political climate "zero nuclear weapons" is merely a rhetorical goal, whether the rhetorician is the President of the United States or a spokesperson of the peace movement. With the spread of nuclear weapons and nuclear technology the call for physical abolition of all nuclear weapons without regard for the political, moral, and psychological changes that must accompany radical disarmament merely heightens anxiety and breeds cynicism.

Since we have long passed the point at which putting the weapons physically out of reach would make us much safer—to avoid an utterly catastrophic holocaust more than 95 percent of present stockpiles would have to be destroyed—most people have lost sight of what disarmament is supposed to achieve. Because we cannot visualize an alternative road to security except through stockpiling arms, we focus on the risks of disarmament rather than the advantages. Even the most minimal arms agreements involve the issue of transferring trust from weapons we do not understand and cannot see but believe in to shadowy foreign leaders whom we have been taught to distrust. Since the purposes of disarmament are unclear and the implications uncertain, most people prefer staying with the world we know or think we know to entering a world in which we put our trust in the sanity and decency of people rather than in the power of machines.

There has been no disarmament because the assumptions of the arms race have been almost universally accepted. Most people, including most people who favor disarmament, accept the premise that more weapons mean more security, that alternative systems of security not based on making hostages of hundreds of millions of people are utopian, and that the survival of the United States as a sovereign actor in the world justifies mass murder, poisoning of the earth, and the hideous mutation of the human species. We do not seem to be able to generate the moral passion to rid the world of arms, because we ourselves are psychologically dependent upon them.

Soviet Blackmail

The standard nightmare for which our national-security strategy is designed is a Soviet attack or Soviet blackmail. If we fall short of the magic number of nuclear weapons, it is argued, Kremlin leaders may think that they would suffer "only" ten million or twenty million or fifty million casualties if they push the button; they may then conclude that running the world with the United States out of the way would be worth it.

"We do not seem to be able to generate the moral passion to rid the world of arms."

There is nothing in Soviet behavior, history, or ideology to suggest that the model of the Soviet leader waiting by the button until the computer predicts an "acceptable" casualty level is anything but a convenient fantasy to support an unending arms race. It is said that it is a harmless fantasy, a kind of insurance policy against Armageddon. But, unlike an insurance policy, the arms race directly affects the risk. By preparing for an implausible war we make other scenarios for nuclear wars—wars by accident and miscalculation—far more probable.

Anyone who ponders the elaborate system of war prevention we have erected—people in submarines submerged for months waiting for the world to destroy three hundred cities or more with a touch of a button, banks of computers that are expected to behave significantly better in communicating critical information than those that produce the billing foul-ups in department stores, cool rational leaders whom we expect to make the most agonizing decisions in a crisis without information or sleep—can understand why a growing number of scientists state flatly that if the arms race continues nuclear war is now inevitable.

A Practical Alternative

What is a practical alternative for the 1980s to a national security strategy based on escalating the arms race? Arms limitation agreements can create a positive political climate in which it becomes possible to move toward an alternative security system. But only if certain requirements are met. The first requirement is that the agreement make both sides feel more secure. Since partial limitations on nuclear weapons may appear to favor one side or the other, as the opponents of SALT II have alleged, the more comprehensive the limitations the more stable the agreement. Second, the new arms relationship should have clear economic payoffs for both sides. Third, the principle of "rough equivalence" should be extended not only to numbers and characteristics of weapons systems, but to other aspects of the military relationship, including the right to acquire bases and to threaten the homeland of either power from such bases. Fourth, the explicit purpose of the agreement should be to remove ambiguities about intentions.

The more agreements require significant internal changes in both societies, the better reassurance they provide. Clear political commitment in the direction of demilitarization is not easy to reverse and thus offers the most reliable indication of national intentions. A substantially emptier parking lot at the Pentagon or at the Ministry of Defense in Moscow, or the conversion of defense plants provide a better index of national intentions even than satellite photos of missile silos, as important as they are. If the Soviets' consumer production began getting the priority attention now available only to the Soviet military-industrial complex, and their tanks began to look as dowdy as their hotel elevators, one could reasonably conclude that something important had happened. A serious program of conversion would require the leaders of both sides to confront powerful interests with a bureaucratic and ideological commitment to the arms race. That in itself would be impressive evidence of a turn toward peace....

It is now more important than ever before to offer an explicit, simple, and comprehensive agreement for prohibiting the further deployment of either Soviet or American military forces in other countries. We need mutually agreed-upon restriction on what each superpower can do with its military power which would outlaw future Vietnams, Dominican Republics, Chiles, Angolas, Czechoslovakias, Hungarys, and Afghanistans. We should offer the Soviets a broad agreement that embodies the principle of equality on which they have long insisted—clear ground rules which inhibit both the U.S. and the U.S.S.R. and symbolize their mutual understanding that the use of military force by the superpowers or by their proxies in the Third World is now too dangerous. Ideological competition will go on but within the confines of the new rules needed to avoid confrontation and war.

Downplay the Military

Both superpowers have much to gain by downplaying the military factor in world politics to the greatest possible extent. In an escalating worldwide arms race both superpowers will continue to lose influence as global politics become increasingly unmanageable and chaotic....

"The call for physical abolition of all nuclear weapons...merely heightens anxiety and breeds cynicsm."

Given the realities of world power and the parallel reflex response in Washington and Moscow, there is no way out of the national-security dilemma as it is now being defined. To build a world consensus to discourage Soviet interventions, however, the U.S. must commit itself to cease further military interventions of its own. The essential characteristic of a stable relationship with the Soviet Union is clarity. An arms race never provides clarity, because any buildup of offensive forces or such an ambiguous "defensive" weapon as the anti-ballistic missile creates anxiety in the adversary, even if the weapon is procured as a "bargaining chip" for negotiation or as a counterweight to weapons on the other side. Detente, as it developed in the years 1972–79, is also too ambiguous a relationship to endure. On both sides expectations were frustrated. The Soviets received neither the massive infusion of technology and credits they had been led to expect nor the clear acceptance of their equal status as a nuclear power. The American people, having been led to believe by Nixon and Kissinger that detente was a U.S. diplomatic triumph, were surprised by the continuing Soviet buildup and the Kremlin's increasingly interventionist policy. The "principles" of coexistence were so general that they easily accommodated radically different interpretations in Washington and Moscow. The lesson to draw from the failure of detente is not that coexistence is impossible— there is no alternative—but that the terms must be spelled out in the most precise terms.

Richard J. Barnet is the author of The Lean Years: Politics in the Age of Scarcity, Global Reach: The Power of the Multinational Corporations, *and of six other books.*

"The existence of a British nuclear force has actually hindered SALT."

Britain Should Disarm Unilaterally

Dick Nettleton

Despite detente, despite negotiations on arms limitations, the arms race goes on.

In mid-1972 the USA and the USSR had 5890 and 2170 strategic nuclear warheads respectively. By mid-1973 the figures had increased to 7040 and 2260. By mid-1974 they were 7960 and 2600. In the last twelve years the number of strategic warheads has increased more than tenfold, and their combined explosive power more than fivefold. Announced American plans indicate that by 1983 they may have as many as 20,000 strategic warheads.

And then there are the tactical nuclear weapons. The USSR has about 3500; the USA, according to evidence given at a Congress hearing, has "tens of thousands" in Europe....

Since 1969 the USA and the USSR have been conducting Strategic Arms Limitation Talks, generally known as SALT. Many people have great hopes that this process will eventually lead to nuclear disarmament.

But as yet it shows no sign of doing so. The major problem with SALT is that it is, as its title proclaims, only about arms *limitation*—it does not even go as far as reduction.

Instead of ending the arms race, it lets it proceed within certain defined limits. But so far those limits have only dealt with numbers of missiles and bombers—they have not been imposed upon the numbers of warheads.

Since you get hit by the warheads, not by whatever launches them, it is the warheads which should be limited. Until they are, the arms race will continue to accelerate. But even when the warheads are limited, that will not be enough—it will still be possible to replace them with better ones.

The real need is to reduce arms levels. Until this is accepted, the only practical effect of SALT will be to divert the arms race into new paths.

Dick Nettleton, *The Case for Nuclear Disarmament*. London: Campaign for Nuclear Disarmament, 1975.

It is, of course, better to have the USA and the USSR negotiating than not; it is true that the atmosphere is much better between the two states than it was in the fifties and sixties. But until this political detente is matched by military detente, we cannot even begin to feel safe.

In Britian we are still spending over £300 million per year on having nuclear weapon 'status.' This may be only 10% of the annual military budget, but it is plainly stupid to be wasting money on this hardware when we cannot afford to build enough homes.

Despite detente, nuclear war has come closer. And with that change has come the growing threat of nuclear proliferation—the spread of nuclear weapons to yet more countries. The more countries that have the Bomb, the greater the danger that it will be used.

It is not just a question of nuclear disarmament being as necessary as it was when CND was founded—it is more necessary, and more urgent, than ever....

Britain is a small island—with cities packed closely together, and bases near some cities, it is a perfect target. Whatever we threaten to do to another nuclear power, we know that little effort would be expanded by that power in utterly annihilating Britain.

Nuclear Graveyard

Britain is already weak. A dozen large warheads would turn it into a nuclear graveyard. So however powerful the British nuclear force were, it could never act as a convincing deterrent, *because a threat to use our weapons is a threat to commit suicide.*

Our nuclear force does not, and never can, protect us. And it makes precious little difference to the 'balance' of fire-power between East and West. If it disappeared tomorrow it would hardly be missed; in fact the Pentagon would probably heave a sigh of relief, as the additional complications of targeting and deploying a force which is nominally under independent control cannot be worth the few extra bangs it might provide....

The acquisition of the Polaris fleet cost over £300 million. It cost £39 million a year to maintain. We do not know for sure how much money is spent on paying, feeding and training the crew, housing their dependents and providing education; maintaining base facilities; maintaining the V-bombers and providing similar services for their crews. We do not know for sure how much money is spent on research and development for nuclear weapons, or on replacing the warheads, which deteriorate very quickly. We do not even know if the maintenance cost is supposed to include the cost of operating the damn things.

"It is in Britain's own interests to get rid of its nuclear weapons."

We do not know for sure—and the fact that the Government never makes it clear how much is spent on these areas means it is a pretty significant amount. A reasonable estimate of the costs involved in being a nuclear power totals about £350 million per year.

The expenditure of all this money does not make us safe. On the contrary it turns us into a prime target, and carries a built-in risk of accident.

Nuclear disarmament would not diminish our security—it would improve it. And by releasing funds, natural resources and, perhaps most importantly, great talent for other areas, it would make us stronger.

All previous arms races have ended in war. All the fine weapons and theories of defense, the guarantees of security, could not then prevent thousands of lives from being lost. There is no reason to suppose that this arms race will be any different. Our only security is in ending the arms race.

Dick Nettleton is vice-chairman for the Campaign for Nuclear Disarmament in Great Britain.

"Even nations not particularly noted for the wisdom of their statecraft did not stray into the ultimate folly [of unilateral disarmament]."

viewpoint **53**

Britain Should Not Disarm Unilaterally

Walter F. Hahn

A theme in the "peace movements" on both sides of the Atlantic is preemptive disarmament or disarmament-by-example. The strength of this theme varies from the outright "unilateralists" in Great Britain, who want to purge their country of all nuclear weapons, to the more "modest" American advocates of a "nuclear freeze."

Nevertheless, a common denominator is the notion that even if the men in Moscow should turn a blind eye and deaf ear to disarmament or arms restraint, the Western nations ought to show the way. Sooner or later, so the reasoning runs, the Soviet leaders will yield to the logic of reining in nuclear arms and/or be shamed into following the Western lead.

When the dangers of one-sidedness are described to "peace movement" members, the standard refrain is: "Why not try something that has not been tried before? Besides, what conceivably could be more dangerous than a continuing nuclear arms race?"

Examples of Folly

Well, it's true enough that history is not exactly bulging with examples of unilateral disarmament—a fact that suggests that even nations not particularly noted for the wisdom of their statecraft did not stray into the ultimate folly. There is one recorded example, but we have to go far back into antiquity.

For the interesting story that follows, all too revelant to today, we are indebted to the late Brigadier General Donald Armstrong, a soldier-scholar who was fascinated by the study of antiquity, not only for what it tells about our wellsprings but for the light it sheds upon the contemporary stage.

General Armstrong's book, *The Reluctant Warriors,* is unique as an exercise in applied history. In the volume, General Armstrong not only recounts the Third Punic War between Rome and Carthage, but he draws explicit parallels to the U.S.A.- Soviet confrontation of modern times.

Weary of Confrontation

The particular story begins in 149 B.C., when Rome and Carthage had logged nearly 100 years of cold and hot war. But now the Carthaginians, prosperous in the pursuit of trade and weary of the sacrifices of conflict and confrontation, debated the question: "Why continue?" Should they "expose their country to war and its terrors, or, not daring to face the attack of the enemy, yield unresistingly to every demand?"

The Carthaginians opted to sue for peace. They entered into negotiations with the Romans, who opened with the demand for 300 children of the noblest Carthaginian families as hostages. If the Carthaginians complied and promised "to obey their orders in other respects, the freedom and autonomy of Carthage would be preserved."

The Carthaginians obliged, amid the laments of bereaved mothers who, according to Appian, predicted "that it would profit the city nothing to have delivered up their children."

The next Roman demand followed apace: "If you are sincerely desirous of peace, why do you need arms? Come, surrender to us all your weapons and engines of war, both public and private." The Carthaginians complied, turning over the complete armor for 200,000 men, innumerable javelins and some 2,000 catapults, along with the ships of their navy. Had not the Romans promised to respect their freedom and autonomy?

Then came the ultimatum from Rome, which read in part: "Bear bravely the remaining command of the Senate. Yield Carthage to us, and betake yourselves where you like within your own territory at a distance of at least 10 miles from the sea, for we are resolved to raze your city to the ground."

Despite the entreaties of the Carthaginian ambassadors, the Romans refused to soften the ultimatum.

Walter F. Hahn, "Disarmament: An Ancient Story." Pamphlet available from Americanism Educational League, Freedom Center, PO Box 5986, Buena Park, CA 90622.

The news triggered a "scene of blind, raving madness" in Carthage. This was understandable, for the Carthaginians were asked to give up not only their city, but their vaunted livelihood in the tradewinds of the Mediterranean.

In desperation, despite their lack of arms, the Carthaginians declared war on Rome. For three years, fighting with makeshift weapons, they resisted the siege of their city, but the odds against them proved too great. The Romans took Carthage and obliterated the city, selling the surviving Carthaginians into slavery.

> "Should they expose their country to war and its terrors or...yield unresistingly to every demand?"

There is a footnote to the story. In the Carthaginian debates over the best course to follow vis-a-vis Rome, the pro-accommodation faction had argued, among other things, that surely Rome's appetite for conquest was satisfied and that the Romans undoubtedly wanted surcease from the protracted conflict as much as did Carthage. And did not the strident voices in the Roman Senate testify to Roman disunity, notwithstanding Cato the Elder's thunderings: "Carthage must be destroyed!"?

History records that the Roman Empire did collapse under the weight of its surfeit and internal contradictions. But by the time this transpired—some five centuries later—it was of no help to the Carthaginians!

Walter Hahn is editor-in-chief of Strategic Review. *This article was awarded a 1983 George Washington Honor Medal by Freedom Foundation at Valley Forge.*

"You do not have to be an Isaac Newton to understand the first law of the nuclear arms race—every action by one side will be matched by an equal and opposite reaction by the other side."

Pro: The Kennedy-Hatfield Resolution

Edward M. Kennedy

Our proposal calls for a mutual and verifiable freeze on the testing, production, and further deployment of nuclear warheads, missiles and other delivery systems with the Soviet Union, followed by major stabilizing reductions in the nuclear arsenals on both sides.

We recognize the distance that the Reagan Administration has come on this issue in recent weeks and months. We welcome the President's new and more affirmative attitude towards arms control. The Administration's movement on this issue is a tribute to the growing effectiveness of another movement of great importance—the nationwide grassroots campaign to stop the nuclear arms race by achieving a nuclear weapons freeze.

The prevention of nuclear war is not only the great issue of our time, but perhaps the greatest issue of all time. Today the two superpowers possess the equivalent of one million Hiroshima bombs—an amount equal to four tons of T.N.T. for every man, woman, and child presently living on this planet.

Like building blocks stacked one upon the other in a child's playroom, the nuclear weapons buildup has lifted all of us to higher and higher levels of danger. Inexorably, we are moving toward the point where the slightest accident or miscalculation could bring the whole structure tumbling down, and plunge our two nations and the world into nuclear holocaust. The Kennedy-Hatfield Resolution insists that we must stop the nuclear buildup now, before we reach the point of nuclear no return.

The President has now spoken about the need to restrain nuclear arms. But my basic concern over the President's plan is that his START proposal does not stop the nuclear arms race; it merely channels it into a new direction. It permits the continued testing, production, and deployment of the MX missile, the Trident II missile, the Cruise missile, the B-1 bomber, the Stealth

Edward M. Kennedy, testimony presented on May 11, 1982 before the Senate Committee on Foreign Relations. He and Senator Mark Hatfield authored S.J. Res. 163.

bomber, and other advanced nuclear weapons. Indeed, the Reagan plan does not cover bombers or Cruise missiles at all—a loophole big enough to fly a fleet of bombers through, with each plane carrying more destructive force than all the bombs dropped in World War II.

While the United States builds more, the Soviet Union will not be standing idle. They have their own new weapons on their own drawing boards—including the Typhoon submarine and a follow-on generation of missiles beyond the current SS-18s and SS-19s.

As recent history demonstrates, the Soviets are prepared to match us every step and every missile of the way in the futile but increasingly dangerous quest for nuclear superiority. You do not have to be an Isaac Newton to understand the first law of the nuclear arms race—every action by one side will be matched by an equal and opposite reaction by the other side.

I believe that a nuclear weapons freeze is the most effective way to halt the nuclear arms race now, so that we can finally begin to run it in reverse. The fundamental question which I ask is the fundamental question that citizens in communities across the country are asking in ever-increasing numbers: Mr. President, why not start with a freeze as the first step toward arms control?

We do not enter a freeze or reduction of nuclear arms because we like the Soviets or they like us—but because both of us prefer existence to extinction.

A nuclear weapons freeze has the clear advantage of bypassing endless, irresolvable arguments about which side is ahead. Too often, we find that equality is in the eye of the beholder. In fact, both sides today are at essential parity. Each side, even after absorbing a first strike, can destroy the other many times over. The United States can make the Soviet rubble bounce all the way from Moscow to Vladivostok, and the Soviets can make our rubble bounce all the way from the Potomac to the Pacific. The Kennedy-Hatfield Resolution accepts this condition of parity; it calls for a mutual freeze now, with mutual reductions to follow, in the interest of preventing mutual annihilation.

At best, the Administration must anticipate protracted negotiations with the Soviets over any such proposal. Now, in this posture, a nuclear freeze could well make all the difference to the success or failure of the Reagan plan. A freeze is the only idea which can stop the spiral of nuclear arms development in the near term, and avoid the self-defeating delays of long-term negotiations over arms reductions.

A freeze agreement would be a nuclear weapons firebreak. Once armaments and technological advances are stopped at present levels, the two superpowers can negotiate phased and balanced reductions. President Reagan has called for one-third reductions in ballistic missile warheads. The Kennedy-Hatfield Resolution calls for across-the-board reductions "through annual percentages or equally effective means." George Kennan, our former ambassador to the Soviet Union and our foremost expert on that country, and Admiral Hyman G. Rickover, Director of Naval Nuclear Propulsion under seven presidents, have argued eloquently and compellingly for deep cuts of at least 50 per cent in the nuclear armories of both sides. These cuts could be achieved by the end of this decade if we mutually agree to reasonable reductions of seven percent a year. This is the approach proposed in the Kennedy-Hatfield Resolution.

"We do not enter a freeze or reduction of nuclear arms because we like the Soviets or they like us—but because both of us prefer existence to extinction."

Finally, a freeze will enhance, not reduce, our overall national security. It will halt the development of more powerful Soviet rockets and block their further deployment of existing weapons. It will prevent one side from perfecting its capacity for a first strike against the other by prohibiting the testing and production of such destabilizing weapons; the result will be a substantial reduction in the fear of a U.S. or Soviet pre-emptive attack. And a freeze will also permit additional resources to be allocated to our conventional military forces, where we do need to do more.

Opponents of a freeze claim that the Soviets would have no incentive to reduce their arsenals after a freeze. They call for building new weapons systems, in order to pile up bargaining chips for later negotiations with the Kremlin.

The arms race has been needlessly and heedlessly perpetuated by this bargaining chip theory, because both sides inevitably feel forced to match new and threatening developments with their own. A decade ago, MIRVs were defended as a bargaining chip during the SALT I talks. The United States continued to deploy them, and then we were told that they were too important to bargain away.

Combination Approach

The Administration says that it wants to go beyond a freeze and do better. But with $100 billion worth of new weapons now in prospect over the next five years, the Administration is still far short of a freeze. I believe the best arms control approach is not to brandish an arms race as a means of achieving arms reduction, but a combination of three important steps:

First, the Administration should pledge unequivocally that it will abide by the limits of the SALT II Treaty, so long as the Soviets also do. The President has been unwilling to give such a pledge thus far.

Second, in order to prevent massive build-ups on either side during prolonged negotiations for reductions, the Administration should propose to the Soviet Union a mutual and verifiable nuclear weapons freeze.

Third, the Administration should seek to negotiate major reductions in all aspects of nuclear forces, not simply in one or two elements of those forces.

Past arms control agreements have been defective, because they have failed to prevent quantum leaps in the sophistication of weaponry. The Vladivostok accord and the SALT II Treaty permitted the development of cruise missiles. The military planners saw the loophole and decided to rush through it with a new weapons system in which they had previously shown only minimum interest.

Where there is a loophole, it will almost certainly be exploited. Where a new system is permitted, it will inevitably be pursued, in order to prevent the adversary from gaining an advantage. A comprehensive freeze, put in place before reductions talks begin, will plug past loopholes and prevent future ones by blocking any further additions to current nuclear arsenals.

Opponents of a nuclear weapons freeze also claim that a freeze is not a practical idea, because it will be difficult to verify. I believe that just the opposite is true. In fact, a freeze may well be easier to verify than a complex arms reduction agreement.

In a matter of months, the two superpowers, assuming their goodwill, could reasonably work out satisfactory verification procedures for a freeze. Members of the Reagan Administration, supporters of the Jackson-Warner Resolution, and other critics of the Kennedy-Hatfield Resolution who claim that a freeze is unverifiable are exhibiting a surprising inconsistency in their logic—they say they will support a freeze tomorrow, after we build some more today. So they too must believe that a freeze actually can be verified.

Strict Verification

In fact, the Kennedy-Hatfield Resolution does not require trust by one side for the other. Every element of the freeze depends on strict verification. What cannot be verified will not be frozen. But there are many experts who agree that a freeze is adequately verifiable.

It may be that some form of on-site inspection will be necessary to verify production and to check certain limited aspects of testing. To presume that the Soviets will not permit any such inspection overlooks the record of the comprehensive test-ban treaty negotiations, now postponed by the Reagan Administration, where the Soviets have agreed to the principle of on-site verification. Even areas where there may be verification questions, such as some areas of production, do not present serious difficulties, since verification in other areas will assure overall enforcement of the freeze.

"My basic concern over the President's plan is that his START proposal does not stop the nuclear arms race; it merely channels it into a new direction."

Critics of the freeze sometimes confuse it with the Soviet proposal for a European freeze. The Kennedy-Hatfield Resolution rejects a freeze in Europe alone. Our proposal is for a global freeze. In case of a Soviet nuclear attack on NATO, the United States could call on its entire nuclear arsenal to respond. For any Administration to suggest that it no longer relies on this option would signal a major and destabilizing change in NATO policy, in which Europe would no longer enjoy the protection of America's nuclear umbrella.

On the critical issue of ending the nuclear arms race now and reducing the arsenals of nuclear annihilation, I believe the Kennedy-Hatfield Resolution provides a vital alternative, and I urge the committee to approve it. Whether we prevail at first or not in this cause, and no matter how long it may take, I will continue to stand, to speak and to work for a nuclear weapons freeze—and so will millions of citizens in every section of the country. The American people want to stop the arms race before it stops the human race.

Edward M. Kennedy is the Democratic senator from Massachusetts.

"An immediate nuclear freeze. . . would. . .be an acceptance of the 'unbelievable Soviet armada that is aimed against us.'"

Con: The Jackson-Warner Resolution

Kenneth Rush

I welcome S.J. Res. 177. In concise, yet most cogent words, it demands an American initiative in arms control that would reinforce the safety and security of all mankind.

The President has taken the initiative along the lines called for in that Resolution. As he said, we must seek agreements which are verifiable, equitable, and militarily significant.

There are some others who would pursue other paths. Arms control cannot be achieved by catchy slogans. As the President said: "Agreements that give only the appearance of arms control breed dangerous illusions." There are proponents for an immediate freeze on the production of any further nuclear weapons. But this would accept the very disparities in nuclear strength which are of serious concern to ourselves and our allies. As the independent International Institute for Strategic Studies recently noted, with regard to theater nuclear systems, "even with the inclusion of Poseidon on the Western side, and the continued exclusion of Soviet strategic systems, the balance is distinctly unfavorable to NATO and is becoming more so." Moreover, is not a freeze at equal and sharply reduced and verifiable levels, as urged by the Jackson-Warner Resolution, a more stable solution than one at present levels?

As a former Ambassador to the Federal Republic of Germany and to France, I never fail to try to consider fully the views of our European allies. The rejection of the concept of an immediate nuclear freeze by Chancellor Schmidt was immediate and categorical. It would, as he said, be an acceptance of the "unbelievable Soviet armada that is aimed against us."

This leads me to an important point, Mr. Chairman. There has been much public attention to the mass public demonstrations of concern in Europe—and more recently here at home—at the dimensions of a possible nuclear holocaust, and the horrors of nuclear war, and

Kenneth Rush, speech before the Senate Committee on Foreign Relations, May 12, 1982.

with worry that some government might believe that limited nuclear war could be a prudent option.

Everyone abhors the prospect of nuclear war. But mere abhorrence is not enough. The essential question is how to prevent the outbreak of any major war which might escalate to nuclear weaponry. In other words, how to keep the peace.

The Answer

And the answer is: deterrence. The concept of deterrence at lower levels is fully preserved by S.J. Res. 177, and thus supports the Alliance policy. To quote the German Foreign Minister, Mr. Genscher:

> "Along with deterrence and defense, arms control and disarmament are integral parts of the Alliance's security policy. The arms control policy aimed at achieving a stable balance of forces at the lowest possible level, a policy which the Federal Government has helped to shape, is also intended to make an effective contribution to prevent war and safeguarding peace.". . .

Since we are faced with the necessity of living with nuclear weapons, with all their risks, let us make a virtue of necessity and continue to preserve, expressly and without ambiguity, such deterrent effect as can be obtained from our strategic strength.

In a recent study by the NATO Working Group of the Atlantic Council, which Brent Scowcroft and I co-chaired, we said:

> "As long as nuclear weapons exist, and general strategic parity prevails, the risk of Allied first use of nuclear weapons in response to armed attack by the Warsaw Pact, particularly in times of confusion and anxiety or as a measure of last resort, simply cannot be excluded from the thinking of the Soviet planners. The loss of escalatory control appreciably reduces the readiness with which NATO would be prepared to initiate use of tactical or theater nuclear weapons; at the same time, it does not go so far as to necessarily reduce that chance to zero. If large scale Soviet conventional attack were met with a stubborn and sustained conventional defense but nevertheless was at the point of prevailing, the Soviets could not but be uncertain that such a resolute enemy

would not turn to nuclear weapons as a measure of last resort. In such circumstances, with the conquest of a viable Western Europe no longer possible, and with the survival of the Soviet regime and homeland at risk, the Soviet planners simply would not have the ability to guarantee a reasonable chance of success.''

And let us not forget one cogent fact that is stressed in the NATO study. The USSR now has ''the potential capability to destroy most of the United States' ICBM silos while NATO''—(including the U.S.)—''by contrast, does not have a corresponding capability against the Soviet Union's ICBM silos. . . .'' Surely, Mr. Chairman, when the START talks commence, S.J. Res. 177, with its call for equal and reduced levels of nuclear armaments, will demand a solution of this imbalance *downward*, rather than by having to respond to it by entering into a further escalating arms race in survivable land based weaponry. The President's proposal asks that this be reduced downward by at least one-third of all current levels.

In the same vein, the Intermediate Nuclear Force (INF) talks in Geneva present the opportunity to move either upward or, preferably, downward.

Imbalance of Power

The new generation of Soviet SS-20 nuclear missiles place the population and infrastructure of Western Europe and the military forces of NATO under the guns of the Soviets. With these new and more accurate weapons, the Soviets might make the mistaken judgment that they could threaten our allies without fear of any retaliatory attack on their territory, especially if they did not threaten to attack U.S. forces or territory. The result has been to shake the confidence of the European Allies in being able to stand up to the Soviets, in light of the pressure provided by this prime example of an imbalance of power.

"An immediate freeze. . .would accept the very disparities in nuclear strength which are of serious concern to ourselves and our allies."

There are only two ways to bring things back into balance. The first choice—vastly to be preferred—is through arms control arrangements, such as the Reagan proposal at the Geneva talks for a ''zero option'' which would eliminate this sort of weapons for both sides. Should that fail, the alternative is to build a new NATO missile force in Europe to put the Soviet missiles in check and disperse the shadow of nuclear blackmail from Western Europe. Such a force need not match the Soviets weapon for weapon; its function would rather be only to frustrate Soviet exploitation of a risk-free situation by making it too costly an option to pursue.

There is, of course, one other choice. By resigning

themselves and letting the Soviets dominate the situation, the Allies could avoid the costs and tensions of competition with the Soviets. But only at the expense of their cherished heritage of freedom from external domination—domination by a police state which cannot tolerate and must suppress liberty. How the Poles would have welcomed the chance to reject that choice!

Words of Hope

S.J. Res. 177 wisely avoids specifics. But it charts a general course that cannot but appeal to all peoples—the Soviets as well as ourselves—as principles to be vigorously pursued. As our government responds to this call, I warmly hope that it is understood that we thereby totally reject the false concept that arms control agreements are not of importance to the security of our country. Let us truly search for a stabilizing agreement with the Soviets that will benefit all the world, not only our two nations. It is my hope that we never be inflexible at the negotiating table so long as we stay within the parameters of security. These are wise words of hope and, at the same time, caution in Ambassador ''Chip'' Bohlen's valuable memoirs:

> ''Although I see no bridge that can be built between the ideological commitments of the Soviet Union and the United States; and insistence on protecting the independence of its allied countries, it does not follow that the two superpowers are on a collision course. *Both governments deeply believe that a nuclear war is unthinkable.* Neither would set out on a course that would lead to mutual suicide. . . .If Moscow lost a war, the whole house of cards could come tumbling down. For this reason, war is to be avoided. Therefore, *I do not see any circumstance under which the Soviets would deliberately embark on World War III. Circumstances might develop along the peripheries of the lines of power, however, which, step by step, could lead to a confrontation in which neither country would back down. . . .*
>
> ''This fear of war is another reason why *the Kremlin has been serious about disarmament. . . .*There are too many sections'' (in SALT I) ''open to varying interpretations, and, as we have seen, *the Kremlin always takes advantage of loose drafting to evade the spirit of treaties.''* (Emphasis added)

In conclusion let me share with you one aspect of the question of arms control that has increasingly given me concern.

The questions of arms control and of defense capability are inseparable and equally important aspects of our national security, and should go hand in hand. However, they get separate and disproportionate attention before the Congress. I would very much hope that as hearings transpire on the defense aspect of our policy, they could as thoroughly look at the arms control aspects, since both are part of our foreign and security policy.

Kenneth Rush is chairman of the board of directors for the Atlantic Council of the United States.

"The fundamental error of the religious pacifists is the notion that the United States and the Soviet Union are equally guilty of endangering peace."

A Nuclear Freeze Would Endanger the US

Phyllis Schlafly

No peace movement has ever prevented war. The freezeniks cannot cite a single example in 6,000 years of recorded history when a peace movement or a weapons-freeze movement ever prevented war. That's because a peace movement promotes peace *only* in peaceful countries, but promotes war in aggressive countries.

On the other hand, history affords us many examples of peace movements starting wars. The weapons-freeze movement of the 1930s, culminating in the Munich ("peace in our time") agreement, stopped the arms race in the peaceful countries (England and Europe) but encouraged the arms race in the warlike countries (Nazi Germany and Japan). The weapons freeze of the 1930s *started* World War II.

Nuclear Freeze won't protect us against any of the threats of the nuclear-space age. It won't protect us against the Soviet weapons' overkill; they already have enough nukes to kill 100 million Americans several times over. It won't protect us against the Russians' cheating on their agreements; they always have and they always will.

Nuclear Freeze can't protect us against international terrorists such as Qaddafi or Castro. It cannot protect us against accidental war—against some Dr. Strangelove pushing the button.

Nuclear Freeze can't protect us against Mutual Assured Destruction (the MAD doctrine). Nuclear Freeze provides absolutely no defense against attack.

Nuclear Freeze can't protect us against the danger posed by proliferation of nuclear weapons among a dozen countries. Although those who watched the 1980 presidential TV debate couldn't believe Jimmy Carter when he said that proliferation was Amy's principal worry, it nevertheless is a concern to those who do understand what it means.

Phyllis Schlafly, "Freeze or Anti-Freeze and High Frontier," *The Phyllis Schlafly Report,* October 1982.

Nuclear Freeze won't stop the arms race; the Russians will go right on racing. Nuclear Freeze would send this signal to the Russians: "Brezhnev, keep racing. America is giving up." That's why a nuclear freeze increases the risk of nuclear war; if we freeze now, we may fry later.

The nuclear freeze people want to turn the clock back to the pre-nuclear age. They are trying hard to "put the genie back into the bottle." They are like the nations that tried to defend themselves with bows and arrows after gunpowder was invented.

Nuclear Freeze is based on the threat of inevitability and the psychology of fear. Americans should not succumb to that kind of scare propaganda. Nothing is inevitable except death and taxes. President Franklin D. Roosevelt warned us, "The only thing we have to fear is fear itself."

America is the great "can-do" nation. We sent a man to the moon and have already conquered technological challenges of staggering and sophisticated size. We should not let the fearmongers tell us that the human race is doomed and that it is impossible to defend ourselves.

"Freeze" is a bad word and a risky condition. Why would anyone want our machines to be frozen? What our country needs is "ANTI-FREEZE"—a safeguard against the elements, and a real defense against all the dangers of the nuclear age.

Fortunately, American technology has developed an "anti-freeze" defensive system that can preserve American freedom and independence. It is called "High Frontier." It is a system of space platforms (like the space shuttle). High Frontier can prevent war and save lives. Nuclear Freeze, on the other hand, can't do either one.

Phony Morality

The nuclear freeze advocates are currently making a tremendous effort to capture the emotions of church-going Americans. By wrapping themselves in the Bible and words such as "peace" and "morality", the freezeniks hope to chill Americans into pacifism.

A handy summary of their arguments appears in a little flier called "To Be or Not To Be in a Nuclear Age...That is the Question" published by the Christophers, an ecumenical, platitudinous organization which popularized the 20th century use of the ancient saying "it is better to light one candle than to curse the darkness."

The Christophers used to have a respectable reputation for presenting current moral issues factually and objectively. The "To Be" tract costs the Christophers their credibility. Because its arguments are typical of what is being said in the freezeniks' "peace offensive" in the churches, they are worth examining.

"It's time we face the truth that the real danger in the world is not nuclear weapons, but Soviet possession of nuclear weapons."

"To Be" falsely states: "A nuclear war is an unjust war." The truth is that the world's first nuclear war was a *just* war. We didn't start it; we were the victim of a sneak bombing attack at Pearl Harbor in 1941. The sunken battleship *U.S.S. Arizona* in Pearl Harbor still contains the remains of some 1,100 American sailors. American servicemen were subsequently the victims of the horrible Bataan March and other atrocities. Tens of thousands of American GIs gave their lives in fierce battles at Iwo Jima, Okinawa, and the Philippines.

In 1945, hundreds of thousands of American servicemen were awaiting orders to the Pacific to fight island by island to end the war against Japan. U.S. plans projected a million American casualties. Those one million Americans were saved when America's use of the atom bomb at Hiroshima and Nagasaki enabled us to end the war far more quickly, with far less loss of American lives, than battling with conventional weapons.

"To Be" falsely states: "Every nuclear arsenal implies a commitment to destroy innocent men, women and children indiscriminately." The United States has a great nuclear arsenal, but the fact is that we have absolutely NO commitment to destroy innocent men, women and children.

We absolutely proved in the years when we had total supremacy over every other nation in the world, and could have used nuclear weapons to achieve any military or political objective we chose, that our nuclear arsenal was a commitment to keep the peace and to protect the security of the Free World.

The section called "What Can I Do?" shows that the authors of "To Be" are either out of touch with the real world or are trying to lead gullible people down the primrose path. "To Be" states: "Learn about the peace efforts of the UN. Founded in 1945 'to save succeeding

generations from the scourge of war,' the UN has both promise and possibility."

Telling people that the United Nations can prevent war and bring peace is about like telling a child to believe in the tooth fairy. The UN did nothing to stop the sneak attacks on South Korea, Hungary, Czechoslovakia, South Vietnam, or Afghanistan, or to stop the killing and persecution that followed those attacks.

The fundamental error of the religious pacifists is the notion that the United States and the Soviet Union are equally guilty of endangering peace by possessing nuclear arsenals. That concept is historically false, intellectually ignorant, and a gross libel on America. Yet, "To Be" smugly asks the identical question about both America and Russia: "Can the claim that a first strike will never take place, be trusted?"

For two and half decades, from 1945 to about 1970, the United States had a first-strike capability against every other nation in the world, including Russia. We proved conclusively that America could be trusted NOT to use a first-strike capability when we had it.

But Soviet possession of a nuclear arsenal is very difficult. How much would you trust the Communists when they have a first-strike capability against us? Are you willing to risk yours and your children's security on that trust?

It's time we face the truth that the real danger in the world is not nuclear weapons, but Soviet possession of nuclear weapons.

Italicized quotations from the Bible are sprinkled throughout this propaganda flier, such as "Those who live by the sword will die by the sword." The flier fails to quote other relevant passages from the Bible. "He that hath no sword, let him sell his garment and buy one." Luke 22:36 "Beat your plowshares into swords, and your pruning hooks into spears; let the weak say, I am strong." Joel 3:10.

Those who are urging a freeze on U.S. weapons are trying hard to co-opt the high ground of morality. But it won't wash. The Bible gives us the key to peace in Luke 11:21: "When a strong man armed keepeth his palace, his goods are in peace." That's why our Founding Fathers gave the U.S. Government the constitutional obligation to "provide for the common defense."

Communist Praises an Archbishop

Herbert Aptheker, chief theoretician of the Communist Party, doesn't often quote from or praise a speech by a Catholic clergyman. When he does, it is purposeful and newsworthy.

In the Communist newspaper, the *Daily World*, of September 3, 1981, Aptheker writes glowingly about a June speech given by the Catholic Archbishop of Seattle, Raymond Hunthausen, to the Pacific Northwest Synod of the Lutheran Church in America. Aptheker is so enthusiastic because "the Archbishop appeals in his address for disarmament—unilateral disarmament." The full text of the remarkable speech, printed both in

Christianity and Crisis of August 17 and in the August *Catholic Worker*, confirms that the Archbishop said this: "As followers of Christ, we need to take up our cross in the nuclear age. I believe that one obvious meaning of the cross is unilateral disarmament."

The launching of one of our Trident submarines was what triggered the Archbishop's plea for us to lay down our arms in the face of the Soviet military threat. He called the Trident (which made its maiden voyage in Puget Sound) "the Auschwitz of Puget Sound." The Archbishop recommended civil disobedience: he called on American citizens to promote disarmament by refusing to pay their income taxes.

Listen to the Archbishop's words (which Aptheker accurately described as "radical"): "I would like to share a vision of still another action that could be taken, simply this—a sizeable number of people in the State of Washington, 5,000, 10,000, ½ million people refusing to pay 50% of their taxes in nonviolent resistance to nuclear murder and suicide. I think that would be a definite step toward disarmament."

Aptheker correctly points out that the Archbishop's speech was notable for "a complete absence of the usual clap-trap about a Soviet menace." Instead, the Archbishop discovered a new menace: "nuclear arms" (which he claims enable the United States to indulge in "exploitation" of other countries and "global terror"), and the "arms corporations" (which, he asserts, have "paralyzed" our government).

"We face the moral risk of seeing our freedom destroyed if the moralists confine their condemnations only to things in the abstract."

Before Archbishop Hunthausen (or any other clergyman) sounds off with any more slurs on the United States, or calls for civil disobedience in order to induce a U.S. surrender to the Soviet Union, he should study the great work of one of the outstanding 20th century Catholic theologians, Charles Cardinal Journet of Switzerland. In his definitive 1964 article entitled "The Conscience of a Christian About Nuclear Arms," he declared: "If the non-Communist bloc unilaterally disarmed, it would give the world to the Soviet Empire and would betray all the holy values, temporal and spiritual, which we ought to defend: this would be the evil of betrayal."

Cardinal Journet eloquently defended the moral right of the West to work for peace by stockpiling nuclear weapons. He defended the right of the West to "produce atomic weapons in the hope never to have to use them, but just to build a deterrent against the threat of the enemy." He pointed out clearly that "we cannot hope *not*

to use them unless we are actually ready to use them."

Cardinal Journet pointed out that if "Christians succeed in imposing unilateral disarmament upon their bloc, the Soviets, by the threat of war, would hold the world in their hands.... We face the moral risk of seeing our freedom destroyed if the moralists confine their condemnations only to things in the abstract and if they refuse to face up to actual conditions."

The Folly of Freeze Without Inspection

"But we can't trust the Communists," say the opponents of a nuclear freeze. "We don't have to," answer the freezeniks; "we can monitor Russian compliance with satellites and other technical means, which can now read a license plate in Moscow."

The answer is simply false. You don't need to be a scientist to see why; all you need is common sense.

Spy satellites in space can take pictures of objects exposed to the lens of the camera. But they cannot take pictures of items under cover of a roof or camouflage or clouds. Factories have roofs. When secret weapons come out of the factories for field testing so that cameras can photograph them, it is too late.

When a new assembly line starts up, the spy satellite cannot know what is its rate of production, or which version of a certain missile is being produced, until the finished missiles roll out the door.

Spy cameras cannot look into a missile and count how many warheads are present. The Soviets can increase or decrease the number of warheads in a nose cone without our knowing about it and without additional testing.

The Russians consistently code radio signals from their test missiles to be sure that we cannot monitor the precise characteristics of their missiles and warheads.

Satellite cameras cannot monitor the testing of nuclear warheads because that is done underground. We try to monitor underground live testing by seismic devices, but that is very unprecise. The Russians can use dummies in their tests which may be very different from live warheads, and the quantity of fissionable material in the warheads can be easily disguised or hidden.

The nuclear freezeniks claim that Russian cheating on a freeze or an arms-control treaty would be unlikely because the risk of detection would be considerable, the price of detection would be great, and the benefits of small-scale cheating would be negligible. To the contrary, all those assertions are false.

As we have seen above, the risk of detection is small and the benefits are great. Moreover, the "price" of detection is non-existent. Who would set the price and demand payment?

For ten years, the Soviets have consistently cheated on SALT I, and they haven't paid any price at all. In the name of detente, the U.S. State Department has turned a deaf ear to the mountain of evidence of cheating. Even if our diplomats were of a mind to file complaints, the Standing Consultative Committee is made up of equal numbers of representatives from both sides, so all votes would end in a tie.

On-site inspection is a simple answer to the problems of verification and compliance. But the Russians refused to allow it in SALT I, they never agreed to it in principle, and they never will.

President Reagan has made it clear that we must have bona fide inspection as part of any START agreement. We should never retreat from that position because, without it, any arms-control agreement or freeze is a farce.

The Soviets have a closed society and they mean to keep it that way. The Russians remain opposed to on-site inspection because they have something to hide.

Who Profits from Nuclear Freeze?

Cui bono?—the Latin phrase meaning "for whose benefit?"—is a good guide to assist discovery of the perpetrator of any crime. When a dastardly deed is done, finding out who made money out of it or who received the benefit is a good rule of investigation.

Look at the current nuclear freeze campaign that appeared to be born fully grown and garbed for war (like Athena from Zeus' head). Common sense should tell us that nothing grows spontaneously from the grassroots unless seeds were sown and nourished.

To find out who sowed the seeds and watered them, *cui bono?* Who profits from the nuclear freeze? It's obvious that the beneficiaries are (1) the Soviets and (2) the consortium of special interests that want to divert federal monies from national defense to social-welfare spending programs.

"The components of the rally were skillfully drawn from the organizations that know how to lobby to keep the spigot of federal funds flowing."

It, therefore, should come as no surprise that the organizers of the June 12, 1982, Rally, which demanded "an end to insane nuclear weapons production," also laced their literature with another principal purpose: "the transfer of monies from military spending to social spending."

For the purpose of press coverage, the rally was stage-managed to be simply a broad-based disarmament demonstration at the time of the UN Special Session on Disarmament. However, the components of the rally were skillfully drawn from the organizations that know how to lobby to keep the spigot of federal funds flowing to organizations that have grown accustomed to feeding at the public trough.

Here is how the rally organizers made their appeal to groups that are interested in receiving federal funds far more than they are interested in questions of war and peace, freeze or anti-freeze. "We invite your organization and its affiliates to join with us in promoting nuclear disarmament and a transfer of funds from military spending to meeting human needs.... We are reaching out to and working with many groups, both on the local and national levels, who have not necessarily worked on these specific issues. It is clear that the time is right to make these connections."

It is clear that a major objective of the nuclear freeze campaign is to launch a political attack on Ronald Reagan's efforts to cut non-defense federal spending. The special-interest groups who profit from a high level of domestic welfare programs have rallied their lobbyists to resist reductions in federal spending by any demogogic tactic they can devise.

The other beneficiary of the nuclear freeze campaign is the Soviet Union. It should be obvious that, if the United States is persuaded not to build the weapons necessary to catch up with the Russians, the men in the Kremlin will be able to maintain their margin of superiority with its capacity for nuclear blackmail.

Appealing to the "good faith" of the men in the Kremlin to reduce their nuclear weapons to the level of ours has about as much chance of succeeding as the Children's Crusade of the 13th century—or of Billy Graham's sermons in Moscow.

Phyllis Schlafly is a leading New Right activist. This article was taken from her newsletter The Phyllis Schlafly Report.

"The weapons that the other side is about to build are far more threatening than anything that is already in the arsenal on either side."

viewpoint **57**

A Nuclear Freeze Would Improve US Security

Richard J. Barnet

Clearly, the number-one health issue for the planet is the question of our very survival as a species. It is no longer a startling statement to conclude that the species, the race, humanity itself, is in danger—in danger principally from the very instruments that we human beings have devised to preserve and protect us. That is probably the first dilemma of our present security situation, one that requires us to rethink the making of national security: what security is both individually and collectively for people today, and what it will take to think our way through to a less insecure environment. We can take some encouragement from the knowledge that the human animal shows remarkable capabilities for adaptation. Areas such as the environment, for example, offer some limited good news, although not nearly enough. When we saw that Lake Erie was dying, we found it could be reversed; when we saw that London was dying from the fumes, it could be reversed. But we have not begun, as a nation, as a group of citizens, to take the action that would reverse the very serious security problem that we face: with each additional nuclear weapon, the nuclear threat becomes more of a menace to the security of each of us.

Why do we seem incapable of seeing in time the dreadful contradictions, the dilemmas of our security system?

Why is it that a man like Admiral Rickover can spend a lifetime making weapons and, on his retirement, make the stunning statement—a most welcome statement, however belated—that the United States is overspending itself on defense and creating the conditions for its own destruction, and that he wished he could have sunk most of the ships that he had spent his lifetime building?

Why is it that President Eisenhower, at the end of his career, would say something very similar about the irrational momentum of the military-industrial complex?

Richard Barnet, "Fantasy, Reality and the Arms Race," *American Journal of Orthopsychiatry*, October 1982. Copyright © 1982 the American Orthopsychiatric Association, Inc. Reproduced by permission.

Or, why is it that General MacArthur could talk so eloquently, again at the end of his career, about the madness of war, any kind of war, in the world that we had built?

And why is it that we have spent so much money on the military—about 2.5 trillion dollars, I calculate, since 1945—and are contemplating spending in the next four years an amount that approaches in dollars what we spent over generations?

The dollar, of course—thanks to the inflation caused in large part by military spending—is not what it was, but the Administration plans to spend 1.6 trillion dollars in the next four years. So we are talking about a figure approaching two trillion dollars just in the period that this Administration will be in office. Yet it is manifestly clear that, having spent this money, we are less secure than we were when the process began. The people of the United States are, in objective terms, less secure; more missiles are facing the United States today than there were twenty years ago, or ten years ago, or five years ago; and there is still no defense against the nuclear weapons in the hands of other nations. We have created a situation in which we are not only objectively less secure, but we feel less secure; that is perhaps the most significant new development of the past four or five years.

A recent national Gallup Poll reported the extraordinary finding that some 47% of the respondents believed that nuclear war is likely within five years. When asked by the pollster if they really understood what that meant, with the question, "What are your personal chances of survival in such a war?" the overwhelming majority came out with the view that their chance for personal survival was less than fifty-fifty.

Trapped by Language

What does it mean to a nation that as a result of its security policies—the war-prevention system for which we spend so much money—almost half the country thinks it will fail within a very short period of time, and that when it fails, they will die? What does that mean to the security and power of the nation? What does it do to our capacity as a people to adapt to the reality that we face? I suspect that we find ourselves unable to grasp the danger because it is all too unpleasant to think about; so most of us do not, at least not at the conscious level. We are trapped by the very language we have developed. The way we have devised to talk about security plays havoc with logic and with our own possibilities for saving our civilization.

"We use beguiling metaphors such as 'shield,' as in the 'nuclear shield.' But there is no shield."

The word "defense" is itself the ultimate irony: at almost the very moment in 1947 when we changed the name of the War Department to the Department of Defense, we lost the capacity to defend the nation. In 1967, we had a Secretary of Defense who made public for the first time some of the grisly arithmetic of nuclear war. One hundred nuclear weapons falling on either the United States or the Soviet Union, in the high-kiloton range, would destroy something like 40 million people on either side and destroy two-thirds of the industrial capacity. The United States today has an arsenal of nuclear weapons of about 30,000 of all kinds; the Soviet Union, about 20,000. So we are talking about a situation in which neither side can possibly defend itself in the traditional sense. The dictionary definition of "defense" is "to ward off, to protect"; and we use beguiling metaphors such as "shield," as in the "nuclear shield." But there is no shield. And when we thought seriously about building an actual shield, an antiballistic missile, the prospect was so absurd, so costly, so technologically beyond our capacity, that we abandoned it; we made one of our few agreements with the Russians based on that fundamental perception on both sides that there could not be a defense in the traditional sense. Yet day after day, we go on using that word.

What they really mean by defense, they explain if we press the point, is deterrence—war prevention. There, again, we are asked to hark back to a long history that we have left behind us, the history of some ten thousand years of our species, in which the idea that you prepare for war to get peace perhaps had some plausibility. The idea that it was better to have more bows and arrows than less, more tanks and planes than less, had a certain plausibility.

But we are now again in the extraordinary situation where producing more weapons not only does not make a war less likely, but makes it more likely. Not only does it fail to create more security for the people who are ostensibly being protected by the weapons, it creates less security in very specific ways. The weapons that both

we and the Soviet Union are building today are increasingly so-called counterforce weapons: they are weapons designed to strike other weapons, and they are highly accurate, programmed by very complex communication systems and computers to strike quickly to reduce the reaction time on both sides....

Justifiable Apprehension

This development has demonstrated beyond doubt that we are unable to control the arms race as a technological problem, that there is no technological solution to the arms race, and that there is no way in which this war-prevention system can work other than by a massive, political intervention into this technological process. Today the war-prevention system is closer to a breakdown than it has ever been. The weapons that the other side is about to build are far more threatening than anything that is already in the arsenal on either side. And that is not only because the weapons are inherently more dangerous—they are—but each new weapon carries with it a declaration of intentions. Each side asks, "Why is the other side building on top of the 30,000, on top of the 20,000? Knowing what 100 weapons will do, what are they doing this for?" So the very momentum of the arms race, as it continues at whatever level, is extremely destabilizing because it creates justifiable apprehension on both sides.

Thus, there is no military balance, and there never can be one. That is another one of those words that is flung at us in the newspapers and in government documents. There is no such thing as a military balance in the first place, because neither side in an uncontrolled arms race will permit it to happen. We will spend our trillion and a half dollars; the Russians will spend theirs. Make no mistake, the notion that was presented in the presidential campaign, and hinted at by the President subsequently, that somehow the Soviet Union would opt out of an arms race if we really challenged them with this massive expenditure, has been belied by everything we know in their 65-year history. That is one of the myths on which this false security system rests, because otherwise there is no denouement in this continuing arms race except war. We are presented with a false reassurance about the Russians collapsing under the pressure of the arms race to push us on to make the "final" effort to achieve security. We have been told this again and again, ever since the arms race began.

It is not surprising, therefore, that the American people do not feel safe, and that below the surface, below the easy sense of fatalism and acceptance that characterizes so many Americans, is a deep-seated apprehension and crippling fear, which in itself seriously undermines the security of our nation.

Refreshing Security

The time has come to redefine what we mean by security. The foreign policy of the United States is now clearly in crisis. We face the most dangerous moment in our national history since the Second World War, and the weapons build-up does not make it any less dangerous. Chairman Brezhnev of the Soviet Union recently expressed the same view. We are heading toward an all-out arms race, the consequences of which we do not understand. Our government is engaged in a massive military build-up without any demonstration that it has either a political or a military strategy that would carry out the stated objectives.

It is important, in strictly economic and technical terms, to look much more closely at what we mean by a military build-up. It is not true that even when you spend large amounts of money for the Department of Defense that you are even increasing military hardware. So much waste, so much superfluous spending is included in the billions that we provide to the Department of Defense that it is very difficult to point to additional military capabilities. We are spending a great deal of money, for example, to take some battleships out of mothballs, battleships that are highly vulnerable to even a primitive enemy attack. Is that an increase in military capabilities? We have followed the rather stunning policy of providing highly sophisticated rockets to some of the very countries we hope to impress by sending into their waters ships that are totally vulnerable to those same missiles. There are, throughout the military budget, contradictions that need to be addressed and that even raise questions about whether such a swollen military establishment actually provides increased military capabilities. But, even more important, the relationship between these new military capabilities, if they exist, and the political options or purposes that these capabilities would supposedly serve is becoming increasingly unclear.

"The arms race...is extremely destabilizing because it creates justifiable apprehension on both sides."

Thus we have come to the point of obsolescence with regard to another traditional word that we use: war. The whole idea of war is to use violence in a controlled way for political objectives. We have reached the point where a nuclear war is certainly a threat to commit suicide; it is beyond politics, it has burst politics. It is also clear that many of the other ways in which we purport to use our military power—so-called conventional war strategies—create such dangers of a nuclear escalation that they, too, carry with them a very uncertain basis for extending or projecting the power of this nation.

We have ceased to understand the political change in the world that has occurred since what I would call "the first nuclear age." In the first nuclear age, the United States had either a monopoly or a near monopoly of nuclear weapons. The world was pretty much under the political control of decision-makers in two cities in the world, Washington and Moscow, divided between the

spheres of influence of those two powers. Today, that is not the case. Today, there are many more nations with nuclear weapons as a result of actions that the United States and the Soviet Union have taken. Power is more and more diffused by sending in sophisticated hardware to countries that we hope thereby to control.

We have created the situations where our own influence has been greatly reduced and threatened. It is not only the United States that has had this experience. The U.S. sent 20 billion dollars to the Shah—the result: a nation that considers itself an enemy of the United States. The Soviet Union sent billions to Egypt, to Sudan, to Indonesia—nation after nation, they have been thrown out and their influence undercut. The traditional notion that we can use the arms economy to buy influence in the old way—and it worked in the old days—no longer is possible. At a time when the Soviet Union is more isolated than it has been since the Second World War, the United States is now devoting its diplomatic energies to isolating itself. The web of relationships that the United States developed with other industrial nations all over the world is seriously frayed. Europe and Japan are no longer clients of the United States, but they are still being treated as such. This failure to understand changes in the real world, the complex reality that we face, seriously undermines the security of the American people.

The Real Problems

We do not face the real problems that confront us; there is little hope of significant recovery of the economic momentum that characterized that very brief period that historians will call the "Pax Americana," that period that Henry Luce said would be the "American Century." It was the American century between 1945 and 1971, and it has been over for more than ten years, but we have not caught up with what has happened. If we do not reform the world monetary system; if we do not find a new set of ground rules for the world economy to operate under; if we do not solve the problems of world debt, of what is happening in the Third World, of massive unemployment around the world which directly impinges on the American economy (our workers are part of a global pool, and what happens around the world directly affects what happens here), if we do not address these problems and direct our energy to their solution instead of to the insoluble problem of finding the technological answer to security in the arms race, we will be in ever-increasing trouble. But the present Administration sees these problems as annoying byproducts of the United States-Soviet confrontation and seems to ignore them as the security threat that they are.

A security policy that would work for the United States, that would promote the stability that this nation needs, must rest on a stable relationship with the Soviet Union. Whatever we may think of the Russians there are only two relationships to have with them: one is a stable relationship based on shared interests in preserving the species and civilization; the other is war....

When we begin to see Soviet consumer production getting the priority attention now available only to the Soviet military, and their tanks looking as dowdy as their hotel lobbies, then I think that we will believe that something important has been done. When they begin to see that we have a real sense of what our security problem is, and that we are actually dealing with our security problem, they will be reassured. We live in a time when our security, in fact, increases their security, and their security increases ours.

"We are presented with a false reassurance about the Russians collapsing under the pressure of the arms race."

An observer from space looking down at Washington, D.C.—the city where the decisions are made to spend the trillions to counter the Russian threat, or the Nicaraguan threat, or the Libyan threat, or whatever—would be astounded by our failure to act on much less hypothetical menaces nearer home. Our capital city, in which I have lived for more than 20 years, is an advanced state of social dissolution. This is not an exaggeration. Large numbers of persons are ill-housed and ill-fed. More than a dozen persons have frozen to death on the streets of Washington this year. Crime is so widespread that fear stalks the city everywhere; you cannot have a middle-class conversation without talking about fear, and in the neighborhoods of the poor the shadow of crime hangs over daily life all the time. The drug trade is so pervasive that the underground economy, millions of dollars over which neither the government nor legitimate business has any control, is the only growth industry in town. The education system is in such shambles that we have seriously crippled a large part of a whole generation to deal with these incredibly complex problems that we face, as Americans and as members of the species.

The observer from space would see this situation in other cities too, and would absolutely wonder why it is that we seem unable to deal with the far more plausible threats that face us, why we seem obsessed, transfixed by distant and highly implausible dangers while immediate social and economic problems threaten to undermine our very culture, even if we manage to avoid stumbling into nuclear war. Billions of dollars are going into combating unlikely threats with a defense and security strategy that is fundamentally, literally, incredible. Americans are becoming more and more insecure because we are putting our money and our energy into combating these remote threats instead of addressing what is really bothering us.

Indeed, to marshall the funds and the talents to meet the remote threats, we are diverting the energy and resources we need to deal with challenges to our survival as a free society. Unless we begin to address these problems, we will find ourselves more and more unable to face reality, and as we fail to face reality, we will find ourselves sucked more and more into the nuclear fantasy. Our 200-year history has exerted far more influence in the world than our weapons have. A democratic system, however imperfect, stuggling to achieve humane values, offering unprecedented levels of consumption for ordinary people has excited hope around the world; but, increasingly, the leaders of other nations are coming to the conclusion that neither the United States nor the Soviet Union has the ideas for the times that we live in, that both nations are frozen in the past. At a dangerous time, the great menace that we face is not the Russians—although they could push that button at any time, and there is nothing we can do about it—but the fact that we ourselves will scare ourselves into impotence and possibly oblivion because we have forgotten what we are doing here and why we became a nation.

Richard J. Barnet is a Senior Fellow at the Institute for Policy Studies in Washington, D.C.

Negotiate First, Then Freeze

David Martin

The enormous confusion that the nuclear freeze movement has been able to generate is indicated by the fact that, on November 2, variously worded freeze referenda passed in eight out of nine states plus the District of Columbia, and 27 out of 29 cities and counties. Clearly, this is an issue that we are going to have to address in the interests of sanity and survival.

Apparently everyone thinks a nuclear freeze would be a good idea, including the nuclear protest movement, the Soviet Politburo, and President Reagan. The basic questions that have to be answered are: on what terms, and with what safeguards?

The position of the Administration is that before it enters into final negotiations for a freeze on nuclear-weapons levels, it considers it essential, as a preliminary, to agree on targets for across-the-board reductions in nuclear weapons. Phase I of its proposed schedule calls for reducing the total number of warheads on both sides to five thousand, from the present level of 7,500 on the Soviet side and slightly more on the American side. This would result in a correlative reduction in throw-weight. No more than half the remaining ballistic-missile warheads would be on land-based missiles. Phase I also calls for reducing the number of ballistic missiles on both sides to equal levels—an approximate reduction of 50 per cent. In the second phase, we would concentrate on achieving reductions in overall throw-weight, again with the target of approximate parity. After verifying these reductions, we could then enter into final negotiations for freezing nuclear arms at the new levels.

This approach is rejected by most of the nuclear-freeze movement because, in their eyes, it demands too many concessions from the Soviet side to make it practical. This is true, even though certain segments of the movement suggest that they too believe in a verifiable

freeze. However, a closer examination of their various declarations indicates that, with few exceptions, they would like to see us freeze now and negotiate later.

The perils of freezing before negotiating can be illuminated by a careful study of the history of the freeze on nuclear weapons technology—nominally a moratorium on atmospheric testing—to which we committed ourselves at the end of October 1958. There are many points of similarity between the "freeze that was," and the kind of freeze that a lot of enthusiastic activists—most of them innocent, but many of them less than innocent—are trying to push us into today.

Then, as now, the pressure for a freeze was generated by what was, on the surface, a broadly based international movement. Then, as now, this movement enjoyed the support of churchmen, professionals, women's organizations, trade unions, and civic organizations by the dozen. But then, as now, the movement was also supported by such notorious Communist fronts as the World Peace Council and the National Lawyers Guild; indeed, common sense suggests that only the Communist apparatus could have provided the degree of international coordination displayed by both movements.

Then, as now, the principal instrument was fear—then the understandable fear of atmospheric contamination and strontium 90 in babies' milk; today the understandable fear of a worldwide holocaust if both sides resort to the weapons they have in their possession.

Then, as now, the movement served Moscow's strategic objectives. Then the objective was to impose a freeze on American research and development in the field of nuclear weapons in order to enable the Soviets to catch up technologically. Now the purpose is to impose a freeze on deployment as well as on research and development in order to enable the Soviets to achieve qualitative, on top of their present quantitative, superiority in nuclear weaponry.

The Honor System

The earlier freeze began on October 31, 1958, when the U.S. completed a series of nuclear tests in the atmosphere. Simultaneously with the final test, the Eisenhower Administration declared it planned to observe a voluntary one-year moratorium on atmospheric testing. The Soviets responded by saying that they would do likewise. Thus began a moratorium based not on any formal agreement, but simply on the presumption that both sides would honorably observe it while negotiations proceeded on a formal test-ban treaty.

Once we had entered into this voluntary one-year moratorium, fear of an adverse international reaction made it difficult for us to terminate it. With a brief interruption in 1961, this honor-system moratorium lasted until the Limited Test Ban Treaty went into effect in October 1963. We had been fastidiously adhering to this unpoliced and unverifiable moratorium. But, on September 1, 1961, Khrushchev unilaterally violated the moratorium by staging a massive series of atmospheric tests, culminating in the explosion of a 58-megaton monster on October 20. There were some ringing statements at the time about Communist perfidy, and our delegation walked out of the Geneva Conference as a demonstration of our outrage. Some six months later we staged a series of atmospheric tests of our own—much more limited than the Soviet series. Even before that, in November 1961, we had gone back to the conference table at Geneva, where we continued to make concessions. And after our own little test series, we again reverted to scrupulous observance of the letter and spirit of the honor-system moratorium.

"The right to peace is obviously a collective, albeit unenforceable, right within the category of human needs."

There were very few critics of the moratorium on nuclear testing, Republican or Democratic, when President Eisenhower entered into it in September of 1958. Senator Thomas J. Dodd of Connecticut did take the floor of the Senate to denounce it as "the most egregious bipartisan act of folly in the history of the Republic." But the critics were sparse, because most politicians lived in fear of being portrayed as a monster who didn't care about strontium 90 in babies milk.

By embarking on the moratorium, Eisenhower created a situation from which the U.S. found it virtually impossible to extricate itself—despite grave suspicions that the Soviets were not abiding by their part of the agreement. It also placed great pressure on the Administration and on our negotiators to make repeated concessions to the Soviets in order to achieve a treaty that at least provided for a plausible—or salable—degree of verification. At the same time, it made the Soviets more inflexible by giving them their principal objective without their having to submit to the constraints that a treaty might have imposed.

U.S. Concessions

Dr. Jerome Wiesner of MIT, who served as a science advisor to both Eisenhower and Kennedy, has argued repeatedly that it was American inflexibility that resulted in the breakdown of the comprehensive test-ban negotiations of 1958 to 1963. In fact, to be any more flexible than we were in Geneva from September 1958 to June 1963, we would have had to be invertebrates. The American side yielded on point after point after point. The Soviets, for their part, although they made some concessions on minor technical points, did not budge on any issue of substance. Indeed, they repeatedly reneged on positions they had previously agreed to.

Let me run through a partial list of the numerous concessions we made to the Soviets in order to achieve a comprehensive test-ban agreement that could justify the nuclear freeze.

Moratorium: We agreed to the unpoliced moratorium in the face of the long Soviet record of broken treaties and agreements. This violated what had up until then been a cardinal principal of our approach to disarmament—that every step toward disarmament had to be accompanied by appropriate and adequate means of verification.

Monitoring Stations: The initial American position when the Geneva Conference first convened in 1958 was that the enforcement of a comprehensive test-ban treaty would require a network of eight hundred stations worldwide. We then agreed on a formula with the Russian scientists that called for 180 stations worldwide, of which 21 would be inside the Soviet Union. By August 1962 we were down to eighty stations worldwide, of which eight to ten were to be in the Soviet Union.

In 1958, it was agreed that the monitoring stations would be manned by non-nationals of the countries in which they were located—that is, there would be international inspection. In August 1962 we accepted the Soviet proposal that each country would designate its own nationals to man the monitoring stations located in its territory, but under international supervision. By February 1963 we were prepared to accept national monitors without international supervision.

Control mechanism: In 1958 we envisioned a control body in which Britain, the United States, and the Soviet Union—the countries then in possession of nuclear weapons—would be represented and no nation would have the right of veto. By August 1962 we had accepted the Soviet position that the negotiations on the test-ban treaty should be merged with the 18-nation Disarmament Conference then going on in Geneva; that the Western and Communist nations should have equal representation (four for each side) on the control commission set up to oversee the implementation of the Comprehensive Test

Ban Treaty; that there should be five neutral nations on the commission. The operating budget, the appointment of the executive officer, the dispatch of investigative teams, and many other matters were made subject to veto by a requirement for unanimity on the part of the United States, the Soviet Union, and Great Britain.

On-Site Inspection: Our opening position in Geneva was that both sides should have the right to inspect all unidentified seismic events above the magnitude of five kilotons and 20 per cent of the unidentified events below five kilotons. By February 1961 we were down to twenty on-site inspections per annum; by May 1961 we were down to 12; by December 1962 we were down to eight or ten. Such an arrangement would have reduced the chances of identifying and verifying any underground test to very close to absolute zero.

Kennedy's Choice

While all of this was going on, the United States lived up to the very letter of the honor-system moratorium—or of the nuclear freeze, to give the arrangement its modern appellation. Indeed, we *more* than lived up to our commitment. The original declaration spoke only of atmospheric testing, leaving us free to conduct underground tests. Over the first two and a half years of the agreement, we conducted only a few small underground tests—it was anything but a vigorous program. But at the end of January 1961, we announced that even these tests would be terminated. In deference to the possibility of negotiating a comprehensive test-ban treaty, we not only stopped all testing and dismantled our testing facilities, but we virtually halted basic nuclear-weapons research. As President Kennedy put it on March 2, 1962:

> ...in actual practice, particularly in a society of free choice, we cannot keep top-flight scientists concentrating on the preparation of an experiment which may or may not take place on an uncertain date in the future. Nor can large technical laboratories be kept fully alert on a standby basis waiting for some other nation to break an agreement. This is not merely difficult or inconvenient—we have explored this alternative thoroughly, and found it impossible of execution.

The Soviets, not surprisingly, did not freeze their research-and-development program. On the contrary, they stepped up their research and expanded their testing facilities. Finally, when all the preparatory work had been done, they let go in September-October 1961 with their mammoth series of atmospheric tests, which demonstrated that they had wiped out the estimated five-year lead we had until then enjoyed in the general field of nuclear-weapons technology, and that the Soviet military establishment now had a clear and massive primacy in super-megaton technology.

Such was the history of our first experience with a nuclear freeze. The record of those Geneva negotiations should be carefully studied, for they provide a prime example of how *not* to negotiate with the Russians. In the course of those negotiations, we made many mistakes. But the initial and central act of imprudence from which all of our other mistakes flowed was the decision to freeze our nuclear-weapons development program while we pursued negotiations for a larger and permanent agreement on nuclear testing.

These basic arguments were stated with surprising eloquence by Representative Les Aspin (D., Wis.), an inveterate Pentagon critic, in a letter to the editor of the *Washington Post* on April 15, 1982. Said Representative Aspin:

> ...A freeze clamps down on the strategic issues that make Kremlin planners sweat, but it doesn't address those issues that make American planners sweat....
> ...For us to get what we want, we need both a freeze *and* reductions. For the Soviets to get what they want, all they need is a freeze. At that point, there is no incentive for them to talk about reductions.
> ...The Soviets will have every incentive to hold religiously to the freeze while stonewalling on the reduction talks....

"The campaign against the...neutron bomb was extremely successful."

These are some thoughts on which our American bishops would do well to ponder before they enshrine the nuclear freeze as a moral imperative that would invalidate all considerations of nuclear strategy or the requirements of diplomacy or the survival of the free world.

David Martin served for almost twenty years on the staff of the United States Senate. His latest book is Patriot or Traitor: The Case of General Mihailovich.

"Now is the time to freeze the arms race in its tracks, to stabilize the balance of terror and to proceed toward reductions."

Freeze First, Then Negotiate

James L. Hart

Since President Carter withdrew the second Strategic Arms Limitation Treaty (SALT II) from consideration by the Senate in 1979, the debate over nuclear weapons policy has intensified. Both the Reagan Administration and the critics of its policy agree that the long-range goal must be reductions, and drastic reductions at that, in the arsenals of both the United States and the Soviet Union. The means to achieving this goal are the current subject of intense debate.

The Reagan Administration contends that the Soviet military buildup over the past two decades represents an unprecedented threat to United States national security. The United States lead in strategic nuclear weaponry, they assert, has been overcome. In some areas the Soviets have actually achieved superiority and threaten to achieve a first-strike capability by the middle of the decade.

In order to enter negotiations with the Soviets from a position of strength, the Administration has initiated the largest peacetime buildup in American history. Weapons programs carried over from previous administrations, such as the MX missile, Trident and the cruise missile, have been accelerated. Other programs abandoned by previous administrations, such as the B-1 bomber, have been restored to a significant place in strategic planning.

Despite misgivings in NATO countries, plans remain to deploy intermediate range Pershing II missiles in Western Europe unless the Soviets agree to dismantle their SS-20's. And the deterrent policy of mutual assured destruction (M.A.D.) continues to recede in the discussions of strategic planners, to be replaced by talk of counterforce, first-strike and limited nuclear war.

The opposition to current strategic policy arises from a diverse group of old peace organizations, church groups and dissident members of the national security establishment. They advance, in various combinations,

James L. Hart, ''The Case for a Freeze on Nuclear Arms,'' *America* October 23, 1982. Reprinted with author's permission.

arguments that the arms race is morally indefensible, economically destructive and that it decreases rather than enhances national security.

This diverse opposition advances various options to current policy. Some call for a return to the SALT II treaty with the aim of putting a cap on the arms race before proceeding to reductions in strategic arsenals. Others are pressing the President to offer the Soviet Union a mutual freeze on the testing, production and deployment of nuclear weapons, effectively halting the arms race in its track and eventually reversing it. Still others argue that the time is ripe for the United States to take a unilateral initiative by making a measured reduction in its nuclear arsenal and inviting a Soviet response.

Within the last year the proposal for a mutual freeze has emerged as the focus of opposition to the current policies. The freeze campaign has scored dramatic success at the grassroots level by winning the endorsement of 10 state legislatures and hundreds of town meetings in New England. An initiative to place the proposal on the November ballot in California gained twice the number of required signatures. Even the narrow defeat of a freeze resolution in the United States House of Representatives was widely interpreted as evidence of the movement's growing political strength.

Despite, or perhaps because of, its broad popular appeal, the freeze proposal is often dismissed as a simplistic response to the complexities of the arms control debate. Supporters of the Administration have denounced it as ''bumper-sticker arms control.'' The President himself insists that an immediate freeze would undermine American security by preserving a ''definite Soviet margin of superiority'' in strategic nuclear weaponry. Even some who sympathize with the freeze campaign consider the proposal to be primarily symbolic in value and an effective vehicle for maintaining political pressure on an administration not otherwise inclined toward serious negotiations with the Soviet Union.

Serious Strategy

Nevertheless, the freeze proposal has been advanced by its proponents as a serious strategy for arms control. It deserves to be evaluated on its own merits as a measure to enhance national and international security. The founding document of the movement, the "Call to Halt the Nuclear Arms Race," calls on the United States and the Soviet Union to adopt a "mutual freeze on the testing, production and deployment of nuclear weapons and of missiles and new aircraft designed primarily to deliver nuclear weapons" as an "essential, verifiable first step toward lessening the risk of nuclear war and reducing nuclear arsenals."

The nuclear arms race began with the cold war. As relations between the United States and the Soviet Union deteriorated in the late 1940's, the Truman Administration decided to counter the Soviet advantage in conventional forces by deploying a formidable arsenal of the new atomic weapons. The American monopoly in nuclear weapons was, of course, short-lived. The first Soviet test of an atomic bomb in 1949 indicated their determination to follow the American lead. Since then, the arms race has proceeded on a consistent pattern of action and reaction, with the United States maintaining a lead in most areas. A look at the dates of some of the most significant developments indicates the pattern:

	United States	Soviet Union
Atomic Bomb	1945	1949
Hydrogen Bomb	1952	1953
Intercontinental Ballistic Missile (ICBM)	1958	1957
Submarine-Launched Ballistic Missile (SLBM)	1960	1968
Multiple Warhead Missile	1964	1973
Re-entry Vehicles (MIRV)	1970	1975

This momentum of action and reaction has continued through a series of arms control agreements. The two SALT treaties, for instance, have permitted not only marginal increases in the size of the respective nuclear arsenals but also substantial qualitative improvements. A classic example of the missed opportunities to halt the momentum of the arms race is the failure of the negotiations on the SALT I Treaty in the late 1960's and early 1970's to prevent the deployment of the then new MIRV technology. MIRV's, multiple independently targetable re-entry vehicles, permit one ballistic missile to strike several distinct targets. The negotiators for the United States were reluctant to surrender an American lead in a new technology that promised significant strategic advantages. The Soviets were unwilling to concede American superiority in this area by concluding an agreement that would forestall the development and deployment of their own MIRV's.

The result was that, within the limits of SALT I on numbers of delivery vehicles, each side proceeded with deployment of MIRV's. SALT II established ceilings on the number of missiles with MIRV's, but these limits were above the level of MIRV's actually deployed at that time. The United States had placed more MIRV's in its arsenal of sea-launched ballistic missiles, while the Soviets have deployed a more substantial arsenal of MIRV's on land-based missiles. The number of warheads on Soviet land-based missiles, together with continuing improvements in accuracy, have created the present concern over the vulnerability of American land-based missiles to destruction by a Soviet first strike. In other words, the infamous "window of vulnerability," which provides the Reagan Administration with the justification for development and deployment of the MX missile, exists because of the failure of previous agreements to break the momentum of the arms race.

"The Reagan policy is thus likely to intensify the momentum of the arms race."

Repeating Mistakes of the Past

The Reagan Administration has failed to learn from this history and seems ready to repeat the mistakes of the past. The Administration proposes to build up the American strategic arsenal in order to give the Soviets an incentive to agree to deep cuts in nuclear weapons. In reality the Soviets are unlikely to tolerate the deployment of the MX, Trident or cruise missiles without taking equivalent steps. And they are equally unlikely to accept Mr. Reagan's proposals in the current Strategic Arms Reduction Talks, since these proposals call for deep reductions in areas of Soviet strength without compensating reductions in areas of relative American strength. The Reagan policy is thus likely to intensify the momentum of the arms race, with consequences I will consider in a moment. A negotiated agreement to freeze arsenals at current levels would, on the other hand, halt both the quantitative and qualitative advances in the arms race.

The current discussion of the "window of vulnerability," "first strikes" and "limited nuclear war" indicate that the arms race is entering a qualitatively new stage. Both the Soviet Union and the United States are now developing and deploying a new generation of weapons with greater reliability and accuracy. These new "counterforce" weapons include the improved Minuteman II, the MX and the Trident II on the American side, and the Soviet SS-18, SS-19 and SS-20. The combination of great power and accuracy that these weapons possess allows them to pose a threat to a new range of targets, including missile silos, military command and control centers and other "hard" or protected targets.

At first glance, the full deployment of the new generation of counterforce weapons might appear to be a positive step. No longer would deterrence depend upon the threat of retaliation against the cities and industrial centers of an enemy, but upon the capability to destroy his military structure. The confidence in these weapons is the basis of statements by some Administration officials about fighting and winning a limited nuclear war, meaning a war which terminates short of strikes against population centers. The Pentagon's new five-year defense plan includes the first strategy for fighting a protracted nuclear conflict with the Soviet Union. American defense policy will be to prevail in such a conflict by "decapitation," strikes at Soviet political and military leadership and lines of communication.

> *"President Reagan's assertion that the Soviet Union possesses a definite margin of superiority simply does not stand up to close examination."*

These new developments in weapons technology and strategic policy are in reality highly dangerous because they would undermine the fragile stability of deterrence. Deterrence has always depended upon the confidence of each side that enough of its nuclear arsenal and command and control structure could survive a first strike to be able to deliver a devastating strike in retaliation. Full development and deployment of a counterforce capability by each side would destroy that confidence and destabilize the strategic balance. Such a situation would increase the incentive to launch first in a time of crisis rather than risk the loss of a significant portion of one's strategic nuclear arsenal to a first strike by the other side.

As a result, the strategic balance would rest on a hair trigger, and each side would be tempted to adopt a policy of launch-on-warning, compounding the possibility that accident or miscalculation could set off a nuclear conflict. And despite talk by some defense experts of "surgical strikes" against purely military targets, it is virtually certain that counterforce strikes would cause tens of millions of civilian casualties in the United States and the Soviet Union, with no guarantee that such a conflict would not escalate into strikes against cities.

No Window of Vulnerability

A mutual window of vulnerability in which both the United States and the Soviet Union are exposed to a crippling first strike by the other side is still several years away. The dangerous instability of that situation can still be avoided if both sides move quickly toward a freeze agreement. This is an especially propitious moment for such an agreement, for there now exists a relatively stable balance in strategic weaponry. This balance is variously described as "rough parity," "essential equality" and "asymmetrical equivalence."

President Reagan's assertion that the Soviet Union possesses a definite margin of superiority simply does not stand up to close examination. The Soviet Union has indeed closed the gap over the last decade; in some specific areas they can even be said to be "ahead." But on balance neither side possesses any clear superiority at present. The United States maintains a narrow lead in the number of strategic nuclear warheads deployed. The Soviet Union has a larger arsenal of land-based missiles that carry more warheads than American ICBM's.

But the United States possesses a vastly superior fleet of ballistic missile submarines. Not only do American Polaris and Poseidon submarines carry more warheads than the Soviet submarines, but they also operate at a much higher state of readiness.

The strategic forces of the two superpowers are, in other words, asymmetrical. They select different priorities in the long-range strategic planning of the respective military establishments. Each strategic system has it weaknesses as well as its compensating strengths. But the balance will remain a stable one so long as each side is only partially vulnerable and neither side can pose the threat of a "disarming" first strike against the other.

The next few years will be a critical period in the nuclear arms race. The United States and the Soviet Union are poised at a moment of danger and opportunity. The danger is that the deployment of the new generation of counterforce weapons will intensify the momentum of the arms race, upset the fragile balance of deterrence and compound the danger of actual conflict. The opportunity is presented by the temporary existence of rough parity. So long as parity exists the dynamic momentum of the arms race can be halted and then reversed without either side being forced to surrender clear superiority or to concede inferiority. Now is the time to freeze the arms race in its tracks, to stabilize the balance of terror and to proceed toward reductions. Such an opportunity may not come again.

James L. Hart, S.J., is an associate chaplain at Loyola University in New Orleans, Louisiana.

"Humanity's survival is the greatest moral issue of our time and only a citizen's movement. . .could pressure governments to put down nuclear weapons."

viewpoint**60**

A Nuclear Freeze Is the Greatest Peace Issue

Mary Ellen Leary

Part of the message in those surprisingly large demonstrations in Europe against super-power nuclear rivalry pitched on the mid-continent turf was exasperation that the American public does not show parallel concern about the likely outcome of a nuclear build-up. The marches, parades, and speeches appealed to governments to forbear, but quite as much, they aimed to awaken world opinion. Certainly American opinion.

Well, the yeast has spread. A ferment is at work. In its own fashion the American response to nuclear hazard is taking shape. That shape promises to be political. It could prove more potent than peace marches.

In California, where law-making by popular will is the style and easy recourse to the ballot with powerful social issues has often pioneered national political movements, petitions are circulating now to put before voters next November a call for a bilateral "freeze" on all nuclear weapons by the U.S. and the USSR.

The "freeze" idea has been circulating among various states for the past couple of years. It grew from exasperated U.S. delegates at the UN's 1978 special session on disarmament. As Harold Willens put it, "It became clear if we relied on governments to end the arms race, humanity would be obliterated. We saw that governments were locked into face-saving positions of rivalry they could not escape. We felt that humanity's survival is the greatest moral issue of our time and that only a citizen's movement that reached past governments could pressure governments to put down nuclear weapons."

The idea has already drummed up enough U.S. support to get favorable resolutions through the Massachusetts and Oregon legislatures and win unanimous approval in the New York state assembly. It prompted large town-meetings in New Hampshire and Vermont. Last March, the "freeze" proposal drew people from

Mary Ellen Leary, "Nuclear Freeze, Bishops and Nobel Laureates," *Commonweal*, January 29, 1982. Reprinted with permission.

thirty-four states to a conference in Washington, D.C. to fashion strategy for a four-year drive to build public support. The event hardly figured as news. Attention was riveted on the totally contradictory thrust of the new administration, sizing its military budget dramatically upward, intent on reversing the slippage in weaponry, wariness, and nuclear sophistication which President Reagan perceived as the careless legacy from previous administrations.

An Expression of Public Will

Admittedly, the nuclear "freeze" initiative has no enforcement leverage. Even if overwhelmingly approved, it has no legal status in Washington or in Moscow. It is merely an expression of the public will; or, rather, of a public hope, at a time when hope is on the decline.

Without muscle, is it meaningless? Many think so. But the view of its supporters is that such an expression has an innate power of its own and can influence world opinion, as the demonstrations have done. The California outcome, either of signature-gathering by April 22 or of vote-winning by November 1982 is unpredictable, though insiders are aglow with confidence. This is the first time political action on this issue of nuclear weapons has been brought to the level of the ordinary voter.

Some points to note: This is a bilateral appeal, not a call for unilateral action by the U.S. It is not a "peace" movement. It does not ask disarmament nor even touch upon the issue of conventional arms, of defense budgets, of conscription, of the morality of war, of defense expenditures versus social needs. It focuses simply and exclusively on the horror implicit in mounting numbers of nuclear weapons and asks a bilateral end to this fuel for world incineration.

The measure states that there exists "substantial and growing danger of nuclear war between the United States and the Soviet Union which would result in millions of deaths. . . ." This arsenal it says reduces national security rather than increasing it. So, "to reduce the threat of nuclear war" it calls on the leadership of both nations to reach an agreement "to halt the testing, production and further deployment of all nuclear weapons in a way that can be checked and verified by both sides." As a first step, it asks the government of the U.S. to propose such an agreement to the government of the Soviet Union. Obviously the whole move anticipates other steps would follow: gradual nuclear disarmament, more negotiations, perhaps a diminished militarism. But the single focus here is on getting a halt, a "freeze."

"Just being born gives one a stake in opposing nuclear weapons."

Last summer, such a proposal would have seemed impertinent and naive, given the pell-mell rush to enhance U.S. military readiness. To most Americans it still may seem so. But European governments took seriously the alarms expressed by their citizens and in November President Reagan also responded. Whether or not some element of Soviet self-interest lurked in the background, the basic sincerity of those demonstrations affected German opinion and Bonn leadership and led President Reagan to his olive-branch speech, so unexpected the world is still weighing its import.

Halt New Weapons

But that new presidential overture and even the present arms control negotiations do not satisfy "freeze" advocates. They persist in calling for a complete halt in new weapons development, in testing, in deployment. Everything. Stop right now! Raising this cry in the context of the on-going military rivalry would seem absurd, if it were not so universal a sentiment, so elemental a cry by mankind for survival. The power of that instinct is what the California campaign aims to rally and the ballot issue becomes a substantial instrument, a unifying center.

Two steps are involved. The first is well along. Even before the Dec. 1 formal start, literature was printed, pamphlets readied, a logo devised, organizations planned, supportive endorsements gathered. Funds, roughly $200,000, are being raised. Ready to go with "petition parties" around the state in December, volunteers are seeking half a million signatures. California law requires 346,000 properly registered voters must endorse a measure, to qualify it for the ballot: the half-million names will cover inaccurate or unregistered signers. Normally, volunteer efforts fall by the wayside. Getting so many names in so large a state is a staggering task. But public response looks promising.

Second step will be pursuit of favorable votes, once the proposal is on the ballot. Next summer, while Con-

gress struggles with the national budget and attention is sharpest on military spending, California's quest for new governor, new U.S. Senator and new layers of other state officials promises to be intermeshed with the nuclear weapons issue.

A number of forces converge at this moment to propel the "freeze" campaign, forces not usually united in a voter appeal. These include: Catholic bishops, a growing number of politically active physicians, scientists including a number of Nobel Prize winners, and environmentalists. All have exceptionally strong bases in California. This combination, together with recruitment of minorities, labor, women's groups and businessmen provides a network reaching far beyond the habitual zealots and campus activists expected to figure in peace movements. Quite unlike the Vietnam war protests, the drive starts out with an air of respectability. Such was apparent when those involved in the initial announcement at a state capitol press conference included San Francisco's Archbishop John R. Quinn, University of California Nobel Laureate Donald Glaser, along with one of the "freeze" initiators, Mr. Willens.

Crime Against God

Although Archbishop Quinn was not the first Catholic bishop to voice alarm at the nuclear arms race as a "crime against God and humankind," his remarks on Oct. 4, the Eight Hundredth anniversary of St. Francis of Assisi, had an electric effect, not only on the astonished congregation in his great Cathedral (who rose spontaneously to applaud) but on many others in the church.

"A 'just' nuclear war is a contradiction in terms," he said. "Nuclear weapons are not simply conventional weapons on a large scale. They are qualitatively of a whole different order of destructiveness. Their tremendous explosive force, as well as their enormous and terrible side effects, will irrevocably alter our ecological system, genetic structure for generations to come, and the fundamental fabric of our social system. . . ." The teaching of the church is clear, nuclear weapons and the arms race must be condemned as immoral."

Archbishop Quinn's commitment to work for a bilateral end to nuclear weapons and his specific advice to his own diocese to undertake work and prayer in that direction dramatized the church's involvement. He has already appointed three new diocesan employees to educate parishes and parochial schools full time on the nuclear threat and on the "freeze" initiatives. Cardinal Timothy Manning of Los Angeles has also spoken out. "Some maniac of a man," he said, may press the proper buttons, "and there will come an end to all time, for all the living and the dead. Is there no stopping this madness?" Other, though not all, California bishops have joined. The National Conference of Catholic Bishops meanwhile have a study of nuclear war underway, due to be completed next fall. The issue hovered noticeably over their recent meeting, so many bishops have already protested in other states against "this madness". . . "certain suicide". . . "folly of unbelievable dimensions."

Catholic bishops are not the only religious group involved, only the most unexpected. Core of the campaign is a religious network: the American Friends' Service Committee, the Ecumenical Peace Institute, Clergy & Laity Concerned, Pax Christi, a host of Unitarian, Lutheran, and Episcopal churches and numerous Jewish groups. Beyond formal endorsements, they have provided volunteers, organizers, and funds. In addition, the drive includes many of the usual liberal organizations, the American Civil Liberties Union, various Democratic clubs and some labor unions. Efforts are underway to engage minorities, a logic the military budget underscores.

Another Layer of Support

The very locale of the campaign's headquarters suggests another layer of support. It is at 5480 College Avenue, Berkeley, where the store-front offices neighbor other "cause" and "issue" centers, along with wine and cheese shops, antique stores, bike and ski stores, all in the hospitable university ambience. Campus backing is a given. Scientists are prominent among the campaign's endorsements. This issue even stirs students from their apathy.

Down the street is Berkeley's Sierra Club office. This expansion environmental group, and its rival, Friends of Earth, have recently committed themselves to the "freeze" drive. Remarked Pam Nichols, who left the Sierra Club to become northern "freeze" manager, "Just being born gives one a stake in opposing nuclear weapons." The one group rejected as sponsors—politicians. Californians for a Bilateral Nuclear Arms Freeze want no one from government aboard, and no partisan influence.

Despite the singular focus on nuclear dangers and resistance to being classed as just another peace movement, the initiators of this drive come, logically enough, from past war protests. The key figures are three. Willens, a wealthy Los Angeles businessman, chairman of Factory Equipment Corp., has been active in various liberal causes, such as the McCarthy and McGovern presidential races, the Center for Defense Information and the Business Executives Against the Vietnam War. But quite apart is his passionate repugnance at nuclear weapons. In World War II as a Japanese translator for the U.S. Marine Corps, he was among the first Americans to view Hiroshima and Nagasaki after the bombs fell. "I was deeply moved at the time," he says. "But I didn't realize until later just how moved. . . ."

Working with him are Steve Ladd, San Francisco head of the War Resisters' League, a far younger activist whose University of California involvement in Vietnam war protests led him to a life-time dedication. Third is Ian Thiermann, a retired Los Angeles businessman, long-time Quaker and pacifist.

Beyond Ability to Heal

Thiermann's rare contribution came as a response to a conference staged by Physicians for Social Responsibility, a fast-growing national organization of the medical fraternity speaking out to prevent massive human damage which they recognize would be beyond doctors' ability to heal. So moved was Thiermann at the doctors' calm catalogue of the catastrophe inevitable after a nuclear bomb blast, that he with the aid of his film-maker son, super-imposed actual photographs from Hiroshima and Nagasaki over the taped track of conference speakers and the result was the overwhelming documentary, *The Last Epidemic*, which has gripped audiences all across the country and shocked the media into attention. This film and the intervention of the medical world is a powerful factor in the California drive.

Several local units of Physicians for Social Responsibility have refused a Pentagon request for systematic identification of hospital and medical facilities in their area available in the event of future military need, which the government anticipates, in its request, would be more massive in numbers and in trauma than ever before experienced in the U.S. In refusing to participate in such pre-planning, the physicians have replied that the request makes a false assumption, misleading the public, by its implication that any treatment would be possible after a nuclear exchange. Archbishop Quinn urged Catholic hospitals in his diocese to consider that response themselves.

Not all peace advocates support the "freeze" initiative. For instance, in Berkeley, Robert Pickus, president of World Without War Council, which works to enlarge international understandings, scoffs at such a movement, built so obviously on fear. He considers the "freeze" proposal an indirect boost for the Soviets, a subtle assault on President Reagan and an erosion of U.S. military readiness.

Another World Without War activist, George Weigel of Seattle, columnist for the Catholic *Northwest Progress*, derides the "peace bishops" for repeating "errors of a failed peace movement" and for "fracturing" the Catholic community. Weigel's group would entice the Soviets into step-by-step conciliations, but it is still occupied with framing the steps.

Nevertheless, the stark simplicity of the "freeze" appeal reaches past political nuance and subtleties of international bargaining to stir a primitive clamor for humanity's survival, which may be the only response adequate to the apocalyptic threat. At this level, the common man may wish to cast a vote.

Mary Ellen Leary is a journalist who lives on the West Coast.

"We must not be so blinded by the prospects of a future Armageddon that we overlook the people of Third World countries who are already being mowed down."

viewpoint **61**

A Nuclear Freeze Is Not the Greatest Peace Issue

David Dellinger

The instinct for survival is basic to all forms of life. We are currently seeing a spectacular expression of that instinct throughout Western Europe and the United States in wave after wave of public opposition to nuclear weapons. It is a response to the overwhelming probability that continuation of the arms race will result in a nuclear holocaust, whether through computer error, political miscalculation or some deadly combination of fear, national self-righteousness, greed and stupidity.

The same species-defending instinct is unmistakably asserting itself in the Soviet Union and Eastern Europe, where people are becoming increasingly aware of the peril and have been encouraged by the rise of large-scale opposition movements in the West. In the Soviet countries the forms taken have been more muted because the forms of repression are more massive—so far—than in the United States and Europe. But recently, 4,000 East Germans gathered in Dresden to express their concern about the dangerous weapons and foreign policies of both East and West.

While hailing these developments, we must recognize that there are grave dangers in the anti-nuclear movement itself, unless we act with our heads as well as our hearts. I don't mean the dangers cited by the Reagan Administration and military officials, who are blinded by their devotion to profits, power and the nation's super power status. The danger I am describing is illustrated by the case of a man who is driving through a small town and suddenly finds himself confronted by a huge truck barrelling down the middle of the road. Unnerved by the prospect of a head-on collision, he swerves sharply to the side and mows down six people on the sidewalk.

Overall Context

In reacting to the nuclear peril, we must not ignore the overall context in which it exists. We must confront both

Dave Dellinger, "Expanding the Horizons of the Anti-Nuclear Movement," *Common Ground*, Fall 1982. Reprinted with author's permission.

nuclear lunacy and the other, closely-related perils that daily afflict ourselves and other people. In particular, we must not be so blinded by the prospects of a future Armageddon that we overlook the people of Third World countries who are *already* being mowed down at an alarming rate by so-called conventional weapons. These weapons range from U.S. and Soviet bombs, helicopter gunships and instruments of torture to forms of violence that are just as deadly but not conventionally classified as weapons. I mean the domination of Third World economies and governments, the rape of their resources, the pollution of their environments and the murderous exploitation of their labor by U.S.-based transnational corporations, backed by the C.I.A., the State Department and the military.

Twelve million babies a year—more than thirty thousand a day—die in developing countries before their first birthday, while their resources are depleted by profit-seeking corporations and the demands of the U.S. arms industry and the Pentagon for strategic minerals and other raw materials. Between thirty-five and forty million people have died in the "limited" wars that have taken place since World War II. Ninety-five percent of these wars have been fought in developing countries, with foreign powers intervening in most of them, and 79% of the interventions carried out by Western nations (*World Military and Social Expenditures*, Ruth Sivard).

I was thrilled by the numbers, spirit, music, signs and banners, and even most of the speeches, at the June 12 Disarmament Rally in New York. But my joy was offset by the knowledge that while the inspiring demonstration was taking place, Israeli planes were scattering death and destruction on Palestinian and Lebanese civilians with cluster bombs, phosphorous, and other obscene, non-nuclear weapons. These armaments were paid for by U.S. taxpayers and supplied free of charge to the Israeli invaders. To compound the tragedy, young Israelis brought up in the aftermath of the Nazi holocaust were being killed as they imposed a new holocaust on young

Palestinians (and their families) who were brought up in exile and longing for a homeland.

Disrupting Unity

Yet there were some who argued that it would disrupt the unity and mar our day of triumph to mention this "lesser" problem or these "lesser" deaths. In a follow-up meeting in my home state of Vermont, an anti-nuclear organizer warned that to include a speaker from the Committee in Solidarity with the People of El Salvador (CISPES) in a forthcoming rally might scare away some of those who favor a nuclear freeze but don't want to hear about other issues. In March, several peace groups that have emphasized the need for a single-issue nuclear freeze movement stretched a little to endorse a national demonstration in favor of cutting off U.S. military aid to El Salvador, but objected to having speakers who would stress the connections with U.S. racism at home and abroad. As if failure to root out racist—and for that matter sexist—practices and attitudes were not one of the reasons "little" genocidal wars and oppressions get legitimized, or at least tolerated.

"Between thirty-five and forty million people have died in the 'limited' wars that have taken place since World War II."

I respect the people who sincerely argue that the road to peace is to get out the largest possible numbers by avoiding "controversial" issues. But they lack a necessary understanding of the institutional and psychological linkages that join these "other" wars and daily violations of human life and dignity to the nuclear horror. They overlook the ability of the government to coopt a movement that does not make these connections—the same way it coopted the anti-bomb movement of the late '50s and early '60s by signing a limited test ban treaty. The treaty shut off mass protests for several crucial years while the government proceeded full speed ahead with its nuclear arms program and expanded its military aggression in Vietnam.

Even before the multiplication of omnicidal nuclear weapons threatened to divert our attention from the reasons these and other weapons are made, the poet Kenneth Patchen spoke ruefully of the anti-war movement of his day: "The trouble is they want to get rid of war without getting rid of the causes of war."

Warring "Little by Little"

We should never forget that small wars are apt to grow into big ones. And we should be aware that the nuclear holocaust will most likely result from a conflict over which superpower controls some Third World country's (or region's) natural resources, markets and labor—not from a desire by either Cold War rival to take over the homeland of the other and rule its people. Besides, "limited" wars are not limited for the people who die in them, or their surviving children, parents or lovers. What would it say about the moral integrity of the peace movement (or, for that matter, its political astuteness) if after a timely concentration on the suicidal nature of nuclear war it settled into a position that ignored thousands of deaths because they are not millions—or, to be more accurate, because they become millions little by little rather than in a few apocalyptic hours or days? Or worse, what if the peace movement accepted, however sadly, the death of millions so long as it did not include our own, or members of our country, race or culture? What is the difference between that and the willingness of certain North American policymakers to sacrifice Europe, if need be, in the supposed interests of the United States?

Continued spread of information on the insanity of nuclear war is critical. It wakes us up to the urgency of our plight and begins to sensitize us to the less spectacular but comparable insanity of the institutions that have brought such weapons into being and threaten to use them. The last administration said that it would resort to military force, if necessary, to protect "our" oil in the Middle East. It couldn't get eight helicopters safely into Iran and back, yet informed us that it would be able to manage a "limited" nuclear war without letting it get out of control. The present administration's Director of the U.S. Arms Control and Disarmament Agency, Eugene V. Rostow, has stated that "Japan, after all, not only survived but flourished after the nuclear attack....Some predict that there would be ten million casualties on one side and one hundred million on the other. But that is not the whole of the population." If that isn't an attempt to prepare the American public to go along with plans for a First Strike, so that "we" will lose "only" ten million while "they" lose a hundred million, what is it?

Their Plight and Ours

Meanwhile, the institutions and attitudes that threaten us are already destroying large numbers of people in other parts of the globe with whom our lives are inextricably linked. Connections must be made between their plight and ours. Most Americans have been conditioned by the media, the pollsters and the multi-million-dollar electoral campaigns posing as exercises in democracy, to be suspicious of political ideas outside the narrow range of conventional approaches that are debated so furiously and often meaninglessly by "our" leaders in Washington. These suspicions have been increased by the overblown rhetoric, narrow dogmatisms and lack of compassion of certain Left sects. So we need to be both cautious and sensitive to people's fears and past negative political experiences as we probe the links.

But at the heart of the grassroots upsurge of anti-nuclear sentiment are the beginnings of a readiness to think new thoughts, engage in previously deplored actions and search for new solutions to the mess we are in. One way or another, our slowly awakening, although still inadequate, consciousness of the nuclear danger must be extended so that we understand its roots in other wars, whether they are carried out by overt military action or through other forms of violence and oppression.

The Middle East Connection

Two of the linkages with the war in the Middle East were emphasized for me on a trip to Israel and Lebanon in late 1979. The Israeli town of Metulla sits on the border which separates Israel from the "promised" land of Lebanon and the territory in Lebanon that was being held in escrow for the Israelis by Lebanese war lord Major Sa'ad Haddad and his "Christian" armies. In Metulla I interviewed both Major Haddad and Colonel Yoram Hamuzrahi, the Israeli officer in charge of liason between the Israeli armies and Haddad's forces. Apart from observing that Hamuzrahi gave the orders and Haddad jumped when he gave them, I learned that the salaries of Haddad's soldiers are paid, and their weapons supplied, by Israel. This means that both are paid by the United States. I also heard some chilling words from Colonel Hamuzrahi. They were spoken in anguish, after hours of probing discussion, but also with bottom-line cynicism and terrifying implications:

> When it comes to policy, every government in the world would sell their mother, their brother and their sister in order to advance their own interests. Why should Israel be any different?...We are not going to yield an inch to the Arabs, even if it means atomic flames in New York.

I realized a second connection in West Beirut during an interview with Yassir Arafat. Another North American who was present asked Arafat if he was worried about the Jewish lobby in Washington. After carefully rephrasing the question to substitute the word Zionist for Jewish, Arafat replied, "I am not nearly so worried by the Zionist lobby in Washington as I am by the U.S. lobby in Israel."

"While the inspiring [anti-nuclear] demonstration was taking place, Israeli planes were scattering death and destruction on Palestinian and Lebanese civilians."

I thought of this later when I learned that Washington showed obvious foreknowledge of what Israel was planning to do four days *before* the long-planned Israeli invasion of Lebanon, and two days before the attempted assassination of the Israeli ambassador in London that served as a pretext for the invasion. The U.S. Navy had already begun moving aircraft carriers and other ships (the U.S.S. Kennedy, the U.S.S. Eisenhower and their escorts and taskforces) to supporting positions off the coast of Lebanon and near the island of Crete. And U.S. Marines and other landing forces were ordered to assemble in Rota, Spain and to prepare to proceed by sea toward Lebanon.

United States officials may complain, from time to time, about the crude style and blunt rhetoric of Israeli Prime Minister Menachem Begin, Defense Minister Ariel Sharon, and Foreign Minister Yitzhak Shamir, much as they used to complain about Thieu and Ky in Saigon during the U.S. war in Viet Nam. High U.S. officials may even sincerely regret the "excesses" of these leaders. But it has been U.S. policy, through a series of Republican and Democratic regimes, to build an overwhelming strike force in Israel, capable of monstrous blitzkriegs not related to the security of the Israeli people. The U.S. government has consistently supported racist, expansionist policies, not out of love for the Israeli people, not because Israeli actions benefit the American people, and certainly not in search of peace or justice.

David Dellinger is currently working with the Vermont Coalition for Jobs, Peace, and Justice. He is a longtime anti-war activist.

Peacekeeping Should Be Left to Professionals

William J. McGill

Rarely in history has it been possible for any nation to dictate peace to all its adversaries and neighbors. The *Pax Romana*, i.e., the Roman peace, lasted in the Mediterranean for nearly 500 years two thousand years ago, but eventually Rome fell. It was undermined by an array of internal weaknesses and assailed by a plethora of unrelenting enemies. Many in this country now seem to believe that America came close to the preeminence of imperial Rome during the years after World War II but frittered away its opportunities by failing to assert strong leadership. There are good reasons to doubt this view of history and I myself am skeptical of attempts in the 1980s to rewrite the history of the postwar era.

It seems more plausible to acknowledge that peacekeeping in today's world is an extremely subtle psychological art and that we have not done too badly given our many internal economic and social problems. Peacekeeping in this professional sense requires that diverse political objectives and potentially deadly adversaries be played off against each other in a balance so delicate that any major effort by one party of interest to disturb the balance, causes all the other parties of interest to move at once to restore it before armed conflict occurs. The Congress of Vienna in the early 19th century, the creation of the European Economic Community, and the detente with the People's Republic of China in our own time are examples of this subtle psychological art form. Each served the cause of world peace extremely well for extended periods of time. Eventually with changing circumstances and changing politics, such structures tend to become creaky and collapse. They must be periodically rebuilt, sometimes (but not always) out of the ruins of war.

The most ambitious attempt in our own time, the Charter of the United Nations and the organization constructed to implement it at the San Francisco conference in 1945 is now generally acknowledged to be a failure.

William McGill, "Keeping the Peace," *Vital Speeches of the Day*, September 15, 1982. Reprinted with permission.

The U.N. has become a captive of the Third World bloc of nations. The organization on which we once pinned so much of our hope for the world's future no longer serves to diminish the bitter rivalry between the United States and the Soviet Union; it has become a forum in which the Third World exploits that rivalry to its own advantage.

Uncontrolled Expansion

As the weaknesses and incompetence of our international peacekeeping machinery became evident in the decades following World War II, ruthless dictators throughout the world were tempted to seize by force what they failed to achieve by negotiation. Our continuing inability to control such conflicts has been a problem but by no means the only problem. The uncontrolled expansion of nuclear weapons to ridiculous levels of overkill, and the intense competition between the great powers, the U.S. and the Soviet Union, for ideological dominance of the planet have also proved to be major problems. These frightening developments in an international environment chronically incapable of controlling or directing events, have begun recently to give rise to intense public anxiety on a worldwide scale.

Politically innocent demonstrators are taking to the streets not just in this country but in Western Europe and Japan as well, shouting demands for a freeze on nuclear weapons. There are of course no peace demonstrators in the Soviet Union or the People's Republic of China insisting on similar renunciation of their own nuclear armaments. The leaders of those countries regard such demonstrations as subversive and forbid them.

But if Russia and China were free, we can well imagine that demonstrators would be there in large numbers as well. It would, I think, be a grave mistake to see these worldwide manifestations of anxiety merely as evidence of a communist plot. It is much more than that. We must never become so hardened as to ignore or misconstrue the obvious anguish of millions who stand to suffer if nuclear war should come.

Still, reason ought to tell us that street demonstrations and slogans are no substitutes for intelligence or hard work. It is not enough merely to pressure for peace. We must also be prepared to construct it in intricate and subtle patterns of international agreements. Humankind's perverse nature will never be altered by slogans. Overwrought demonstrators must somehow realize that the world crushes inexperienced and naive idealists. Idealism has to be learned with intelligent planning and great quantities of caution if it is ever to become truly effective for building a better world. Most of all, the reality of a durable peace requires that we accept progress in small steps. People who demand nothing less than total psychological and spiritual change are doomed to a life of predictable frustration.

"It is not enough merely to pressure for peace. We must also be prepared to construct it in intricate and subtle patterns of international agreements."

It is a fact that our doctrines of deterrence, the so-called MAD principles of mutually assured destruction, evolved in the nuclear era after 1945, weak and primitive though they are, have probably been the single most important factor in keeping the peace between the U.S. and the Soviet Union for the past 35 years. We cannot risk the loss of such deterrence even as we acknowledge the anguished pleas of an anxious public. Most demonstrators who plead for peace have no idea what they propose to get us into. Their approach is largely emotional whereas the solutions to the great problems of our age must be acts of the mind. . . .

Nothing truly significant can be wrought without emotional commitment, but commitment unaccompanied by thought leads to mob rule. We need solutions not slogans.

All of us can expect to be bombarded in the media with reports of mass peace demonstrations during the months ahead. News of conflict on behalf of peace is a natural for selling newspapers and TV time. But as we listen and read, we ought to reserve a certain skepticism for people who shout simplistic formulas without offering a clear view of the machinery by which the peace is to be kept. That machinery is the only substantive question.

Peace Agenda

What is the machinery supposed to do? We need to strengthen our ability to deter any aggressor; discipline our own zealots, and there are plenty of them, who want to bomb other societies back to the stone age; find common interest with the Soviet Union and China in preventing the spread of nuclear weapons to ambitious dictators in the Third World; sit down with the Soviets to write a carefully-drawn treaty that will put a stop to the uncontrolled arms race between East and West without threatening either deterrence or the national security of either party. The building of effective machinery for achieving these and related policy objectives is difficult but it and it alone constitutes the peace agenda for the Eighties.

We have to face it. Peacemaking in today's world is not an occupation for amateur do-gooders unable to make their way in an environment filled with terrorists and bomb throwers. Our peacemakers must be tireless, strong and determined in their efforts to resolve conflicts. Like Anwar Sadat they may have to give up their lives.

I will close these brief remarks with a touching story illustrating the urgency of devising the machinery for peace. Forty years ago a great naval battle was fought in the central Pacific near the island of Midway on June 4-5, 1942. It proved to be decisive in frustrating the Japanese warlords' ambition to become the dominant military force in the western Pacific. After Midway, Japan's war in the Pacific was inevitably lost.

The account of that battle in which a relatively small American naval force, badly battered after the disaster at Pearl Harbor six months earlier, managed nevertheless to rout a much larger Japanese armada is a gripping tale in itself. If you wish, you can read about it in Walter Lord's excellent book *Incredible Victory*.

My story deals with two extraordinary young men who gave up their lives. One was Lieutenant Commander John Waldron, leader of Torpedo Squadron 8, a collection of twenty ancient attack planes based on the carrier Hornet. At about 10 a.m. on the morning of June 4th Waldron led his squadron into the concentrated firepower of the entire Japanese strike force of four carriers encircled by dozens of protecting warships. Torpedo 8 came in at low level where there was almost no chance of survival. Only one man came through alive. Waldron, the brave leader, perished.

But the vehemence and daring of Waldron's attack drew the Zeroes protecting the Japanese carriers down to water level, permitting a large force of American dive bombers to slip in at high altitude unobserved and unchallenged. Within ten minutes three of the Japanese carriers were reduced to a shambles and sinking. The tide of battle was turned completely by the unexampled bravery of Torpedo 8.

In the afternoon of that same day Lieutenant Joichi Tomanaga, commander of the Japanese air attack on Midway, took off from the only remaining carrier, Hiryu, to lead a hastily conceived strike against the carrier Lexington. The Japanese carriers had suffered terribly through the morning. Hundreds of planes were lost and many more were severely damaged. Lieutenant Tomanaga's aircraft sustained serious damage to one of

234

its wing tanks. He refused all pleas by his subordinates to trade planes. There were none in reserve. The Lieutenant took off knowing that with insufficient fuel he would never make it back. He was seen to disappear as his group of torpedo planes swept in on the Lexington in a determined attack that injured her fatally.

Cruel Losses

And so these two brave young men, one American and one Japanese, lie buried in the Pacific within a few miles of each other. In life neither one knew the other; neither spoke the other's language. But in death they lie together as brothers, lost on the same day, in the same place, and essentially in the same way.

What a great pity that they never knew one another; and what a pity that the political leaders of their time were unable to prevent the war in which they gave their lives. The world needs brave young men like Waldron and Tomanaga, not to mention the thousands of others who were lost along with them. What a pity that so many brave young men have had to die in all the wars that might have been prevented.

In simple language, if we fail in our responsibility to create the means by which peace may be preserved, then many other brave young men will also have to die; and not just young men, but young women, children, and old people as well. The impact of modern war on civilian populations is overwhelmingly cruel because of major advances in the technology of warfare, and especially because of the capability of mass destruction associated with modern thermonuclear weapons. This time our entire civilization is at stake.

"Our doctrines of deterrence. . .have probably been the single most important factor in keeping the peace between the U.S. and the Soviet Union for the past 35 years."

The commitment to peace and the responsibility to preserve the peace are matters that can now no longer be postponed. You are free to march and chant slogans, or you can seek out and support those who will offer inventive and determined proposals for building the machinery of peace. Which is it to be? I have no doubt what your answer is. God bless you all and keep you safe.

William J. McGill is President-Emeritus of Columbia University.

"To those who say that arms control should somehow not be politicized, that it should be left to the tender mercies of the experts, I say, 'Nonsense.'"

Peacekeeping Is the Citizens' Responsibility

David Durenberger

Someone once said that Congress doesn't run, it waltzes. That person must have been thinking about arms control. Look at what has been happening to the nuclear freeze resolution in the House of Representatives. They have waltzed all over it, and still come up empty-handed.

If it were up to Congress alone, I suppose the issue would have disappeared. But it hasn't. And the reason is that people like you have continued to apply pressure, forcing Congress and the Administration to come to grips with the question of arms control. . . .

It should be apparent from the outset that, simply at the technical level alone, arms control is an enormously complex topic with few easy answers. In part, that's because it concerns a topic which we really don't know much about—preventing a nuclear war. It's difficult to prove the existence of a negative, so we can all draw different lessons from history about when wars were prevented and why. The fact that something didn't happen is no proof that we caused it not to happen. Just as important, of course, we don't really understand nuclear war, since there has never been one. So from the outset, we all should admit that the topic is vital but ultimately not subject to rigorous tests of evidence.

In short, we have a great deal of expertise on which to draw when it comes to the technical details. But we have very little expertise on which to draw when it comes to proving the case for or against a given proposal. This means that in large part each of you will rely on your own moral reasoning when grappling with this topic. In doing so, we must all recognize that there is no concrete evidence that our judgment or that of those who disagree with us is either wrong or right. A recognition of our need for understanding is the beginning of wisdom on this subject, and it is therefore vital that we do everything possible to hear out the views of others. As the Catholic Bishops have noted in their

pastoral letter, we need "not only conviction and commitment, but also civility and charity."

To those who say that arms control should somehow not be politicized, that it should be left to the tender mercies of the experts, I say, "Nonsense." Let's dismiss from the outset the notion that arms control is above politics. It *is* politics, just as a debate over health policy is politics. If war is too important to be left to the generals, and health policy too important to be left to the physicians, then arms control is too important to be left to the arms controllers.

There is a second facet of arms control which makes it inherently political—contradictory goals. We're all familiar with the statement that arms control seeks to achieve decreased defense expenditures, a decreased likelihood of war, and—if all else fails—a decreased death toll in the event that conflict should break out. But let's not forget that these goals can be and almost always have been contradictory. If we pursue one, we hamper another, for instance when we argue that civil defense measures can make war more, not less, likely.

There is a larger dilemma as well. Arms control is not a substitute for defense policy. But neither is it the opposite of defense policy. It is a necessary corollary of our entire approach to international security. This means that we cannot afford to oversimplify the topic, either by ignoring the compelling need to prevent nuclear war or by ignoring the equally compelling need to resist the menace of Soviet totalitarianism. . . .

Essence of Politics

This kind of dilemma—the management of contradictory goals and the necessity to guard our flanks while moving forward—is also the essence of politics. Politics is nothing more or less than trying to find a solution to diverse and often contradictory goals. That is a truism. For instance, former Secretary of Defense Melvin Laird —whose background was in the Congress—recognized that he could never engender support for the SALT I

David Durenberger, "Domestic Politics of Arms Control," April 30, 1983.

Treaty without appealing to the conservatives. SALT I, after all, froze launcher levels at a point which gave the Russians a numerical advantage. So he stressed that our lead in MIRV technology offset the Russian lead in launchers, and he moreover conditioned his public support for SALT on full-scale modernization of the strategic forces. In doing this, he laid the groundwork for our later doctrine of Essential Equivalence. He managed thereby to find a way to bring together people with opposing goals. He resorted to compromise.

But a second truism about politics is that politics is the business of getting government to respond to some pressing issue, at least as that issue is defined by the citizenry. We are certainly familiar with this in arms control. The campaign to stop the B-1, which had gained momentum throughout the early 1970's, pressured Jimmy Carter into making cancellation of that weapon a part of his campaign platform in 1976. On the other hand, the entire issue of the window of vulnerability took on larger-than-life dimensions because a number of people repeatedly focused the attention of a few politicians on the issue of heavy Soviet ICBM's. The result was that the campaign of 1980 was dominated by a discussion of the window of vulnerability. Now our START agenda is focused on addressing this concern. In the past two Presidential campaigns, in other words, persistent pressure by a few dedicated people has significantly shaped our arms control posture.

There is a third truism about politics, however. That is that the first two truisms can conflict with each other. One person's compromise is another person's cop-out, which means that the cycle begins all over again. We are witnessing that right now, with the discussion about the MX missile.

President Reagan tried to compromise on the MX by opposing the "racetrack" basing scheme while putting the missile into interim hardened silos pending a final basing dicision. Those concerned about ICBM vulnerability immediately criticized the decision, led by Senator John Tower. Those concerned that the accuracy of the MX is destabilizing also criticized the decision, led by Senator Mark Hatfield. Intensely motivated people, in other words, were not satisfied with any portion of the initial MX decision. Since late 1981, we have been trying to find something new which can satisfy all concerns—vulnerability, control of defense expenditures, instability, and arms control talks. I'm not sure we will succeed. . . .

The first political reality is *avoidance of the topic*. This phenomenon is understandable, but it does a disservice to the goal of controlling and reducing arms. We cannot control what we will not confront.

Most people have a sensible attitude of repugnance toward weaponry, particularly weaponry of mass destruction. It is horrifying to listen, as I have, to weapons specialists glibly talking about such things as prompt radiation fatalities, uranium-jacketed bomb cas-

ings, and all the other esoterica of today's weaponry. There is something almost pornographic about the intensity with which a few Dr. Strangeloves approach the topic.

But it is just as disturbing to see people totally avoid the topic for fear that they will get their hands dirty. . . .

Not long ago, a good friend of mine refused to participate in the launching ceremonies for the submarine *Minneapolis-St. Paul.* He stated that as an ordained minister, he could not countenance the idea of christening a vessel which might kill people. I didn't press the point, but I fear that this kind of thing can lead us to avoid our own responsiblities as citizens to learn about security policy and arms control. It risks leaving policy in the hands of a few high priests, trained in tortuous logic to think tanks and ordained in some back room of the Pentagon or of High Frontier.

> *"Politics is the business of getting government to respond to some pressing issue, at least as that issue is defined by the citizenry."*

A second reality is that *attention spans are short.* I have repeatedly welcomed the new and dramatic public concern over nuclear weapons. It is overdue, and it puts the kind of pressure needed on politicians. But I must confess that I am terrified that the attention being paid today may fade away tomorrow. It has happened before, and it can happen again. A corollary concern is that I hope we won't spend too much time reinventing the wheel.

Parallel Issues

There are some astonishing parallels between today's issues and the issues which the public debated in the late 1950's and early 1960's. It was then that mass demonstrations in Europe expressed deep concern over American intermediate range missiles that could strike Russia from the continent in the space of a few minutes. Air bases were surrounded by human chains of demonstrators. Fear was expressed that the U.S. might initiate a war resulting in the destruction of Europe and eventually the world. Articles were published to remind us of the need for invulnerable systems in order to preserve deterrance. In short, when we went through the controversy over the Titan, Thor, Jupiter and Bomarc missiles, we raised many of the same points now being raised about the Pershing and Cruise missiles. Why didn't we learn? And why don't we remember? . . .

Yet, already there are signs that the intensity of the issue may be fading from the public mind. A recent CBS television news show focused on this year's town meetings in New Hampshire. Last year, those meetings concerned arms control, and people were discussing it daily, This year, the issue is acid rain.

A third reality is that *abstraction often dominates specifics.* This is hardly news to an audience of attorneys. But it is very pertinent to the politics of arms control. Until we can get a specific proposal to consider, we in government are unlikely to go beyond the level of nostrums. Yet, ironically, as we get into specifics on any subject, we often find that our imagined consensus breaks down. The great merit of abstractions is that we can all agree on them. We can all agree, for instance, that nuclear war would be the worst catastrophe in history, and that we should bend our efforts toward preventing it. But how? There, we run into difficulties.

Recently, a Roper Organization survey resulted in some very dismaying but hardly surprising findings concerning public support for a nuclear freeze. The findings basically state that a freeze means different things to different people. Only 9 percent of those sampled oppose a freeze outright. But 36 percent favor a freeze if the Soviets first cut back their forces to a level equal to ours—in other words, reduce now, freeze later. Twenty percent, on the other hand, favor a freeze today, with reductions later. Fourteen percent favor a freeze if we first build up, and 10 percent favor a freeze after we have gained outright superiority. . . .

One of the tragedies of arms control in the past few years was President Carter's inability to recognize this point. He touched a number of fundamental chords in the American public during his 1976 campaign because of his sincerity and because we were looking, after years of Vietnam and Watergate, for something new. Moreover, he probably came to office with a better technical understanding of arms and arms control policy than any recent President. Yet his equivocation—and the widespread perception of his equivocation—resulted in a series of arms control failures. . . .

"I have repeatedly welcomed the new and dramatic public concern over nuclear weapons. It is overdue, and it puts the kind of pressure needed on politicians."

On the other hand, President Reagan understands better than most people the role of leadership style in setting the public agenda. He has been able to mobilize the public over and over again, to the bafflement of his critics who have not seen such uniquely personal leadership in many years. Yet he has done so with perhaps the least sophisticated grasp of arms and arms control policy of any President in fifty years. Many of his senior advisors on the subject are equally untrained. . . .

The fifth political reality is that *ideology often overrides practicality.* This is true enough among the general public and among public interest lobbies, so I won't belabor you with still more cautionary notes about letting the best become the enemy of the good. But is is true to an unrecognized degree within the Congress as well.

To say that is a bit contradictory, for I have been emphasizing thus far that Congress tends to react to pressure rather than to stake out a set of rigid positions. That's true for the institution, but it does not hold true for all individuals. Unfortunately, as we learned last December when we suffered through a massive filibuster over the issue of gas taxes, one or two determined ideologues can set the agenda for an entire legislature. . . .

The sixth and final reality is obvious, and it follows from all the rest: *Governments resort to lip service and word games as a first response to pressure for a consensus.*

With all due respect to Jan Kalicki and Senators Kennedy and Hatfield, I am struck by how deliberately the current freeze resolution has used vague or ambiguous terminology. I am not suggesting that the authors and sponsors of this or other resolutions like last year's Jackson-Warner bill are being cynical or insincere. They are not. I am suggesting, however, that politicians find it necessary to resort to compromise over *language* when they are seeking to pick up votes. That's the nature of bargaining. . . .

In arms control, as in politics, bedfellows are often strange. But if we ignore this reality—if we pretend that arms control can, does, or should occur in a vacuum defined by technicians—we will lose what we seek: a policy of security based on public support. There is no arms control without politics. We may not like the results, but that simply calls for more rather than less political input. The challenge of knowledgeable input is yours.

David Durenberger is the Republican US senator from Minnesota.

"Public opinion itself, when it is not artificially aroused by some passionate feeling of pride or unjust frustration, opts for peaceful solutions."

Dialogue Is Essential for Peace

Pope John Paul II

On the threshold of the new year 1983, for the 16th World Day of Peace, I present you this message on the theme "Dialogue for Peace, a Challenge for Our Time."

I am addressing it to all those who are, on the one hand, a people responsible for peace: those who preside over the destiny of peoples, international officials, politicians, diplomats. But I am also addressing it to the citizens of each country. All are in fact called by the need to prepare true peace, to maintain it or to re-establish it on solid and just foundations.

Now I am deeply convinced that dialogue—true dialogue—is an essential condition for such peace. Yes, this dialogue is necessary, not only opportune. It is difficult, but it is possible, in spite of the obstacles that realism obliges us to consider.

It therefore represents a true challenge which I invite you to take up. And I do this without any other purpose than that of contributing, myself and the Holy See, to peace, by taking very much to heart the destiny of humanity, as the heir of the message of Christ and as the first one responsible for that message, which is above all a message of peace for all men.

I am sure that in this I am voicing the basic aspiration of the men and women of our time. Is not this desire for peace affirmed by all leaders in their good wishes to their nations or in the declarations which they address to other countries?

What political party will abstain from including in its program the quest for peace? As for the international organizations, they were created to promote and guarantee peace, and they maintain this objective in spite of setbacks.

Public opinion itself, when it is not artificially aroused by some passionate feeling of pride or unjust frustration, opts for peaceful solutions. In addition, more and more movements work—even with a lucidity or sinceri-

ty that can sometimes leave much to be desired—so that people will realize the need to eliminate, not only all war, but everything which can lead to war. Citizens, in general, wish for a climate of peace which will guarantee their search for well-being, particularly when they find themselves faced—as in our own days—by an economic crisis which threatens all workers.

But it would be necessary to go to the logical conclusion of this aspiration, which is happily very widespread: Peace will not be established, nor will it be maintained, unless one takes the means. And the means par excellence is to adopt an attitude of dialogue, that is of patiently introducing the mechanisms and phases of dialogue wherever peace is threatened or already compromised, in families, in society, between countries or between blocs of countries.

The experience of history, even recent history, shows that dialogue is in fact necessary for true peace. It would be easy to find cases where the conflict seemed fatal, but where war was avoided or abandoned because the parties believed in the value of dialogue and practiced this dialogue in the course of long and honest discussions.

On the contrary, where there have been conflicts—and contrary to a widespread opinion, one can, alas, number more than 150 armed conflicts since the Second World War—it was that dialogue did not really take place, or that it was falsified, made into a snare, or deliberately reduced. The year which has just ended has once more offered the spectacle of violence and war. People have shown that they preferred to use arms rather than to try to understand one another.

Yes, side by side with signs of hope, the year 1982 will leave in many human families a memory of desolation and ruin, a bitter taste of tears and death.

Now, who then would dare to make light of such wars—some of which are still going on—or of states of war, or of the deep frustrations that wars leave behind? Who would dare, without trembling, to envisage even

Pope John Paul II, World Day of Peace message delivered January 1, 1983.

241

more extensive and much more terrible wars which still threaten?

Is it not necessary to give everything in order to avoid war, even limited war (thus euphemistically called by those who are not directly concerned in it), given the evil that every war represents, its price which must be paid in human lives, in suffering, in the devastation of what would be necessary for human life and development, without counting the upset of necessary tranquility, the deterioration of the social fabric, the hardening of mistrust and hatred which wars maintain toward one's neighbor?

Political Strength of Dialogue

And today when even conventional wars become so murderous, when one knows the tragic consequences that nuclear war would have, the need to stop war or to turn aside its threat is all the more imperious. And thus we see as more fundamental the need to have recourse to dialogue, to its political strength, which must avoid recourse to arms.

But some people today who consider themselves realists are doubtful about the possibility of dialogue and its effectiveness, not least when the positions are so tense and irreconcilable that they seem to allow no space for any agreement. How many negative experiences, how many repeated setbacks, would seem to support this disillusioned viewpoint.

And yet, dialogue for peace is possible, always possible. It is not a utopia. Moreover, even when dialogue has not seemed possible, and when one has come to the point of armed confrontation, has it not been necessary, after all—after the devastation of war, which has shown the power of the conqueror but has resolved nothing regarding the rights which were contested—has it not been necessary to seek for dialogue?

To tell the truth, the conviction I am affirming here does not rest on this fatality, but upon a reality: on a consideration of the profound nature of the human person. Those who share the Christian faith will be more easily persuaded of this, even if they believe in the congenital weakness and sin which has mocked the human heart since the beginning.

But every person, whether a believer or not, while remaining prudent and clearsighted concerning the possible hardening of his brother's heart, can and must preserve enough confidence in man—in his capacity of being reasonable, in his sense of what is good, of justice, of fairness, in his possibility of brotherly love and hope, which are never totally perverted—to aim for recourse to dialogue and the possible resumption of dialogue.

Yes, people are finally capable of overcoming divisions, conflicts of interests, even if the oppositions seem radical ones—especially when each party is convinced that it is defending a just cause—if they believe in the virtue of dialogue, if they agree to meet face to face to seek a peaceful and reasonable solution for conflicts.

It is even more necessary that they should agree to begin again to ceaselessly propose true dialogue—by removing obstacles and by eliminating the defects of dialogue which I shall speak about later—and to travel to the end this single road which leads to peace, with all its demands and conditions.

I therefore consider it useful to recall at this point the qualities of true dialogue. They apply in the first place to dialogue between individuals. But I am thinking also and especially of dialogue between social groups, between political forces in a nation, between states within the international community. They also apply to dialogue between the vast human groupings which are distinguished from one another and which face one another on the levels of race, culture, ideology or religion.

So students of warfare recognize that most conflicts find their roots here, at the same time as being connected with the great present-day antagonisms of East-West on the one hand, North-South on the other.

Dialogue is a central and essential element of ethical thinking among people, whoever they may be. As an exchange, of communication between human beings that language makes possible, it is in fact a common quest.

Basically, it presupposes the search for what is true, good and just for every person, for every group and every society, in the grouping one is a member of or in the grouping which presents itself as the opposing one.

"Dialogue between nations must be based on the strong conviction that the good of the people cannot be finally accomplished against the good of another people."

It therefore first of all demands openness and welcome: that each party should explain its thoughts, but should also listen to the explanation of the situation as the other party describes it, sincerely feels it with the real problems which are proper to the party, its rights, the injustices of which it is aware, the reasonable solutions which it suggests.

How could peace become established while one party has not even taken the trouble to consider the conditions of the other party's existence?

To engage in dialogue thus presupposes that each party should accept the difference and the specific nature of the other party. It also presupposes that each party should become really aware of what separates it from the other, and that it should assume it, with the risk of tension that comes from it, without renouncing through cowardice or constraint what it knows to be true and just. For that would result in a shaky compromise.

And, on the other hand, one should not attempt to reduce the other party to a mere object, but should consider the party to be an intelligent, free and responsible subject.

Dialogue is at the same time the search for what is and remains common to people even in the midst of tensions, opposition and conflicts. In this sense, it makes the other party a neighbor. It accepts its contribution, it shares with it responsibility before truth and justice. It is to suggest and to study all the possible formulas for honest reconciliation, while linking the just defense of the interests and honor of the party one represents to the no less just understanding and respect for the reasons of the other party, as well as the demands of the general good common to both.

Furthermore, is it not more and more obvious that all the peoples of the earth find themselves in a situation of mutual interdependence on the economic, political and cultural levels? Anyone who attempted to free himself from this solidarity would soon suffer from it himself.

Finally, true dialogue is the search by peaceful means for what is good. It is the persistent determination to have recourse to all the possible formulas of negotiation, mediation and arbitration; to act in such a way that the factors which bring people together will be victorious over the factors of division and hate. It is a recognition of the inalienable dignity of human beings.

It rests upon respect for human life. It is a wager on the social nature of people, on their calling to go forward together, with continuity—by a converging meeting of minds, wills, hearts—toward the goal that the creator has fixed for them. The goal is to make the world a place for everybody to live in and worthy of everybody.

The political virtue of such a dialogue could not fail to bear fruit for peace. My esteemed predecessor Paul VI devoted a large part of his first encyclical, *Ecclesiam Suam,* to dialogue. He wrote:

"Openness to dialogue which is disinterested, objective and frank, is in itself a declaration in favor of free and honest peace. It excludes pretense, rivalry, deceit and betrayal" (*AAS 56,* 1964, p. 654). This virtue of dialogue demands of the political leaders of today much clear-sightedness, honesty and courage, not only with regard to other peoples, but with regard to the public opinion of their own people. It often presupposes a true conversion. But there is no other possibility in the face of the threat of war.

And once again, it is not an illusion. It would be easy to quote those of our contemporaries who have gained honor by practicing it thus.

Obstacles to Dialogue

On the other hand, it seems to me salutary also to condemn particular obstacles to dialogue for peace.

I am not speaking about the difficulties inherent in political dialogue such as the frequent difficulty of reconciling concrete, opposing interests. There is also the frequent difficulty of emphasizing precarious conditions of existence without pointing to injustice properly speaking, on the part of others. I am thinking of what damages or prevents the normal process of dialogue.

I have already let it be understood that dialogue is blocked by an a priori decision to concede nothing, by a refusal to listen, by a claim to be—oneself and only oneself—the measure of justice. This attitude can conceal quite simply the blind and deaf selfishness of a people, or more often the will to power of its leaders.

"True dialogue is the search by peaceful means for what is good."

It also happens that this attitude coincides with an exaggerated and out-of-date concept of the sovereignty and security of the state. The state then runs the risk of becoming the object of unquestionable worship, so to speak. It runs the risk of justifying the most questionable undertaking. Orchestrated by the powerful means at the disposal of propaganda, such worship—which is not to be confused with properly understood patriotic attachment to one's own nation—can inhibit the critical sense and moral sense of the more aware citizens and can encourage them to go to war.

For all the more reason one must mention the tactical and deliberate lie, which misuses language, which has recourse to the most sophisticated techniques of propaganda, which deceives and distorts dialogue and incites to aggression.

Finally, dialogue is fixed and sterile when certain parties are fostered by ideologies which in spite of their declarations are opposed to the dignity of the human person, to his or her just aspiration according to healthy principles of reason, of the natural and eternal law (cf. *Pacem in Terris, AAS 55*, 1963, p. 300), ideologies which see the motive force of history in struggle, which see the source of rights in force, that see in the discernment of the enemy the ABC of politics. Or, if it still exists, the dialogue is a superficial and falsified reality. Therefore it becomes very difficult, not to say impossible. There follows almost a complete lack of communication between countries and blocs. Even the international institutions are paralyzed. And the setback to dialogue then runs the risk of serving the arms race.

However, even in what can be considered an impasse to the extent that individuals support such ideologies, the attempt to have a lucid dialogue still seems necessary in order to unblock the situation and to work for the possible establishment of peace on particular points. This is to be done by counting upon common sense, on the possibilities of danger for everyone and on the just aspirations to which people themselves largely adhere.

Dialogue for peace must be established in the first

place on the national level in order to resolve social conflicts, in order to seek the common good. While bearing in mind the interests of different groups, the common effort for peace must be made ceaselessly—in the exercise of freedoms and duties which are democratic for all thanks to the structures of participation and thanks to the many means of reconciliation between employers and workers—by respecting and associating the cultural, ethnic and religious groups which make up a nation.

Unfortunately, when dialogue between government and people is absent, social peace is threatened or absent; it is like a state of war. But history and present-day observation show that many countries have succeeded or are succeeding in establishing ways of truly working together to resolve conflicts that arise within them, or even of preventing the conflicts by acquiring truly effective means of dialogue. They also enact legislation which is in constant evolution, and which appropriate jurisdictions cause to be respected for the common good.

If dialogue has shown itself to produce results on the national level, why should it not be so on the international level? It is true that the problems are more complicated, the parties and interests in question are more numerous and less homogeneous. But the means par excellence always remains honest and patient dialogue.

Where this is missing between nations, every effort must be made to restore it. Where it is insufficient, it must be perfected. Dialogue should never be set aside by having recourse to the force of arms to resolve conflicts.

And the great responsibility engaged here is not only that of the opposing parties, whose passion it is difficult to control. It is also and much more the responsibility of more powerful nations which fail to help these others to restore dialogue, which push them into war or which tempt them by arms trading.

Dialogue between nations must be based on the strong conviction that the good of the people cannot be finally accomplished against the good of another people: All have the same rights, the same claims to a worthy life for their citizens. It is essential to make progress in overcoming artificial divisions inherited from the past and the antagonism of blocs. Greater recognition must be given to the increasing interdependence of nations.

The Object of International Dialogue

If one wishes to state exactly the object of international dialogue, one can say that it must be notably concerned with the rights of man, with justice between peoples, with economics, with disarmament and with the common international good.

Yes, it must be directed toward the recognition of individuals and human groups in their specific nature, in their original character, with the area of freedom they need, and notably the exercise of their basic rights.

On this subject, one can hope for an international juridical system more receptive to the appeals of those whose rights are violated. And one can hope for jurisdictions which have effective means of making their authority respected.

If injustice in all its forms is the first source of violence and war, it goes without saying that, in a general way, dialogue for peace cannot be dissociated from dialogue for justice on behalf of peoples who suffer frustration and domination by others.

Dialogue for peace will also necessarily involve a discussion of the rules which govern economic life. For the temptation to violence and war will always be present in societies where greed and the search for material goods impels a wealthy minority to refuse the mass of people the satisfaction of the most elementary rights to food, education, health and life (cf. *Gaudium et Spes,* 69). This is true of every country; but also in the relationships between countries, especially if bilateral relations continue to be prevalent.

It is here that openness to multilateral relationships, notably in the framework of international organizations, brings an opportunity for dialogue which is less burdened by inequalities and therefore more favorable to justice.

Obviously the object of international dialogue will also concern itself with the dangerous arms race in such a way as to reduce it progressively, as I suggested in the message I sent to the United Nations Organization last June, and in conformity with the message that the learned members of the Pontifical Academy of Sciences took on my behalf to the leaders of the nuclear powers.

"The temptation to violence and war will always be present in societies where greed and the search for material goods impels a wealthy minority to refuse the mass of people the satisfaction of the most elementary rights to food, education, health and life."

Instead of being at the service of people, the economy is becoming militarized. Development and well-being are subordinated to security. Science and technology are being degraded into the auxiliaries of war.

The Holy See will not grow weary in insisting upon the need to put a stop to the arms race through progressive negotiations, by appealing for a reciprocity. The Holy See will continue to encourage all steps, even the smallest one, of reasonable dialogue in this very important sphere.

But the object of dialogue for peace cannot be reduced to a condemnation of the arms race; it is a question of searching for a whole more just international order, consensus on the more equitable sharing of goods, services, knowledge and information, and a firm determination to order these to the common good.

I know that such a dialogue of which the North-South dialogue forms a part is very complex; it must be resolutely pursued, in order to prepare the conditions for true peace as we approach the third millennium.

After these considerations my message is intended to be above all an appeal to take up the challenge to dialogue for peace.

I address it in the first place to you, the heads of state and government! May you be able, in order that your people may know real social peace, to permit all the conditions for dialogue and common effort which, when justly established, would not compromise but would favor, in the long term, the common good of the nation in freedom and independence! May you be able to conduct this dialogue on equal terms with the other countries, and help parties in conflict find the paths of dialogue, of reasonable reconciliation and of just peace!

I also appeal to you, the diplomats, whose noble profession it is, among other things, to deal with disputed points and to seek to resolve them through dialogue and negotiation, in order to avoid recourse to arms, or to take the place of the belligerents. It is a work of patience and perseverance which the Holy See values all the more in view of the fact that it itself is engaged in diplomatic relationships by which it wants to see dialogue adopted as the most suitable means of overcoming differences.

I wish above all to repeat my confidence in you, the leaders and members of international organizations, and in you, the international officials! In the course of the last 10 years, your organizations have too often been the object of attempts at manipulation on the part of nations wishing to exploit such bodies. However it remains true that the present multiplicity of violent clashes, divisions and blocks on which bilateral relations founder, offer the great international organizations the opportunity to enter upon a qualitative change in their activities, even to reform their own structures on certain points in order to take new realities into account and to enjoy effective power.

Whether they are regional or worldwide, your organizations have an exceptional chance to seize—to regain, in all its fullness—the mission which is theirs by virtue of their origin, their charter and their mandate; to become the places and instruments par excellence for true dialogue for peace.

Far from allowing themselves to be overcome by paralyzing pessimism and discouragement, they have the possibility of affirming themselves still more as centers of encounter where one can envisage the most audacious questioning of the practices which today prevail in political, economic, monetary and cultural exchanges.

I also make a particular appeal to you who work in the mass media! The sad events which the world has experienced in recent times have confirmed the impor-

tance of enlightened opinion in keeping a conflict from degenerating into war. Public opinion, in fact, can put a brake on warlike tendencies or, on the contrary, support these same tendencies to the point of blindness.

Now, as those responsible for radio and television broadcasts and for the press, you have an ever more preponderant role in this sphere. I encourage you to weigh your responsibility and to show with the greatest objectivity the rights, the problems and the attitudes of each of the parties in order to promote understanding and dialogue between groups, countries and civilizations.

Finally, I must address myself to every man and woman and also to you, the young: You have many opportunities to break down the barriers of selfishness, lack of understanding and aggression by your way of carrying on a dialogue, every day, in your family, your village, your neighborhood, in the associations of your city, your region, without forgetting the non-governmental organizations. Dialogue for peace is the task of everyone.

And now, I exhort you especially, the Christians, to take your part in this dialogue in accordance with the responsibilities that are yours: to pursue them with the openness, frankness and justice called for by the charity of Christ; to take them up again ceaselessly, with the tenacity and hope which faith enables.

"Public opinion, in fact, can put a brake on warlike tendencies or, on the contrary, support these same tendencies to the point of blindness."

You also know the need for conversion and prayer, for the main obstacle to the establishment of justice and peace is to be found in man's heart, in sin (cf. *GS*, 10), as it was in the heart of Cain when he refused dialogue with his brother Abel (cf. Gen. 4:6-9).

Jesus has taught us how to listen, to share, to act toward other people as one would wish for oneself, to settle differences while one travels together (cf. Mt. 5:25), to pardon. And above all, by his death and resurrection, he came to deliver us from the sin which sets up one against the other, to give us his peace, to break down the wall which separates the problems.

That is why the church does not cease to implore the Lord to grant people the gift of his peace, as the message of last year emphasized. People are no longer vowed to not understanding one another or to being divided from one another, as at Babel (cf. Gen. 11:7-9). In Jerusalem, on the day of Pentecost, the Holy Spirit caused the first disciples of the Lord to rediscover, beyond the diversity of languages, the royal road to peace in brotherhood. The church remains the witness of this great hope.

May Christians be ever more aware of their vocation to be, against winds and tides, the humble shepherds of that peace which, on Christmas night, God entrusted to us!

And, with them, may all men and women of good will be enabled to take up this challenge for our time, even in the midst of the most difficult situations; that is to say, may they be enabled to do everything in order to avoid war and to commit themselves for this purpose, with increased conviction, to the path which removes the threat of war: dialogue for peace!

Pope John Paul II was elected head of the Roman Catholic Church in 1978.

"One of the functions of civil disobedience is to expose the choices, and then leave persons free to decide and to live or die with the consequences."

Actions Will Bring Peace

Dean Snyder

Last summer I became one of those who have committed civil disobedience to protest this nation's nuclear weaponry policy—a growing number, as the newsletter of the National No-Nukes Prison Support Collective has reported. During the six-month period of March-September 1982, there were 3,481 arrests of activists (including protesters against nuclear power plants, a small minority). Although arrests made in New York City on June 14 during the mass blockage of the UN missions of nations possessing nuclear weapons accounted for about half of the total, these people ran a relatively low risk of serious punishment. Still, 1,476 of those arrested throughout the country in that six-month period spent some time in jail as a result of their acts of civil disobedience. It seems to me that this many persons willing to risk prison in order to express their condemnation of U.S. nuclear war preparations is significant—certainly a more significant number than relatively scant popular media coverage would seem to indicate.

I was one of five members of a Philadelphia Christian peace group who chained shut the doors of the General Electric Space Division headquarters in Valley Forge and then celebrated the Christian holy meal behind the closed doors before the police got to us. At this particular plant, GE—which is the country's fourth largest war contractor, drawing $6 million a day from the federal treasury—produces satellites for the Defense Satellite Communications System III (DSCS III). Designed to withstand a nuclear attack and go on functioning, these satellites are essential to the Pentagon's "command, control and communications" modernization program, known as C^3. The system is being built to enable the U.S. to conduct a so-called "protracted" nuclear war. Colin Gray, an adviser to President Reagan, testifies to this: "The C^3 modernization story doesn't make any sense if you're not thinking along these lines

[of protracted nuclear war]. . . .If you only need your forces to go bang on day one, who cares about survivability of satellites?"

DSCS III is not only a reflection but a specific implementation of an aggressive U.S. nuclear war policy. That this policy really exists is substantiated by *Los Angeles Times* reporter Robert Scheer in his new book *With Enough Shovels: Reagan, Bush and Nuclear War* (Random House), an amazing collection of public statements and quotes from Reagan and members of his administration. The perception, says Scheer, is of nuclear war as "not only a war that can be won, but as a war consistent with the preservation of civilization."

A week after our arrest at GE, what was to have been a pretrial hearing somehow became, in the unpredictable way the courts work in this country, our actual trial. Without being permitted to testify about the nature of the work done in GE's Valley Forge plant or, for that matter, about much else, we were found guilty of criminal trespass, a summary offense. The sentence was a $200 fine each (which we do not intend to pay) or 30 days' imprisonment (about which we apparently have little choice). A friendly law professor has advised us that, under the legal codes of Pennsylvania, we should be able to argue in court that our actions were legally justified, since they constituted an attempt to avoid the harm, evil and catastrophe of the crime being committed by GE, and so we have decided to appeal the sentence. As to whether the criminality of nuclear weaponry production can finally be argued in court, we shall see.

Interpreting Our Actions

Over the past months we have been asked to interpret our actions at General Electric both to basically friendly groups, such as church social-action organizations, and to quite hostile audiences, such as on radio call-in shows. In some ways it has been easier to understand the response of those who strongly con-

Dean Snyder, "Civil Disobedience: What it Means," *The Christian Century.* Copyright 1983 Christian Century Foundation. Reprinted by permission from the April 27, 1983 issue of *The Christian Century.*

demn what we did. They appear to believe sincerely that this nation is totally benevolent and that the Soviets are demonic. They are convinced that the Soviets intend to bury us—literally—and therefore it would be better to bury them *and* ourselves rather than risk defeat.

With these folk, who have bought the propaganda used to justify the allocation of well over $2 billion a year of public monies to General Electric, our task has been relatively clear and simple, if not always successful. We quote George Kennan a lot, so as to suggest that the Soviets may not have webbed toes and tails. We encourage people to wonder how our nuclear weapons systems could be merely defensive when the U.S. has persistently initiated new technologies several years before the U.S.S.R. had them.

"Perhaps the peace movement needs to listen to Thoreau when he points out that people who have 'an undue respect for the law' become 'the agents of injustice.'"

We point out that our government may not always have been honest with us about the status of the arms race, citing Daniel Ellsberg's statement that, at the time of the Cuban missile crisis when there was supposed to be a missile gap favoring the Soviets, they possessed exactly *four* ICBMs. If the audience is Christian, we propose that they at least wrestle with the meaning of faith in a Christ who chose not to return evil for evil but who unilaterally disarmed himself on the cross.

If the reception from audiences of this kind has not been exactly friendly, we have at least been able to understand their perspective and why, given their assumptions, our action at GE was threatening to them. In addition, we hope it has been possible to raise some questions in their minds about the official justifications of the arms race on the part of national leadership.

More difficult to understand are the reactions of people who operate from basically the same reading of reality that we do: a belief that the United States is uniquely responsible for the arms race (and that, until quite recently, it was hardly fair to call it a race at all); a belief that there is in the Soviet Union a diversity of opinion, including a strong aversion to nuclear war and the desire to avoid it (as demonstrated by a history of Soviet restraint in the face of U.S. provocation); a belief that nuclear weapons and warfare systems are illegal according to both international and national law (see the statement "The Illegality of Nuclear Weapons," by the Lawyers Committee on Nuclear Policy) and are immoral according to every religious and human definition of decency and justice. And yet these people are opposed to, and offended by, civil disobedience.

In this regard, it is refreshing and instructive to reread Henry David Thoreau's classic essay "On the Duty of Civil Disobedience" and to identify with Thoreau's bewilderment at the way basically like-minded people reacted to his resistance against slavery and U.S. imperialism in Mexico. He characterizes what is at stake as a matter of "manhood"—today we would say "what it means to be human." Sarcastically suggesting that the census count of his day was in error, he asks, "How many men [and women] are there to a square thousand miles in this country? Hardly one."

What It Means to Be Human

Let us build on Thoreau's understanding. If we drive past the GE plant in Valley Forge again and again, and know (or even suspect) the nature and significance of the activity conducted there, and then if we treat *that* space and *that* work as inviolable and protected by law, we become—each time we drive by—something less than women and men. To grant the bomb a right to exist and to respect the guise of legality and the institutions of punishment which protect its existence is to forsake our humanity.

From this perspective, what the courts and judges decide about our actions in resistance to what we believe to be a genocidal evil is irrelevant. Whatever they decide about us, there is a larger issue at stake. Our understanding of what it means to be human requires that we refuse to allow gross inhumanity to be perpetrated in our midst and in our names without announcing our opposition with our persons, nonviolently but firmly and unmistakably. This is what Thoreau called "cast[ing] your whole vote, not a strip of paper merely, but your whole influence." Here, protest is a religious and human concern, a matter of personal salvation in its best and largest sense. Thus, the legalities of the matter are beside the point.

Thoreau also states that "those who, while they disapprove of the character and measures of a government, yield it their allegiance and support are undoubtedly its most conscientious supporters, and so frequently the most serious obstacle to reform." He concludes that dissent without civil disobedience is consent. To suppose that an evil can be challenged by changing the law or by the manipulation of the political system alone is to become complicit in the assumption that the evil is legal and politically mandated.

In our case, the question would be this: While we are working politically to alter U.S. nuclear war policy, is that policy acceptable in the meantime? If our political efforts to reverse the arms race do not succeed for five years or ten or 20, will we continue to pay our taxes and keep off GE's property? If we do, we are supporting and cooperating with the bomb's guise of legality. Following Thoreau, where gross lawlessness and immorality are pretending to be legal and are protected by institutions of law, the only appropriate response is to deny the pretense by disregarding and defying the law and its institutions.

I understand Thoreau to be saying that civil disobedience is not a political strategy, the relative merits of which can be weighed in comparison to one campaign or another. He does affirm the efficacy of civil disobedience for political change, but in the face of such horrendous crimes as slavery (or, in our case, nuclear war preparations) civil disobedience is, first and foremost, a moral and human duty. To refuse to withdraw one's cooperation from a government (or corporation) engaging in such crimes and covering them with the guise of legality, and instead to try to change the government only through petitions and such, is actually to support the evil we claim to despise. We are accepting and assuming the government's (or corporation's) right to engage in such evil in our names and on our behalf.

One objection commonly raised to this sort of argument in support of civil disobedience is advanced by such persons as Abe Fortas and Sidney Hook, along with large numbers of others who, although working for disarmament, disapprove of civil disobedience. They take the position that the legal and political channels for the righting of wrongs in our society are adequate, and therefore civil disobedience is not warranted—this is, after all, a democracy. Thoreau answers this objection by contending that it is simply "not necessary that he should do something wrong" while working through due process to change it. At issue is the evil we knowingly tolerate while trying to figure out the appropriate political procedures and strategies to change it.

In the case of U.S. nuclear war policy, the above objection seems to me an extreme misreading of our situation. The U.S. is not a simple democracy, but a political system based on power held by vested interests. General Electric is one, and, though only the fourth largest Department of Defense contractor, it realizes an income of $6 million a day from the continuing escalation of the arms race. No matter what our political schemes—and some have been impressive of late—we must still decide whether or not we will cooperate with the bomb and the numerous vested interests it serves.

Accepting Personal Responsibility

Another objection holds that civil disobedience is counterproductive because it alienates people, especially when it includes such acts as blood-pourings and the damaging of weaponry hardware. It is quite true that some people do become alienated—precisely because civil disobedience moves the issue of U.S. nuclear war policy from the arena of politics to that of personal responsibility. One is challenged by the option of civil disobedience to accept personal responsibility rather than allow one's morality to be determined by legal codes and societal norms.

Those who believe we should be careful not to alienate people, it seems to me, are assuming that there is some way to effect change other than by requiring persons to make decisions and then to act on them. Perhaps people can be tricked into doing away with the

bomb if only we are nice to them, or perhaps we can sneak something past them if they are in a good mood. One of the functions of civil disobedience is to expose the choices, and then leave persons free to decide and to live or die with the consequences.

I remain puzzled as to how individuals and groups can agree that U.S. nuclear war policy is illegal and immoral and yet insist that civil disobedience is an inappropriate response. In Richard Falk's opinion, "the fundamental distress bound up in this nuclear national security state is one of idolatry." When America is regarded as totally benevolent and beyond criticism, that is the idolatry of nationalism. When force and military might, rather than justice and righteousness, are seen as the source of our security, that is the idolatry of militarism.

And when obedience to the law is placed above personal responsibility and results in compliance with evil, that is the idolatry of legalism. Perhaps the peace movement needs to listen to Thoreau when he points out that people who have "an undue respect for the law" become "the agents of injustice."

There is an old Methodist preacher's story about a millionaire who, on discovering that he was about to lose his entire fortune, became despondent. So he got into his limousine and said to his chauffeur: "James, I have decided to commit suicide. Drive the car over the nearest cliff."

"We point out that our government may not always have been honest with us about the status of the arms race."

One might add a contemporary midrash to this story: James was so used to following instructions that he was halfway to the cliff before he realized what was about to happen and suddenly awoke to the injustice of it all. At that point he took one hand off the wheel to write a letter to his congressperson. This slowed down his driving enough so that he managed to seal and stamp the letter just as the car crashed on the rocks at the base of the cliff.

It is clear, given the numbers of those arrested for engaging in civil disobedience, that more and more of us are finding ourselves unable to cooperate with a government that is drawing closer and closer to the likelihood of nuclear holocaust. We suspect that the effectiveness of the peace movement may depend not on political astuteness but on the willingness to state clearly and boldly that U.S. nuclear war preparations are immoral and illegal.

Dean Snyder is the Protestant campus minister to Drexel University in Philadelphia and a member of the Brandywine Peace Community.

"The Soviet Union...has done everything in its power to foment public opinion against all new U.S. strategic theater and tactical nuclear weapons."

viewpoint **66**

Soviets Have Infiltrated the US Peace Movement

An interview with John Barron in *Human Events*

Q. *Mr. Barron, in your explosive* Reader's Digest *article, "The KGB's Magical War for Peace," you say the KGB is concentrating on one of the largest "Active Measures" campaigns mounted since World War II. "Its objective is to secure military superiority for the Soviet Union by persuading the United States to abandon new weapons systems that both American political parties and numerous strategists judge essential to Western military security. The name of the game is 'nuclear freeze.'"*

First, what do you mean by "Active Measures"? And second, what kind of convincing proof is there that the Soviets initiated a freeze campaign or are manipulating it?

A. In Soviet or KGB jargon, the term "Active Measures" embraces a wide range of activities, all undertaken to influence public opinion and thereby the policy of government. These measures include overt propaganda; covert propaganda; the incitement or staging of mass demonstrations; the usage of what the KGB calls agents of influence, that is, people who under Soviet direction are advocating policies that benefit the Soviet Union, pretending they're doing so for some other purpose, the usage of forgeries, fabrications and even, in some instances, the commission of acts of terrorism, sabotage and, in the past, assassination.

Q. *Do they have a department specifically called that?*

A. As a matter of fact, they do. Service A of the First Chief Directorate of the KGB is responsible for conceiving and coordinating the clandestine phase of Active Measures. It's important to understand, however, that *all* of the resources of the Soviet state are concentrated and orchestrated into a campaign once it begins. Literally, everybody from Brezhnev, and now Andropov, on down plays a part if anyone can play a part. Every resource at the disposal of the state is invoked.

John Barron, "The Soviet Role in the Peace Movement," *Human Events*, December 4, 1982. Reprinted with permission.

Q. *But what kind of evidence is there that the Soviets initiated a freeze campaign?*

A. I would balk at stating that the Soviets initiated it. The idea of a nuclear freeze is an old one. It has been bandied about over the years. But there is conclusive, specific and overwhelming evidence that the Soviet Union, through its international front organizations such as the World Peace Council, the National Peace Councils (like the U.S. Peace Council), which are subsidiaries of the World Peace Council, the KGB, and through a variety of subsidiary fronts with which various Soviet instrumentalities maintain relations, has done everything in its power to foment public opinion against all new U.S. strategic theater and tactical nuclear weapons.

Beginning with the enhanced radiation warhead, going through the theater missiles in Europe and the B-1 and MX, they have certainly done all that they could do to fuel and direct the disarmament campaign in the West and the freeze in particular, which really began in the United States in the spring of 1981.

Q. *On February 23 of last year, Brezhnev called for a freeze. Are you saying that that call was somehow the catalyst for the freeze movement?*

A. I would only cite the record which anyone who wishes may examine. At the Soviet Party Congress on February 23, Brezhnev issued the first call for a nuclear freeze—a cessation of development and deployment of all new nuclear weapons. That would encompass every major weapons system the United States for years has planned to offset what our strategists perceive to be a serious imbalance in our relative strategic strengths.

The enhanced radiation warheads, i.e., the neutron bomb, the MX missile, the Trident submarine, a new manned bomber, the cruise missile, the Pershing IIs—everything would be frozen. The purpose, clearly, was to leave the Soviet Union with the new advanced weapons that *it* has emplaced but deny equivalent weapons to the U.S. and NATO. While they're calling for a freeze, incidentally, they continue to deploy these lethal new weapons, particularly the medium-range SS-20 missile against Europe.

On March 20, 1981, less than a month after his call—this official call from the Party Congress in Moscow—there convened at Georgetown University the first national strategy meeting of the nuclear freeze campaign. Perhaps that is coincidence. It is a fact, though, that until Brezhnev issued the call, nothing had really happened in the United States. There had been a great ongoing campaign in Europe, but only after the call from Brezhnev did things begin to happen here.

Now, at this meeting in Georgetown, there were a series of workshops at which each phase of the campaign that ensued was outlined, discussed and planned. I make that statement on the basis of a copy of the agenda of the program which we obtained, and furthermore upon interviews by our researchers with some of the participants who affirmed that what the agenda stated would be discussed *was* discussed. *The New Mobilizer*, a publication for the Mobilization for Survival, an umbrella organization including many of the old peace groups, suggests there were a number of other Soviets there. The record available to us, that is, the official agenda, identified only two.

"Kapralov mixed with the crowd, urging them on in their efforts to halt U.S. production of new weapons."

Q. *What exactly did the gathering call for? Did they say Congress should pass a nuclear freeze resolution, that we have to organize specific peace groups around the country?*

A. The fundamental objective was to persuade the United States to agree to a nuclear freeze.

Q. *Were they basically embracing what Brezhnev had outlined on February 23? Was that their basic proposal?*

A. Yes—a total nuclear freeze on the development and deployment of new nuclear weapons. And suddenly they discussed in marvelous detail just how they were going about promoting this freeze. And they have proceeded to do exactly what they planned to do.

Q. *Who was at the meeting, and what organizations were represented?*

A. The agenda lists a variety of organizations. The Institute for the Study of the U.S.A. and Canada, a front of the Soviet International Department which oversees Soviet Active Measures, was represented. Members of the Women's International League for Peace and Freedom, the Institute for Policy Studies, along with members of the Coalition for a New Foreign and Military Policy, Clergy and Laity Concerned and the American Friends Service Committee were among those listed as participants.

On Saturday, March 21—and I'm still referring to the official agenda—the assembled discussed how to get the freeze passed. Activists were taught about "Congressional District/Petitions Approach," "Referendum/State Legislator Approach," "How to Approach Middle America" and "Working with the Religious Community," etc. This was a seminal gathering, the one that catapulted the freeze campaign into existence.

Q. *At least two Soviet representatives you say attended. Who are they, and what role did they play in the conference?*

A. Oleg Bogdanov, an International Department specialist in Active Measures, flew in from Moscow. He has been to the United States several times and has identified himself in different ways at different times. On this occasion, he posed as a representative of the Institute for the Study of the U.S.A. and Canada, which is headed by Georgi Arbatov. I reiterate that this organization is a front of the International Department for the conduct of Active Measures. A number of its staff members, however, are regular officers of the KGB. And they collaborate with the International Department in promoting mass movements such as the nuclear freeze.

Yuri Kapralov is probably the more important and more interesting. Kaprolov is a KGB officer working out of the Washington residency of the KGB.

In examining his background, we find that he was first abroad in the late 1960s in the KGB residency in Cairo. He spoke Arabic and English well. His knowledge of Arabic and English suggests that he was probably dispatched to Cairo to work against English speaking people in Egypt. He subsequently drifted into the peace movement, acquired some superficial expertise, at least the knowledge of the jargon of disarmament, arrived in the United States in the summer of 1978 and remarkably, a short time later, was an invited speaker at the first disarmament conference at the Riverside Church in New York. This Riverside Church had that year engaged Cora Weiss as its disarmament director.

Promoting Disarmament

Q. *The same Cora Weiss connected with Women Strike for Peace and the anti-war movement?*

A. Yes. Kapralov, incidentally, has participated in a variety of "peace" and "disarmament" forums. Promoting disarmament has been his specialty; it's his field of responsibility.

What role did he and Bogdanov play at the Georgetown meeting? Well, Bogdanov was listed as a panel member on "SALT and the Soviet Response," while Kapralov talked about the Soviet disarmament position generally. Kapralov mixed with the crowd, demonstration in Lisbon—a demonstration, incidentally, urging them on in their efforts to halt U.S. production of new weapons. The correspondent for *The New Mobilizer* who had written about the gathering characterized Kapralov's statements as "very impressive."

Q. *You also mentioned in your article—on the same day that the nuclear freeze strategy conference was held—that the International Physicians for the Prevention of Nuclear War held its first annual conference. Can you describe a few things about this group? How did this fit into the whole strategy of the nuclear freeze campaign?*

A. Well, I think the coincidence is at least interesting. Brezhnev issues his call. Less than a month later we have the meeting at Georgetown beginning on March 20. Again on March 20 at Airlie House in Virginia we have a meeting of another group which was organized in part, I think, at the initiative of Brezhnev's personal physician.

However, the Soviet delegation to this physicians' conference was not headed by a physician at all but by Georgi Arbatov, a candidate member of the Politburo and head of the Institute for the Study of the U.S.A. and Canada! The Americans sent physicians who were seeking, I believe honestly, to find a way to prevent the catastrophe of nuclear war. But Arbatov is not a physician and had no medical data to contribute. But he had a lot to say, and what he did say is that deterrence doesn't work any more. He didn't explain why not.

Why doesn't it work? Have we had a nuclear war, are we about to have one? No. He also said that the United States was responsible for everything that has happened and, in fact, said that the Russians consider that the first nuclear bomb dropped on Hiroshima was aimed as much at them as at the Japanese.

Q. *You say in your article that among the most important Soviet fronts in the current "peace" campaign is the World Peace Council. How does it fit into this picture of the nuclear freeze movement?*

A. The World Peace Council is a principal international front organization of the International Department of the Central Committee of the Communist Party of the Soviet Union. It was actually organized in 1949 but first emerged in Paris in 1950 to foment ban-the-bomb propaganda at a time when the Soviets had not armed themselves with nuclear weapons. They had tested them, but they didn't have them. So the strategy was to persuade us to abandon them.

WPC was evicted from Paris—for subversive activity. They retreated to the Bloc countries, then set up shop in Austria. And they were tossed out of *there* for subversion. They went into a period of relative quiescence until 1968 when they reemerged in Helsinki, this time to promote sentiment against American involvement in Vietnam. A number of governments beyond our own have labeled the WPC as a Soviet subversive front.

The president of the WPC is Romesh Chandra, an Indian Communist, an old-time, controlled, witting

Soviet agent. He frequently appears in the company of KGB officers, *senior* KGB officers. The whole record of the WPC is one of unfailing support of any and every Soviet cause, including the invasion of Afghanistan.

Q. *They publicly supported the invasion of Afghanistan?*

A. Oh, yes. One would think that an organization genuinely interested in peace would protest, at least demurely, actions which endanger peace—the clandestine emplacement of Soviet missiles in Cuba, the murderous suppression of the Hungarian uprising, the invasion of Czechoslovakia, the suppression of the fledgling trade union movement in Poland and the invasion of Afghanistan. But no, they've not had one word of criticism, however mild, against any of these actions.

In fact, Chandra himself is almost embarrassingly slavish in his praise of all things Soviet. Then there's the question of finances. The WPC has refused to make its books public. The WPC tried to upgrade its status with the United Nations, which recognizes it as a non-governmental body, but the British, I believe, pointed out that anyone seeking this higher status has to show that they're not financed or controlled by any government, and the WPC refused.

"Chandra himself is almost embarrassingly slavish in his praise of all things Soviet."

World Peace Council

Q. *But the U.S. recognizes it anyway?*

A. Yes.

Q. *How influential is this group?*

A. The World Peace Council, its subsidiaries and their off-shoots which send people into the streets of Europe, provide the hard cadre who organize meetings, who get things done, who draw good people into the streets and create an illusion that the world is up in arms against whatever the United States is advocating at the moment. So to that extent, and particularly in the campaigns since 1977, the World Peace Council has been rather effective.

Chandra has claimed credit for influencing President Carter's decision not to produce the enhanced radiation warhead or so-called neutron bomb. And the Soviet Union is sufficiently satisfied with the services of the World Peace Council that it pours vast sums of money into its maintenance.

Q. *Does it influence American lawmakers?*

A. Whether it has influenced congressmen I can't say, but it has at least persuaded congressmen to join its representatives in meetings and to march with them.

Q. *Which ones have marched with them?*

A. Well, Rep. Gus Savage of Illinois led a WPC

which the Portuguese Socialist party and labor unions boycotted on the grounds that it was pro-Soviet.

When Romesh Chandra led a delegation to Washington and was received at the U.S. Capitol, Rep. John Conyers of Michigan said, "You have joined to give us courage and inspiration" in our fight against the neutron bomb. Now, I don't know if Rep. Conyers really derived his courage and inspiration from Chandra or from one of Chandra's escorts at this meeting, a gentleman named Radomir Bogdanov.

This man had an interesting past. He spent much of his career as a KGB officer in New Delhi when the KGB residency there was developing Chandra as one of the great Soviet agents of influence. He was a friend and protege of Gen. Boris Solomatin, who became chief of the KGB in Washington and then in New York.

Back in Moscow, Col. Bogdanov reincarnated himself as Dr. Bogdanov, a scholar, at the Institute for U.S.A. and Canada. He accompanied Chandra to this meeting at the Capitol and delivered a speech which we found out about, incidentally, only by reading back issues of *The Daily World*. The *World* characterized the speech as the most heart-rending and inspiring of all the talks there. So I don't know whether Rep. Conyers drew his inspiration from Chandra or the KGB colonel, Bogdanov.

Q. *A number of peace groups in the U.S., including WILPF, have members on the WPC.*

A. There is no question about that, and there is also no question that the U.S. Peace Council, which is headed by an American Communist, Michael Myerson, is simply an offshoot of the World Peace Council, and I don't think it pretends to be otherwise. I don't think it would take issue with that characterization.

Q. *What have been some of its most effective campaigns?*

A. The campaign against the enhanced radiation weapon, or the neutron bomb, was extremely successful. Communist spokesmen have boasted that this is one of the most significant and successful political action compaigns since World War II. They themselves claim credit for generating a public climate in which President Carter, despite recommendations of his senior security advisers, decided not to deploy, not to develop the so-called neutron bomb.

They did this by implementing the basic strategy they are continuing to follow today. One, this new weapon is supposedly "ghastly" and "barbaric." It will push mankind closer to the precipice of nuclear war. Now, that argument will not withstand dispassionate scrutiny. Nevertheless, anyone would be a fool not to be afraid of having mankind pushed to the brink of nuclear war, and so people become scared. The Active Measures campaign succeeded marvelously in grotesquely distorting the nature of this enhanced radiation warhead, which is solely a defensive weapon and has no utility as an offensive one.

Tactical Nuclear Weapons

The situation was this. We have some 7,000, maybe 9,000, tactical nuclear weapons stored in Europe. They are terribly destructive weapons, the equivalent in destructive force—or much greater in destructive force—to those dropped in Japan. If you were to use those in Europe, you would blow up many innocent people and much of the countryside we're trying to defend. They really aren't credible deterrents because the Soviets, knowing us, very much doubt that we would, for example, blow up German cities to stop Soviet tanks. It doesn't make sense.

It became feasible in the mid-1970s, however, to perfect a weapon that does relatively little physical damage. What it does do is emit neutrons which flash with the ease of light passing through a window through the thickest of armor and kill tank crews.

The Soviets or the Bloc had amassed more than 22,000 tanks, a figure that has now risen to 45,500. This was an intimidating force. It was meant not to attack but to cow, to wrest concessions from the West and to fragment the alliance which has kept peace ever since World War II. This weapon, which causes quite limited physical damage depending on the altitudes at which it is detonated, which leaves no lingering radiation, was a credible deterrent.

You could use it against mass formations of armor without killing people in cities or civilians a good distance away. Its deployment would do much to nullify the psychological threat as well as the military threat of all this great mass of Soviet armor. You wouldn't use it in a city—there would be no purpose. It was made to nullify concentrations of armor, and armor to be effective has to be concentrated.

The Soviets didn't want it built, so they say this weapon threatens the peace. If you are for this weapon, you are for war. If you're against this weapon, you're for peace. And through mass demonstrations which were not necessarily reflective of public opinion—informed public opinion—they created an illusion that the world was up in arms against this inhumane, barbaric new American weapon which they characterized as the ultimate capitalist weapon because it killed people while preserving property.

It was interesting that in the press coverage of the time, all the references were to the bomb killing people—not soldiers in tanks.

John Barron is the senior editor of Reader's Digest. *He is the author of the best-selling* KGB: The Secret Work of Soviet Secret Agents. *President Reagan has cited his work as proving that communists are involved in the nuclear freeze campaign.*

"The anti-freeze campaign. . .is to instill the fear that the freeze movement is Soviet-inspired and manipulated by agents and their dupes."

The Rumor of Infiltration Is a Smear Campaign

Frank Donner

The American past offers nothing in the way of anti-government protest comparable to the nuclear freeze movement in numbers, geographic scope, social and economic diversity, extent of organization involvement and depth of commitment.

The proposal for a mutual freeze—on the testing, production and deployment of nuclear weapons and of missiles and new aircraft designed primarily to deliver nuclear weapons, as an essential, verifiable first step toward reducing the risk of nuclear war—is supported by more than 276 city councils around the nation. In addition, 446 New England town meetings, 56 county councils, 11 state legislatures from Hawaii to New York and one chamber of 6 other state legislative bodies have voted to endorse the freeze. More than 2.3 million people from rural, semirural, suburban and urban areas have signed freeze petitions circulated by a host of organizations and coalitions—many local ad hoc committees, others national and long active in the peace movement....

It is only one measure of the depth of support for the freeze in the land that it inspired the largest demonstration in the history of the United States, the gathering of nearly a million people in New York City last June 12 on the occassion of the United Nations second special session on disarmament....

Fearmongers in High Places

It is plain that the instincts and convictions of the freeze supporters are rooted solidly in the American tradition of liberal humanism, a social vision reflecting a concern for the lives and fates of others. The critics and opponents of the freeze, however, the paladins of unlimited weaponry, are committed to the modern secular religion of a long, twilight struggle with the Soviet Union in which our ultimate victory is assured by our moral superiority. At bottom this is a conflict

Frank Donner, "But Will They Come? The Campaign to Smear the US Peace Movement," *The Nation,* November 6, 1982. *The Nation Magazine,* Nation Associates Incorporated © 1982.

between a constituency tormented by the vision of worldwide death and destruction and one for whom nuclear confrontation is worth risking to achieve the conquest of the Soviet Union and world domination.

The anti-freeze campaign relies in large part on the use of fear, the most efficient weapon in the American political arsenal. One of its goals, which the right has been pressing for years, is to instill the fear of Soviet aggression so as to gain support for nuclear confrontation and its preparations; but another, newer goal—and in these days an increasingly important one—is to instill the fear that the freeze movement is Soviet-inspired and manipulated by agents and their dupes. This is unquestionably a risky gambit, given the scope and diversity of the movement and a climate generally unreceptive to McCarthyite Red-baiting, but the Reagan Administration and its allies in Congress and along the Far Right obviously feel that the unprecedented outpouring for peace demands an all-out response.

The President himself has joined in the fray. In a speech to a veterans' group in Ohio on October 4, he said the freeze campaign, a movement "that's sweeping across the country," is "inspired by not the sincere, honest people who want peace, but by some who want the weakening of America and so are manipulating honest people and sincere people." (Subsequently rebuked for Red-baiting, he replied he "did not have any Americans in mind." This, it should be noted, repeats an earlier Administration charge that the Soviet Union controls the European peace movement.) The "dupe" formulation is designed, of course, to make Reagan's attack more credible in view of the immense size of the domestic movement, the unassailable political, professional and religious credentials of the freeze activists and the pitifully depleted ranks of the U.S. Communist Party. Because the dupe charge pays lip service to the sincerity of the duped innocents, it has become the armature for the anti-freeze movement, both

255

its "respectable" sectors and its more garish nativist counterparts.

Finding plausible links between these domestic dupes and their Soviet masters is the task assigned to the New Right. Its most prominent spokesman is Jeremiah Denton, Senator from Alabama and head of the Security and Terrorism Subcommittee of the Senate Judiciary Committee....

Publicists on the Far Right

The main movers of the anti-freeze campaign—those who feed the likes of Denton—are ideologues and publicists on the Far Right. They serve a considerable network of groups and lobbies and foundations and think tanks, and their views are expressed by any number of columnists and commentators and journals and newsletters, but to a remarkable degree the key themes pour out from a small coterie of true believers.

Chief among them is a veteran Red-hunter (and a protege of right-wing Representative Larry McDonald), John Rees. Rees, who has been the publisher of a periodical called *Information Digest* since 1968 and is the Washington correspondent for the John Birch Society's weekly, *The Review of the News,* also had a career as a spy. In the late 1960s, he and his wife—she subsequently joined McDonald's staff—penetrated the left community in Washington, D.C. Later, while disguised as a cleric, he posed as a member of a group contesting a Georgia utility company's proposed nuclear plant.

Until the mid-1970s, Rees was shunned by mainstream Red-baiters as an extremist, serving as a foil, if you will, for their "moderate" credentials. The Birch forces were the only ones to see him as "an internationally respected investigative journalist." Today, however, even the *National Review* calls his reporting on the peace movement "meticulously documented," and his authority as a reliable source is glibly assumed by publications such as *Barron's* and *Reader's Digest.*

Rees became a leader of the anti-freeze pack with the publication, accompanied by his own typically hugger-mugger annotations, of a memorandum dated February 21 to philanthropist Stewart Mott from an aide, Anne Zill. Although it was referred to by the Far Right media as a zealously guarded secret document wrested from its subversive source by skillful deception and derring-do—inserting it in the *Congressional Record,* McDonald mentioned how "Mr. Rees had uncovered this Moscow directed 'Peace' offensive strategy"—the memorandum had in fact already been distributed to at least 150 people.

The Zill memorandum was nothing more than a description of the organizational components of the peace movement, with an introduction on its transformation from a rather despairing campaign into a creative, energetic enterprise, but Rees managed to give it a heavily subversive slant. After a reference to the Women's International League for Peace and Freedom,

for example, Rees wrote: "In the U.S., the W.I.L.P.F. has been thoroughly penetrated by members of the Communist Party, U.S.A.; it has had a program for the past 20 years of exchange visits of Soviet and U.S. 'peace activists.'" Not only that, but "the W.I.L.P.F. works closely with the World Peace Council and its sister front, the Women's International Democratic Federation," and, as anyone on the right knows, "the World Peace Council is a wholly owned subsidiary of the Soviet Union."

Indeed, the W.P.C. does seem to serve as the *fons et origo* of the entire right-wing analysis. Based in Helsinki, Finland, it is said to be—by no less than Reagan himself ("Oh, those demonstrations," he said in a television interview, "these are all sponsored by a thing called the World Peace Council, which is bought and paid for by the Soviet Union")—the main channel of Soviet propaganda and the Rasputin of the European disarmament movement. The fact that the W.P.C. is recognized by the United Nations as a nongovernmental organization and has been invited to participate in official discussions on disarmament and colonialism does not seem to diminish its sinister character.

"Because the dupe charge pays lip service to the sincerity of the duped innocents, it has become the armature for the anti-freeze movement."

The American affiliate of the W.P.C. is the United States Peace Council, cast not only as the link to the domestic peace movement but as its main fomenter and guide. The Peace Council, which has chapters across the country, has some Communist Party members in its midst, but it also has members from Congress, state legislatures, city councils and legal and religious groups....

Ree's grotesque linkage of virtually all disarmament and freeze initiatives to Soviet Communism has been sanctified by articles from other true believers in more respectable rightist organs such as *The Wall Street Journal, The American Spectator, Barron's* and *Reader's Digest.* Perhaps the most influential and widely cited articles in this genre are "The Building Blocks of the Freeze Movement," a *Wall Street Journal* piece by Dorothy Rabinowitz, a contributor to *Commentary* since the late 1960s, and Rael Jean Isaac and Erich Isaac's long article in *The American Spectator,* "The counterfeit Peacemakers: Atomic Freeze." Both articles appeared on the eve of the June 12 freeze demonstration and were clearly intended to discredit the demonstrators by subversifying the rally's principal sponsors. . .

Disinformation at "Reader's Digest"

However skillful—or bizarre—the polemics of *The Journal* and *The American Spectator,* the master of the ingenious smear is *Reader's Digest.* For the last year it has been raising the specter of the Soviet nuclear menace. In June it ran an article on how radicals influence antiwar groups, which—though generously conceding that the "small minority of communists in the peace movement do not control it"—made the point that the movement's success would reduce the United States "to an isolated second-rate power." In August it published "The Russian Knife at America's Throat," an overheated warning of a massive Cuban buildup "turning this client state of the Soviets into a serious threat to U.S. security." (And this from a journal which, it will be recalled, was hailed by Susan Sontag in February of this year as more reliable source "about the realities of Communism" than *The Nation* or *New Statesman.*)

"The Digest's biggest gun to date was fired in October, in a book segment. . .by John Barron."

But the *Digest's* biggest gun to date was fired in October, in a book segment, "The KGB's Magical War for 'Peace.'" It was written by John Barron, a senior editor of the *Digest* and the author of an earlier book on the K.G.B., *KGB: The Secret Work of Soviet Secret Agents*—a work that is widely understood to have been based on material fed to Barron by former C.I.A. superspook James J. Angleton.

In an opening blurb we are warned that the "patriotic, sensible people who make up the peace movement have been penetrated, manipulated and distorted to an amazing degree by people who have but one aim—to promote Communist tyranny by weakening the United States." Barron, it assures us, documents the "secrecy, forgery, terrorism and fear" used to implement this plot. Barron does nothing of the kind. The greater portion of his article deals with alleged K.G.B. capers in Europe; when he talks about the United States, he gives us warmed-over Rees, only now all the Soviet actors are "KGB agents."

For example, he describes a conference in March 1981 at Georgetown University to plan freeze organizing strategy. The conference was reportedly attended by 275 to 300 delegates from thirty-three states and Britain, and two invited guests from the Soviet Union. One, Barron says, was a specialist in hanky-panky ("Active Measures"), the other a K.G.B. agent with a cover of Soviet Embassy counselor. "Thus, little more than two miles from the White House, the K.G.B. helped organize and inaugurate the American 'nuclear freeze' campaign. While many civic and church groups of unassailable repute were to join in advocating the 'freeze,' in terms of the strategy and organization of the drive, this little-noted conference at Georgetown was a seminal

meeting." Faulty logic aside, nowhere do we find a syllable of proof for these claims—nor an answer to the puzzle of why Russians would endanger their credibility in peace circles by deploying two spies who could be exposed by the likes of John Barron.

But that is only half the story. According to Barron, "U.S. counterintelligence identified more than 20 Soviet agents endeavoring to influence elements of the peace movement, particularly leaders in religion, labor and science. . . . The Soviets supplemented the labors of their New York and Washington residencies by sending people from the Center"—that's K.G.B. headquarters in Moscow—"into the United States on temporary assignment." Again Barron fails to provide any sources for this startling information (C.I.A.? F.B.I.? N.S.A.?), surely something we would expect from a reputable journalist writing in a magazine of huge circulation.

The Mobilization for Survival Coalition predictably comes in for attack, though Barron has nothing to add to the standard smears and distortions except to describe Terry Provance as a W.P.C. "activist" and an "energetic leader." The best Barron can do is to tell of an M.F.S. conference last December in Milwaukee where one organizer said that a coalition "makes it easier to call out more people to demonstrate" and where "in workshops, allies of the revolutionary Weather Underground lobbied for terrorism in general." This supposedly "climactic strategy session" came up with the sinister idea of forming "task forces to write letters to newspapers and importune elected officials in behalf of the nuclear freeze and against major American weapons systems."

Barron also takes a swipe at the sponsors of the freeze resolutions in Congress. After all, they knew the resolutions would not be binding, yet they went ahead and thus "significantly augment[ed] the Soviet campaign to prevent the United States from producing the weapons that would ensure a balance of strategic power." This strange, purely political, jab suggests Barron may have friends in the White House as well as in the C.I.A.

The question of Barron's provenance is not academic. Those familiar with intelligence operations in Europe have reported that Western intelligence agencies, desperate to check further defections to the peace cause from such pillars as the churches and the Social Democratic parties, have mounted a full-scale disinformation campaign there. For example, Coalition for Peace Through Security, a British group linked to the deceptively named Committee to Prevent Nuclear War (it is actually a right-wing group in Washington, D.C.), has played a key role in various "dirty tricks" attacks on the British Campaign for Nuclear Disarmament. And a skillfully forged letter on the stationery of the International Fellowship of Reconciliation, presumably the work of an intelligence agency, was sent to at least thirty European newspapers. Expressing concern over "the alarming rise of pacifism in Western Europe," the forgery went on to deplore the young people "who turn a blind eye to the Soviet nuclear buildup in Europe [and] blame the United States for the arms race and the danger of war."

Given Barron's past performances, one may wonder whether he is not part of a disinformation campaign in this country. After all, the C.I.A. did admit in June—in a statement filed in connection with the settlement of a Freedom of Information Act lawsuit—that it had been using journalists not only to gather information but also to promote and disseminate C.I.A.-inspired or-produced stories in support of U.S. foreign policy.

Frank Donner, author of The Age of Surveillance, *is a longtime specialist on the activities of the American right.*

"The Soviet-Peace Council-Freeze disinformation campaign is being launched...to divide and isolate the biggest peace movement the world has ever seen."

The US Peace Council Is Independent

Michael Myerson

For some time and in some quarters of our movement, it has been a common assumption that the World Peace Council is a "front" for the Soviet Union and its Communist Party, if not the KGB; and that ipso facto, the U.S. Peace Council is also a "front" of a foreign agent, albeit twice removed. The reasoning is that the Soviet Peace Committee, led in large part, as are all Soviet institutions, by Soviet Communists, is a firm supporter and collaborator with the WPC. Some even say it "pulls the strings."

To supplement the case against the USPC is its inclusion of U.S. Communists, moreover, *known* Communists, in its leadership. Such was the reasoning that led the Coalition for a New Foreign and Military Policy—which includes such U.S. affiliates of international bodies as Democratic Socialists of America, the National Council of Churches, War Resisters League, and Women's International League for Peace and Freedom—to deny membership to the U.S. Peace Council two years ago....

The same point has come up so often in recent months within the Freeze movement and the June 12th Coalition as to deserve some response....

It is worth noting that when the first Cold War was waged in the late 1940s, liberal forces such as the Americans for Democratic Action launched the political equivalent of preemptive first strikes. In order to avoid being accused of being communists, they became the best anti-communists. (Not that it worked, for it never does. They were accused of communism anyway.)... History may, but needn't, repeat itself, with the Left being barred from progressive organizations and coalitions in times of Cold War in order to please the Cold Warriors.

It isn't necessary in this space to make a brief for the U.S. Peace Council. Those with whom we have worked in our short three-year existence are aware of our

modest contributions and sometimes instrumental role building grassroots support for the Transfer Amendment; organizing trade union committees on economic conversion; building community support for SALT II; helping initiate the National Network in Solidarity with Nicaragua and the Committee in Solidarity with the People of El Salvador; organizing street demonstrations and helping build national conferences in support of the people of Namibia and South Africa and for sanctions against the Pretoria regime; initiating a national campaign to free Nelson Mandela; leading the demonstrations against the Chinese invasion of Vietnam; building grassroots opposition to the Cruise and Pershing II missiles and the neutron bomb; leading the peace movement in support of last year's Solidarity Day demonstration in Washington, and, for 18 months, playing a key role in the development of the June 12 demonstrations; and, sometimes almost alone within the peace movement, organizing against U.S. military adventurism in the Middle East, including U.S. collaboration with Israeli and right-wing Arab plans to dominate the peoples of the region.

Throughout, we have made a concerted effort—also often nearly alone within the peace movement—to build the Peace Council among working people, on a multiracial, multinational basis in our leadership and our base. In the course of doing so, we have discovered that there is often a correlation between redbaiting and racism. Both ideological props serve the same master in dividing people against themselves instead of uniting them in their common struggle.

Sharing Leadership

Even within the peace movement, some folks are threatened by the notion of sharing leadership, i.e. decision-making power, with (not to say, taking leadership from) Blacks and Latinos and Arab, Asian, and Native Americans. When Blacks and Puerto Ricans assume leadership in the Peace Council, they are said to

Michael Myerson, "An Open Letter to the Peace Movement," *The Daily World*, November 25, 1982.

be "used," which is a polite way of saying that they are too stupid to decide for themselves what they want and with whom. It is an endemic problem in our movement, worthy of some consideration, if we are to discover the organized force capable of defeating the military-industrial complex which holds us all hostage.

"We clearly understand that some will publicly distance themselves from a position which acknowledges the United States government as the responsible party for the arms race."

We indicated at the beginning of this letter that the Soviet-Peace Council-Freeze disinformation campaign is being launched at the same time by the same people who have undertaken the greatest arms build-up in history precisely to divide and isolate the biggest peace movement the world has ever seen.

It behooves us to understand not only from whom the red-baiting comes, but whom it serves and to what purpose. In this regard, let us come to the heart of the matter: the World Peace Council, based in Helsinki, Finland, with whom the U.S. Peace Council works, enjoys the participation on all levels of the Soviet Peace Committee (a non-governmental organization) as well as national committees in 125 other countries and virtually every national liberation movement, e.g. SWAPO, the ANC of South Africa, the PLO, the FMLN/FDR of El Salvador, etc. (Actually, it is incorrect to say that the U.S. Peace Council is *affiliated* with the WPC. In fact there is no structural relationship between the two bodies and certainly no WPC participation in U.S. Peace Council policymaking.)

What is rarely noted is that the WPC enjoys as well the participation on all levels, including in its top leadership, in addition to members and leaders of Communist parties, members and leaders of Social Democratic parties, Christian Democratic parties, Labor parties, Socialist parties, independent government parties, and members of no party at all....

It says something about the provincialism, chauvinism, and narrow-mindedness of our body politic and even our peace movement that only here in the United States is Communist participation in leadership read to be the same as "domination." If the WPC reflects any international body nearly precisely, it is the United Nations, 98% of whose views it shares, whose officials participate in every WPC meeting, and for whose non-governmental organizations section it serves as vice-president.

For most of this century, our country has careened between legal and extra-legal methods to delegitimize communism as a political force. In most industrialized countries, including those of NATO and the Common Market, Communist parties are considered quite a normal part of the political landscape....The U.S. Peace Council is one organization which rejects the characterization of Communists as sinister foreign agents and welcomes the participation of Communists alongside all others as legitimate peace activists. Obviously, this makes us part of some "international conspiracy" and even foreign agents ourselves.

Moreover it is our belief that peace cannot be won by the peace movement of our country alone, or even by the combined might of all of the peace movements in all of the NATO countries and Japan. Our peace movement, like all great social movements, harbors many ideologies, many and varied experiences, many points of view, all of which make common cause on those essential things upon which we can agree. One cannot be in the peace movement and insist on full agreement on most points....For example, there is a strong current of pacifism within our peace movement, including several organizations which are pacifist. The U.S. Peace Council works closely with many of these organizations. We have great admiration for the pacifist tradition, for their sense of moral outrage, for their militant active opposition to the arms race. Still, we are not a pacifist organization as such....

The Soviet Myth

Our struggle is too important, too precious to our survival, to be led down false paths. We have in mind particularly the only surviving ideological prop of the arms race—let it be said clearly—the myth of the Soviet threat. In our peace movement of many ideologies and points of view, one does not have to like communism or socialism or the way the Soviet system works to understand what Averill Harriman and Armand Hammer and George Kennan and other opponents of that system have known for years, which is that the Soviets want peace.

Unlike our own military establishment, the Soviets haven't a single nuclear weapon based in another country, and certainly none along our borders. The Soviets have unilaterally renounced the first use of nuclear arms and the concept of fighting a limited nuclear war, and have called such concepts criminal.

Such concepts are of course at the heart of current U.S. military policy. The U.S. is developing new forms of chemical warfare and space warfare and has begun to produce the neutron bomb. The Soviets have called for the abolition of chemical warfare, space warfare and the neutron bomb. The United States is placing up to 450,000 troops of its Rapid Deployment Force in the Persian Gulf and the Indian Ocean, within striking distance of the Soviet Union. Compare this to the outcry upon the "discovery" in 1980 of 2,500 Soviet instructors who had been in Cuba for 17 years with the agreement of the United States; or the use of unverified reports of Soviet arms to Nicaragua, which serve as the rationale for U.S. military aid to the dictatorships of Central America.

The Soviets have ratified SALT II and are ready to move to SALT III and reductions. The U.S. has not and is not. The U.S. within NATO is moving to deploy first-strike missiles in their countries five minutes striking distance from Moscow and Leningrad. Again, the Soviets have no nuclear weapons outside their borders, not to mention this hemisphere. The Soviets support the comprehensive test ban while the U.S. has broken off longstanding CTB negotiations. The Soviets call for mutual reduction of any single weapon or all weapons, while our government raises the ante on spending, foreign bases and new weapons systems. The Soviets call for making whole regions of the globe free of nuclear weapons and foreign bases while the U.S. builds new bases in every region.

When we in the U.S. Peace Council—who have a range of viewpoints regarding the Soviet political system—make the above set of observations, we are accused of arguing ''that the blame for the arms race lay wholly with the United States'' (the quote, which might have come from any of a dozen publications, is from the June 1982 *Democratic Left*) as if it is so obvious as to be axiomatic that the two major nuclear powers are equally responsible. We confess: we believe that the first country to develop atomic bombs and the only one to drop them on human beings; the first to develop hydrogen bombs, forward-based delivery systems, ICBMs, MIRVs, submarine-based missiles, etc., the only one to develop the neutron bomb; the one that has, at each point including the present, escalated the arms race; the first to develop military alliances against its adversary and the only one to surround its adversary with nuclear weapons and place nuclear weapons in the hands of its allies; the only to, as a matter of policy, prepare for and refuse to renounce a nuclear first-strike; the only one to dismiss the concept of a bilateral nuclear freeze, is indeed the one responsible for the arms race.

Of course some hold that if the USSR was really for disarmament it would disarm, unilaterally if need be, but those who so argue did not experience 22 million deaths in the last war, several million more from foreign invasions (including U.S. troops) earlier in this century, nor are they surrounded by hundreds of hostile bases with thousands of nuclear weapons owned by governments which are willing and anxious with plans in hand to use them to destroy the USSR.

We do not insist on other organizations sharing our estimates and analyses as the criterion for winning *bona fides* as a ''legitimate'' peace organization. We do insist though that ours is at least as legitimate a point of view, as honestly arrived at as any other and political conformity must not be a litmus test for ''acceptability.'' We clearly understand that some will publicly distance themselves from a position which acknowledges the United States government as *the* responsible party for the arms race, even if they know better. They feel that only by going along with anti-Sovietism can they preempt red-baiting and calling into question their patriotic credentials.

Mutual Self-Interest

A much larger number, probably the majority of our peace movement, are simply opposed to the Soviet system and let that interfere with their judgment on Soviet foreign policy. But one needn't like communism or socialism or the way the Soviet system works to understand that it is a matter of mutual self-interest and survival to halt, reduce, and eliminate nuclear arms. Disarmament and survival are the issues, not the two social systems. It is not a matter of presenting bills to one another, a peace movement form of ''linkage'': ''Before we Americans will renounce first use, you Soviets must write the ACLU credo into your constitution and stop your activities in Afghanistan.'' After all, the Soviets never demanded that the U.S. make mandatory full employment and free medical care and education as constitutional rights and implementation of UN sanctions against South Africa and Israel as prerequisites to its own unilateral renunciation of first use. Time is too short and the dangers too great to allow ourselves to be held hostage to our biases and preferences.

''One cannot be in the peace movement and insist on full agreement on most points.''

These, in sum, are the approaches our organization takes in regard to U.S.-Soviet relations, which are at the heart of the arms race. Others will of course differ. It should go without saying but perhaps does not: We are a fully autonomous organization, as much so as any other component of our peace movement. Our leadership, elected at a biannual national conference, reflects our diversity. Quite apart from the multiracial, multinational composition of our board—a majority of which is non-white, making it unique among U.S. peace organizations—we include a number of elected Democratic Party officials, Democratic Socialists, independents, members of the Citizens Party and other local independent parties, and, yes, Communists. We resent any suggestion that we are at least dupes if not agents of anyone. Moreover, those whom we represent, not only in the Peace Council, but in our communities, our unions, our legislatures, our churches, would take great offense at any such suggestion....

Finally, our experience in working with USPC members who belong to the Communist Party has shown them to be as honest, hard-working, thoughtful and dedicated to the cause of peace as anyone else....We are convinced that within a movement as diverse and varied as our peace movement, it's best to take each other on face value with a sense of mutual respect and trust and a spirit of cooperation in the task to which we are all committed—building a world free of the threat of nuclear war and of all wars.

Michael Myerson is executive secretary of the U.S. Peace Council. The viewpoint above comes from an open letter to the U.S. peace movement.

"The creation of a front allows the Communist Party to win sympathy among people who would otherwise have nothing to do with it."

The US Peace Council Is a Soviet Front

Ronald Radosh

An old problem is back. Activists in the nuclear freeze movement are faced, whether they like it or not, with the question of what attitude they should take toward Communists and Communism. They want the White House to engage in serious arms control negotiations, which is an essential goal. While working toward that goal, they are receiving overtures from American Communists who espouse unity in a common effort, but whose own private agenda is quite different.

One might have thought that the experience of decades would have settled this issue long ago—indeed, as long ago as 1924, during the third-party campaign of Senator Robert M. LaFollette. After working to support LaFollette as part of a broad coalition, the Communists received new orders from Moscow and suddenly condemned him as a Fascist. LaFollette concluded in a public letter that Communists had joined his campaign only "to disrupt it," and warned, "To pretend that the Communists can work with the progressives is deliberately to deceive the public."

After World War II, liberals faced the issue again when the remnants of the wartime Popular Front supported Henry A. Wallace's 1948 Presidential campaign. Wallace's "Gideon's Army" believed that there were "no enemies on the Left," that liberals and Communists had to work together and maintain unity against the conservative drift. Americans for Democratic Action, the American Civil Liberties Union, the New York State Liberal Party, and many other liberal groups disagreed, contending that the Communists' antidemocratic ideology and their subservience to Soviet policy were flatly incompatible with liberal goals—and that liberal organizations were not only within their rights to exclude them but had a moral obligation to do so. This did not prevent right-wing extremists from continuing to attack such organizations as Communist, but it deprived such charges of much of their force.

Today the issue has reappeared, with the Reagan Administration and its right-wing allies Red-baiting the entire nuclear freeze movement. The President himself started the attacks, proclaiming in December 1981 that antiwar demonstrations "are all sponsored by a thing called the World Peace Council, which is bought and paid for by the Soviet Union." Far-right author and researcher John Rees followed suit, stating that "the Soviet Union is running the current worldwide disarmament campaign through the K.G.B. and…the World Peace Council," and that U.S. peace activists were "up to their necks in this effort." And there were more such attacks. Of course all this is nonsense: the vast majority of those who campaigned and voted for freeze resolutions in November have never even heard of the World Peace Council.

Obscure Group

The right's tactic of using this relatively obscure group to undermine the peace movement has not worked. The American press has been sharp in exposing the paucity of the allegations, particularly in challenging the President's recent assertion that "foreign agents" instigated the freeze movement. Even a cursory look at the Nuclear Weapons Freeze Campaign shows that the U.S. Peace Council, the American branch of the World Peace Council, is not part of its elected leadership. It is not to be found on its National Committee or on the smaller executive and strategy committees. On the other hand, major organizations such as the Presbyterian Church are officially involved, and one suspects that it is this kind of popular support that really upsets the White House.

If Communists and U.S. Peace Council members are involved in working for the freeze on a local level, their participation is too minimal to have any political meaning. Yet they are trying to play a more active part. Indeed, just as the right needs to paint the freeze movement as pro-Communist, so do the Communists

Ronald Radosh, "The Peace Council and Peace," *The New Republic,* January 31, 1983. Reprinted by permission of The New Republic, © 1983 The New Republic, Inc.

need this Red-baiting to gain them attention and legitimacy. A new generation of activists naively responds to the problem with their own kind of illogic. If the attack on the peace movement through the U.S. Peace Council is McCarthyism, they reason, the rejection of the U.S. Peace Council must also be McCarthyism.

It is this attitude, newly emerging, that allows such an old-fashioned Communist front as the U.S. Peace Council to gain a following among old left peace groups such as Women's Strike for Peace and the Women's International League for Peace and Freedom. These groups were themselves incorrectly attacked by Senator Jeremiah Denton as Communist fronts. But it would be correct to describe their leaders as unfailing fellow travelers of the type that flourished in the 1940s and 1950s. The brochure of the U.S. Peace Council's national conference is adorned with ads from both the various locals and the national office of the W.I.L.P.F.

"Just as the right needs to paint the freeze movement as pro-Communist, so do the Communists need this Red-baiting to gain them attention and legitimacy."

Perhaps the best example of how the new breed of fellow travelers reacts to Soviet policy can be found in their response to the Soviet invasion of Afghanistan. It never occurred to them to react first with an outright condemnation of the invasion—to say nothing of offering their moral support to an indigenous liberation movement struggling for self-determination. They argued that the Soviet invasion was not a cause for alarm. After all, Afghanistan was already a client state of the Soviet Union, and the Afghani rebels were composed of barbarians—wife-beaters who objected to imposed progressive measures such as elimination of the bride price. You simply could not, as *Nation* correspondent Fred Halliday argued, compare the Afghan rebels to the heroic Vietnamese Communists. One group was composed of Marxist guerrillas, the other of "ultraconservative tribesmen" who need to be brought into the modern world under progressive Soviet tutelage. Thus the Soviet invasion was to be applauded, not condemned.

Red-baiting helps the Communists gain a hearing. How this works is revealed in a recent special issue of *The Nation*, in which Frank J. Donner writes that the U.S. Peace Council is simply a peace group with chapters around the country; it has "some Communist Party members in its midst, but it also has members from Congress, state legislatures, city councils and legal and religious groups." Donner makes the U.S. Peace Council sound like a broad-minded chapter of the Rotary Club. But the fact is the U.S. Peace Council was established by the American Communist Party two years ago as a

vehicle to consolidate its "peace work," and as a way to reach the newly emerging broad peace movement with pro-Soviet arguments.

"Open Letter"

In December the U.S.P.C.'s executive director, Michael Meyerson, a longtime Communist Party activist and a member of its Political Committee, issued a long "Open Letter" on "The New 'Red Scare,' " which the U.S.P.C. mailed to every major peace group. As Meyerson's letter describes the U.S.P.C., it is simply an independent group of peace activists. It has "known Communists in its leadership," but that is because it rejects anti-Communism and refuses to bar the "Left" from "progressive organizations and coalitions in times of Cold War in order to please the Cold Warriors." (Meyerson ignores the possibility that the peace movement might have its own reasons for wanting to bar Communists.) He offers another argument for Communist "participation": that Communists bring "a sometimes missing sense of organization, direction, and ideological cohesiveness." He points with pride to years of "peace activities" on the part of Communist "quintessential Americans," like William Z. Foster and Benjamin Davis, the two most hardline Stalinists ever to rise from the ashes of American Communism. Meyerson's list of Communists smoothly excludes the "peace activities" of the Party's most popular and long-standing leader, Earl Browder—who went to prison for his peace campaign during the Nazi-Soviet pact, and who was purged in 1945 for prematurely advocating the detente the Party now supports. Meyerson ends his "Open Letter" by extolling the virtues of his Party comrades: "Our experience in working with U.S.P.C. members who belong to the Communist Party has shown them to be as honest, hard working, thoughtful and dedicated to the cause of peace as anyone else."

Except, that is, when the cause of peace is espoused within the Soviet Union. I asked Meyerson what he thought of the independent peace activists who were arrested after demonstrating in Red Square on June 12. He regretted the suppression, he said, but he characterized the brave group as "not a peace movement," but a tiny band "seeking passports to emigrate to Israel." When I asked him if there had ever been a Soviet action to which the U.S.P.C. might object, Meyerson recalled Nikita Khrushchev's testing of a 58-megaton bomb in 1961, which ended a three-year moratorium on Soviet and American above-ground testing. "That probably wasn't necessary," he said with a sigh. I reminded him that at the time, Communists and their allies in the peace movement rushed to defend these tests, claiming that they were necessary to match America's strategic superiority. "They probably weren't good Communists," he retorted. "Good Communists," it seems, should have been able to see through Khrushchev's revisionism and adventurism.

Meyerson, like Reagan, claims that the U.S.P.C. has played a major role in the nuclear freeze movement, a conclusion directly at odds with the December 9 report of the House Select Committee on Intelligence. "We run it [the freeze campaign] in West Virginia," he told me. He went on to say—falsely, it turns out—that Randall Forsberg, who originally formulated the freeze idea, traveled to Moscow as part of a U.S.P.C. delegation. Forsberg told me that she went to Moscow as an individual, and then, as part of a group put together by the U.S.P.C., attended a dubious meeting with the official Soviet Peace Committee. Forsberg says she refused to sign the statement Meyerson had drawn up as a press release on the eve of the group's departure from Russia, and adds that she bluntly told him that she would not "be a propaganda tool for the Soviet Union." Forsberg stressed that she was fully aware that the Soviet Peace Committee was actually a state-run group, not a "non-governmental" body as claimed by the U.S.P.C. The U.S. Peace Council, Forsberg says, is "completely anti-American," a group whose members see nothing wrong "on the other side." They hew only to "the current line in the Soviet Union." They are simply a "pro-Soviet organization," and there are a lot of other people in the peace movement in the United States who feel the same way about them."

Forsberg's assessment of the U.S.P.C. is accurate. Meyerson's "Open Letter" invites anyone to join, as long as they understand that "the Soviets want peace." The U.S.S.R. is described as a power that takes unilateral steps toward disarmament; only the United States, in U.S.P.C. eyes, has ever "escalated the arms race." There is a lengthy attack on NATO's proposed deployment of Pershing missiles in Europe, but not a word about the actual Soviet buildup of SS-18 and SS-20 nuclear missiles targeted on Western Europe.

The U.S.P.C. stresses that "the struggle for disarmament is indivisible from the struggles for independence and self-determination," except when the struggling takes place in Afghanistan or Poland. Only in Central America and the Middle East is liberation looked for. The U.S.P.C. is certainly unique among peace groups to list as a main demand "defeat for the Camp David accord," which, it argues, was designed to neutralize Egypt so that Israel could carry out "genocide" against the Arab peoples. The U.S.P.C. is clear that it only supports "legitimate movements of national liberation," such as the P.L.O.

"Peace" in Its Title

But why a U.S. Peace Council, when the American Communists can peddle their line through their own Party? Because the creation of a front allows the Communist Party to win sympathy among people who would otherwise have nothing to do with it. Thus the brochure of the U.S.P.C.'s 1981 National Conference contains an ad from "Friends of Iowa," which appears to

be signed by virtually every peace-minded minister and church activist in that Midwestern state. The nuances of the U.S.P.C.'s positions are of little interest to these good people; it is enough for them that the organization has "peace" in its title and is a proclaimed opponent of Ronald Reagan.

The U.S.P.C. has also obtained a good share of political support from elected black leaders, including State Senator Julian Bond of Georgia, Representative John Conyers of Michigan, and Gus Newport, the mayor of Berkeley, and a co-chairman of the U.S. Peace Council. Conyers declined to discuss the issue, and Bond did not return repeated phone calls. But Mayor Newport strongly endorsed the U.S.P.C.'s positions. Only the United States, he told me, takes steps to gain superiority when in fact it "has even more [arms] than the Soviet Union." I asked him about the SS-20s, and he responded that any expressions of concern about them had to be in the context of understanding that "our foreign policy is the worst in the world." Western Europeans, he argued, felt threatened because the U.S. was "dictating that missiles be deployed on their shores." These missiles, he said, gave the Soviet Union "justification to deploy the SS-20s."

I read to Newport the wise words of E.P. Thompson, the British social historian turned peace leader. "Martial law in Poland is not only an internal matter," Thompson writes. "A defeat for freedom in Poland will be a devastating defeat also for peace." Newport sees it differently (as does Meyerson, who told me he had "great respect for Thompson, but he is wrong"). Newport said that he supports workers' movements, but added that the smashing of Solidarity was used by Reagan to distract attention from the smashing of PATCO; moreover, the "labor movement in Britain took a position against Solidarity." They had "sent people over there to investigate the situation" and they had not viewed the Polish movement favorably. Finally, Newport said that American peace groups that rejected working with the U.S.P.C. "have received a lot of money from the Rockefeller Foundation and places like that."

"The U.S. Peace Council, Forsberg says, is 'completely anti-American.'"

There have been two different responses to the efforts of the U.S.P.C. to gain entry into the peace movement. Two years ago, the influential Coalition for a New Foreign and Military Policy met to discuss the U.S.P.C.'s application for affiliation. (The groups affiliated with the coalition include the National Council of Churches, the United Hebrew Congregations, the Democratic Socialists of America, and the War Resisters League.) Admirably, after long and heated debate, its board voted 18 to 4, with four abstentions, to reject the U.S.P.C.'s request. According to the minutes of the meeting, the majority decided that it had to make clear that "the positions the Coalition takes that are critical of the U.S. government and its policies come from our own independent analysis and conclusions and are not influenced by organizations that may have associations of some sort with a foreign power." Particular concern was expressed that the U.S.P.C.'s affiliation with the World Peace Council meant that they were "completely dominated by the Soviet Union."

New York Freeze Rally

This response was not repeated, however, by the June 12 Rally Committee that put together the massive New York City freeze rally. The U.S.P.C. had one seat on its executive committee, and four other seats were held by Communists or fellow-travelers who officially represented their unions but were backed for admission by the U.S.P.C. Yet the committee refused a seat to the Democratic Socialists of America, on the ground that they are a "political grouping." The U.S.P.C. was able to get the committee—whose members were keen on unity—to tone down the official rally call so that it was not equally addressed to both the United States and the Soviet Union. In its own literature, the U.S. Peace Council described June 12 as a day in which Americans would be demanding action to "reduce *our* arsenals." (My emphasis.)

"Those in the peace movement who wish to rid its ranks of Communists are not McCarthyites."

At the executive committee meetings, Meyerson argued that the rally should include such demands as a call for an end to U.S. intervention in Central America. This was part of what he terms a "serious attempt to address the question of...U.S. interventionism, and the racist consequences of the arms race." The rally itself ended up hearing from at least one speaker who contended in his speech that "there can be no disarmament without the independence of Puerto Rico."

Obviously, some of the rally committee board members who welcomed the U.S.P.C. to their ranks did not privately agree with Meyerson. But they implicitly adopted the mushy logic that all enemies of American militarism are their friends, even if these new allies actively support Soviet militarism. Perhaps these individuals should listen to the advice of E.P. Thompson, who has related an incident that occurred at the end of a speech he gave at the Riverside Church peace conference last year. A Soviet citizen rose to speak on behalf of the World Peace Council. This man praised Thompson for his critique of NATO defense strategy, but criticized him for not defending the Soviet SS-20s.

Thompson comments:

To allow the Western peace movement to drift into collusion with the strategy of the World Peace Council—that is, in effect, to become a movement opposing NATO militarism only—is a recipe for our own containment and ultimate defeat. This will also meet with a refusal in Eastern Europe...where much public opinion is utterly jaded with official 'peace-loving' propaganda, and where state sponsored Peace Committees have never, throughout their whole thirty-year existence, fluttered an eyelash in protest against any action of Soviet militarism.

The only beneficiaries of Communist involvement in the peace movement are the two groups that would like to see a pro-Soviet peace movement in the United States: the Reagan Administration on the one hand, and the Communists and fellow-travelers on the other. Ironically, these two forces think of each other as mortal enemies; in fact, both are enemies of an effective peace movement. The desire to do something about the nuclear danger is faultless. So is the desire to protect civil liberties. But there is no good reason to collaborate with Communists, and plenty of reason not to. Those in the peace movement who wish to rid its ranks of Communists are not McCarthyites. There is a difference between Red-baiting, which must be rejected, and anti-Communism, which is a moral and political necessity. Unless the peace movement understands this, it will sink into oblivion.

Ronald Radosh is co-author with Joyce Milton of The Rosenberg File: A Search for the Truth.

"Ever since its first proposal on prohibiting nuclear weapons, the Soviet Union has insisted that nuclear disarmament should be a top-priority task."

The Soviets Initiate Peace Treaties

Novosti Press Agency Publishing House

The alarming development of events in the world today calls imperatively for urgent measures to prevent nuclear war, which would be disastrous for mankind. In view of this *the Soviet Union submitted to the 36th session of the UN General Assembly in 1981 a proposal that a Declaration on the Prevention of Nuclear Catastrophe be adopted. The adopted Declaration states that the first use of nuclear weapons would be the gravest crime against humanity.* At the same time the Declaration condemned all doctrines admitting the possibility of such use as running counter to the laws of human morality and to the lofty ideals of the United Nations.

At the Second Special Session of the UN General Assembly on Disarmament in June 1982 the Soviet Union took a step of exceptional importance by unilaterally undertaking not to be the first to use nuclear weapons. If the other nuclear powers follow the Soviet Union's example, the likelihood of nuclear war will be reduced to naught and the entire military and political situation in the world will change radically for the better.

The Soviet Union insists also on the necessity of all states pledging themselves not to use force or the threat of force in relations with one another. In connection with this the Soviet Union *advocates the conclusion of a world treaty on the non-use of force in international relations. It submitted the draft of such a treaty for consideration by the United Nations back in 1976.*

Anxious to prevent a nuclear war, the Soviet Union proposed at the 37th session of the UN General Assembly in 1982, as a first step in this direction, that all the nuclear states freeze the production and deployment of nuclear weapons and their delivery vehicles and the production of fissionable materials for building nuclear weapons of various types. . . .

Back in 1946 the Soviet Union submitted to the UN Atomic Energy Commission a draft convention prohibiting the production, use and stockpiling of atomic weapons and

Disarmament, The Main Soviet Proposals. Moscow: Novosti Press Agency Publishing House, 1983.

providing that within three months from its entry into force all atomic weapons were to be destroyed. . . .

Ever since its first proposal on prohibiting nuclear weapons the Soviet Union has insisted that nuclear disarmament should be a top-priority task.

In 1978, at the First Special Session of the UN General Assembly on Disarmament, the Soviet Union came forward with a sweeping initiative on stopping the nuclear arms race and on nuclear disarmament. It proposed that an international agreement be reached on discontinuing the manufacture of all types of nuclear weapons and on gradually reducing their stocks until they were completely eliminated. . . .

Proposing that the limitation and reduction of nuclear weapons should cover all such weapons and in the first place strategic and medium-range ones, the Soviet Union favoured an agreement that the first step in arms reduction should be a major one.

The Soviet Union attaches great importance to measures aimed at reaching agreement with the United States on limiting and reducing strategic weapons, which constitute the core of the military might of both sides.

In 1972, as a result of Soviet-American talks on the limitation of strategic armaments, two important documents were signed—the Treaty on the Limitation of Anti-Ballistic Missile Systems and the Interim Agreement on Certain Measures with Respect to the Limitation of Strategic Offensive Arms (SALT-1).

Under the terms of the Treaty, which is of unlimited duration, the Soviet Union and the United States pledge themselves not to deploy ABM systems on their territories and to limit themselves to a specific number of such systems and an agreed number of anti-missile launchers.

The Interim Agreement, concluded for a term of five years, imposed specific limitations on the number and type of intercontinental ballistic missile (ICBM) fixed launchers, submarine launched ballistic missile (SLBM) launchers and modern ballistic missile submarines.

The question of verification was resolved successfully. The parties agreed that the observance of the Treaty and the Agreement would be verified with the help of national technical means.

In 1979 the Soviet Union and the United States signed a Treaty on the Limitation of Strategic Offensive Arms (SALT-2), which establishes equal ceilings for nuclear weapon delivery vehicles and provides for a reduction of existing nuclear armaments. To lessen the danger presented by the qualitative arms race, the treaty considerably limits the modernization of strategic offensive systems and the development of new systems. The SALT-2 Treaty establishes a mutually acceptable balance of Soviet and American interests, based on the principle of equality and equal security. Full implementation of the documents signed in Vienna would create new opportunities for ending the build-up of nuclear missile arsenals and ensuring their effective limitation in both type and number. The United States, however, torpedoed the entry of the treaty into force.

"In the opinion of the USSR, for these talks to lead to agreement, firstly, they must really pursue the aid of limiting and reducing strategic arms. . . .Secondly, the sides must conduct the talks with account of their legitimate security interests."

The Soviet Union attaches great importance to the current strategic arms limitation and reduction talks with the United States. The very fact that they are being held is of undoubted positive significance. But this alone is not enough. There must be a desire on both sides to search for mutually acceptable decisions. In the opinion of the USSR, for these talks to lead to agreement, firstly, they must really pursue the aim of limiting and reducing strategic arms and not serve as a cover for continuing the arms race and disturbing the existing parity. Secondly, the sides must conduct the talks with account of their legitimate security interests and strictly in keeping with the principle of equality and equal security. Finally, everything positive that has been achieved in this sphere must be preserved. The Soviet Union has, in addition, proposed that with the beginning of the talks the numbers of strategic weapons be frozen and that their modernization be maximally limited. While the talks proceed no actions should be undertaken which would destabilize the strategic situation. Specifically, the USSR has proposed the stage-by-stage reduction of the total number of the ICBM and SLBM launchers and heavy bombers of both sides to 1,800 each, that is to say, *lowering by 25 per cent the initial ceiling on these weapons* put by the SALT-2 Treaty.

Prohibition of Nuclear Tests

It is the Soviet Union's opinion that complete and general prohibition of nuclear weapon tests is one of the pressing tasks in limiting the arms race. These tests result in improvements in nuclear weapons, in the appearance of new types of these weapons and hence in an escalation of the arms race. This process leads to the destabilization of the strategic situation, for the new weapons by virtue of their characteristics hardly lend themselves to control.

The Soviet Union was the first nuclear power to express its support for terminating nuclear tests and to include the question of prohibiting them in its disarmament programme. *Back in May 1955 it submitted to the United Nations a proposal that all states possessing nuclear weapons should undertake to halt nuclear tests.*

In 1963, on the Soviet Union's initiative, the Treaty Banning Nuclear Weapon Tests in the Atmosphere, in Outer Space and Under Water was concluded. At present 110 states are parties to the Treaty, which was the first major success in the work to curb the arms race. It limited to a certain extent the opportunities for further improving nuclear weapons.

In 1974 the USSR and the USA signed the Treaty on the Limitation of Underground Nuclear Weapon Tests, which provided for the renunciation by the sides of tests of the most powerful and dangerous types of nuclear weapons and the limitation of the number of underground nuclear weapon tests outside the scope of the prohibition to a minimum. The sides agreed on the use of national technical means of verification. Through the fault of the United States the Treaty has not yet entered into force.

In 1976 the USSR and the United States concluded the Treaty on Underground Nuclear Explosions for Peaceful Purposes, which put specific ceilings on the power of both single and multiple nuclear explosions for peaceful purposes. The observance of the provisions of the Treaty is guaranteed by national technical means of verification, the exchange of information about planned explosions, and the provision of access to the site of the explosion by the side conducting an explosion to the other side. Regrettably, the United States is being slow about carrying the Treaty into effect.

High on the agenda today is the question of the cessation of all nuclear weapon tests by all states. The draft of an appropriate treaty was worked out by the Soviet Union and submitted to the UN in 1975. The Soviet initiative was approved by the overwhelming majority of UN member states, but the Western powers and China did not support the proposal, and talks on the general and complete prohibition of nuclear weapon tests did not start then.

In 1977, on the Soviet Union's initiative, the USSR, the USA and Britain began trilateral talks to work out a treaty on the general and complete prohibition of nuclear weapon tests. In the course of the talks, for the sake of reaching accord, the Soviet Union made a number of major compromises. It declared its readiness to agree to a moratorium on nuclear explosions for peaceful purposes as well as to the prohibition of all nuclear weapon tests for a specific time. It also agreed that the future treaty should come into effect even if at first only three of the five nuclear powers signed it. The main provisions of the treaty were agreed upon, and its signing seemed to be around the corner. But because of the West's abrupt turn towards stepping up military preparations the trilateral talks stopped making progress, and at the end of 1980 they were unilaterally broken off by the Western side. . . .

Back in 1957 the Soviet Union put forward an initiative to conclude an agreement on the non-proliferation of nuclear weapons. In a memorandum on partial disarmament measures submitted to the 12th session of the UN General Assembly it proposed that the nuclear weapon states undertake not to transfer atomic and hydrogen weapons to other states and military blocs.

In 1965, taking the same approach, *the Soviet government submitted to the UN a draft Treaty on the Non-Proliferation of Nuclear Weapons.*

In 1968 Soviet-United States talks that started in the autumn of 1966 led to the signing of the Treaty on the Non-Proliferation of Nuclear Weapons, which has now been acceded to by about 120 states. By the Treaty the states possessing nuclear weapons pledged themselves not to transfer to anyone such weapons or other nuclear explosive devices, while the states not possessing nuclear weapons undertook not to produce and not to acquire such weapons and devices. With a view to verifying compliance with these obligations the non-nuclear-weapon states parties to the Treaty were to conclude with the International Atomic Energy Agency (IAEA) agreements on guarantees providing for the establishment of the latter's control over all their nuclear activities.

In response to the wishes of many non-nuclear-weapon countries and hoping to strengthen the non-proliferation regime, the Soviet Union expressed its readiness—as an act of good will—to place some of its peaceful nuclear installations—several atomic power stations and research reactors—under the IAEA control. . . .

Security of Non-Nuclear States

The further strengthening of the non-proliferation regime depends to a certain extent on what guarantees states which voluntarily renounce the production and acquisition of nuclear weapons will have that such weapons will not be used against them.

Attached to the Treaty on the Non-Proliferation of Nuclear Weapons are international documents pertaining to guarantees of the security of non-nuclear-weapon states parties to the Treaty. In June 1968 the governments of the USSR, the USA and Britain made special statements in the UN Security Council reaffirming their intention, as permanent members of the Security Council, to press for immediate actions by the Council to ensure support to a non-nuclear-weapon state party to the Treaty which became a victim of aggression or threat of aggression with the use of nuclear weapons. An appropriate resolution was adopted by the Security Council.

"The Soviet Union has. . .proposed that with the beginning of the talks the numbers of strategic weapons be frozen and that their modernization be maximally limited."

At the same time many non-nuclear-weapon states continue to urge that the nuclear powers assume an obligation not to use nuclear weapons against them. In furtherance of these legitimate wishes, *the Soviet Union stated at the First Special Session of the UN General Assembly on Disarmament in 1978 that it would never use nuclear weapons against the states which had renounced the production and acquisition of these weapons and did not have them on their territory.* The Soviet Union also declared its readiness to conclude relevant special agreements with any of the non-nuclear-weapon states, and called upon the other nuclear powers to follow suit and assume similar obligations. In the same year, at the 33rd session of the UN General Assembly, the Soviet Union proposed concluding an international convention on the strengthening of guarantees of the security of non-nuclear-weapon states. In the autumn of 1980 it proposed in the UN that, as a first step towards concluding an international convention, all nuclear-weapon states should make similar statements on the non-use of nuclear weapons against the non-nuclear-weapon states which did not have such weapons on their territory. These statements could subsequently be approved by an authoritative decision of the Security Council.

The Soviet Union holds that the establishment of nuclear-free zones in different regions of the world would contribute to strengthening the non-proliferation regime and hence to reducing the threat of nuclear war.

The question of creating nuclear-free zones has existed since the 1950s, when the Soviet Union and other socialist countries came forward with the ideas of establishing zones free from nuclear weapons in specific regions of the world. *Early in 1956 the Soviet Union submitted to the United Nations its proposal on establishing a zone of limitation and inspection of armaments, including limitation and inspection of the deployment of all types of atomic and hydrogen weapons, in Central Europe.*

In the late 1950s and early 1960s, following the example of the Soviet Union and other socialist countries, many states proposed that nuclear-free zones be created in the Balkans, the Mediterranean region, Northern

Europe, Africa, the Middle East, Latin America and other regions.

As the USSR sees it, any agreement on nuclear-free zones should ensure in reality that the territories of states in these zones become completely free from nuclear weapons, and rule out any loopholes for the violation of the non-nuclear status of the zones. . . .

In 1978, proceeding from its principled stand in favour of setting up zones free from nuclear weapons, the Soviet Union became a guarantor of the Treaty for the Prohibition of Nuclear Weapons in Latin America, so far the only international agreement on making a specific region a nuclear-free zone. . . .

As we know, in the course of the discussions in Scandinavian countries about setting up a nuclear-free zone, the idea has been expressed that the Soviet Union's consent to assume certain additional obligations with regard to the part of its territory adjoining the zone would promote the establishment of such a zone. In this connection Leonid Brezhnev noted that the guarantees that nuclear weapons would not be used against countries included in the zone were for those countries undoubtedly the principal and most important obligation that the Soviet Union was prepared to assume. But this did not preclude the possibility of considering some other measures which would apply to the part of Soviet territory in the region adjoining the nuclear-free zone in Northern Europe. The Soviet Union, Leonid Brezhnev said, was prepared to discuss this question with the countries concerned.

"High on the agenda today is the question of the cessation of all nuclear weapon tests by all states."

There is a direct link between the question of setting up nuclear-free zones and the Soviet proposal, submitted to the UN in 1978, on non-stationing nuclear weapons on the territories of states where there are no such weapons at present. . . .

The Soviet Union has invariably supported the attempts of the littoral states of the Indian Ocean to turn this region into a zone of peace where all foreign military bases would be dismantled and where no one would threaten the security, independence and sovereignty of the littoral countries.

In 1977-78 the Soviet Union had bilateral talks with the United States on limiting and subsequently cutting down on military activities in the Indian Ocean. But these talks were broken off by the US as they ran counter to the militarist policy of the United States in that region. . . .

The need to devise reliable safeguards against the appearance of new weapons of mass destruction is dictated by the fact that the arms race, which formerly involved mainly increases in number, is now tending more and more towards qualitative improvement of armaments and developing fundamentally new types of destructive weapons. With rapid scientific and technological progress, new types of weapons may appear in the foreseeable future, and their effects may not only be comparable to nuclear weapons, they may also far exceed them.

In view of the trends in and prospects for the development of new scientific and military research, *the Soviet Union came forward in 1975 with a proposal on banning the development and manufacture of new types of weapons of mass destruction and new systems of such weapons and submitted the draft of an appropriate international agreement.*

Since then the UN General Assembly and the Disarmament Committee have constantly concerned themselves with this problem. Initiatives in this have been coming from the Soviet Union, which has repeatedly submitted proposals on individual questions and in 1977 submitted a revised draft agreement taking into account the considerations and wishes of other participants in the talks. The main feature of the amended draft is that a comprehensive agreement on banning the development and manufacture of new types and systems of weapons is supplemented by a provision on the possibility of concluding separate agreements on the prohibition of specific types of such weapons.

At its 36th session in 1981 the UN General Assembly adopted, on the proposal of the USSR, an appeal to the states to make, as a first step towards concluding a comprehensive agreement, statements that they renounced the development of new types and systems of weapons of mass destruction, with a view to such statements being subsequently approved by a Security Council decision. . . .

Arms in Outer Space

The Soviet Union offers a reasonable alternative to military rivalry in outer space, that of international co-operation in its peaceful exploration and use.

A quarter of a century ago, after the launching of the world's first artificial satellite the USSR, at that time the only space power, raised the question of banning the use of outer space for all military purposes without exception.

Since then the Soviet Union has consistently advocated making outer space an area where states would peacefully co-operate. *In 1967, with the active participation of the Soviet Union, the Treaty on Principles Governing the Activities of States in the Exploration and Use of Outer Space, including the Moon and Other Celestial Bodies was concluded.* It prohibits placing in orbit nuclear and other weapons of mass destruction.

Limitation of military use of outer space was also the objective of Soviet-American talks (1978-1979), frozen by the American side, on anti-satellite systems.

In 1981 the Soviet Union made a proposal in the United

Nations on concluding an international agreement on the prohibition of the stationing of weapons of any kind in outer space and submitted the draft of an appropriate treaty.

The Soviet Union sees steps to limit and reduce armed forces and conventional armaments as intrinsically connected with nuclear disarmament measures.

In 1946 the Soviet Union was the first to raise in the UN the question of the general regulation and reduction of armaments and armed forces. In 1948 it proposed that the permanent members of the Security Council reduce, as a first step, their ground, naval and air forces by one-third within one year. In May 1955 it submitted to the UN a comprehensive plan on reducing armaments which envisaged, among other things, reducing the armed forces of the USSR, the United States and China to 1-1.5 million and those of Britain and France to 650,000 in the course of 1956.

In the mid-1950s and early 1960s the Soviet Union regularly made considerable unilateral reductions, amounting to more than 3 million men, of its armed forces.

Reduction of Military Budgets

A reduction of the military expenditures of states could be a serious brake on the arms race. The Soviet Union has always attached great importance to this question.

In 1973 the Soviet Union submitted to the 28th session of the UN General Assembly a proposal on the reduction of the military budgets of states permanent members of the UN Security Council by 10 per cent and utilization of part of the funds thus saved to provide assistance to developing countries.

Over the past few years, hoping to secure progress in solving the question of reducing military budgets, the Soviet Union has made its proposal more specific, expressing its readiness to agree to reduce the military expenditure in absolute figures, not in percentage. It was suggested that the first step should be a freeze on military budgets. . . .

Disarmament

Of special importance is the problem of limiting nuclear armaments in Europe. The Soviet Union has taken practical steps testifying to its desire to reach accord with the United States on this question. It is known to have unilaterally stopped further deployment of medium-range missiles in its European part. Moreover, it is reducing a part of these weapons. Finally, it is not additionally deploying medium-range missiles beyond the Urals, from where they could reach Western Europe.

The Soviet Union is ready to agree, in the course of the Soviet-American talks on the limitation of nuclear armaments in Europe, on the complete renunciation by both sides of all types of medium-range weapons. It is prepared to go further and agree on completely ridding Europe of both medium-range and tactical nuclear weapons. If the West is not yet prepared for radical decisions, the USSR would agree to a gradual but considerable mutual reduction of the number of medium-range nuclear weapons.

The Soviet Union is ready, among other things, to agree that it should retain in Europe only as many missiles as are kept there by Britain and France—and not a single one more.

"The Soviet Union holds that the establishment of nuclear-free zones in different regions of the world would contribute to strengthening the non-proliferation regime and hence to reducing the threat of nuclear war."

The Warsaw Treaty countries favour also a number of steps which would strengthen the political and legal foundation of the observance on the continent of the principle of the non-use of force or the threat of force. This is the aim of the socialist countries' 1976 proposal that all states signatories of the Helsinki Act undertake not to be the first to use nuclear weapons against one another. *In 1979 the Soviet Union proposed that agreement be reached on no first use of both nuclear and conventional armaments*—in other words, that something like a non-aggression pact be concluded among the participants in the European conference. In January 1983 a new major proposal was put forward at the meeting of the Warsaw Treaty Political Consultative Committee to the effect that a treaty on the mutual renunciation of the use of military force and maintenance of peaceful relations be concluded between the Warsaw Treaty member-states and the NATO countries. . . .

An outstanding initiative for peace was displayed by the Soviet Union when it submitted to the 14th session of the UN General Assembly, on September 18, 1959, its Declaration on General and Complete Disarmament. It proposed disbanding all armed forces, destroying weapons of all types, halting military production, dismantling military bases and discontinuing allocations for military purposes. Implementation of these proposals would remove the very possibility of war, for the states would be deprived of the means of waging it.

A major step forward in the development of this Soviet programme was made with the submission to the Disarmament Committee in 1962 of the draft treaty on general and complete disarmament under strict international control. This detailed draft provided for three stages of general and complete disarmament over five years.

Novosti Press Agency is the national press agency of the USSR. It voices the official ideas of the Soviet Union.

"The USSR had violated every treaty it had ever signed with exception of a treaty made with Hitler to invade Poland at the beginning of WWII."

The Soviets Violate Treaties

Cardinal Mindszenty Foundation

On March 16, 1982, Soviet Premier Leonid Brezhnev announced a "unilateral moratorium" on the stationing of medium-range missiles west of the Urals, saying it was meant to set a "good example" for the United States. This much-publicized promise of a missile "freeze" would last, said Brezhnev, until the Soviet Union and the U.S. reached an agreement on reducing such weapons in Europe or NATO gave up plans for deploying Pershing 2 and cruise missiles in Western Europe. Brezhnev, of course, never mentioned Soviet SS-20 missiles already in place, aimed at the west, which caused NATO's request for the Pershing and cruise missiles.

Brezhnev's promised "moratorium" proved to be a hoax. For more than two months following the USSR's "unilateral freeze" the Soviets moved 15 additional medium-range SS-20 missiles in place for a total of 315 SS-20s with 945 nuclear warheads, over 70 per cent of which are aimed at Europe.

But the Kremlin would never be the first to use those weapons, promised Premier Brezhnev in a speech he dispatched Ambassador Andrei Gromyko to read at the U.N. Special Disarmament session in New York. The USSR "assumes an obligation not to be the first to use nuclear weapons" Gromyko solemnly pledged. This, he said, was intended to raise the level of trust between the U.S. and Soviet nuclear powers.

For those with short memories—and the Soviets assume most Americans are so inclined—this was the same Andrei Gromyko who sat in the White House on October 18, 1962 and solemnly assured President John F. Kennedy that the Soviets had not placed offensive nuclear weapons in Communist Cuba, when Kennedy had U-2 photographs in his desk drawer showing Soviet missiles already in place around Havana.

In 1963, the U.S. and Soviets signed a nuclear test ban treaty which prohibited the placing of nuclear

"Trusting the Communists, A History of Treaty Violations." *The Mindszenty Report*, August 1982. Reprinted with permission.

weapons in space. "This treaty is an important step in the progressive development of international law" said then-Ambassador Arthur J. Goldberg. "It reduces the danger of conflict and promotes the prospects of cooperation in the newest and most unfamiliar of all realms of human activity."

Less than twelve months later the U.S. Secretary of Defense, Robert McNamara, revealed that the Soviet Union had developed and tested a system to put nuclear bombs in orbit over the United States. What about the Soviets' promise not to do so in their signing of the outer space treaty? U.S. officials eager to excuse Soviet violations haggled: the system as tested never made a complete pass around the Earth, so it was not really "in orbit" and thus did not violate the outer space treaty.

In May 1972, Brezhnev reportedly personally pledged to President Richard Nixon that the USSR would not build mobile intercontinental ballistic missiles. On November 2, 1977, the *New York Times* revealed that the Soviets had not only built these missiles but they were capable of reaching targets in the U.S. This was in clear violation of Brezhnev's solemn promise to a U.S. President, in addition to a violation of provisions in the SALT I treaty, signed by the Soviets, on fixed ICBM launchers.

On August 6, 1981, columnist William Safire reported on a conversation between Brezhnev and Gromyko, intercepted by U.S. intelligence, showing how the Soviets were already planning to cheat on SALT I by concealing a "main missile" that had never been mentioned in SALT negotiations. This turned out to be the Soviet SS-19 which came as a surprise to U.S. officials including U.S. Secretary Henry Kissinger who termed the concealment "sharp practice" on the part of the USSR.

With U.S. disarmament activists insisting on an immediate moratorium to all nuclear weapon systems research, development and deployment, the U.S. and Soviets are discussing new disarmament proposals leading to an arms reduction treaty agreeable to both sides and to the entire world. This raises a serious question: if the Soviets have cheated on previous arms agreements, can they be trusted to comply with future treaties? What, in fact, is the Soviet record on not only arms agreements but other promises made by the Kremlin over the years?

Broken Promises

In 1956, the U.S. Senate Internal Security Subcommittee published a detailed study of "Soviet Political Agreements and Results" which showed that the USSR had violated every treaty it had ever signed with exception of a treaty made with Hitler to invade Poland at the beginning of WWII.

According to this document, the Soviets broke more than 100 major treaties with other countries in a period of a little over 35 years. Since the Senate study, the USSR has gone on breaking promises and agreements, including such outrageous acts as violating the United Nations collective treaty to keep peace by invading Czechoslovakia in August 1968 and, more recently, threatening military action against Poland to suppress the free-trade-union Solidarity movement.

How have the western nations responded to repeated Soviet treaty violations? Two months after the USSR and four other Communist satellite countries invaded Czechoslovakia—in violation of not only the U.N. charter, but also the Warsaw Pact alliance and a bilateral alliance each had with the Czechs—both major candidates for president of the U.S. pledged in their campaigns to seek Senate ratification of a nuclear nonproliferation treaty with the USSR and its co-invaders of Czechoslovakia.

Here are a few examples of Soviet treaty violations from more than 100 such examples:

- **December 4, 1917**—The Soviets signed a treaty recognizing the independence of the Ukrainian Republic.
  December 24, 1918—Recognition of the Ukrainian Republic cancelled and Soviets invaded the independent Republic.

- **April 12, 1920**—USSR signed a treaty recognizing the independence of Lithuania. **August 11, 1920**—USSR signed a similar agreement recognizing the independence of Latvia.
  June 15, 1940—Soviets invaded and annexed Lithuania. **June 16, 1940**—Soviets invaded and annexed Latvia.

- **October 14, 1920**—USSR signed a treaty recognizing Finland and its boundaries.
  May 12, 1940—USSR invaded Finland and annexed large portions of Finnish territories.

- **February 4, 1945**—USSR signed the Yalta Agreement promising "free elections of governments

responsible to the will of the people" of post-WWII Europe.
August 1982—Until now, no free elections have ever been permitted in all the captive nations controlled by the USSR.

- **July 17, 1945**—USSR agreed at Potsdam that "Germany must be treated as a single economic unit (and that) freedom of speech, press, and religion shall be permitted.
  August 1982—Until now, the USSR has violated the Potsdam promise by isolating East Germany from West Germany and, in **August 1961,** permitting construction of the Berlin Wall in Soviet-controlled East Berlin.

"The Soviets broke more than 100 major treaties with other countries in a period of a little over 35 years."

- **June 26, 1945**—USSR, in signing the U.N. charter agreed to abide by such articles as Article 25 which stated that all member nations agreed "to accept and carry out the decisions of the Security Council."
  June 25, 1950—The U.N. Security Council called on all member states to "render every assistance to the United Nations in the execution of this resolution (to defend South Korea) and to refrain from giving assistance to the North Korean authorities."
  July 27, 1953—To this date, when an armistice was signed, the USSR gave no assistance to the U.N. in Korea, and every assistance possible to the North Korean Communists. The Korean armistice forbade "the introduction into Korea of reinforcing aircraft, weapons and ammunition" and called for inspection by the Neutral Nations Commission. The USSR introduced advanced-type aircraft and weapons to North Korea and refused inspection by the Neutral Nations Commission.

- **March 31, 1958**—USSR Supreme Soviet promised to abolish further testing of nuclear weapons if all other countries would do likewise. The U.S. discontinued nuclear testing.
  September 1 through October 30, 1961—USSR conducted more than 50 nuclear weapons tests, including tests of weapons 2½ times more powerful than any ever tested by the U.S.

- **July 23, 1962**—USSR signed Geneva treaty "guaranteeing peace, freedom and neutrality of Laos."
  April 1963—Soviet-supplied Communist forces gain control of half of Laos. **June 18-26, 1969**—60 Russian-made PT-76 tanks are used in an effort to

take over all of Laos.

- **SALT decade (1969-79)**—U.S. (among other actions during strategic arms treaty negotiations on SALT I and II) froze ICBM forces and SLBM forces, scrapped over 250 B-52 bombers, deactivated anti-ballistic missile system, canceled B-1 bomber production. Soviets in the same period spent over $100 billion more than the U.S. on strategic offensive forces and weapons.

History of Subversion

The Soviet history of broken promises and treaties with the U.S. goes back to 1933 when, in exchange for recognition of the new Soviet government, the USSR promised not to engage in subversion in the U.S.

"It will be a fixed policy," the Soviets agreed, "to refrain, and to restrain all persons in government service and all organizations of the Government of under its direct or indirect control, including the organizations in receipt of any financial assistance from it, from any act overt or covert liable in any way whatsoever to injure the tranquility, prosperity, order, or security of the whole or any part of the United States, its territories or possessions, and—in particular—from any act tending to incite or encourage armed intervention, or any agitation or propaganda having as an aim, the violation of the territorial integrity of the United States, its territories or possessions, or the bringing about by force of a change in the political or social order of the whole or any part of the United States, its territories or possessions."

In addition, the Soviets promised not to permit "residence on its territory of any organizations or group. . .which has as an aim. . .the preparation for the overthrow of, or the bringing about by force of a change in, the political or social order. . .of the United States." The Soviets signed this agreement on November 16, 1933, when the U.S. established official U.S. recognition of the Russian Bolshevist government.

"In Communist ethics, it is not wrong to break a treaty. A good Communist has the affirmative duty to do so, if by so doing he benefits the Communist cause."

One month later, in December 1933, the Soviets violated this agreement by sponsoring a conference of evolving world Communist parties at which it was resolved to work toward overthrowing the governments of capitalist countries by force, propaganda and agitation. From the day the USSR and the U.S. signed the treaty recognizing Communist Russia, the Soviets have systematically violated their "non-subversion" promise by—among other things—conducting espionage through their trade missions, agitating and propagandizing against U.S. domestic and foreign policy through the

subservient U.S. Community Party, and using the Soviet Embassy as a base for spying and collecting secret intelligence information.

Treaties as Weapons

Can we ever trust the leaders of the Soviet Union to honor a treaty? Not unless it serves their immediate or long-range goals—and then subject to cheating at the same time. How the Soviets—and all Communists—interpret the meaning of treaties was explained best, perhaps, in Laurence W. Beilenson's book, "The Treaty Trap" (Public Affairs Press), now out-of-print but considered the definitive word on the history of the performance of political treaties. Here is how Beilenson compares the Communist and non-Communist difference:

"While Christian ethics have had small influence on the performance of treaties by western nations, the fact that Christian rulers have been taught from boyhood that it is wrong to break a promise has exercised some restraint. In the western democracies, there is another restraint on the political leader because of his concern for the political fortunes of his party and himself. In the open society of the United States, when the President breaks a treaty, he will be criticized, and his party will lose votes because of the criticism. In the Soviet Union, that restraint is missing. Since the rulers control the press and other media, the criticism will neither be read or heard. Moreover, in Communist ethics, it is not wrong to break a treaty. A good Communist has the affirmative duty to do so, if by doing so he benefits the Communist cause. This is inherent in the ethics of Leninism."

Where a western leader might have thoughts about the immorality of breaking a treaty, Beilenson points out, Lenin excused the good Communist from such concerns by redefining morality and ethics:

"But is there such a thing as Communist ethics?" Lenin asked in a 1920 speech. "Of course, there is. . . .In what sense do we repudiate ethics and morality? In the sense that they were preached by the bourgeoisie, who declared that ethics were God's commandments. We. . .do not believe in God. . . .We say that our morality is entirely subordinated to the interests of the class struggle of the proletariat. . . .We say: Morality is that which serves to destroy the old exploiting society and to unite all the toilers around the proletariat, which is creating a new Communist society. . . .For the Communist, morality consists entirely of compact united discipline and conscious mass struggle against the exploiters."

The teachings of Lenin have never been forsworn by any Communist leader who followed him, Beilenson notes, so Lenin's blueprint for Communist action is still the ultimate word today and guides the rulers of the Soviet empire.

The Communist theory that treaties are made to be broken was spelled out by Lenin in 1918 in a secret meeting of the Bolshevik Party Congress. Beilenson explains that Lenin and his chief aides were discussing Soviet signing of the treaty of Brest-Litovsk in which the USSR promised not to agitate against Germany following WWI:

"Bukharin and the Left Communists had charged that the Soviet government had hampered its efforts to promote a German revolution by its promise not to agitate in the Treaty of Brest-Litovsk. In urging ratification of the treaty, Lenin answered: 'Yes, of course, we are violating the treaty; we have violated it thirty or forty times. . . .'"Lenin went on to say that it didn't matter, only that care should be taken that the Soviets were not caught very soon violating this particular treaty.

Treaties are weapons as far as the Communists are concerned. "A diplomat's words *must* contradict his deeds—otherwise, what sort of a diplomat is he?" asked Stalin. "Words are one thing—deeds something entirely different. Fine words are a mask to cover shady deeds. A sincere diplomat is like dry water or wooden iron."

"It is ridiculous not to know the history of war, not to know that a treaty is the means of gaining strength," said Lenin ("Reply to Debate on War and Peace" [1919] *Selected Works,* International Publishers, Vol. VII, p. 309), ". . .the history of war shows as clear as can be that the signing of a treaty after defeat is a means of gaining strength. . . ."

SALT Violations

There has been a tendency of American negotiators to look the other way and excuse the Soviets in violating treaties, and even more so in complying with such arms control agreements and treaties as the Limited Test Ban Treaty, the Threshold Test Ban Treaty, the Biological Warfare Convention and SALT I and SALT II. Of the latter, while the U.S. Senate failed to ratify, President Reagan has promised to comply with SALT II provisions as long as the Soviets do likewise. The Soviets, on the other hand, say they are not bound to comply until the U.S. ratifies SALT II, giving them all the benefits and none of the obligations of the treaty.

Evidence has now been gathered in a startling new study published by the Texas Policy Institute (6250 Westpark, Suite 110, Houston, TX 77057, $3 per copy) that the Soviets have consistently violated arms reduction treaties and other agreements on disarmament. Entitled "The Bitter Fruit of SALT: A Record of Soviet Duplicity," its author, David S. Sullivan—Harvard University cum laude, former CIA official—is considered one of the most knowledgeable experts on Soviet violations of SALT.

Sullivan documents 14 examples of Soviet negotiating deceptions in SALT I and II and 30 cases of other arms control treaty violations, including the practice of camouflaging all Soviet strategic forces which deliberately interfere with so-called "U.S. technical means" of verifying any Kremlin cheating on arms agreements. These "U.S. technical means"—satellites, surveillance spacecraft and such—supposedly make sure that the Soviets are complying with the "nuclear freeze" being proposed by U.S. and other disarmament activists.

Anyone who reads Sullivan's study carefully will realize that to the Communists arms control is a weapon of political conflict. In his words: "If arms control is ever to be able to contribute to U.S. national security interests, a wholly new beginning must be made and completely rethought, new theories and principles developed. Arms control thinking must accept the reality that the Soviets have entirely different and hostile objectives in negotiations which so far have been fundamentally incompatible with those of the U.S. The Soviets have disdain and contempt for those Americans who believe arms control is a cooperative process."

"'A diplomat's words must *contradict his deeds—otherwise, what sort of a diplomat is he?' asked Stalin."*

U.S. and world security would be far better served by an acceleration of unilateral U.S. strategic program designed to restore U.S.-Soviet strategic military parity, Sullivan concludes. "The world was far safer during the Cold War years of U.S. strategic superiority, before the U.S. invented SALT to its own disadvantage."

These are words that must be impressed on the minds of U.S. negotiators looking for some breakthrough to reverse the arms race as a move towards world peace—peace that comes not from man but, as Pope John Paul reminds us—from God.

The Cardinal Mindszenty Foundation conducts educational and research activities concerning communist objectives, tactics and propaganda. The Foundation sponsors study groups, speakers clubs, conferences and films.

"Children should learn to live in harmony with themselves and their peers so they will enter the adult world with the sense that reconciliation, instead of war, is the road to peace."

Peace Begins in the Classroom

Gordon Oliver

Following the explosion in 1945 of the world's first nuclear bomb at a New Mexico test site, Albert Einstein made a remark that was to become famous. The bomb, he said, "has changed everything save our modes of thinking, and we drift toward unparalleled catastrophes."

His words are truer today than 37 years ago. The ultimate nuclear disaster seems to loom ever closer, while we remain paralyzed and incapable of finding peaceful ways to solve the problems that haunt us as a community of nations. We continue to enhance our differences more than our similarities, and to rely for security more on weapons than on mutual trust and respect.

So, how do we change our "modes of thinking"? In parochial and public school classrooms across the nation, teachers are searching for ways to begin that essential process. Their approaches have been refreshingly varied, but they are almost always based on the same fundamental concept: that children should learn to live in harmony with themselves and their peers so they will enter the adult world with the sense that reconciliation, instead of war, is the road to peace.

The idea that schools should teach children how to get along is hardly new. Teachers have always admonished students against fighting and arguing and reprimanded those who did resort to violence. What has changed, though, is that teachers involved in the development of peace education programs now make a link between peace among peers and peace in the world.

That idea imbues teachers with a new sense of urgency about not only ending youthful disputes but also developing new ways for students to resolve conflicts without resorting to force. For older students, the issue of conflict resolution on the school grounds can lead to discussions of world conflict resolution and the complexities of international war and peace issues, as part of a peace education curriculum.

Peace education for older students in most cases also means controversial issues of nuclear weapons policy and the justification for nuclear war are discussed directly. These discussions might include such topics as the use of civil disobedience tactics in protest of nuclear weapons.

Balanced Presentation

This does not mean, however, that peace education is synonymous with a pacifist or even arms reduction viewpoint. The emphasis in most peace education programs is on a balanced presentation of viewpoints so students are able to make their own decisions. In a typical discussion in Seattle on national defense, for instance, students are likely to hear about the concept of "peace through strength" that is promoted by the current administration, alongside a discussion of the notion of unilateral disarmament advocated by Archbishop Raymond Hunthausen.

In part because Hunthausen has helped elevate the conflict in defense policy viewpoints to the front pages, Seattle and western Washington offer a good representative sample of current thoughts and strategies in peace education. The region has an intense interest in nuclear weapons issues because of its abundant military installations and the dominant presence of the Boeing Corporation, a major military supplier. In the Seattle area some powerful and respected peace organizations have developed, bolstered by Protestant and Catholic leaders who refuse to allow the moral issue of nuclear weapons policy to be ignored.

But even against that strong background of public interest, peace education is only beginning to take root to a significant degree this school year. Seattle's Immaculate High School, an inner-city Catholic school, ran a highly praised program until the institution was forced to close 18 months ago because of funding problems.

The closure was a critical factor in Hunthausen's decision to fund a three-year position of peace and justice coordinator for secondary schools. The archbishop further fueled the peace education movement last fall

Gordon Oliver, "Teaching Peace to Our Children," *National Catholic Reporter*, December 24, 1982. Reprinted by permission of the National Catholic Reporter, PO Box 281, Kansas City, MO 64141.

277

when he delivered a speech at a diocesan educators' conference which one teacher recalled as "a mandate for peace education."

In local elementary school districts, momentum for peace education could emerge from the recent "Target Seattle" symposium on nuclear weapons. As part of the 10-day series of speeches and activities, Target Seattle offered workshops for educators on how to discuss nuclear war or teach about it through direct or indirect means.

The workshops and a subsequent volunteer effort to initiate a conflict resolution program in city schools has been endorsed by the Seattle school board and the local teachers union, and the Seattle school district has provided space in an elementary school for a volunteer-run resource center on peace education material.

"Teachers...now make a link between peace among peers and peace in the world."

Educators invariably mention the Immaculate High School program as the Seattle area's model for peace education. Holy Names Sister Mary Lila Gary, a former religion instructor at Immaculate, recalled that the peace education program there was successful "largely because it was a goal of the whole school. An atmosphere of peace is very important," she said.

Such an atmosphere could be achieved because the structure of the peace education program was clear to all faculty members, she said. "If an issue such as the Nestle boycott came up, it could be discussed in religion or social studies classes and not be considered unusual," she said.

The program encompassed a multitude of cultural awareness and peace education topics, discussed in classrooms and in special school assemblies and activities. And one-quarter of the school year was devoted to discussion of the peace education topics in the religion curriculum, she said. The school also had its own conflict resolution committee that was "very effective" in handling student conflicts, she said.

Gradual Integration

Now at Eastside High School in the Seattle suburb of Bellevue, Gary is working with others to develop a different approach to peace education that fits into that school's program. Peace education concepts are being integrated into the curriculum gradually as the community and faculty understand and accept the concepts of peace education, and the program establishes credibility, she said.

The Eastside peace education program, housed mainly in the religion department curriculum, is centered on an annual peace education day which covers four different topics in a four-year cycle. The topics—hunger awareness, multicultural awareness, peaceful alternatives to violence and global interdependence—serve as

springboards for discussion and activities for a period of weeks, Gary said. The peace education concept in the school is also flexible enough to allow for discussion and activities related to current topics—for instance, students were given "extra credit" if they attended parts of the Target Seattle symposium, Gary said.

Another school that receives heavy praise for its program in peace and justice is the Jesuit-operated Bellarmine Preparatory School in Tacoma. The school's program is based heavily on social justice activities, and its extensive community service program has been chosen as one of five in the nation—and the only Catholic school—to serve as a model "service learning program" for the federal volunteer agency VISTA.

The school's community service director, Joan Fleet, said more than 200 students enrolled last year in elective community service classes. They worked for 28 agencies, more than half of them nonprofit. According to Fleet's statistics on the program's impact, the students averaged five hours a week of volunteer work for a total of 13,465 volunteer hours, at a savings to agencies of $47,117 in personnel costs based on minimum wage salaries.

The program advances students' understanding of peace by teaching them about justice, Fleet contended. "They've heard all the theories. They know all about religion and faith. This gives them a chance to use it," she said. But programs involved in political change in peace-related areas are not listed among agencies students may serve under the community service program, she said. Instead, a student who expresses interest in a political issue—Fleet uses world hunger as an example—is urged to adapt that issue to a service-oriented activity, such as working at a local soup kitchen.

"Don't tell me what's wrong. I want to do something that will make it better," Fleet said. "I made peace signs in the '60s and we still have wars." Fleet said controversial issues such as Hunthausen's disarmament stand are open for classroom discussion but the other side of such issues also is presented to students.

At the diocesan level Dr. Anthony Gnanarajah recently has assumed the position of coordinator of peace and justice education for secondary schools. Gnanarajah is encouraging educators in the diocese's nine secondary schools to develop an "integrated approach" to peace education that introduces the concept in such unlikely places as the math and physical education departments. Math teachers, for instance, should begin using examples of world resource distribution or world poverty as samples in math equations instead of the traditional apples and oranges, Gnanarajah said.

"Generally these concepts have been taught in religion and social studies classes," he said. "That's not enough. I'm advocating shared responsibility. After all, we are one ministry of Christ." Gnanarajah is giving in-service workshops and promoting peace education in various forums in the community, but schools will not receive an edict from the diocese to integrate the concepts into their curriculums, he said. Of further assistance to educators will be a diocesan peace and justice center, now being developed through the Catholic Charities office, which will provide literature and ideas to schools, noted the center's new director Kathleen Smith.

A much different situation exists in local public schools, whose peace education activists look with envy at the state of development of the concepts by their Catholic school counterparts. Many public schools teachers received their first introduction to peace education through the Target Seattle workshops. Along with knowledgeable presentations by other teachers, workshop participants received impressive packets of background material on nuclear war and on discussing the issue with children.

When Viewpoints Clash

In the sessions for secondary school teachers, emphasis was placed on direct discussion of the issues of nuclear war tied with game-playing where students learn how conflict develops and can lead to war when viewpoints clash.

Ron Timmons, a member of the Seattle chapter of Educators for Social Responsibility, said the nuclear war peril is not only the fault of the government, but also the fault of public schools for failing to provide students with the concepts of peace.

Issues of peace and justice remain the same, obviously, for elementary students as for secondary students, but the approaches to teaching those issues differ vastly. Recent studies indicate that young children suffer from increasing anxiety because of their heightened awareness that a nuclear bomb could end their world, and teachers in Seattle frequently mentioned that growing anxiety. One of the recent Target Seattle speakers, child psychiatrist Dr. John Dunne, urged parents not to expose children to the grisly details of nuclear war's impact at too young an age. Six- and seven-year-olds can be "shaken up" by improperly handled discussions, and even 10- to 12-year-olds have trouble with the subject because in their pre-puberty stage their emotions are already close to the surface, Dunne said.

Indirect methods of handling the topic were encouraged. Songs about peace, for instance, help children to imagine what the world would look like if we learned to get along, said Marcia Berman, a visiting singer from Los Angeles. And games—the traditional tool of elementary teachers—can be fashioned in ways that encourage cooperation and nonviolence.

An elementary teacher in Portland, Patricia Fellers, began working on peace education issues six years ago and has become one of the most popular speakers in the Northwest for education conferences. Fellers stumbled into the field with grant money from the U.S. Bicentennial in 1976; that led to a magazine on peace education and finally a complete curriculum guide. The guide now is being revised and improved, she said, and interest is burgeoning: "It's an idea whose time has

definitely come."

Fellers has outlined a five-point definition of peace education that includes: creation of a positive self-image; building of a spirit of community; an awareness of world problems; a recognition of global plurality and independence, and action. She also has developed a conflict resolution strategy, currently in use in Holy Redeemer School where she teaches sixth grade students. That strategy also includes five steps: students state the problem; teacher restates the problem; students and teacher decide on a course of action; they suggest what can be done to avoid a repeat situation, and they seek reconciliation—a handshake.

Fellers' program also includes discussion of death and dying, so students learn not to fear death or to reduce their fear. And she adds a "world pledge of allegiance," written by students, to the morning ritual after the U.S. pledge of allegiance.

Before she began peace education under that name, Fellers recalled, she had students play a classroom game called "apartment" which has remained a profound lesson in peace and war for her ever since.

Students each had their own designated "apartment" marked by tape on the floor, and the first two days were idyllic harmony in the imaginary community. The joyous life was once disrupted by the turmoil of the outside world, when an announcement came over the classroom loudspeaker asking prayers for students in a school that had been bombed in fighting in the Middle East during the 1967 six-day war.

"Peace education concepts are being integrated into the curriculum gradually."

By the game's third day, however, the harmony broke down. Students began to break rules that had been created by unstated consensus, and doors were posted with warnings of fines for anyone who entered the "apartment" without knocking. Benches that had been used for sitting in the park became barricades and the community deteriorated quickly into a "totally armed camp," she said. Fellers said she called off the game and asked the students to consider what had happened.

"Then a little voice said 'We almost had a war. We're just as bad as the Arabs and Israelis,' " she said. "Then they really understood for the first time what that war was all about."

Fellers and other Catholic school teachers say a simple point in peace education is to give the students some home in the midst of increasing terror of war and depression among young people, and to assure them of God's love for them.

"We need to show them that there's hope and that there are things we can do," she said. "As Christians, we need to tell them that no matter what happens, God will take care of you. At the same time, they should know that we are stewards and we have a responsibility to try to change things."

Gordon Oliver is a freelance writer.

"Its objective is poisonous: to brainwash American public school students through misinformation...on the need for peace at any cost."

viewpoint **73**

The Peace Curriculum Brainwashes Students

Charlotte Iserbyt

Would not our violence-wracked planet rejoice if the Soviet Union's Ministry of Education developed a peace-oriented conventional and nuclear disarmament program for Soviet Schools, a program that through psychological teaching techniques would undo the anti-American bias instilled in Communist youth over the years?

Believe it or not, the U.S. Department of Education has, knowingly or unknowingly, allowed just this to happen in American schools, vis-a-vis American students' attitudes toward war, peace and the Soviet Union.

On Dec. 5, 1980, a few weeks prior to President Reagan's inauguration, the Department of Education approved a program for use in the nation's schools entitled "Facing History and Ourselves." Approval means that the program can be listed as "exemplary" in the Department of Education's National Diffusion Network catalog entitled "Educational Programs That Work," which local schools use to assist them in selecting programs.

"Facing History and Ourselves" deals with the history of 20th Century genocide, human behavior and the issue of nuclear war from the liberal-left viewpoint. And a spinoff program entitled "Decision-Making in a Nuclear Age"—not federally funded but developed by the same person who had gained valuable experience developing "Facing History and Ourselves," at taxpayers' expense—is an extremely popular curriculum (in use in 250 schools across the country) recommended by Educators for Social Responsibility and other left-wing disarmament groups opposed to the Reagan Administration's national security policies. (Educators for Social Responsibility lists the U.S. Peace Council, an arm of the Soviet-controlled World Peace Council, as a resource organization for nuclear disarmament curriculum materials.)

Charlotte Iserbyt, "Education Department Pushing Disarmament Programs," *Human Events*, May 21, 1983. Reprinted with permission.

Yes, this spinoff program does fit the title of the NDN catalog. It is, unfortunately, a program "that works." Its objective is poisonous: to brainwash American public school students through misinformation, scare tactics and psychological techniques on the need for peace at any cost through disarmament and a nuclear freeze.

As a former Department of Education employee and the person who recommended in December 1981, to no avail, that "Facing History and Ourselves" be removed from the NDN catalog, I continue to wonder what more evidence the White House needs to convice it that all is not well in the Department of Education.

Evidence presented to the White House by loyal Reaganauts (most of whom have either been fired or have resigned) has been ignored, and the Department continues merrily on its bureaucratic way, becoming bigger and more powerful every day.

No Place for Brainwashing

I am opposed to federal support for curriculum development, be it under a Reagan or Carter administration. There is no place for federal support of right or left-wing ideological brainwashing in America's public schools. This problem of curriculum development is the prime reason the Department should be abolished, and not replaced by a foundation or anything else.

Secretary Terrel Bell will defend federal support by saying curriculum is developed by local schools, etc. That is true. However, in order for curriculum to be listed in the NDN catalog it has to be approved by federal bureaucrats who hold a certain political philosophy.

Recently I attended a conference, sponsored by the Maine chapter of Educators for Social Responsibility, in Augusta, Maine, which was billed as "Teaching Decision-Making in the Nuclear Age" (title lifted from the NDN spinoff program).

The objective of the conference was to train teachers in the implementation of nuclear/disarmament/peace education programs, including the above-mentioned

"Decision-Making in a Nuclear Age" curriculum, in Maine schools.

Maine's Commissioner of Education, Harold Raynolds, unabashedly and against the better advice of Maine citizens and some officials in his own Department, accepted the invitation to be the keynote speaker. Not only did he make pro-freeze comments and support the teaching of disarmament curriculum, he also lashed out at President Reagan for his recent comments at the meeting of Evangelicals and in his recent TV broadcast to the American people on the state of U.S. defenses.

Disarmament Activists

I spent eight unforgettable hours attending workshops which included frightening films, propaganda regarding interdependence, and instruction on psychological strategies to bring about attitudinal change in students (future voters), so they can go out into their communities as pro-freeze disarmament activists.

Although the media did their usual hatchet job on the President's excellent speech, most adult Americans undoubtedly understood the importance of his message. In this connection, however, a warning is in order.

The White House has for too long ignored the importance of elementary and secondary education, as it relates to the political attitudes of future voters.

Does the White House think that the implementation in America's public schools of left-wing political programs such as "Facing History and Ourselves" and its spinoff curriculum, "Decision-Making in a Nuclear Age" is unimportant? The White House had better start concentrating on issues other than those dealing with tuition tax credits and prayer in the schools, important as some may feel they are.

It should check into what the National Diffusion Network, whose strength has been significantly increased during the Reagan Administration, recommends to local schools as "exemplary."

It should question Secretary Bell on the educators' definitions of such terms as core curriculum, excellence, dissemination, evaluation, basic skills, decision-making, higher order critical thinking skills, character education, international/global education, gifted and talented education, community education, and computer-assisted-instruction. If the White House is a conservative White House, it will be shocked to learn that these programs are not at all what their innocent-sounding titles imply.

Best Interests of Children

The White House has allowed the situation at the Department of Education to deteriorate so drastically that major surgery is required. For the umpteenth time (a plea from all of your most ardent supporters): please replace Secretary Bell with someone who shares the conservative philosophy that helped get you elected, and who is dedicated to serving the *best* interests of our children in a free society, not the *special* interests of the bureaucrats who feed at the trough of bigger and bigger

budgets for federal, state and local education programs.

I am tired of having to publicly defend President Reagan every time he is attacked by members of the educational establishment. When is the President going to come to the defense of those who continue, through thick and thin, to defend him and his policies?

When is the President going to override the recommendations of his White House advisers (who have revealed that they know absolutely nothing about education) and accept the advice of his most ardent supporters, including many teachers, who are well informed on this important subject?

I am still awaiting a reply to a letter I wrote last July to the President which went into great detail regarding the situation in the Department of Education. I know that the President read my letter, made notes in the margins, and requested Ed Meese to take action on it.

Why, after nine months, two follow-up letters to Mr. Meese, neither of which was answered, and finally a special totally useless trip to Washington to inquire about the status of my letter, have I had no reply? Why, indeed?

"The White House has for too long ignored the importance of elementary and secondary education, as it relates to the political attitudes of future voters."

The White House should take note of the most recent edition of *Education Week* (one of the leading educators' journals), in which the following quote is found:

"He who Laughs…more confident and relaxed Secretary of Education has been making appearances at hearings and meetings around the country recently. Terrel H. Bell, who has frequently exhibited a troubled, harried countenance as he defended the Reagan Administration's education plans, is said by associates to have emerged triumphant from the Administration's latest internal budget deliberations. He is benefiting, they say, from the new 'moderate' stance on education issues taken by the Administration."

I do not recall the President promising his supporters in 1980 "a moderate stance on education issues." What he promised was a conservative stance and a drastic step: to abolish the Department of Education; and what he led us to believe was that there was *no* role for the federal government in education. That's right, Secretary Bell. I said, "no federal role."

Charlotte Iserbyt served on the Reagan transition team in 1980 and then as special assistant to the assistant secretary of the Office of Educational Research and Improvement at the Department of Education.

"There is no strength in weakness, but there is strength in a clearly voluntary renunciation of power."

viewpoint **74**

Eliminate Aggression to Achieve Peace

Roland H. Bainton

I take as a point of departure a remark of my grandson. He said to me, "Grandpa, the difference between me and you is that when you were my age you thought you might live to grow up. I am not so sure that I will."

That a sense of doom should pervade a whole culture is nothing new. The early Christians thought the world was about to end. At the close of the Renaissance, Erasmus said, "This is the worst century since that of Christ. I see no hope but for the coming of the Lord Jesus."

Today, for other reasons, there is profound doubt as to whether our civilization can survive the end of the century. It is partly due to the success of our technology. Success usually introduces new problems, which then have to be confronted. Obviously, there has occurred a diminution of the world's resources by reason of an increase in population. We are caught up in an energy crisis. It is not insoluble, because we still have the sun, the winds, the tides, and the heat inside the earth. But we will have to bend our efforts toward utilization of these energy sources in a world where there are more people who live longer. We are simply in a tighter situation now than ever before.

But the greatest threat to survival lies in our improved capacity to destroy ourselves. There have been three major crises in the history of the Western world. The first was the period of the Emperor Augustus and the birth of Christ. Rome had conquered the then known world, and enslaved the people. Slavery was never more extensive or worse than it was in the age of Augustus. The roads were clear, but the gods were dying, and the old agricultural morality was declining. Out of that ferment arose Christianity, which had formative influence on the development of Western civilization. In

Roland H. Bainton, "Taking a Risk for Peace," *The Center Magazine, No. 408.* Reprinted with permission.

the second major crisis, the Christian hegemony cracked during the period of the Reformation, and wars of religion ensued. Yet out of that period came a new dynamism. Today we face a third major crisis because of our ability, never before possessed, to make the globe uninhabitable and largely to exterminate the human race. Our great fear is war.

Yet we are in a quandry. Nobody wants war but we are not sure how to avoid it. The old answer has been that if you want peace, prepare for war. *Si vis pacem, para bellum.* One must be so strong that no one will dare attack. Ideally, that tactic produces the balance of power, where each of a group of powers is powerful enough to resist an attack from another. It has worked in part for brief periods of time in history. During the course of their existence, the Greek city-states adjudicated about ninety disputes by arbitration. Nevertheless, they so fought each other that they were overrun, first by Macedon, then by Rome. The Renaissance period in Italy also provides an example. The Italian city states of Venice, Milan, Florence, Naples, and Rome had reduced war to something of a summer sport. Their purpose was not to kill but to capture as many as possible, and then count the chips and settle down for the winter. That reduced war to a degree, but there persisted enough fighting to weaken Italy, allowing the French to invade and sweep her into the vortex of European politics.

The eighteenth century saw, for a period, political equipoise among England, Spain, France, Italy, and the German states. War was somewhat more humane, partly because better financed. Armies were paid and did not have to ravage the countryside. The leaders of mercenary troops did not want to lose their men, so they spent whole summers maneuvering around to see which one would get tired first. If the armies did run into each other, the commanders would exchange invitations to fight until someone fired a salvo and the battle began.

283

Balance of Power

But the outcome was the French Revolution and Napoleon. The balance of power did not work for long. It never has, and it never can, because each party to the balance of power is trying to sway it in its own direction. If one gets more powerful than the rest, a coalition of the weaker states will form to overpower it. The balance is always in turmoil, always shifting. During the Second World War, I heard a political scientist in this country say, "We should never beat Japan too badly; we'll need her against China. We should never beat Germany too badly; we'll need her against Russia. Never make friends, only allies." The art of diplomacy continues to be the art of deception. All are striving to do each other in, and if somebody touches the wrong button, there may be a conflagration.

Some say that in place of the balance of power we have a new version, the balance of terror. They argue that the terror is so awesome that it is restrictive. No power wants to turn loose the weapons we possess because we know how devastating the results will be. Ex-military men claim that war is obsolete as a way of settling international disputes. No side can gain a victory. Universal devastation is the result. In the face of this danger, some say that we should merely be prepared to use weapons of such force so we will not be attacked. But we would not actually use them.

"Our greatest threat to survival lies in our improved capacity to destroy ourselves."

That means bluffing, and a bluff is likely to be called. Again, the wrong button may be pushed, setting things off. It is also extremely doubtful, if tension becomes acute, that any weapon one has will not be used. The British admiral, Lord Fisher, in the First World War, said that trying to limit armaments is like trying to fight with one arm behind your back: when the fighting gets tough, that arm comes out damned quick. If we have destructive force and we are pushed, we will almost certainly make use of it.

But suppose it is never used? In that case, the armaments pile up, waiting "to be used if," and armaments are unproductive production. We start with one pile. It is superseded by a better pile, and a better pile, and a better pile. The outmoded parts may be sold off to the other countries of the world, thereby increasing the danger.

If we don't destroy ourselves by warfare, we may all end in universal bankruptcy. That, in its turn, may bring the appeal to the strong man, the Hitler or the Mussolini or the Stalin. Or it may result in a universal communism where government takes over in an attempt to regulate all of these matters. But we may just simply bring ourselves to a thorough-going impoverishment by getting ready to "defend ourselves if."

It makes no sense. The time has come when the idealistic objections to war and the pragmatic considerations coincide. As a pacificist, I would say war is wrong. And as a liberal, I would say it is foolish. The pragmatic and the idealistic perspectives at last join in opposing the arms race.

What, then, is to be done about it? In the political sphere, nothing would be more effective than a little by little renunciation of power—the very opposite of building strength for protection. There is no strength in weakness, but there is strength in a clearly voluntary renunciation of power. If any nation would dare to take the risk of cutting back its arsenal, of possessing a little less than the other side, it might have an enormous result and bring the other side to follow suit. Of course, it is a risk. But we are confronted with risks in all directions. At least it is a risk in the interest of peace.

The great enemy of our time is distrust. We are all conspiring with one another against each other. We are all deceiving one another. We are afraid of the Russians, and not without reason, because of their attempts to entrench themselves in the Persian Gulf, in Africa, and in Cuba. They equally distrust us because of our treatment of Chile and Guatemala and Nicaragua, our military base in the Caribbean, and our economic measures against Cuba. We are all playing the same game and all distrusting one another. If only one would take the idealistic risk of trust, it might turn out to be utterly pragmatic.

Then there is the question of public opinion about disarmament. I speak here partly as a churchman, for I am concerned about the role of the church, but I speak also as a citizen, a member of society. There are, I think, three possible responses to the nuclear arms debate. One is to pull out. Remove yourself from the whole dirty mess. Set up a little community which lives harmoniously within itself, like the Quakers, the Amana colony, or the Shakers. Pursue an ideal life, supported by agriculture and by handicrafts for your own consumption. The current Bruderhof movements in our society are movements of withdrawal. They are modern parallels to monasticism, which is also experiencing revival in this country. The idea is to wash one's hands of the question and to live in a reasonable and harmonious fashion, in the hope that maybe it will have some influence on our society. But it has never had a great influence. Medieval monasticism worked for the monks, but it did not have much effect on the society as a whole.

Another option is the way of domination, the theocracy. The papacy in the thirteenth century came close to being the arbiter of Europe. Savonarola tried it in Florence. Calvin in a measure tried it in Geneva, and there have been other Calvinist regimes. None lasted long. One can hardly impose an idea upon an entire population. So, while withdrawal does not affect the whole, theocracy invites resistance and it collapses.

All that remains is to be in but not of the world; to participate, and yet to do so within certain moral limits. That creates a division within an idealistic body, be it a church or a liberal group, or whatever you please. It exposes the difference between the prince and the prophet. The prince is the prime minister, the king, the president—the one who is responsible as executive for an entire population. Such a person, if he is an idealist, can never realize his entire program. One king of Poland said, " I am the king of sheep and goats, and if I paid no attention to the goats, they would butt me out." That does not mean that an idealistic prince must go against his conscience. He had better resign when he reaches that point. But he will never be able to put over what he regards as a completely idealistic program.

"The balance of power did not work for long. It never has, and it never can."

The prophet, on the other hand, is in a position to advocate the unadulterated ideal. He may be a journalist, he may be a writer, he may be in any walk of life. He may be a candidate for the Presidency, with no chance of being elected, who uses the process an an opportunity to educate the public.

Collaboration

The prince and the prophet can collaborate. There is an example in the case of the abolition of slavery in England, where the executive was William Pitt and the prophet was William Wilberforce. They were close friends, though they had some friction because Wilberforce wanted Pitt to make antislavery the main issue at every session of Parliament. Pitt knew that if he tried he would be ousted, and unable to put across other liberal legislation. But Wilberforce, a member of Parliament with no executive responsibility, hammered on that one issue. He had an assistant who continually collected data about how slaves were captured, transported, and sold in the slave trade. He kept bringing that evidence in, session after session, and hammering it home. After thirty years, Parliament agreed to abolish the slave trade—but only the trade. The British dominions could still buy slaves from the Spaniards or the French. So, the agitation kept on for another twenty years. On the day before Wilberforce died, Parliament voted one million pounds sterling to indemnify the slaveholders and emancipate all the slaves in the British dominions. Eight hundred thousand were emancipated. The prophet and the prince had collaberated, and symbolically, Pitt and Wilberforce were buried in Westminster Abbey, side by side.

The distressing element in the story is that it took fifty years. We do not have that much time. Our only hope is that we may have more prophets who will succeed in influencing public opinion to the point where the executive can do that which is both right and sensible.

Ultimately, the question of disarmament and the peace of the world rests on how one understands the purpose of human life. Though the point will never be universally recognized, I ask myself the same question I heard posed by a churchman from East Germany recently. He asked, "Is security the chief end of mankind? Would it not be better to be wiped out than to survive by becoming more brutal than the beasts?"

Roland Bainton is professor of ecclesiastical history at Yale University. He is the author of more than thirty books, including the biography of Martin Luther, Here I Stand.

"As long as there are humans, there will be conflicts; but...conflicts can be resolved in non-violent ways."

Mediate to Solve International Conflict

Milton C. Mapes, Jr.

Imagine a world at peace. No more war, no more revolutions, no more terrorism, no more sending our sons and grandsons off to slaughter one another. Imagine a world in which the threat of nuclear annihilation no longer exists. Imagine what a world this could be.

An impossible dream? Not any longer. Not now. Because for the first time in history, we have within our grasp an alternative means of resolving human conflict— an alternative to force and violence....

Over 35 years ago humanity gained the power to destroy itself. The power to preserve itself has not come as easily. But today, thanks to an emerging discipline called ''conflict resolution''—a new way to deal with human conflict—we have that power. Scientists are developing and applying effective methods for resolving conflict without resort to violence.

Conflict resolution is being recognized as a new field of study that integrates knowledge drawn from many other disciplines. It has teachable principles of analysis and proved techniques of its own.

In other words, it is now feasible to organize peace learning and conflict resolution into an academic program, which is why a national peace academy has suddenly become a very practical and possible goal.

Fine, but does conflict resolution really work? Is it really practical—or is it still in the ''theory'' stage? Let me tell you about a few instances when it was put to the test—and passed. No doubt you heard the news stories at the time, but you may not have been aware of the role conflict resolution played.

> During the Hanafi Muslim takeover in Washington, experts in conflict resolution got involved early and probably saved the lives of fifty hostages.
> At Wounded Knee, expert intervention prevented the already violent FBI-Indian confrontation from escalating into another Indian war.

Milton C. Mapes, Jr., direct mail letter by National Peace Academy Campaign, 110 Maryland Ave. NE, Washington, DC 20002.

> Over three dozen prison-riot situations in the past two years were defused by professionals of the Community Relations Service using conflict resolution techniques (sadly, no such experts were involved at Attica).
> In 1965, the intervention of one mediator achieved a near-miracle of peace-making in the Dominican Republic after President Johnson's action there.

Most labor disputes are settled by means of conflict resolution techniques. And these arts and skills achieved at Camp David what traditional diplomacy could not—a peace treaty between Israel and Egypt.

Conflict resolution assumes that as long as there are humans, there will be conflicts; but that conflicts can be resolved in non-violent ways. I can imagine no plan for peace better attuned to the realities of the world.

Sadly, one of these realities is that when nations prepare for war, war is what they usually get. If we want a peaceful world, shouldn't we prepare for peace?

Peace-Loving Nation

We are, we say, a peace-loving nation. What we want most for the world, for our children and grandchildren, is peace. We already have four national academies devoted to maintaining peace through military capability and skill. Wouldn't it make sense also to have at least one national academy devoted to research and training in non-military approaches to peace making—to the development of the affirmative arts and skills of peace?

Suppose the United States Academy of Peace were to be established. What exactly would it do?

It would commit the world's most powerful nation to a long-term search for the means and methods of peace, without in any degree weakening our military capabilities. Can you picture any single act that would do more to excite hope in the hearts of the world's billions, or do more for America's image—and for our pride in our own country?

Congress is considering historic legislation that would make the Academy a reality—but its passage is far from certain. Sen. Matsunaga of Hawaii (one of 53 co-sponsors of the Senate bill) explained the mission of the Academy:

"The Academy would perform research on its own and fund research at other institutions...it would provide graduate and postgraduate educational programs...and continuing education services such as seminars and workshops for individuals and organizations in both public and private sectors and it would publish the results of its research."

Ideally, a large portion—perhaps up to 25%—of the long-term students would come from foreign countries (several of which have expressed interest in starting their own peace academies.)

The Peace Academy would select top-notch people from all walks of life, give them the finest training possible in the techniques of peacemaking, then send them back into society, here and abroad.

They would move on to positions in government, private organizations, foreign service, armed forces, corporations, labor unions, and international organizations.

Peacemaking Experts

Ultimately there will be worldwide a reserve of experts in peacemaking who will work for creative alternatives to violence—and who will be available to cool off trouble spots before they reach the explosive point.

As centuries-old conflicts go unresolved in our world... as terrorism remains an active threat...as nuclear weapons become more and more available—the work of the Peace Academy may be crucial to the survival of us all. Sen. Randolph of West Virginia put it this way:

"We do not have the luxury of waiting. We must realize that...continuing wars of greater devastation will be, in a sense, a part of our collective failure if we fail now to pass this legislation. Through men and women trained and educated at the Academy, we can do at least part of the job of stopping untold human misery, untold suffering, and an untold loss of life on this earth...."

Would it be worth the cost? We must keep in mind that preparing for and engaging in conflicts is terribly costly to society. The Peace Academy could contribute to bringing these enormous costs down, and therefore must be regarded as one of the most cost-effective proposals ever put before Congress.

As Congressman Dan Glickman has noted, "Peace is good business and good government finance."

Congress originally liked the concept well enough to create a Commission to hold hearings and study the idea. The Commission's conclusions: the Peace Academy would be timely, necessary and cost-effective, *more* than just a "visible symbol of the nation's constant and historic purpose of promoting peace among nations." It based its findings on the realization that "peace requires knowledge, judgement, and skill no less complex than that which is required for war."

Milton Mapes is executive director of the National Peace Academy campaign.

Influence Public Policy Through Citizen Dissent

Raymond Lucker

I want to bring up an issue which is creating great interest today, namely dissent from public policy and civil disobedience.

All of us know and accept the principle that any citizen in a democracy may disagree with an existing law and seek to have it changed. Our Christian sense may recognize that an existing policy is unfair or that it could be improved. It is our duty as citizens and as Christians to work for the passage of just laws.

So we are concerned about and work to change our laws affecting equitable taxation, human rights, abortion, land use, environmental pollution, prayer in the public schools, tax support for children attending parochial schools, and a host of other issues that touch our lives and beliefs.

We use peaceful and non-violent means to get our ideas before the public and before our elected representatives. We write articles and letters, give speeches, participate in discussions, debates and conventions. We see that on most issues there can be legitimate differences of opinion. We work for consensus and compromise.

Now suppose a law or public policy is such that I cannot in conscience accept it. There are some issues on which, as a Catholic, as a follower of Jesus Christ, I cannot compromise.

The policy of this country on abortion is wrong. We do not have to accept or participate in that policy. Suppose the Diocese of New Ulm owned a hospital. If government regulations or law said that we would have to allow abortions in that hospital since it was the only hospital in the area, we would have to disobey. It might mean that the hospital would have to be closed. I would go to jail rather than be forced to participate in or cooperate with an abortion.

Raymond Lucker, "Tax Resisters Have Right to Avoid Madness," *The Catholic Bulletin*, April 7, 1983. Reprinted with author's permission.

There have been many instances in history where Catholics and other Christians disobeyed a law rather than violate their conscience. They used non-violent means and were willing to pay the consequences. Frequently their witness was what got an unjust law or sinful public policy changed.

Early Christians were put to death rather than worship the Roman emperor as divine. They disobeyed civil law rather than their conscience. When the empire disintegrated Christians were ready to bring a new life into Europe.

St. Thomas More, chancellor of England, would not support his king, Henry VIII, when he declared himself head of the Church of England.

Many Polish people today engage in countless acts of non-violent protest against a ruthless communist government.

Disobeying Unjust Laws

Dr. Martin Luther King and his followers disobeyed unjust laws, refusing to ride in the back of the bus, refusing to accept segregation in education, housing and public facilities. They went to jail. Some were beaten and killed. Through their non-violent protest they brought about changes in a grave social evil.

Members of the Witnesses of Jehovah believe that saluting the flag is a violation of the First Commandment. They were beaten and jailed for refusing to obey a law requiring school children to salute the flag. Ultimately their position was upheld by the U.S. Supreme Court.

Hundreds of thousands of Americans are working to change the interpretation of the Constitution which allows abortions taking life away from the unborn. We have a right to dissent. We must dissent. The issue is not going to go away.

Another issue which is not going to go away is the escalating arms race and the use of nuclear weapons in defense of our country.

The church has consistently taught that acts of war deliberately directed against innocent non-combatants are gravely wrong. No one may participate in such an act. Thus a soldier would have to disobey orders if commanded to shoot civilians. No one could participate in obliteration bombing of cities. Here dissent would lead to disobedience, disobedience of human law in favor of obeying God's law.

One can be a good Catholic and be a conscientious objector. That is, one has a right to object to all war and also the right to object to a particular war. This right is acknowledged by our government and protected by law, even though the government may demand some form of alternative community service.

"One can be a good Catholic and be a conscientious objector."

There are some who refuse to pay their taxes on the grounds that their tax money is used for weapons and for war preparation. They are disobeying the law. They are ready to pay the consequences. I do not personally hold that position. But they do have the right to hold it. I thank them for their witness.

I believe that the arms race is evil and that among other things is diverting valuable resources from the poor and from human services.

I believe that using nuclear weapons against civilian populations or threatening to so use them is evil. I believe that the very possession of nuclear weapons as long as we are making no sustained commitment to achieve multilateral disarmament, is evil.

I do not want to contribute to this madness. What I do is take such a small salary that I no longer pay income tax. I make sure that my annual salary each year is no more than $3,600. This is no special hardship; my needs are few. I have no family to support. I am free to contribute to the poor.

Each of us in our own way must respond to the Lord's call. This is one way for me.

Raymond Lucker is a bishop of the Roman Catholic Church.

290

"Exactly what human values...what national interests, are worth defending with weapons of genocidal destruction?"

Recognize Nuclear War as Suicide

James Avery Joyce

Human rights have recently been extended far beyond their earlier connotation as duties "owed" to individuals by a national government or, at least, by the community. Such rights are normally enforceable if and when they are violated by authority or by other individuals. In short, a human right is a legally enforceable claim.

International lawyers, however, are now debating whether there exists a so-called "third generation" of human rights. This idea was recently introduced by Karel Vasak, former director of the Institute of Human Rights at Strasbourg. Arguing that "human rights" is a constantly developing concept, Vasak cites civil and political rights as the first generation in this development; economic, social and cultural rights as the second; and now a third generation under the generic heading of "rights to solidarity." Within this category he includes the right to development, to environment, to the ownership of the common heritage of humankind (i.e., the ocean floor), the right to communication and to peace.

But other human rights specialists, such as A. H. Robertson, formerly director of human rights for the Council of Europe, have argued that the "rights to solidarity" should not be characterized as human rights at all. Robertson advances two reasons for this position: human rights apply to the individual, whereas the rights to solidarity are collective; and human rights can be secured by law, but this is not the case with the new rights.

Another participant in this debate is Carl Aage Norgaard of the University of Arhus, a Danish member of the European Commission of Human Rights. In an unpublished statement, Dr. Norgaard sums up the present situation in a very interesting way:

"It is generally agreed that the concept of "Human Rights" is a developing one. This has often been stressed by the

James Avery Joyce, "Is There a Right to Peace?" Copyright 1983 Christian Century Foundation. Reprinted by permission from the February 24, 1982 issue of *The Christian Century*.

European Commission and Court of Human Rights when applying the rules of the European Convention regarding civil and political rights. This involves that new aspects of life, new situations or conflicts, which were not and could not be foreseen when the Convention was drafted, should be included in the existing articles of the Convention by interpretation, which means that the rules will be clarified and developed. This is, however, a usual legal process known by all judicial organs applying the law.

Norgaard concludes that

in spite of the fact that the traditional concept of Human Rights has certain clear characteristics, it could be argued that the concept ought to be generally expanded to include the "new rights" in question, because they are as important and fundamental as the traditional Human Rights, and the need for promotion and understanding of these rights is of an overwhelming importance for mankind."

New Rights

But Robert Pelloux, professor emeritus of the University of Lyons, takes a more pessimistic view, arguing that the "new" rights are not "true" rights. He warns that by adding them to the well-publicized list of "fundamental rights and freedoms" which was accepted as public world law in the Universal Declaration of 1948 and its subsequent Conventions, we risk diluting the "true" rights and place them at the mercy of changing policy decisions.

As this debate proceeds, some specialists in human rights law have suggested that it might be useful to rethink the whole process of innovation that the United Nations system constantly presents to us. In the light of the vast economic and technological changes that the UN has already contributed to the global system of what Vasak calls "solidarity," it is now possible to classify the basic human standards into three broad categories: rights (individual), needs (collective) and uses (world law).

Each of these categories has its own potential legal order; e.g., the 1948 Declaration and subsequent Covenants; the New International Economic Order (NIEO) and various General Assembly resolutions on the rights and duties of states; and the Law of the Sea Convention, covering, among other things, "the right of peaceful passage through international straits." Although they overlap and are all termed "rights," the international institutions and processes for implementing them require that they receive separate consideration on their own merits. That examination cannot be pursued further here; but, if such a division of rights is valid, then the right to peace is obviously a collective, albeit unenforceable, right within the category of human needs. Could there be a greater human need today than peace?

The collective right to peace demands such a basic approach—in fact and law—that we can no longer afford to regard it merely as a sentimental concept or to confine it to an intellectual category of human rights. After all, the moral and legal rule established by the UN is itself a "peace" system. This global order is founded on the opening principles set out in the 1945 Charter:

> To reaffirm faith in fundamental human rights, in the dignity and worth of the human person, in the equal rights of men and women and of nations large and small, and...
> To promote social progress and better standards of life in larger freedom,

AND FOR THESE ENDS

> To practice tolerance and live together in peace with one another as good neighbors....

But since at least 1949, when NATO was created, there has existed a parallel system based on entirely different standards. This is a militant regime operating on a set of principles which, to be frank, represents the institutionalization of violence. It is, in short, the war system. Thus, growing up side by side within our lifetime, there are two rival orders, each claiming the loyalty and dedication of humankind. The UN world order is based on human rights and the toleration of national, ideological, cultural and social differences. The rival "defense" alliances seek to eliminate those very differences by using military techniques based on modern weaponry.

This might seem to be a far too sophisticated way of looking at today's global confrontations. But these are the facts of our time, even though they are often simplified in captions like East/West, North/South, rich/poor. These conflicts are well publicized in the news media of all countries and are reasonably understood by most people. Yet the basic war/peace confrontation has been given so little attention that its position within the international law of human rights has hardly been grasped by the general public or even by political leaders.

The moral and legal implications of this dilemma are too startling to be faced openly in national policies. This is why we ignore or repress them and talk instead about deterrence. But we fail to realize that nuclear deterrence is a freak doctrine that has put an end to what was once called national defense. Consequently, political leaders and military men continue to advocate these new weapons of mass destruction without regard to their

incompatibility with the international law of human rights, let alone the norms of civilized life on this planet. Worse still, until recently these weapons have been accepted by public opinion as legitimate and essential means of defense. From time to time, however, individuals like Nobel Peace Prize laureate and unaligned UN spokesman Sean MacBride have condemned the use of nuclear and other weapons of mass destruction as an "international crime." Yet little study has been done to define the nature of the crime or to identify criminal responsibility within the terms of the Genocide Convention.

Human Rights

In light of the human rights standards—rights that have received almost unanimous acceptance from the UN member states—it is becoming obvious to the average person that planning a nuclear war against a neighboring country is a horrendous crime against all humanity. The question is one I posed in my book *The War Machine:* "Exactly what human values,...what national interests, are worth defending with weapons of genocidal destruction? Where are human rights, when millions of human beings are reduced to mathematical coefficients on nuclear targets?"

"Until recently these weapons have been accepted by public opinion as legitimate and essential means of defense."

This protest of conscience is not mere rhetoric. The daily speeches and writings of admirals and generals and defense ministers overlook one essential thing: the Convention on the Prevention and Punishment of Genocide is still world law. It is specific and was intended to be specific. It had its birth in the Nuremburg principles by which the criminals of World War II were judged and condemned. But the Convention has also become a net for catching the criminals who plan a *third* world war. Its language is precise. I need only cite part of Articles II and III (my italics):

Article II: In the present Convention, genocide means any of the acts, committed *with intent to destroy,* in whole or in part, a national, ethnic, racial or religious group, *as such:*
   (a) Killing members of the group;
   (b) Causing serious bodily or mental harm to members of the group....
Article III: The following acts shall be punishable:
   (a) Genocide;
   (b) Conspiracy to commit genocide;
   (c) Direct and public incitement to commit genocide;
   (d) Attempt to commit genocide;
   (e) Complicity in genocide.

There are no reciprocity clauses in the Convention, nor are there theories of self-defense or immunity embedded in it. The crime is absolute and definable. Nuclear weapons as means of mass destruction, it could be argued, might plausibly be neutral *in themselves.* But when they are used, or intended to be used, to destroy a "national group," they become the crime of genocide. The two most vital terms in the Convention—which is now international law, even for countries that have not yet ratified it—are the phrases "with intent to destroy" and "as such." What happens if we have the "intent to destroy" the Soviet Union as a national group "as such"? The crime of genocide, a term which as been bantered about for 30 years, has suddenly become recognized as an act of national policy that is condemned by the common will of humankind.

"We fail to realize that nuclear deterrence is a freak doctrine that has put an end to what was once called national defense."

But there has recently arisen a corollary of this situation. The unilateral repudiation of using nuclear weapons against the Russians or any other national group is a valid political policy sustained by moral law and upheld by international law as well. In other words, the Genocide Convention has given the campaigns for unilateral and absolute disarmament a basis in both public morality and human rights law. The fast-growing peace movements in Britain, the Netherlands, Germany, Scandinavia and elsewhere have assumed a legal sanction in human rights law.

This is, as I say, a new legal situation which neither politicians nor average citizens fully understand. The right to peace becomes more challenging as nuclear weapons become more immoral and more savage. It is not surprising that growing numbers of perceptive people are realizing this and voicing their opposition. Kenneth Greet, president of the British Methodist Conference, has addressed the Methodist community and call support for nuclear weapons a sin. The Netherlands Inter-Church Council, Pax Christi and numerous other religious movements are totally opposed to nuclear weapons and repudiate their use by their own governments, irrespective of what other governments do. But where are the lawyers' organizations in this great crusade?

The next stage in our pilgrimage is not only to exorcise the mortal sin of nuclear genocide, but to promote the nascent right to peace both as a human right and as a moral imperative to ensure humanity's survival.

Dr. Joyce, a British attorney and economist, is a consultant to the Human Rights Division of the United Nations in Geneva, Switzerland.

Form a Think Tank for Peace

Claes Nobel, interviewed by James Bolen

NEW REALITIES: How did you, a member of the world-renowned Nobel family, come to settle in the United States?

NOBEL: I came here in 1959 to acquire business training, and for various reasons decided to stay. Although I am still a Swedish citizen, I now live in Milwaukee, where I first settled.

It wasn't too long after I arrived in this country that I discovered it was far more conducive to my business lifestyle and goals, as well as my other interests. These other interests eventually manifested as the Earth Aid Society, a non-profit foundation I started in 1974 because of my concern for the rapid deterioration of the environment. The first years of Earth Aid Society, then, were focused on environmental, ecological, and population issues.

NEW REALITIES: That has now changed, hasn't it?

NOBEL: Yes. But only in the sense of priorities. I still feel very strongly about the environment, whether it is the pollution of the oceans, the atmosphere, or our rivers, not to mention the very soil in which we grow our food.

In the last few years, however, a much more immediate and urgent issue has taken precedent over everything else for me, one that affects every living creature on this planet, and time is running out....

NEW REALITIES: And that is....

NOBEL: Nuclear war. We each have our own personal resources—time, a little extra money, energy, friends, supporters—and I assessed mine and realized that I had to make a choice. I knew I could not be truly effective with more than one issue, though both tugged at me so strongly.

But the more I thought about the possibility of a nuclear war—no matter how remote it seemed or might be for others—the larger it loomed in my mind that our

James Bolen, interview with Claes Nobel, *New Realities*, March 1982, © 1982, New Realities.

planet, despite already being gradually destroyed by pollution and misuse of its resources, was already on fire with the insanity of huge nuclear arsenals and continuing proliferation. By this I mean we are storing up nuclear weapons, and distributing them, all over the earth at a fantastic rate. Just a little spark is all it will take to set the whole thing off, with no way to stop or undo it after it starts.

And the situation is simply getting worse, not better. Just recently I saw a story in the *New York Times* with this headline: "76% in Poll Say Nuclear War is Likely in a Few Years." That should be enough to scare anyone into action.

It's also been projected that in just five short years—now a wink of an eye—over a dozen more countries will have these terrible weapons. Starting a nuclear war will be in the hands of almost anyone. Who will be in charge of these machines of destruction? Who in these countries will be in control of this awesome power with the capability of beginning a holocaust that will totally destroy the human race?

NEW REALITIES: It sounds like you think we're doomed, that there's no hope left.

NOBEL: If I truly did, I wouldn't be doing what I'm doing.

In truth, I see a great deal of hope and a positive side to all of this emerging—a genuine solution. At work all over the world, more and more people are becoming convinced that spiritual growth is the only answer. They are committed to it.

I too am now committed, despite my earlier years as an agnostic.

NEW REALITIES: What changed your thinking?

NOBEL: A few years ago, I began taking a second look at all religions—particularly Christianity—not as a born-again Christian, but more as one who has had a spiritual renewal. I was struck by the common thread that runs through them all, that the true way to outer peace is first through inner peace and inner wisdom.

From my extensive global travels and contacts, I also discovered that there are a great many intelligent men and women all over the world striving to bring us to our senses about the insanity of nuclear proliferation.

This is what Earth Aid Society is now all about. We want to help bring all of these people together to work on one great project for peace, which involves informing people throughout the world about what can be done to save ourselves and the planet.

NEW REALITIES: What kind of project?

New Manhattan Project

NOBEL: We like to think of it as a New Manhattan Project, with the sole objective of finding the Source of Life, rather than the source of death, which is the atomic bomb.

As you know, it was the Manhattan Project in the 1940s that first split the atom, giving birth to the Bomb. So we envision a New Manhattan Project of the 1980s that will put the unleashed genie of death back in the bottle by focusing the attention of millions on this problem, compared to only a few thousand that first time.

The only similarity of this new one to the first Manhattan Project, which has been called the largest single organized human effort in history, is that it should be even greater. The U.S. Government knew that the Allies had no choice but to enter the race with Nazi Germany for the worst possible prize.

But now, the world is facing an even worse challenge today and there is no real effort being made to meet the challenge. Surely we cannot reasonably expect to undo the damage—or potential damage that such an effort made possible—by doing less. Common sense tells us that a much greater effort will have to go into the New Manhattan Project if we expect it to achieve success.

The idea for this came about several years back as a natural consequence of realizing that it was lack of wisdom that brought about our present world predicament. Unfortunately, the word wisdom can seldom be applied to any political leader of our generation; yet it is only through wisdom that we can hope to find peace.

NEW REALITIES: Exactly how would such a project give us this wisdom?

NOBEL: Through the real laboratory—the human body and mind—with its nervous system, brain, thought and creative process, seat of being. . .the access to all wisdom.

The idea is to marshall the creative genius and support of our best brains throughout the world in science and religion—as well as the esteemed thinkers and leaders in other fields—which has been the dream of our philosophers from earliest times. In just this century, with the advances made by science since Einstein, Heisenberg, Planck, and others, the possibility of working together for lasting world peace is very real—within our very grasp.

What we are seeking to understand is the insight and guidance we get from within, including knowledge of the Life Force we all share—call it life energy, prana, shakti, bioenergy, or whatever. If we spent as much time and effort on the scale and order of the original Manhattan Project in trying to understand the spiritual nucleus of life—the seat of our wisdom and being—rather than the material nucleus of the atom, we would surely succeed. We're not talking about anything new here, but only updating and expanding on something that's been around since the dawn of history.

NEW REALITIES: And then what?

NOBEL: Simultaneous with this would be an effort to inform everyone around the world of the aim of the project. This part of it is perhaps even more important than any other.

"The true way to outer peace is first through inner peace and inner wisdom."

Unlike the first Manhattan Project, which was carried out in absolute secrecy, this research would be open. The media would be given free access to all data, progress, and findings from the very inception, and it would be urged to publish and broadcast everything. Public discussion and the free flow of information are absolutely essential. So the success of a project such as this depends on revealing what has always been held secret.

To me then, it is not a question of whether there will be something like a New Manhattan Project to bring a balance back to ourselves and our planet, with spiritual science offsetting material science. It is only a question of *when*. The clock is ticking away faster than ever. All men and women of good will should act now, before it is too late.

NEW REALITIES: But what will this do for the masses? Do you intend to organize everyone around the world into one big protest?

Spiritual Experience

NOBEL: Our goal is not to disrupt social institutions or governments. We simply wish to help bring about a change in their basic thinking, by bringing to light the validity of spiritual experience. This whole area of human potentiality needs to be put on a scientific footing. It has to be acknowledged and discussed by our leading thinkers—scientists, philosophers, religious leaders—and then presented to the world to show that this is a natural, normal part of all of us. It holds the key to our very survival and well-being.

Already, polls taken in this country show that half of the population has had some kind of a religious experience at least once in their lives, and that some 80 percent are searching for "inner meaning." So we must now attempt to understand what kind of mechanism is involved, just as science now tries to understand other phenomena of the mind.

NEW REALITIES: Then you don't think that this is already being adequately handled by the traditional and new religions?

NOBEL: With all due respect to all the worlds' religions and spiritual organizations, the effort is insufficient in view of the current state of the world. It is hardly dealt with or discussed on a public, nonsectarian basis. And when it is, it is never at the depth it should be.

Again, and I'm repeating myself to emphasize my point, what is needed is to have our finest minds focus their attention on what is called "mysticism." There has to be an opening up of the mind, and the fastest way to bring this about is through wide-spread dissemination of the kind of information and facts that would come to light in a scientific investigation of mystical experience.

How can consciousness or the human race take a quantum leap if we continue to rely solely on the intellect for all our knowledge of the universe? The mental health of the race—and its very survival—requires that such information be made widely known. That's why the media is indispensable to the successful outcome of a spiritual research project such as we are talking about.

Essentially, millions of people must become involved in one way or another to change current thinking.

NEW REALITIES: Yet there are those who would probably say that such a project is a waste of time and resources, and that your sense of urgency about nuclear war is more like doomsdaying and borders on hysteria. Hasn't this been said about every new weapon from the bow-and-arrow to machine guns and even dynamite? Haven't we always been able to contain or limit ourselves?

NOBEL: The difference is that our military and scientific leaders know that nuclear weapons are not in the same category. They are light-years beyond anything in the conventional arsenals. One mistake, one error or deliberate spark is all it will take to ignite the whole world.

"Sixty percent of all the world's scientists are currently engaged in work on military projects."

The urgency, we feel, is that the project we're proposing is the fastest, safest, and sanest way to bring about a balance between the all-annihilative force of the nuclear missiles and the wisdom we have within us to defuse them forever.

Most people don't realize that some 60 percent—60 percent!—of all the world's scientists are currently engaged in work on military projects. Again, where's the balance?

NEW REALITIES: You feel all of our problems, then, are the result of this imbalance?

NOBEL: Yes, which is mostly due to an industrialized society—not inherently bad in itself—which has distracted us from that part of ourselves we call the spirit, the soul. The result is that we're out of balance; we're governed solely by our intellect, which has become the major influence in our lives, instead of our intuitive side. The problems we face today are the direct outcome of this imbalance.

It is now time for us to seek for the source of inner guidance if we are to make the right choices from here on out. We must pay attention to our intuition or inner voice, which we seldom do because our intellect and ego dismiss it as having no basis in fact or substance in truth.

Through my own searches and observations on a global basis over the years, I've come to the conclusion that the only thing that will save the race is this "little inner voice." We must let it speak, we must let it be heard, and we must learn to listen. But this is much more difficult than we think. If it were not so, then all those who meditate would be in basic agreement with one another. But this isn't the case.

NEW REALITIES: What is this inner, intuitive source or voice to you? What do you call it?

Co-Creators with God

NOBEL: Well, I'm quite comfortable with calling it God, which seems as good a name as any. Yet it has also been referred to as the higher self, the soul, the atman, and so on. But it really doesn't matter what we call it, although acknowledging its existence, paying attention to it, and making use of the wisdom it offers does.

I have also come to believe that we are co-creators with God, and that our very thoughts often manifest into actions. If our thoughts are not controlled, if there are too many fearful and destructive ones, then this negativity can sometimes manifest in our lives.

This brings me back to the greatest concern today: world peace. Unless we have peace within ourselves and constantly in our thoughts; unless we have peace among ourselves as individuals and in our communities; and unless we have peace on the highest level, which is among nations; then the present world situation will continue to deteriorate into a world war. You don't have to be a prophet or a genius to see that is where we're headed.

I'm also convinced that we must not turn our back on this evil, which has to be recognized and rooted out wherever it is found. We've got to change our thought patterns and our very belief systems in this regard.

So the basic necessity of a New Manhattan Project at this point—for all human beings—is to focus upon these critical concerns.

NEW REALITIES: Why don't you just go directly to the media and the world arena with all this and make your appeal?

NOBEL: That isn't the way it works. New ideas have to struggle to be born and accepted, peace won't come by ignoring the unprecedented preparations for war.

For example, recently I watched a television program in which William F. Buckley, Jr., was interviewing the British writer Malcolm Muggeridge. They both said they very much enjoy talking about mysticism, about Christ, but the moment they brought up the subject, especially at social gatherings, their friends looked at them as though they had lost a few marbles, or worse. Buckley said one could not use the word Christ more than twice a year without risking being the "Christ" himself. Meaning, of course, that he would be branded either a lunatic or blasphemous. So it remains a problem even for intellectuals of Mr. Buckley's stature, not to mention our leading authorities in science and other fields, to discuss this subject on a very serious, rational basis. It's still very much taboo.

NEW REALITIES: How do you hope to overcome this syndrome, this taboo?

NOBEL: Earth Aid Society would like to see persons like Mr. Buckley, Bill Moyers, Dick Cavett, Carl Sagan, Isaac Asimov, and hundreds of other writers, broadcasters, media personalities, etc., discuss mystical experience. I am totally convinced that when this happens we'll see a dramatic leap in consciousness, a switch to a positive pattern of thinking that will reshape our future into a fully positive, peaceful one.

"We're governed solely by our intellect…instead of our intuitive side."

Nearly a century ago, Englishman James Allen wrote a beautiful, inspirational book, *As A Man Thinketh*, on this very notion. Among other things it contained the following poetic observation:

> *"Mind is the Master power that moulds*
> *   and makes.*
> *And Man is Mind, and evermore he*
> *   takes*
> *The tool of Thought, and, shaping*
> *   what he wills*
> *Brings forth a thousand joys, a*
> *   thousand ills:—*
> *He thinks in secret, and it comes to*
> *   pass*
> *Environment is but his looking-glass."*

That observation by Allen was never truer than it is today.

That's why we want to reach the millions of people all over the world about this.

NEW REALITIES: What makes you so sure it will work?

NOBEL: Because it has worked, and worked well, in many other instances.

For example, it was once taboo to talk about sex, that is, in trying to understand it in a mature, healthy way. But that has changed, and there is a more healthy attitude about it now. To be sure, there are excesses, there always are. But even the excesses of a few would fade away if genuine spiritual experience were to become the topic of the day. We are entering a New Age. We cannot continue to behave and think in the old ways. The Bible says that the Truth will set us free. No man or woman should ever fear truth.

How can we act responsibly without knowing the facts? Naivete about any subject—including mystical experience—is most dangerous. A New Manhattan Project would end this naivete for all time.

NEW REALITIES: Then you really do think it will work.

NOBEL: Along with many others, I am staking my name and resources on it. We believe it is the only way to end the overhanging threat of a nuclear holocaust that confronts every single one of us.

Claes Nobel is the great-grandnephew of Alfred Nobel, founder of the prestigious Nobel prizes for distinguished service to humanity.

"If those of us who protest the injustice of our system were instead to withdraw our support from the system, then change would begin."

Follow Gandhi's Example to Peace

Shelley Douglass

Gandhi used to tell his followers that *swaraj*, home-rule for India, would come only when every Indian exercised *swaraj*, self-rule, in his or her own life. The dependence of India upon the British, he said, was the sum of the dependence of each Indian upon British cloth, British thought, British custom, British government. British rule continued because Indians felt powerless to remove it, and because by their actions they in fact rendered themselves powerless. Gandhi was able to bring about a nonviolent freedom struggle insofar as people were able to see the truth in this insight of his: the imposition of British rule was made possible by Indian cooperation, and could be ended by noncooperation. Indians had to learn to respect themselves, to throw off the limitations of untouchability and of their own reverse racism; Indians had to learn to govern their own desires for wealth and property; Indians had to refuse to surrender to their centuries of conditioning to caste divisions so that they could work together for freedom.

For the Gandhian movement protest was not enough. One could not stand by shouting objections as a major miscarriage of justice occurred. Violence did not meet the case; violence did not recognize the responsibility of Indians for their own problems, and so would not change anything at the deepest level. What Gandhi called for and sometimes achieved was a struggle within each person's soul to take responsibility for the evil in which it was complicit, and having taken responsibility, to exercise self-control and begin to change. The Salt March to the sea and the magnificent control exhibited by demonstrating Indians grew slowly from humble roots: the scrubbing of latrines in the face of social taboo, the sharing of gold jewelry by the wealthy, living and eating together in defiance of caste regulations, wearing Indian *khadi* (homespun) to withdraw support from the British economic empire. These actions and many others were

symbolic of the deep change brought about by the Gandhian movement, a change in which people acknowledged their own responsibility for the wrong they sought to change, and thus in changing themselves were able to change their situation.

When violence broke out during the freedom struggle and later during partition, it happened because that vital insight was lost for a time. People again located the source of evil outside of themselves and tried to eliminate it with force. Gandhi's fasts and teachings were then concentrated on taking responsibility for the violence he might have caused, and calling people to take steps to stop their own violence. He understood that in giving up our own responsibility for evil we also give up the possibility of changing it. Gandhi's refusal to see the British as solely responsible for the situation of India was the key to Indian independence.

Struggle for Social Change

I believe that Gandhi's insistence upon recognizing our cooperation with evil and withdrawing it, is essential to the struggle for social change and nuclear disarmament in which we are engaged today. So often people feel powerless to create change—the leaders of political parties, the generals, the multinational executives, and such groups and persons are held responsible for our situation, and they do not listen to the voices of the poor and the disenchanted. This is true, of course. Governments and corporations exist to hold power or make a profit, and they rarely listen to polite words of protest. If our hope for change rests upon reasonableness of any government or economic system, then our hope is slim indeed.

The underlying fact that we tend to overlook is that while systems do not listen to people very well, they are made up of the very people to whom they do not listen. The existence of a given system depends upon the cooperation of all those who do not benefit from it and all who are hurt by it, as well as upon the smaller

Shelley Douglass, "The Power of Noncooperation," *IFOR Report*, April 1983.

number of people who gain status or wealth from it. If those of us who protest the injustice of our system were instead to withdraw our support from the system, then change would begin.

There are some logical steps to be taken in recognizing our responsibility and withdrawing our complicity. First, we have to know what it is that is wrong enough to justify such a step; secondly, we need to know how we are involved in supporting it; third, how we can best withdraw our support; fourth, what do we do with the support withdrawn from the system?

"When violence broke out during the freedom struggle…it happened because that vital insight was lost for a time."

Involvements with the nuclear system vary. Because Kitsap County, where we are living, is overwhelmingly military in its nature, the decision to noncooperate here is for many a decision to leave a job. For others it has been a decision to help distribute Ground Zero's disarmament leaflets despite military prohibitions, to criticize waste and dishonesty in the Navy itself, or simply to refuse to accept the stereotypes so prevalent now of who and what "protesters" are, and try instead to hear and share with us.

Payment of Taxes

For people not so directly involved with the military, the most obvious connection with nuclear policy is often the payment of taxes. Refusing all or part of our taxes, or paying them under protest, is a direct way to withdraw our cooperation with the making of nuclear weapons. For some, refusal to pay taxes has meant a re-examination of their convictions and life-style. They have had to become more open to uncertainty and more reliant upon faith for security as they wait to see what action will be taken by the courts. For others, the decision to live below the taxable income level has helped them to become less dependent upon the consumer goods that we take for granted. In reducing their income level to avoid financing nuclear weapons they have also begun to move out of the consumer society that necessitates these weapons.

As people refuse to give their money to the state to finance weapons they are able to take personal responsibility for the use of their money, channeling it to a soup kitchen, a child care center, a social change project that expresses their commitment to peace and justice. Sharing of one's substance for the good of all becomes more powerful when it is done with personal involvement.

Noncooperation may include marches, vigils and tax refusal, but it includes also an inner dimension: the refusal to allow our minds to be manipulated, our hearts to be controlled. Refusing to hate those who are identified as enemies is also noncooperation.

The discipline of nonviolence requires of us that we move into the various forms of noncooperation. We will probably move slowly, one step at a time. Each step will lead to another step; each step will be a withdrawal from support of what is wrong and at the same time a building of an alternative. Negativity is never enough. It is not enough to oppose the wrong without suggesting the right. Our religious roots can help us here, with their insistence on confronting the evil within ourselves and on our unity with all peoples.

New Kind of Power

The difficult thing about nonviolence is that it is a new kind of power to us, a new way of thinking. Even as we resist the structures in our society that separate us from others, we incorporate those structures in our own minds. Nonviolence becomes not only a process of resisting our own unloving impulses. Jesus' injunction to remove the beam from our own eye before presuming to treat our sisters' and brothers' eyes, and his direction to overcome evil with good can point our way. It is true that we resist what we understand to be evil. The system does evil. But the individual people who make up the system are people like you and me: combinations of good and evil, of strength and weakness. To hate people is to incorporate part of the evil that we resist. We must learn instead to love the people while we confront the system with our lives.

At the base of love for those caught within an evil system is the understanding that we are they: that we too are caught in the same system. Just as people in the peace movement have important insights and criticisms for people in the military, military folk have crucial insights to share with us. No one person owns the truth—each one has a piece of it, as Gandhi said, and if we can put all our pieces together we may find a bigger truth. Recognizing our own complicity in an evil system means that we can take responsibility for it through noncooperation. It also means that we can confront our own failures, forgive ourselves, and from that process learn compassion. We can be honest enough to admit our own imperfections and our lack of certainty, and accept the same in other people.

Just as we do not have to hate Russian people or Chinese people, we do not have to hate those who stand against our beliefs within our own country. We can be friends. We can work together in ways acceptable to all of us: to feed the hungry, to help at a school, to plan a liturgy, to sponsor activities for our children, to encourage freedom and creativity. As we work together we can get to know each other, and when that happens we can begin to explore our feelings about disarmament with mutual acceptance. Even when we feel that the people who range themselves against us have become close-minded or unreasonable, we do not have to retaliate in kind. We can find the places in ourselves where we are close-minded and unreasonable, and understand the fear behind such feelings. We can forgive and refuse to be drawn into a cycle of hate and fear. It is possible to hold out the hope of community to all people, and to work at conflicts within our communities and neighborhoods in the same spirit that we would like to bring to international conflict.

"Noncooperation…includes…the refusal to allow our minds to be manipulated, our hearts to be controlled."

The new power of nonviolence comes from taking responsibility: personal responsibility for our own lives, and our share of responsibility for the country and the systems in which we live. The power of nonviolence lies in facing ourselves with love and compassion while honestly confronting our own evil, and then in facing the evil of our country honestly, while confronting it with love and compassion. Nonviolence is an invitation to nurture the good, to confront the evil, and in doing so to build a new community which will bear in it the best of the old.

Shelley Douglass is a minister of the United Church of Christ. She works at Ground Zero, a disarmament project on the Pacific coast of the U.S.

"The military forces of the United States shall not be used against any other people except by direct affirmative vote of a majority of all citizens."

Put War to a Vote

Philip S. Foner

In seeking to depreciate the significance of the numerous nuclear freeze resolutions adopted by voters in the last election, President Reagan charged that their sponsors were dupes of the Soviet Union. Certainly these misguided souls were straying into an area—national security—where decision-making is best left to the experts.

Actually, the idea of citizens voting on questions relating to war is not new in this country. Back in 1916, proposals that a national referendum be held before the United States declared war were widely discussed. One of the most vocal champions of the idea was Allan L. Benson, the Socialist Party candidate for President that year.

Believing that wars are caused by capitalist nations competing for markets, Benson proposed removing the power to declare it from governments and placing the decision in the hands of the voters. He suggested the following constitutional amendment:

> The military forces of the United States shall not be used against any other people except by direct affirmative vote of a majority of all the citizens of the United States more than 18 years of age. The word "citizens" shall be construed to include women as well as men, but the reservation to the people of the sole right to declare offensive war shall not be construed as any limitation upon the duty of Congress and the President, hereby imposed, to resist invasion, or upon American warships to defend themselves if attacked.
>
> War shall be proposed only by a majority vote of both houses of Congress, by the legislatures of more than half of the states, or by petition of 30 percent of the population more than 18 years of age. War having been proposed, a general election to determine the question shall be called to take place not less than 60 days or more than six months from the date of the proposal.

Benson's amendment did not withhold from Congress or the President the power to respond to an attack by a foreign aggressor, but they could do so only in the event of an actual invasion. Mere unfriendly acts were not

enough; if the government wanted to respond to these with military force, it must seek the voters' approval.

To make the parlor patriots and barroom generals think twice, Benson added a codicil to his amendment, enjoining the President, in the event of war, to call up first those who had voted in favor of it. And he singled out for special attention the war hawks of the press, the podium and the halls of Congress:

> Every writer, public speaker, and public official who shall advocate war shall, forthwith upon such advocacy, notify the President thereof, conviction of failure to do so being punishable by imprisonment for not less than five years nor more than ten. In the event of war following such advocacy within five years, such persons shall be required to go to the front as common soldiers and remain in the thick of the fight until the end of the war, unless sooner killed or incapacitated by wounds. If wounded, such persons, upon recovery, shall be sent back to the front if the war be still in progress.

War Referendum

On April 30, 1916, the Republican Senator from Wisconsin, Robert M. LaFollette, introduced his own version of the war referendum in the Senate. LaFollette's bill called for the director of the Bureau of the Census to distribute ballots "whenever the President shall sever diplomatic relations with any foreign Government." The ballot would read:

> Shall the United States declare war against the Government of _____ (name of country) with which Government the President has severed diplomatic relations?
> Yes_____   No_____

The census director would be responsible for counting the ballots, and he would report the results to Congress. Speaking in favor of the bill, Republican Senator Moses Edwin Clapp of Minnesota declared on May 5, 1916:

> We have today peace societies, and their motives are grand and worthy, but we shall have permanent peace on this earth only when that time comes that the great, broad equation of humanity, composing the nations of the earth, shall declare whether there shall be peace or war, and when that broad equation includes not only those who must bare

Philip S. Foner, "Putting War to a Vote," *The Nation*, January 29, 1983. *The Nation Magazine*, Nation Associates Incorporated © 1983.

their breasts to the battle storms on the battlefield, but shall include the womanhood of the nations who must bear their share of the burden and the sacrifice of war.

Mr. President, this proposed measure takes from Congress no power whatsoever. If this Nation should be threatened by war, if, as a matter of defense, it is unwise to await the action of a submission to the people of the question, no one would doubt but that Congress would promptly and efficiently respond to the demand for defense and to repel invasion; but it does contemplate that in this matter of declaring war, when time shall permit of the submission of the question, that the great rank and file of this Republic shall be heard in some effective manner, so far as affecting the presentation of their sentiments upon that question.

"We shall have permanent peace on this earth only when. . .humanity. . .shall declare whether there shall be peace or war."

Thus, the antiwar referendum has an honorable history in this country. Now, when the increasing likelihood of a nuclear holocaust puts everyone at risk and when the Administration calls for first-strike weapons and discusses nuclear war-fighting capabilities, the need for citizens to have a voice in the matter is more urgent than ever. Benson and LaFollette's proposals did not stop World War I, but their modern counterparts may help prevent World War III.

Philip S. Foner is professor emeritus of history at Lincoln University.

"By their cost alone armaments kill the poor by causing them to starve."

Convert Military Budgets into Food

Alfred Kastler

With the prudence and restraint to be expected of a scientist, I must express my pessimism regarding the future of the human race, in view of the present attitude of governments.

The advancement of culture depends on the survival of the human race, and I think that this is the most agonizing problem confronting us. I also think that there is a very close relation between the assistance that can be given to the Third World and the armaments race.

There is no need to be a great scholar or great prophet to see that the human race is rushing toward its suicide. When the two superpowers—the United States and the Soviet Union—proposed a treaty on the non-proliferation of nuclear weapons to the other nations a few years ago, they morally undertook to follow, of course, disarmament. This undertaking has not been respected, for what have they done since then? In spite of the Geneva talks which have been dragging on for years, in spite of the Vladivostok meeting, all they have done is to institutionalize and intensify the arms race.

Three Bombs Per Day

While we are discussing culture, the United States of America is manufacturing three hydrogen bombs per day to maintain the balance of terror, as is the Soviet Union. These bombs will be used to arm multiple-head missiles. Hundreds of submarines armed with these weapons are constantly ploughing the seas, awaiting the order to fire.

The Hiroshima bomb destroyed a city with its one hundred thousand inhabitants. A single hydrogen nuclear head will suffice to wipe out the area of greater Paris with its ten million inhabitants. Soon the stock of these weapons on both sides will have reached a total of 10,000. Will there be a nuclear war between the United States and the Soviet Union? I don't think so, for

Alfred Kastler, "The Challenge of the Century," *The Bulletin of the Atomic Scientists,* September 1977. Reprinted by permission of *The Bulletin of the Atomic Scientists,* a magazine of science and public affairs. Copyright © 1977 by the Educational Foundation for Nuclear Science, Chicago, IL 60637.

dissuasion is effective.

While this mad race continues—this challenge to morality denounced by Albert Schweitzer, which is also increasingly a challenge to human intellegence—another process is dominating the future of the human race on this planet: the population explosion.

There are today four billion human beings on the Earth. About one billion enjoy a reasonable standard of living in the industrialized countries; about 2.5 billion in the Third World have a standard of living which averages about 5 percent of ours, though there are considerable inequalities.

The lower the standard of living, the higher the birth rate. That appears to be a sociological law. Among us the population stagnates; in the so-called developing countries it doubles in a quarter of a century. By the end of the twentieth century, we shall be one billion well-off people confronted by five billion of the Third World. I'm sorry, but there won't be five billion. Food supplies will be unable to keep up with the increase in population; at least one out of five will have died of hunger by then. Out of the four billion who remain, half will be young people for whom, in our market economy and even with the development of industrial farming in the underdeveloped countries, there will be neither work nor food.

Will they be content to die without protest? Certainly not; there will be a revolt. And we should not forget that, even if they have not enough to eat, they will have weapons because, as we know, they in turn spend 12 billion dollars every year on armaments. One billion well-fed people will therefore be confronted by four billion who are starving. The billion well-fed people in a state of panic will have 10,000 hydrogen bombs.

Blissful Ignorance

I leave it to the artists and film producers to imagine the scenario, which has a 99 percent chance of becoming fact unless there is a radical change of attitude in the meantime on the part of governments. But even supposing the governments remain in blissful ignorance, you will say, "There is still public opinion." I believed that too. I believed it until last May when I learned of the result of the referendum in Switzerland. The Swiss federal government had suggested giving assistance to the Third World; the majority of the Swiss people refused it. This is a matter for regret, but I think it is symptomatic and is merely a reflection of the attitude of the average citizen in Europe, who is completely ignorant of the situation in which mankind finds itself today.

Thus, I think that the first duty for us intellectuals, whether we are scientists or men of letters, philosophers or artists, is to try to save the human race with culture and not to impose our culture on people who, we think, have none. And it is our duty to make the citizens of our countries conscious of the situation in which mankind is placed, for at present they are utterly ignorant of it.

"Military expenditures throughout the world have now reached $300 billion a year. . . .As compared with it, the annual budget of UNESCO is. . .one three-thousandth of the amount."

At this point I would like to quote something which gives me grounds for hope—an extract from a 1976 declaration by the Holy See in reply to a U.N. survey on the role of the United Nations in the field of disarmament:

> The massive budgets allocated to the manufacture and stock-piling of weapons is tantamount to misappropriation of funds by the 'managers' of the large nations or favoured blocks.
> The obvious contradiction between the waste involved in the over-production of military devices and the extent of unsatisfied vital needs (developing countries and the marginal and poor elements in rich societies) is in itself an act of aggression which amounts to a crime, for even when they are not used, by their cost alone armaments kill the poor by causing them to starve.

Further on, this document adds:

> The armaments race has become a cumulative process, which has its own dynamics, independent of any aggressive feelings, and which escapes the control of States. It is a machine gone mad.

This, then, was the statement from the Holy See. I am not a Catholic and I do not always agree with the steps taken by the Vatican. But I must say that, as scientists and intellectuals, we must be fully in agreement with this statement and it is our duty to raise the alarm.

Military expenditures throughout the world have now reached $300 billion a year. This is a vast sum which represents an enormous potential of human labor. As compared with it, the annual budget of UNESCO is $80 million—one three-thousandth of the amount. In other words, if all the nations of the world, including those of the Third World, agreed to reduce their military budgets by 1 percent, this would make it possible to increase UNESCO's budget thirtyfold. A comparison of this sort reveals how ridiculous is the effort made by the rich nations to further education, science and culture as against the effort they make to develop their means of destruction.

No Scientific Obstacle

I state categorically that it would be scientifically possible to change this situation.

In spite of my pessimism, I perceived a gleam of hope on the occasion of a journey I made on behalf of UNESCO to Mali several years ago. I went to preside over the first research theses prepared by young physicists at the College of Education set up by UNESCO in Mali. There I saw a building, half of which had been built with financial assistance from the United States and half with aid from the Soviet Union. I met members of the teaching staff—one from Poland, one from Yugoslavia, two from France, one from Scotland and one from Canada. I was very pleased to note that these people coming from countries with different ideologies were capable of working together to assist a country of the Third World. But what might not be achieved if this effort could be multiplied by ten or by a hundred? I say that, scientifically and technically, it is possible.

I spoke just now of a reduction of military budgets by 1 percent, but it would not be unreasonable to suggest 10 percent. I do not believe that such a reduction would have the slightest effect on the security of any of the developed countries, but it would make it possible to change the situation enormously in the Third World. In the space of a generation, it would be possible to promote agriculture, and to develop sources of energy in these countries—poor in fossil resources but rich in solar energy—which are inexhaustible and without pollution.

There is no scientific or technological obstacle to changing the entire future of humanity; the only obstacles are psychological and social. It is essential to cause a radical change in the attitude of governments which must be preceded by a change in the attitude of the public. And it is up to us intellectuals to pursue these ends if we want this new economic and social order to assert itself and the men and women on our planet to survive.

Alfred Kastler, a 1966 Nobel laureate and a member of the Institute of France, is emeritus professor of physics, University of Paris.

Overview:
The Bishops and the Bomb

Time Magazine

The official summary of the bishops' pastoral letter on war and peace was released on June 9, 1983. The full text of that summary is contained in viewpoint 83.

In another age the meeting would have been held in seclusion and secrecy. Last week, however, 276 bishops of the Roman Catholic Church in the U.S. were debating in the full glare of TV lights and under the gaze of an international press corps. A few years ago precedent would have dictated that division among the prelates be suppressed, lest the faithful be scandalized. But many of the bishops who assembled for the annual meeting of the National Conference of Catholic Bishops in Washington, D.C., were openly wondering if their ideas were right for the church, or for the nation. And the document that the bishops debated, instead of being couched in the traditional terms of moral certitude, asked Catholics not to read and obey, but to weigh and consider the conclusions, much as had the bishops themselves. Both the candid, probing manner of the debate and the topic of their discussion reflect the enormous changes that are sweeping through the Catholic Church in America.

The document under discussion was the draft of a pastoral letter, addressed to 51 million American Catholics, on the morality of nuclear war. In it, the bishops are seeking to develop a theology of peace that challenges some of the fundamental assumptions and defense strategies of every American Administration, and most of the Western world, since the beginning of the nuclear age. The bishops' key attack is on the doctrine of nuclear deterrence. They acknowledge that the U.S. threat to use nuclear arms in response to a Soviet assault might prevent the outbreak of war, but they nonetheless conclude that the policy is unsatisfactory because it created, and keeps in place, a balance of ter-

ror that all too easily could lead to a holocaust. They are also offended by the cost of maintaining deterrence, which they say takes money away from programs for the poor. In addition, the bishops call for a nuclear freeze, which is opposed by the Administration and many experts, who argue that it would preserve Soviet nuclear superiority. The bishops also urge the Administration to work actively for a disarmament agreement with Moscow.

Doubting that any nuclear war can be limited, the bishops oppose the first use of nuclear weapons by the U.S. To deter the Soviets from using their superior conventional forces in an invasion of Western Europe, the U.S. has kept open the option of using nuclear weapons before the Soviets do. The bishops also criticize the deployment of new MX missiles on the ground that they would quicken the arms race. The Administration insists that the U.S. needs the MX to counter new Soviet weaponry. Surveying the broad sweep of the bishops' document, Archbishop Edward A. McCarthy, 64, of Miami said last week, "Cataclysmic threats demand dramatic responses. We need to demonstrate that waging peace has become a high priority of the church of the Prince of Peace in this 20th century crisis."

With the endorsement of Pope John Paul II, a Vatican panel declared in September that prevention of nuclear war "is the greatest moral issue humanity has ever faced and there is no time to lose." But just how should centuries of Christian theological teachings about war be applied to the realities of the current arms race? For two years the U.S. bishops have struggled with that question. The climax of their debate coincided with events that dramatized the relevance of their talks: a change of leadership in the Soviet Union, the passage of various nuclear referendums at this month's elections, and crucial discussions on U.S. defense spending.

Since the debate about the morality of atomic weapons began in 1945, U.S. Protestants have led the way, in both mounting demonstrations and developing theology. The pastoral letter, which will be formally issued next May after further revision, is by far the strongest and most dramatic Christian challenge to the structure of U.S. nuclear strategy.

A Watershed for Catholicism

Moreover, the antinuclear crusade is a watershed for U.S. Catholicism. As a group, American bishops were almost jingoistic in their endorsements of U.S. foreign policy. Today dozens of the prelates are avowed pacifists. On nuclear morality and other social issues, says the Rev. Michael Campbell Johnson, Rome-based head of the Jesuits' Commission for Justice and Peace, the American bishops "may at last be slightly out in front of the [world] church as a whole." Some feel they may be too far out in front. New York's Terence Cardinal Cooke, 61, warned his colleagues last week that the nuclear issue has "great potential for seriously dividing our church and nation."

The pastoral letter was drafted by a committee of five bishops, whose views on nuclear strategy range from hawkish to openly pacifist. The chairman of that committee in many ways exemplifies the new spirit of American Catholicism. He is the Most Rev. Joseph Louis Bernardin, 54, Archbishop of Chicago As head of the nation's largest archdiocese (2.4 million members), Bernardin is expected to be added to the ten American Cardinals when Pope John Paul II names new members of the Sacred College. Bernardin has been a close colleague of the Pope's since they served together from 1974 to 1978 on the Vatican's international council for the Synod of Bishops.

Bernardin is greatly respected by his fellow American bishops, in part for his ability to work out compromises on controversial issues. Soft-spoken and mild-mannered, he has a knack of achieving his goals without causing commotion or rancor. Says a top Catholic clergyman, in admiration: "When Bernardin makes waves, they're always smooth waves."

The choice of Bernardin to chair the nuclear panel was made in 1980 by Archbishop John Roach of St. Paul and Minneapolis, 61, president of the U.S. bishops' conference since 1980. Says Bernardin of his delicate assignment: "We don't expect everyone to accept our conclusions, but we believe we must think this thing through to the end."

At the start of the debate, Cardinal Cooke, who is also military vicar to Catholics in the armed forces, called for stronger emphasis on the righteousness of "defense against unjust aggression," more realism about Communism and more reaction from bishops in other Western nations who are "anxious about their own defense." Another conservative, New Orleans Archbishop Philip Hannan, 69, argued that his colleagues should scrap the document entirely because it ignores the evils of Soviet Communism.

Hannan was followed by Seattle's Archbishop Raymond Hunthausen, 61, an avowed pacifist who advocates unilateral U.S. disarmament. He is also risking federal indictment by refusing to pay half his income taxes as a protest against the Administration's defense spending. Hunthausen last year called the missile-carrying Trident submarine, based near his city, "the Auschwitz of Puget Sound," but on this occasion his rhetoric was less outrageous. "To many my message seems like foolishness," he said, "but to me, it is simply the Gospel of Jesus Christ."

"The church must be a participant in protecting the world and its people from the specter of nuclear destruction."

Philadelphia's influential Archbishop, John Cardinal Krol, 72, is liberal on disarmament and conservative on church discipline and doctrine. He suggested that the pastoral letter should more clearly acknowledge a nation's right to resist attack and tyranny from unjust aggressors by all means that are morally licit.

The Issue of Deterrence

The most difficult issue in the draft was a statement on the morality of nuclear deterrence. Here the bishops took their guidance from a message by John Paul to a United Nations General Assembly disarmament session last June. The Pope had written: "Under present conditions, 'deterrence' based on equilibrium—certainly not as an end in itself but as a stage on the way to progressive disarmament—can still be judged morally acceptable. However, to ensure peace it is indispensable not to be content with a minimum which is always fraught with a real danger of explosion." The question facing the bishops was whether they should be more specific than the Pope.

In the midst of the discussion, the White House launched a carefully wrought defense of its nuclear policies. What deeply concerned the Administration was fear that the bishops' criticism of nuclear deterrence would encourage the peace movement in the U.S. and abroad and build pressure for unilateral rather than mutual disarmament. That, in turn, might undermine U.S. efforts to negotiate arms limitations agreements with the Soviets.

The Administration's case was made by National Security Adviser William Clark, a Catholic layman. In an open letter to Bernardin, he said that the White House agreed with the Pope's stand and, indeed, with much of what the bishops were saying. But Clark said that he and President Reagan were "especially troubled" that the draft ignored American proposals "on achieving steep reductions in nuclear arsenals, on reducing conventional forces and, through a variety of verification and confidence-building measures, on further reducing the risks of war." Clark noted that the Soviets had mounted a huge arms buildup during the past decade when the U.S. was holding down arms spending. He also argued that it was perfectly moral for the U.S. to make certain that "our deterrent forces remain sufficiently strong and credible to assure effective deterrence." The goal, he said, is "to prevent war and preserve the values we cherish." As for the bishops' stance on the MX, the Administration argues that their opposition to the development of more sophisticated weapons would reduce the prospects of limiting a nuclear war.

The bishops also had to face the terrible paradox of deterrence: it is based on fear and therefore cannot work if one side or the other can be absolutely certain that nuclear weapons will never be used. This point was advanced by William V. O'Brien, a political scientist at Georgetown University, who noted in the *Washington Quarterly* that "deterrence without credible intention to carry out the deterrent threat will not be effective."

A Divided House

The bishops were divided on whether or not the nuclear button should ever be pushed in defense of the U.S. On the final day of their meeting, the bishops debated the document in a plenary session for two hours, then voted, with only four nays, to hold a special conference in Chicago on May 2 and 3 to polish and issue a final nuclear policy statement. Bernardin's committee will be getting written comments from the bishops and reactions from the Vatican, which has followed the discussions with keen interest, as well as from bishops in Western Europe who are somewhat worried by what they see as the Americans' leftward drift.

"The comments I have received. . .indicate the great potential which this draft has for seriously dividing our church and our nation."

The final debate made it obvious that the committee has much work still to do. Despite an overwhelming consensus on the basic thrust of the document, the bishops want a stronger biblical and theological rationale for their conclusions. There is likely to be more acknowledgment of U.S. disarmament efforts and further recognition of the Soviet threat. On the key question of the morality of nuclear deterrence, the bishops will be trying to refine their position. Under sharp press questioning in Washington, Bernardin acknowledged

that the current text is ambiguous on whether it is ever moral to use nuclear weapons. An earlier draft had said it was possible to use them in retaliation, but only if aimed at military targets. That section was dropped because the bishops decided that any nuclear confrontation would escalate to all-out war. The current version strongly suggests that such conflicts could not be contained, and thus that no use of nuclear weapons could ever be morally sanctioned.

While the bishops were weighing their words, some priests, nuns and lay people have been challenging nuclear might with deeds. At Groton, Conn., nine Catholic protesters were sentenced this month for trying to damage a nuclear submarine. In Denver, two nuns have been convicted of forging Government passes to enter Rocky Flats nuclear weapons plant and place signs saying DACHAU and DEATH FACTORY. Sister Frances Russell of Cheyenne, Wyo., is coordinating a tristate coalition to protest probable deployment of MX missiles in the area. The veteran radical Catholic, Jesuit Father Daniel Berrigan, faces a 5-to-10-year sentence for damaging warhead cones in Pennsylvania. "In the 1960s we went to jail alone," he marvels. "Now there are bishops at our side and Jesuits putting up bail."

To be sure, the activists on antinuke picket lines represent a small minority of American Catholics. Nonetheless, many people both inside and outside the church are wondering how it is that bishops who only a few years ago praised the Lord and passed the ammunition are now backing what some see as a pacifist-tinged cause.

Several factors are involved. One is the impact of Pope John XXIII, who succeeded the sternly anti-Communist Pius XII in 1958. Pope John sought to reach some measure of accommodation with the repressive regimes of Eastern Europe to help the church survive. He also said total nuclear disarmament was essential, and summoned that watershed meeting in the history of the 20th century church, the Second Vatican Council. Among other things, the council called upon Catholics to take a more active role in promoting social justice in Christ's name. Many of the bishops who participated in last week's debate freely admit that Vatican II was a turning point in their lives. Said St. Paul's Roach: "It was really the mind and spirit of the council that I have tried to assimilate and absorb."

That emphasis on social justice, particularly the abolition of war, was carried forward by Pope Paul VI in his memorable 1965 address to the United Nations, where he pleaded: "No more war! War never again!" John Paul II is equally fervent. In a dramatic and symbolic speech at the Hiroshima memorial, he demanded that humanity make a "moral about-face" from war.

There was also a change in the leadership of the church in America. The old-fashioned autocratic Cardinals whose pride was in building new parishes and schools gradually gave way to men with a more pastoral, people-oriented outlook. Pope Paul is given much credit for orchestrating the change. He once remarked to his Secretary of State, Jean Cardinal Villot, "Don't American Catholics understand what vast power they have, and what a responsibility? Increasingly that power devolved on bishops who rejected a monarchical style of ruling, were open to ecumenical contacts with Protestants and more readily accepted the advice of new priests' senates and lay parish councils.

The new breed of bishops also has a strong sense of collegiality and a willingness to follow leadership regardless of rank. Bernardin and Roach, despite their relative youth, probably have more influence among their fellow prelates these days than do the Cardinals as a group. Other emerging leaders in the hierarchy include Archbishops James Hickey of Washington, 62; John May of St. Louis, 60; and Rembert Weakland of Milwaukee, 55. All these men were advocates of a nuclear freeze even before the Bernardin committee issued the text of the pastoral letter. Krol, the leading figure among the older hierarchs, is staunchly in agreement.

"Many bishops. . .feared that the new Administration might blunder its way into nuclear war."

American Catholicism has also undergone some profound internal changes. In the age of immigration, Catholics essentially were strangers in a predominantly Protestant land. Reacting to nativist charges that their spiritual loyalty to Rome was somehow more important than political loyalty to their new homeland, Catholic immigrants and their children sometimes attempted to be superpatriots.

Des Moines Bishop Maurice Dingman, 68, explains the change: "We have gone from being a fortress church to a lighthouse church. When we were an immigrant church, we put a wall around the people, and we did a good job of protecting them. We maintained their faith. But we could no longer stay in our shelter. We let down the drawbridge and crossed the moat, and we're out in the mainstream of America."

Some bishops point out, with a bit of exasperation, that they have in fact taken provocative positions on major political issues in the past, although without catching the public eye as they have on nuclear arms. The Bishops' Program anticipated New Deal labor and welfare laws 14 years before the inauguration of Franklin D. Roosevelt, and the hierarchy spoke out strongly against racial injustice in 1958, early in the civil rights struggle.

Through this period the hierarchy continued to back U.S. foreign policy. The Viet Nam War at first paralyz-

ed and then catalyzed the bishops. They called upon the U.S. to end the war in 1971. The bishops argued that any good that could be gained from the fighting was outweighed by the destruction of human life and moral values. One high Vatican prelate believes that many American bishops, feeling they had spoken out too late on the war, "may be compensating now by taking a strong stand [on nuclear weapons]. The Viet Nam experience also influenced them to take a close look at American involvement in other areas."

Church and State

In January 1973, the bishops were shaken by a second event, the Supreme Court decision allowing abortion on demand in most circumstances. This legal challenge to the age-old Catholic teaching that abortion is equivalent to murder forced the bishops to adopt a style of political propaganda and maneuver that, until then, had been more characteristic of liberal Protestants. For Catholicism, the abortion decision was a bold attack on human life and dignity. The radical change produced reflection upon other "life" issues, especially the arms race. Says Bernardin: "If you take a strong stand against abortion as the unjust taking of human life, then you cannot remain indifferent to nuclear warfare."

The bellicose rhetoric of the Reagan campaign alarmed many bishops, who feared that the new Administration might blunder its way into nuclear war. Many bishops became more active in various antinuclear efforts. In November 1980, the bishops authorized the Bernardin committee to begin work on the pastoral letter. Pressed by mounting local demands to help the poor and the unemployed, key church leaders like Roach also assailed Reagan's $1.5 trillion defense buildup. The ensuing antinuclear wave in Western Europe and the U.S. has strengthened the bishops' commitment.

There may have been other subtle factors at work. Liberal Jesuit Sociologist John Coleman suggests that the bishops almost instinctively grasped the arms race as a moral issue because they needed ro restore their "credibility" with the laity, which had eroded because the hierarchy had no choice but to support Pope Paul's unpopular (and widely ignored) ban on birth control.

The bishops' growing interest in political action was also increased by their involvement with the church in Latin America. There bishops, priests and nuns have embraced the social liberalism of Pope Paul and Vatican II, siding with the poor against the oligarchies. A tempering influence on Latin American clergy was Pope John Paul's admonition that they should not get directly involved in politics. But the general effect of the church's activism in Latin America was to encourage the U.S. bishops not only to become more aggressive politically in the U.S., but to take strong policy stands on human rights in the hemisphere.

During the past year, the U.S. bishops and Protestant

activists of like mind strongly opposed Reagan Administration policy in El Salvador. The bishops demanded that the Administration cut off military aid to El Salvador, arguing that it only escalated the violence, much of which has been engendered by the Government. Two weeks ago Archbishop Roach called for an end to U.S. military involvement in Guatemala because of that nation's human rights atrocities. Nonetheless, the gap between the bishops and the White House on policy in Central America has narrowed slightly. The Administration has seemingly become more sensitive to human rights violations in El Salvador, while Roach has joined Reagan in denouncing oppression by the Marxist Sandinista regime in Nicaragua.

Church Involvement

The range and volume of pronouncements by the U.S. bishops on social issues have increased enormously in recent years. The bishops or their spokesmen have issued at least 200 statements since 1966, when the hierarchy reorganized itself into two bodies: the National Conference of Catholic Bishops, a strictly ecclesiastical body, and the U.S. Catholic Conference, the civic and service agency of the bishops. Depending on the issue, the bishops may sound like sanitized Moral Majoritarians or Kennedy Democrats. Besides familiar stands (for tuition tax credits to help private-school parents; against mercy killing, sleazy TV shows and the religious vacuum in public schools), the bishops have taken distinctly liberal stances on welfare, crime, prisons, housing, national health insurance, world food policy, South Africa and the Panama Canal treaty (the bishops were strongly influenced by calls of support from Archbishop Marcos McGrath of Panama City). The bishops have backed both Israel's right to exist and Palestinians' "right to a state."

Next year the bishops will take up a topic that is potentially as divisive as abortion or nuclear weaponry. A committee led by Milwaukee's Archbishop Weakland is conducting a thoroughgoing moral evaluation of capitalism. The bishops have already advocated the redistribution of economic wealth in the U.S., and have blamed Third World poverty on an exploitive U.S. economic policy and multinational corporations. Conservative critics find this an appallingly simplistic view of economic realities, amounting at best to a kind of global sentimentality and at worst to a repetition of left-wing propaganda platitudes. Last week, without specifically mentioning Reaganomics, a bishops' panel denounced "current policies which attempt to solve America's economic ills at the expense of the poor and unemployed."

As the bishops argue their case against nuclear arms in the months ahead, they will contend that this stance is consistent with the tradition of church teaching on war. Until the Bomb, Christianity's approach to war had remained fundamentally unchanged for centuries.

The earliest Christians refused all military service because they thought Jesus' love-thy-neighbor teachings mandated pacifism, and because Rome required idolatrous vows. Christianity became an established religion in the 4th century and soon embraced St. Augustine's "just war" theory, expanded in later centuries by Thomas Aquinas and other theologians.

"The council also said that it was morally right for Catholics to be pacifists."

The traditional conditions for a morally justifiable war, which are generally accepted by non-Catholics as well as Catholics, are that it be declared by a legitimate authority, for a righteous cause, with good intention, as a last resort, and waged with limited means. The two criteria for conduct of a just war that are especially pertinent to today's nuclear debate are "discrimination" (no direct killing of innocent civilians) and "proportion" (a war's devastation must not exceed the evil it seeks to overcome). Nuclear pacifists argue that these two factors necessarily rule out atomic warfare.

Vatican Involvement

In 1954 Pope Pius XII cautiously approved the use of atomic, bacterological and chemical weapons, but forbade these methods if they "entirely escape from the control of man" or cause the "annihilation of all human life within the radius of action," Pius, who denounced saturation bombing even before the inferno of Hiroshima, declared that wars of righteous aggression, in order to punish an offense or to recover territory, could no longer be justified because modern weaponry had become so devastating. Wars of national self-defense, however, were still permitted.

At Vatican II, a coalition of U.S. and European bishops persuaded the council to accept, grudgingly, the idea of nuclear deterrence. *The Pastoral Constitution on the Church in the Modern World,* promulgated in 1965, declares: "Since the defensive strength of any nation is considered to be dependent upon its capacity for immediate retaliation, this accumulation of arms. . .serves, in a way heretofore unknown, as a deterrent to possible enemy attack. Many regard this as the most effective way by which peace of a sort can be maintained between nations at the present time."

The council also said that it was morally right for Catholics to be pacifists, denounced the costly arms race and called for disarmament, "not unilaterally" but at an "equal pace," and "backed by adequate and workable safeguards." The bishops at Vatican II further declared, "Any act of war aimed indiscriminately at the destruction of entire cities or extensive areas along with their population is a crime against God and man himself." The World Council of Churches, which represents 350 million Protestant and Orthodox Christians, had said much the same thing four years earlier.

The U.S. bishops' peace offensive began with a pastoral letter in 1976. It declared that modern conflict "is so savage that one must ask whether war as it is actually waged today can be morally justified." The bishops said that no Christians can "rightfully carry out orders or policies requiring direct force against noncombatants." Then came this key statement: "As possessors of a vast nuclear arsenal, we must also be aware that not only is it wrong to attack civilian populations but it is also wrong to threaten to attack them as part of a strategy of deterrence." The bishops were applying the traditional teaching that it is as wrong to intend to commit an evil act as it is to commit it. In 1979, testifying on behalf of the hierarchy before the Senate Foreign Relations Committee, Cardinal Krol went further. He flatly ruled out use or "declared intent" to use nuclear weapons under any circumstances, presumably because masses of civilians would inevitably be involved.

> *"Some critics charge that the bishops are usurping the proper role of the laity."*

The final phase in the evolution of peace theology was the formation in 1980 of the Bernardin committee. Archbishop Roach skillfully chose the membership of the five-man committee to span the spectrum of the bishops' thinking on nuclear arms. The most liberal member of the committee is Auxiliary Bishop Thomas Gumbleton, 52, of Detroit, who heads Pax Christi, a movement with strong pacifist inclinations. A total of 57 bishops belong to the organization. Gumbleton's hawkish opposite on the committee is Bishop John O'Connor, 62, who runs the church's military ministry for Cardinal Cooke. The committee is rounded out by two moderates: Bishop Daniel P. Reilly, 54, of Norwich, Conn., and George A. Fulcher, 60, Auxiliary Bishop of Columbus.

The Committee Begins

Beginning work in July 1981, the Bernardin committee held 14 hearings and heard from 36 witnesses, including Secretary of Defense Caspar Weinberger and his predecessor, Harold Brown, SALT Negotiator Gerard Smith, as well as theologians, Bible scholars, physicians and peace protestors. Bernardin sent a copy of the first draft of the committee's report to the Pope, who is said to have approved it.

When news of the text's dovish stance leaked last June, National Security Adviser Clark wrote fellow Catholics asking them to press the Administration views upon the bishops. The topic doubtless came up when Clark and President Reagan lunched with the Pope's top aide, Agostino Cardinal Casaroli, in Hartford on Aug. 3. On Sept. 13, Weinberger sent Bernardin a carefully worded statement making the same points that Clark made later. In October, retired General Vernon Walters, a State Department troubleshooter, quietly visited Rome to brief Pope John Paul on the Administration's position on nuclear strategy, among other matters. The White House campaign changed the view of neither the bishops nor the Pope.

The anguished discussion of the bishops in Washington about the morality of nuclear deterrence reflected only part of a far broader debate that is building about the proper place of the bishops and the church they serve in the modern world. The debate involves a number of respected Catholic thinkers. The four main points currently at issue:

A few critics make the flimsy charge that the bishops' activism, particularly their zealous support for measures that would overturn the Supreme Court's abortion ruling, violates the consitutional principle of church-state separation. Not only is there no clear legal bar against such efforts, but just about every U.S. denomination has entered politics at one time or another. Says Archbishop Roach: "We may never allow the separation of church and state to be used to separate the church from society." Former Defense Secretary James Schlesinger disagrees with the bishops' view on deterrence, but says: "Some laymen would like the bishops to confine their discussion to kissing on the first date. Bishops have as much right to comment as anybody else."

Rabbi Balfour Brickner, a longtime social-action official for Reform Judaism, has battled Catholic officialdom on abortion. Yet he says of the nuclear issue, "They let us carry the ball alone for too long. Bring on the bishops!" But Archbishop Peter Gerety, 70, of Newark, warns, "We have to make clear that we are not trying to write legislation or elect politicians." In some cases bishops have veered close to doing both on the abortion issue.

The Bishops' Competence

Numerous critics argue that writing detailed prescriptions on nuclear strategy is simply beyond the bishops' scope of knowledge. At least one bishop is inclined to agree. Peoria's Edward O'Rourke, 65, thinks the clergy are experts on moral principles, but not always on how to apply them: "I'm not confident we bishops have the ability to tell the President of the U.S. how to get the world out of the dangerous position in which it finds itself. If I were that wise, I wouldn't be sitting here in Peoria." Says Catholic Layman Robert Spaeth, liberal arts dean at St. John's University, a Catholic school in Minnesota: "I don't exercise much independence on matters like the infallibility of the Pope, but if a bishop tells me the MX missile is bad, that's *my* field."

In an interview with TIME, Archbishop Bernardin said the technical competence question "makes me smile. There are many people who write about these issues, newspaper editors, for instance. Are they really expert in a technical sense in every field they write about? They write on the basis of study, on the basis of their conversations with people. The same thing is true of us bishops. We do not present ourselves as experts in nuclear warfare or in nuclear armaments, but we do want to share with our people, and all people of good will, what we have learned and what we think the moral implications are."

Some critics charge that the bishops are usurping the proper role of the laity. Quentin Quade, executive vice president of Jesuit-run Marquette University, says the real issue is not "more or less activism, but who is responsible for putting these values into practice." Quade deduces from Vatican II that the clergy are supposed to preach principles and the laity are supposed to apply them. Michael Novak, a Catholic philosopher and theologian who is perhaps the most quoted opponent of the bishops' pastoral, thinks that "they are suffering from hubris, taking on vocations that aren't theirs."

The Bishops' Aides

Some conservatives argue that the bishops are largely endorsing documents drafted by the Washington staff of the U.S. Catholic Conference, which Catholic rightists consider to be unfairly tilted to the left. The favorite target of the conservatives is Father J. Bryan Hehir, 41, onetime Harvard student of Henry Kissinger, who has been in charge of the conference's office for international justice and peace since 1974. Hehir, who makes no secret of his liberal tendencies, often testifies before Congress on such topics as amnesty for draft resisters, disarmament, world food policy, and human rights violations in Chile and South Korea. He is the top adviser for Bernardin's committee on nuclear arms as well as for the committee on capitalism.

Bernardin dismisses the criticism that he and his peers are prisoners of their staffs ("It's kind of offensive and demeaning"). Hehir readily defends the bishops' campaign: "Protecting human dignity is a thoroughly Gospel task. It can't be done outside the political arena. That's why the church does it. It's not trying to impress people with being *au courant*."

Secularization

One criticism of the bishops echoes a complaint that conservative Protestants have long registered against their ecclesiastical leaders: in speaking out on every conceivable issue, the church runs the risk of losing sight of its essential task—to preach the Gospel message. "Some people will feel we have lost our spirituality," admits Cleveland's Bishop Anthony Pilla, 50, who nonetheless supports the pastoral letter, with some reservations.

In a new 206-page critique of the bishops' social policies, Political Theorist J. Brian Benestad of the University of Scranton argues that by subtly secularizing the church, the bishops are surrendering their most

effective strategy for changing society. It is papal teaching, he argues, that evangelism and the spiritual education of individuals must be the church's primary way of reforming society.

"Some people say we shouldn't talk politics and that we should address ourselves to truly religious issues," Bernardin answers. "Well, it's not as simple as all that. It's our responsibility to address the moral dimension of the social issues we face. These issues, of course, do have a political dimension as well as a moral dimension. I don't deny that, but that doesn't mean we're not permitted to talk about them. But our perspective must always be from the moral or ethical dimension. I reject out of hand that we have taken a leftward swing. What we are trying to do is focus on the teaching of the Gospel as we understand it, and to apply that teaching to the various social issues of the day. Our central theme is our respect for God's gift of life, our insistence that the human person has inherent value and dignity."

What impact will the bishops' words on weapons have? "It's too early to say what activism will mean in the broader American context," says Harvard Political Scientist Stanley Hoffmann. "Certainly in terms of numbers alone to Catholics represent a potent political force. In part it depends on what they do with the pastoral letter. If it's stuck in a file cabinet some place, the long-term effect will be minimal."

"You can't move through the water this fast without a lot of turbulence around the edges."

The bishops, of course, have no intention of filing away their forthcoming pastoral letter. But the day is long past when the bishops, or even the Pope, can tell the American Catholic community what to think, let alone how to act. On the issue of abortion, linked so closely by the bishops to that of nuclear arms, surveys by the National Opinion Research Center show that 77% of Catholics think that the law should permit abortion for a danger to the mother's life, and 44% for social reasons, such as a family's poverty. American Catholics widely disregard the Pope and bishops on birth control. Says Loyola University of Chicago Psychologist and ex-Priest Eugene Kennedy: "You can't deliver a Catholic vote on anything any more—Catholics are not one isolated bloc with homogeneous interests."

But if the bishops cannot persuade skeptical Catholics to join their stand against nuclear arms, both the White House and nuclear-freeze advocates believe that they can become a potent force in shaping and influencing what is likely to become an increasingly important political issue in the months ahead. Says Archbishop Oscar Lipscomb of Mobile, 51, with some trepidation: "We are going to divide America over this issue. But the people of America have shown resilience. They can work through it and heal us."

Lipscomb and many other bishops talk of the need to begin a dialogue on the issue of the morality of nuclear arms. The importance of the pastoral is that it is not an authoritarian fiat, but basically an invitation to lay Catholics, as well as to priests and nuns, to join the bishops in the kind of anguished soul searching that produced the document. It is that openness, that tentative quality of the pastoral, that appeals to Sister Mary Evelyn Jegen of Chicago, national coordinator of Pax Christi. Says she: "I see that the bishops are caught because they've got three hats on. They're trying to deal with this issue as theologians, as pastors and as public figures. But the fact that they're trying, and to some extent succeeding, shows the health and strength of the church. And the open consultation with others, their willingness to listen and learn—that's so *new*."

Concern with Humanity

Father Theodore Hesburgh, 65, president of the University of Notre Dame, is not worried about the debate within the church over the propriety of the bishops' actions. Says he: "You can't move through the water this fast without a lot of turbulence around the edges." The situation, he thinks, is stabilizing. And Hesburgh praises the pastoral characteristics of today's bishops: their concern with humanity as well as with doctrine. "They embrace what is good," says Hesburgh, "and a little imperfection too. They know that it's better to encourage little flowers than to sweep the ground clean. It's exciting to be a priest in the middle of an exciting development: the blossoming of the Gospel in new ways."

"Peace has never been achieved, even for a while, by moral inspiration alone."

Says Bishop Gumbleton: "We're offering this as a guide to conscience, not the way it was done in the past: 'We know best. This is the answer.' We are trying to engage the whole church in the same process the committee went through." Gumbleton's colleague, Bishop Reilly, agrees: "We aren't claiming this is Almighty God handing down the truth from the mountain as with Moses. It's the bishops of the U.S., trying to apply the teachings of Jesus Christ to issues never faced before by the human family."

The Catholic Church, and indeed all churches, has preached peace across the centuries and has never achieved it. That is no reason why they should not continue to preach the message and to try to change mankind. That is their vocation. But peace has never been achieved, even for a while, by moral inspiration alone. It has always required the highly imperfect, compromise-ridden and impure actions of political leaders. The dilemma potentially posed by the bishops' strivings is that reaching for the best could undermine the good, and that striving for the ideal might undermine the practical.

Time *magazine published this article as part of a special issue on The National Conference of Bishops pastoral letter.*

314

> *"We do not perceive any situation in which. . .nuclear war on however restricted a scale can be morally justified."*

The Bishops' Pastoral Letter: A Summary

National Conference of Catholic Bishops

The U.S. bishops released the official summary of their 1983 pastoral letter on war and peace June 9. During their May 2-3 meeting in Chicago, the bishops voted to defer action on the official summary until after the meeting. A draft reflecting the changes in the pastoral adopted during the Chicago meeting was later mailed to the bishops, who were asked to comment and vote on it. In the summary, the bishops synthesize main points of the pastoral letter, pointing to the difference between its universally binding principles and those principles that allow for a diversity of opinion. The bishops discourage readers of the pastoral letter from using passages out of context and from using brief portions of the document "to support positions it does not intend to convey." The experience of preparing the pastoral letter, says the summary, made the bishops aware of "the range of strongly held opinion in the Catholic community on questions of both fact and judgment concerning issues of war and peace." The bishops urge "mutual respect among individuals and groups in the church as this letter is analyzed and discussed." The full text of the summary follows.

The Second Vatican Council opened its evaluation of modern warfare with the statement: "The whole human race faces a moment of supreme crisis in its advance toward maturity." We agree with the council's assessment; the crisis of the moment is embodied in the threat which nuclear weapons pose for the world and much that we hold dear in the world. We have seen and felt the effects of the crisis of the nuclear age in the lives of people we serve. Nuclear weaponry has drastically changed the nature of warfare, and the arms race poses a threat to human life and human civilization which is without precedent.

We write this letter from the perspective of Catholic faith. Faith does not insulate us from the daily challenges of life, but intensifies our desire to address

them precisely in light of the Gospel which has come to us in the person of the risen Christ. Through the resources of faith and reason we desire in this letter to provide hope for people in our day and direction toward a world freed of the nuclear threat.

As Catholic bishops we write this letter as an exercise of our teaching ministry. The Catholic tradition on war and peace is a long and complex one; it stretches from the Sermon on the Mount to the statements of Pope John Paul II. We wish to explore and explain the resources of the moral-religious teaching and to apply it to specific questions of our day. In doing this we realize and we want readers of this letter to recognize that not all statements in this letter have the same moral authority. At times we state universally binding moral principles found in the teaching of the church; at other times the pastoral letter makes specific applications, observations and recommendations which allow for diversity of opinion on the part of those who assess the factual data of situations differently. However, we expect Catholics to give our moral judgments serious consideration when they are forming their own views on specific problems.

The experience of preparing this letter has manifested to us the range of strongly held opinion in the Catholic community on questions of both fact and judgment concerning issues of war and peace. We urge mutual respect among individuals and groups in the church as this letter is analyzed and discussed. Obviously, as bishops we believe that such differences should be expressed within the framework of Catholic moral teaching. We need in the church not only conviction and commitment, but also civility and charity.

While this letter is addressed principally to the Catholic community, we want it to make a contribution to the wider public debate in our country on the dangers and dilemmas of the nuclear age. Our contribution will not be primarily technical or political, but we are convinced that there is no satisfactory answer to the human problems of the nuclear age which fails to consider the moral and religious dimensions of the questions we face.

Although we speak in our own name as Catholic bishops of the church in the United States, we have been conscious in the preparation of this letter of the consequences our teaching will have not only for the United States, but for other nations as well. One important expression of this awareness has been the consultation we have had, by correspondence and in an important meeting held at the Vatican (Jan. 18-19, 1983), with representatives of European bishops' conferences. This consultation with bishops of other countries and, of course, with the Holy See has been very helpful to us.

Catholic teaching has always understood peace in positive terms. In the words of Pope John Paul II: "Peace is not just the absence of war. . . .Like a cathedral, peace must be constructed patiently and with unshakable faith" (Coventry, England, 1982). Peace is the fruit of order. Order in human society must be shaped on the basis of respect for the transcendence of God and the unique dignity of each person, understood in terms of freedom, justice, truth and love. To avoid war in our day we must be intent on building peace in an increasingly interdependent world. In Part III of this letter we set forth a positive vision of peace and the demands such a vision makes on diplomacy, national policy and personal choices.

While pursuing peace incessantly, it is also necessary to limit the use of force in a world comprised of nation states, faced with common problems but devoid of an adequate international political authority. Keeping the peace in the nuclear age is a moral and political imperative. In Parts I and II of this letter we set forth both the principles of Catholic teaching on war and a series of judgments based on these principles about concrete policies. In making these judgments we speak as moral teachers, not as technical experts.

I. Some Principles, Norms and Premises of Catholic Teaching

A. On War

1. Catholic teaching begins in every case with a presumption against war and for peaceful settlement of disputes. In exceptional cases, determined by the moral principles of the just-war tradition, some uses of force are permitted.

2. Every nation has a right and duty to defend itself against unjust aggression.

3. Offensive war of any kind is not morally justifiable.

4. It is never permitted to direct nuclear or conventional weapons to "the indiscriminate destruction of whole cities or vast areas with their populations" (The Pastoral Constitution on the Church in the Modern World, 80). The intentional killing of innocent civilians or noncombatants is always wrong.

5. Even defensive response to unjust attack can cause destruction which violates the principle of proportionality, going far beyond the limits of legitimate defense. This judgment is particularly important when assessing planned use of nuclear weapons. No defensive strategy, nuclear or conventional, which exceeds the limits of proportionality is morally permissible.

B. On Deterrence

1. "In current conditions 'deterrence' based on balance, certainly not as an end in itself, but as a step on the way toward a progressive disarmament, may still be judged morally acceptable. Nonetheless, in order to ensure peace it is indispensable not to be satisfied with this minimum, which is always susceptible to the real danger of explosion" (Pope John Paul II, Message to U.N. Special Session on Disarmament, 8; June 1982).

2. No *use* of nuclear weapons which would violate the principles of discrimination or proportionality may be *intended* in a strategy of deterrence. The moral demands of Catholic teaching require resolute willingness not to intend or to do moral evil even to save our own lives or the lives of those we love.

"The arms race is one of the greatest curses on the human race."

---

3. Deterrence is not an adequate strategy as a long-term basis for peace; it is a transitional strategy justifiable only in conjunction with resolute determination to pursue arms control and disarmament. We are convinced that "the fundamental principle on which our present peace depends must be replaced by another, which declares that the true and solid peace of nations consists not in equality of arms, but in mutual trust alone" (Pope John XXIII, "Peace On Earth," 113).

C. The Arms Race and Disarmament

1. The arms race is one of the greatest curses on the human race; it is to be condemned as a danger, an act of aggression against the poor and a folly which does not provide the security it promises (cf. Pastoral Constitution on the Church in the Modern World, 81; Statement of the Holy See to the United Nations, 1976).

2. Negotiations must be pursued in every reasonable form possible; they should be governed by the "demand that the arms race should cease; that the stockpiles which exist in various countries should be reduced equally and simultaneously by the parties concerned; that nuclear weapons should be banned; and that a general agreement should eventually be reached about progressive disarmament and an effective method of control" (Pope John XXIII, "Peace On Earth," 112).

D. On Personal Conscience

1. Military Service: "All those who enter the

military service in loyalty to their country should look upon themselves as the custodians of the security and freedom of their fellow countrymen; and when they carry out their duty properly, they are contributing to the maintenance of peace" (Pastoral Constitution on the Church in the Modern World, 79).

2. Conscientious Objection: "Moreover, it seems just that laws should make humane provision for the case of conscientious objectors who refuse to carry arms, provided they accept some other form of community service" (Pastoral Constitution on the Church in the Modern World, 79).

3. Non-violence: "In this same spirit we cannot but express our admiration for all who forgo the use of violence to vindicate their rights and resort to other means of defense which are available to weaker parties, provided it can be done without harm to the rights and duties of others and of the community" (Pastoral Constitution on the Church in the Modern World, 78).

4. Citizens and Conscience: "Once again we deem it opportune to remind our children of their duty to take an active part in public life, and to contribute toward the attainment of the common good of the entire human family as well as to that of their own political community. . . .In other words, it is necessary that human beings, in the intimacy of their own consciences, should so live and act in their temporal lives as to create a synthesis between scientific, technical and professional elements on the one hand, and spiritual values on the other" (Pope John XXIII, "Peace On Earth," 146; 150).

II. Moral Principles and Policy Choices

As bishops in the United States, assessing the concrete circumstances of our society, we have made a number of observations and recommendations in the process of applying moral principles to specific policy choices.

"Decisions about nuclear weapons are among the most pressing moral questions of our age."

A. On the Use of Nuclear Weapons

1. Counterpopulation Use: Under no circumstances may nuclear weapons or other instruments of mass slaughter be used for the purpose of destroying population centers or other predominantly civilian targets. Retaliatory action which would indiscriminately and disproportionately take many wholly innocent lives, lives of people who are in no way responsible for reckless actions of their government, must also be condemned.

2. The Initiation of Nuclear War: We do not perceive any situation in which the deliberate initiation of nuclear war on however restricted a scale can be morally justified. Non-nuclear attacks by another state must be resisted by other than nuclear means. Therefore, a serious obligation exists to develop morally acceptable non-nuclear defensive strategies as rapidly as possible. In this letter we urge NATO to move rapidly toward the adoption of a "no first use" policy, but we recognize this will take time to implement and will require the development of an adequate alternative defense posture.

3. Limited Nuclear War: Our examination of the various arguments on this question makes us highly skeptical about the real meaning of "limited." One of the criteria of the just-war teaching is that there must be a reasonable hope of success in bringing about justice and peace. We must ask whether such a reasonable hope can exist once nuclear weapons have been exchanged. The burden of proof remains on those who assert that meaningful limitation is possible. In our view the first imperative is to prevent any use of nuclear weapons, and we hope that leaders will resist the notion that nuclear conflict can be limited, contained or won in any traditional sense.

B. On Deterrence

In concert with the evaluation provided by Pope John Paul II, we have arrived at a strictly conditioned moral acceptance of deterrence. In this letter we have outlined criteria and recommendations which indicate the meaning of conditional acceptance of deterrence policy. We cannot consider such a policy adequate as a longterm basis for peace.

C. On Promoting Peace

1. We support immediate, bilateral, verifiable agreements to halt the testing, production and deployment of new nuclear weapons systems. This recommendation is not to be identified with any specific political initiative.

2. We support efforts to achieve deep cuts in the arsenals of both superpowers; efforts should concentrate first on systems which threaten the retaliatory forces of either major power.

3. We support early and successful conclusion of negotiations of a comprehensive test ban treaty.

4. We urge new efforts to prevent the spread of nuclear weapons in the world and to control the conventional arms race, particularly the conventional arms trade.

5. We support in an increasingly interdependent world political and economic policies designed to protect human dignity and to promote the human rights of every person, especially the least among us. In this regard we call for the establishment of some form of global authority adequate to the needs of the international common good.

This letter includes many judgments from the

perspective of ethics, politics and strategy needed to speak concretely and correctly to the "moment of supreme crisis" identified by Vatican II. We stress again that readers should be aware, as we have been, of the distinction between our statement of moral principles and of official church teaching and our application of these to concrete issues. We urge that special care be taken not to use passages out of context; neither should brief portions of this document be cited to support positions it does not intend to convey or which are not truly in accord with the spirit of its teaching.

In concluding this summary we respond to two key questions often asked about this pastoral letter:

Why do we address these matters fraught with such complexity, controversy and passion? We speak as pastors, not politicians. We are teachers, not technicians. We cannot avoid our reponsibility to lift up the moral dimensions of the choices before our world and nation. The nuclear age is an era of moral as well as physical danger. We are the first generation since Genesis with the power to threaten the created order. We cannot remain silent in the face of such danger. Why do we address these issues? We are simply trying to live up to the call of Jesus to be peacemakers in our own time and situation.

What are we saying? Fundamentally, we are saying that the decisions about nuclear weapons are among the most pressing moral questions of our age. While these decisions have obvious military and political aspects, they involve fundamental moral choices. In simple terms, we are saying that good ends (defending one's country, protecting freedom, etc.) cannot justify immoral means (the use of weapons which kill indiscriminately and threaten whole societies). We fear that our world and nation are headed in the wrong direction. More weapons with greater destructive potential are produced every day. More and more nations are seeking to become nuclear powers. In our quest for more and more security we fear we are actually becoming less and less secure.

In the words of our Holy Father, we need a "moral about-face." The whole world must summon the moral courage and technical means to say no to nuclear conflict; no to weapons of mass destruction; no to an arms race which robs the poor and the vulnerable; and no to the moral danger of a nuclear age which places before humankind indefensible choices of constant terror or surrender. Peacemaking is not an optional commitment. It is a requirement of our faith. We are called to be peacemakers, not by some movement of the moment, but by our Lord Jesus. The content and context of our peacemaking are set not by some political agenda or ideological program, but by the teaching of his church.

Ultimately this letter is intended as an expression of Christian faith, affirming the confidence we have that the risen Lord remains with us precisely in moments of crisis. It is our belief in his presence and power among us which sustains us in confronting the awesome challenge of the nuclear age. We speak from faith to provide hope for all who recognize the challenge and are working to confront it with the resources of faith and reason.

"We support efforts to achieve deep cuts in the arsenals of both superpowers."

To approach the nuclear issue in faith is to recognize our absolute need for prayer: We urge and invite all to unceasing prayer and works of penance for peace with justice for all people. In a spirit of prayerful hope we present this message of peace.

The US bishops released the official summary of their 1983 pastoral letter on June 9, 1983.

"History is more on the side of the bishops who challenge our anti-Soviet obsession than on the side of their critics."

viewpoint 84

The Bishops' Proposal Could Bring Peace

Edward Cuddy

The American bishops have stepped into a hornet's nest with their eyes wide open. For two centuries, the United States Government could count on their automatic support for the nation's wars. But no more. Their pastoral letter, "The Challenge of Peace," declares the conservative writer, Erik von Kuenhelt-Leddhin, promises to do "nothing less than place the American Catholic Church in opposition to the nuclear strategy of the United States."

Christian morality, according to the first two drafts of the pastoral letter drafted by the National Conference of Catholic Bishops, permits no nuclear destruction of civilian populations, not even in retaliation for Soviet destruction of American cities. It allows no nuclear attack on military targets which could devastate nearby populations; no first use of nuclear weapons, not even to repulse a conventional attack. The bishops grudgingly tolerate nuclear deterrence, the cornerstone of American strategy, but only as a temporary condition while seeking progressive disarmament. But they virtually nullify this limited concession by opposing the very threat to inflict nuclear destruction on the enemy.

The pastoral document goes beyond mere criticism of our nuclear policy. It challenges the sacred dogmas that have inspired our cold war: that American power is the guarantor of freedom in a world threatened by Soviet aggression. The Russian threat is real, the bishops admit. Yet, with equal force, they fault the "competing ambitions" of both superpowers for pushing the planet to the brink of disaster. They condemn that "form of anti-Sovietism" which paralyzes peacemaking, along with the "obsessive perception" of "irrational" Soviet leaders "striving insanely for world conquests." The Russians are not "monstrous" but "human beings created in the image and likeness of God," they assert, amid dire warnings that our own "hardness of heart" can cement the world into a dangerous status quo.

Edward Cuddy, "The American Bishops and the Soviet Threat," *America,* April 16, 1983. Reprinted with permission of author.

"God bless the Catholic bishops," declares Southern Baptist leader, Foy Valentine, echoing many activists who have longed for American Catholicism to puts its muscle into the antiwar movement. Elsewhere, however, the churchmen have scraped raw nerves. "Uninformed, unrealistic and morally irresponsible"—that's how philosopher Sidney Hook labels the episcopal document. It ignores "the guiding dogmas of Communist theory and practice" and the "history of Soviet aggression." Its opposition to nuclear retaliation, he fumes, exposes America to becoming "first red, then dead." Mr. Hook's rancorous reaction is shared by many citizens, including a vocal group of conservative Catholics who would save both church and state from the idealistic bishops. Phyllis Schlafly, convinced that America's atom bomb was a gift from "a wise God," detects a streak of cowardice in the pastoral and predicts that most American Catholics will never give in to "loving the Russians." "The bishops are pushing us down the road of appeasement and surrender," declares Michael Novak, a point seconded by two dozen Catholic Congressmen in a public letter to the American hierarchy. White House aides have hinted loosely that "foreign agents" may have influenced the authors of the pastoral letter.

Are the Bishops Right?

The final draft is due in May. Designed primarily to help Catholics form a mature conscience, secondarily to shape public opinion, it stands as an open invitation, not only to ponder the morality of our nuclear strategy, but to re-examine our anti-Soviet obsessions and the nature of the Russo-American power struggle. Already powerful pressures have surfaced to press the bishops to dilute the final draft. The finished product, claims a consultant to the bishops, will remain 95 percent unchanged. But, "the hawks will win insofar as the bishops will sharpen their criticism of the Soviets, focusing more on their aggressive policy." Should the

Catholic leaders bend to this pressure?

A quick glance at history lends currency to the bishops' hawkish critics. The growth of the Russian state from the modest Duchy of Muscovy in the 15th century to the sprawling empire that straddles the Eurasian land mass today reflects the expansionist drive in Russian history. Obsessed with their own security, Soviet leaders have endangered the security of others. The repressive governments in Eastern Europe and the Soviet buildup of nuclear and conventional forces testify to the reality of the threat. American diplomacy, however flawed, has played a significant role in checking Soviet power. One cannot lightly dismiss the thoughtful criticism of both liberals and conservatives that nuclear arsenals have prevented all-out war between the superpowers. The pastoral letter, claims *The New Republic*, weakens deterrence—"the only responsible attitude toward nuclear weapons that has so far been conceived."

"Events in the early 1960's tend to confirm the bishops' inference that the very strategy of deterrence has accelerated the arms race."

Nevertheless, a critical study of history can buttress the political theology of the pastoral letter. Soviet behavior in the nuclear age can be understood only against the background of Russian history, a 300-year struggle to keep pace with the superior military technology of the West. This feature—so salient in Russian experience, so obscure in American consciousness—must inform our response to the bishops' stunning challenge to American diplomacy and the mindset that supports it.

Ever since the days of that famous "Westernizer," Peter the Great (1682-1725), the Russians have been in a technological contest with Western powers. As leaders of a nation assaulted repeatedly by Western European nations, Peter was dominated by one conviction: Either adopt Western technology or perish at Western hands. His policies paid off at Poltava in 1709, when Russian forces, armed with Western-type weapons, defeated the Swedish army and launched their own nation as a major force in European politics.

Thanks to the industrial and military programs of Peter and his successors—along with the bitter Russian winter and the brilliant strategy of her military leaders—the Czar's forces were able to repel Napoleon's invading army in 1812. But then the industrial revolution swept across 19th-century Europe, and Russia's enemies opened a wide technological lead. Japan, a sliver of a nation which had adopted Western technology and weaponry, inflicted a startling defeat on the Russians in the war of 1904-05. Then came catastrophic World War I when the poorly armed forces of the Czar were mauled by the Kaiser's armies, powered by the humming factories of the continent's dominant industrial power. Defeat came amid staggering results: millions of casualties at the front, strikes and riots at home and, finally, the upheaval which swept the tottering Czarist regime into the debris of history and ushered the Bolsheviks to power.

A View of History

The Great War revived harsh lessons, learned long before, under Peter the Great. The people groaned when Joseph Stalin imposed his strenuous program of heavy industry and military production in 1928. But there could be no slackening of the tempo, he told the 16th Party Congress. "Old Russia" had suffered "continual beating" for "falling behind." Either Russia catches up to the advanced countries, "or they crush us," he warned.

Modernization, Soviet style, was a bone-crushing, ruthless enterprise, generating rebellion and bloody repression. But when the German armies came again in World War II, the Russians were already. Along a 1,000-mile front, the Nazi armies, three million strong—the most formidible military machine ever assembled—hurtled across the Russian border, their advanced guns, tanks and aircraft blitzkrieging Russian troops deep into the interior. At bloodsoaked Stalingrad, Soviet forces held the line. Backed by a torrent of howitzers, machine guns, Katyusha rockets, modern tanks and aircraft pouring from their factories, they launched the great counteroffensive that would help destroy the Nazi war machine.

Victory brought no rest for the Russians, however. The atomic ashes of Hiroshima marked a new, terrifying stage in their perennial race with the West, this time with the nuclear-powered Americans setting the pace.

Although Americans generally blame the cold war on the ruthless Soviet takeover of Eastern Europe after 1945, many historians are convinced that defense, not global conquest, was the basic passion spurring Soviet expansion. For centuries, Eastern Europe had been Russia's exposed flank, the turbulent corridor through which Poles, Swedes, Frenchmen and Germans had repeatedly battered the homeland. Twenty million deaths in World War II drove home the point: Soviet security depended on Soviet control over the power vacuum that was Eastern Europe.

However much we attribute the cold war to Soviet aggression, the Catholic bishops are on solid historical grounds when they indict "both the U.S. and the U.S.S.R." as "the players" in the dangerous game of "superpower rivalry." Indeed, the United States "was the first to build and use" atomic weapons, the bishops remind us, and the bombing of Hiroshima and Nagasaki constituted a "butchery of untold magnitude." From the outset, we enjoyed a commanding lead in atomic weaponry against an enemy that had suffered repeatedly from technologically superior powers. In the Eisenhower years, Secretary of State John Foster Dulles talked glibly of "massive retaliation" while the United States wove a web of alliances that ringed the Soviet Empire from Western Europe to East Asia. In the process, Russia's nightmare, West Germany, was rearmed and incorporated into a nuclearized NATO command structure.

Washington's sabre rattling came at a bad time—just when the Soviet Union was vibrating to the power struggle between its dovish premier, Georgi Malenkov, and his hawkish opponent, Nikita Khrushchev. Malenkov wanted to cut military production in favor of consumer goods. But these were disastrous policies, charged Pravda, while enemies "were hatching plans for a new world war." Anxieties stirred by American diplomacy helped tip the balance toward the more belligerent Khrushchev in his bid for power.

Events of the 60's

Events in the early 1960's tend to confirm the bishops' inference that the very strategy of deterrence has accelerated the arms race. John F. Kennedy arrived at the White House after thumping the Republicans for permitting a "missile gap" favoring the Soviets. That "missile gap," as it turned out, actually favored Washington. Yet the Kennedy Administration, as its Defense Secretary Robert F. McNamara admitted recently, used the myth to charge full steam ahead in the arms race. The United States "opened an enormous lead over the Soviet Union in I.C.B.M.'s and Polaris missiles" triggering a "massive Soviet effort to catch up," claims historian Robert Divine. "The nuclear arms buildup of the sixties. . .thus became Kennedy's grimmest legacy."

"By the end of the 1970's the spirit of detente was ebbing before a resurgence of Soviet-American tensions."

The Cuban missile crisis of 1961 threw the frenzied arms race into high gear. That showdown, so many Americans believe, was President Kennedy's finest hour. Khrushchev's reckless effort to install nuclear missiles in Cuba was stopped cold by a resolute President whose skillful diplomacy removed the threat while avoiding war.

But there is a Russian side to the story. Eighteen months earlier, the United States had tried to overthrow Fidel Castro through the ill-fated invasion that ended in the disaster at the Bay of Pigs. Since Cuba had already turned to the Soviet Union for support, Khrushchev was on the spot. A second, more successful invasion would dramatize his inability to protect an ally against Yankee aggression. Convinced that another invasion was coming "unless we did something," he resorted to nuclear missiles as "the most tangible and effective deterrent to further aggression." Moreover, Khrushchev was only following the American example, he reports in his memoirs. From American bases in Europe and Turkey, "Our vital industrial centers were directly threatened by planes armed with atomic bombs and guided missiles tipped with nuclear warheads. . .and now they would learn just what it feels like to have enemy missiles pointing at you."

Edward Cuddy is professor of history and government at Daemen College, Amherst, N.Y.

"[The Bishops] will not truly reduce the danger. They will truly reduce our capacity to deter it."

The Bishops' Proposal Encourages War

John P. Lehman, Jr.

The proposed pastoral letter on nuclear arms by the Committee on War and Peace of the National Conference of Catholic Bishops has elicited a good deal of attention and comment.

Because nuclear war would threaten all of civilization, the bishops reason that nuclear deterrence could be justified only on the basis of a paradox: the use of evil (the threat to use nuclear weapons) in order to prevent greater evil (the actual use of nuclear weapons). Faced with this paradox, the bishops then offer proposals to reduce the immorality of deterrence by reducing the numbers of nuclear weapons and their role in preventing war.

Oddly enough, it is possible to agree completely with the letter's assertions about the moral paradox of deterrence and to disagree completely with its specific recommendations to reduce the danger of war. That is because the letter's points on the moral paradox are logical and well-founded in moral philosophy, while many of the recommendations are neither well-informed nor logical. What is worse, if adopted, such recommendations could lead directly to immoral consequences.

The bishops' conclusions about the moral problem of deterrence are far from new. The threat to take human life in order to preserve it has always been a central dilemma; the nuclear era raises this dilemma to global proportions but does not change its essential moral significance. Except for the pacifists, most philosophers—and most nations—have reasoned that self-defense was a moral risk worth taking compared to the immorality of submission to aggression, with its certain loss of innocent lives and liberty. Nearly 40 years of experience with nuclear deterrence have not changed this conviction. The pacifist argument continues to be refuted by the behavior of the aggressor or totalitarian regimes. The bishops agree reluctantly with this proposition, even in the nuclear era, when they accept the moral paradox as a justification for deterrence.

This real problem with the bishops' letter then is not with the moral paradox of deterrence, but rather the means proposed by the bishops to reduce it.

The Bishops' Strategy

1. In their discussion of nuclear strategy, the bishops reduce deterrence itself to an empty incantation. They reject the strategy of retaliation against population centers as an immoral act of revenge. At the same time, they decry the development and deployment of weapons with "hard target kill" capability, that is, weapons capable of destroying other weapons rather than civilian populations. But if we will not retaliate to attack by an act of revenge (destroying the Soviet cities) or an act of strategy (destroying the Soviet weapons), then how do we deter?

2. American strategy has long been predicated on the concept of Mutual Assured Destruction, which essentially holds both the U.S. and Soviet populations hostage to retaliation. President Reagan, recognizing the moral obliquity of such a strategy, is trying to move the U.S. away from the hair-trigger (and hair-raising) implications of such a nuclear posture. U.S. forces are therefore being given greater capability to attack Soviet forces rather than Soviet population centers, hoping to reduce collateral damage from nuclear attack in the process. But the nuclear freeze advocated by the bishops would arrest this change—in effect, freezing us in the very posture of Mutual Assured Destruction that the bishops oppose.

3. The bishops' endorsement of a mutually verifiable "freeze" on testing and deployment, even if it could be brought about, supposes that deterrence is a static concept. In some respects, the Soviets now field a force more numerous, more modern and more capable than our own. The freeze does not arrest this trend—the U.S.

John P. Lehman, Jr., "The U.S. Catholic Bishops and Nuclear Arms," *The Wall Street Journal,* November 15, 1982. Reprinted by permission of *The Wall Street Journal,* © Dow Jones & Company, Inc., 1982. All Rights Reserved.

B-52s and the current submarine force will face retirement and obsolescence in fairly short order whether there is a freeze or not, thereby eroding the sufficiency of our deterrent. Hence, and arrangement that halts the U.S. effort to develop and deploy more modern weapons will not only confirm the Soviet advantages, it will increase them.

Our Deterrent Is Essential

4. The erosion of our deterrent is hardly the basis for mutual disarmament though it is surely a step toward unilateral disarmament—which the bishops oppose. It is an odd strategy indeed that expects the Soviets to negotiate fair and deep reductions when every day of a freeze would improve their own position.

As for the recommendation that the U.S. take unilateral risks to elicit a constructive Soviet response, we have had more than a decade of arms-control efforts based on American restraint. The facts of the relative strengths of both sides today, compared to 1970, indicate that these risks have been run to no obvious benefit for the stability of deterrence or effective arms control.

5. "First use" of battlefield nuclear weapons in Europe is rejected by the bishops because of the dangers of escalation. Instead, we are advised that a conventional attack should be resisted by conventional means. But the bishops should have considered that the true objective of deterrence in Europe is the prevention of war itself. The uncertainty of NATO's response, including the possibility of escalation, is an essential part of that deterrence. Moreover, the bishops do not seem to have realized that conventional forces take far more of society's resources than do nuclear weapons, a fact that imposes its own heavy moral choices. (Was the slaughter of the Somme really more moral than the bombing of Hiroshima?)

"In their discussion of nuclear strategy, the bishops reduce deterrence itself to an empty incantation."

---

6. The issue of attacking military targets in or near civilian areas is another manifestation of the moral paradox. In this instance, however, the bishops believe that they can oppose such attacks on the ground that civilian losses will be disproportionate, despite the clear intention to attack only military installations. Have the bishops considered, however, that the practical moral consequence of such a prohibition will be to encourage our adversaries to locate their forces in or near civilian areas? In a still broader application, how do the bishops propose to deal with terrorism, when getting at the terrorist risks the lives of "civilians"—the hostages or the bystanders? Or does the prohibition only apply to nuclear terrorism?

7. The bishops' opposition to weapons with hard-target kill capability, strategic planning for a nuclear warfighting capability and limited or tactical nuclear warface is absurd in terms of the basic argument. One cannot complain about the immorality of nuclear war because of its unlimited impact and then oppose the development of a strategy or a technology that seeks to limit its impact.

In summary, the bishops have said something true and something new. The trouble is that what is true—the paradox of deterrence—is not new, and what is new—proposals to reduce the paradox—are not true. They will not truly reduce the danger. They will truly reduce our capacity to deter it.

John P. Lehman, Jr. is Secretary of the Navy.

> *"Nuclear war theory and nuclear war itself run counter to two fundamental . . . ideas that have influenced Catholic thinking on questions of war and peace."*

The Bishops' Approach Is Sound

Marcus Raskin

As one of his first acts of the new year, Pope John Paul II announced the elevation of eighteen bishops to the College of Cardinals. Among them was Archbishop Joseph Bernardin of Chicago, chairman of the Bishops' Committee on War and Peace, which prepared the Pastoral Letter on War and Peace, the church's strongest condemnation yet of nuclear weapons. The letter, which draws upon extensive testimony from expert witnesses as well as theological discussions among the bishops, caused consternation in the Reagan Administration. Vernon Walters, the President's roving ambassador, was dispatched to the Vatican to convey Reagan's displeasure. But the main effect of this overture was to strengthen the draft statement, which must be approved by the National Conference of Catholic Bishops.

The White House's discomfiture comes as no great surprise. The pastoral letter hurls a direct challenge at the most basic assumptions of the modern national security state. The bishops advocate arms control as a way of easing international tensions, halting nuclear proliferation, reducing conventional forces and encouraging the development of peaceful exchanges between potential adversaries. They call for a cutback in arms sales and the establishment of multilateral controls over arms exports. The pastoral letter advocates deep cuts in the nuclear arsenals of both superpowers, a verifiable nuclear freeze, a comprehensive test-ban treaty and procedures to prevent accidental nuclear exchanges. The bishops denounce the MX missile, oppose any nation acquiring a first-strike capability and characterize planning for limited nuclear war as morally repugnant. And they favor maintaining a clear distinction between nuclear and nonnuclear weapons. In sum, the Pastoral Letter on War and Peace is far more comprehensive than any previous statement by the church, the Second Vatican Council or the Pope regarding

Marcus Raskin, "War, Peace and the Bishops," *The Nation,* January 29, 1983. *The Nation Magazine,* Nation Associates Incorporated © 1983.

nuclear war and the arms race.

We have no illusions that the pastoral letter will immediately win unanimous approval. Rarely do pronouncements of church policy go unchallenged from within or by secular critics without. Nevertheless, when religious figures of such stature speak out on a fundamental issue affecting the future of humankind, their words should have considerable impact. And the letter does not confine itself to matters of policy; included is a section detailing what both government officials and private citizens can do about the arms race right now.

The Absurdist Position

The moral dimension of the church's case against nuclear armaments can surely withstand the assaults of its opponents. For all that the advocates of counterforce and deterrence have to offer is a future under the present balance of terror, with the ever-present risk of the ultimate holocaust. The defenders of the nuclear status quo represent what I shall call the *absurdist* position; it is predicated on an antimorality and an antihumanity, involving preparation for a war that could cause the extinction not only of one's enemies but of one's own people as well.

The absurdist approach threatens nuclear war in local disputes. It calls for building weapons of mass destruction, devising strategies for their use, planning nuclear Auschwitzes, numbing every shred of moral sensitivity and abandoning the principle of proportionality of means to ends that should guide enlightened statecraft. According to the bishops, this absurdist position has

> strained our moral conception. May a nation threaten what it may never do? May it possess what it may never use? Who is involved in the threat each superpower makes: government officials? or military personnel? or the citizenry in whose "defense" the threat is made?

The bishops argue that nuclear war theory and nuclear war itself run counter to two fundamental although sometimes opposing ideas that have influenced Catholic thinking on questions of war and peace. The first is pacifism; the second is the doctrine of "just war." The bishops treat pacifism with far more seriousness and respect than the church has in the past. No longer is nonviolence a dangerous philosophy to be relegated to the fringes of theology. "The pacifist option" is now to be considered by Catholics. Although they do not openly advocate pacifism, the bishops endorse it as a politically and morally acceptable choice, and they single out for praise peace activists like Dorothy Day and Martin Luther King Jr.

As for the doctrine of just war, the letter points out that it was not meant to condone all war. Indeed, the bishops say, rather than contradicting the pacifist viewpoint, the just-war doctrine springs from the same basic tenets of Christianity, namely:

> We should do no harm to our neighbor; our enemy is the key test of whether we love our neighbor; and the taking of even one human life is a prospect we should consider in fear and trembling.

The just-war theory originated in St. Augustine's teaching that to protect the innocent it may be necessary to do harm to the enemy. Augustine's view was expanded by St. Thomas Aquinas to include the right of self-defense. But "butchery of untold magnitude," as Pope Paul VI characterized the atomic bombings of Hiroshima and Nagasaki, would fail to meet either philosopher's standard.

According to the bishops, there are seven criteria to be used in determining whether a war is a just one or not. There must be a real possibility of injury to the innocent and a real threat to life and human rights. There must be a "right intention," which means that efforts to reach a peaceful solution must continue during the conflict. And there must be an "avoidance of unnecessarily destructive acts or imposing unreasonable conditions" (e.g., unconditional surrender).

Military violence is to be used by a nation only after all "reasonable means of redress have been pursued." There should be proportionality of means to ends. And national leaders must ask themselves if going to war is a lesser evil than not doing so.

Finally, the bishops say, wars must employ "just means." That is, the lives of civilians must not be endangered. The concept of just means directly contradicts the modern doctrine of total war, under which nation-states seek, through political centralization and technology, to involve civilians on both sides as combatants. Nuclear weapons have become an instrument of the total state, which seeks power as an end in itself.

Just War and Nuclear War

How does nuclear war measure up to the bishops' just-war criteria? Not surprisingly, they conclude that it fails all of their moral tests. In such a war, a nation-state knows no limits and arrogates to itself the power of life and death over all human life on the planet. As they put it: "The destructive potential of the nuclear powers threatens the sovereignty of God over the world which He has brought into being. We could destroy His work."

Having established that proponents of nuclear war can draw no support from the just-war theory, the bishops then consider if there are any circumstances, short of total war, in which national leaders and their military commanders might use nuclear weapons. Stating that under the nonviolent tradition the church "would oppose all use of nuclear weapons under any conditions," the bishops imply that it would reach the same conclusion under the just-war tradition. After all, total, or counterpopulation, warfare was denounced by Pope Pius XII in the 1950s because it meant "the pure and simple annihilation of all human life within the radius of action." The Second Vatican Council called such warfare a "crime against God and man himself meriting unequivocal and unhesitating condemnation." This condemnation was also leveled at nuclear retaliation, for "no Christian can rightfully carry out orders or policies deliberately aimed at killing non-combatants."

"The present tragedy demands new national security policies. . .and the pastoral letter offers much that will be helpful in formulating them."

This represents a startling political change for the American Catholic Church, which, in the days of Francis Cardinal Spellman, supplied religious and ideological support for the cold war, including support for the weapons to be used in what was regarded as almost a holy war against Russia.

The bishops specifically condemn the first use of nuclear weapons. They also criticize NATO policy on tactical nuclear weapons because it authorizes field commanders to use such weapons in the event of a Soviet invasion of Europe. The bishops heard testimony from various experts that commanders would not be able to control or limit the use of nuclear weapons once they had crossed the threshhold. The result, of course, would be an extraordinary loss of life in Europe and genetic damage to future generations. (American and Soviet doctors have estimated that casualties in the first weeks of a nuclear war in Europe would be between 160 million and 180 million.)

One issue that is not adequately addressed in the bishops' letter is the use of nuclear weapons in conflicts in the Third World. The likelihood of the Soviet Union retaliating if the United States intervened with nuclear weapons in a local conflict is not great, but what of their use by nations other than the superpowers? For example, what if Chile used nuclear weapons against Argentina? Could local wars escalate into regional holocausts?

Although the danger of such escalation is not dealt

with, the bishops do call for the proscription of "limited" nuclear war, and they ask if the term has any meaning. Can there really be discriminate targeting? Wouldn't civilian casualties still run into the millions? Wouldn't organized society collapse in a limited nuclear exchange?

In a recent speech former Secretary of Defense Robert McNamara suggested a "no-use" nuclear policy, and he called for the institution of high-level communications links between Moscow and Washington to facilitate such an agreement, or to limit any war that broke out despite these measures. But this seems a variant on the familiar control and management approach. Under this approach, those who wanted to limit nuclear war through arms control and arms management ended up justifying new weapons systems on the ground that they were "invulnerable" (and thus better "deterrents") or new command and control systems which merely provide leaders with more options for using nuclear weapons. "Control" meant finding ways to use nuclear weapons either in limited wars or as "bargaining chips." Thus, while the public debate concerns deterrence, the arms manufacturers, civilian strategists and military planners continue to talk about how to use nuclear weapons in "limited" and "controlled" ways. Rather than how to prevent war, the focus is on deterrence—an essentially passive notion—and on setting supposedly prudent limits on weaponry. Under deterrence, there is a "reasonable" answer to the question "How much is enough?"

Five Moral Problems

As for deterrence theory itself, the bishops raise five moral problems: "(1) the possession of weapons of mass destruction; (2) the accompanying threat and/or intention to use them; (3) the declared, or at least not repudiated, willingness to use such weapons on civilians; (4) the moral significance of the prevention of use of nuclear weapons through a strategy which could not morally be implemented; and (5) the continued escalation of the nuclear arms race with its diversion of resources from other needs."

"The use of strategic nuclear weapons and the declared intent to use them are equally wrong."

The bishops conclude that the use of strategic nuclear weapons and the "declared intent to use them" are equally wrong. Deterrence cannot be an end in itself. It must be accompanied by moves toward disarmament. If a nation does not pursue disarmament negotiations, according to the bishops, "the Catholic Church would certainly have to shift [its position] to one of uncompromising condemnation of both possession and use of such weapons."

The bishops' comments on deterrence are rather murky. One reason for this is that despite their doubts that it will avert nuclear war, they are trying to be "practical" and recognize that most political leaders are unable to think in any other terms.

Deterrence is, of course, a *psychological* construct. The assumption is that one nation can be made to fear another nation because of the latter's superior military power. To Realpoliticians like that great nineteenth-century statesman Henry Kissinger, military power must be used or threatened to achieve national political gains.

The defenders of the deterrence theory argue that nuclear weapons have kept the peace between the superpowers since 1945, but is this so? When the United States had a nuclear monopoly following World War II, the absence of a Soviet deterrent did not lead to a preventive war against Russia—a course advocated by several top generals and certain elements in the Central Intelligence Agency (not to mention Bertrand Russell). In 1960, the proponents of deterrence thought that 100 or 200 strategic weapons on American submarines were quite adequate to deter the Soviet Union. Now defense planners say 10,000 American warheads are not sufficient. Yet there is no evidence that the Russian population has increased to the same degree in the interim. Deterrence has not discouraged other nations from coveting nuclear weapons. As the bishops put it, deterrence has "not, in fact, set in motion the process of disarmament. On the contrary, under its impulse there has been almost unlimited acceleration in building arms."

As an alternative to deterrence, the bishops propose "building peace as the way to prevent war." They call for unilateral initiatives by the United States, which they hope would encourage a Soviet response. As an example of such an initiative they suggest a U.S. pledge to forgo deployment of first-strike weapons like the MX.

A Just Defense

The present tragedy demands new national security policies that moral leaders and their supporters can embrace, and the pastoral letter offers much that will be helpful in formulating them. One might criticize the bishops' interpretation of the just-war theory, which makes acceptable wars in which damage to noncombatants can be minimized. And they are hundreds of years late in acknowledging that pacifism is a viable, humane and sometimes necessary option. One is still left with the question of how to find a satisfactory political and moral course of action. The peoples of the world want neither mass destruction nor limited wars, but they do want a *just defense*.

By a just defense I mean a mode of social protection that recognizes the nation-state's role in the protection of its citizens, recognizes that international institutions such as the United Nations also have such a role, and accepts the principle that governments and people must operate according to moral standards of conduct and not surrender to the madness of proliferating military technology. A just defense requires establishing ways for nations to properly exercise their right of self-defense. Its use should be limited to times when a nation is attacked, and the means should be circumscribed by international law. Military measures that cause ecological damage on an international scale and harm future generations, for example, should be proscribed. Citizens would be obligated to withdraw support from their own governments if they used an unjust defense system—such as nuclear weapons. However, potential aggressors would be put on notice that the nation's people will never submit to them and will continue the struggle through appropriate measures.

The willingness of the church fathers to prescribe a sort of nuclear code of morality for Catholics should cause great alarm among those who hold the reins of power in this country. The withdrawal of the church's blessing from the actions of America's leaders is a novel experience. It is something we would expect from the church in Latin America or Poland—certainly not from the church in the United States.

Whether or not one admits it, the role of religion as a political force is increasing all over the world. The reason is obvious. Science has not brought spiritual progress. It has *decentered* people and driven them to look for roots, for a compass by which to steer their course in an alien world. The search for fundamentalist roots, whether in Lynchburg, Virginia, or Qum, Iran, is a profound symptom of the failure of modernism. This failure is reflected in the bishops' statement that the function of sovereign states is to keep "order and authority in the political community." They cannot speak to the deeper moral obligations of the human community. That is the role of religion.

The bishops' idea of developing Christian cells to confront a "neopagan society" does not mean a call for passivity. It is a call for beginning a series of public confrontations of the kind that Catholic peace activists like the Berrigan brothers pioneered during the Vietnam War and have resumed. The bishops call on people to "move from discussion to witness and action." Possibly the bishops will relate their opposition to nuclear war to the church's position on abortion. Nuclear weapons can destroy future generations; nuclear war is mass abortion. Thus, they may unite "prolife" groups and antinuclear groups—two constituencies that have heretofore been far apart.

The bishops are aware that there are problems in the world other than nuclear weapons. They allude to imperialistic spheres of influence and crushing poverty. They recognize that these problems are connected to the arms race. They suggest that the wastefulness of the arms race is one cause of the dislocations in the world economic system. They speak of mutual needs among the earth's people. Here their thinking is a bit shallow.

Without a clear definition of need, enormous disparities and structural injustice will continue. A rich person's needs are not the same as those of a poor person. Consequently, the issue becomes how to define need broadly enough to encompass equality and social justice. The Catholic Church will have to confront directly the problem of class.

But for the time being, for the bishops, for all of us, "no single issue transcends the need to prevent nuclear war." The bishops conclude with advice to a variety of people—workers in defense industries, parents, priests, young people, scientists and public officials. They ask them to reexamine their daily activities in the light of their letter. And in so doing, they risk creating political turbulence in the name of humanity. Thank God.

Marcus Raskin, a senior fellow at the Institute for Policy Studies, is a member of the editorial board of The Nation *magazine.*

The Bishops' Approach Is Unrealistic

Rupert J. Ederer

Before getting involved in making moral statements about nuclear war and nuclear weaponry, the Catholic Bishops of the United States had best prepare by doing two things. First, they had better rid themselves of any illusion that our political leaders are likely to pay serious attention to what they say. Ours is not an "age of faith" but a post-Christian, therefore neo-barbaric age. The difference between politicians on all sides at present, and for that matter between them and Hitler and Stalin, is a difference of degree and not of kind. Pragmatic secularism is the order of the day and, all pious protestations notwithstanding, only residual traces of real humanism coat the surface. We need scarcely drag out the ho-hum attitude toward the annual murder of millions of human beings in the womb worldwide to prove this point here, need we? So whatever comes of the forthcoming episcopal declaration on nuclear war will simply be an exercise of the provincial *Magisterium* which, so long as it remains within the lines already drawn by the Papal *Magisterium*, will still be legitimate and important, because it will bind the consciences of Catholics. That, ultimately, is why the next step is so necessary.

In dealing with the complex issue of how our nation should prepare to defend itself against an avowed enemy, the Bishops must make sure that they have equipped themselves with the best information available. That includes knowledge of the general guidelines provided in traditional Church teaching on war and self-defense, as well as what has been said by the Supreme *Magisterium* in the specific context of the post-Hiroshima era. It is just possible that the outstanding Popes whom our Church has been blessed with in recent times have already said all that needs to be said in given circumstances. In that case, what provincial Hierarchies may have to say would be redundant and superfluous at best; and at worst it may simply muddle

Rupert J. Ederer, "On War and Peace," *The Wanderer*, February 17, 1983. Reprinted with permission.

or even pervert the teaching of the Papal *Magisterium*.

So far as traditional Catholic teaching is concerned, we know that a nation has a right to defend itself against unjust aggression; and we ought to know also that every citizen has an obligation to help defend his nation according to his capacities. Thus, for example, obedience to conscription laws and paying the extra taxes which wars normally require are actions demanded by legal justice. And legal justice is equally as binding as simple commutative justice, as in buying and selling. Indeed, legal justice presents an even more urgent obligation in given situations, because it is a part of social justice in that it involves the common good and not simply the good of some individual, as is the case with commutative justice.

That, for example, is why I may turn the other cheek when an aggressor threatens me individually; but I may not do so when unjust aggression threatens my country. In the latter case, turning the other cheek constitutes a violation of legal justice, not to mention social charity which in this case takes the form of patriotism, that is, love of country. And my action may all too easily be simply a cloak for cowardice. Recent Popes in their social teachings have made clear the right of nations to defend themselves as well as the obligations of individuals to contribute to this defense. Pacifism has never been acceptable in Catholic teaching, although the quest for peace, and specifically for justice which is the only durable basis for peace, has always been in the foreground of Catholic social teaching.

In addition to the general teaching on the right of self-defense, whether by an individual or by a nation, Catholic doctrine has also provided certain criteria governing the just war. These are traceable at least so far back as to the great genius of St. Thomas Aquinas. They include the conditions that: 1) the war is authorized by the legitimate government; 2) there is a sufficient or just cause, such as defense, even though an offensive war may also be just, for example, to enact just punishment for a grievous wrong committed by another nation; 3) the war is conducted in a just manner. Rational behavior suggests additional criteria such as the assumption that all peaceful means for resolving the dispute have been exhausted; that there has to be a reasonable prospect for a successful outcome of the war; and that the foreseeable havoc wrought by the war not constitute a worse evil than the injustice which is being repelled.

The modern pacifist urge suggests, among other things, that nuclear warfare is *per se* unjust because of any unlikelihood that the end achieved by war would outweigh the horrendous destruction involved overall, and because it is never just conduct to wage indiscriminate war directly on civilian populations. In this regard the limitations of provincial Hierarchies became apparent during World War II when direct indiscriminate warfare, conventional as well as nuclear, was used routinely by all sides. Yet, by and large, only the Papal *Magisterium* in the person of Pope Pius XII denounced such warfare by whomever, while national Hierarchies confined themselves to accusing the other side.

"Do Bishops know enough about these matters to make such valid moral judgments about them?"

Now, oddly enough, there is a reverse tendency in the United States to fire moral broadsides against one's own country. This may be due to the frustrating awareness that the other side will pay no attention anyway; and there may even be less valid reasons. It is precisely because the other side will pay no attention to moral preaching by, say, the American Bishops that the latter have to be especially careful. Although our public officials will probably not take seriously their moral pronouncements, there is still the matter of what the significant Catholic percentage of our population will feel constrained to do or not do because of what their Bishops have to say. Their actions could expose our country to a weakening of its defense, and that could be an immoral, not to mention a disastrous eventuality.

An Important Distinction

Certain things are necessary, therefore, before proceeding further on this course. First of all, distinctions have to be made between the use of nuclear weapons and all-out nuclear warfare. That implies an adequate knowledge of the logistics and ballistics of nuclear weaponry and warfare. The existence of nuclear weapons presents us with at least the theoretical possibility that these may be used selectively with predominantly military objectives in mind. On the other hand, they may be used in an all-out effort to destroy

the enemy nation, which matter has, in effect, already been ruled on by the Papal *Magisterium*. Because it involves direct indiscriminate warfare against civilian populations, such a war would be unjust, quite aside from the prospects of whether the damage resulting would or would not outweigh the injustice which led to the war. The latter consideration is already speculative and therefore probably less compelling than the former. To weigh the possible physical damage from all-out nuclear war against the possible moral damage from, say, worldwide subservience to Soviet serfdom, is an exercise we may therefore spare ourselves. Now if national Hierarchies choose to reaffirm what the Papal *Magisterium* has already stated long ago and repeatedly, that is their prerogative. It may be a useful magisterial exercise on their part, even though it may be as ineffectual, unfortunately, as the repeated Papal pronouncements have been to date.

The second possibility now becomes the all-important consideration. What about limited use of nuclear weapons? Here the question of adequate knowledge about nuclear ballistics and logistics moves into the foreground as essential in arriving at valid moral judgments. Do Bishops know enough about these matters to make such valid moral judgments about them? Are they justified in making gratuitous assertions to the effect that there can be no limited nuclear war and therefore that all nuclear weapons must be banned? As moral teachers their role is not to speculate about what may or may not happen. That is the role of prophets. Moral teachers must make judgments on what could or may happen. Since it is distinctly possible that nuclear weapons may be used to achieve limited military objectives, moral teaching is properly entitled to consider this possibility and judge its morality.

The Falkland Lesson

The Falkland Islands War provided a glimpse of how nuclear weaponry could have been used to achieve limited military objectives. Suppose for the moment, that Argentina's cause was just and that it possessed nuclear missiles. Even the non-military mind can perceive of how Argentina could have used even just one or two well-placed missiles to put the British naval task force out of action. Naval task forces or even individual aircraft carriers are well worth the expenditure of nuclear missiles, given the unfortunate case where war has, in fact, broken out. How the British would have responded is, of course, the other side of the grim scenario. If they retaliated by obliterating Argentinian population centers, the war would have been grossly unjust, with Britain guilty of the injustice and Argentina guiltless but devastated. On the other hand, Great Britain could also have acted with a limited nuclear action, for example, to destroy Argentinian missile sites in anticipation of their possible use against its fleet. Warfare would then be reduced to limited nuclear dimensions and could at least conceivably remain within the strictures of "just war." That the risk of escalation is indeed great does not eliminate the possibility of limited nuclear action. Therefore the need for moral judgment regarding it is still present. In fact, this imaginary episode points up the need for a moral statement about the placement of missile sites away from population centers. What must also be considered here is the fact that nuclear missiles have maximum destructive force when exploded above the surface, which is also when radioactive fallout is minimized. That type of explosion was used in Hiroshima and Nagasaki, where the actions were immoral in any case, because the bombs were directed indiscriminately against civilian populations. But the point is that for use against military objectives, maximum damage is normally what is sought, so that the added moral complication of widespread radioactive fallout may not be a factor.

"The Bishops had better remember that the entire nuclear issue is no longer simply a matter of us vs. them."

What emerges from this speculative scenario in no way adds up to a consoling removal of the risk factor involved in the limited nuclear exchange. However, it opens up the possibility, if not the necessity, of admitting that the retention of nuclear weapons as such can still be moral. There is no moral obligation on our part to tell anyone, let alone a hostile power, what our nuclear missiles are intended for. The dilemma which seems to be driving some toward irrational judgments stems from the now discredited strategy of "mutually assured destruction," so appropriately designated as MAD. Ironically, even if we choose to announce to the Soviets, for example, that we would use our nuclear arsenal only against military objectives, and if we sincerely meant it, they would most likely not believe a word of what we said so that the nuclear weapons would still have the desired deterrent effect. Preposterous as this may seem, the Soviets' own incredulity and cynicism would thus work to our great advantage. What we have there is simply another reflection of a world gone mad.

We Cannot Disarm

All such analysis may seem heartless and grim to morally sensitive people. It goes without saying that the position in which our modern world finds itself is absurd and immoral. Far better if the countless billions in money and material which nations feel compelled to spend for "defense" could be used to bring the poor nations into the 20th century. Then, among other things, the rich nations could also again enjoy the economic prosperity which otherwise eludes them. That is the goal which all recent Popes have urged, and it is the one to which the great and sensitive Pope Paul VI devoted an entire encyclical (*Progressio Populorum*, 1967).

But unfortunately, the world is not listening to the Mother and Teacher of nations in such matters. The deadly weapons are here; they proliferate rather than diminish in number and potency. Nations stand face to face as enemies, not as Christian neighbors. To advocate unilateral nuclear disarmament, therefore, is not only irrelevant but irresponsible, and ultimately immoral. On the other hand, to advocate such disarmament by all parties is not new, and it is valid and moral even if ineffective. Thus, our Bishops had better think carefully before they decide to go beyond what our alert and prophetic Papal *Magisterium* has already done and done well, whether or not anyone was listening. And they had also better remember that the entire nuclear issue is no longer simply a matter of us, i.e., the United States, vs. them, i.e., the Soviet Union. Many countries now have nuclear arsenals; and this includes some minuscule but fractious and volatile nations.

Rupert J. Ederer is professor of economics at the State University College of Buffalo, N.Y.

"First-strike nuclear weapons are immoral and criminal."

Nuclear Weapons Are Immoral

Raymond G. Hunthausen

Disarmament is a subject I have thought about and prayed over for many years. I can recall vividly hearing the news of the atomic bombing in Hiroshima in 1945. I was deeply shocked. . .at the news that a city of hundreds of thousands of people had been devastated by a single bomb. Hiroshima challenged my faith as a Christian in a way I am only now beginning to understand. That awful event and its successor at Nagasaki sank into my soul, as they have in fact sunk into the souls of all of us, whether we recognize it or not.

I am sorry to say that I did not speak out against the evil of nuclear weapons until many years later. I was especially challenged on the issue by an article I read in 1976 by Jesuit Father Richard McSorley, titled "It's a Sin to Build a Nuclear Weapon." Father McSorley wrote:

The taproot of violence in our society today is our intention to use nuclear weapons. Once we have agreed to that, all other evil is minor in comparison. Until we squarely face the question of our consent to use nuclear weapons, any hope of large scale improvement of public morality is doomed to failure.

I agree. Our willingness to destroy life everywhere on this earth, for the sake of our security as Americans, is at the root of many other terrible events in our country.

I was also challenged to speak out against nuclear armament by the nearby construction of the Trident submarine base and by the first-strike nuclear doctrine which Trident represents. The nuclear warheads fired from one Trident submarine will be able to destroy as many as 408 separate areas, each with a bomb five times more powerful than the one used at Hiroshima. . . .Trident and other new weapons systems such as the MX and cruise missile have .such extraordinary accuracy and explosive power that they can only be understood as a build-up to a first-strike capability. First-strike nuclear weapons are immoral and criminal.

Raymond G. Hunthausen, speech delivered to the Pacific Northwest Synod of the Lutheran Church, June 12, 1981.

They benefit only arms corporations and the insane dreams of those who wish to "win" a nuclear holocaust.

I was also moved to speak out against Trident because it is being based here. We must take special responsibility for what is in our own back yard. And when crimes are being prepared in our name, we must speak plainly. I say with a deep consciousness of these words that Trident is the Auschwitz of Puget Sound.

A Situation to Despair

Father McSorley's article and the local basing of Trident are what awakened me to a new sense of the Gospel call to peacemaking in the nuclear age. They brought back the shock of Hiroshima. Since that reawakening five years ago, I have tried to respond in both a more prayerful and more vocal way than I did in 1945. I feel the need to respond by prayer because our present crisis goes far deeper than politics. I have heard many perceptive political analyses of the nuclear situation, but their common element is despair. It is no wonder. The nuclear arms race can sum up in a few final moments the violence of tens of thousands of years, raised to an almost infinite power — a demonic reversal of the Creator's power of giving life. But politics is itself powerless to overcome the demonic in its midst. It needs another dimension. I am convinced that a way out of this terrible crisis can be discovered by our deepening in faith and prayer so that we learn to rely not on missiles for our security but on the loving care of that One who gives and sustains life. We need to return to the Gospel with open hearts to learn once again what it is to have faith. . . .

I am told by some that unilateral disarmament in the face of atheistic communism is insane. I find myself observing that nuclear armament by anyone is itself atheistic, and anything but sane. I am also told that the choice of unilateral disarmament is a political impossibility in this country. If so, perhaps the reason is that we have forgotten what it would be like to act out of faith. But I speak here of that choice not as a political platform — it might not win elections — but as a moral imperative for followers of Christ. . . .

To ask one's country to relinquish its security in arms is to encourage risk — a more reasonable risk than constant nuclear escalation, but a risk nevertheless. I am struck by how much more terrified we Americans often are by talk of disarmament than by the march to nuclear war. We whose nuclear arms terrify millions around the globe are terrified by the thought of being without them. The thought of our nation without such power feels naked. Propaganda and a particular way of life have clothed us to death. To relinquish our hold on global destruction feels like risking everything, and it is risking everything — but in a direction opposite to the way in which we now risk everything. Nuclear arms protect privilege and exploitation. Giving them up would mean our having to give up economic power over other peoples. Peace and justice go together. On the path we now follow, our economic policies toward other countries require nuclear weapons. Giving up the weapons would mean giving up more than our means of global terror. It would mean giving up the reason for such terror — our privileged place in the world.

How can such a process, of taking up the cross of nonviolence, happen in a country where our government seems paralyzed by arms corporations? In a country where many of the citizens, perhaps most of the citizens, are numbed into passivity by the very magnitude and complexity of the issue while being horrified by the prospect of nuclear holocaust? Clearly some action is demanded — some form of nonviolent resistance. Some people may choose to write to their elected representatives at the national and state level, others may choose to take part in marches, demonstrations or similar forms of protest. . . .

"The nuclear arms race can sum up in a few final moments the violence of tens of thousands of years."

I would like to share a vision of still another action that could be taken: simply this—a sizeable number of people in the State of Washington, 5,000, 10,000, 500,000 people refusing to pay 50 percent of their taxes in nonviolent resistance to nuclear murder and suicide. I think that would be a definite step toward disarmament. Our paralyzed political process needs that catalyst of nonviolent action based on faith. We have to refuse to give incense — in our day, tax dollars — to our nuclear idol. On April 15 we can vote for unilateral disarmament with our lives. Form 1040 is the place where the Pentagon enters all of our lives, and asks our unthinking cooperation with the idol of nuclear destruction. I think the teaching of Jesus tells us to render to a nuclear-armed Caesar what that Caesar deserves — tax resistance. And to begin to render to God alone that complete trust which we now give, through our tax dollars, to a demonic form of power. Some would call what I am urging "civil disobedience." I prefer to see it as obedience to God.

What We Can Do

I must say in all honesty that my vision of a sizeable number of tax resisters is not yet one which I have tried to realize in the most obvious way — by becoming one of the number. I have never refused to pay war taxes. And I recognize that there will never be such a number unless there are first a few to give the example.

I fully realize that many will disagree with my position on unilateral disarmament and tax resistance. I also realize that one can argue endlessly about specific tactics, but no matter how we differ on specific tactics, one thing at least is certain. We must demand over and over again that our political leaders make peace and disarmament, and not war and increased armaments, their first priority. We must demand that time and effort and money be placed first of all toward efforts to let everyone know that the United States is *not* primarily interested in being the strongest military nation on earth but in being the strongest peace advocate. We must challenge every politician who talks endlessly about building up our arms and never about efforts for peace.

We must ask our people to question their government when it concentrates its efforts on shipping arms to countries which need food, when it accords the military an open checkbook while claiming that the assistance to the poor must be slashed in the name of balancing the budget, when it devotes most of its time and energy and money to developing war strategy and not peace strategy. . . .

The nuclear arms race can be stopped. Nuclear weapons can be abolished. That I believe with all my heart and faith, my sisters and brothers.

Raymond G. Hunthausen is Archbishop of the Roman Catholic Archdiocese of Seattle. This viewpoint was taken from a speech he delivered to the Pacific Northwest Synod of the Lutheran Church on June 12, 1981.

"There are greater evils than the physical death and destruction wrought in war."

Nuclear Weapons Are Not Immoral

William A. Stanmeyer

In 1981 the ageless debate over the morality of war took on new urgency as the Reagan Administration sought to bolster sagging American military capability at the same time as some vocal Christian bishops and other clerics began preaching a new gospel of unilateral disarmament. These events took place in a context of heightened world tensions exacerbated by the Soviet Union's relentless assertion of *Realpolitik* in Poland, Central America, and Afghanistan. Christian laymen of powerful intellect were puzzled by the problem. It is likely that an enormous philosophical schism has opened betwen laymen who understand geopolitics and clerics who do not. Yet their ignorance does not deter them from pronouncing first-strike anathemas on policies for which many of their co-religionists had voted.

There is danger, first, that the word peace will suffer the same fate, through the systematic distortions of television and pulp magazines, as the word love already has suffered. Just as a gushy feeling of momentary togetherness is not true love, neither is the mere absence of war the same as true peace. On this point the modern pacifist position is highly vulnerable, for its routine refusal to discuss the connection among freedom, justice, and peace misstates the just war theory and, in purported rebuttal of the theory, manages only to bury the wrong corpse.

Immoral Order

True humane peace must include substantial human justice. But true justice for human beings must include extensive civic freedom and a political order that protects individual rights against the state. As St. Augustine observed, "peace is the tranquillity of order"—and *at root this order is moral, not merely physical.* Every totalitarian regime represses essential human rights and thus violates the moral order at its root. When a govern-

William A. Stanmeyer, "Toward a Moral Nuclear Strategy," *The Policy Review,* Summer 1982, issue No. 21. Reprinted with permission.

ment purposefully destroys the order of justice and subordinates all individual rights to the ruling elite's will to power, it declares war, in fact if not in word, against its own citizens. Like the Polish martial law regime imposed in December, 1981, such governments destroy the moral dimension of the order they impose, leaving only the physical quiet in the streets and silence in the camps: an empty shell, the fake "peace" of a jail filled with innocent prisoners. This is the counterfeit tranquility of immoral order. As John Courtney Murray wrote 20 years ago in a brilliant analysis deserving close study today:

> "There are greater evils than the physical death and destruction wrought in war. And there are human goods of so high an order that immense sacrifices may have to be borne in their defense. . . .The tradition of reason has always maintained that the *highest value in society is the inviolability of the order of rights and justice."*

The pacifist silence on the results of unilateral American disarmament—e.g. immediate helplessness to defend, say, Israel against likely Soviet attack; eventual surrender of the United States itself to Soviet domination—vitiates the entire pacifist-unilateral-disarmament argument. It reduces what should be moral analysis to a eudemonic calculus of material profits and losses. Surrender as a step to a worldwide Gulag is thus seen as better than war to preserve freedom. It is implied (though rarely argued clearly) that because to preserve one's physical life is the greatest good, it is better to live for a bit longer in an unjust society without freedom than to die sooner fighting to establish or preserve a just society with freedom.

Confusing the Material and the Spiritual

It cannot be stressed enough that morality is not some sort of reverse body-count: as if that nation is more "right" which brings about the death of fewer people than the nation which brings about the death of more people. The pacifist who tolerates radical or fundamental political immorality so as to avoid the pain and death of war confuses the material and the spiritual. If one decided the immorality of a nation's entry into war solely by the physical deaths it would cause, the North's entry into the Civil War was not moral, and neither France (for a short time, until defeated) nor England (for a long time, until victorious) fighting World War II was acting morally. In each case, they could have reduced the killing by the simple expedient of quick surrender—and acquiescing in what even the pacifist, one hopes, would admit was an even greater moral evil than the damage self-defense brought in its wake.

Those who take up arms in defense of justice, law, and humane order are the true defenders of peace; for justice at times needs the protection of force, and peace itself must sometimes be defended against violation. Among the good things human society can accomplish "there are some human goods"—surely justice is among them—"of such importance for the human community that their defense against an unjust aggression is without doubt fully justified. Their defense is even an obligation for the nations as a whole, who have a duty not to abandon a nation that is attacked."

Christianity and Peace

Military power is a function of both technical capability and moral stamina or will. When Christian bishops lead the laity to believe that Christ's teaching condemns what the layman's instincts tell him is legitimate self-defense, the bishops create a kind of cognitive dissonance or spiritual tension among their followers, whose will to resist unjust aggression weakens in proportion to their moral confusion. This weakness will eventually translate, through the ordinary processes of a democratic republic, into national policy. Thus when a bishop attacks the Trident submarine as immoral, he may, in time, destroy it as effectively as if he had sabotaged it with a physical bomb. It follows that the Department of the Navy is entitled to take defensive philosophical measures against such spiritual attacks: to point out that they are faulty philosophy and incorrect theology.

The peace proposed in the Christian scriptures cannot be simply translated into the peace of worldly arrangements. We have Jesus' own words:

"Peace is what I leave you; it is *my own* peace that I give you. *I do not give it as the world does.* Do not be worried and upset; do not be afraid."

The spiritual peace is the tranquility of soul of the just man who fears not the future, who worries not about weapons and wars—even if he be a soldier in battle—because through faith God is with him. The man or woman who confuses the cessation of military hostilities (an external, political, measurable event in the public life of nations) with the internal and personal sharing in the untroubled spirit of Christ is a person who looks to political and public events to provide the peace promised by Jesus. Yet Jesus' own words tell us

that *His* "own peace" is *not* to be found in political and public events and thus will not be found in political-public disarmament. The fact that physical disarmament is not Christ's route to His peace is evident also from *Matt. 24.4:* "You are going to hear the noise of battles close by and the news of battles far away; but do not be troubled. Such things must happen."

The Difference Between Force and Violence

In a statement on peace in October, 1980, the Episcopal bishops of the United States asserted: "...we are compelled to say that never before has it been so clear that reason forbids the use of violence, or the threat of it, as a means of securing one society against another."

"Limited nuclear war is, morally, permissible if one respects the injunction not to will directly the destruction of innocent civilians."

They imply that "reason"—moral philosophy—has always forbidden "violence" or its threat even in legitimate self-defense, and that this truth is clearer today because of nuclear weapons. Yet this denial of the right of self-defense was *never* Christian moral teaching. Moreover, the confusion created by the deliberate use of the nuanced word, *violence*, when the more neutral word, *force*, would do, is almost dishonest and begs the question. In the criminal codes of every state an affirmative defense against the charge of illegal use of deadly force usually appears under the heading, "Use of Force in Self-Defense." Books on ethics commonly deal with the question of moral "use of force." Therefore precise reasoning should begin with the distinction: power applied against another person or nation is neutral; the reasonable use of power is to be called force; the unreasonable use of power is to be called violence.

The Episcopal bishops' pronouncement would have made deterrent use of military force against Germany in 1940 "forbidden" by "reason." This position is a prescription for surrender to any tyrant who has a big army and small scruples.

To account for this confusion one must understand that the pacifist mentality has never been able to bridge what to it seems two irreconcilable opposites: the evil in using force to protect rights and the evil in surrendering rights to the aggressor. Lacking a principled theory by which to distinguish when the use of power is right and when it is wrong, the pacifist simply assumes that because it is sometimes wrong, it is always wrong. And because it is easier for the imagination to dwell on the physical evils consequent upon self-defense than for the mind to perceive the moral evils consequent upon failure to defend, the pacifist, when discussing U.S. defense, conveniently neglects to consider what surrender will do to his family and his country. Yet what the KGB and those generals who recently brought "peace" to Poland would do if they were to get their hands on us should clearly be part of any moral equation.

The Right of Self-Defense

Because the evils of warfare are indeed horrendous, I know of no easy way to turn the imagination, with the mind, to the more abstract—but crucial—level of moral reasoning, save to start with analogous person-to-person questions. Since social or political morality is an extension, with appropriate qualifications, of private morality, the traditional moralist must begin with the perennial doctrine of *individual* right-of-self-defense against unjust attack. And because pacifists are usually highly idealist and sometimes religious persons (who confuse a counsel with a commandment), the most compelling example goes along these lines:

A sadistic perpetrator of child-abuse, who has admitted killing six children, kidnaps your neighbor's five-year-old little girl. Luck combined with some detective skill enable you to discover them just at the moment the kidnapper is about to murder the child. The only way to prevent her death is to shoot the kidnapper. You may do so, and neither the legal system nor traditional moral reasoning would find any fault or wrong in your action. (You also may do so if the intended victim were yourself or some other adult.)

"It is reasonable to expect American surrender to the Soviets logically will follow from unilateral disarmament."

This example, which is universally admitted, deserves analysis. Note that there is a physical evil that the rescuer commits: he kills the kidnapper. But this is not a moral evil. As a matter of fact, *not* to save the child when one could have done so is itself a serious moral evil: i.e., not to cause a physical evil (death-of-kidnapper) is immoral because it is a conscious refusal to defend the moral order being violated in the suffering victim. The reason lies in the clash of rights. Though the kidnapper, as a human being, has a general "right to life," by denying that right in the innocent child, he denies it universally. (He claims, in effect, that *he* has the "right" to torture and kill in any case; or, more likely, he claims in effect that there simply is no moral order of rights but "the law of the jungle"—in which case there is no moral order to protect him, either.) Another expression of the argument is to approach the problem as a *collision of rights.*

"By the very fact that the assailant's attack is unjust,

his right to life yields to that of the person attacked. The right to life of the two parties is no longer equal, but the aggressor temporarily loses his right to life by his aggression. Killing in itself is not wrong, but what makes it wrong is its *injustice,* the invasion of another man's right. If that right is extinguished, there is no injustice present to make the act of killing wrong."

In his preoccupation with externals, the pacifist generally misses the point that killing *in itself* is not a moral evil unless it is unjust. This confusion of the physical and the moral is not unlike the confusion between force and violence. It leads some pacifists to connect the anti-war and anti-abortion movements in a mistaken belief that because both are "pro-life" they both have the same moral philosophy, as if physical life and not moral innocence were the central point.

The conditions for legitimate self-defense using deadly force are these: 1) the motive must be self-defense alone; 2) force must be used only at the time of the attack; 3) when there is no other way of preventing the evil; 4) and in proportion to the evil: no more injury may be inflicted than is necessary to avert actual danger. These points apply to warfare as well.

The Just War Theory

Correct application of the just war theory will lead to four related conclusions. First, *the Mutual Assured Destruction strategy is probably immoral,* if we grant the usual distinction between "innocent" civilians and "non-innocent" military, since the strategy uses the directly willed (intentional) killing of civilians as a means to the good end of national survival.

Second, *the Counterforce strategy is moral,* since one wills the destruction only of combatants and only permits collateral harm to civilians. A corollary is that limited nuclear war is, morally, permissible if one respects the injunction not to will directly the destruction of innocent civilians.

Third, *an ABM defensive strategy,* designed to destroy incoming enemy missiles and planes, *is undoubtedly moral.* Indeed, it is to be preferred. From unclassified documents it appears that the state of the art is far enough along to make anti-ballistic defensive systems entirely feasible. To render our homeland and worldwide bases relatively invulnerable would create immense advantage for our offensive weapons systems, thus enabling us to reduce our expenditures for such systems and, if ever needing to use them, to apply them surgically to counterforce purposes.

Fourth, because a Counterforce strategy limits and does not will civilian death, and because an ABM defense prevents civilian deaths, it is immoral *not* to substitute such approaches for the dubiously moral MAD strategy. And, in proportion as someone could influence public policy toward a strategy such as ABM defense which both protects freedom and preserves innocent lives, but instead urges policies that will do neither—as do the unilateral-disarmament Christians—he shares in the immorality of those who could do good but instead counsel evil. I will summarize the reasoning that leads to these conclusions in the following paragraphs.

Simply put, the just war theory requires: 1) lawful authority, which means the decision is by government and not private parties; 2) just cause, which includes (a) sufficient proportion, (b) last resort, and (c) fair hope of success; 3) right intention; 4) right use of means. Murray adds that in the nuclear age there are new corollaries: (1) all wars of aggression, whether just or unjust, fall under the ban of moral proscription; but (2) *a defensive war to repress injustice is morally admissible both in principle and in fact.*

The major objections to the just war theory are these: first, it is said that there is no adequate proportion between the harm America's weapons will inflict on Russia, should war break out, and the values we would preserve here. Second, even if proportion existed, some claim it is impossible to avoid the direct and intentional killing of millions of people we have no right to kill—i.e., the "good end" of self-preservation does not justify the "evil means" of directly willing ultimate evil for innocent people. Third, even if there be proportion and no direct willing of numerous deaths of innocents, supposedly we have no fair hope of success—i.e., "in a nuclear war, nobody wins."

Let me deal with these objections. As to proportion: as I have already argued, this cannot be solved by simply comparing the numbers of deaths on each side. However awful the prospect of countless Russian and American deaths, the central question is spiritual, not material. We must attempt to balance the moral-spiritual evil suffered by Western civilization in choosing surrender instead of self-defense, against the moral-spiritual evil entailed in defending one's country and civilization. While individual claims of private citizens for life are a factor, here, the prime point is the structural rectitude and moral values of each society as a whole. And it is reasonable and moral to seek to prevent an entire civilization—the West—from consignment to the Gulag for an unknown number of generations. There are fates worse than death. (Further, the Just Social Order with, so many of the clergy tell us, immense governmental payments to the poor, will not occur under tyranny: *all tyrannies are poor nations, because the precondition of prosperity is freedom.* Moreover, as the essential condition of civil rights, religious activity, intellectual growth, and a just public order, freedom must be defended lest we yield our children and the whole world to the tyrant for centuries to come.) The quiet of a conquered people is compulsory acquiescence in immense moral evil: *a permanent public "order" that is radically and essentially unjust.* Further, it is reasonable to expect American surrender to the Soviets logically will follow from unilateral disarmament. Those clergy who preach such disarmament but do not admit this

result subtly insinuate a deceptive *political* judgment as premise to their moral conclusion. They presume either (a) that life will go on in America as before we disarmed; or (b) that even if we disarmed, we would not have to surrender. Both premises are arrant nonsense, a fact which probably explains why they are scarcely ever urged openly.

Ends-Means Analysis

The second objection, based on the correct principle that the end does not justify the means, overlooks the corollary. Someone *may* act using a neutral or good means, even if as a side-effect he brings about *foreseen but unintended* evils. Here we must examine Mutual Assured Destruction and "massive retaliation." If we assume a sharp dichotomy between civilians and military personnel, then the massive retaliation against Soviet cities will be immoral, even if, as is manifest, the Soviet Empire as a society lacks structural values claiming our respect. For innocent civilians as individuals, collectively aggregating millions, have a right to live which we may not deliberately abort. But since the *moral evil* lies in the *will* and not the event, self-defense with nuclear weapons is permissible under a strategy, such as Counterforce, that does not use the direct and intentional killing of masses of civilians as a means to the end of self-preservation. Further, antiballistic (ABM) or laser defensive strategy to destroy incoming enemy ICBMs far enough out in space that no civilians are harmed at all meets *every* criterion of the just war. Both strategies are quite permissible under ends-means analysis.

"Many of the 'peace bishops' have made up their minds without considering all the alternatives."

Indeed, the silence of the disarmament bishops on the immense life-saving potential of such a defensive strategy belies their asserted concern for the moral imperative to limit nuclear war. The imperative arises from the moral duty to respect innocent human life; consequently, strategies and weapons which are discriminating in their targets, controllable in their effects, or removed from civilians in their theater of use, have moral priority. Such are space-weaponry systems. In my judgment, silence about the moral superiority of such weapons calls into serious question either the knowledge or sincerity of the unilateral disarmament lobby—as does the disdain it and some bishops show toward civil defense measures. At least one bishop has urged hospital administrators under his authority to refuse cooperation with any Defense Department planning for nuclear emergencies. One is at a loss to perceive how religious leaders, who purport to be outraged at the immorality they discern in widespread civilian deaths, can refuse to assist in practical steps to limit and prevent the deaths they claim to abhor. Or, on a more general level of moral-military strategy, how they can reject military measures which would deter the enemy from attacking cities or at least redirect their assault to military targets.

What Winning Means

One fears that the refusal to consider ABM space weapons and civil-defense hospital planning arises from an emotional desire to justify depicting the problem as so horrendous and intractable that the *only* "solution" is to throw up one's hands in surrender, stop reasoning about messy calculations like strategy and proportionality, and embrace a sloganized procrustean solution—unilateral disarmament—that needs no further analysis and admits no extended qualification. This is bumper-sticker politics, not moral argument. It is a mirror image of the stereotypical "hawk's" presumed reaction to a political-military crisis such as the Iranian hostage situation: "Nuke 'em!" But the tradition of reason deserves a better witness from men whose Church set up great universities where once students blended the philosopher's logic and casuistry with the scientist's and lawyer's care for fact and nuance. My impression is that many of the "peace bishops" have made up their minds without considering all the alternatives. The possibility that defensive measures could bring a future war clearly within the rules of the just war theory would undercut their *a priori* conclusion. Not wanting to rethink their position, as they are not really interested in fact or nuance, they close their minds to the strategic and moral superiority of military-civilian defense. Needless to say, self-inflicted blindness to a moral alternative to assertedly immoral actions renders objection to those actions hollow—and raises serious doubt whether the self-blinded should guide the rest of us.

"It is naive to assume that unilateral American disarmament will embarrass the Russians."

The final objection is that nobody will win. But this ignores the crucial fact that *the West has already won.* For the past 30 years, its nuclear deterrent has both prevented a war breaking out *and* preserved Western civilization from the moral and spiritual evil of Soviet domination. The fact should make clear that the notion of victory is not a simple one, but a question of political, military, and sociological judgment, upon which bishops speak with no special authority. There are different definitions of victory and, consequently, different moral attitudes that are appropriate in each case. The Soviets, masters of utilitarian calculus, are far less pessimistic; they construe "winning" to mean sur-

vival of their political control, plus the ability to impose their will on us. If by "winning" we mean no American cities are destroyed, then, because our presidents and bishops have left us defenseless by not building ABMs, we cannot "win" if an all-out nuclear war breaks out. But that is only one possibility and, on the experience of the last 30 years, the least likely possibility. (It might, of course, become more likely if the "peace movement" undermines the strategic foundations of that 30 years' peace.

If by "winning," however, we mean preserving the moral-spiritual values of our society free at last from the tyranny the Soviets would impose; then winning may well be possible. As a political matter the Soviet Empire has a weak underbelly: the seething restiveness of the captured peoples (*vide* Poland). The loyalty of the Warsaw Pact armies in a long war is seriously in doubt. Thus anticipated disruption of Soviet political-military control of their own peoples during war is a major deterrent; it is possible, given the "correlation of forces," that the prospect of U.S. interdiction of the chain-of-command could so disrupt and delay Soviet aggression in Western Europe that the leadership would avoid the risk. Moreover, it is obvious that an "all-out" war will cause even greater disruption—and consequent possible overthrow of the regime—than a "limited war." Thus the assumption that the Soviets' preferred option is total war is controvertible; indeed, it is quite possible to conceive a scenario in which the nuclear exchange is minimal—Sir John Hackett has done just that in his extraordinary book on the Third World War—or even avoided altogether as both sides restrict themselves to conventional war from motives of prudence.

"Peace in our Time"

My final point is that it is naive to assume that unilateral American disarmament will embarrass the Russians into doing the same. History teaches the opposite: as Hitler demonstrated, a power vacuum invites attack. Prudence mandates that Americans follow a course most likely to reduce hostilities to manageable levels: that is, to convince the Soviets of our ability to prevent them from winning. But insofar as we fail to modernize our weapons and even disarm those we have, we send just the opposite signal. As we stumble out of the arms race they run all the harder, and their overt imperialism intensifies in direct proportion to the spread of pacifism in America. The preachers of disarmament bear a frightening resemblance to Neville Chamberlain, who boasted that his adroit mix of negotiation and compromise had achieved "peace in our time." May they not get the same results as he did?

As a matter of morality, it is immoral to refuse to consider the evil consequences of an ostensibly good course of action. Yet the disarmament lobby will not discuss the moral evil of American surrender necessitated by its military helplessness. It is immoral not to help prevent genocide, yet unilateral disarmament will so weaken the United States that we could do nothing to prevent genocide against Israel if the Soviets embarked upon, or encouraged, such a war in the Middle East. It is immoral not to consider alternatives that will both preserve peace and freedom and protect civilian lives, yet the disarmament lobby is utterly silent when it could urge building defensive ABMs to knock out incoming Soviet missiles, thus sparing millions of innocents in both America and Russia the military application of the MAD theory.

Truly the preachers of the Apocryphal Gospel of assured peace without sacrifice do prophesy a false vision.

William A. Stanmeyer is a law professor associated with the Delaware Law School and the Lincoln Center for Legal Studies.

"Those who argue that risking the use of nuclear weapons is inherently immoral, fail to discuss the immorality of risking the imposition of life without any human rights."

viewpoint **90**

Nuclear War May Be Necessary

John W. Gofman and Egan O'Connor

The yearning to survive the nuclear age is obviously a natural, healthy goal. However, the goal of *surviving with human rights* is obviously a morally superior goal to mere survival.

Nuclear weapons happen to be one of the current technologies employed in the ages-old pull and haul among slavery, slaughter, mere survival, and survival with human rights. The primitive technology of decapitation is another current technology (Cambodia). Historically, it has never required nuclear weapons for the enemies of human rights, hereafter called "bullies" to slaughter defenseless non-combatants. The fact that, in the nuclear age, even mothers and babies find their own lives on the line is disgusting, but not new.

Those who argue that *risking* the use of nuclear weapons is inherently immoral, fail to discuss the immorality of *risking* the imposition of life without any human rights on ourselves and future generations. We have seen several such societies in our lifetimes; they have not been fantasies in Nazi Germany, Soviet Russia, Pol Pot's Cambodia, Idi Amin's Uganda, El Salvador, and other unhappy lands.

We mean societies where survival itself is commonly made dependent on morally bankrupt behavior, such as collaboration with the bullies. . .societies where informants and betrayals abound, where mistrust, fury, and corruption are the norms. . .societies where the integrity of whole professions is corrupted to the core, by judges who defend and apply laws violating human rights, by scientists who publish state-serving untruths, by physicians who terrorize dissidents by forcing mind-damaging drugs into them. We shall call these "slave societies".

Bully-Control: A Moral Imperative

To prevent the moral bankruptcy which can occur and has occurred in modern slave societies, those who

John W. Gofman and Egan O'Connor, "On the Morality of Weapons," reprinted with authors' permission.

cherish life and human rights must do whatever is necessary to achieve Bully-Control. This is a moral imperative, and is not related to the particular tools available to bullies, from contracting collars for child-decapitation (in Cambodia) to nuclear bombs.

By definition, bullies do not share our ideas about individual human rights, about everyone's *equal* right to be free from human coercion, or about the sanctity of contract (whose sanctity facilitates voluntary rather than coercive relations among humans). Therefore, can we protect ourselves from current or future bullies by practicing "conflict resolution" with them, or by making treaties with them? We have strained, unsuccessfully so far, to find a *sound* affirmative case for either.

Nor are bullies effectively controlled by the alleged "power of powerlessness." When the Nazis saw their defenseless victims, stripped naked, standing meekly before mass graves which they had dug for themselves, the victims' utter powerlessness did not overwhelm the Nazis with sensations of mercy. The Nazis blasted them to oblivion.

Force *is* required to achieve Bully-Control. Although we wish with all our hearts that it were *not* so, the evidence and logic for that assertion are overwhelming. Wishful thinking, the enemy of successful science, is also the enemy of successful survival, and must be avoided.

A Proposal for Reducing Force

Since force is *required* to achieve Bully-Control, it is *morally* right to use force against bullies, and morally wrong *not* to do so, because failure to stop bullies means (a) that you fail to help the current victims, and (b) by letting bully-behavior "pay", you guarantee the appearance of even more and bigger bullies, and the destruction of even more innocent life and human rights. Morality aside, negligence about Bully-Control increases your *own* risk of enslavement or slaughter because of (b).

And let us never forget that agreeing to be enslaved "for a while" (surrender) does *not* guarantee your own survival. A bully who has the inclination and power to enslave you, also has the power to slaughter you, after perhaps unspeakable physical and moral degradation, at a time of his own choosing. Need we draw pictures from Auschwitz, the Soviet Gulag, Uganda, Cambodia, El Salvador?

Human history shows failure after failure to achieve Bully-Control, largely thanks to wishful thinking. Now a vociferous movement is suggesting that peace can never by.achieved by military force. We call that wishful thinking. We suggest that peace—by which we mean Bully-Control and the preservation of individual human rights, or civilization—will *always require* the willingness to use force to control and eliminate bullies. The level of such force could one day be very *low,* if we humans dedicate ourselves to stopping bullies anywhere on the planet while they are just aspiring, small-time bullies. We work for that vision of peace and liberty.

But up to now, humankind has not been dedicated to Bully-Control. Obstacles in addition to wishful thinking have been illiteracy, isolation, and grinding poverty, followed by the diabolical modern doctrine of non-interference in "sovereign" states, no matter what atrocities are committed there. This doctrine permits well-armed and big-time bullies to come into existence (e.g., past and future Hitlers), and consequently, the doctrine guarantees that the preservation and restoration of human rights will require big-time military force belonging to non-bullies, and sometimes big-time human sacrifice.

Fifty-five million humans—mostly innocent—died in World War Two. Yet it did not have to happen that way. Much of the suffering could have been prevented had we used force on Hitler the moment he committed his *first* violations of human rights; the imposition of yellow armbands upon the Jews should have been enough to trigger Bully-Control measures. Was it *moral,* and was it smart in terms of our *self*-interest, to have abstained so long from crushing him? We think not.

First-Rate Weaponeers

Big-time bullies have both the will and the means to develop the newest and most fiendish weapons which technology permits. Had Hitler gotten his V-2 rockets a little sooner, the fate of millions of innocent English might have been very different. The lesson is this:

Those whose goal is *survival with human rights* had better attract the best brains they can into research and development of ever-new weapons, had better expound the morality of such work, and had better support weapons and force which are superior to those of existing and potential bullies. We think this is a general principle which will still be valid hundreds of years from now.

The current claim that more nuclear weapons and new types of weapons *necessarily* (note the emphasis) in-

crease the likelihood of holocaust needs challenging because it is not true. More of the right kind of weapons could *decrease* the probability of both nuclear holocaust and loss of human rights through nuclear blackmail.

However, in the contest between bullydom and human rights, one aspect which tends to tip the balance in favor of bullies is the fact that they can rely on the extreme reluctance of good people ever to *use* weapons causing mass-slaughter, no matter what outrages the bullies commit. The very decency of good people can leave human rights without a credible defense. Today, if good people refuse to use nuclear weapons, they are unilaterally disarmed no matter how many such weapons they possess.

This terrible problem needs facing by all people of goodwill. Let us support weaponeers in the refinement of *bully-focal* weapons—that is, credible weapons whose use could eliminate the violators of human rights *without* causing slaughter on a massive scale. Furthermore, since *suicide* is quite simply not an effective method of Bully-Control, people of goodwill today need to develop *defenses* against potential nuclear bullies. Who needs first-rate weaponeers? Anyone whose goal is *survival with human rights.*

The Defense of Human Rights

The defense of human rights against bullies is an essential consumer-service to ourselves, and a moral duty to future generations, who can be born free if we do the right thing. If funding this really important human need takes 6% or 26% of our Gross National Product for a while, the military budget may be a bargain in historical terms. There have been plenty of times in history (and now in Afghanistan) when people had to put *all* their efforts into defending themselves from a murderous invader, while scratching for barely enough food to survive.

In the past, bullies were fought off with piles of stones, with spears, with gun powder, with tanks, with bombers. The technologies of force have evolved and will always evolve. Today they include machetes and bayonets, toys which explode, helicopter gunships, germs, chemicals, mind-damaging drugs, and nuclear bombs. We believe coherent debate about nuclear and other weapons, and their morality, will *begin* only after the citizens have debated, "What is meant by the term, Peace Movement? What should be its goals?

A genuine Peace Movement could turn out to be very different, both morally and practically, from a Nuclear Freeze Movement, a Disarmament Movement, a Weapons-Lab Shut-Down Movement, or a Surrender Movement.

John W. Gofman and Egan O'Connor head the Commission for Nuclear Responsibility.

"Given its ultimacy and indiscriminacy, nuclear warfare is inherently, irredeemably unjust, regardless of who uses it for what purposes."

Nuclear War Cannot Be Justified

Lloyd J. Averill

One of the most promising developments in the moral awareness of the Christian community, and of the nation at large, is the abandonment by members of the Roman Catholic hierarchy of a traditional "just war" doctrine, at least as it applies to the use of nuclear weapons.

It could hardly have come at a more propitious moment, given the apparent readiness of the president and his advisors to move toward nuclear confrontation. It ought to become the occasion for all of us to reappraise the "conventional wisdom" of nuclear-arms apologetics, particularly at three points:

1. *The notion that nothing really new has been added to warfare by the introduction of nuclear weaponry is as mistaken as it is dangerous.*

In *Newsweek*, columnist George Will argued recently that, after all, the Thirty Years' War laid waste large areas of Europe by cruder means, that World War I carnage was accomplished without benefit of nuclear technology, and that the fate of Dresdeners in World War II demonstrated that civilians can be held hostage even by weapons of lesser scope.

Yet surely we must conclude that something utterly, shudderingly new *has* burst upon us when the arms of war not only maim and kill their immediate victims but inject mutation and death into human genes; when explosives not only devastate earthbound structures but threaten the atmosphere itself; when noncombatants a world away, although unaware of the battle, are held hostage by the uncontrollable nature of the elemental fury propelled into the winds.

Nuclear weapons *are* different from conventional arms, not only in scope but also in the instant totality of their destructiveness. Our ability to create outright death and deadly contamination, panic and epidemic on a *global* scale takes not the leisurely 30 years of 17th century devastation, not yet the nearly 300 days of Ver-

dun's rage, nor even the three days of Dresden's horror, but bare *seconds*. And those who emerge will only euphemistically be called "survivors."

That quantum leap in terror transmogrifies everything we thought we knew about justice and warfare, and renders established moral and tactical considerations obsolete. That is why the Catholic bishops can no longer appeal to traditional teaching about a "just war." Given its ultimacy and indiscriminacy, nuclear warfare is inherently, irredeemably unjust, regardless of who uses it for what purposes.

2. *Any expectation that commanders on either side will find it possible to wage a "limited" nuclear war exhibits a misplaced confidence in military restraint.*

While there are differences in destructive force among the nuclear weapons in Soviet and American arsenals, the smallest among them has the largest implicit within it. The battlefield has its own irresistible logic of escalation. Even when our adversaries could not retaliate in kind, American commanders still found one ghoulish nuclear "demonstration" at Hiroshima insufficient, and offered the world a second at Nagasaki. With present retaliatory capability, it is simply not credible that commanders will not feel obliged to inflict the maximum cost on an enemy, whether for tactical advantage or for sheer revenge; for blood vengeance in the face of even certain defeat is as much a part of our received military tradition as is the pursuit of victory.

Who Decides

The choice we must make is this: to give our proxy to military commanders to determine, within the logic of battle, what is and is not the moral use of a range of power never before commanded, with a consequence that has never before existed; that by their decision, the battlefield may instantaneously become the world. Or, understanding that morality is always the first victim of warfare, *to set the moral limits before the battle begins.*

3. *There is moral casuistry in arguing that it is acceptable to possess what it is not acceptable to use.*

George Will insisted in the *Newsweek* article that while the *use* of mass-destruction weapons cannot be "approved," their *possession* can be "tolerated" if they are intended to hold in check some adversary's "intolerable evil." But to "tolerate" nuclear arms in our kind of split-second world is in fact to approve their use *in advance*, under whatever circumstances and to whatever ends they may be used. Simple madness of the sort hauntingly portrayed in the film *Dr. Strangelove* will not be the worst of it; nor will simple malevolence. Irreversible catastrophe may be deployed, from Moscow or Washington, by the sanest, best-informed and best-intentioned but nevertheless *mistaken* judgment, under the pressure of bare minutes in which to decide between restraint and holocaust.

Indeed, the world is closer than ever before to the creation of an ultimate "Doomsday Machine." Recent reports indicate that the Soviets may have concluded that it will be necessary to set their own missiles for virtually automatic response to any apparent threat, given the reduction in their warning time which will result from American deployment of ground-hugging missiles in western Europe.

"To 'tolerate' nuclear arms in our kind of split-second world is in fact to approve their use in advance."

Furthermore, nuclear rhetoric tempts us to a distorted view of where "intolerable evil" lies, as if it resided only in our adversaries. We know better than we have ever known that there is a capacity for deception and moral recklessness in the highest offices of our land, which can hold all of us hostage to evil acts committed in the all-justifying name of national self-interest. If we have more confidence in the moral restraint of our own leaders than of our adversaries, the more serious question is whether any frail human system can bear the awful weight of such power.

In any case, if the moment again comes when a decision is made to use our nuclear weapons, you and I will not be asked in that moment to approve, any more than we were invited to pass sentence on Hiroshima and Nagasaki before the bombers took off. The only kind of moral responsibility open to us is to determine, ahead of time, the kinds of power that we will give to our leaders, *and to tolerate no more than we are prepared to approve.*

The chief moral problem, for us no less than for our adversaries, is how to adapt an old nature to a new situation. Said John Cotton in 1656: "Let all the world learn to give mortall man no greater power than they are content they shall use, for use it they will."

Lloyd J. Averill is an independent consultant to colleges and universities in Kalamazoo, Michigan.

"Both the United States and the Soviet Union could emphasize defense in and of itself, and might head toward a state of mutual assured survival."

viewpoint **92**

Overview: High Frontier

Newsweek

Legend has it that around 200 B.C., the Greek scientist Archimedes devised engines of war that for three years held the Romans at bay in their siege of his native Syracuse. One such weapon, made of mammoth concave mirrors, focused fiery sunlight onto Roman warships off the coast and set them afire whenever they approached within bowshot of the city's walls. If true, Archimedes had invented the prototype of a weapon that may someday revolutionize war: the laser cannon. Last week President Reagan invoked the idea of using concentrated light as a weapon not against ships, but against the most awesome weaponry of our time—nuclear missiles. Space-based defensive systems, the president suggested, could "pave the way for arms-control measures to eliminate [nuclear] weapons themselves."

The idea is unquestionably alluring: orbiting laser weapons that could intercept aircraft and missiles within seconds after launch, making ballistic warfare all but obsolete and replacing weapons designed to kill people with weapons that kill weapons. The strategic doctrine that underlies the balance of terror would be turned on its head. No longer would the best defense be a good offense. Rather, both the United States and the Soviet Union could emphasize defense in and of itself, and instead of reeling toward mutual assured destruction, might head toward a state of mutual assured survival. The president cautioned that such a plan "will take years, probably decades," and may not be realized until the next century. But Reagan said current technology has attained a level of sophistication that makes such wonders possible, and his aides likened the endeavor to develop them to John F. Kennedy's 1961 commitment to put a man on the moon by 1970.

Technology Needed

Unfortunately, it may well be impossible to achieve. Apart from its staggering costs, the chief obstacle to the "Star Wars" scenario is that the needed technology does

not yet exist. Reagan's vision of a brave new anti-ballistic world stretches the limits of scientific credulity. If American technology could produce an ABM system that that was 95 percent effective—a rate most experts regard as a practical impossibility—that would still mean that 1 out of every 20 missiles would get through. Moreover, anti-satellite systems and powerful "space mines" could destroy defensive battle stations before they could fire. And like all other weapons systems, a space-based ABM system would be vulnerable to counter-measures—a pre-emptive strike to blind or destroy the space station, for example.

How much progress has been made in laser technology? Research has been under way since the early 1960s, but until very recently, laser-based strategic defense was a "subcritical" issue. The Pentagon is currently working on a three-part space-based project: the development of a powerful chemical laser, a mirror capable of reflecting its beam with precision over thousands of miles and an aiming mechanism for the laser beam. But not until 1987 will the Defense Department find out whether the project is even feasible enough to go forward with a prototype. Among the ABM possibilities on the drawing boards:

Chemical lasers. These would derive their energy from the spontaneous combustion of hydrogen and fluorine—and are the most advanced of the systems now being developed. But they also have the biggest problems: the chemicals used in the reaction are highly combustible and corrosive, and they emit light in a less effective region of the spectrum.

Mirrors in space. Ground-based lasers would send a beam to giant mirrors in the sky, which in turn would reflect the beams at attacking missiles. The problem with this approach is that when a laser beam operates within the atmosphere, it heats the air through which it passes. The heated air defocuses the beam, causing less energy to reach the target. What's more, such a device would be a fair-weather weapon. What happens when you try to blast an intense laser beam through a heavy rainstorm? Steam.

Particle-beam weapons. These accelerate protons or ions. Using these charged atomic particles, these weapons could bore into targets, causing structural damage, disrupting electronics and detonating fuel or explosives. These weapons are still in the conceptual stages.

Nuclear-pumped X-ray lasers. The lasers use energy derived from a small nuclear explosion to slam a brutally intense pulse of X-rays against an enemy missile. Before the detonation, as many as 50 laser rods would be aimed at individual targets; the launched missiles would be obliterated by the impact of the X-rays when the blast occurred. Of all these weapons, the X-ray laser appears to be the most promising and the one President Reagan may well be counting on to ''give us the means of rendering these nuclear weapons impotent and obsolete.'' Although information on the X-ray laser remains classified, the Lawrence Livermore National Laboratory reportedly created an X-ray pulse with the system in a recent underground test in Nevada. The president's chief science adviser, George A. Keyworth II, however, conceded last fall that while it ''is an embryonic technology that should be pursued aggressively, I don't see any clear-cut systems application at this time. It's premature. It's at the science stage.''

''Each superpower could fire a nuclear warhead into space and explode it, unleashing an ''electromagnetic pulse'' that might damage whatever is nearby.''

A space-based laser ABM system may, in fact, prove too complex to work. While it may be possible to develop a laser defense against manned long-range bombers, notes Robert S. Cooper, director of the Defense Advanced Research Projects Agency, the problem becomes far more complicated when the targets are ballistic missiles. The defense system would require a surveillance mechanism to detect the launching of enemy salvos, a method to determine whether they were unfriendly and, of course, a highly precise aiming system to zap the target. Long-range bombers, which must spend 5 to 10 hours en route to their targets, give defensive systems plenty of time to zero in; to hit a missile, however, the ABM system would have only a few hundred seconds while the target is being launched. (The individual warheads, which separate from the missile after the boost stage, must be hard enough to withstand re-entry into the atmosphere, and are therefore much more difficult to destroy.) ''I've devoted my life to systems and to the technology that goes into systems,'' said Cooper recently, ''and my judgment is that we now cannot manage the complexity of the kind of system that

we're talking about.''

Verification Difficult

There is also the problem of verifying kills—the system's ability to determine whether its laser has destroyed the target. ''Do you assume that if the laser has been pointed at the target for a calculated sure-kill time that destruction can be assured?'' asks Wallace D. Henderson, vice president for systems integration at BDM International Corp., which does classified laser research for the Defense Department. Henderson points out that to be wholly effective, a laser space station should be able to determine that it has hit one target before re-aiming at another. But that is very difficult, he says. ''It may be several seconds before a mortally wounded booster departs sufficiently from a ballistic trajectory to be declared no longer a threat.'' By that time, the system may have lost its chance to refocus on another threat.

Finally, the space stations themselves would be vulnerable. The killer satellite, an orbiting kamikaze designed to destroy enemy satellites by pulling up next to them and exploding, is a formidable weapon against space-based ABM stations as well. The Soviets have had anti-satellite (ASAT) capability for about a decade and are believed to have a considerable lead in satellite and laser technology. (Defense Department officials estimate the Soviet high-energy laser program is three to five times the size of America's.) Although both the Soviet ASAT and the American version now in development are effective only against low-orbiting targets, it is conceivable that an ASAT could be equipped with lasers to attack higher altitude targets such as ABM stations. More simply, each superpower could fire a nuclear warhead into space and explode it, unleashing an ''electromagnetic pulse'' that might damage whatever was nearby.

The specter of space mines and ASAT's equipped with high-energy lasers greatly complicates the task of operating an ABM system. As Henderson points out, protection of our bases would seem to require the establishment of ''keepout'' zones in space large enough to negate the effects of space mines. Space stations would have to be hardened to withstand possible laser attack—yet another technological challenge. According to Henderson, ''these questions of operational utility and feasibility call for detailed consideration before greatly increasing emphasis on laser-system technology. It could be embarrassing to spend billions to demonstrate the adequacy of technology to support development of a space high-energy laser system that could be operationally marginal or easily defeated.''

Still, there are those who believe these technological and operational glitches can be overcome. Edward Teller compares Reagan's decision to push ahead with ABM research to Roosevelt's decision to build the atomic bomb. ''In both cases, [the president] took a strong stand which in the former case was decisive and which in the present case I hope will be decisive,'' Teller told

Newsweek's William J. Cook. "This decision, I hope, will convert the cold war into real peace. That is clearly the intention—and it is very much more than wishful thinking because there are real proposals, real possibilities behind it."

"This decision, I hope, will convert the cold war into real peace....There are real proposals, real possibilities behind it."

That is one view. Another was voiced last fall by a Reagan defense expert who suggested that laser weapons are a highly questionable cure: "The high-energy laser is to warfare what laetrile is to cancer." But Reagan may have reached for the stars because he believed that only a 21st-century solution could break the nuclear deadlock. The question is whether his is a workable dream—or whether the ABM system will remain as mythical as Archimedes's mirror machine.

Newsweek *published this article as part of a special issue on the High Frontier.*

"The 'security' promised by Reagan's space wars program [is] not the security of peace, but the security of American victory in a nuclear war rendered all but inevitable."

High Frontier Accelerates the Arms Race

Michio Kaku

The "space wars" speech delivered by Ronald Reagan on March 23 may represent the most enormous gamble of his Administration—and of our lives. In committing the United States to the development of massive space-based antiballistic defense systems, Reagan raises the stakes of the contest between American and Soviet weaponry to a level all but unimaginable.

One possible outcome, offered by Reagan, is attractive: This country will be perpetually protected from nuclear devastation by Soviet missiles. Another possible outcome, feared by many scientists and strategic thinkers, is disastrous: The arms equilibrium between the two superpowers will be disturbed to the point where a nuclear first strike becomes inevitable.

In either event, Reagan's laser-beam proposal, which the Soviet Union immediately denounced as a violation of the 1972 Antiballistic Missile Treaty, must be understood as a profound departure from the balance-of-terror doctrine that has prevailed for the past three decades. Reagan's speech sets the arms race on a wholly uncharted course.

The strategic rationale underlying the space wars proposal can be found in a glossy, 175-page document called *The High Frontier* (published last year by the right-wing Heritage Foundation). Here, retired Lieutenant General Daniel O. Graham, former director of the Defense Intelligence Agency, advocates a policy of "ensured survival" to replace the current doctrine of "assured destruction," which leaves the United States vulnerable to wholesale destruction by Soviet nuclear warheads.

To ensure survival, Graham recommends a system of 400 satellites that would constantly circle the globe, armed with a lethal array of energy beams capable of shooting down Soviet missiles within five minutes of their launching. The energy beams would consist of light (driven by hydrogen fluoride lasers), particle beams (of charged or neutral subatomic particles), X-rays (driven by an atomic explosion and focused by lasers), microwaves, and EMP (electromagnetic pulse generated by a nuclear detonation).

In addition, Graham would have the Pentagon deploy killer satellites capable of blinding or destroying Soviet satellites in outer space, as well as ground-based "energy cannons" capable of knocking down enemy missiles before they reach their targets in the United States. A massive civil defense program would also be developed, just in case any Soviet missiles managed to penetrate the antimissile arsenal.

The U.S. military point with pride at the advances in laser technology that have supposedly placed satellite antiballistic missile systems within reach—at a research cost of about half a billion dollars. They cite a test conducted five years ago in San Juan Capistrano, California, where a hydrogen fluoride laser was used to blast three antitank missiles traveling through the air at 450 miles per hour.

However, the military efficacy of space weapons, let alone their advisability as a new stage in the arms race, is a matter of much dispute. It is no great feat, critics note, for ground-based lasers to shoot down airborne antitank missiles. It is much easier to destroy a slow-moving, preprogrammed missile that is easily tracked by radar than to intercept from outer space thousands of Soviet missiles launched simultaneously and speeding at thousands of miles per hour over a vast area. The feasibility of space wars weapons against targets of this sort has never been demonstrated.

It took an entire building to house the 300-watt power supply for the San Juan Capistrano tests. A genuine laser cannon could require from 100 billion to one trillion watts, and might entail placing several nuclear power plants in orbit—an impractical assignment at best.

Furthermore, the space-based beams can easily be neutralized by inexpensive countermeasures. Warheads coated with highly reflective paint can diminish the

Michio Kaku, "Wasting Space," *The Progressive,* June 1983. Reprinted by permission from *The Progressive,* 409 East Main St., Madison WI 53703. Copyright © 1983, The Progressive, Inc.

usefulness of laser beams. Decoys and chaff can confuse radar. For every ruble the Soviets might spend on such cheap diversions, the United States would have to spend millions of dollars on devices that can differentiate between real warheads and duds. And there is always the possibility—some would say the likelihood or even the certainty—that the Soviets would destroy U.S. satellites with killer satellites or space mines of their own.

"The mere perception by one side that the other has achieved a first-strike capability or a foolproof ABM system may suffice to provoke nuclear war."

Finally, it may be that the laws of physics simply rule out the successful development of space weaponry. Because a satellite takes ninety minutes to complete an orbit around the Earth, only a fraction of the laser fleet would be in position to act in case of an enemy attack. Within a few minutes, the small number of satellites must locate enemy missiles with pinpoint accuracy, separate out the decoys and dummies, focus the destructive beam long enough to destroy a warhead, confirm the kill, and repeat the process hundreds or thousands of times. It may be impossible to do all that.

What makes the new space war strategy such an ominous development, though, is not the high cost, dubious effectiveness, or great vulnerability of the weaponry, but the potential escalation of the arms race to a new, destabilizing level.

The mere *perception* by one side that the other has achieved a first-strike capability or a foolproof ABM system may suffice to provoke nuclear war. The Soviet Union, understandably fearful that the United States is preparing a knock-out first strike, could decide to jump the gun and fire first. Former U.S. strategic arms negotiator Paul Warnke has said, "There is no question in my mind that we could have a war in space within a decade unless we devise a treaty that will stop it." And a war in space would inevitably become a war that devastates the Earth.

Accelerating the Arms Race

Neither the skepticism of most scientists nor the profound misgivings felt by many strategic analysts seems to have had any impact on President Reagan. His preoccupation is with the Soviet Union and the possibility that it may forge ahead in the arms race. For him, the space wars scenario seems to hold out the hope of perpetual, foolproof protection for the United States.

The Soviet military might entertain similar visions. For decades, both superpowers have secretly studied the black arts of antisatellite (ASAT) and ABM warfare, hoping to find security on the ground by placing the proper weaponry in space.

When the Soviets launched their first Sputnik in October 1957, the United States immediately embarked on a crash program called SAINT (for satellite interceptor). SAINT was abandoned in 1962 only because nuclear-tipped ASAT missiles based on Kwajalein Atoll and Johnston Island in the Pacific seemed to offer a more promising way of attacking Soviet space satellites. Though the use of such missiles was explicitly banned by the Outer Space Treaty of 1967, they were kept in place until 1975, when the Pentagon came to the embarrassing realization that the electromagnetic pulse generated by nuclear detonations would wreak indiscriminate havoc among American as well as Soviet satellites.

Today, the U.S. ASAT program calls for use of an F-15 fighter jet equipped with a miniature rocket that is capable of soaring 200 miles into outer space and homing in on Soviet satellites. The rocket, called the MHV (miniature homing vehicle), is now undergoing final flight tests.

In addition, the Space Shuttle has increasingly taken on a role as a space wars weapon. Its heavy involvement in military applications dates back to May 13, 1978, when President Carter signed Presidential Decision Memorandum Thirty-seven, calling for "activities in space in support of [the U.S.] right of self-defense, thereby strengthening national security, the deterrence of attack, and arms control agreements." With substantial funding from the military budget, the Space Shuttle now serves as a vehicle for beam-weapon experimentation. The Soviets have protested, to no avail, that this violates existing treaties.

ASAT systems will be ready for deployment in the 1990s, but beam weapons are at a less advanced stage and their current status is shrouded in secrecy. We do know that the Defense Advanced Research Projects Agency (DARPA) set up Project See Saw as long ago as 1958 to investigate particle beam ABM systems. After more than a dozen years of exploratory work, See Saw was abandoned in 1972 when researchers concluded that the costs of such weaponry would be prohibitive.

In the 1970s, the Army started its own program, first called Sipapu (a Native American word for "sacred fire") and later renamed White House. The Navy set up the mysterious Chair Heritage Project, which runs a test series called Dauphin at the Lawrence Livermore weapons laboratory in California.

X-Ray Lasers

Three years ago, Dauphin dispelled the long-held assumption that it was impossible to generate X-ray lasers. In the first successful test of its kind, Dauphin demonstrated that a small underground nuclear charge could be used to pump an X-ray laser at a wavelength of .0014 microns. This breakthrough helped persuade the Pentagon and the Reagan Administration that an elaborate space wars program might be feasible. In X-ray laser, a nuclear detonation creates huge numbers of soft

X-rays that can be channeled through hundreds of laser tubes into directed X-ray beams. When used in space, however, the nuclear explosion kills the satellite itself, so a laser cannon of this sort can be used only once.

Predictably, we know even less about the Soviet Union's space war efforts than about our own Government's, but there is no doubt that the Russians, too, have explored techniques of destroying enemy satellites. Instead of using conventional jet fighters to launch ASAT weapons, the Soviets have been experimenting since 1968 with maneuverable satellites capable of firing conventional charges to destroy enemy vehicles in space.

On April 13, 1976, Cosmos 814 was borne aloft on an F-1M missile launched from the sprawling Tyurantam space port. After only one orbit, Cosmos 814 maneuvered within striking distance—one kilometer—of the previously launched Cosmos 803. It was a stunning display of satellite virtuosity, and it prompted President Ford to approve funding for the Pentagon's MHV program.

Still, Soviet ASAT efforts cannot be construed as a serious threat to the security of the United States. The Soviet weapons can effectively be directed only against low-altitude satellites in orbit at 200 miles or less, while most important U.S. communications satellites are in synchronous orbits at 20,000 miles—beyond the reach of either Cosmos or MHV. What's more, Soviet killer satellites are unsophisticated machines, able to home in only on carefully preprogrammed dummy satellites locked into special orbits.

Soviet efforts to manipulate satellites in outer space can easily be tracked on radar, but the progress of space beam research on the ground is a matter of speculation and interpretation of aerial reconnaissance.

The Reagan Administration's claims that the Russians are "ahead" in laser ABM technology rests almost exclusively on a single scrap of disputed evidence. In 1972, Major General George Keegan, then in charge of the $3 billion-a-year U.S. Air Force intelligence apparatus, alleged that satellite photos of a Soviet base sixty kilometers south of Semipalatinsk proved beyond doubt that the Russians were out in front in development of particle beam weaponry. Keegan cited four large holes in the ground and two spherical structures that he described as energy storage tanks for particle beams.

Keegan's assertions were investigated by the Central Intelligence Agency, which decided his evidence was marginal and inconclusive. The CIA skeptics designated the Soviet facility as URDF-3, for "unidentified research and development facility number three," leaving Keegan virtually alone in insisting that the Soviets had a twenty-year jump on the United States. It was only with the advent of the Reagan Administration that Keegan's charges started receiving a respectful hearing, and the retired general recently put in a return appearance on the CBS Television *Sixty Minutes* program.

Obstacles to Weapons

The hard-line scientists who have played a role in persuading the Reagan Administration to commit itself to space wars are no fools. They are aware of the doubts voiced by their colleagues and they understand the formidable obstacles that stand in the way of effective satellite weapons. They surely realize that no laser ABM system will ever be able to destroy all Soviet missiles immediately after launch, and that a failure rate of even 1 per cent would inflict catastrophic damage on targets in the United States.

Why, then, are they pushing the ABM system, and why is the Administration heeding their advice? The answers are to be found in the arcane theories and peculiar ratiocinations of the Nuclear Warfighting strategists.

The laser ABM, with all its limitations, may have effective applications in conjunction with the launching of a preemptive first strike.

"The Russians, too, have explored techniques of destroying enemy satellites."

The Nuclear Warfighters reason that an American first strike, no matter how successful, could never destroy all of the Soviet retaliatory force. That's where the space weapons would come into play: The 10 to 20 per cent of Soviet missiles that might manage to escape a U.S. first strike could be shot down by a laser ABM system. In Nuclear Warfighting jargon, this is called Strategic Defense.

The arithmetic is simple: The Soviet Union has about 8,000 strategic warheads aimed at targets in the United States. In the near future, the land-based MX missile and the submarine-launched Trident II will be accurate enough to drop two hydrogen bombs on each of the Soviet SS-18 and SS-19 missile silos.

Still, there are some uncertainties: To what extent will magnetic and gravitational anomalies over the North Pole divert the attacking U.S. missiles from their flight paths? Until the missiles actually are sent on their course, no one will know. It must also be assumed that at least 10 percent of the Soviet nuclear submarine fleet will survive a first strike. In sum, there is a likelihood that about 1,000 of the 8,000 Russian warheads would still be available to retaliate against the United States.

With all its faults, the laser ABM system can reasonably be expected to handle most of those remaining 1,000 Soviet warheads. The few missiles that might elude both the first strike and the laser ABM provide the rationale for the Administration's new emphasis on civil defense and relocation plans; the purpose of such programs is to preserve U.S. industrial capacity for the "post-attack era."

State Department consultant Colin S. Gray, one of the

Nuclear Warfighters, has neatly summed up the doctrine:

"The United States should plan to defeat the Soviet Union and to do so at a cost that would not prohibit U.S. recovery. Washington should identify war aims that in the last resort would contemplate the destruction of Soviet political authority and the emergence of a postwar world order compatible with Western values....A combination of counterforce offensive targeting, civil defense, and ballistic missile and air defense should hold U.S. casualties to approximately 20 million, which should render U.S. strategic threats more credible."

"The laser ABM...may have effective applications in conjunction with the launching of a preemptive first strike."

The objective, in other words, is not merely a first strike—though that is an essential component—but a comprehensive mix of first-strike targeting, antimissile weaponry, and civil defense measures that will guarantee, in the Administration's view, that the United States will "prevail" in a nuclear exchange.

That is the "security" promised by Reagan's space wars program—not the security of peace, but the security of American victory in a nuclear war rendered all but inevitable.

Michio Kaku is a professor of nuclear physics at the Graduate Center of the City University of New York and is director of the Institute for Peace and Safe Technology. He is co-author of Nuclear Power: Both Sides.

"The debate over space weaponry should go beyond the question, 'Is testing such systems permissible?' to the question, 'Is the international law we have...in the world's interest?'"

High Frontier
Will Not Accelerate the Arms Race

Walter McDougall

How should we approach the bizarre, mortal issues raised by the prospect of space-based ABM technology? The public discussion of space weaponry has already been sullied by calculated hysteria meant less to reveal real demerits of the new technologies than to prevent publicity of their potential merits. Thanks to media sensationalism, a misinformed public either applauds inanely at the prospect of Atari's Missile Command game coming to life, or else deplores the plot of Pentagon Darth Vaders to annex space to their Empire. Before serious debate can commence, some slogans must be put to rest. The fact is that in the topsy-turvy canopy of space, our gut reactions are not trustworthy. Sometimes the world is upside-down.

1. *Laser weapons will militarize space.* This is the war-cry of journalists and others who want to preserve the virginity of outer space from the rapine of terrestrial militarists. It is not a new sound in the heavens, but an echo from the post-Sputnik era when men of good will hoped to keep cold-war rivalry out of the newly opened territory of space, and thus not repeat the failure to control atomic power at the outset. But there was a superstitious undertone in the "space for peace" chorus: even though the Russians' ICBMs, and not their stubbornly secret space program, were the true threat, there was something scary about Red moons overhead carrying heaven knew what. In time, the U.S. and the USSR concluded that bombs in orbit were too messy, and the Partial Test Ban Treaty (1963) and the Outer Space Treaty (1967) banned testing and deployment of weapons of mass destruction in outer space. But there were other military uses of space, and from the beginning the "space for peace" cry was as futile as if it had been shouted in the vacuum of space itself.

Already Militarized

Space was militarized even before Sputnik I soared in

October 1957, and is irreversibly so after 25 years. If it were not enough that satellite launchers were usually military missiles, or that civilian space technologies were often identical to those needed for defense, then the very necessity of military satellite systems to support strategic missile forces ensured the militarization of space. In order to aim ICBMs for any purpose other than the crudest city-busting, in order to protect them, in order to avoid paranoid over-estimation of the enemy's capability and to monitor his technical progress—in other words, in order to perform essential support functions in the missile age—we (and the Soviets) had to push quickly for satellite systems in the service of military geodesy, surveillance, communications, meteorology, infrared early warning, and electronic ferreting.

In the case of the United States there was a premium attached to spy satellites because of the closed nature of Soviet society. We needed, and still need, secure means of surveillance more than the Soviets do—not because we are devious and aggressive, but because they are. Indeed, the U.S. spy-satellite program was begun a year before the Space Age was born.

So what is new about laser anti-missile systems? It is the prospect of *active* as opposed to *passive* military space systems. There has not yet been a shot fired in anger in the serenity of space. A-SATs seem especially provocative, because an attack on enemy satellites would probably never occur without signaling nuclear war. But this is to confuse cause and effect. Men on earth may start nuclear wars; machines in space do not. But what if a laser shot down a spacecraft by accident? This would be grave indeed, but far less serious than the accidental launch of a nuclear warhead, the prospect we live with today. In any case, why is it more important to protect pristine space, where nothing lives, than the crowded earth? But the most elementary fact is that once military assets are placed in space, they inevitably become targets. Space *is* militarized, and to prevent somehow the extension of active weaponry to space—to keep it a

Walter McDougall, "How Not to Think About Space Lasers," May 13, 1983, *National Review.* © 1983 by National Review, Inc., 150 East 35th Street, New York, NY 10016. Reprinted with permission.

sanctuary for passive military systems—would simply be to protect the strategic status quo. This suggests a second misconception impeding fruitful debate.

2. *Don't rock the MAD boat.* MAD—mutual assured destruction—is the missile-age gospel, sanctified by Robert McNamara in 1965 and preached by a generation of politicians, pundits, and political scientists. Why it held sway for so long will be an interesting problem for historians. The ascendancy of liberalism was certainly a factor, since MAD permitted the U.S. to freeze nuclear delivery systems for 15 years, cut arms spending sharply during years of Soviet buildup, and relegate military history, strategy, and leadership to the category of the disreputable. Since nuclear weapons had "changed the world," history was irrelevant. Since war was now unthinkable and a credible deterrent all that was needed, strategy was obsolete. Since defense variables were now quantifiable (megatonnage, throw-weight, circular error probability, etc.), human factors and provocative military "virtues" were atavistic. Such corollaries to MAD appealed to the technocratic mind.

"There is reason to believe that strategic arms would be better controlled, the balance more secure, and the risks lower in an ABM world."

To be sure, our doctrine has never been purely MAD. If a leak or a federal court ever spills the Single Integrated Operational Plans (SIOP) from the Sixties and Seventies, they should show that U.S. priorities always included military targets in the Soviet Union. We may have had one strategy for public consumption, and another—a mix of counterforce and countervalue—in reality. MAD, let us recall, requires that if the Soviets strike first at our missile, bomber, and submarine bases, the President may respond by flinging what warheads remain at Russian cities. This, of course, invites a final, fatal blast at our cities. Would any President order Armageddon out of spite? If the answer is "not likely," then what has been the rationale of MAD?

Its logic derived first from the technological determinism that says nuclear weapons changed warfare forever. The nature of the beasts—small, cheap, very destructive, and impossible to repel—gave an advantage to the attack and counterattack unique in history. No matter how devastating one's first blow, retaliation was swift and certain, and thus a "big war" unthinkable. Indeed the nuclear age has been one of 38 years of "strategic peace"; five more years and we break the record of 1871 to 1914. Whether this was due to nukes, to deterrence, or in fact to American superiority is a haunting question.

Yet once the peace-keeping value of MAD was assumed, a second justification emerged. As Henry Kissinger put it in Brussels in 1979, "[This] school of thought to which I myself contributed...considered that strategic stability was a military asset;...the historically amazing theory developed that vulnerability contributed to peace and invulnerability contributed to risks of war." The goal was not, therefore, to escape from the balance of terror, but to prevent its destabilization. Chief among destabilizers was ABM. Despite the fears of a Soviet missile defense (the Tallinn Upgrade), Red China's ICBM tests, and the maturation of Safeguard technology, ABM failed in this country both because of its costliness and because of MAD fears of destabilization.

ABM and Deterrence

Now ABM is back. Despite SALT and America's strategic snooze, the Soviets continued to build far beyond what they needed for stable deterrence. SALT II accordingly died, the SALT I ABM treaty is currently open for review, and space-based laser or other systems now hold out hope of an effective and clean technology for the defensive mission. We all hope that START (Strategic Arms Reduction Talks) will succeed in reducing arsenals, but non-nuclear defensive systems do not necessarily conflict with that hope. Ultimately, arms reduction and ABM have the same aim: the end of terror.

This time, however, the country must not only debate the risks and merits of ABM, it must also put MAD on trial. Even assuming MAD was a salutary doctrine for the early missile age, why is it assumed that that age will last forever? Critics have applied to space-based lasers the fallacy of the last move—that every technological fix inevitably triggers a counter-fix. True enough, but technological advance can be stopped, if at all, only by universal political will. We must always try to marshal that will, but meanwhile how could we preserve MAD in the face of continued Soviet buildups? Build another thousand missiles and put them out to sea, in zany shell-game silos, or into space? Go to any extreme to preserve our freedom to incinerate Russian cities? There is reason to believe that strategic arms would be better controlled, the balance more secure, and the risks lower in an ABM world, laser or otherwise, than in a MAD one.

Consider the possibilities. The first scenario is that the superpowers agree to ban space weaponry, i.e., ABM is rejected again. This avoids the risks of transition, but preserves the risks inherent in an offensive strategic environment. The second is that both superpowers achieve a space-based ABM capability simultaneously. This would be ideal, for it would usher in another stable world, but one in which stability would derive from the certain *failure* of a first strike, rather than the certain *success* of retaliation. How long this technical regime might then last is anybody's guess. But if there is ever a time to muster the political will to freeze the strategic moment, let it come then, not now.

Enforcing Arms Control

The third and fourth scenarios involve the U.S. or the

USSR's deploying space-based ABMs first. This would surely mean gross imbalance. But if the U.S. is first, we will have won another chance not only to demonstrate our restraint, but to coax the Soviets and the world to accept an enforceable regime of arms control, the regime we failed to win during our atomic monopoly. Finally, there is the chance that the Soviets will acquire this technology first. The risks that would entail should suffice to motivate all Americans to see that it does not come to pass.

Of the four scenarios, the one that most disturbs critics of laser ABMs is the third. They fear that if the U.S. began to deploy, the Soviets would feel forced to pre-empt. As suggested above, this contradicts the argument that laser ABMs are easily countered and hence wasteful, but it also ignores the fact that by the time such a system is deployed, in the 1990s, the traditional U.S. deterrent will have been reinforced sufficiently to cover the deployment of space systems. The last historical purpose of the retaliatory doctrine could be to shelter the transition to a new, mature nuclear age cradled in space.

3. *The scientists are the only ones we can trust.* Maybe no one believes this any more, but many still act as if they do, out of what I call the Law of Selective Deference. This holds that experts with supporting testimony are self-interested. After Sputnik we wanted to trust the experts who crowded into every corner of the Federal Government. When the technocratic promise of the 1960s soured—our technology having failed to save Third World democracy, the inner cities, and the American dollar—technical experts lost credibility. This was especially so in defense. Many people took for granted the meanness of government white-coats with their connections to weapons labs, hawkish senators, and the military-industrial complex.

Politics of Weaponry

There was never room for honest disagreement between an Edward Teller and a Barry Commoner. But, sadly, one cannot always trust expert debate on a question such as space weaponry even when all parties share a concern for strong, economical defense. Aside from turf-protecting, paradigmatic thinking, envy jealousy, and academic politics, scientists also entrench themselves around specific technologies and doctrines. A career DOD official, frustrated over what he saw as foot-dragging on lasers, attributed it to the fact that Carter's top defense aides all had backgrounds in nuclear physics: "...charged-particle beams and high-energy lasers upset the technology monopoly of weapons created in World War II for offensive strategy. Tremendous power and prestige has [sic] accrued to those whose background is in nuclear-weapons design and they are now in policy-making positions....It is very difficult to be statesmanlike when everything you've learned can be overturned by new technology in which the defense can predominate" (*Aviation Week & Space Technology,* July 28, 1980).

Is this charge justified, or is it the grumbling of one

engaged in a tenuous line of research? We may hope that high officials will always overcome the temptation to "spike" new ideas for personal motives. Yet revolutionary weapons often met stony resistance from hierarchies in the past. Can we not expect the same phenomenon today? Our major weapons decisions in recent decades have been made by officials who cut their teeth on nuclear bombs and missiles. Beam weapons are in the same relation to their lifework as dive bombers were to battleships or machine guns to the cavalry, or missiles to the big bombers.

"There is the chance that the Soviets will acquire this technology first. The risks that would entail should suffice to motivate all Americans to see that it does not come to pass."

There is certain to be polarization over space lasers and other ABMs within the labs, the Pentagon, and the nation. We must listen carefully to expert testimony, but also note whence it comes.

4. *Space weapons are against the law.* Another common complaint against plans for prototype A-SAT or ABM weaponry is that it is illegal: aren't there treaties against that? The answer is: only for the time being. SALT I obliged signatories not "to interfere with national technical means of verification" (spy satellites) or "to develop, test, or deploy ABM systems which are sea-based, air-based, or mobile land-based." Thus space is a high frontier, but not a lawless Wild West. Nevertheless, failing extension of SALT I or a new ABM/A-SAT pact, there could be no ban on devices capable of destroying spacecraft and missiles.

The prospect for future negotiations is dim. The A-SAT talks adjourned in Vienna, the Soviets having persisted in killer-satellite experiments and insisted that the Space Shuttle is a form of A-SAT in need of control. Moscow asked that the issue be placed on the UN docket, but that means nothing. What law there is concerning space-based weaponry will unravel if either side jettisons SALT I (which can always be done on six months' notice). Would this be a disaster? Perhaps, perhaps not. We have tended to assume that arms control is an irreversible "process." Why should it not go into reverse, or start up new paths in an altered technical and political environment? The debate over space weaponry should go beyond the question, "Is testing such systems permissible?" to the question, "Is the international law we have, or project, in our and in the world's interest?"

5. *Space weapons mean a new arms race.* The threat of a new arms race, somehow more terrible because "in space," ignites concerned laymen. This judgment assumes that there was an old arms race that somehow

355

stopped, and will stay stopped unless the space cadets get their way. One need not cover this ground again: the Soviets never stopped racing, lately we have been losing, and advanced technology has always been the trump that saves us from becoming far more of a garrison state than we are. In this context, space based lasers appear as a fruitful technology in which our comparative advantage may be best exploited and our social values, born of an insular, liberal strategic tradition, best preserved. Of course, any large defense program must be judged on its merits, but there is no question of starting a new arms race.

"The Soviets never stopped racing, lately we have been losing, and advanced technology has always been the trump that saves us from becoming far more of a garrison state."

Why build such machines, though, except to fight nuclear wars? Hasn't the human race used every weapon it has ever built? The makings of a straw man are here for either side of the debate.

Walter McDougall is a professor of diplomatic history at the University of California, Berkeley. His second book, The Heavens and the Earth: The Political Roots of the Space Age, *will be published by Basic Books.*

"The message is both dramatic and very easy to understand. It tells the Kremlin's new Himmler that in wanting to protect ourselves, we have no desire to annihilate. . .the USSR."

viewpoint **95**

High Frontier Is the Best Defensive Weapon

Patrick Dillon

Unquestionably, President Reagan's timely announcement of a High Frontier defense system was a brilliant political and strategic maneuver. It places the United States squarely into a checkmate position vis a vis the Soviet dictators and has succeeded, in one sweeping stroke, in putting the lie to the sham, peaceful quackery that the Kremlin has so assiduously been disseminating over the past several decades.

Frankly, I'm surprised they fell so easily into exposing themselves for what they really are—a cruel and evil clique of power hungry bandits intent on turning the world into one giant Gulag. If I had been Andropov, I would have passed Reagan's new initiative by with hardly more than an offhand comment that the Soviet Union seeks only friendly co-operation with other nations and rejects all forms of aggression. This would have taken some of the political wind out of the President's sails preserving, at least for the time being, the tattered fabric of Moscow's peaceful posturings.

Evidently, this was just too much for the Politburo to cope with and, instead, they screamed like stuck pigs with little thought given to the effect of their violent reaction on a world that has now received a privileged glimpse of what lies in their black hearts.

Effective Threat

It matters little how far we or they are advanced in the technicalities of an anti-ballistic missile umbrella. This will come in good time. What is important is that Reagan has pulled the rug out from under the Kremlin's carefully laid strategy of thermo-nuclear blackmail. This is a vital element in the U.S.S.R.'s three point plan for the emasculation and final destruction of the United States, viz., external encirclement, internal demoralization, nuclear blackmail leading to progressive surrender.

Andropov's howls of anguish remind me of a chat I

Patrick A. Dillon, ''President's High Frontier Message Is Clear,'' *The Union Leader*, April 14, 1983. Reprinted with permission.

once had with an insurance adjuster who told me that if a client accepted his loss settlement with equanimity he knew, instinctively, that he had not done his job properly. On the other hand, if the client protested loudly, then he was certain his offer had been right on target.

Let us examine the ramifications of the President's initiative. First and foremost it gives the West much needed surcease from the growing fear of an endless escalation in nuclear throw weight that many perceive can only lead to the final Armageddon. Secondly, the realization of a viable non-nuclear system of disposing of incoming Soviet missiles IN SPACE before they reach American soil removes from them an important psychological weapon. Part of their policy for world domination requires that we remain vulnerable and fearful of the awesome destructive capacity of their nuclear strike force. Finally, of course, the ultimate effectiveness of their massive missile buildup will now be rendered partially redundant and greatly reduced for the purpose for which it was originally intended. Perhaps this is what they are really screaming about.

What the President has told the world, loud and clear, is that we in the West only wish to defend ourselves against being incinerated—by whom? Well, certainly not the Samoans.

The message is both dramatic and very easy to understand. It tells the Kremlin's new Himmler that in wanting to protect ourselves, we also have no desire to annihilate the peoples of the U.S.S.R. although, God knows, the way some of them are treated, many might be looking forward to some quick end to their miserable lives.

I have no doubt that the leaky sieve of our scientific community will make it easy for Moscow to remain in step with any progress we make in the construction and operation of our High Frontier umbrella. But that is really of no consequence in as much as if they attempt to neutralize our defenses in space—quite harmless non-nuclear devices—they will only succeed in confirming to the world at large that their attitude is aggressive and destructive. It is hard to preach peace and seek to bury your opponent at the same time. None of this means that either side will be entirely free of risk and start dismantling its nuclear strike force. I predict however that it will gradually diminish and, by updating, become more selective and accurate.

Long-Awaited Reprieve

Naturally, no defense system is completely foolproof, but if it can stop 90 percent of a first strike several miles up in space, we stand a far better chance of survival down here at a 10 percent hit level. Again, it will be the same old Mexican stand-off but with some significant improvements over the present horrors of Mutual Assured Destruction. At least Mutual Assured Defense is a step in the right direction up and away in the bright blue yonder where the devastating blasts of nuclear warheads can do a deal less harm to the life of this planet.

"No defense system is completely foolproof, but if it can stop 90 percent of a first strike. . .we stand a far better chance of survival."

A final word about the 21st Century. Much of the technology associated with the High Frontier deterrent will indeed take on the flavor of "Star Wars" with armored space ships zapping each other with particle beam lasers. At least this will give us Earthlings a long awaited reprieve from living under the daily terror of nuclear warfare down here in our own back yards. There is, of course, also the hope that, having reached the zenith of its despotism, the Soviet Empire will collapse in the morass of its own sterility.

Patrick Dillon writes frequently for the Union Leader.

"Our technological superiority should be applied to the difficult art of space weaponry to regain and hold strategic superiority."

High Frontier Is a Dangerous Offensive Weapon

Kurt Gottfried

ASAT, yet another acronym, has begun to invade the news columns. One is told that it is an antisatellite—a device that can destroy a satellite. But that still leaves many unanswered questions.

How does an ASAT differ from an antiballistic missile, or ABM, a device that can destroy an intercontinental ballistic missile, or ICBM, in flight? Satellites are much more fragile than ICBM's and stay in orbit for weeks. ICBM's are vulnerable for only a few minutes, so striking a swarm of them is a prodigious problem. Therefore, even an ineffective ABM could be a wonderful ASAT.

Do treaties allow ABM's? The 1972 ABM treaty does not permit the field testing of the laser ABM's alluded to by the President in his "Star Wars" speech. To quote the Arms Control Impact Statement the President sent to Congress in April, "The ABM treaty prohibition on development, testing and deployment of spacebased ABM systems applies directly to directed-energy technology," that is, to lasers, etc.

Treaty Violations

Are ASAT's forbidden by treaties? Existing treaties impose no effective restraints on ASAT development or testing, even though there is a relationship between ABM's and ASAT's. Since an ABM system could, in its infancy, already be an effective ASAT, it could masquerade as such to evade the ABM treaty. By the same token, a program to develop only ASAT's could be misperceived as a budding ABM by the other side. ASAT's could therefore trigger enormous buildups of offensive missiles, which is precisely what the ABM treaty was designed to prevent.

What are the attitudes of the super powers to weapons in space?

The Administration will not resume negotiations on limiting ASAT's. This stance is perfectly consistent with

its long-range strategy, as laid down in the Defense Guidance, the Pentagon's five-year master plan. The plan assumes that the United States must be able to "prevail" in nuclear war; therefore, it must be able to "deny the enemy the use of his space systems" and "insure that treaties and agreements do not foreclose opportunities to develop these capabilities."

The White House wants to renegotiate the ABM treaty to allow space-based ABM's, as it made clear yet again on June 18 in an amicable response to a speech by Foreign Minister Andrei A. Gromyko. Are the superpowers on the same wavelength for once?

They are not. The Kremlin has used every opportunity to suggest an interest in ASAT arms control and opposition to new-fangled ABM's, as exemplified by a remarkable advertisement in *The New York Times* by leading Soviet scientists attacking space-based ABM's.

Expensive and Dangerous

Why do the two Governments take opposite sides on what seems to be only a technical issue? The Administration's motives were spelled out in the Defense Guidance and more recently by the White House: Our technological superiority should be applied to the difficult art of space weaponry to regain and hold strategic superiority. While Soviet motives are hard to assess, they are probably the other side of the same coin: A healthy respect for American technology and a fear that an arms race in space would be terribly expensive and hazardous. Indeed, they must now see that the major accomplishment of their inept 15-year ASAT project has been to justify an American program that is about to produce a much more potent weapon.

Does that not mean that the Administration's policy is best suited to American interests? Speaking first of ASAT, the United States, with its forces spread across the globe and facing a secretive adversary, relies heavily on satellites for communication and intelligence. In contrast, Soviet forces are mainly on or close to the

Kurt Gottfried, "A Backfiring Weapon," *The New York Times,* July 21, 1983, © 1983 by The New York Times Company. Reprinted by permission.

Eurasian landmass and depend primarily on land-based and airborne communications. The United States would therefore be the loser if both sides acquired effective ASAT's.

Soviets Unable to Respond

But will the Soviet Union ever build effective space weapons? The United States has usually been first with sophisticated weapons: nuclear bombs, multiple independently targetable missiles, or MIRV's, submarine-based missiles, etc. The Soviet Union has always followed suit. Often their weapons are blunderbusses compared with American designs, but that does not make them less lethal. And in the case of ABM's, it is far more difficult to build a missile defense than to circumvent and overwhelm it.

"The Soviets 'must now see that the major accomplishment of their inept 15-year ASAT project has been to justify an American program.'"

In short, the Administration's military space policy rests on the assumption that, for the first time, the Soviet Union will not be able to respond effectively to a major threat to its security. Whether or not this conjecture is correct is not essential. If right, we can look forward to desperate Soviet reactions at least as dangerous as the Cuban missile crisis; if wrong, we can look forward to a standoff at a drastically reduced margin of safety.

Kurt Gottfried is a professor of physics and nuclear studies at Cornell University and is director of The Union of Concerned Scientists.

"The economic benefits of a strong U.S. commitment to the exploitation of space for both security and industry are potentially very great."

viewpoint 97

High Frontier Is Affordable and Improves Security

William Armstrong

In order to fulfill the objectives of the High Frontier concept, including rapidly closing the "window of vulnerability," creating the concrete basis for a new strategy of Assured Survival, and opening space for economic growth, the following list of urgent requirements is presented.

The requirements for military systems to implement the High Frontier concept are these:

A point defense for U.S. ICBM silos which, within two or three years, at a cost less than that of superhardening, can destroy any confidence the Soviets might have in a first strike against our deterrent.

A first-generation spaceborne ballistic missile defense, deployable in five or six years at a cost not exceeding that of the original MX-MPS system and capable of significant attrition of a Soviet strategic missile attack in the early part of trajectory.

A second-generation space defense system, deployable within 10 or 12 years and capable of attacking hostile objects anywhere in near-Earth space with advanced technology weaponry (e.g., lasers).

A utilitarian manned military space control vehicle, deployable within the next six to eight years and capable of inspection, on-orbit maintenance, and space tug missions wherever satellites can go.

A civil defense program of sufficient scope and funding to take advantage of the proposed active missile defenses and thus add to U.S. deterrent strength.

The primary requirements in core space technology and nonmilitary applications are:

Improved space transportation, designed to lower the cost-per-pound in orbit to under one hundred dollars.

A manned space station in low Earth orbit as soon as practicable. It would allow low cost, efficient development and testing of both civilian and military system elements and would constitute a first step toward a similar manned station at geosynchronous orbit.

William Armstrong, "Defense of America," *Congressional Record,* June 14, 1983.

Development work on reliable, high-capacity energy systems in space, initially to power other space activities, and eventually to provide electrical power to any spot on Earth.

Preparatory development of a selected number of promising commercial business opportunities. Government efforts should focus on encouraging the transformation of these "seed" efforts into independently viable commercial operations as soon as possible. . . .

Costs

The total costs of the High Frontier concept over the next five or six years in outlays of constant dollars might be on the order of $20 billion. Through 1990 the total costs in constant dollars would probably be about $35 billion—a figure that compares favorably with what would have been the total cost of MX—MPS in its original configuration. It also compares favorably with the Apollo-Moon landing program, and strikingly so if the inflation rate of the past 12 years is considered.

If one considers possible tradeoffs in programs no longer needed or lowered in priority by the existence of an effective strategic defense, the real costs of the High Frontier programs are lower. For instance, the $2.5 billion now earmarked for superhardening of existing missile silos and for deploying more complex point defenses need not be expended. There are other possible tradeoffs such as repositioning of SAC airfields, reducing the urgency of theater nuclear force upgrade in Europe, C^3 improvements, and so forth. Thus real (or net) costs over the next 10 years for High Frontier could be well under $50 billion total.

Finally, there is a reasonable chance for sizable cost offsets from industry and Allied participation in the most expensive aspects of the High Frontier effort—nonmilitary applications. This is especially true if a vigorous effort to tap solar energy is emphasized. Several nations have already stated their willingness to assist in such an effort. Such nongovernment input would further reduce the real costs of the concept.

In any case, costs to the U.S. taxpayer of implementing High Frontier will certainly be lower than those involved in other approaches to solving urgent security issues, e.g., MX—MPS. The High Frontier approach, therefore, cannot be characterized as unrealistically expensive.

Military Impacts

The mere announcement of a bold, new U.S. initiative along the lines of the High Frontier concept would have beneficial impacts at home and abroad. The fulfillment of the urgent requirements noted above would have even more far-reaching impacts.

"If one considers possible tradeoffs in programs no longer needed or lowered in priority. . .the real costs of the High Frontier programs are lower."

On the purely military-strategic side, we would be moving away from the unstable world of terror balance to one of Assured Survival—a much more stable condition. We would provide answers to U.S. and Allied security problems not involving the amassing of ever larger stockpiles and ever more expensive deployments of nuclear weapons.

By creating a proper balance between strategic offense and strategic defense, we broaden the options for strategic retaliatory systems. A great deal of the counterforce, damage-limiting function of our strategic forces can be shouldered by the defensive systems. Cruise missiles become a more attractive option in a new strategic setting that includes defenses against ballistic missile attack. Proliferation of cruise missiles on land, sea, and air platforms may become a feasible alternative to expensive ballistic missile or bomber options.

Perhaps most important to our military efforts as a whole, the High Frontier concept would restore the traditional U.S. military ethic. The military man's role as defender of the country has always been the tie that has bound him to the supporting citizenry. Strategies of the recent past, such as MAD, which deny that role have seriously weakened that bond. A commitment to a new strategy consistent with the military rationale of the average U.S. citizen could greatly ease problems in all facets of U.S. security efforts.

Political Impacts

The potential for public support of this concept is enormous. If the military and nonmilitary aspects of High Frontier are effectively harnessed together, broad segments of the U.S. body politic are likely to rally in support. Recent elections have demonstrated the widespread desire for improved defenses. There is a remarkably large support base, primarily among younger people, in the form of space enthusiasts. And there is general disillusionment with the doctrines and strategies of the past.

The High Frontier concept will even convert or confuse some of the conventional opponents of defense efforts and technological innovations. It is harder to oppose nonnuclear defensive systems than nuclear offensive systems. It is impossible to argue effectively for a perpetual balance of terror if it can be negated by new policies. It is hard to make environmentalist cases against space systems.

Even those naysayers whose basic concern is disarmament will be hard pressed to make a case against High Frontier, the ABM Treaty notwithstanding. It is not necessary to abrogate the ABM Treaty to commit to High Frontier programs.

The High Frontier spaceborne defensive systems fall into the category described in the treaty as "systems based on other principles" which are "subject to discussion" with the Soviets. Point defense systems can be selected that are so different from ABM systems, as defined in the treaty, that they too could be considered as not covered. Indeed, some silo-defense systems can be considered "dynamic hardening"—a substitute for reinforced concrete—rather than an ABM. Further, the current ABM Treaty is scheduled for review in 1982, and the United States could propose any amendments deemed necessary to accommodate strategic defensive decisions.

A U.S. commitment to the High Frontier concept does not necessitate rejection of arms negotiations with the Soviets. It does, however, mean that future negotiations would proceed on a different philosophical basis. Rather than continue to pursue agreements which attempt to perpetuate a balance of terror and MAD, our negotiating efforts would be dedicated to achieving a stable world of Mutual Assured Survival. . . .

Proposed Statement of U.S. Policy

The United States and its Allies now have the combined technological, economic, and moral means to overcome many of the ills that beset our civilization. We need not pass on to our children the horrendous legacy of "Mutual Assured Destruction," a perpetual balance of terror that can but favor those most inclined to use terror to bring down our free societies. We need not succumb to ever gloomier predictions of diminishing energy, raw materials, and food supplies. We neet not resign ourselves to a constant retreat of free economic and political systems in the face of totalitarian aggressions. The peoples of the Free World can once again take charge of their destinies, if they but muster the will to do so.

In April 1981, the Space Shuttle Columbia made its dramatic maiden voyage into space and back safely to Earth. This event was not merely another admirable feat of American space technology. It marked the advent of a new era of human activity on the High Frontier of space. The Space Shuttle is a development even more momentous for the future of mankind than were the completion of the transcontinental railway, the Suez and Panama Canals, or the first flight of the Wright brothers. It can be viewed as a "railroad into space" over which will move the men and materials necessary to open broad new fields of human endeavor in space and to free us from the brooding menace of nuclear attack.

This is an historic opportunity—history is driving us to seize it. . . .

Further, we can place into space the means to defend these peaceful endeavors from interference or attack by any hostile power. We can deploy in space a purely defensive system of satellites using nonnuclear weapons which will deny any hostile power a rational option for attacking our current and future space vehicles or for delivering a militarily effective first strike with its strategic ballistic missiles on our country or on the territory of our Allies. Such a global ballistic missile defense system is well within our present technological capabilities and can be deployed in space within this decade, at less cost than other options that might be available to us to redress the strategic balance.

We need not abrogate current treaties to pursue these defensive options. A United Nations Treaty prohibits the emplacement of weapons of mass destruction in space, but does not prohibit defensive space weapons. The ABM Treaty requires discussion among Soviet and U.S. representatives of any decision to proceed with defensive systems "based on other principles" such as space systems. We should initiate such discussions and propose revisions, if necessary, in the ABM Treaty which is scheduled for review in 1982.

Defense Against Attack

Essentially this is a decision to provide an effective defense against nuclear attack for our country and our allies. It represents a long-overdue concrete rejection by this country of the "Mutual Assured Destruction" theory, which held that the only effective deterrent to nuclear war was a permanent threat by the United States and the Soviet Union to heap nuclear devastation on the cities and populations of each other. The inescapable corollary of this theory of MAD (perhaps the most apt acronym ever devised in Washington) was that civilian populations should not be defended as they were to be considered hostages in this monstrous balance of terror doctrine. The MAD doctrine, which holds that attempting to defend ourselves would be "destabilizing" and "provocative," has resulted not only in the neglect of our active military and strategic defenses and our civil defense; it has also resulted in the near total dismantlement of such strategic defenses as we once had.

For years, many of our top military men have decried the devastating effect the MAD theory has had on the nation's security. In fact, our military leaders have,

over the years, denied its validity and tried within the limits of their prerogatives to offset its ill effects. But those effects are readily evident. The only response permitted under MAD to increased nuclear threats to the United States or to its Allies is to match these threats with increased nuclear threats against the Soviet Union. Further, a U.S. strategy which has relied at its core on the capability to annihilate civilians and denied the soldier his traditional role of defending his fellow citizens has had a deleterious effect on the traditional American military ethic, and on the relationship between the soldier and the normally highly supportive public.

This legacy of MAD lies at the heart of many current problems of U.S. and Allied security. We should abandon this immoral and militarily bankrupt theory of MAD and move from "Mutual Assured Destruction" to "Assured Survival." Should the Soviet Union wish to join in this endeavor—to make Assured Survival a mutual endeavor—we would, of course, not object. We have an abiding and vital interest in assuring the survival of our nation and our allies. We have no interest in the nuclear devastation of the Soviet Union.

"Most important to our military efforts as a whole, the High Frontier concept would restore the traditional U.S. military ethic."

If both East and West can free themselves from the threat of disarming nuclear first strikes, both sides will have little compulsion to amass ever larger arsenals of nuclear weapons. This most certainly will produce a more peaceful and stable world than the one we now inhabit. And it will allow us to avoid leaving future generations the horrendous legacy of a perpetual balance of terror.

What we propose is not a panacea that solves all our problems of national security. Spaceborne defense does not mean that our nuclear retaliatory capabilities can be abandoned or neglected. The United States will still maintain strategic offensive forces capable of retaliation in case of attack. The Soviets, while losing their advantage in first-strike capabilities, will still be able to retaliate in case of attack. Nor does our approach to the strategic nuclear balance eliminate the need to build and maintain strong conventional capabilities.

We Americans have always been successful on the frontiers; we will be successful on the new High Frontier of space. We need only be as bold and resourceful as our forefathers.

William Armstrong is a senator from Colorado. He supports the High Frontier project.

"High Frontier...will draw off a large proportion of the scientific...talent from a civilian economy that desperately needs the new research."

viewpoint 98

High Frontier Is Expensive and Endangers National Security

Patrick Callahan

In ordering a program of research and development toward a system of antimissile defenses, President Reagan is acting upon motives that are unexceptionable. Our national psyche and conscience would be greatly relieved if freed from the risk of sudden nuclear destruction and from the evil of threatening to commit the mass murder that would be nuclear retaliation. Sadly, the good intentions of the President do not provide sufficient justification for the program he has authorized. The decisive criterion for any governmental action must be the goodness of its results. And there are good reasons to expect that the effort to create a system of antimissile defenses will not bring the hoped for benefits and may be counterproductive for security.

Although much of the technology to be developed is still at the early stages of inception, it is clear that some of the problems that plagued earlier proposals for ballistic missile defenses—the Safeguard and Sentinel ABM systems—would not apply to the program the President has in mind. The old ABM technology could be swamped by proliferating the number of warheads. The new technology, relying on weapons having the speed of light and guided by powerful radars and microcomputers, probably could be made invulnerable to such overloading tactics. It should be possible to have nearly instantaneous evidence whether a laser or charged-particle beam has destroyed its target. The weapon should then be able rapidly to readjust its aim, if it missed, or to acquire another target. Such weapons would also not be as inherently dangerous as ABM missiles, which in themselves were small nuclear weapons.

Many of the devastating flaws in Sentinel and Safeguard, though, will still plague the systems using newer technology.

To begin with, it is worthwhile to recall the severe criteria for a successful missile defense. The tremendous power of nuclear weapons means that defense systems must be perfect. If the Soviet Union were to launch its 7,500 missile warheads, and if a missile defense system were able to destroy 99 percent of them (which would be a phenomenal rate of success compared to any previously deployed weapon since the sword) fully 75 warheads would land on American targets. Even if the defense were aided by a 50 percent failure rate of Soviet systems, that would still mean 37 nuclear explosions on our territory. Since the detonation of even one of these weapons near a population center would be an unimaginable disaster, the proponents of the new missile defense systems must promise perfect success. Anything less does not merit serious consideration.

There is, however, little reason to expect that the proposed systems will be able even to approximate a high level of success. The historical record is replete with wonder-weapon concepts that never delivered what they promised. This has especially been the case with high technology weapons that by their nature cannot cope with contingencies or situations unanticipated by their designers. Is there any reason to suspect that these weapons using the highest of the high technologies would not be just as prone to such oversights and glitches?

Unsolvable Problems

If anything, one should suspect that these weapons will be more prone to slippage between plan and performance. How can such weapons be tested in realistic settings? In all likelihood, they will be too large to be launched into space in one piece; are we going to launch their components and then send technicians into space to assemble them? If we do that, are we then going to launch ballistic missiles into space to see if they will be shot down? And if the antimissile systems fail on their first tests, how are we going to make adjustments when the weapons are in outer space? Clearly, a realistic testing program, even if it were technically feasible, would be prohibitively expensive. So what the President proposes to do is create a

Patrick Callahan, "The Delusion of Defense—Once Again," *America*, April 30, 1983. Reprinted with author's permission.

weapons system that will have to be deployed without any valid checks to see if it could perform its assigned mission under fire.

Let us suppose, for sake of argument, that the barriers to testing can be overcome and a system is deployed. How do we conduct ordinary maintenance on systems in outer space? How do we repair things in outer space? Perhaps this problem can be solved, but it would seem reckless to presume that it can be. Especially given the high performance standards the system will have to meet, it probably is reasonable to presume that a workable system would rarely be able to work up to specifications.

"Expensive technology already has cut away many of the resources needed to keep the armed forces trained and adequately equipped and supplied."

Since neither we nor the Soviets could ever be certain that a missile defense system would be effective, the defense of the United States would still have to rest ultimately upon the deterrent threat of nuclear retaliation. This is precisely the condition from which President Reagan nobly wants to free us.

Creating New Dangers

An even more fundamental flaw exists in the President's vision of hope. It tries to heal what essentially is a political wound—the military insecurity that abides in a politically anarchic international system—with a technological band-aid. Even if the desired systems could work, they could only provide protection if the Soviet Union did not make a counterresponse. Could any scenario be less plausible than the Soviet Union taking the development and deployment of such a system passively? In fact, the Soviets could and probably would deal with such an American program in three different ways. One would be to match the American program with a missile defense system of their own. A second would be to devise ways to neutralize the American system. Among the possibilities would be using antisatellite systems to attack the elements of the American system, or jamming or confusing the radar and computer-based target acquisition components of the system, or shielding their missiles with reflective materials to deflect laser beams. The possibilities are limited only by the inventiveness of Soviet technicians. A third way the Soviet Union could deal with the American system would be to shift its nuclear forces to bombers and cruise missiles which, because they stay in the lower atmosphere, are not vulnerable to space-based systems. Another way to state this point is this: The President's proposed new program would add another facet to the arms race that the de-

fense is guaranteed to lose, because it must beat every move of the offense, whereas the offense must win on only one facet of the competition to negate the value of the defense.

In response to the criticisms voiced above, an advocate of the President's proposal could argue that even if such a defense system did not work perfectly, it might save some lives in case deterrence failed, and so it ought to be adopted for that reason. That point would be valid only if the development and deployment of such a system did not create new dangers. But it does. One is the economic burden it will impose on the economy and ultimately on the national defense. This is a major research and development program being contemplated. It will be funded, in all likelihood, by deficit spending. This will be a drag on renewed economic growth. But the deficit funding is the least serious economic disadvantage of the proposal. It will draw off a large proportion of the scientific and engineering talent from a civilian economy that desperately needs the new research and development if it is to stay competitive with the rest of the world. Together, these two economically undesirable side effects will also weaken the country's defenses by reducing the economic base for the armed forces in future decades.

Dependence on Technology

A second disadvantage is that it will continue and probably exaggerate a serious distortion in our current military configuration. Expensive technology already has cut away many of the resources needed to keep the armed forces trained and adequately equipped and supplied. The result is a need to rely increasingly and unwisely on the threat to use nuclear weapons. The development of a missile defense system and the arms race it will set off will only deepen that dependence.

A third danger is the greatly increased risk of instability that will develop once both the superpowers have packed outer space with the components of an air defense system and with antisatellite systems and with hunter-killer satellites and with whatever other kinds of exotic technology get invented. Under those circumstances, there will be constant tension and fear because each country could gain a significant military advantage by a sneak attack with its forces in place. That would give each a powerful incentive to attack first, especially in a crisis.

And the final danger is that the promise of a missile defense creates the false hope of an easy solution to the problem of nuclear weapons. It distracts us from grasping the central truth of our time—the only way to remove the threat of the bomb is to remove the bomb—and distracts us from the hard political measures needed to bring about any degree of disarmament.

The delusion of defense, then, is the ultimate danger, and the sooner we all become aware of it, the better.

Patrick Callahan is an assistant professor of political science at De Paul University in Chicago.

"What America needs today is not a blueprint for a flashy space weapon but a policy of abolition: we must abolish nuclear weapons."

viewpoint **99**

High Frontier Increases the Need for a Freeze

Sidney Lens

Before President Reagan's televised speech March 23 on the military budget, White House aides urged him not to include the "Star Wars" scenario in his comments. Their reasoning was that it would divert attention from the main point he was trying to make: that his request for a $239 billion armaments budget was justified because the Soviet Union was a persistent and growing military threat.

Reagan turned down the suggestion. Perhaps his instincts told him that what he had to say about the great Russian conspiracy was too thin to convince many people, and that a diversion—especially one painted in utopian terms—was precisely what was needed. In any event, it was his description of a dreamlike defensive weapon that would shoot down Soviet missiles "before they reached our own soil or that of our allies" that captured the headlines. The argument that we needed an increase in military spending of 10 per cent plus inflation—upwards of $30 billion—was less than convincing, but not too many people noticed.

Soviets More Ahead

The substance of the president's claim was that the Russians are moving ahead of us. In the past decade and a half, he said, the Soviets "have built up a massive arsenal. . .that can strike directly at the United States." The fact is that in the past decade and a half, *both* powers have built up a massive arsenal. In 1968 the United States had 4,200 strategic nuclear warheads, the Soviets 1,100; today we have 9,300, they have 7,300—an increase of 5,100 for us and 6,200 for them.

What those figures prove is not that we need "more," but that we should have negotiated a freeze or a cutback in 1968, before our escalation sparked their escalation. Former Secretary of Defense Robert McNamara—by no means an apologist for the Kremlin—told the *Los Angeles Times* in 1982 that the Soviet buildup of the

Sidney Lens, "What the President Didn't Tell Us," Copyright 1983 Christian Century Foundation. Reprinted with permission from the May 4, 1983 issue of *The Christian Century*.

1960s and 1970s was a "reaction to the earlier U.S. military buildup and to rumors that the U.S. was preparing to strike first at the Soviet Union. . . .If I had been the Soviet secretary of defense I would have been worried as hell at the imbalance of forces."

As proof that the Russians are plunging ahead of us, Reagan produced a graph showing that the most recent new missile in our arsenal, the Minuteman III, was introduced in 1969, whereas the Soviets have developed and produced five new missiles since then. It sounded frightening, as though we had become militarily impotent.

But while it is true that we haven't built a new type of missile, we introduced the MIRV (multiple independently targetable re-entry vehicle) in 1970, so that land-based missiles which once carried only a single warhead now carry three, and those on submarines, as many as 14. Of greater importance, our weapons now have guidance systems such as the MARV and the MARK 12-A, which make them at least twice as accurate as Soviet weapons. This development is of the utmost importance, for if the accuracy of a weapon is doubled, its "kill" capability increases by eight times.

Comparisons Difficult

The difficulty in making nuclear comparisons is that each side has different weapons for different strategies. Reagan made much ado about Soviet superiority in intermediate-range missiles. They had 600 before, he said; they have added hundreds of the new SS-20s—whereas the United States still has no such weapons at all in Europe, "none." "So far," he chided, "the Soviet definition of parity is a box score of 1,300 to nothing in their favor."

The president omitted a few pertinent facts, however. One is that the U.S. has a large number of F-111 airplanes in Britain capable of raining hundreds of nuclear bombs on the Soviet Union. Our allies, Britain and France, also have a few hundred warheads each (mostly on submarines), capable of hitting the Soviet Union. And although most of our 7,000 tactical nuclear warheads in Europe do not have the range to reach Soviet soil, we have a couple of dozen submarines in the Atlantic, Pacific, Mediterranean and Indian oceans which have at least 3,000 warheads targeted on the U.S.S.R. all the time—plus 2,000 more in home ports.

Our 41 nuclear submarines are invulnerable—which means that, unlike the situation with land-based missiles, no way has yet been found to track them down and destroy them. The Soviets also have nuclear submarines, of course, 61 of them, but almost all of their missiles carry single warheads; few are fully MIRVed. Thus the ratio in the United States' favor is nearly five to one—5,000 submarine-launched warheads for us, a thousand or 1,200 for them. Moreover, most Soviet ships of this class are in port; they have only 400 nuclear weapons at sea at any given time.

"There were nine occasions when limited nuclear war was planned or threatened . . . .For Reagan to imply that only the Soviets contemplate using armed force. . .is more than a gross exaggeration."

To emphasize how menacing the Soviet threat has become, Reagan showed classified pictures of a Soviet intelligence-gathering facility in Cuba, run, he said, by 1,500 Soviet technicians, and another in western Cuba for long-range Soviet reconnaissance. He also showed a 10,000-foot airstrip on the island of Grenada (population 110,000) being built by Cuba with Soviet help. These three facilities are supposed to represent a grave threat to American security.

A little reflection indicates how out of focus such claims are. The Russians may or may not have two bases and one airstrip near American soil. But the U.S. has had bases with nuclear weapons flush up against Soviet territory, in Turkey, for decades. Our troops and ships are ensconced in 400 major and 2,000 minor bases around the world, most of them part of a great circle around the Soviet Union. No nation in history has ever been encircled with more firepower than the Soviet Union is today—and we are tightening that circle constantly.

American Threats

Reagan implied that our military machine is benevolent, for defensive purposes only; the Soviets' is malevolent, for offense. "Some people may still ask, 'Would the Soviets ever use their formidable military power?' Well, again, can we afford to believe they won't?" He pointed to Afghanistan and Poland, two instances in which the Soviets come off badly. But he omitted our own interventions in Lebanon, the Dominican Republic, Vietnam, our hundreds of covert CIA actions and—most grave—the 12 known occasions when the United States has considered or threatened limited or total nuclear war.

The first such instance, reported by Senator Henry Jackson more than 30 years after the event, occurred in 1946, when President Harry Truman gave Soviet Ambassador Andrei Gromyko a 48-hour ultimatum for the Russians to get out of two provinces in Iran, or have the Soviet Union itself atom-bombed. In October 1962 we again threatened nuclear war against the Soviet Union because it had placed missiles in Cuba. And in 1973 the superpowers almost came to a nuclear exchange when the Israelis were slow to observe a cease-fire in the Yom Kippur War.

Then there were nine occasions when limited nuclear war was planned or threatened: twice during the Korean War (once by Truman, once by Eisenhower); once in Vietnam, when we offered three nuclear bombs to France to use in China and the Viet Minh; a second time in Vietnam when our marines were surrounded at Khe Sanh; and yet a third time when Nixon sent secret messages through intermediaries that he would use nuclear weapons against North Vietnam unless the Vietnamese came to terms by November 1969. We weighed using the bomb to force the communists to join a tripartite government in Laos, to defend Quemoy and Matsu islands against China, during the Berlin blockade and during the 1957 "Lebanon crisis." Given this history, for Reagan to imply that only the Soviets contemplate using armed force and nuclear weapons—whereas we are quiescent—is more than a gross exaggeration.

The president failed to make a case for his requested $30 billion boost in the 1984 military budget, even from the point of view of a hawk. He didn't mention that we already have enough strategic warheads to destroy all 218 Soviet cities with a population of 100,000 or more at least 40 times over; and that the only purpose additional weapons might serve would be, in Winston Churchill's phrase, to "make the rubble bounce."

Reagan's Utopia

The real purpose for the $1.7 trillion Reagan buildup contemplated over the next five years, and for the Star Wars scenario, is something the president hinted at but didn't dare spell out. Reagan's utopian proposal called for a speedup in research and development of *defensive* weapons, laser and particle-beam weapons, which at some future time would be able to shoot Soviet weapons from the sky before they came close to us. At that point, said Reagan, we would have "assured survival," and we would not have to rely on our ability to retaliate after a first strike by the Russians. We would be safe at all times, and the danger of nuclear war would be over. He further implied that we would no longer need our present offensive weapons arsenal.

It sounded beautiful, like a child's fantasy come true. Although it was immediately denounced as a pipe dream, particularly in Europe, it undoubtedly seemed reasonable to many people; it probably even helped Reagan in his quest for more defense dollars.

But the idea of a physical defense against nuclear weapons is not something new. In 1945 seven University of Chicago scientists, including Nobel laureate James Franck, told the Truman administration that it was not likely that science would find a physical defense against nuclear weapons such as antitank guns against tanks or antiaircraft guns against planes. For a decade and a half some physical defense was still possible; a few airplanes carrying nuclear weapons could be shot down by anti-aircraft guns. But with the coming of the intercontinental ballistic missile (ICBM), traveling at 16,000 miles an hour, physical defense became impossible—at least for the time being. Lyndon Johnson wheedled $1.9 billion from Congress to develop an antiballistic missile (ABM), and Nixon extracted a few billion more. But for a variety of reasons the ABM could not do the job; Nixon grudgingly admitted that an effective ABM was "not now within our power."

Double Suicide

In the absence of physical defense, neither side could win an actual nuclear war. Each might totally destroy the other, but could not prevent being destroyed itself in a retaliatory strike. Any exchange would become a "double suicide," in General Douglas MacArthur's famous phrase. The strategists therefore concentrated on two types of defense that were not physical: psychological defense and civil defense. The psychological defense was called "deterrence" or "balance of terror"; each side had to convince the other that it was crazy enough to commit suicide to thwart the other's ambitions. Civil defense meant hiding from the weapons' effects, in bomb shelters, fallout shelters, through the evacuation of cities and most recently through another evacuation program, called "Crisis Relocation." The first three plans died quickly after they were proposed; crisis relocation is still official policy, but it carries no weight with the public.

Through all these years the idea of a physical defense did not die. In recent times it has been associated with a strategy called "disarming first strike." In the latest scenario, the U.S. would place "killer satellites" in space using the space shuttle; they would hunt down and kill Soviet communications, early-warning and navigational satellites. The Soviet command would then be rendered deaf, dumb and blind. It could not retaliate in any coherent fashion.

That is where Reagan's new wonder weapons come in. If the Soviets nonetheless decided to retaliate at random, our laser-beam weapons aboard low-orbit satellites—or other beam weapons from the ground—would destroy Russian missiles almost on launch. The Soviets would be effectively disarmed, and we could force them to do our bidding. In the parlance of right-wingers this is called "Finlandization": the Kremlin would be converted into a pliant, subordinate state, much as Finland is today to the Soviet Union.

Physical and Technological Problems

The problems with this strategy are monumental. First of all, the feasibility of the beam weapons themselves is questionable. Experts like Kosta Tsipis of MIT call the program "wasted money," sure not to work. "Charged-particle beams," he says, "are forbidden, so to speak, by the laws of nature. The magnetic field of the Earth would bend the beam. You would never be able to concentrate [the particles] enough to hit anything." As to neutron beams, they could be better aimed but could easily be frustrated "as they come near the target." The same is true of laser beams, according to another scientist, Richard P. Van Duyne of Northwestern; they could be diffused by shrouding "the missile in a cloud of dust particles."

Even the father of the "high-frontier" strategy, from whom Reagan acquired most of his Star Wars ideas, the retired Lieutenant General Daniel O. Graham, concedes that deployment of beam weapons in global defense systems "is too far in the future." Moreover, quite a few Soviet warheads—despite what Reagan implied—would still get through. Graham says the plan is not "a panacea which solves all the problems of our national security. Spaceborne defense does not mean that our nuclear retaliatory capabilities can be abandoned or neglected." The Soviets, he admits in an article for the right-wing Heritage Foundation's *National Security Record* (June 19, 1982), would lose some of "their advantages in first-strike capabilities," but "would be able to retaliate in case of attack."

In other words, with all the new space technology decades from now, we might gain some strategic advantage, but the arms race would continue, this time in space—and with all the uncertainties that attend it on earth.

"Reagan was right. . . .The danger we face is monumental. . . .Not even a space weapon will cure it."

In any case, the problems of 1983 cannot be solved by projecting a space wars scenario for the year 2008. In the meantime, each side is furiously building its arsenal, and shouting that the other is untrustworthy. The U.S., for instance, is projecting 100 new B-1 bombers, 100 MX missiles, 15 Trident submarines, 464 ground-launched and 8,348 air- and sea-launched cruise missiles, 108 Pershing II missiles, 1,280 neutron bombs and two new aircraft-carrier battle groups—and the U.S.S.R. is no doubt matching us bomb for bomb. Also in the meantime, other nations are gaining the capability of making nuclear weapons—100 nations are expected to be members of the "nuclear club" by the year

2000—and the danger of a nuclear war beginning in a "small" conventional war—say, between Iran and Iraq —is growing apace. Germany and Japan can begin producing nuclear weapons within a couple of months after they make the decision to; if the present trade frictions intensify, the possibility that other great powers will join the nuclear club mounts.

Against this background, Reagan's speech is seen not as a plea for strategic arms reduction but for making the U.S. so overpowering that Moscow would have no alternative but to cry uncle. That is the hope—though not the likelihood.

Arms Race Needs End

The arms race can be ended only by ending it. That means an immediate freeze without quibbling over the niceties of "verification." Better still is Jerome T. Wiesner's proposal for a "unilateral moratorium." Wiesner, a member of the National Security Council under Kennedy, suggests that we stop producing more nuclear weapons on our own, then invite the Russians to do the same. If they do, we would reduce our stockpiles by a certain percentage and again invite Moscow to match our effort, until there was complete disarmament.

"With all the new space technology decades from now, we might gain some strategic advantage, but the arms race would continue."

Simultaneously we would have to disabuse ourselves of the ideological basis for the cold war—namely, that "you can't trust the Russians." That thesis is irrelevant and obstructive. It is true that we cannot trust the Russian government, but then, we cannot trust *any* government, including our own. Nor should we. Whether we like the Soviet system or not, we and the Soviet people have a common destiny: finding a means of surviving together.

What America needs today is not a blueprint for a flashy space weapon but a policy of abolition: we must abolish nuclear weapons. That would not mean scrapping those instruments of death tomorrow morning, but it would mean a *commitment* to do so, and taking certain unilateral initiatives (such as a freeze) while negotiating a quick timetable for abolition.

Reagan was right on one thing. The danger we face is monumental. The sickness is malignant. Not even a space weapon will cure it.

Sidney Lens is senior editor of Progressive *magazine. His most recent book is* The Maginot Line Syndrome: America's Hopeless Foreign Policy.

"High Frontier would add nothing to the country's offensive arsenal and thus renders the whole disarmament debate moot."

High Frontier Eliminates the Need for a Freeze

Gregory Fossedal

It's called High Frontier. It's a new national strategy. And it gives President Reagan the opportunity—in one bold stroke—to: (1) slam shut the window of U.S. military vulnerability; (2) fast-thaw the nuclear freeze movement; (3) preserve America's narrowing technological lead in space; and (4) greatly limit the damage from any Soviet first-strike attack.

The President can accomplish all this within five years using existing technology, at a total cost to the taxpayer of only $10 billion dollars a year.

Mr. Reagan's new political possibility is the result of the new scientific possibilities in space using American micro-technology. And the timing is perfect: Just as the nuclear freeze debate begins, the Heritage Foundation has completed work on a study which details just how a missile defense system could work.

Disarmament Becomes Moot

Headed by former Defense Intelligence Agency chief Daniel Graham, a team of defense and space technology officials drew the blueprint for a "High Frontier" shield against a Russian nuclear attack. High Frontier would rely on a multilayered series of cheap, simple devices to filter out "at least 95 percent" of a Soviet launch, according to Graham and his staff of more than 20 experts. These devices include:

—Orbiting satellites that intercept Soviet missiles as they come off their pads into outer space;

—Ground-based anti-missile systems that defend against missiles which manage to leak through the double-wave of satellite attacks;

—And, civil defense measures to protect population centers from the small number of missiles that might reach their targets.

The High Frontier system could be constructed using the space shuttle and other existing technology over a five year period. No laser beam lead times, no Star

Wars assumptions.

Armed with the detailed Heritage study, plus supporting assessments from a number of government agencies that have confirmed its findings, President Reagan would have the secret weapon needed to undercut the nuclear freeze crusade. High Frontier would add nothing to the country's offensive arsenal and thus renders the whole disarmament debate moot.

But there are several hurdles. One may be the Pentagon establishment, some of whose members fear a loss of turf if High Frontier gains status as the approach of the 80s. Graham's Heritage report carries a specific recommendation that the project be given independent status, which is critical to quick implementation of the program and construction of the system. Lower-level defense bureaucrats may resent the new approach and try to undermine the system's technical credibility with an overload of negative scientific data.

Moreover, conservatives inside and outside the Pentagon may worry that the High Frontier project will be pushed by liberals as an alternative, rather than a supplement, to a necessary buildup in conventional and strategic forces. More than one program has been embraced in the past during development stages, then dumped when ready for construction.

That, Graham says, is why the system must have guaranteed funding over several years, and be constructed quickly to avoid overruns and political second-guessing.

Opposition Supports MAD

Perhaps the biggest obstacle to High Frontier is the intellectual and political community that has built up a huge stake in the continuation of the Mutual Assured Destruction (MAD) doctrine, the unstated U.S. nuclear strategy since the 1960s. Under the MAD doctrine, nuclear war becomes "unthinkable," and defense expenditures beyond a certain point irrational. As long as

Greg Fossedal, ''Exploring the High Frontier,'' *Conservative Digest*, June 1982, pp. 22-43. Copyright © 1982 by Viguerie Communications, June 1982. 7777 Leesburg Pike, Falls Church, VA. $18/yr.

each side retains enough firepower for a second-strike, the deterrent remains.

The MAD concept made construction of a defense system unnecessary and even dangerous according to the small academic community which hammered out strategic concepts. Unless a system were perfect, it was argued, it would be provocative—tempting a first-strike by the Russians, who would fear the same from us once our defense was completed.

"None of the present systems at the present or foreseeable state of the art would provide an impenetrable shield over the United States," Defense Secretary Robert McNamara complained in 1962. "Were such a shield possible, we would certainly build it." Well, of course, no perfect defense is ever possible—not from nuclear weapons, not from a bullet.

Arms Control Irrelevant

But the High Frontier concept, by shielding almost everyone, is the political dynamite that could explode the whole MAD doctrine. Arms control negotiations would be irrelevant, because it wouldn't matter what the Soviet Union did with their arms.

"Imagine what voters would say if offered a choice between the freeze and High Frontier. . . .The potential coalition. . . extends from Jerry Brown to Senator Jesse Helms."

Detente would be unnecessary, because influencing Soviet arms spending would no longer be a goal. Instead, the United States could focus full attention on Soviet terrorism, chemical warfare, military intervention, and conventional buildup.

Replacement of the deterrence strategy with a doctrine of Assured Survival would not only free up U.S. foreign policy and military planning, it might turn the grass-roots nuclear freeze movement inside out.

Much ado has been made about the small-town voters in Vermont and marchers in New York who supported a "verifiable, mutual freeze." When polled, however, the same people admitted that the Soviet Union could not be trusted to participate. What people seem to be saying, then, is that they want a fresh alternative to the current nuclear debate.

Broad Base Support

Imagine what those voters would say if offered a choice between the freeze and High Frontier. The potential coalition for High Frontier extends from Jerry Brown to Sen. Jesse Helms.

One caveat for the Reagan administration is that such broad coalitions can be built either way. If the President doesn't seize the Heritage concept, it could be co-opted by a Sen. Gary Hart and aimed right back at conservatives. A second caveat: There may be no technological time to waste. The Russians will begin deployment of their own satellite crafts within the next decade.

If the United States fails to develop its own core technologies—through High Frontier, the space shuttle, and other projects—America could find itself outflanked in the ultimate theatre of action—space—wondering how its leaders allowed it to squander an advantage in science and innovation that should belong to the West.

Gregory Fossedal is a columnist for the Washington Times *and a Special Consultant for the Heritage Foundation's High Frontier project.*

glossary

Acronyms

The following acronyms are used throughout this book.
Definitions ending in an asterisk are further explained in the
glossary of terms which begins on the next page.

ABM	Antiballistic Missile*
ACDA	US Arms Control and Disarmament Agency
AFSATCOM	Air Force Satellite Communications System
ALCM	Air-Launched Cruise Missile*
ASAT	Antisatellite
ASM	Air-to-Surface Missile
ASW	Anti-Submarine Warfare
ASSW	Anti-Strategic Submarine Warfare
AVF	All Volunteer Force
AWACS	Airborne Warning and Control System
BMD	Ballistic Missile Defense
BMEWS	Ballistic Missile Early Warning System
BWC	Biological Weapons Convention
C³	Command, Control, and Communications
CBR	Chemical, Biological, Radiological
CBU	Cluster Bomb Unit
CCD	Conference of the Committee on Disarmament
CEP	Circular Error Probability
CMC	Cruise Missile Carrier*
CTB	Comprehensive Test Ban
DCS	Defense Communications System
DEW	Distant Early Warning
DMZ	Demilitarized Zone
DOD	Department of Defense
ENDC	Eighteen-Nation Disarmament Conference
EW	Electronic Warfare
FEMA	Federal Emergency Management Agency
FOBS	Fractional Orbital Bombardment System
FY	Fiscal Year
GCD	General and Complete Disarmament
GDP	Gross Domestic Product*
GLCM	Ground-Launched Cruise Missile*
GNP	Gross National Product*
IAEA	International Atomic Energy Agency*
ICBM	Inter-Continental Ballistic Missile*
IRBM	Intermediate-Range Ballistic Missile
INF	Intermediate-Range Nuclear Forces

JCS	Joint Chiefs of Staff
MAD	Mutually Assured Destruction*
MAP	Military Assistance Program
MARV	Maneuverable Re-Entry Vehicle
MIRV	Multiple Independent Re-Entry Vehicle*
MLRS	Multiple Launch Rocket System
MRBM	Medium-Range Ballistic Missile
MRV	Multiple Re-Entry Vehicle*
MT	Metric ton, Megaton
NASA	National Aeronautics and Space Administration (USA)
NATO	North Atlantic Treaty Organization*
NCA	National Command Authority
NPT	Treaty on the Non-Proliferation of Nuclear Weapons
PTBT	Partial Test Ban Treaty
REM	Roentgen Equivalent Man*
RPV	Remotely Piloted Vehicle
RV	Re-Entry Vehicle*
SAC	Strategic Air Command
SALT	Strategic Arms Limitation Talks*
SAM	Surface-to-Air Missile
SCAD	Subsonic Cruise Armed Decoy
SLBM	Submarine Launched Ballistic Missile*
SLCM	Submarine-Launched Cruise Missile
SRAM	Short-Range Attack Missile
SSN	Nuclear-Powered Attack Submarine
START	Strategic Arms Reduction Talks*
TTBT	Threshold Test-Ban Treaty
TNF	Theater Nuclear Forces
TOA	Total Obligational Authority*
USA	United States Army
USAF	United States Air Force
USAFR	United States Air Force Reserve
USAR	United States Army Reserve
USMC	United States Marine Corps
USMCR	United States Marine Corps Reserve
USMM	United States Merchant Marine
USN	United States Navy
USNR	United States Naval Reserve
USREDCOM	US Readiness Command
USSR	Union of Soviet Socialist Republics*
WRS	War Reserve Stocks
WTO	Warsaw Treaty Organization

Terms

air burst nuclear explosion in which the detonation takes place in the atmosphere and the fireball does not touch the ground

anti-ballistic missile (ABM) defensive missile which destroys incoming ballistic missiles or their warheads

ABM treaty agreement between the US and USSR to permanently limit each side to two ABM deployment areas with restrictions on the deployment of ABM launchers and interceptors. Also known as SALT I agreements

air-launched cruise missile (ALCM) missile that is launched from an aircraft

arms control process of limiting or reducing arms to lessen the risk of conflict and to reduce the consequences of a conflict should it occur

atom smallest part of an element that has all the chemical properties of that element

Backfire name of a modern Soviet supersonic bomber that would be used in a theater or naval strike

ballistic missile missile whose propulsion system consists of rockets which burn early in the flight of the missile. After the rockets burn out, the payload coasts on to the target on a "ballistic trajectory" like a bullet fired from a rifle

basing mode type of housing for nuclear missiles. Various basing modes proposed for the MX missile are silos, underground capsules, or a movable track system

bilateral action taken equally by two sides or countries

blast wave tremendously high pressure wind resulting within a fraction of a second after a nuclear explosion

Bolshevism political philosophy of the radical Marxists who seized the Russian government in 1917. Often used as a synonym for communism

broken arrow code name for an accident involving nuclear weapons; used by the Defense Department

circular error probability accuracy estimate of a weapon using the radius of a circle to predict where 50 percent of the missiles are likely to hit

civil defense survival preparation program used to protect civilians in the event of an attack or natural disaster

Comprehensive Test Ban proposal to abolish nuclear weapons testing below as well as above ground

containment policy attempt by the US to "contain" communism, through financial and military aid to countries viewed as vulnerable to its influence, and by the encirclement of military bases and forces

counterforce nuclear strikes or strategies against other nuclear weapons to nullify them

countervalue nuclear strikes or strategies against nonmilitary targets such as population centers, industry, and resources

critical mass least amount of fissionable element that can sustain a chain reaction

cruise missiles small, unmanned airplanes carrying nuclear warheads. They can be launched from airplanes, trucks, ships, or submarines

cruise missile carrier (CMC) aircraft used for launching a cruise missile delivery system. The vehicle which delivers weapons to their targets

Department of Defense part of the US government which regulates the military services and is responsible for defending the nation

deployment spreading out or distributing something, particularly military forces and arms

detente relaxation of international tension between the Cold War adversaries, usually brought about by a treaty or agreement

deterrence condition in which a strategic power is dissuaded from attack because the potential victim could retaliate effectively

escalation stepping up, increasing, intensifying

Eastern Europe European countries most closely connected—geographically, philosophically, and politically—with the Soviet Union

fallout radioactive particles that fall to the ground downwind from a nuclear explosion

fireball spherical hot ball (10,000,000 degrees F) that is formed after a nuclear bomb is exploded in the atmosphere. It rapidly expands and then cools to become a mushroom-shaped cloud

fission process that occurs when an atom's nucleus breaks into two smaller pieces and several neutrons

fractionation division of the payload of a missile into several warheads

fratricide theory that supports basing MX missiles closely together because, if attacked, the first incoming missile detonation would send up a wall of radiation and debris that would destroy or deflect other attacking warheads

freeze immediate halt to building weapons; prelude to disarmament

fusion process that occurs when two nuclei of a light element such as hydrogen fuse together to form a nucleus of a heavier atom

gamma rays rays of energy similar to x-rays but having a shorter wave length and potentially more damaging to the material they penetrate

gross domestic product (GDP) total monetary value of all goods and services produced in a country in a year, excluding imports and exports

gross national product (GNP) total monetary value of all goods and services produced in a country in a year

ground-launched cruise missile (GLCM) cruise missile launched from ground installations or vehicle

ground zero area of ground directly beneath a nuclear explosion

guidance equipment on board a missile which measures the position, speed, and direction and directs the missile toward its desired destination

half-life amount of time a radioisotope needs for half of its nuclei to become nuclei of other atoms by emitting radiation

hardness resistance of a possible target to the effects of enemy nuclear weapons. The often-discussed hardness of missile silos is usually measured in pounds-per-square-inch (psi) of blast pressure

hard target weapon that is protected against a nuclear blast through structural hardening, such as the ICBM silos

hawk slang term for people who believe in a strong military defense and an aggressive stance toward other countries

hegemony leadership or dominance

holocaust devastation, destruction

imperialism policy of extending governmental rule and influence over foreign countries

inertial navigation computerized system of navigating a missile that adjusts the navigational path to ensure the missile will arrive on target

intelligence networks agencies that gather information, often secret, often acquired by subterfuge, about other governments

Intercontinental Ballistic Missile (ICBM) long-range missile based on the continental United States which has sufficient range to attack most or all of the Soviet Union, or a Soviet missile with corresponding capability

International Atomic Energy Agency (IAEA) organization that monitors nuclear activities to reduce the proliferation of nuclear weapons

ionization static electricity that occurs among atoms of material that are exposed to radiation

isotope variant of an element that results when the number of neutrons in the element is increased or decreased

Joint Chiefs of Staff chairman and the heads of the Armed Services (Army, Navy, Air Force) who advise the President about defense policy

Kremlin building that houses the executive branch of the Russian government; also used as a synonym for that branch

launcher equipment required to launch a missile. ICBM launchers can be either fixed or mobile

launch on warning usually used to mean a launch of missiles after one side receives electrical signals from radars, infra-red satellites, or other sensors that enemy missiles are on the way, but before there have been nuclear detonations on its territory

megaton explosive power equivalent to one million tons of TNT

military-industrial complex term used by President Eisenhower to describe the joint effort of the military and the defense industry in creating new weapons

multiple independent re-entry vehicle (MIRV) system missile capable of carrying two or more re-entry vehicles which can be directed individually toward separate targets. The targets for a single missile can be spread over a wide area which is often called the "footprint" of the missile, depending on the range to which the missile is targeted

mutual assured destruction (MAD) nuclear deterrence theory based on the idea that if one country strikes with nuclear weapons, the second country will cause reciprocal retaliatory damage

multiple re-entry vehicle (MRV) ballistic missile with several warheads which cannot be separately targeted

MX missile "light ICBM" under the terminology of SALT II, approximately the same size as the Soviet SS-19 ICBM

Nonproliferation Treaty agreement first signed in 1968 to prevent the spread of nuclear weapons. Nations without nuclear weapons agreed to continue without them. Those nations with nuclear weapons agreed to work to prevent their spread and to aid in the development of peaceful uses of nuclear energy

North Atlantic Treaty Organization (NATO) strongest nuclear military alliance that is opposed to the Warsaw Pact. It includes Belgium, Britain, Canada, Denmark, France, Greece, Iceland, Italy, Luxembourg, the Netherlands, Norway, Portugal, Turkey, the United States and West Germany

neutron bomb relatively small bomb that destroys body tissue with its high-speed neutrons but does very little damage to land or buildings

nuclear survivability ability of a missile to withstand a counter-attack and find its way to its target in spite of other nuclear weapons it may encounter

nuke slang term for nuclear, often referring to nuclear weapons

omnicide killing everything; annihilation

overkill ability to destroy a target more than once

pacifism opposed to war and violence

parity equality

Partial Test Ban Treaty treaty that prohibits testing nuclear weapons in the atmosphere, in outer space, or underwater. The United States, Britain, and Russia agreed to the treaty in 1963. Since then 109 other countries have signed the treaty

particle beam weapons weapon that produces an intense beam of subatomic particles such as electrons

payload total weight of the re-entry vehicles carried by a single missile

Peacemaker missile another term for the MX missile, coined by President Reagan, because the missile would be used to keep the peace with the Soviet Union

penetration aids equipment, such as decoys, carried along as part of a missile's throw-weight, specifically to assist the re-entry vehicle to get through ballistic missile defenses

Pentagon building that houses the US Department of Defense; used as a synonym for military policy and policy makers

preemptive first action; to do something before someone else gets a chance

radiation energy waves and particles produced in atomic fission or fusion which damage living tissue

priority targeting choosing the most vital targets to be destroyed first

pro forma according to form; in form only, not actual

proxy forces military personnel and equipment which purport to belong to the country they are fighting for but which, in fact, are funded and commanded by an outside country for its own purposes of influence and power

radiation, delayed gamma rays and electrons that are emitted from the debris of a nuclear explosion for a long period

radiation, initial intense and deadly flash of gamma and x-rays that are emitted in a nuclear explosion

radiation sickness serious illness caused by radiation damage to the gastro-intestinal tract

rearmament acquiring and building up an arsenal after a period of having few arms or weapons, or having slowed down in their production and accumulation

reciprocity to be able to fire back what is given or its equivalent

re-entry vehicle (RV) shell around a warhead, generally in the shape of a cone or modified cone, which protects the missile warhead during its re-entry through the earth's atmosphere

Roentgen Equivalent Man (REM) term used to measure the potential impact of radiation exposure on human cells

soft target target such as a population center that is not protected against the effect of a nuclear weapon

Strategic Arms Reduction Talks (START) arms control negotiations proposed by President Reagan. Negotiations involving intercontinental missiles reduction

Strategic Arms Limitatons Talks (SALT) series of negotiations between the US and USSR, begun in 1969, attempting to limit the production, acquisition, maintenance, and use of strategic weapons

Soviets governing officials or the people of the Soviet Union

strategic weapons weapons that are intended for distant targets such as another continent

submarine-launched ballistic missile (SLBM) ballistic missile launched from a nuclear submarine

tactical weapons nuclear weapons that are intended for an intermediate-range target

Third World developing nations, especially of Asia, Africa, and South America, not aligned with either the NATO nations or the Warsaw Pact nations, considered as a potential force to be wooed by both groups

terminal guidance guidance system in which the missile or its re-entry vehicle "looks" at the ground near the target and homes in

theater weapons nuclear weapons that are intended for a target as close as a few miles away

thermal radiation heat resulting from a nuclear explosion

thermonuclear weapons nuclear weapons that require very high temperatures for detonation of a fusion reaction

throw-weight useful weight which a ballistic missile can place on a trajectory toward its target by the boost or main propulsion stages of the missile. It includes such items as re-entry vehicles, targeting devices and penetration aids

Total Obligational Authority (TOA) money that the US Defense Department has in addition to its yearly budget. It is left over from the previous year or from the sale of inventory

totalitarian government with strong authoritarian control concentrated in a single political party

triad expression used to explain the concept that the US has three separate, and in some ways roughly equal, types of strategic nuclear forces—land-based ICBMs, sea-based SLBMs, and bombers

unilateral action done by only one person, group, or nation

Union of Soviet Socialist Republics (USSR) group of fifteen politically connected nations in Eastern Europe and Northern and Western Asia, of which Russia is the largest

verification total process of determining compliance with treaty obligations in the context of safeguarding national security

warhead part of a missile system that explodes and causes damage to the target

warning indications from any of a wide variety of sources that another nation intends to start hostilities. The term ''strategic warning'' is often used to mean indications hours or days in advance that attack is definitely planned, while ''tactical warning'' means evidence (usually from radar or other electronic systems) that enemy warheads are actually on the way and will arrive in a matter of minutes

Warsaw Pact strongest nuclear military alliance that is opposed to NATO. It includes the USSR, Bulgaria, Czechoslovakia, East Germany, Hungary, Poland and Romania

window of vulnerability term used by President Reagan in 1981 to describe what he believed was the US's inability to defend itself in the event of a surprise attack

zero option US proposal to refrain from basing missiles in Western Europe on condition that USSR remove its existing missiles from there

organizations

American Committee on East-West Accord
109 Eleventh St. SE
Washington, DC 20003
(202) 546-1700

The purpose of the Committee is to reduce tensions (and thereby the possibility of nuclear confrontation) between East and West by strengthening public understanding of strategic arms agreements and mutually beneficial programs in science, culture and trade. It publishes the bimonthly *East/West Outlook*.

American Defense Preparedness Association
Rosslyn Center
1700 North Moore Street
Arlington, VA 22209
(703) 522-1820

The ADPA was founded to improve the performance of the industrial base in support of the Armed Forces and to promote awareness of the need for a strong defense posture among the American people. In the past 64 years, the association has grown to 52 chapters comprising 33,700 members. It publishes the *National Defense* journal.

American Enterprise Institute for Policy Research
1150 17th Street NW
Washington, DC 20036
(202) 862-5800

The Institute, founded in 1943, is a conservative think tank that researches a number of issues, including foreign policy and defense. A subscription to *Foreign Policy and Defense Review*, published bi-monthly, costs $18 a year.

American Friends Service Committee
1501 Cherry Street
Philadelphia, PA 19102
(215) 241-7000

The Religious Society of Friends (Quakers) founded the Committee in 1917, but it is supported and staffed by individuals of all major denominations. Its purpose is to relieve human suffering and to find new approaches to world peace and nonviolent social change. It is a co-recipient of the Nobel Peace Prize.

Americanism Educational League
P.O. Box 5986
Buena Park, CA 90622
(714) 828-5040

The League, founded in 1927, campaigns on behalf of private owner-ship of property, strong national defense, strict crime control and limited government conducted within balanced budgets. It periodically publishes position papers and pamphlets on national defense issues.

Arms Control and Disarmament Agency
U.S. Department of State
Washington, DC 20451
(202) 632-3597

This government agency publishes information on disarmament treaties, ongoing negotiations and other arms control issues. It occasionally does studies on the military balance and annually publishes *World Military Expenditures and Arms Transfers*.

Arms Control Association
11 Dupont Circle NW, Suite 900
Washington, DC 20036
(202) 797-6450

This non-partisan association, founded in 1971, does research on practical and theoretical questions of arms control. A subscription to *Arms Control Today*, published eleven times a year, costs $25, $10 for students.

Cardinal Mindszenty Foundation
P.O. Box 11321
St. Louis, MO 63105
(314) 991-2939

This anti-communist organization was founded in 1958 to conduct educational and research activities concerning communist objectives, tactics, and propaganda through study groups, speakers, conferences and films. It publishes the monthly *Mindszenty Report* and *Red Line*.

Center for Defense Information
Capitol Gallery West
600 Maryland Avenue SW
Washington, DC 20024
(202) 484-9490

The Center, founded in 1972 as a non-partisan research organization, provides up-to-date information and analyses of the US military. A subscription to *The Defense Monitor*, published ten times a year, is included in its annual $25 membership fee.

Center For War/Peace Studies
218 E. 18th Street
New York, NY 10003
(212) 475-0850

The Center was originally founded in 1966 as a program of the New York Friends Group. It carries out in-depth studies of global problems, including arms control. A subscription to *Global Report*, published four times a year, is included in its annual $20 membership fee. Students may subscribe for $5 a year.

Christian Anti-Communist Crusade
P.O. Box 890
227 E. Sixth Street
Long Beach, CA 90801
(213) 437-0941

The Crusade, founded in 1953, sponsors anti-subversive seminars "to inform Americans of the philosophy, morality, organization, techniques and strategy of Communism and associated forces." Its newsletter, published semi-monthly, is free.

Coalition For A New Foreign and Military Policy
120 Maryland Avenue NE
Washington, DC 20002
(202) 546-8400

The Coalition, founded in 1976, united 44 national religious, labor, peace, research and social action organizations working for a "peaceful, non-interventionist and demilitarized U.S. foreign policy." It works to reduce military spending, protect human rights and promote arms control and disarmament. A subscription to *Coalition Close-Up*, published quarterly, and other publications, is included in its annual $20 membership fee.

Committee For Nuclear Responsibility
Box 11207
San Francisco, CA 94101

The Committee, founded in 1971, proposes ways to eliminate nuclear power and nuclear arms. It publishes occasional papers and flyers on nuclear issues.

Committee on the Present Danger
1800 Massachusetts Avenue NE
Washington, DC 20036
(202) 466-7444

The Committee, founded in 1976, describes its functions as directing attention to the unfavorable military balance between the United States and the Soviet Union. It publishes occasional papers dealing with this issue.

Congressional Budget Office
Office of Intergovernmental Relations
House Annex #2
2nd and D Streets SW
Washington, DC 20515

The CBO is an agency of Congress established to review the budgetary implications of various programs. Budget issue papers consider a host of narrow issues, but also very broad strategic analyses. Write for a list of publications. All CBO publications can be received free.

Council for a Livable World
100 Maryland Avenue NE
Washington, DC 20002
(202) 543-4100

The Council, founded in 1962, is a public interest group which raises funds for Senatorial candidates who work for arms control, and which lobbies on arms control and military budget issues. It publishes study papers and fact sheets on issues of foreign policy and arms control.

Council For the Defense of Freedom
P.O. Box 28526
Washington, DC 20005
(202) 371-6710

The Council, founded in 1951, is concerned about "the mortal danger we face if we do not stop communist aggression." Its weekly paper, *The Washington Inquirer*, repeatedly deals with the arms race and "our failure to take measures to overcome our lack of preparedness." A subscription is $20 a year.

Council On Economic Priorities
84 Fifth Avenue
New York, NY 10011
(212) 691-8550

The Council, founded in 1969, disseminates information on a number of economic issues, including military contracting and spending. Its newsletter, published eight to twelve times a year, is included in its annual membership fee of $15 a year. Students may join for $7.50 a year. Also included with membership are several studies and reports.

Department of Defense
Office of Public Affairs
Public Correspondence Division
Room 2E 777
Washington, DC 20037

Write for a list of publications and an order form.

Educators for Social Responsibility
23 Garden Street
Cambridge, MA 02138
(617) 492-1764

The objective of this disarmament organization is to help children and adults deal with their feelings about the threat of nuclear war, and ultimately to end the nuclear arms race. It develops curriculum materials, workshops, school and community-based education projects.

Fellowship of Reconciliation
Box 271
Nyack, NY 10960
(914) 358-4601

FOR, founded in 1915, is a pacifist organization, made up of religious pacifists drawn from all faiths. It "attempts, through education and action, to substitute nonviolence and reconciliation for violence in international relations." It publishes pamphlets, books, cards and the monthly *Fellowship* dealing with disarmament and nonviolence. A subscription to *Fellowship* is $6 a year.

Foreign Policy Association
205 Lexington Avenue
New York, NY 10016
(212) 481-8450

The Association, founded in 1918, is a non-partisan educational organization that deals with foreign policy issues. It publishes a wide range of publications dealing with foreign policy.

Ground Zero
806 15th Street NW, Suite 421
Washington, DC 20005
(202) 638-7402

This group, which draws its name from the point of detonation of a nuclear weapon, is a nonpartisan nuclear war education project funded primarily by foundations. Through its educational materials and programs, it encourages citizens to consider strategies for preventing nuclear war. It publishes the *Report From Ground Zero* monthly.

The Heritage Foundation
214 Massachussetts Avenue NE
Washington, DC 20002
(202) 546-4400

The Foundation, founded in 1974, is "dedicated to limited government, individual and economic freedom and a strong national defense." It publishes research in various formats on national defense. A subscription to *National Security Record*, published monthly, is $25 a year.

Institute For Defense and Disarmament Studies
2001 Beacon Street
Brookline, MA 02146
(617) 734-4216

The Institute, incorporated in 1980, was founded "to study the nature and purposes of military forces and the obstacles to and opportunities for disarmament." It publishes an annual survey of *World Military Forces & Disarmament Opportunities* and other disarmament materials.

Institute For Policy Studies
1901 Q Street NW
Washington, DC 20009
(202) 234-9382

The Institute, founded in 1963, is a research and public education center which publishes a variety of books, reports and issues papers on international affairs. Write for a catalog of its publications.

Moral Majority
305 Sixth Street
Lynchburg, VA 24504
(804) 528-0070

This conservative political movement was founded in 1979 by Rev. Jerry Falwell to respond to developments that indicate a "moral decline" in America. Among the issues it advocates is deterrence of a nuclear war by a strong American defense.

National Peace Academy Campaign
110 Maryland Avenue NE
Washington, DC 20002
(202) 546-9500

This campaign was founded in 1966 for indviduals interested in the establishment of a United States Academy of Peace, a federally chartered, non-governmental institution providing research and training in conflict resolution. Its objective is to persuade Congress to establish such an institution as recommended by the congressionally authorized Peace Academy Commission.

Nuclear Control Institute
1000 Connecticut Avenue NW, Suite 406
Washington, DC 20036
(202) 822-8444

The Institute is a nonprofit educational organization working to prevent the spread of nuclear weapons through commercial nuclear power and research programs. It seeks to prevent civilian nuclear programs from following technological paths that will lead to the development of nuclear weapons.

Nuclear Information and Resource Service
1346 Connecticut Avenue NW
Washington, DC 20036
(202) 296-7552

The NIRS provides information, advice, materials, and speakers to people trying to halt nuclear activities or promote alternatives to nuclear power. Its publications include *Legislative and Regulatory Alert*, *Groundswell*, and several fact sheets and pamphlets.

Pax Christi USA
6337 W. Cornelia Avenue
Chicago, IL 60634
(312) 736-2114

Founded in 1973, Pax Christi is a Roman Catholic peace movement, dedicated to "building peace and justice by exploring and articulating the ideal of Christian nonviolence." It works for disarmament, a just world order, selective conscientious objection, education for peace and alternatives to violence. It publishes occasional papers and a quarterly newsletter which can be obtained by making a voluntary contribution.

Physicians For Social Responsibility
639 Massachusetts Avenue
Cambridge, MA 02138
(617) 491-2754

This organization of medical doctors has more than 100 chapters in cities throughout the country. The group holds periodic symposia to alert people to the medical consequences of nuclear war. Founded in 1979, annual membership is $30 and student membership is $10.

Rockford Institute
934 North Main Street
Rockford, IL 61103
(815) 964-5053

The Institute is a nonprofit research center devoted to the study of the cultural dynamics of a free society. It publishes three periodicals, *Chronicles of Culture, The Rockford Papers* and *Persuasion At Work,* as well as occasional special papers and monographs.

Rocky Flats Action Group
1428 Lafayette Street
Denver, CO 80218
(303) 832-4508

This joint project of American Friends Service Committee and the Fellowship of Reconcilitation was founded to build a constituency for disarmament and for ending all nuclear threats. Its goals include the closing and conversion of the Rocky Flats nuclear weapons plant in Denver, CO. It is currently coordinating a campaign and Nuclear Weapons Facilities Task Force, which works to freeze construction of weapons and weapons facilities.

Saint Joan Peace Institute
316 Pennsylvania Avenue SE, Suite 203
Washington, DC 20003
(202) 544-0353

The Institute is a division of Eagle Forum Education and Legal Defense Fund, a national educational organization headed by Phyllis Schlafly.

SANE
711 G Street SE
Washington, DC 20003
(202) 546-7100

SANE was founded in 1957 "to bring about negotiated settlement of international disputes and major cuts in arms spending." Its membership fee of $20 a year, $10 for students, includes action alerts, issue analyses and a subscription to *Sane World* which is published monthly.

Soviet Embassy
Information Department
1706 18th Street NW
Washington, DC 20009

Speeches and statements on disarmament and Soviet foreign policy are available. It is best to ask for a specific speech or publication.

Union of Concerned Scientists
26 Church Street
Cambridge, MA 02238
(617) 547-5552

This advocate organization was founded in 1969 to voice concern on the impact of advanced technology on society. It has conducted independent technical studies on nuclear power plant safety, radioactive waste disposal options, and the nuclear arms race. It conducts an active public education program including nationwide UCS-sponsored events, periodic television and radio appearances and publishes a quarterly entitled *Nucleus.*

US Government Accounting Office
Document Handling and Information Services Facility
P.O. Box 6015
Gaithersburg, MD 20760

The GAO reviews the general efficiency of government administration and particular procurement programs. It is a good source of authoritative critiques of Pentagon programs. Write for the *Monthly List of GAO Reports,* which includes an order form. A single copy of any GAO report is free.

War Resisters League
339 Lafayette Street
New York, NY 10012
(212) 228-0450

WRL, founded in 1923, is a national pacifist organization opposed to armaments, conscription and war. *WRL News,* published every other month, is free. *Win* magazine is $20 a year.

bibliography

Books

Paul Abrecht &
Ninan Koshv, eds.
Before It's Too Late: The Challenge of Nuclear Disarmament. Geneva, Switzerland: World Council of Churches, 1983.

Ruth Adams & Susan
Cullen, eds.
The Final Epidemic: Physicians and Scientists On Nuclear War. Chicago: The Educational Foundation for Nuclear Science, 1981.

Robert C. Aldridge
The Counterforce Syndrome: A Guide to U.S. Nuclear Weapons and Strategic Doctrine. Washington, DC: Institute for Policy Studies, 1978.

Stephen E. Ambrose &
James A. Barber, Jr.,
eds.
The Military and American Society. New York: The Free Press, 1972.

Richard J. Barnet
Real Security: Restoring American Power in a Dangerous Decade. New York: Simon & Schuster, 1981.

Petr Beckman
The Health Hazards of Not Going Nuclear. New York: Ace Books, 1980.

Laurence W.
Beilenson
Survival and Peace in the Nuclear Age. Chicago: Regnery/Gateway, Inc., 1980.

Patrick M. Blackett
Studies of War: Nuclear and Conventional. Westport, CT: Greenwood, 1978.

Boston Study Group
Winding Down: The Price of Defense. San Francisco: Boston Study Group, 1982.

Harold Brown
Thinking About National Security. Boulder, CO: Westview Press, 1983.

Richard Burt, ed.
Arms Control & Defense Postures in the Nineteen-Eighties. Boulder, CO: Westview, 1982.

Cambridge University
The Nuclear Revolution: International Politics Before and After Hiroshima. New York: Cambridge University Press, 1981.

James Chance
Solvency: The Price of Survival. New York: Random House.

Michael Clarke and
Marjorie Mowlam,
eds.
Debate on Disarmament. Boston: Routledge & Kegan Paul, 1982.

Andrew Cockburn
The Threat: Inside the Soviet Military Machine. New York: Random House, 1983.

S.T. Cohen
The Neutron Bomb: Political, Technological & Military Issues. Cambridge, MA: Institute for Foreign Policy Analysis, 1978.

John M. Collins
U.S.-Soviet Military Balance. New York: McGraw-Hill, 1980.

*Congressional
Quarterly*
U.S. Defense Policy. Washington, DC: Congressional Quarterly, 1980.

M. Dando &
B. Newman, eds.
Nuclear Deterrence: Implications & Policy Options for the 1980s. Atlantic Highlands, NJ: Humanities, 1982.

Thalit Deen and
Earl S. Browning
How to Survive a Nuclear Disaster. Piscataway, NJ: New Century, 1981.

Robert W.
DeGrasse, Jr.
Military Expansion, Economic Decline. New York: Council on Economic Priorities, 1983.

Theodore Draper
Defending America. New York: Basic Books, 1977.

Thomas H. Etzold
Defense or Delusion? New York: Harper & Row, 1982.

James Fallows
National Defense. New York: Random House, 1981.

Lawrence Freedman
The Evolution of Nuclear Strategy. New York: St. Martin, 1981.

Joseph D. Douglas &
Amoretta M. Hoeber
Soviet Strategy for Nuclear War. Stanford, CA: Hoover Institution Press, 1971.

Alan Geyer
The Idea of Disarmament: Rethinking the Unthinkable. Aurora, IL: Caroline House, 1982.

Samuel Glasstone &
Philip J. Dolan, eds.
The Effects of Nuclear Weapons. Washington, DC: Department of Defense, 1977.

Geoffrey Goodwin
Ethics and Nuclear Deterrence. New York: St. Martin, 1982.

Peter Goodwin
Nuclear War: The Facts of Our Survival. New York: The Rutledge Press, 1981.

Daniel O. Graham
High Frontier: A New National Strategy. Washington, DC: The Heritage Foundation, 1982.

Daniel O. Graham
Shall America Be Defended? New Rochelle, NY: Arlington House, 1979.

Ground Zero
Nuclear War: What's In It For You? New York: Pocket Books, 1982.

Ground Zero
What About the Russians—And Nuclear War? New York: Pocket Books, 1983.

Robert Heyer
Nuclear Disarmament. New York: Paulist Press, 1982.

Fred Kaplan
The Wizards of Armageddon. New York: Simon & Schuster, 1983.

Peter Karsten, ed.
The Military in America. New York: The Free Press, 1980.

Arthur M. Katz
Life After Nuclear War. Cambridge, MA: Ballinger Publishing, 1982.

Cresson Kearney
Nuclear War Survival Skills. Aurora, IL: Caroline House, 1981.

Edward Kennedy &
Mark Hatfield
Freeze! How You Can Help Prevent Nuclear War. New York: Bantam Books, 1982.

George F. Kennan
The Nuclear Delusion. New York: Pantheon, 1982.

Christopher A. Kohm
The ABC's of Defense. New York: Foreign Policy Associaton, 1981.

Christopher A. Kohm,
ed.
U.S. Defense Policy. Chicago: H.W. Wilson Company, 1982.

Sidney Lens
The Day Before Doomsday. Boston: Beacon Press, 1977.

Sidney Lens
The Maginot Line Syndrome: America's Hopeless Foreign Policy. Cambridge, MA: Ballinger, 1983.

Robert Jay Lifton
and Richard Falk
Indefensible Weapons. New York: Basic Books, 1982.

N. Luzin	*Nuclear Strategy & Common Sense.* (Progress Publishers, USSR) Chicago: Imported Publications, 1981.	Marion Anderson	*"The Empty Pork Barrel."* Available for $2.00 from Employment Research Associates, 400 South Washington Ave., Lansing MI 48933.
L.W. McNaught	*Nuclear, Biological & Chemical Warfare.* Elmsford, NY: Pergamon, 1982.	Jeffrey G. Barlow, ed.	*"Reforming the Military."* Available for $3.00 from the Heritage Foundation, 513 C Street NE, Washington, DC 20002. 1981.
Samuel B. Payne, Jr.	*The Soviet Union and SALT.* Cambridge, MA: MIT Press, 1980.	Bureau of Public Affairs	*"Security and Arms Control: The Search for a More Stable Peace."* Available from the Bureau of Public Affairs, US Department of State, Washington, DC 20520. 1983.
Jeffrey Record	*NATO's Theater Nuclear Force Modernization Program: The Real Issues.* Cambridge, MA: Institute of Foreign Policy Analysis, 1981.		
John P. Rose	*The Evolution of US Army Nuclear Doctrine 1945-1980.* Boulder, CO: Westview, 1980.	Committee on the Present Danger	*"Has America Become Number 2?"* Available from the Committee on the Present Danger, 1800 Massachusetts Ave. NW, Washington, DC 20036. 1983.
Phyllis Schlafly and Admiral Chester Ward	*Kissinger on the Couch.* New Rochelle, NY: Arlington House, 1975.	Congress of the United States	*"Defense Spending and the Economy."* Congressional Budget Office. Available from the Superintendent of Documents, US Government Printing Office, Washington, DC 20402. 1983.
Jonathan Schell	*The Fate of the Earth.* New York: Alfred A. Knopf, 1982.		
SIPRI	*The NPT: The Main Political Barrier to Nuclear Weapon Proliferation.* New York: Crane-Russak Company, 1980.		
Stockholm International Peace Research Foundation	*Armaments and Disarmament in the Nuclear Age.* Atlantic Highlands, NJ: Humanities Press, 1976.	Marta Daniels and Wendy Mogey	*"Questions and Answers on the Soviet Threat and National Security."* Available for $1.00 from the American Friends Service Committee, 1501 Cherry St., Philadelphia, PA 19102. 1981.
Richard Taylor and Colin Pritchard	*The Protest Makers: The British Nuclear Disarmament Movement.* Elmsford, NY: Pergamon, 1980.	Midge Decter	*"Is the West in Danger?"* Available from the Rockford Institute, 934 North Main St., Rockford, IL 61103.
E.P. Thompson and Dan Smith, eds.	*Protest and Survive.* New York: Monthly Review Press, 1981.	Civil Defense Preparedness Agency	*"Protection in the Nuclear Age "* Department of Defense. Available from the Public Information Service, Bureau of Public Affairs, Department of Defense, Washington, DC 20520. 1977.
W. Scott Thompson, ed.	*From Weakness to Strength: National Security in the 1980s.* San Francisco: Institute for Contemporary Studies, 1980.		
James L. Tyson	*Target America.* Chicago: Regnery/Gateway, 1981.	Robert DeGrasse, Jr. and Others	*"The Cost and Consequences of Reagan's Military Buildup "* Council on Economic Priorities. Available for $2.50 from the International Association of Machinists and Aerospace Workers, Room 1007, 1300 Connecticut Ave. NW, Washington, DC 20036. 1982
Unipublishers	*Comprehensive Study on Nuclear Weapons.* New York: Unipublishers, 1981.		
William R. Van Cleave	*Strategic Options for the Early Eighties.* White Plains, MD: Automated Graphics Systems, 1979.		
Kurt Waldheim	*Nuclear Weapons: Report of the Secretary-General of the United Nations.* Brookline, MA: Autumn Press, 1981.	Department of Defense	*"Soviet Military Power."* Available for $6.50 from Superintendent of Documents, US Government Printing Office, Washington, DC 20402. 1983.
Jim Wallis	*Waging Peace.* New York: Harper & Row, 1982.		
Lewis W. Walt	*The Eleventh Hour.* Ottawa, IL: Caroline House Publishers, 1979.	Samuel T. Francis	*"The Soviet Strategy of Terror."* Available from the Heritage Foundation, 513 C St., NE, Washington, DC 20002. 1981.
Western Goals	*The War Called Peace: The Soviet Peace Offensive.* Alexandria, VA: Western Goals, 1982.	Colin S. Gray	*"Strategy and the MX."* Available for $2.00 from the Heritage Foundation, 513 C Street, NE, Washington, DC 20002. 1980.
Laird M. Wilcox	*One Hundred Secret Hiding Places in Your Home.* Kansas City, MO: Editorial Research Service, 1980.	Fred Charles Ikle	*"What It Means to Be Number Two."* Available for $1.00 from Ethics and Public Policy Center, 1211 Connecticut Ave. NW, Washington, DC 20036.
Agatha S. Wong-Fraser	*The Political Utility of Nuclear Weapons: Expectations & Experience.* Lanham, MD: University Press of America, 1980.		
		Fred Kaplan	*"Mutual Delusions: Soviet and American Thinking on Fighting and Winning a Nuclear War."* Available from the Council for a Livable World Education Fund, 11 Beacon Street, Boston, MA 02108.

Pamphlets

		Ambassador Kennedy	*"Nuclear Nonproliferation: Our Shared Responsibility."* Current Policy #446. Available from the Public Information Service, Bureau of Public Affairs, Department of State, Washington, DC 20520.
American Friends Service Committee	*"Makers of the Nuclear Holocaust."* Available for $1.25 from AFSC, 1660 Lafayette, Denver, CO 80218. 1981.	National Conference of Catholic Bishops	*"The Challenge of Peace: God's Promise and Our Response."* Available from the National Catholic News Service, 1312 Massachusetts Ave. NW, Washington, DC 20005. 1983.
James R. Anderson	*"Bankrupting America."* Available for $3.00 from Employment Research Associates, 400 South Washington Ave., Lansing, MI 48933. 1982.	Novosti Press Agency Publishing House	*"Suicide for Europe?"* Available from the Soviet Embassy, Information Department, 1706 18th St. NW, Washington, DC 20009.

Organization of the Joint Chiefs of Staff	*"United States Military Posture for FY 1984."* Available from the Superintendent of Documents, US Government Printing Office, Washington, DC 20402.
Progress Publishers	*"How to Avert the Threat to Europe."* Available from the Soviet Embassy, Information Department, 1706 18th St., NW, Washington, DC 20009. 1983.
Ronald Reagan	*"Progress in the Quest for Peace and Freedom."* Current Policy #455. Available from the Public Information Service, Bureau of Public Affairs, Department of State, Washington, DC 20520.
Phyllis Schlafly	*"The Pastoral Letter on War and Peace We Wish the Bishops Had Written."* Available for $5.00 from the Saint Joan Peace Institute, 316 Pennsylvania Ave. SE, Suite 203, Washington, DC 20003. 1982.
Ruth Leger Sivard	*"Military Budgets and Social Needs: Setting World Priorities."* Available for 50 cents from Public Affairs Pamphlets, 381 Park Ave. S, New York, NY 10016. 1977.
Ruth Leger Sivard	*"World Military and Social Expenditures, 1982."* Available for $5.00 from World Priorities, Box 1003. Leesburg, VA 22075. 1982.
Edward Teller	*"For America's Defense: The Unmanned Vehicle System."* Available from the Americanism Educational League, P.O. Box 5986, Buena Park, CA 90622.
Union of Concerned Scientists	*"The Arms Control Debate."* Available from the Union of Concerned Scientists, 1384 Massachusetts Ave., Cambridge, MA 02238.
Ben J. Wattenberg	*"The Cost of America's Retreat."* Available from the Ethics and Public Policy Center, 1211 Connecticut Avenue NW, Washington, DC 20036.
Young Americans for Freedom	*"Zero Option."* Available free from YAF, Box 1002, Woodland Rd., Sterling, VA 22170. 1982.

Periodicals

E. Abrams	"Nuclear Weapons: What Is the Moral Response?" *Department of State Bulletin,* December 1982.
Gordon Adams	"Congress Begins the Debate," *The Bulletin of the Atomic Scientists,* April 1983.
Robert C. Aldridge	"The Pentagon's Secret First-Strike Plans," *The American Atheist,* May 1983.
America	"Deterrence: The Dialogue Continues," February 5, 1983.
Richard J. Barnet	"Dancing in the Dark," *The Progressive,* April 1982.
Richard J. Barnet	"Of Cables and Crises," *Sojourners,* February 1983.
John C. Bennett	"Countering the Theory of Limited Nuclear War," *The Christian Century,* January 7-14, 1981.
William F. Buckley, Jr.	"Questions and Answers on the Right," *National Review,* May 28, 1982.
The Bulletin of the Atomic Scientists	June 1982. Numerous articles on the nuclear arms race.
Glyn G. Caldwell and Others	"Mortality and Cancer Frequency Among Military Nuclear Test (Smoky) Participants," *Journal of the American Medical Association,* August 1983, Volume 250, No. 5.

Christiantiy and Crisis	January 18, 1982. Special issue on nuclear arms and disarmament.
Christianity Today	"A Proposal to Tilt the Balance of Terror," April 9, 1982.
Mike Clark	"Inflation and the Arms Race," *The Other Side,* January 1982.
Commonweal	August 13, 1982. Special issue on Catholic bishops and nuclear weapons.
John R. Connery	"The Morality of Nuclear Warpower," *America,* July 17, 1982.
Conservative Digest	June 1982. Section on the High Frontier and conservative reactions to the peace movement.
Current	July/August 1982. Section on nuclear weapons and war.
Current History	May 1983. Entire issue devoted to the Soviet-American arms race and arms control.
Arnoud de Borchgrave	"A Strong America: Key to World Peace," *New Guard,* Winter 1980-82.
Defense 83	A monthly magazine published by the Department of Defense to provide official and professional information to commanders and key personnel on matters related to defense policies.
The Defense Monitor	A magazine published ten times a year by the Center for Defense Information.
Robert DeGrasse, Jr., & William Ragen	"Megabucks for the Pentagon," *Inquiry,* April 26, 1982.
Richard D. DeLauer	"Countering the Soviet Threat," *Defense,* June 1983.
Department of State Bulletin	May 1982. Section on arms control, including visual atlas of current military forces.
Engage/Social Action	February 1983. Special section on the arms race and militarization.
Gregory A. Fossedal	"The Defense Build-Up That Isn't," *Conservative Digest,* September 1982.
J. Garvey	"The Bishops & the Critics," *Commonweal,* January 14, 1983.
Leslie H. Gelb	"A Practical Way to Arms Control," *New York Times Magazine,* June 5, 1983.
Billy Graham	"A Change of Heart: Billy Graham on the Nuclear Arms Race," *Sojourners,* August 1979.
Billy Graham	"Peace: At Times a Sword and Fire," *Christianity Today,* December 17, 1982.
Raoul Girardet	"Neutralism and Pacifism," *NATO Review,* Number Five, 1982.
Darel Grothaus	"The Danger in Chirps and Mutters," *Sojourners,* March 1983.
Darel Grothaus	"Scared to Death," *Sojourners,* February 1983.
Harvard Nuclear Study Group	"The Reality of Arms Control," *The Atlantic Monthly,* June 1983.
Hugh B. Hester	"Dare to Face the Cause," *The Churchman,* June-July 1983.
William P. Hoar	"It's Time for a Tough American Foreign Policy," *American Opinion,* April 1981.
Fred Charles Ikle	"What It Means to Be Number Two," *Fortune,* November 20, 1978.
The Internationalist	March 1981. Special issue on the nuclear arms race.
A.S. Jefferson & Douglas Mitchell	"The State of the Army," *New Guard,* Summer 1980.
Robert C. Johansen	"Numerical Insecurity," *The Atlantic Monthly,* August, 1983.

Kermit D. Johnson	"The Sovereign God and 'the Signs of the Times,'" *The Christian Century*, August 17-24, 1983.
Henry Kissinger	"A New Approach to Arms Control," *Time*, March 21, 1983.
Michael T. Klare	"An Open Letter to the U.S. Peace Movement," *The Witness*, June 1983.
Michael T. Klare	"The Weinberger Revolution," *Inquiry*, September 1982.
Andrew Kopkind	"The Return of Cold War Liberalism," *The Nation*, April 23, 1983.
Sidney Lens	"Unfathomable Risk," *The Progressive*, June 1983.
B.G. Levi	"The Nuclear Arsenals of the US and USSR," *Physics Today*, March 1983.
McCall's	"The Fear That Haunts Our Children," May 1982.
Robert A. Manning	"America's Newest Tripwire," *Inquiry*, January 1983.
Jonathan Marshall	"Who's Afraid of Defense Reform?" *Inquiry*, August 1982.
Lester Mondale	"Atomic War—The Way to Win," *The Churchman*, January 1982.
Mary Morrell	"Blue Sky for Defense," *Engage/Social Action*, April 1982.
The Nation	"The New Arms Technology and What It Means," April 9, 1983.
National Defense	A monthly magazine published by the American Defense Preparedness Association.
National Security Record	A monthly magazine published by the Heritage Foundation.
New Guard	Fall 1982, Special section on nuclear arms control.
Michael Novak	"Nuclear Morality," *America*, July 3, 1982.
Joseph A. O'Hare	"One Man's Primer on Nuclear Morality," *America*, July 3, 1982.
Verne Orr	"Report to the Shareholders of Defense," *Vital Speeches of the Day*," January 1, 1983.
Michael Parenti	"More Bucks from the Bang," *The Progressive*, July 1980.
The People	"U.S.-Soviet Nuclear Debate: An Exercise in Deception," *The People*, May 28, 1983.
Eric Pooley	"A Separate Peace: East German Pacifists Call Their Own Tune," *The Progressive*, March 1983.
M.G. Raskin	"War, Peace and the Bishops," *Nation*, January 29, 1983.
Ronald Reagan	"Peace and National Security," *Department of State Bulletin*, March 1983.
Robert B. Reich	"Hi-Tech Warfare," *The New Republic*, November 1, 1982.
John J. Rhodes	"The Far Side of the Hill," *Foreign Affairs*, Winter 1982/83.
Alvin Richman	"Public Attitudes on Military Power, 1981," *Public Opinion*, December/January 1982.
C.A. Robinson, Jr.	"Defense Budget Presses Nuclear Effort," *Aviation Week Space Technology*, January 31, 1983.
Douglas Roche	"The Machinery of Peace," *Vital Speeches of the Day*, August 1, 1983.
John P. Roche	"The Anti-Nuke Strategy," *National Review*, February 1982.
Eugene V. Rostow	"Arms Control Fever," *National Review*, August 19, 1983.
R.J. Rummel	"The Freedom Factor," *Reason*, July 1983.
Science Digest	November 1982, Special section on nuclear scenarios and solutions.

Charles L. Schultze	"Economic Effects of the Defense Budget," *The Brookings Bulletin*, Fall 1981.
George Shultz	"U.S. Foreign Policy: Realism and Progress," *Department of State Bulletin*, November 1982.
Bent Sorensen	"Redefining Defense," *The Bulletin of the Atomic Scientists*, August/September 1981.
R.L. Spaeth	"Debating Disarmament with Catholic Bishops," *Vital Speeches of the Day*, January 15, 1983.
John Steinbruner	"Arms and the Art of Compromise," *Brookings Review*, Summer 1983.
Lloyd G. Shore	"Can Nuclear Weapons Be Abolished?" *Bulletin of the Atomic Scientists*, December 1980.
Strobe Talbot	"Playing for the Future: Is the US Making the Right Moves Toward Moscow in Arms Control?" *Time*, April 18, 1983.
Time	"Reagan for the Defense," April 4, 1983.
Mikhail Tsypkin	"The Conscripts: The Soviet Union," *Bulletin of the Atomic Scientists*, May 1983.
Suzanne C. Toton	"Peacemaking Put in Context," *America*, August 13, 1983.
John W. Vessey, Jr.	"The Unrelenting Growth of Soviet Military Power," *Vital Speeches of the Day*, May 15, 1983.
Louis J. Walinsky	"Coherent Defense Strategy: The Case for Economic Denial," *Foreign Affairs*, Winter 1982/1983.
Thomas J. Watson	"Man Against War," *Arms Control Association*, January 1982.
Caspar W. Weinberger	"The Reality of the Soviet Threat," *Defense*, June 1983.
Caspar W. Weinberger	"We've Been Overspending, But Not for Defense," *U.S. News & World Report*, November 23, 1981.
Caspar W. Weinberger	"Why We Must Have a Nuclear Deterrent," *Defense/83*, March 1983.
The Witness	June 1982. Special issue on the Christian's response to nuclear weapons.
Albert Wohlstetter	"Bishops, Statesmen, and Other Strategists on the Bombing of Innocents," *Commentary*, June 1983.

index